Business Plans Handbook

(...)

Business Plans Handbook

A COMPILATION OF ACTUAL BUSINESS PLANS DEVELOPED BY BUSINESSES THROUGHOUT NORTH AMERICA

VOLUME

12

Lynn M. Pearce,
Project Editor

THOMSON
✦
GALE

Detroit • New York • San Francisco • New Haven, Conn. • Waterville, Maine • London • Munich

THOMSON

GALE

Business Plans Handbook, 12th Volume

Lynn M. Pearce

Project Editor
Lynn M. Pearce

Product Design
Jennifer Wahi

Composition and Electronic Capture
Evi Seoud

Manufacturing
Rita Wimberley

LIBRARY OF CONGRESS CATALOGING-IN-PUBLICATION DATA

ISBN 0-7876-6682-3
ISSN 1084-4473

Printed in the United States of America
10 9 8 7 6 5 4 3 2 1

Contents

Highlights vii

Introduction ix

BUSINESS PLANS

Beauty Salon
Salon Flora 1

Campground
California RV & Campgrounds 15

Car Wash
Platinum Car Wash 23

Concrete Coating Company
Techno–Coatings USA 37

Custodial Cleaning Company
Spic and Span 45

Daycare
Childhood Dreams Inc. 49
Ziggle Zag Zip Daycare/Childcare 55

Dentist's Office
Fremont Dental Office 61

E–Commerce Website Producer
Internet Capabilities 65

Entertainment Production, Distribution, and Performance Company
Mentonic Hero Inc. 71

General Staffing Company
GENRX LLC 83

Go–Cart Designer and Supplier
Speedy Go–Carts 91

Home Inspection Company
Home Inspectors Are We 95

Information Technology Personnel Agency
Rekve IT Staffing 99

Online Payment Services
Exactor Technologies, LLC 109

CONTENTS

Online Woodworking Manufacturing & Retailing
U–nique Woodworking 119

Plumbing Service
Matt's Plumbing and Air Conditioning 125

Senior Care Facility
Hearts and Hopes Senior Home 131

Sports Bar and Grille
Stone Oak Sports Bar & Grille 137

Sports Tournament Organizer
Scramble Sports Tournament Series 163

APPENDIXES

Appendix A
Business Plan Template 207

Fictional Plan 1 - Food Distributor 213

Fictional Plan 2 - Hardware Store 217

Appendix B
Associations 221

Consultants 223

SBA Regional Offices 238

Small Business Development Centers 239

Service Corps of Retired Executives Offices 244

Venture Capital & Financing Companies 268

Appendix C
Glossary of Small Business Terms 329

Appendix D
Cumulative Index 353

Highlights

Business Plans Handbook, Volume 12 (BPH-12) is a collection of actual business plans compiled by entrepreneurs seeking funding for small businesses throughout North America. For those looking for examples of how to approach, structure, and compose their own business plans, BPH-12 presents 20 sample plans, including plans for the following businesses:

- Beauty Salon

- Campground

- Car Wash

- Concrete Coating Company

- Custodial Cleaning Company

- Daycare

- Dentist's Office

- E–Commerce Website Producer

- Entertainment Production, Distribution, and Performance Company

- General Staffing Company

- Go–Cart Designer and Supplier

- Home Inspection Company

- Information Technology Personnel Agency

- Online Payment Services

- Online Woodworking Manufacturing & Retailing

- Plumbing Service

- Senior Care Facility

- Sports Bar and Grille

- Sports Tournament Organizer

FEATURES AND BENEFITS

BPH-12 offers many features not provided by other business planning references including:

- Twenty business plans, each of which represent an owner's successful attempt at clarifying (for themselves and others) the reasons that the business should exist or expand and why a lender should fund the enterprise.

- Two fictional plans that are used by business counselors at a prominent small business development organization as examples for their clients. (You will find these in the Business Plan Template Appendix.)

- A directory section that includes: listings for venture capital and finance companies, which specialize in funding start-up and second-stage small business ventures, and a comprehensive listing of Service Corps of Retired Executives (SCORE) offices. In addition, the Appendix also contains updated listings of all Small Business Development Centers (SBDCs); associations of interest to entrepreneurs; Small Business Administration (SBA) Regional Offices; and consultants specializing in small business planning and advice. It is strongly advised that you consult supporting organizations while planning your business, as they can provide a wealth of useful information.

- A Small Business Term Glossary to help you decipher the sometimes confusing terminology used by lenders and others in the financial and small business communities.

- A cumulative index, outlining each plan profiled in the complete Business Plans Handbook series.

- A Business Plan Template which serves as a model to help you construct your own business plan. This generic outline lists all the essential elements of a complete business plan and their components, including the Summary, Business History and Industry Outlook, Market Examination, Competition, Marketing, Administration and Management, Financial Information, and other key sections. Use this guide as a starting point for compiling your plan.

- Extensive financial documentation required to solicit funding from small business lenders. You will find examples of: Cash Flows, Balance Sheets, Income Projections, and other financial information included with the textual portions of the plan.

Introduction

Perhaps the most important aspect of business planning is simply doing it. More and more business owners are beginning to compile business plans even if they don't need a bank loan. Others discover the value of planning when they must provide a business plan for the bank. The sheer act of putting thoughts on paper seems to clarify priorities and provide focus. Sometimes business owners completely change strategies when compiling their plan, deciding on a different product mix or advertising scheme after finding that their assumptions were incorrect. This kind of healthy thinking and re-thinking via business planning is becoming the norm. The editors of Business Plans Handbook, Volume 12 (BPH-12) sincerely hope that this latest addition to the series is a helpful tool in the successful completion of your business plan, no matter what the reason for creating it.

This twelfth volume, like each volume in the series, offers genuine business plans used by real people. BPH-12 provides 20 business plans used by actual entrepreneurs to gain funding support for their new businesses. The business and personal names and addresses and general locations have been changed to protect the privacy of the plan authors.

NEW BUSINESS OPPORTUNITIES

As in other volumes in the series, BPH-12 finds entrepreneurs engaged in a wide variety of creative endeavors. Examples include a proposal for a bar/grill, a sports tournament, and a carwash. In addition, several other plans are provided, including an e-commerce website designer, both a general and an IT staffing company, a dental office, a home inspection company, and two separate business plans for a daycare center.

Comprehensive financial documentation has become increasingly important as today's entrepreneurs compete for the finite resources of business lenders. Our plans illustrate the financial data generally required of loan applicants, including Income Statements, Financial Projections, Cash Flows, and Balance Sheets.

ENHANCED APPENDIXES

In an effort to provide the most relevant and valuable information for our readers, we have updated the coverage of small business resources. For instance, you will find: a directory section, which includes listings of all of the Service Corps of Retired Executives (SCORE) offices; an informative glossary, which includes small business terms; and a cumulative index, outlining each plan profiled in the complete Business Plans Handbook series. In addition we have updated the list of Small Business Development Centers (SBDCs); Small Business Administration Regional Offices; venture capital and finance companies, which specialize in funding start-up and second-stage small business enterprises; associations of interest to entrepreneurs; and consultants, specializing in small business advice and planning. For your reference, we have also reprinted the business plan template, which provides a comprehensive overview of the essential components of a business plan and two fictional plans used by small business counselors.

SERIES INFORMATION

If you already have the first eleven volumes of BPH, with this twelfth volume, you will now have a collection of over 260 real business plans (not including the one updated plan in the second volume, whose original appeared in the first, or the two fictional plans in the Business Plan Template Appendix section of the second, third, fourth, fifth, sixth, and seventh volumes); contact information for hundreds of organizations and agencies offering business expertise; a helpful business plan template; more than 1,500 citations to valuable small business development material; and a comprehensive glossary of terms to help the business planner navigate the sometimes confusing language of entrepreneurship.

ACKNOWLEDGEMENTS

The Editors wish to sincerely thank the contributors to BPH-12, including:

- Brett Bachelier, Mark Chase, and Justin Renshaw
- Michele Bussone, Alpha Quadrant Inc.
- Christopher Clay, BusinessandMarketingPlans.com
- Tim Hayden and Larry Weiss, Cook School of Business, Saint Louis University
- Gerald Rekve, Corporate Management Consultants

The editors would also like to express their gratitude to both Lisa Bastian, CBC, of Bastian Public Relations, and Jerome Katz of the Cook School of Business at Saint Louis University. Both individuals have been instrumental in finding and securing high–quality, successful business plans for inclusion in this publication.

COMMENTS WELCOME

Your comments on Business Plans Handbook are appreciated. Please direct all correspondence, suggestions for future volumes of BPH, and other recommendations to the following:

Managing Editor, Business Product
Business Plans Handbook
The Gale Group
27500 Drake Rd.
Farmington Hills, MI 48331-3535

Phone: (248)699-4253
Fax: (248)699-8052
Toll-Free: 800-347-GALE
E-mail: BusinessProducts@gale.com

Beauty Salon
Salon Flora

34 Destin St.
Naples, Florida 34102

Staff at BusinessandMarketingPlans.com

This business plan was created for two highly trained, veteran hair stylists with an established client base and lots of business savvy. They sought capital to open an upscale salon to further serve the styling needs of regional customers. This plan raised $70,000 for the company's owners.

EXECUTIVE SUMMARY

Salon Flora is a beauty salon dedicated to providing customer satisfaction with excellent service, quality products, and an enjoyable atmosphere at an excellent price/value relationship.

Nature is not something you can hold onto–it is something we are borrowing from our children; we must do our part to keep the balance in life. We strive to keep balance in our clients' life by supplying services and products that enhance physical appearance and mental relaxation. We will maintain a friendly, fair, and creative work environment which respects diversity, ideas, and hard work.

To achieve our objectives, Salon Flora is seeking $70,000 in additional loan financing. This loan will be paid back from the cash flow of the business and will be collateralized by the assets of the company. It will be backed by the character, experience, and personal guarantees of the owners.

Financial highlights for the first three years of operations

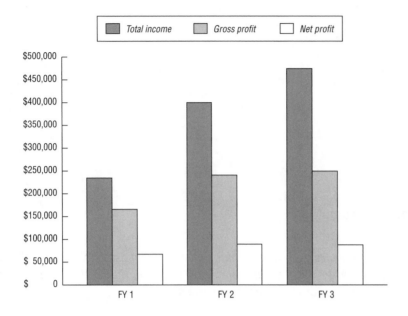

Keys to Success

The keys to success in our business are:

- Location, Location, Location: providing an easily accessible location for customers with plenty of off street parking.

- Environment: providing an environment conductive to relaxation and professional service.

- Convenience: offering clients a variety of services in one setting, and flexible business hours.

- Reputation: superior personal service reputation of the owners/managers and other "stylists."

BUSINESS OVERVIEW

Company Summary

Salon Flora is designed to enhance each client's image and outlook. We specialize in restoring balance to the body and mind through the *HairFlux* philosophy of beauty, wellness, care for the environment and our passion for service and retail. We will provide a unique experience for our guests. We treat each client as if they were a guest in our home, offering a cup of *HairFlux's* comforting tea and a cozy robe to change into. Our outstanding stylists will benefit from ongoing *HairFlux* education classes both in the salon and at other choice locations.

Start-up summary

Start-up summary table

Start-up expenses	
Legal	$ 1,000
Stationary	$ 100
Rent (deposit)	$ 6,720
Utilities	$ 100
Phone	$ 50
Total start-up expenses	**$ 7,970**
Start-up assets	
Cash balance on starting date	**$28,030**
Total current assets	$28,030
Long-term assets	
Leasehold improvements	$45,000
Equipment (chairs, mirrors, etc)	$19,000
Total long-term assets	$64,000
Total assets	**$92,030**
Owner's equity	
Alan Wolvin	$15,000
Yvette DeVito	$15,000
Total owner's equity	**$30,000**
Total current liabilities	$ 0
Long-term liabilities	
Loan	$70,000
Total long-term liabilities	**$70,000**
Loss at start-up	(**$ 7,970**)
Total liabilities and owner's equity	**$92,030**

Products & Services

Salon Flora is considered an upscale beauty salon. We will offer a wide range of services that include:

- Hair: Precision cuts, relaxers, perms, colors, color correction, shampoo, conditioning, curling, re–constructing, weaving, waving, and a patented hair straightening system

- Skin Care: European facials, body waxing, and massage

- Provide added value services to each of our guests, such as: a stress–relieving scalp treatment, stress–relieving hand massage, and make–up touch–up after each service

- Retail *HairFlux* products so that the client can reproduce their enhanced appearance.

Sales forecast table

Annual sales forecast	FY 1	FY 2	FY 3
Sales			
Owners	$ 47,800	$ 48,800	$ 48,800
Stylist retail sales	$ 69,070	$156,180	$189,399
Treatment room rent	$ 10,800	$ 14,400	$ 17,280
Treatment rooms retail sales	$ 23,780	$ 54,120	$ 65,621
Station rental	$ 89,000	$132,000	$158,400
Total sales	**$240,450**	**$405,500**	**$479,500**
Cost of goods sold			
Owners	$ 22,167	$ 29,721	$ 35,851
Stylist retail sales	$ 32,031	$ 95,119	$139,141
Treatment room rent	N/A	N/A	N/A
Treatment rooms retail sales	$ 11,028	$ 32,961	$ 48,208
Station rental	N/A	N/A	N/A
Total cost of goods sold	**$ 65,225**	**$157,800**	**$223,200**

Competition

There are a number of salons in our area; however none will be like Salon Flora. Salon Flora will set itself apart from other beauty salons. We will offer over twenty-five years of combined hair care experience, weekly education to our staff, added value services and a full line of *HairFlux* products. Our business atmosphere is a relaxing one where clients can kick back and be pampered.

Soft drinks will be offered to clients as they enter for service.

GROWTH STRATEGY

The major market for our products and services is singles, couples, and families within but not limited to a twenty–mile radius. The owners/managers have clients that travel twenty to ninety miles, and many plan their business around their hair care needs. Salon Flora has easy access from a main highway with plenty of parking, a rarity in the downtown business district. Our service is for individuals but might be beneficial for companies and corporations, through incentive programs, such as business make over or promotional services.

We will also promote bridal packages through local hotels and associated business and day–of–beauty packages complete with lunch and door-to-door limousine service, if desired. *HairFlux Corporation* will offer our services through their 800 phone number, website, and corporate store at the nearby Shady Oak Mall, along with our own Salon Flora website. We will concentrate on the Palma county area in southern Florida.

Marketing & Sales

Our marketing strategy is a simple one: satisfied clients are our best marketing tool. When a client leaves our business with a new look, he or she is broadcasting our name and quality to the public.

Most of our new clients are referrals from existing clients. We reward clients for referrals with free shampoo and/or conditioner. Distribution of coupons for a free gift with product purchases or services at the salon "grand opening" celebration will strengthen customer loyalty.

We will publish ads in local publications and magazines to promote our staff, services, and retail products. The publications we will work with are:

- *Best Images:* a full color, bi–monthly advertising magazine with a 100,000 home circulation in the regional area. This full page, color ad will cost $4,000 and reach potential upper–income clients.

- *All the News Magazine:* a trusted reference for business and shopping resources, with a home circulation of 50,000 in the nearby coastal areas. These full–page color ads cost $1,115 for an inside page, and $3,000 for front cover. These ads will reach potential clients with $50,000 to $150,000 incomes.

- *Yellow Pages:* We will also place ads in the Yellow Pages which have the entire county circulation.

- We will also have our own Salon Flora–*HairFlux Institute* website. This website is always available for stylists and guests. Information on current promotions, upcoming events, education and links to the *HairFlux Corporation* are instantly available.

MANAGEMENT SUMMARY

Salon Flora is a *HairFlux* concept salon. The upscale brand recognition of *HairFlux* enhances the reputation of the salon. Salon Flora will be organized and managed in a creative and innovative fashion to generate very high levels of customer satisfaction, and to create a working climate conducive to a high degree of personal development and economic satisfaction for our staff.

Training classes to help improve employee product knowledge and skills will be conducted on a regular basis. As the business grows, the company will consider offering an employee benefit package to include health and vacation benefits for everyone.

Management Team

Yvette and Alan have both been independent contractors for a combined thirty-two years, and have the experience, passion, and working knowledge to get the job done.

Alan F. Slinger

Owner/Manager/Artistic Director. Alan has been in the beauty industry for eighteen years and brings a large variety of experience to this venture; upon graduating from Monique Beauty College in 1990 he worked for one of New York's leading salons, helping with education and platform work for both *HairFlux* and *Matrix/Logics Corporations*. He was also a part-time Artistic Educator with *Matrix/Logics*, responsible for color and hair cutting classes in New York City. His previous experiences consist of commercial, retail stores, management, construction and manufacturing. Alan's retail management experience and general business knowledge grounds him in the realties of running a successful business. He loves dealing with people, and has the drive, ambition, and discipline to manage the business and its employees. This career is his life, his calling.

Yvette Cruz

Owner/Manger: Yvette Cruz was born in Barcelona, Spain, forty years ago. She is the second child of nine. She began her career by mentoring her three cousins.

At age 21, she moved to the United States. After finishing her education at Monique Beauty College she went to work in her cousin's salon. Cruz is involved in various activities in the world of beauty. She is responsible for the designing and marketing of a specialty tool called the *Color–Wandz*, created to expedite the stylist time in color services. She has worked with the *HairFlux* product line for the past eleven years as an independent contractor, and also has been involved in many global events for *HairFlux*. She is a firm believer in donating her artistic talents for various events.

Personnel Plan

The personnel plan calls for a receptionist starting in the second year. The receptionist will answer phone, book appointments, and receive payments for services and products. There will be eleven hair stylists, one artistic director/owner, one stylist/owner, two part–time assistant stylists, one esthetician and a massage therapist. Everyone but the receptionist and assistants will be independent contractors, and will pay a weekly fee for their station or treatment room.

Annual personnel plan

Sales	FY 1	FY 2	FY 3
Receptionist	$0	$30,000	$34,000
Assistant	$0	$ 0	$ 0
Assistant	$0	$11,920	$11,920
Total payroll	**$0**	**$41,920**	**$45,920**

FINANCIAL ANALYSIS

Our goal is to be a profitable business beginning in the second month. The owners and stylists already have an existing client base.

The financials that are enclosed have a number of assumptions:

- Chair rental value is $250.00 per week x 11 chairs = $2,750.00 per week x 52 = $143,000 per year. This figure is not assumed until the end of the first year. Our projections are based on opening with three stylists. We will then add a stylist the second month, the third month, the fourth month, and the sixth month. Salon Flora will then add two more stylists in the eighth month and two more in the tenth month.

- Revenues will grow on chair rental each month and level off at the end of the first year with all chairs rented.

- Revenues will grow at an annual rate near 50% on retail sales in year one.

- Revenues are expected to increase in November and December due to holiday sales at this time of year. We anticipate this increase from gift certificates and increased product sales, and to stay steady throughout the following year to account for the normal flow of new clients coming into the salon and our aggressive marketing program.

- Estimates for sales revenue and growth are intentionally low, while anticipated expenses are exaggerated to illustrate a worst–case scenario.

We have included cost of goods sold in our calculation of net sales because we expect to do a high volume of retail through our salon. However the majority of sales are coming from the services and rental income.

Product sales will be a major part of our business. We are projecting sales of $4,000 a month increasing each month thereafter as we add stylists to the salon. We expect each stylist to sell a minimum of $100.00 per day in retail. We also project the treatment rooms to generate a minimum of $170.00 per day in retail sales. We are certain that in time these services will be a large part of our revenue, but to err on the conservative side, we estimate revenues from these services to be only $3,655.00 a month for the first year.

To assure the initial capital fund lender that the owners are financially stable, personnel tax returns for both partners for the last three years are attached. Another source of collateral is Alan Slinger's home, valued at $500,000 with a payoff balance of $395,000.

Break-even analysis

Break-even analysis	
Monthly units break-even	118
Monthly revenue	
Break-even	$6,514
Average per-unit revenue	$55.00
Average per-unit variable cost	$11.43
Estimated monthly fixed cost	$5,160

Projected Profit and Loss

We expect sales to hit $240,450 at the end of the first year of business, and should increase to more than $479,500 by the third year as the reputation of the salon, its stylists, and services grow. Second year revenues also anticipate having a full staff.

General assumptions

	FY 1	FY2	FY3
Current interest rate	7.00%	7.00%	7.00%
Long-term interest rate	7.00%	7.00%	7.00%
Sales on credit	0.00%	0.00%	0.00%
Tax rate	30.00%	30.00%	30.00%

Annual pro forma profit and loss

	FY 1	FY 2	FY 3
Total Income	**$240,450**	**$405,500**	**$479,500**
Cost of goods sold	$ 65,225	$157,800	$223,200
Gross profit	**$175,225**	**$247,700**	**$256,300**
Gross profit %	72.87%	61.09%	53.45%
Expenses:			
Payroll	$ 0	$ 41,920	$ 45,920
Depreciation	$ 10,900	$ 10,900	$ 10,900
Rent	$ 26,880	$ 26,880	$ 26,88
Utilities	$ 6,000	$ 6,800	$ 7,000
Insurance	$ 1,200	$ 1,200	$ 1,200
Supplies	$ 11,900	$ 11,900	$ 11,900
Advertising	$ 4,200	$ 4,200	$ 4,200
Misc.	$ 840	$ 840	$ 840
Payroll taxes 15%	**$ 0**	**$ 6,288**	**$ 6,888**
Total operating expenses	**$ 61,920**	**$110,928**	**$115,728**
Profit before interest and taxes	$113,305	$136,772	$140,572
Interest expense	$ 4,323	$ 2,958	$ 1,698
Taxes incurred	$ 32,695	$ 35,851	$ 41,662
Net profit	**$ 76,288**	**$ 97,963**	**$ 97,212**
Net profit/sales	**31.73%**	**24.16%**	**20.27%**

First year of operations monthly profits

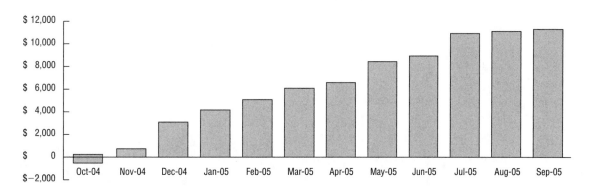

Second year of operations monthly profits

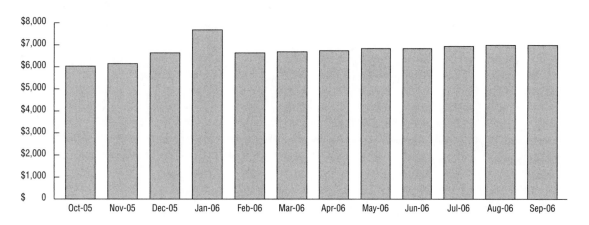

Cash flow

Annual pro forma cash flow	FY 1	FY 2	FY 3
Cash received			
Cash from operations:			
Cash sales	$240,450	$405,500	$479,500
Cash from receivables	$ 0	$ 0	$ 0
Subtotal cash from operations	$240,450	$405,500	$479,500
Additional cash received			
Subtotal cash received	$240,450	$405,500	$479,500
Expenditures			
Expenditures from operations			
Cash spending	$ 0	$ 41,920	$ 45,920
Payments of accounts payable	$153,262	$254,717	$325,468
Subtotal spent on operations	$153,262	$296,637	$371,388
Additional cash spent			
Principle repayment of loan	$ 18,000	$ 18,000	$ 18,000
Change in inventory	$ 20,000	$ 20,000	$ 0
Subtotal cash spent	$191,262	$334,637	$389,388
Net cash flow	**$ 49,188**	**$ 70,863**	**$ 90,112**
Cash balance	**$ 77,218**	**$148,081**	**$238,193**

First year of operations monthly cash flow

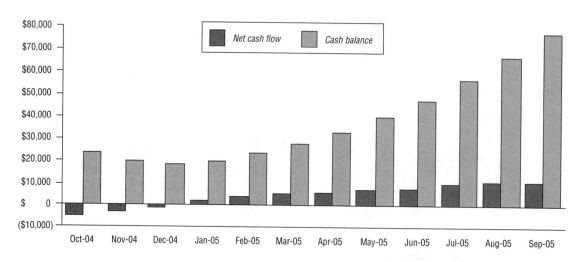

Pro forma balance sheet

Assets	FY 1	FY 2	FY 3
Current assets			
Cash	$ 77,218	$148,081	$238,193
Accounts receivable	$ 0	$ 0	$ 0
Inventory	$ 20,000	$ 40,000	$ 40,000
Total current assets	$ 97,218	$188,081	$278,193
Long-term assets			
Leasehold improvements	$ 45,000	$ 45,000	$ 45,000
Equipment	$ 19,000	$ 19,000	$ 19,000
Accumulated depreciation	$ 10,900	$ 21,800	$ 32,700
Total long-term assets	$ 53,100	$ 42,200	$ 31,300
Total assets	**$150,318**	**$230,281**	**$309,493**
Liabilities and owner's equity			
Current liabilities			
Accounts payable	$ 0	$ 0	$ 0
Total current liabilities	$ 0	$ 0	$ 0
Long-term liabilities			
Loan	$ 52,000	$ 34,000	$ 16,000
Total liabilities	$ 52,000	$ 34,000	$ 16,000
Paid-in capital	$ 30,000	$ 30,000	$ 30,000
Retained earnings	($ 7,970)	$ 68,318	$166,281
Earnings	$ 76,288	$ 97,963	$ 97,212
Total owner's equity	$ 98,318	$196,281	$293,493
Total liabilities and owner's equity	**$150,318**	**$230,281**	**$309,493**
Net worth	$ 98,318	$196,281	$293,493

Monthly sales forecast—fiscal year one

Monthly sales forecast	Oct-04	Nov-04	Dec-04	Jan-05	Feb-05	Mar-05
Sales						
Owners	$ 3,000	$ 4,000	$ 4,800	$ 4,000	$ 4,000	$ 4,000
Stylist retail sales	$ 0	$ 900	$ 4,500	$ 3,600	$ 4,500	$ 5,400
Treatment room rent	$ 0	$ 0	$ 0	$ 1,200	$ 1,200	$ 1,200
Treatment rooms retail sales	$ 0	$ 0	$ 0	$ 1,000	$ 2,000	$ 2,200
Station rental	$ 3,000	$ 4,000	$ 5,000	$ 6,000	$ 6,000	$ 7,000
Total sales	**$ 6,000**	**$ 8,900**	**$14,300**	**$15,800**	**$17,700**	**$19,800**
Cost of goods sold						
Owners	$ 1,391	$ 1,855	$ 2,226	$ 1,855	$ 1,855	$ 1,855
Stylist retail sales	$ 0	$ 417	$ 2,087	$ 1,669	$ 2,087	$ 2,504
Treatment room rent	N/A	N/A	N/A	N/A	N/A	N/A
Treatment rooms retail sales	$ 0	$ 0	$ 0	$ 464	$ 927	$ 1,020
Station rental	N/A	N/A	N/A	N/A	N/A	N/A
Total cost of goods sold	**$ 1,391**	**$ 2,272**	**$ 4,313**	**$ 3,988**	**$ 4,869**	**$ 5,379**

Monthly sales forecast	Apr-05	May-05	Jun-05	Jul-05	Aug-05	Sep-05
Sales						
Owners	$ 4,000	$ 4,000	$ 4,000	$ 4,000	$ 4,000	$ 4,000
Stylist retail sales	$ 6,500	$ 7,200	$ 8,100	$ 9,200	$ 9,420	$ 9,750
Treatment room rent	$ 1,200	$ 1,200	$ 1,200	$ 1,200	$ 1,200	$ 1,200
Treatment rooms retail sales	$ 2,250	$ 2,750	$ 3,000	$ 3,300	$ 3,600	$ 3,680
Station rental	$ 7,000	$ 9,000	$ 9,000	$11,000	$11,000	$11,000
Total sales	**$20,950**	**$24,150**	**$25,300**	**$28,700**	**$29,220**	**$29,630**
Cost of goods sold						
Owners	$ 1,855	$ 1,855	$ 1,855	$ 1,855	$ 1,855	$ 1,855
Stylist retail sales	$ 3,014	$ 3,339	$ 3,756	$ 4,266	$ 4,368	$ 4,521
Treatment room rent	N/A	N/A	N/A	N/A	N/A	N/A
Treatment rooms retail sales	$ 1,043	$ 1,275	$ 1,391	$ 1,530	$ 1,669	$ 1,707
Station rental	N/A	N/A	N/A	N/A	N/A	N/A
Total cost of goods sold	**$ 5,913**	**$ 6,469**	**$ 7,002**	**$ 7,652**	**$ 7,893**	**$ 8,083**

Monthly sales forecast—fiscal year two

Monthly sales forecast	Oct-05	Nov-05	Dec-05	Jan-06	Feb-06	Mar-06
Sales						
Owners	$ 4,000	$ 4,000	$ 4,000	$ 4,800	$ 4,000	$ 4,000
Stylist retail sales	$ 9,500	$10,000	$12,000	$14,400	$12,400	$12,800
Treatment room rent	$ 1,200	$ 1,200	$ 1,200	$ 1,200	$ 1,200	$ 1,200
Treatment rooms retail sales	$ 3,900	$ 4,000	$ 4,100	$ 4,920	$ 4,300	$ 4,400
Station rental	$11,000	$11,000	$11,000	$11,000	$11,000	$11,000
Total sales	**$29,600**	**$30,200**	**$32,300**	**$36,320**	**$32,900**	**$33,400**
Cost of goods sold						
Owners	$ 2,436	$ 2,436	$ 2,436	$ 2,923	$ 2,436	$ 2,436
Stylist retail sales	$ 5,786	$ 6,090	$ 7,308	$ 8,770	$ 7,552	$ 7,796
Treatment room rent	N/A	N/A	N/A	N/A	N/A	N/A
Treatment rooms retail sales	$ 2,375	$ 2,436	$ 2,497	$ 2,996	$ 2,619	$ 2,680
Station rental	N/A	N/A	N/A	N/A	N/A	N/A
Total cost of goods sold	**$10,597**	**$10,963**	**$12,242**	**$14,690**	**$12,607**	**$12,911**

Monthly sales forecast	Apr-06	May-06	Jun-06	Jul-06	Aug-06	Sep-06
Sales						
Owners	$ 4,000	$ 4,000	$ 4,000	$ 4,000	$ 4,000	$ 4,000
Stylist retail sales	$13,200	$13,600	$14,000	$14,400	$14,800	$15,080
Treatment room rent	$ 1,200	$ 1,200	$ 1,200	$ 1,200	$ 1,200	$ 1,200
Treatment rooms retail sales	$ 4,500	$ 4,600	$ 4,700	$ 4,800	$ 4,900	$ 5,000
Station rental	$11,000	$11,000	$11,000	$11,000	$11,000	$11,000
Total sales	**$33,900**	**$34,400**	**$34,900**	**$35,400**	**$35,900**	**$36,280**
Cost of goods sold						
Owners	$ 2,436	$ 2,436	$ 2,436	$ 2,436	$ 2,436	$ 2,436
Stylist retail sales	$ 8,039	$ 8,283	$ 8,526	$ 8,770	$ 9,014	$ 9,184
Treatment room rent	N/A	N/A	N/A	N/A	N/A	N/A
Treatment rooms retail sales	$ 2,741	$ 2,802	$ 2,862	$ 2,923	$ 2,984	$ 3,045
Station rental	N/A	N/A	N/A	N/A	N/A	N/A
Total cost of goods sold	**$13,216**	**$13,520**	**$13,825**	**$14,130**	**$14,434**	**$14,665**

Monthly profit and loss—fiscal year one

Monthly pro forma profit and loss	Oct-04	Nov-04	Dec-04	Jan-05	Feb-05	Mar-05
Total income	$ 6,000	$ 8,900	$14,300	$15,800	$17,700	$19,800
Cost of goods sold	$ 1,391	$ 2,272	$ 4,313	$ 3,988	$ 4,869	$ 5,379
Gross profit	$ 4,609	$ 6,628	$ 9,987	$11,815	$12,831	$14,421
Gross profit %	76.81%	74.47%	69.84%	74.76%	72.49%	72.83%
Expenses:						
Payroll	$ 0	$ 0	$ 0	$ 0	$ 0	$ 0
Depreciation	$ 908	$ 908	$ 908	$ 908	$ 908	$ 908
Rent	$ 2,240	$ 2,240	$ 2,240	$ 2,240	$ 2,240	$ 2,240
Utilities	$ 500	$ 500	$ 500	$ 500	$ 500	$ 500
Insurance	$ 100	$ 100	$ 100	$ 100	$ 100	$ 100
Supplies	$ 900	$ 900	$ 900	$ 1,200	$ 1,000	$ 1,000
Advertising	$ 350	$ 350	$ 350	$ 350	$ 350	$ 350
Misc.	$ 70	$ 70	$ 70	$ 70	$ 70	$ 70
Payroll taxes	$ 0	$ 0	$ 0	$ 0	$ 0	$ 0
Total operating expenses	$ 5,068	$ 5,068	$ 5,068	$ 5,368	$ 5,168	$ 5,168
Profit before interest and taxes	($ 460)	$ 1,559	$ 4,919	$ 6,444	$ 7,662	$ 9,252
Interest expense	$ 408	$ 400	$ 391	$ 382	$ 373	$ 365
Taxes incurred	($ 260)	$ 348	$ 1,358	$ 1,818	$ 2,187	$ 2,666
Net profit	($ 608)	$ 812	$ 3,170	$ 4,243	$ 5,102	$ 6,221
Net profit/sales	−10.13%	9.12%	22.17%	26.85%	28.83%	31.42%

	Apr-05	May-05	Jun-05	Jul-05	Aug-05	Sep-05
Total income	$20,950	$24,150	$25,300	$28,700	$29,220	$29,630
Cost of goods sold	$ 5,913	$ 6,469	$ 7,002	$ 7,652	$ 7,893	$ 8,083
Gross profit	$15,037	$17,681	$18,298	$21,048	$21,327	$21,547
Gross profit %	71.78%	73.21%	72.32%	73.34%	72.99%	72.72%
Expenses:						
Payroll	$ 0	$ 0	$ 0	$ 0	$ 0	$ 0
Depreciation	$ 908	$ 908	$ 908	$ 908	$ 908	$ 908
Rent	$ 2,240	$ 2,240	$ 2,240	$ 2,240	$ 2,240	$ 2,240
Utilities	$ 500	$ 500	$ 500	$ 500	$ 500	$ 500
Insurance	$ 100	$ 100	$ 100	$ 100	$ 100	$ 100
Supplies	$ 1,000	$ 1,000	$ 1,000	$ 1,000	$ 1,000	$ 1,000
Advertising	$ 350	$ 350	$ 350	$ 350	$ 350	$ 350
Misc.	$ 70	$ 70	$ 70	$ 70	$ 70	$ 70
Payroll taxes	$ 0	$ 0	$ 0	$ 0	$ 0	$ 0
Total operating expenses	$ 5,168	$ 5,168	$ 5,168	$ 5,168	$ 5,168	$ 5,168
Profit before interest and taxes	$ 9,869	$12,512	$13,129	$15,880	$16,159	$16,379
Interest expense	$ 356	$ 347	$ 338	$ 330	$ 321	$ 312
Taxes incurred	$ 2,854	$ 3,650	$ 3,837	$ 4,665	$ 4,751	$ 4,820
Net profit	$ 6,659	$ 8,516	$ 8,954	$10,885	$11,087	$11,247
Net profit/sales	31.79%	35.26%	35.39%	37.93%	37.94%	37.96%

Monthly profit and loss—fiscal year two

Monthly pro forma profit and loss	Oct-05	Nov-05	Dec-05	Jan-06	Feb-06	Mar-06
Total income	**$29,600**	**$30,200**	**$32,300**	**$36,320**	**$32,900**	**$33,400**
Cost of goods sold	**$10,597**	**$10,963**	**$12,242**	**$14,690**	**$12,607**	**$12,911**
Gross profit	**$19,003**	**$19,237**	**$20,058**	**$21,630**	**$20,293**	**$20,489**
Gross profit %	64.20%	63.70%	62.10%	59.55%	61.68%	61.34%
Expenses:						
Payroll	$ 4,014	$ 4,094	$ 4,176	$ 4,260	$ 4,345	$ 4,432
Depreciation	$ 908	$ 908	$ 908	$ 908	$ 908	$ 908
Rent	$ 2,240	$ 2,240	$ 2,240	$ 2,240	$ 2,240	$ 2,240
Utilities	$ 500	$ 500	$ 500	$ 500	$ 500	$ 500
Insurance	$ 100	$ 100	$ 100	$ 100	$ 100	$ 100
Supplies	$ 992	$ 1,012	$ 1,032	$ 1,053	$ 1,074	$ 1,095
Advertising	$ 350	$ 350	$ 350	$ 350	$ 350	$ 350
Misc.	$ 70	$ 70	$ 70	$ 70	$ 70	$ 70
Payroll taxes	$ 602	$ 614	$ 626	$ 639	$ 652	$ 665
Total operating expenses	$ 9,776	$ 9,888	$10,003	$10,119	$10,238	$10,360
Profit before interest and taxes	$ 9,227	$ 9,349	$10,056	$11,511	$10,055	$10,129
Interest expense	$ 295	$ 286	$ 277	$ 268	$ 260	$ 251
Taxes incurred	$ 2,680	$ 2,719	$ 2,934	$ 3,373	$ 2,939	$ 2,963
Net profit	$ 6,253	$ 6,344	$ 6,845	$ 7,870	$ 6,857	$ 6,915
Net profit/sales	21.12%	21.01%	21.19%	21.67%	20.84%	20.70%

	Apr-06	May-06	Jun-06	Jul-06	Aug-06	Sep-06
Total income	**$33,900**	**$34,400**	**$34,900**	**$35,400**	**$35,900**	**$36,280**
Cost of goods sold	**$13,216**	**$13,520**	**$13,825**	**$14,130**	**$14,434**	**$14,665**
Gross profit	**$20,684**	**$20,880**	**$21,075**	**$21,270**	**$21,466**	**$21,615**
Gross profit %	61.01%	60.70%	60.39%	60.09%	59.79%	59.58%
Expenses:						
Payroll	$ 4,520	$ 4,611	$ 4,703	$ 4,797	$ 4,893	$ 4,995
Depreciation	$ 908	$ 908	$ 908	$ 908	$ 908	$ 908
Rent	$ 2,240	$ 2,240	$ 2,240	$ 2,240	$ 2,240	$ 2,240
Utilities	$ 500	$ 500	$ 500	$ 500	$ 500	$ 500
Insurance	$ 100	$ 100	$ 100	$ 100	$ 100	$ 100
Supplies	$ 1,117	$ 1,139	$ 1,162	$ 1,186	$ 1,209	$ 1,233
Advertising	$ 350	$ 350	$ 350	$ 350	$ 350	$ 350
Misc.	$ 70	$ 70	$ 70	$ 70	$ 70	$ 70
Payroll taxes	$ 678	$ 692	$ 705	$ 719	$ 734	$ 751
Total operating expenses	$10,484	$10,610	$10,739	$10,870	$11,004	$11,147
Profit before interest and taxes	$10,201	$10,270	$10,336	$10,400	$10,462	$10,467
Interest expense	$ 242	$ 233	$ 225	$ 216	$ 207	$ 198
Taxes incurred	$ 2,988	$ 3,011	$ 3,034	$ 3,055	$ 3,076	$ 3,081
Net profit	$ 6,971	$ 7,025	$ 7,078	$ 7,129	$ 7,178	$ 7,188
Net profit/sales	20.56%	20.42%	20.28%	20.14%	20.00%	19.81%

Monthly cash flow—fiscal year one

Monthly pro forma cash flow	Oct-04	Nov-04	Dec-04	Jan-05	Feb-05	Mar-05
Cash received						
Cash from operations:						
Cash sales	$ 6,000	$ 8,900	$14,300	$15,800	$17,700	$19,800
Cash from receivables	$ 0	$ 0	$ 0	$ 0	$ 0	$ 0
Subtotal cash from operations	$ 6,000	$ 8,900	$14,300	$15,800	$17,700	$19,800
Additional cash received						
Subtotal cash received	$ 6,000	$ 8,900	$14,300	$15,800	$17,700	$19,800
Expenditures						
Expenditures from operations						
Cash spending	$ 0	$ 0	$ 0	$ 0	$ 0	$ 0
Payments of accounts payable	$ 5,699	$ 7,180	$10,222	$10,649	$11,689	$12,670
Subtotal spent on operations	$ 5,699	$ 7,180	$10,222	$10,649	$11,689	$12,670
Additional cash spent						
Principle repayment of loan	$ 1,500	$ 1,500	$ 1,500	$ 1,500	$ 1,500	$ 1,500
Change in inventory	$ 4,000	$ 4,000	$ 4,000	$ 2,000	$ 1,000	$ 1,000
Subtotal cash spent	$11,199	$12,680	$15,722	$14,149	$14,189	$15,170
Net cash flow	($ 5,199)	($ 3,780)	($ 1,422)	$ 1,651	$ 3,511	$ 4,630
Cash balance	$22,831	$19,051	$17,629	$19,280	$22,791	$27,421

	Apr-05	May-05	Jun-05	Jul-05	Aug-05	Sep-05
Cash received						
Cash from operations:						
Cash sales	$20,950	$24,150	$25,300	$28,700	$29,220	$29,630
Cash from receivables	$ 0	$ 0	$ 0	$ 0	$ 0	$ 0
Subtotal cash from operations	$20,950	$24,150	$25,300	$28,700	$29,220	$29,630
Additional cash received						
Subtotal cash received	$20,950	$24,150	$25,300	$28,700	$29,220	$29,630
Expenditures						
Expenditures from operations						
Cash spending	$ 0	$ 0	$ 0	$ 0	$ 0	$ 0
Payments of accounts payable	$13,382	$14,726	$15,438	$16,906	$17,225	$17,475
Subtotal spent on operations	$13,382	$14,726	$15,438	$16,906	$17,225	$17,475
Additional cash spent						
Principle repayment of loan	$ 1,500	$ 1,500	$ 1,500	$ 1,500	$ 1,500	$ 1,500
Change in inventory	$ 1,000	$ 1,000	$ 1,000	$ 1,000	$ 0	$ 0
Subtotal cash spent	$15,882	$17,226	$17,938	$19,406	$18,725	$18,975
Net cash flow	$ 5,068	$ 6,924	$ 7,362	$ 9,294	$10,495	$10,655
Cash balance	$32,488	$39,412	$46,774	$56,068	$66,563	$77,218

Monthly balance sheet—fiscal year one

Pro forma balance sheet	Starting balances	Oct-04	Nov-04	Dec-04	Jan-05	Feb-05
Assets						
Current assets						
Cash	$ 28,030	$ 22,831	$ 19,051	$ 17,629	$ 19,280	$ 22,791
Accounts receivable	$ 0	$ 0	$ 0	$ 0	$ 0	$ 0
Inventory	$ 0	$ 4,000	$ 8,000	$ 12,000	$ 14,000	$ 15,000
Total current assets	**$ 28,030**	**$ 26,831**	**$ 27,051**	**$ 29,629**	**$ 33,280**	**$ 37,791**
Long-term assets						
Leasehold improvements	$ 45,000	$ 45,000	$ 45,000	$ 45,000	$ 45,000	$ 45,000
Equipment	$ 19,000	$ 19,000	$ 19,000	$ 19,000	$ 19,000	$ 19,000
Accumulated depreciation		$ 908	$ 1,817	$ 2,725	$ 3,633	$ 4,542
Total long-term assets	$ 64,000	$ 63,092	$ 62,183	$ 61,275	$ 60,367	$ 59,458
Total assets	$ 92,030	$ 89,922	$ 89,234	$ 90,904	$ 93,647	$ 97,249
Liabilities and owner's equity						
Current liabilities						
Accounts payable	$ 0	$ 0	$ 0	$ 0	$ 0	$ 0
Total current liabilities	$ 0	$ 0	$ 0	$ 0	$ 0	$ 0
Long-term liabilities						
Loan	$ 70,000	$ 68,500	$ 67,000	$ 65,500	$ 64,000	$ 62,500
Total liabilities	$ 70,000	$ 68,500	$ 67,000	$ 65,500	$ 64,000	$ 62,500
Paid-in capital	$ 30,000	$ 30,000	$ 30,000	$ 30,000	$ 30,000	$ 30,000
Retained earnings	($ 7,970)	($ 7,970)	($ 7,970)	($ 7,970)	($ 7,970)	($ 7,970)
Earnings	$ 0	($ 608)	$ 204	$ 3,374	$ 7,617	$ 12,719
Total owner's equity	$ 22,030	$ 21,422	$ 22,234	$ 25,404	$ 29,647	$ 34,749
Total liabilities and owner's equity	$ 92,030	$ 89,922	$ 89,234	$ 90,904	$ 93,647	$ 97,249
Net worth	$ 22,030	$ 21,422	$ 22,234	$ 25,404	$ 29,647	$ 34,749

	Mar-05	Apr-05	May-05	Jun-05	Jul-05	Aug-05	Sep-05
Assets							
Current assets							
Cash	$ 27,421	$ 32,488	$ 39,412	$ 46,774	$ 56,068	$ 66,563	$ 77,218
Accounts receivable	$ 0	$ 0	$ 0	$ 0	$ 0	$ 0	$ 0
Inventory	$ 16,000	$ 17,000	$ 18,000	$ 19,000	$ 20,000	$ 20,000	$ 20,000
Total current assets	**$ 43,421**	**$ 49,488**	**$ 57,412**	**$ 65,774**	**$ 76,068**	**$ 86,563**	**$ 97,218**
Long-term assets							
Leasehold improvements	$ 45,000	$ 45,000	$ 45,000	$ 45,000	$ 45,000	$ 45,000	$ 45,000
Equipment	$ 19,000	$ 19,000	$ 19,000	$ 19,000	$ 19,000	$ 19,000	$ 19,000
Accumulated depreciation	$ 5,450	$ 6,358	$ 7,267	$ 8,175	$ 9,083	$ 9,992	$ 10,900
Total long-term assets	$ 58,550	$ 57,642	$ 56,733	$ 55,825	$ 54,917	$ 54,008	$ 53,100
Total assets	$101,971	$107,130	$114,146	$121,599	$130,985	$140,571	$150,318
Liabilities and owner's equity							
Current liabilities							
Accounts payable	$ 0	$ 0	$ 0	$ 0	$ 0	$ 0	$ 0
Total current liabilities	$ 0	$ 0	$ 0	$ 0	$ 0	$ 0	$ 0
Long-term liabilities							
Loan	$ 61,000	$ 59,500	$ 58,000	$ 56,500	$ 55,000	$ 53,500	$ 52,000
Total liabilities	$ 61,000	$ 59,500	$ 58,000	$ 56,500	$ 55,000	$ 53,500	$ 52,000
Paid-in capital	$ 30,000	$ 30,000	$ 30,000	$ 30,000	$ 30,000	$ 30,000	$ 30,000
Retained earnings	($ 7,970)	($ 7,970)	($ 7,970)	($ 7,970)	($ 7,970)	($ 7,970)	($ 7,970)
Earnings	$ 18,941	$ 25,600	$ 34,116	$ 43,069	$ 53,955	$ 65,041	$ 76,288
Total owner's equity	$ 40,971	$ 47,630	$ 56,146	$ 65,099	$ 75,985	$ 87,071	$ 98,318
Total liabilities and owner's equity	$101,971	**$107,130**	**$114,146**	**$121,599**	**$130,985**	**$140,571**	**$150,318**
Net worth	$ 40,971	$ 47,630	$ 56,146	$ 65,099	$ 75,985	$ 87,071	$ 98,318

Campground

California RV & Campgrounds

41 Waterway Loop
Tenino, California 98589

Gerald Rekve

California RV & Campgrounds will be a fully–equipped, soft activity facility catering to families. It is situated in an area that is a destination spot for tourists looking for a beautiful and safe place to relax and enjoy a range of outdoor activities. There will be campsites for tents as well as fully–equipped RV sites.

EXECUTIVE SUMMARY

Business Overview
California RV & Campgrounds is a new business scheduled to start operations April 15, 2006.

California RV & Campgrounds is situated on the waterfront in Tenino, the gateway to Layout Sound, on the east coast of Los Waterville, California. Initially the business will offer 20 tent sites, each big enough for four people, and 10 fully–equipped RV sites. The campground will also offer a small laundry room, shower room, and recreational activities including: guided cultural hiking tours, summer fishing tours, whale watching tours, mountain biking trails, bird and wildlife viewing, photography, surfing, beach volleyball, picnic tables and barbeques.

Mr. Charles Pearce has cleared the land over the past twelve months. He holds Certificates of Possession on the land and has received a BCR from the Prince Albert Regional Park Partners for this project.

Financing will be sought through First State Bank in the amount of $70,000. When this amount is added to owners' equity of $11,500, a total project budget of $81,500 will be available. These funds will be used to establish the hydro and electrical infrastructure, place the RV pads, equip the office, make improvements to the trailer, and develop materials (brochures, business cards, and a website) to market the campground.

Operations
California RV & Campgrounds will operate year round with 3–5 anticipated permanent RV clients and seasonal tent camping clients. It will be sold as a safe, family–oriented destination that is easily accessible to Mainland and Coastal–region families.

Mr. Pearce already owns an aluminum skip boat (valued at $10,000) which will be used for fishing tours and whale watching tours. Mr. Jack Osborn has a 12 foot by 40 foot trailer (valued at $13,000) on the property which will serve as the office, laundry room, and shower facility for campers. The washer and dryer will be leased at a rate of $150.00 per month.

Upon approval of funding, California RV & Campgrounds will be incorporated for liability reasons. Due to the nature of the business it is not anticipated that California RV & Campgrounds will require an environmental audit.

Management Summary

Mr. Charles Pearce and Mr. Jack Osborn will be the sole owners and operators of the facility. Ms. Wendy Summers will be the company's bookkeeper and Mr. Bill Hamptom, CA will complete the company's annual financials.

With a projected 15% growth per annum, it is anticipated that that the company will hire two seasonal students in the summers within the first five years of operation.

BUSINESS STRATEGY

California RV & Campgrounds has a unique market advantage with a waterfront property in world famous Tenino. Because the property was leased from the government, there are no ongoing lease costs or facility rental costs associated with operations. In addition, the cultural knowledge and skills that both owners and staff bring to the operation will enhance the tourism experience.

California RV & Campgrounds will be located in beautiful Tenino, which is commonly referred to as the gateway to pristine Layout Sound on the West Coast of California. The site is only 4 miles away from the Pacific Rim National Park which features many boardwalks and a world famous old growth swamp. In addition, whale watching is featured in the region, as each year 20,000 Gray Whales migrate past Tenino on their way to their summer feeding grounds in the waters of Mexico. Other regional features include Long Beach where surfers challenge the breakers, natural hot springs in Hot Springs Cove, and the grouping of islands in beautiful Layout Sound where kayakers abound along with scuba divers and underwater divers.

Swamp tours consist of specialized boats equipped for client safety. These boats have both internal viewing areas equipped with air–conditioning as well as small snack vending machines. The outside viewing decks have chairs with seatbelts. Some of the tours take place in alligator–infested areas, so every precaution for client safety is taken.

GROWTH STRATEGY

According to *California Statistics 2002*, tourism is the second largest industry in California and camping represents 13% of this market. Furthermore, tourism revenues in California are up, reaching a new high of $9.2 billion in 2003, a 4.9 percent increase over 2002. The state also enjoyed a record 22.3 million visitors. *California Statistics 2002* also reported that developed camping and hiking—both of which are California RV & Campgrounds' primary attractions—will experience a 49 to 57 percent growth rate from 1995–2050.

A California Tourism study completed in 2002 found that eco–tourism in California generated $995 million in revenue in 2001 and employed more than 13,000 people, an 11% increase from the previous year. The second strongest area in tourism in California is retired tourism. In addition, the U.S Tourism Council also stated that a survey indicates that 25% of the international tourists showed interest in cultural experiences.

Success Factors

California RV & Campgrounds will operate with a strong experienced manager. It has a unique product and world–famous location within a growing and strong tourism market. The seasonality of the business is offset through the promotion and recruiting of long–term permanent RV residents who are conservatively estimated to number only three in the first year of operation.

FINANCIAL ANALYSIS

Item	Cost
20 RV pads	$ 30,000
Office furniture, computer, printer	$ 3,000
Hydro hook ups	$ 50,000
Electrical hook ups	$ 70,000
Incorporation costs	$ 2,500
Specialized boats (lease down payment)	$ 22,000
Marketing: brochures/website/CA	
tourist information centers	$ 4,400
Operating capital	$ 20,000
Total required	$182,000
Less owner equity	− $ 20,000
Total financing required	= $162,000

PRODUCTS & SERVICES

California RV & Campgrounds will be a fully–equipped, soft activity facility catering to families. It is situated in an area that is a destination spot for tourists looking for a beautiful and safe place to relax and enjoy a range of outdoor activities.

Initially the business will offer 20 tent sites, each big enough for four people, and 10 fully–equipped RV sites. The campground will also offer a small laundry room, shower room, and recreational activities including: guided cultural hiking tours, summer fishing tours, whale watching tours, mountain biking trails, bird and wildlife viewing, photography, surfing, beach volleyball, picnic tables and barbeques.

Mission Statement

California RV & Campgrounds will offer high–quality customer service and safe, family–oriented camping facilities as a profit and growth oriented business.

MARKET ANALYSIS

History of the Industry

Camping provides an opportunity to experience nature and the environment firsthand. Campers participate in fishing, hunting, swimming, wildlife viewing, and nature photography activities. Just as importantly, camping helps people escape the stress of urban life while providing physical benefits, including exercise from hiking, swimming and many other activities. Scouts, Girl Guides and many other youth organizations believe that camping instills confidence in youth and offers older campers' opportunities to challenge themselves in unfamiliar surroundings.

Camping takes many forms. In the 19th century, American naturalist and explorer John Muir routinely set off into the woods with little more than a sack of food and a journal to write his thoughts. In the early 20th century, American conservationist and philosopher Aldo Leopold paddled a canoe and rode horseback through the wilderness of the Midwest as a writer.

Modern camping enthusiasts may share the emotions of earlier naturalists, along with their desire to experience nature, but they usually camp in commercial campgrounds which serve as campsites for RVs and backpackers on the outskirts of national and state parks, along highways throughout the United States, and along both coastlines.

Present Conditions

Currently, there are over 230 campsites in California State Parks and numerous private ones, 23% of these on Los Waterville, California. The total number of recreational areas, state parks and ecological reserves equals a little more than 800. Most campsites are either within or next to state parks. State park campsites recorded 2.6 million visits in 2005, down from the year before. Los Waterville Island parks, however, bucked the downward trend with visits increasing by two percent in 2005. Campgrounds on the Island logged 788,888 visits and parks recorded 3.8 million day trips that year. On average, mid–Island campsites record an average of 73,222 overnight visitors each season. Independent campgrounds are generally less feasible due the land lease or purchase costs associated. This unique opportunity for California RV & Campgrounds to compete directly with industry campgrounds is a direct result of no lease or purchase costs associated with the site's Government Leased designation.

The campground business is undergoing some changes to meet consumer demand for a higher level of convenience and a wider choice of recreational activities, which California RV & Campgrounds will be able to fulfill. Studies show that successful campgrounds offer a range of on–site outdoor activities, as well as making the most of opportunities provided by the surrounding wilderness or park areas as California RV & Campgrounds does.

Competition

While the competition is intense on the Island with 45 campsites currently in operation, there is only one campsite listed for Tenino—"Pacific Rafting Adventure Resort". This company is geared more towards extreme adventure tourism and does not cater to the same soft adventure client that California RV & Campgrounds targets and therefore is considered an indirect competitor.

Additional indirect competitors for California RV & Campgrounds are six RV Campgrounds, three of which cater to specific target markets of: golf, fishing, and surfing. Of the remaining three, two are listed as resorts and represent a higher cost product. The sixth campground, Ocean Camp Campground, is considered a direct competitor. Ocean Camp Campgrounds prices are slightly higher; however they do offer a greater variety of site amenities but target primarily RV Campers.

Although competition in the camping sector is intense, sales for the Los Waterville Island industry have increased annually. Because of this, there are plenty of opportunities for newer, high–end campsites with all the facilities and conveniences. To be successful within the industry, a lake or ocean location in a superior natural setting is more important than ever. Proximity to other tourist attractions, such as a nearby town or city, is also an advantage.

OPERATIONS

Location and Facilities

California RV & Campgrounds is easily accessible by Island and Mainland residents, and during peak camping season (May, June, July and August) the campground will take advantage of high volumes of tourists traveling to California Tourist Information Centers.

California RV & Campgrounds will be a 23–acre property featuring 20 tent sites and 10 RV sites. The property is waterfront and will feature Prince Albert Regional Park art designs on the offices/washrooms/laundry room as well as offer culturally–minded hiking tours of the area.

Advertising

The company will advertise the campgrounds through various avenues including the Internet and a prominent ad in a brochure put out by the California Tourist Information Centers. We will take reservations by phone with a 50% deposit, which is the industry standard. Services such as guided cultural hiking tours and fishing tours can be offered at this time and will be undertaken by Mr. Charles Pearce who possesses an excellent knowledge of Prince Albert Regional Park history and culture. These aspects of operations are anticipated to represent less than three percent of overall revenues in the first year of operation. However, as demand for this unique service increases, the company will hire a site secretary to oversee the available services.

An artist will be painting the signs for the camp and the trailer to enhance the Prince Albert Regional Park artistry and unique features of this campground.

OBJECTIVES

Pre–Opening Goals

- Secure loan of $70,000 to develop site.

- Meet with local fire department to discuss fire safety regulations.

- Schedule contracts and contractors to establish infrastructure: water, sewage, and laying RV pads.

- Buy liability insurance.

- Begin minor construction work: paint trailer, install leased coin operated washer/dryer.

- Purchase office equipment, furniture and computer and establish administrative systems.

- Open a merchant's account with a local bank and set up a direct debit and Visa payment system.

- Undertake First Aid Training.

- Create advertising pieces, promotional items, and a waiver form for customers to sign to limit responsibility on the campground.

- Identify internet hosting company to register website name and establish website.

- Establish links with target communities through the California Tourist Information Centers and local Chambers of Commerce.

- Open for business April 2006.

A final compliance inspection under the Fire Services Act and Building Code is scheduled for April 10, 2006. The campsite should be fully operational by April 15, 2006.

Post–Opening Goals (Medium–term)

- Increase market share.

- 10% growth per annum.

- Lease pop machine.

Post–Opening Goals (Long–term)

- Add 20 more RV sites for a total of 30.

- Purchase and rent kayaks and canoes.

- Establish plan to sell convenience items.

MAJOR SUPPLIERS

Supplier/ location	Supplies	Terms
Timmons Construction, Tenino	RV pads	COD
Tenino Regional District, Tenino	Hydro/sewage/water	COD
Valley Gardens, Tenino	Grounds landscaping	COD
Ace Appliances, Coastal BC	Coin operated washer/dryer	5 year lease

CUSTOMERS

California RV & Campgrounds' target customers are from the Greater Los Waterville Regional District and Los Waterville. Studies show California campground visitors are mostly residents of California. The statistics reflect a growing number of American visitors who feel safe traveling in California.

Baby boomers are also a growing market. The average age of campground visitors is 35 to 55. Most visitors have a slightly higher than average disposable income (money to spend after all expenses are paid), with a family income of about $80,000 plus annually. Many visitors to campgrounds are families, with parents ranging from 40 to 55 and children averaging five to 15. This market segment has an annual income of from $60,000 to $80,000. The RV market, mostly retirees, has an average income of $45,000.

The primary market segments for the California RV & Campgrounds are families from the nearby Coastal region and the Lower Mainland area. The Coastal region has a population of 1,449,000, while the surrounding 200 mile radius now has a population of nearly 2.9 million. In California, 6 out of 10 families have children living at home; more specifically, 42% of all families in the state have children between the ages of 6–17. This group will form the majority of clients that are drawn to California RV & Campgrounds.

MARKETING & SALES

California RV & Campgrounds will adopt a strategic marketing campaign which includes: brochures, a California Tourist Information Centers agreement, a website, and networking within the region to schools and the local Chamber of Commerce.

California RV & Campgrounds will promote the campgrounds as a safe, family–oriented camping experience on the beautiful east coast of Los Waterville Island. Features such as fishing expeditions and whale watching will be touted. The guided cultural hiking tours will be advertised as a year long activity, because this area is renowned for its spectacular winter ocean storms.

The company will track the marketing methods to optimize their effectiveness by asking clients how they heard of the camp, maintaining client records, and sending annual postcards inviting former guests to return with a "wish you were here" note signed by the owners. These postcards will also act as the company's brochures and will be designed to the specifications as required by California Tourist Information Centers where they will be placed. The California Tourist Information Center's agreement will allow the company to place their brochures at the tourist information centers where there are very high numbers of tourists and along the ferry routes that bring tourists to the Island.

Further, the company will establish a website targeted to American tourists featuring many regional aesthetic features such as the Gray Whales, artwork images that backdrop the cultural hiking tours and images of the site and the beachfront with brilliant sunsets. Clients may call or email their inquiries or reservations to the campgrounds directly; this will ensure the safety of credit card payments and minimize the initial website costs.

Pricing Strategy and Occupation Rates

California RV & Campgrounds will offer the following services which are competitively priced within the industry for the range of on–site amenities offered:

- 10 fully–equipped RV Site hook–ups at $25.00 per night or $600.00 per month.

- 20 Tent sites at $22.00 per night.

- Guided Cultural Hiking Tours for groups of six or more at $10.00 an hour, per person.

- Fishing Tours for groups of six or more at a rate of $20.00 an hour, per person.

- Boat tours of swamp lands, $10.00 per person for a one–hour tour or $15.00 for a two–hour tour.

Campgrounds are a seasonal business, with modest increases in demand in April and May, a sharp rise in June, and a peak in demand in July and August. September sees a steady decline as the season winds down. August is an especially high camping month, accounting for 33 percent of state campground use. The average length of stay is three to four days. California RV & Campgrounds will take advantage of peak tourist seasons and California Tourist Information Centers tourism traffic. The company will also offer special promotional rates to targeted schools in the Coastal region and Lower Mainland.

The industry has previously been dominated by over 230 state–owned campsites. Today, private campgrounds are on the rise and tend to offer better facilities. During the peak camping season in July and August both public and private campsites are booked to full capacity in an industry where demand outstrips capacity.

During summer peak months it is expected that both RV and tent sites will be with a gradual curve in revenues from April and decline in late October. During the winter months it is conservatively estimated that three RV long–term residents will be booked.

Cultural hiking tours and fishing tours—as untested products—are conservatively estimated to result in less than 3% gross revenue per year. Annual sales are anticipated to increase by 10% per year for the ten RV pads. Due to the limited number of tent sites, annual revenues are not anticipated to increase in this area until the company can expand to develop additional tent sites.

All sales will require a 50% non–refundable deposit, which is industry standard, with the balance due upon arrival. The company will focus on customer service and will offer non–transferable "camping coupons" for their next visit for persons who have any complaints with their camping experience.

Business Feasibility and SWOT Analysis

Strengths

- Government leased land

- Tenino beachfront location

- Cultural component

- Competitive pricing

- Management experience

Weaknesses

- New entrepreneurs

- Limited marketing budget

California RV & Campgrounds will succeed based upon the company's prime location on the waterfront in Tenino, regional tourism draws, competitive pricing and lower operating costs as a result of no land lease or purchase costs. In addition, the company will benefit from the industry experience of Mr. Charles Pearce and the cultural component of operations that establishes a unique market advantage within the industry.

Car Wash

Platinum Car Wash

614 King Dr.
New Fredericksburg, Ohio 45231

Staff at BusinessandMarketingPlans.com

The car wash industry is over 10 billion dollars a year in this nation, and growing along with America's love for their automobiles and SUVs. This business plan is for a car wash that will offer a "superior express wash" at affordable prices. It raised $1 million for the company's owner.

EXECUTIVE SUMMARY

Platinum Car Wash Inc. is an S corporation and owned by Edward Green who is re–locating to New Fredericksburg, Ohio, from Chicago. Mr. Green recently sold the first Platinum Car Wash facility in Chicago to prepare for relocation. This business was profitable throughout his ownership. Mr. Green has successfully maintained profitability in his many business ventures.

Mr. Green will build a new conveyor wash and express oil facility on King Drive in New Fredericksburg. This ideal corner lot (King and Wyoming Blvd.) is at the center of the commercial district. Platinum Car Wash will be located across the street from the only major grocery store chain, a McDonald's, and a busy gas station. Development plans for this commercial district include the construction of a 38–acre Lowes store.

Platinum Car Wash offers customers a full service, automated, conveyor–style car wash, self–service car washing, and full–service oil and lubrication services. Our facilities are well lit, clean and attractive. We have 24–hour surveillance to ensure client well–being and peace of mind. Our prices are considerably more competitive than a standard conveyor car wash, $9.95 versus $15 to $24. Our excellent location gives customers the opportunity to service and maintain their vehicle during typical household errands.

The population of New Fredericksburg is estimated to change from 88,769 to 112,966, resulting in a growth of 27.3% between 2000 and the current year. Over the next five years, the population is projected to grow by 21.5%. The number of households in this area is estimated to change from 33,909 to 43,757, resulting in an increase of 29.0% between 2000 and the current year. Over the next five years, the number of households is projected to increase by 22.5%.

With well over 200 million passenger cars, vans, pick–up trucks and sport utility vehicles out on the roads in the United States, demand for automotive after–market services such as oil and transmission maintenance has grown steadily in recent years. According to *The U.S. Market for Automotive After-market Service Specialists*, a newly published Packaged Facts report available at MarketResearch.com, the number of cars in the U.S. has grown by about one million vehicles per year and the service sectors have seen a corollary expansion.

There are over 30,000 car washes in the United States. The car wash industry is over $10 billion a year in this nation and growing along with America's love for their automobiles and SUVs. It stands to reason that with 16 million or more cars being sold each year in the United States that car washes are good business. Mark Thorsby, executive director of the International Carwash Association, said preliminary findings from a new survey report a decline in home car wash because of lack of time, environmental awareness and technological improvements.

Objectives

·   To achieve first fiscal revenues in excess of $800,000, increasing to $1,000,000 in year six.

·   To achieve net cash flows in excess of $200,000 in the first fiscal year.

Mission

Platinum Car Wash understands that our customers do not want to waste their time or their money. We offer our customers superior services and amenities in a clean, comfortable environment coupled with fair prices. We give our customers value for their money and time.

Keys to Success

·   Experienced ownership and management

·   Newest in POS customer tracking systems and automated car wash technology

·   A successful marketing campaign and materials with experience in implementation

·   Experienced direct sales strategy to build annual fleet maintenance contracts

·   Solid, corner location in a commercial district that is growing

·   New Fredericksburg experienced a growth rate of over 25% for the past five years and is projected to grow in excess of 20% for the next five years

Financial highlights

Financial highlights	FY1	FY2	FY3	FY4	FY5
Total income	$898,350	$943,268	$990,431	$1,039,952	$1,091,950
Gross profit	$484,350	$508,568	$533,996	$ 560,696	$ 588,730
Net profit	$305,440	$329,955	$355,863	$ 383,248	$ 412,196

BUSINESS OVERVIEW

Platinum Car Wash Inc. is an S corporation and is owned by Edward Green who is re–locating to New Fredericksburg, Ohio, from Chicago. Mr. Green recently sold the first Platinum Car Wash facility in Chicago to prepare for relocation. This business was profitable throughout his ownership. Mr. Green has successfully maintained profitability in his many business ventures.

Platinum Car Wash offers customers a full service, automated, conveyor style car wash, self–service car washing, and full service oil and lubrication services. Mr. Green will build a new conveyor wash and express oil and lubrication facility on King Blvd, in New Fredericksburg. This ideal corner lot (King and Lucie Blvd.) is at the center of the commercial district. Platinum Car Wash will be located across the street from the only major grocery store chain, a McDonald's, and a busy gas station. Development plans for this commercial district include the construction of a 38–acre Lowes store.

Start-up summary

Start-up summary table

Start-up expenses	
Construction cost	$ 325,000
Total start-up expenses	**$ 325,000**

Start-up assets	
Pre paid expenses	$ 27,500
Supplies	$ 20,000
Total current assets	**$ 47,500**

Long-term assets	
Land	$ 650,000
Equipment	$ 500,000
Land improvements	$ 150,000
Total long-term assets	**$1,300,000**
Total assets	**$1,347,500**

Owner's equity	
Owners investment	$ 677,500
Total owner's equity	**$ 677,500**

Liabilities	
Current liabilities	
Total current liabilities	**$ 0**

Long-term liabilities	
Loan	$ 995,000
Total long-term liabilities	**$ 995,000**
Loss at start-up	($ 325,000)
Total liabilities and owner's equity	**$1,347,500**

Products & Services

Platinum Car Wash is a conveyor style, automated car wash. This system uses biodegradable non–phosphorus soap and is designed to reclaim and recycle 80% of water used.

Platinum Car Wash offers a superior express wash at a lower price than other full service car washes. We offer amenities for our customers such as free use of automobile vacuum and a two day weather guarantee. If it rains on a freshly washed car, within forty–eight hours, Platinum Car Wash will wash it again free of charge. Platinum Car Wash will also offer self–service wash facilities to capture both the "DIY" market as well as the "DIFM" (do it for me) market.

Platinum Car Wash is also offering a quick oil change service. Customers can accomplish two automobile maintenance chores at one time.

Competition

In the competitive car wash industry, consumers choose a facility based on the quality of the facility and the services offered. Platinum Car Wash offers a superior wash and convenience for our customers by offering both washing and oil changes. Our facilities are well lit, clean and attractive. We have 24–hour surveillance to ensure client well–being and peace of mind. Our prices are considerably more competitive than a standard conveyor car wash, $9.95 versus $15 to $24. Our excellent location gives customers the opportunity to service and maintain their vehicle during typical household errands.

Marketing & Sales

Platinum Car Wash has developed a series of promotional flyers and service outlines to use in building brand awareness and developing fleet contracts with various city agencies.

OPERATIONS

Facility Construction and Maintenance

Mr. Green's long–time success within the car wash industry has built relationships with the manufacturers of car wash equipment and suppliers. These relationships will ensure the timely construction of the facility as well as maintaining proper supply levels for continued customer satisfaction.

Fulfillment

All services offered by Platinum Car Wash are fulfilled onsite. Our hours of operation, staffing requirements and equipment maintenance are tailored to ensure peak efficiency.

Technology

The Platinum Car Wash facility will utilize the very latest in car wash technology. The state–of–the–art conveyor system is the most efficient, environmentally friendly system available. Our POS system is equipped with customer tracking software that will build in-house promotions. Customers will automatically receive oil change reminders and coupons for service.

MARKET ANALYSIS

The following demographic information is provided by Claritas and reflects 2005 statistics:

The population of New Fredericksburg is estimated to change from 88,769 to 112,966, resulting in a growth of 27.3% between 2000 and the current year. Over the next five years, the population is projected to grow by 21.5%. The number of households in this area is estimated to change from 33,909 to 43,757, resulting in an increase of 29% between 2000 and the current year. Over the next five years, the number of households is projected to increase by 22.5%. For this area, 44.8% of the population is estimated to be employed and age sixteen and over for the current year.

The occupational classifications are as follows: 23.3% have blue collar occupations, 58.5% are white collar, and 18.2% are service and farm workers. For the civilian employed population age sixteen and over in this area, it is estimated that they are employed in the following occupational categories: 10.8% are in "Management, Business, and Financial Operations," 16.0% are in "Professional and Related Occupations," 17.6% are in "Service," and 31.9% are in "Sales and Office," 0.5% are in "Farming, Fishing, and Forestry," 12.5% are in "Construction, Extraction, and Maintenance," and 10.8% are in "Production, Transportation, and Material Moving."

Most of the dwellings in this area (83.8%) are estimated to be owner–occupied for the current year. For the entire country the majority of the housing units are owner–occupied (66.7%).

The following chart indicates the growth of different demographic populations segmented by age.

Growth of different demographic populations, segmented by age

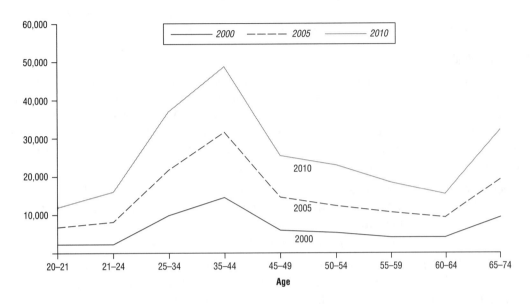

The following chart demonstrates the growth in income by the population of New Fredericksburg.

Growth in income by the population of New Fredericksburg

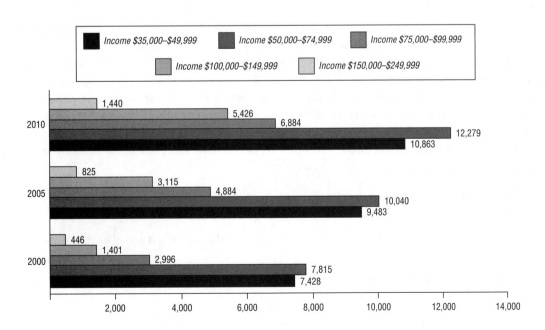

Market Segmentation

Platinum Car Wash has segmented their market into a B–2–B fleet market and the general middle income driving population. The need to maintain and wash an automobile is almost inherent with ownership.

Target Market Segmentation Strategy

Platinum Car Wash will build a strong fleet contract market through direct sales efforts and use of promotional incentives to build brand recognition within the community.

Industry Analysis

With well over two hundred million passenger cars, vans, pick–up trucks and sport utility vehicles out on the roads in the United States, demand for automotive aftermarket services such as oil and transmission maintenance has grown steadily in recent years. According to *The U.S. Market for Automotive Aftermarket Service Specialists,* a newly published "Packaged Facts" report available at MarketResearch.com, the number of cars in the U.S. has grown by about one million vehicles per year and the service sectors have seen a corollary expansion.

"The fact that we now have a larger vehicle fleet than ever before has combined with the growing number of older vehicles and increasing federal and state regulations to create a very healthy market for service specialists," said Don Montuori, Acquisition Editor for *Packaged Facts.* "We predict that the annual growth rate for the market will be at about 4% for the next five years."

The total aftermarket industry had estimated sales of $179 billion in 2001, according to the report and the Automotive Aftermarket Industry Association (AAIA). Of these sales, service repair constituted 69% of all aftermarket expenditures, making it the largest category within the industry. As technology renders automotive products more complicated the percentage of Americans who turn their car over to a professional for repairs and maintenance has grown significantly, resulting in over $123 billion in service sales in 2001 (AAIA figures).

There are over thirty thousand car washes in the United States. The car wash industry is over ten billion dollars a year in this nation and growing along with America's love for their automobiles and SUVs. It stands to reason that with sixteen million or more cars being sold each year in the United States alone that car washes are good business.

Mark Thorsby, executive director of the International Carwash Association, said preliminary findings from a new survey report a decline in home car wash because of lack of time, environmental awareness and technological improvements. With 50% growth in industry share during the past nine years, the industry appears to be attracting former do–it–yourselfers. The average labor cost to operate a typical full–service car wash is 35% of every sales dollar plus another 6% or more for workman's comp and payroll tax. Since the outlook for car wash services is robust, full–service operators and new investors should consider an operating platform that will help them thrive. Many more communities throughout the country are banning driveway washing and other types of car washes that do not conserve fresh water.

Many of the industry metrics are favorable:

• Average revenue for wand–bays has risen from $942 per month in 1991 to over $1,200 in 2004.

• Average revenue and net profits for in–bay automatic has risen by over $1.00 per car since 1991.

• In–bay wash volumes have trended upwards from an annual average of 12,100 cars per year in 1991 to over 21,500 in 2004.

• Exterior–only wash volumes have risen from an annual average of 51,000 cars per year in 1991 to 77,300 in 2004.

- Net profit for exterior–only has risen by over $1.40 per car since 1991.

- Full–service wash volumes have increased by 2,000 cars per year since 1991.

GROWTH STRATEGY

Competitive Edge

The greatest competitive edge Platinum Car Wash has is experienced ownership. Mr. Green has operated a successful car wash and has a deep understanding of how to meet client needs. His fair pricing, strategic experience, solid location and superior facility bring Platinum Car Wash to the forefront.

Advertising

Platinum Car Wash developed a successful marketing mix in the previous location. We will repeat that mix in New Fredericksburg.

We advertise heavily with flyer promotions, local print media outlets and by pairing promotions with local merchants. Our gas station promotions benefit both the station and Platinum Car Wash. A gas station customer purchases a set amount of gas and receives a $4 coupon towards a car wash.

Platinum Car Wash builds strong community ties by washing police patrol cars at no cost to the department. This public relations service builds goodwill for the business and also encourages officers to refer Platinum Car Wash and to use the service for personal vehicles.

Platinum Car Wash will develop a promotions campaign targeting the new local high school. Sponsorships of events and graduation coupons will attract this underserved niche.

Our "good weather" guarantee is a popular promotion. If it rains within forty-eight hours of having your vehicle washed at Platinum Car Wash, we will wash it again free of charge.

Our greatest marketing strategy is our ideal location and the attractiveness of our facilities. We will have outdoor signage and a clean, appealing facility. This attention to detail builds customer loyalty and strengthens brand recognition.

Sales Strategy

Mr. Green will meet with the heads of local agencies and vehicle fleet owners to negotiate service contracts. Currently under consideration are law enforcement service departments, the Department of Environmental Conservation fleet and private limousine or taxi services. Mr. Green was successful in building strong fleet service contracts at the previous Platinum Car Wash location, and anticipates repeating this successful sales strategy in New Fredericksburg.

Sales forecasts

Annual revenue forecast	FY1	FY2	FY3	FY4	FY5
Oil/lube rental income	$ 42,000	$ 44,100	$ 46,305	$ 48,620	$ 51,051
Full service	$756,000	$793,800	$ 833,490	$ 875,165	$ 918,923
Self serve	$ 72,000	$ 75,600	$ 79,380	$ 83,349	$ 87,516
Vending	$ 9,450	$ 9,923	$ 10,419	$ 10,940	$ 11,487
Vacuum	$ 18,900	$ 19,845	$ 20,837	$ 21,879	$ 22,973
Total revenues	**$898,350**	**$943,268**	**$990,431**	**$1,039,952**	**$1,091,950**
Cost of goods sold					
Water/soap/wax	$414,000	$434,700	$456,435	$ 479,257	$ 503,220
Total cost of goods sold	**$414,000**	**$434,700**	**$456,435**	**$ 479,257**	**$ 503,220**

CONSTRUCTION TIMELINE

- Preparation of site for foundation—2 weeks

- Pour footings and construction of shell—4 weeks

- Plumbing and wiring of building—5 weeks

- Installation of equipment—6 weeks

- Blacktop of parking lot and landscaping—1 week

- Total construction time for facility—18 to 20 weeks

MANAGEMENT SUMMARY

Platinum Car Wash is both owned and managed by Edward Green. His experience as a successful car wash owner is invaluable to the success of the new venture. Mr. Green has developed a successful system of marketing, fulfillment and customer satisfaction through previous car wash ownership. These successful systems will be replicated at the new facility.

Management Team

Edward Green has been a successful entrepreneur since 1992. He began with a 2,800 sq.–ft. furniture rental store that expanded from one to five locations in ten years. In 1994, Mr. Green opened the first Platinum Car Wash location and profitably ran the business until he recently sold it to relocate to Ohio. The Platinum Car Wash facility was founded concurrently with ownership of County Line Laundromat, which is still a successful business. Mr. Green opened and owned the Clean It! Laundromat in 1995 before selling the business profitably in 2000. Mr. Green attends the yearly national car wash owners and laundry mat owners' conventions and has developed strong contacts within the industry. He is also a member of the state's car wash and laundromat associations.

Personnel plan

Annual personnel plan	FY 1	FY 2	FY 3	FY 4	FY 5
General employees	$69,120	$72,576	$76,205	$80,015	$84,016
Total payroll	**$69,120**	**$72,576**	**$76,205**	**$80,015**	**$84,016**

FINANCIAL ANALYSIS

Expense forecast

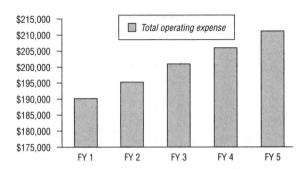

Key financial indicators

	FY 1	FY 2	FY 3	FY 4	FY 5
Sales	$898,350	$943,268	$990,431	$1,039,952	$1,091,950
Gross margin	$484,350	$508,568	$533,996	$ 560,696	$ 588,730
Operating expenses	$190,867	$196,077	$201,547	$ 207,291	$ 213,322

Projected profit and loss

Annual pro forma profit and loss	FY 1	FY 2	FY 3	FY 4	FY 5
Total income	**$898,350**	**$943,268**	**$990,431**	**$1,039,952**	**$1,091,950**
Cost of goods sold	**$414,000**	**$434,700**	**$456,435**	**$ 479,257**	**$ 503,220**
Gross profit	**$484,350**	**$508,568**	**$533,996**	**$ 560,696**	**$ 588,730**
Gross profit %	53.92%	53.92%	53.92%	53.92%	53.92%
Expenses:					
Payroll	$ 69,120	$ 72,576	$ 76,205	$ 80,015	$ 84,016
Depreciation	$ 86,667	$ 86,667	$ 86,667	$ 86,667	$ 86,667
Electric	$ 8,400	$ 8,820	$ 9,261	$ 9,724	$ 10,210
Gas	$ 600	$ 630	$ 662	$ 695	$ 729
Phone	$ 900	$ 945	$ 992	$ 1,042	$ 1,094
Insurance	$ 1,800	$ 1,890	$ 1,985	$ 2,084	$ 2,188
Sanitation	$ 1,080	$ 1,134	$ 1,191	$ 1,250	$ 1,313
Taxes	$ 700	$ 735	$ 772	$ 810	$ 851
Advertising costs	$ 7,200	$ 7,560	$ 7,938	$ 8,335	$ 8,752
Supplies	$ 9,600	$ 10,080	$ 10,584	$ 11,113	$ 11,669
Maintenance	$ 1,200	$ 1,260	$ 1,323	$ 1,389	$ 1,459
Misc.	$ 3,600	$ 3,780	$ 3,969	$ 4,167	$ 4,376
Total operating expenses	**$190,867**	**$196,077**	**$201,547**	**$ 207,291**	**$ 213,322**
Profit before interest and taxes	$293,483	$312,491	$332,449	$ 353,404	$ 375,408
Interest expense	$ 74,710	$ 69,202	$ 63,252	$ 56,824	$ 49,879
Taxes incurred	$ 0	$ 0	$ 0	$ 0	$ 0
Net profit	**$218,773**	**$243,289**	**$269,197**	**$ 296,581**	**$ 325,529**
Net profit/sales	**24.35%**	**25.79%**	**27.18%**	**28.52%**	**29.81%**

Projected cash flow

Annual pro forma cash flow	FY 1	FY 2	FY 3	FY 4	FY 5
Cash received					
Cash from operations:					
Cash sales	**$898,350**	**$943,268**	**$990,431**	**$1,039,952**	**$1,091,950**
Subtotal cash from operations	$898,350	$943,268	$990,431	$1,039,952	$1,091,950
Additional cash received					
Subtotal cash received	**$898,350**	**$943,268**	**$990,431**	**$1,039,952**	**$1,091,950**
Expenditures					
Expenditures from operations					
Payroll	$ 69,120	$ 72,576	$ 76,205	$ 80,015	$ 84,016
Operating costs	$109,790	$106,036	$101,928	$ 97,433	$ 92,519
Cost of sales	$414,000	$434,700	$456,435	$ 479,257	$ 503,220
Subtotal spent on operations	**$592,910**	**$613,312**	**$634,567**	**$ 656,705**	**$ 679,754**
Additional cash spent					
Principle repayment of loan	$ 68,582	$ 74,090	$ 80,041	$ 86,469	$ 93,414
Subtotal cash spent	**$661,493**	**$687,403**	**$714,608**	**$ 743,174**	**$ 773,168**
Net cash flow	**$236,857**	**$255,865**	**$275,823**	**$ 296,778**	**$ 318,782**
Cash balance	**$236,857**	**$492,722**	**$768,545**	**$1,065,323**	**$1,384,105**

Projected balance sheet

Pro forma balance sheet	FY 1	FY 2	FY 3	FY 4	FY 5
Assets					
Current assets					
Cash	$ 236,857	$ 492,722	$ 768,545	$1,065,323	$1,384,105
Pre paid expenses	$ 27,500	$ 27,500	$ 27,500	$ 27,500	$ 27,500
Supplies	$ 20,000	$ 20,000	$ 20,000	$ 20,000	$ 20,000
Total current assets	**$ 284,357**	**$ 540,222**	**$ 816,045**	**$1,112,823**	**$1,431,605**
Long-term assets					
Land	$ 50,000	$ 650,000	$ 650,000	$ 650,000	$ 650,000
Equipment	$ 500,000	$ 500,000	$ 500,000	$ 500,000	$ 500,000
Land improvements	$ 150,000	$ 150,000	$ 150,000	$ 150,000	$ 150,000
Accumulated depreciation	$ 86,667	$ 173,333	$ 260,000	$ 346,667	$ 433,333
Total long-term assets	$1,213,333	$1,126,667	$1,040,000	$ 953,333	$ 866,667
Total assets	**$1,497,691**	**$1,666,889**	**$1,856,045**	**$2,066,157**	**$2,298,272**
Liabilities and owner's equity					
Current liabilities					
Total current liabilities	**$ 0**	**$ 0**	**$ 0**	**$ 0**	**$ 0**
Long-term liabilities					
Loan	$ 926,418	$ 852,327	$ 772,287	$ 685,817	$ 592,404
Total liabilities	**$ 926,418**	**$ 852,327**	**$ 772,287**	**$ 685,817**	**$ 592,404**
Owners investment	$ 677,500	$ 677,500	$ 677,500	$ 677,500	$ 677,500
Retained earnings	($ 106,227)	$ 137,061	$ 406,258	$ 702,839	$1,028,368
Earnings	$ 218,773	$ 243,289	$ 269,197	$ 296,581	$ 325,529
Total owner's equity	**$ 571,273**	**$ 814,561**	**$1,083,758**	**$1,380,339**	**$1,705,868**
Total liabilities & owner's equity	**$1,497,691**	**$1,666,889**	**$1,856,045**	**$2,066,157**	**$2,298,272**

Monthly revenue forecast	Nov-05	Dec-05	Jan-06	Feb-06	Mar-06	Apr-06
Oil/lube rental income	$ 3,500	$ 3,500	$ 3,500	$ 3,500	$ 3,500	$ 3,500
Full service	$63,000	$63,000	$63,000	$63,000	$63,000	$63,000
Self serve	$ 6,000	$ 6,000	$ 6,000	$ 6,000	$ 6,000	$ 6,000
Vending	$ 788	$ 788	$ 788	$ 788	$ 788	$ 788
Vacuum	$ 1,575	$ 1,575	$ 1,575	$ 1,575	$ 1,575	$ 1,575
Total revenues	**$74,863**	**$74,863**	**$74,863**	**$74,863**	**$74,863**	**$74,863**
Cost of goods sold						
Water/soap/wax	$34,500	$34,500	$34,500	$34,500	$34,500	$34,500
Total cost of goods sold	**$34,500**	**$34,500**	**$34,500**	**$34,500**	**$34,500**	**$34,500**

Monthly revenue forecast	May-06	Jun-06	Jul-06	Aug-06	Sep-06	Oct-06
Oil/lube rental income	$ 3,500	$ 3,500	$ 3,500	$ 3,500	$ 3,500	$ 3,500
Full service	$63,000	$63,000	$63,000	$63,000	$63,000	$63,000
Self serve	$ 6,000	$ 6,000	$ 6,000	$ 6,000	$ 6,000	$ 6,000
Vending	$ 788	$ 788	$ 788	$ 788	$ 788	$ 788
Vacuum	$ 1,575	$ 1,575	$ 1,575	$ 1,575	$ 1,575	$ 1,575
Total revenues	**$74,863**	**$74,863**	**$74,863**	**$74,863**	**$74,863**	**$74,863**
Cost of goods sold						
Water/soap/wax	$34,500	$34,500	$34,500	$34,500	$34,500	$34,500
Total cost of goods sold	**$34,500**	**$34,500**	**$34,500**	**$34,500**	**$34,500**	**$34,500**

Monthly pro forma profit and loss	Nov-05	Dec-05	Jan-06	Feb-06	Mar-06	Apr-06
Total income	$74,863	$74,863	$74,863	$74,863	$74,863	$74,863
Cost of goods sold	$34,500	$34,500	$34,500	$34,500	$34,500	$34,500
Gross profit	$40,363	$40,363	$40,363	$40,363	$40,363	$40,363
Gross profit %	53.92%	53.92%	53.92%	53.92%	53.92%	53.92%
Expenses:						
Payroll	$ 5,760	$ 5,760	$ 5,760	$ 5,760	$ 5,760	$ 5,760
Depreciation	$ 7,222	$ 7,222	$ 7,222	$ 7,222	$ 7,222	$ 7,222
Electric	$ 700	$ 700	$ 700	$ 700	$ 700	$ 700
Gas	$ 50	$ 50	$ 50	$ 50	$ 50	$ 50
Phone	$ 75	$ 75	$ 75	$ 75	$ 75	$ 75
Insurance	$ 150	$ 150	$ 150	$ 150	$ 150	$ 150
Sanitation	$ 90	$ 90	$ 90	$ 90	$ 90	$ 90
Taxes	$ 58	$ 58	$ 58	$ 58	$ 58	$ 58
Advertising costs	$ 600	$ 600	$ 600	$ 600	$ 600	$ 600
Supplies	$ 800	$ 800	$ 800	$ 800	$ 800	$ 800
Maintenance	$ 100	$ 100	$ 100	$ 100	$ 100	$ 100
Misc.	$ 300	$ 300	$ 300	$ 300	$ 300	$ 300
Total operating expenses	$15,906	$15,906	$15,906	$15,906	$15,906	$15,906
Profit before interest and taxes	$24,457	$24,457	$24,457	$24,457	$24,457	$24,457
Interest expense	$ 6,426	$ 6,390	$ 6,355	$ 6,318	$ 6,282	$ 6,246
Taxes incurred	$ 0	$ 0	$ 0	$ 0	$ 0	$ 0
Net profit	$18,031	$18,067	$18,102	$18,138	$18,175	$18,211
Net profit/sales	24.09%	24.13%	24.18%	24.23%	24.28%	24.33%

Monthly pro forma profit and loss	May-06	Jun-06	Jul-06	Aug-06	Sep-06	Oct-06
Total income	$74,863	$74,863	$74,863	$74,863	$74,863	$74,863
Cost of goods sold	$34,500	$34,500	$34,500	$34,500	$34,500	$34,500
Gross profit	$40,363	$40,363	$40,363	$40,363	$40,363	$40,363
Gross profit %	53.92%	53.92%	53.92%	53.92%	53.92%	53.92%
Expenses:						
Payroll	$5,760	$ 5,760	$ 5,760	$ 5,760	$ 5,760	$5 ,760
Depreciation	$7,222	$ 7,222	$ 7,222	$ 7,222	$ 7,222	$ 7,222
Electric	$700	$ 700	$ 700	$ 700	$ 700	$ 700
Gas	$50	$ 50	$ 50	$ 50	$ 50	$ 50
Phone	$75	$ 75	$ 75	$ 75	$ 75	$ 75
Insurance	$150	$ 150	$ 150	$ 150	$ 150	$ 150
Sanitation	$90	$ 90	$ 90	$ 90	$ 90	$ 90
Taxes	$58	$ 58	$ 58	$ 58	$ 58	$ 58
Advertising costs	$600	$ 600	$ 600	$ 600	$ 600	$ 600
Supplies	$800	$ 800	$ 800	$ 800	$ 800	$ 800
Maintenance	$100	$ 100	$ 100	$ 100	$ 100	$ 100
Misc.	$300	$ 300	$ 300	$ 300	$ 300	$ 300
Total operating expenses	$15,906	$15,906	$15,906	$15,906	$15,906	$15,906
Profit before interest and taxes	$24,457	$24,457	$24,457	$24,457	$24,457	$24,457
Interest expense	$6,209	$ 6,172	$ 6,135	$6,097	$ 6,059	$ 6,021
Taxes incurred	$0	$ 0	$ 0	$ 0	$ 0	$ 0
Net profit	$18,248	$18,285	$18,322	$18,360	$18,398	$18,436
Net profit/sales	24.38%	24.42%	24.47%	24.52%	24.58%	24.63%

Monthly pro forma cash flow	Nov-05	Dec-05	Jan-06	Feb-06	Mar-06	Apr-06
Cash received						
Cash from operations:						
Cash sales	**$ 74,863**	**$ 74,863**	**$ 74,863**	**$ 74,863**	**$ 74,863**	**$ 74,863**
Subtotal cash from operations	$ 74,863	$ 74,863	$ 74,863	$ 74,863	$ 74,863	$ 74,863
Additional cash received						
Subtotal cash received	**$ 74,863**	**$ 74,863**	**$ 74,863**	**$ 74,863**	**$ 74,863**	**$ 74,863**
Expenditures						
Expenditures from operations						
Payroll	$ 5,760	$ 5,760	$ 5,760	$ 5,760	$ 5,760	$ 5,760
Operating costs	$ 9,349	$ 9,314	$ 9,278	$ 9,242	$ 9,206	$ 9,169
Cost of sales	$ 34,500	$ 34,500	$ 34,500	$ 34,500	$ 34,500	$ 34,500
Subtotal spent on operations	**$ 49,609**	**$ 49,574**	**$ 49,538**	**$ 49,502**	**$ 49,466**	**$ 49,429**
Additional cash spent						
Principle repayment of loan	$ 5,515	$ 5,551	$ 5,586	$ 5,623	$ 5,659	$ 5,695
Subtotal cash spent	**$ 55,124**	**$ 55,124**	**$ 55,124**	**$ 55,124**	**$ 55,124**	**$ 55,124**
Net cash flow	**$ 19,738**	**$ 19,738**	**$ 19,738**	**$ 19,738**	**$ 19,738**	**$ 19,738**
Cash balance	**$ 19,738**	**$ 39,476**	**$ 59,214**	**$ 78,952**	**$ 98,691**	**$ 118,429**

Monthly pro forma cash flow	May-06	June-05	July-06	Aug-06	Sep-06	Oct-06
Cash received						
Cash from operations:						
Cash sales	**$ 74,863**	**$ 74,863**	**$ 74,863**	**$ 74,863**	**$ 74,863**	**$ 74,863**
Subtotal cash from operations	$ 74,863	$ 74,863	$ 74,863	$ 74,863	$ 74,863	$ 74,863
Additional cash received						
Subtotal cash received	**$ 74,863**	**$ 74,863**	**$ 74,863**	**$ 74,863**	**$ 74,863**	**$ 74,863**
Expenditures						
Expenditures from operations						
Payroll	$ 5,760	$ 5,760	$ 5,760	$ 5,760	$ 5,760	$ 5,760
Operating costs	$ 9,132	$ 9,095	$ 9,058	$ 9,020	$ 8,983	$ 8,945
Cost of sales	$ 34,500	$ 34,500	$ 34,500	$ 34,500	$ 34,500	$ 34,500
Subtotal spent on operations	**$ 49,392**	**$ 49,355**	**$ 49,318**	**$ 49,280**	**$ 49,243**	**$ 49,205**
Additional cash spent						
Principle repayment of loan	$ 5,732	$ 5,769	$ 5,806	$ 5,844	$ 5,882	$ 5,920
Subtotal cash spent	**$ 55,124**	**$ 55,124**	**$ 55,124**	**$ 55,124**	**$ 55,124**	**$ 55,124**
Net cash flow	**$ 19,738**	**$ 19,738**	**$ 19,738**	**$ 19,738**	**$ 19,738**	**$ 19,738**
Cash balance	**$ 138,167**	**$ 157,905**	**$ 177,643**	**$ 197,381**	**$ 217,119**	**$ 236,857**

Concrete Coating Company

Techno–Coatings USA

4653 Hidden Knoll
Oxford, Mississippi 38677

Michele T. Bussone

Using this business plan, the owner of a company that uses concrete to restore, protect and beautify surfaces quickly raised $150,000 of the $250,000 he eventually hopes to secure from investors.

EXECUTIVE SUMMARY

Mr. Gary Wright, sole shareholder of Techno–Coatings USA (TCU), wants to borrow $250,000 and spend it over a period of 15 months. These funds will be used to grow his business. He will accomplish this growth by adding three additional crews and a manufacturing component for custom concrete work that will enable him to take on more and larger jobs. Growth is expected to hit $3,000,000 by the end of year 2.

Today's climate is extremely favorable to his type of business. New, larger custom homes are popular; remodeling older homes is still a growing industry and commercial renovations are finding concrete rehabilitation an economical choice while enhancing the appearance of the floors and/or walls.

This growth will require that he fully outfit the new crews; hire supervisors, stock necessary materials and supplies and have operating funds to cover expenses during the training and ramp–up periods.

In return, Mr. Wright will pay 12% interest annually on the investment for a period of five years. Investors can leave their monies in for the full period or withdraw at any time after two years. Since Mr. Wright basically is the company, insurance will be procured and maintained for the life of the investment to cover all monies involved. This insurance will cover both death and inability to perform his job.

Uses of loan	Time needed	Amount
Payment marketing materials and collaterals	Immediate (1–2 months)	$17,000.00
Crew # 2 set-up	Month 4 of year 1	$60,000.00
Added materials	Month 4 of year 1	$15,000.00
Crew # 3	Month 10 of year 1	$60,000.00
Storage building	For end of year 1	$18,000.00
Crew #4	Year 2	$60,000.00
Outfit manufacturing forms, equipment, materials for R&D	Year 1	$20,000.00

COMPANY HISTORY

This is Gary Wright's second year of operation. In that time he has created an excellent reputation for himself and his company based on professional and creative completion of each cement–based overlay project.

His "can–do" attitude has enabled him to set himself apart the average concrete refinishers or painters in the area. Remodeling was the initial area of work, but new home construction soon followed. Commercial renovation is becoming a popular and economical alternative to tile and carpet. Self–leveling overlays offer tremendous benefits that explain the widespread use in many casinos, hotels, restaurants, shopping malls, resorts, theme parks and office buildings.

NOTE: In situations where a concrete slab has cracked, spalled or aged, cementicious overlayment can provide a solution when compared with the time–consuming and cost alternative off ripping out the old slab and pouring new concrete. Self–leveling overlays, flowable, polymer–modified cementicious toppings have the huge advantage of setting within a few hours. Provided they are properly and regularly maintained, self–leveling overlayments will also last indefinitely, which offers a clear advantage over carpet, tile, vinyl and other more traditional floor coverings. Additionally, overlays are considerable less expensive than pricier alternatives such as granite, terrazzo or marble.

In central south Mississippi, Gary is in the forefront with this technology. With the advent of new paints, polymers and techniques, contractors needed some time to figure out what to do with these new products. Despite this, they're still learning and eager to realize the opportunities. Combine this with the improved willingness to spend on home improvements, and Gary has a winning combination.

OBJECTIVES

Gary's goals are to achieve sales of approximately $700,000 in Year 1 and over $3,000,000 in Year 2. He will accomplish this with four crews of experienced contractors primarily from the painting field. By far the majority of his people will be mature workers who realize that this is their last chance to make money and prepare for retirement. It is Gary's intention to retain his employees by creating a two–way commitment that works to everyone's benefit—including but not limited to competitive pay; a simple retirement plan; and recognition/bonuses for work well done.

His long–term goals are to create a niche for TCU in which he can offer new, creative designs and products while his staff performs the daily operations. His artistic designs coupled with the excellent training and execution of staff will ensure business continuity.

The overall objective for TCU is to create a sustainable organization that provides a good living for Gary and allows him to enjoy his family. TCU must also 1) provide a good living for his employees and laborers, and 2) provide a valuable service to home and business owners throughout Mississippi who wish to improve the intrinsic and aesthetic values of their properties.

PRODUCTS & SERVICES

There are three areas for his services: older home remodeling, new home construction and commercial renovation.

There is a great demand for materials and techniques designed to restore, protect and beautify concrete surfaces that have deteriorated due to normal aging, acid rain, salt attack and high traffic. Older homes and commercial buildings with cracks, stains, uneven surfaces or simply needing a face–lift are great candidates. He has even been working with counter tops, sinks and bathtubs for interior drama. Then consider new construction that wants the cost and durability of concrete with the look of tile or natural rock. (See the list of TCU services later in this plan.)

What we are discussing here is the implementation of ideas. Gary's forte is listening to what the customer wants—be it patio, living room floor, building entrance or bathtub—and converting that idea to reality.

His medium is concrete, his palette consists of paints, stains and polymers and his brushes are stamp kits, rakes and brooms. What he creates become integral parts of the buildings and items of pride to their owners.

Gary has taken a conventional business and raised it to an unconventional level; adding beauty and drama to horizontal or vertical surfaces.

MARKET ANALYSIS

Gary currently services a geographical market comprised of central, south Mississippi. His current size limits his range; but so far he has more work than he can handle.

A current list of customers who can keep his current and future crews working regularly is found later in this plan.

Once his crews are trained, jobs can be handled anywhere in Mississippi. A distinct advantage to the services is the fast–track turnaround time on most renovation projects. Even new construction schedules (concrete curing) can be adhered to fairly easily allowing work to be negotiated months out.

Competition

Suppliers of materials are offering paint and concrete contractors training in how to apply their products. Local contractors who used to spend their time repairing concrete in preparation for laying carpet are now being asked to add decorative finishes and skip the carpet.

Suppliers are not moving into the DIY (Do It Yourself) Market as there are too many ways to spoil a job. Warranty issues have always been a concern and even professionals new to the business have problems. Correct substrate preparation is mandatory. Too much moisture content will ruin a job, just as not following specifications exactly!

So competition is limited to the trades, primarily concrete finishing and painting contractors. Except for the largest companies, most contractors are either residential or commercial with little crossover. The larger companies can afford the training charged by suppliers and many will probably have some crews trained for their commercial divisions. Employees of contractors will also be taking jobs on the side. Small contractors may enter with minimal, if any, training. Some of these will "dirty" the business with poor workmanship.

Competition exists—always has, always will. But this is too hot of an area to ignore. Success will depend on two things: marketing and word–of–mouth recommendations.

OPERATIONS

Marketing & Sales

Gary needs to spend more time marketing the business. This is why the first supervisor will be his father–in–law, Sonny. Officially retired from his first career but still full of energy and ideas, Sonny has worked with Gary and understands the business. He also has extensive supervisory experience gained from his previous career. Gary will still design the job and mix the product for it, but will be freed from the routine preparation.

The first resource needed is a color brochure that can be for general distribution. The second resource is a more complete portfolio of jobs with before and after pictures, especially for the larger commercial and custom jobs. Both will require a professional photographer and a layout designer. The third resource will be actual samples of the possible finishes: field stone, brick, tile, acid–stained (with some color differentiation in all categories). As manufacturing starts, a website will aid in promoting the designs and concepts developed by Gary and his crews.

Word–of–mouth advertising has worked well so far in the residential sector. The brochures left behind with satisfied clients can be given out. Gary's work will be to get the brochures out to new–home builders and general contractors as well as to hotel, mall and office building owners and managers.

The promotion will focus on the substantial cost savings as well as quick turnaround time. Gary's time spent in sales will prove invaluable here. He knows his products and how to present them and himself. Armed with cost analyses of the various options his renovation services look really inviting. We must also look at the intangible to be marketed—the skill to create a one–of–a kind solution. The portfolio will assist, but the ability to listen and understand what a client wants and then deliver something a client falls in love with is a real factor here. When we spoke of competition, we also have to look at what separates TCU from the competition, and Gary's ability to work and think "out of the box."

Management Summary

Gary Wright is the only management at this time. He is an experienced Top Sales Achiever with a solid record of performance in setting benchmarks and a proven set of skills that include:

- Excellent Presentation
- Strong Closing
- Sales Process Knowledge
- Relationship Building
- Customer Service
- Staff Training
- Problem Solving
- Market Penetration

His principal personal strengths include a high energy level, an ability to set and attain challenging goals, and a healthy sense of urgency. He is a team leader and team player who can be counted on to attain better than expected results.

From 1996 to 2003, Mr. Wright was employed by Good Deal Enterprises in Jackson, Mississippi. He progressively advanced to positions of increased challenges and responsibilities in support of car sales operations that include: Sales Representative, Sales Manager, and General Sales Manager. In this role, he was selected by senior management to direct the expansion of this dealership from 2 acres to 7 acres and oversaw all aspects of construction. He concurrently hired and trained a staff of 27 personnel that included the sales and support staff. During this time he consistently met established construction goals while continuing to increase sales of new and used vehicles.

Before this, Mr. Wright was employed as a Food Broker for L&M Foods in Writer, Mississippi. While in this position, he aggressively marketed the company's preprocessed meat products to major accounts in Mississippi including Kroger's, H–E–B Grocery Company, Albertsons, Super K–Mart, Super Wal–Mart, and other grocery companies.

Gary's first supervisor will be his father–in–law, put in place to manage his crew. The second crew will be added within four months and will have its own supervisor. Ten months into Year 1 there will be a third crew and supervisor. Six months into Year 2 will be a fourth crew and supervisor. It is planned that most, if not all, supervisors will come from within the crews.

Gary will continue with the basic office functions, and be helped by his wife the first year. He will also continue to be advised by his accountant. In Year 2, a full–time administrator will need to be hired to free additional time for Gary.

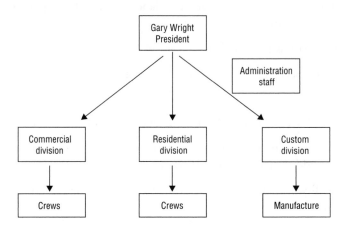

Here is a picture of TCU in five years. Gary is still the primary figure, spokesperson and leader. Each division will have its own manager as well as crews and supervisors. The administration section will have grown to accommodate the accounting and support needs of each division. Crew supervisors, depending on artistic and technical skill levels, will mix their own products for each job. It is not TCU's intention to develop a large organization but to maintain sales in the $10 million range, always with an emphasis on quality production versus quantity.

Financial Analysis

Techno-Coatings USA labor estimates worksheet

Position	Wages	Job starts	Conversion to employee	
Management (Gary)	4,500	Immediate	Immediate	
Crew supervisor 1	2,000	4 months into Y1	Immediate	Father In Law
Crew supervisor 2	3,500/mo	4 months into Y1	Immediate	
Crew supervisor 3	3,500/mo	10 months into Y1	Immediate	
Crew supervisor 4	3,500/mo	6 months into Y2	Immediate	
Replace supervisor (FIL)	3,500/mo	Start Y2	Immediate	
Crew # 1 (original)	Percent of sales	Immediate	Mid Y1	
Crew # 2	Percent of sales	4 months into Y1	1 month into Y2	
Crew # 3	Percent of sales	10 months into Y1	4 month into Y2	
Crew # 4	Percent of sales	6 month into Y2	3 month into Y3	
Crew # 5 manufacture	$15–17/hr	Start Y2	Immediate	

Assumptions:
1. Work crew can cover sales of $850,000
2. Supervisors will be drawn from crews
3. Crews start out as contract labor. If they last 9 months, they will have option for employee status with benefits
4. Crews hired 90 days before needed to allow time for training and ramp up

These expenses will be incurred as crews are added according to schedule.

Assumptions used in the preparation of proformas include:

Labor

- Labor runs 22 percent of sales.

- It is intended to operate with contract labor initially until an individual proves reliable, thoroughly knowledgeable on the job and requests a more permanent relationship with TCU, estimated to be nine months. At that point, they will become employees.

- TCU has been and will continue to take on more mature labor with a history in concrete construction to reduce the basic training time.

- Training is very important in this business because it is custom work.

- Payroll taxes are calculated for Social Security, Medi, TWC (2.7 percent) and FUTA.

Materials

- Materials currently run 18 percent of sales. Assume 19 percent due to recent increases.

- Even though economies of scale will be available at the higher volumes, we are not figuring this into the calculations. This should cover additional increases in costs.

- Sometime in year 2 a storage facility will be purchased and placed on Wright's land to house materials.

Interest

- Interest on the investment is calculated at 12 percent.

Personnel

- Gary Wright, in the first year, will be a full–time working Supervisor until his father–in–law Sonny can take over.

- Gary's father–in–law will work as the supervisor until the manufacturing operation grows. He will then relinquish that responsibility and will be replaced from within if possible.

- Gary will be spending more time mixing project stains for the crews, creating new products and marketing the business.

- A full–time office administrator will be hired to free Gary's time for the start of Year 2.

Description	Interior	Exterior
Concrete acid staining	X	X
Sealing	X	X
Concrete and wood decorative overlay	X	X
Repair overlay	X	X
Concrete counter tops	X	X
Concrete scoring	X	X
Vertical, horizontal decorative overlay	X	X
Floor preparation	X	X
Floor recovery	X	X
Bath tubs and sinks (custom)		

**Overlays: solid semi gloss, tile, stone, slate, brick

Services

Equipment list per crew

Description	Quantity	$ Amount
Trowels, rake, squeegees, etc	misc	500.00
1/2" drills w/paddles	2	400.00
300" Extension cords	2	150.00
4 1/2" Grinders w/blades	4	600.00
7 1/2" Grinder w/blade	1	450.00
Bead blaster	1	4,800.00
Buffer	1	1,000.00
Compressor	1	3,000.00
Concrete polishing kit	1	6,000.00
Crack chaser	1	1,500.00
Enclosed trailer 6 x 12	1	2,800.00
Ford 250/350 XL	1	27,000.00
Generator	1	800.00
Industrial wet vacs	2	400.00
Ligit set Stanley W2664	2	300.00
Maintainer and ladders	2	500.00
Paint gun and air hopper	1	1,700.00
Parking cover	1	500.00
Pumps	2	1,200.00
Rags, buckets, knives, tape, blades, paper	misc	250.00
Sales tax on items		950.00
Sanders w/discs	3	400.00
Stamp kits		4,800.00
		60,000.00

Some equipment may be found second-hand, but only new prices
are listed here.

Suppliers

Our suppliers are located in Mississippi and nearby states.

- Limeracoat

- KP Tile Store

- Kerry Contractors Supply

- Morfilled Polymers

- Lowes and Home Depot of Jackson, Mississippi

Customers

Our customers are all located in Mississippi.

- Gregg Custom Homes

- Sabinal Group

- N–Site Architects

- YP Construction

- Joyous Construction

- Marvin Gregg Homes

- Kenneth Quick Homes

- Purte & Larry

- FMT Management

- Leading Edge Flooring

- Insider Looks
- LL Tiling
- Horizon Green Solutions Inc.
- MS Construction

Custodial Cleaning Company

Spic and Span

1A Prestwick Ln.
Wilshire, Mississippi 39730

Gerald Rekve

A recent college graduate established his own custodial cleaning company after working with a consulting company, analyzing the marketplace, and writing this business plan.

EXECUTIVE SUMMARY

After graduation from Cooke Community College, Mark Hubbard knew he wanted to run his own business. One of Mark's first jobs was working for a cleaning crew. Mark worked in this job for two years, and then one day it hit him. He knew how to make this business more profitable and better for both the owner and the clients he worked for. So Mark proceeded to contact a firm to help with industry research and write the business plan. After doing this, Mark enlisted the help of his family to get the business going. While they are not partners, they helped finance the business. Starting in Year 2, each family member will be paid back their original investment plus 15%. Each of the four family members invested $17,000 to get Mark started in this venture.

Mark set up the company as a limited liability company, and has all four family members on the board of directors, along with one accountant and one lawyer.

MARKET ANALYSIS

Competition

We have reviewed the market and have determined that there is a lot of room for another Custodial Cleaner in the city. The city of Wilshire has a population of 400,000. Its business district is vibrant and prosperous. The GDP for the city puts Wilshire in the top twenty for growth this year. This is fueled by a strong manufacturing sector, since the biotech and computer sectors have been very stable and growing at a slow rate.

Right now there are ten firms listed in the local *Building Owners & Managers Association Directory (BOMA)*, as well as fourteen other firms listed in the local yellow pages. According to the yellow page ads there are only a few that offer services in all business sectors. This is good, because we aim to be a full service firm offering services to all sectors.

Right now there are 8,000 business listed with the city license department. There are 11,000 office spaces, warehouse, and commercial buildings in the city limits. Based on this, we are very confident that the new entrant to the market would be welcome. We made some marketing calls and determined that 40% of the respondents would welcome competitive quotes. We also discovered that the respondents have used a number of different providers but were not satisfied. They were willing to pay a higher rate if they could get reliable suppliers to cleaning services. This was especially a very strong statement from the banking sector. This sector had a total of 149 branches in the city.

Currently, the average cleaning company charged between .22 per square foot to .26 per square foot to clean office and commercial locations. After discussions with a major bank, they told us that if we could clean their 27 branches for a three month trial period with no issues or complaints, they would be more than happy to give us a three year contract. Based on this one contract, this would give us the following single–client revenue potential: 27 locations, with an average of 1500 square feet = 40,500 square feet × .34 per square foot. = $13,770 per month.

While we will grow our business, we have determined to start with our focus on winning this one client and, if we do, we will use this as a foothold to grow our business.

STAFFING

We will be cleaning 27 banks per night; this will include vacuuming, washing windows, cleaning bathrooms etc. Two staff will take 45 minutes to clean the average–sized bank (based on national averages). Therefore, in an eight hour shift starting at 6:00 PM, including travel time, each two–man shift can clean eight banks every night. We will then require the hiring of three two–man shifts to operate the cleaning; the owner will rotate in these shifts to insure quality control is being met.

The average cleaning firm is paying $7.00 per hour for cleaning staff. We will pay $7.25 per hour as a base wage. However, if there are no client complaints for the previous month, we will pay the two–man cleaning crew a bonus of $2.00 per hour. We are very confidant this will insure quality cleaning and low turnover. We want to keep turnover very low, as it costs $125 for each new employee to get bonded and trained. If there are no complaints for the previous six months, we will pay the two–man crew a $400 bonus. This bonus will be reduced by $100 per complaint.

All staffing will be given extensive training before they actually go into the market and clean our clients' offices. We will use a national training model that takes about four days to complete. We will do this in a rented training room within a local hotel.

All staff will be required to be bonded. Having said this, some new hires may not be bonded (i.e. recent bankruptcy victims), and if we have a good feeling about the employee we will absorb the fee for bonding.

All staffing will be required to have a driver's license; however they do not require a vehicle, as we will offer them a company van. This will insure there is never a situation where our staff are stranded or can't make it to a client's job site.

GROWTH STRATEGIES

Strategic Alliances

We will become a member of *BOMA (Building Owners Managers Association)*. This will allow us to connect with all of our potential clients at functions. We believe this will be one of our keys to success. The other key to our success will be referrals from happy clients, so we will work hard to win and keep clients. We will also join the local board of trade and other business associations.

Advertising

We will run ads for our services in the local yellow pages; we will run a sustaining ad campaign in the local business newspaper. This will give us a targeted market advertising approach, with the key to success: winning new long–term clients. There will come a time when these clients will grow us to a point where we have reached a market share that meets our goals.

Products & Services

The cleaning business is as simple as a business can get. All you need to do is keep things clean, using state–of–the–art cleaning products and skills, and as required by the client.

Services Offered

- Office cleaning

- Carpet shampooing

- Warehouse cleaning

- Window cleaning, high–rise

- Shredding of documents (with clients' equipment)

- All general cleaning

- Hazardous waste cleaning (will be added Year 2)

- Crime scene clean up

The rates we charge for this service varies from a per square foot to a flat fee service. An example of flat fee service is crime scene clean up, where we charge a flat fee starting at $995 plus supplies up to $5500. These fees are assigned by the local city purchasing department and each service is given a number in terms of severity by the police department. The higher number gets the higher fee.

EQUIPMENT

Necessary Equipment

- 4 company vans

- 4 complete sets of cleaning equipment

- 20 company uniforms

- Office equipment (laptop computers, maps, etc.)

- 1 carpet steamer/shampooer

- 6 vacuum cleaners

We have also set up an account with a local wholesaler to supply us with large volumes of the required cleaning products at discounted prices.

FINANCIALS

We just bought the company vehicles, allowing us to write them off. We will trade them in every four years or sell them outright while buying new replacement vehicles. These units will serve a couple of purposes: they will provide our image as professional and they will transport our workers to each site without the worry of staff not showing up for work.

- The cost of these bare bone vans are $12,250 each or a total of $49,000

- Specialized cleaning equipment—$2,500

- Vacuums—$4,000

- Uniforms—$1,800

- First month cleaning supplies—$700

- Yellow page ad deposit—$1,200

- Memberships in clubs—$1,400

Total start–up costs—$60,600 plus any employee hiring expense.

After we get the contract signed from the bank for the three month trial we will have thirty days to assemble our staff and equipment. Based on review we can have all the equipment in one week; we will start running ads now to get the hiring process started.

COMPETITION

As mentioned above in the market analysis, we have determined that the competitors in the market are working at a maximum. They are either very happy with their market share or can see the need to expand the market share. This is to our benefit as we move forward. Of all the competitors, there are only four that are affiliated with a national chain, the rest are small independent firms. Having said this, when we called each of them to drop into our accountant's office to offer their services we noted that only the four from the national chain had company vans. The rest of the companies said this was not required. We also noticed that based on their appearance and presentation, we would very quickly be able to take market share away from them.

While we don't want to underestimate our competition, we do believe that sales presentation and appearance will go a long way in selling our services to new clients. We need to separate ourselves from the competition and by doing so will win the high fee contracts.

Daycare
Childhood Dreams Inc.

132 Glenn
West Town, Ohio 44256

Gerald Rekve

Childhood Dreams Inc. was formed in late 2004 by Selma Tramon. Selma had worked in the retail arena for a number of years. After selling her dollar store, Selma realized that she enjoyed children. Selma's children were grown and she wanted to somehow incorporate her love of children into a new business. She enlisted in the help of a consulting firm to develop this business plan and research the daycare industry.

EXECUTIVE SUMMARY

Market Analysis

West Town is a quiet city of 100,000 people. It is an active vibrant community with six high schools and eight junior and preschools. The population is broken down into the following categories:

- 0–5 = 8,000

- 6–10 = 12,000

- 11–18 = 8,000

- 18–29 = 15,000

- 30–45 = 20,000

- 46–65 = 35,000

- 66 + = 11,000

Currently there are sixty–six daycare/childcare facilities in the city, with an average of twelve children per site. There are 38,000 homes in the region, including single–family and multi–family units. The average income per household is $44,230. Last year the average family spent $560 per month on daycare. There were 792 childcare spaces booked last year, at a rate of $25 per child per day. The daily revenue was $19,800.

We called all sixty–six day care facilities and determined that on average there was only 8% vacancy. However, most of the owners told us these would be booked up quickly, as the turnover rate was low.

The local state government provides a $5 per child rebate for families under $36,900 per year in household income. Based on the averages, we will be pricing our daily daycare rate in the $33–38 range.

We did notice in our market analysis that only 12% of the child care providers offered service to the mentally challenged. Most of the child care providers explained that due to the high cost of specialized staffing, they would not get involved in that area. However, upon further research, we determined this perception was incorrect. After calls to the state department responsible for this area, we determined that the state would offer special grants.

Grants from State and Federal Governments

- For each child that is medically challenged, $12 per day over the rate we charge that parent. We cannot charge more than $38.00 per day total.

- Plus a $120 per month special education training needs grant per child

- Plus a food allowance of $9 per day per child

- Plus a special transportation allowance grant of $4–$18 per day per child (the less children you have who meet the requirements the higher the rate you are paid)

- Plus free medical transport for any one of these special needs children, if they require any medical care or transportation by emergency vehicles.

- Plus a monthly mailing of free children's books, as long we take care of special care children.

- Plus a wage incentive grant to hire certified staff to maintain these children, the federal government would pay 59% of the wage of these staff. The going rate for these staff is $18.00 an hour. This means we can hire this person for around $8.20 per hour.

Based on our study and as indicated from the available grants, the mentally challenged population is underserved. Most families of mentally challenged children have the children under the care of a family member or have reduced their work schedule in order to insure their children are managed properly. Based on this specific need, we redirected our efforts from opening a standard childcare daycare facility to creating an office location with typical business hours.

OPERATIONS

Market Analysis

As mentioned in our market analysis, we were able to identify a market opportunity we did not know existed. This allowed us to revise our business planning and direction. In our market analysis we found a few different grants to operate our facility, and we are very confidant that most of the providers in our city were not fully aware of these grants. We feel there is a great opportunity.

Location

We have done a site selection and after reviewing a number of locations, we have made the determination that the best location is the one that follows the this criteria:

- Centrally located

- Free parking

- Ground floor

- Easy walking access to parks, theaters, and other kid–friendly places

- Great lighting for night

- Side area attached to the location, with greenery

- Outside place for gym and play toys

- Large front windows, to generate a lot of light

- Over 3,000 square feet of space at a rate of no more than $1,400 per month

- No unacceptable business types within ten city blocks of the childcare location
- Landlord who will insure the quality of the tenants who share the building. It is important to sign a lease with these protections and understanding of our services, as well the need to offer security to our clients.

Staffing

We will offer child care services six days a week, from 6:00 am to 7:00 pm. This will make it easy for clients to drop of their children as required.

Staff Requirements

- 2 full–time, certified staff
- 8 full–time staff
- 3 part–time staff
- 2 front counter staff (for phone and customers)
- 1 janitorial staff
- 1 accounting staff
- 1 office manager (owner)

Customers

Revenue Opportunities

- Standard childcare
- Challenged children childcare, for both mentally and physically challenged children
- Part–time daycare, for parents who just want to drop their children for a couple of hours

Security

We strongly believe that security is very important for us and our clients. Therefore we have taken extra steps to insure the security of the location and the children and staff.

We will install a complete video surveillance system. Our clients will be able to view their children at any time via the internet secure video link. The clients will be required to register for this service, but this service will be free.

We will have each client check their child in and out each day. The person who picks the child up at the end of the day will be required to be registered. If they are not, they cannot pick up the child. Each child once checked in the morning will be given an ankle bracelet that will send off a unique alarm and will identify which child's alarm is ringing.

We will also pay for a security system for the location. Each staff will be given special training on security, and local law enforcement will be notified of our location.

We will continue to review our security systems so they meet our clients' needs.

Expenses

Furniture/Equipment Needs

- Video surveillance system
- 2 computers
- 1 printer
- 1 fax machine

- 1 software system to keep kids safe
- Play area toys
- 2 office desks
- 1 refrigerator
- 1 cooking stove
- 1 microwave
- Kitchen cabinets
- 20 kids' desks
- Accounting and word processing software
- Educational equipment for the children
- 8 bunk beds for children's nap time
- 10 computers for teaching children

FINANCIAL ANALYSIS

Annual Fixed Costs

Annual Staffing Costs:

- 2 full–time certified staff—$79,040
- 8 full–time staff—$122,880
- 3 part–time staff—$24,960
- 2 front counter staff, for phone and customers—$33,280
- 1 janitorial staff—$14,500
- 1 accounting staff—$29,500
- 1 office manager (owner)—$40,000 + profits

Total annual staffing costs: $344,160 + (8%) $27,532.80 = $371,692.80

Retail Location Costs

- Rent—$16,800
- Heating & Lighting—$7,500
- Telephone—$1,885
- Yellow Page ad—$4,200
- Security System & Monitor—$2,300
- Advertising Costs—$5,000
- Food Items—$4,800
- Misc Items—$4,000

Total Estimated Annual operating costs—$46,485

Note, as part of our negotiation with the landlord, the landlord has agreed to pay for a leasehold improvement to the location, in exchange for a 5 year lease.

Revenue Potential

Based on the market, we have estimated an average of forty–two children per day at $36 per day. This will result in revenue of $471,744 per year. If you factor in the government grants possible for this service, our net profit margin will be higher.

The lease will be signed in March 2007 and it will take approximately one month to complete the necessary renovations. We will be in operation in May of 2007. All applications for the grants have been completed and approved. Our requirement for a $40,000 operating line of credit has already been established. Most of the staff has been hired.

Daycare

Ziggle Zag Zip Daycare/Childcare

1413 Appleby Way
Appleton, Wisconsin 54911

Gerald Rekve

Our vision and mission is simple: provide high quality childcare to families, single mothers, and single fathers in an affordable manner. Using new ideas in childcare management, we will offer field trips, full day services (7 am to 8 pm), and full weekend hours. We will also provide computers, books and other educational services, all in a fun and safe environment. Furthermore, all of our staff will be trained or will hold a child care certificate from a recognized school or college. While there are a number of competitors in the market, none offer the full range of services that we offer, especially for such a competitive price.

EXECUTIVE SUMMARY

Products & Services

Rates

One of the key ingredients to a successful business is understanding our market. We know that we cannot be everything to everyone; however we do feel strongly that when it comes to daycare, we can and will offer services to all income brackets. In fact, government cuts on services to low income people is one of the key motivations for this daycare business.

To this end, we will be the first in this state to offer rates based on income. While it could be argued that this is unfairly biased against higher income families, we would disagree. In fact we are very confidant that higher income families will embrace our approach, because in the long run, we are offering high–end day care to everyone, not just the families that can afford to pay for this service.

We will use the following formula to determine what we charge for our services. Based on the latest income tax return, we will determine the family's gross annual income. Using this figure, the rates are determined by the following schedule:

- Under $25,000 per year = $14.00 per child per day

- $25,000–$40,000 per year = $24.00 per child per day

- $40,000–$75,000 per year = $29.00 per child per day

- $75,000 + per year = $36.00 per child per day

In addition, single mothers with an income below $25,000 annually will be eligible for free bus services. Furthermore, families with more than one child in our care will be eligible for a 30% discount for each additional child off our income–based rates.

Bus service to and from home will be available for a charge of $7.00 per family per day, regardless of the number of children.

MARKET ANALYSIS

Market potential for Ziggle Zag Zip Daycare is based on the number of children in the market. This number is based on the most recent U.S. Census.

According to the census data, there are 2,158 children under the age of 6 years old living in our market area; there is also an additional 2,502 children between the ages of 6 and 12. Therefore there are 4,660 children under the age of 12 years in our area.

Our total market size is 4,660 children x $25 per child per day (an average price point). This means our highest revenue potential is $116,500 per day. In order to determine how much of this market realistically could be converted to our services, we must first understand the market and our competitors.

Competition

We have estimated the number of home–based and unlicensed daycare locations to be about 12, with an average of 4 children per house. Each of these daycares charges from $15–$25 dollars per day. The target market for these home–based daycares is low income homes.

Our focus will be to offer competitive rates to these home–based daycares, with all the added benefits of full–time day care and services like computers, an outside play area, and field trips with parent volunteers.

Other daycares that present competition are those that are registered with the state and follow all the required policies. The average prices of these daycares are $29–$38 per day per child.

Most of these daycares have outside play areas; few have computers for children; and none have transportation for picking children up or taking them to field trips.

The average daycare takes care of 14 children on a Monday to Friday basis. Only 2 of these daycare centers offer weekend or evening childcare. We feel this is a dramatically under–served population based on the large retail and manufacturing sectors that work shift–work up to 18 hours per day.

OPERATIONS

Staffing

Staffing is the most important part of a successful day care. Therefore we will make extra efforts to insure all our staff has the proper training. All our staff will be certified child care workers. Additional training will be provided in the following areas:

• Client management

• Child safety while under our care

• Various classes on different educational methods, etc.

The pay rate will vary from $7–$11 per hour, based on the duties of the staff and the training they bring to our company. The cooks and bus drivers will also act as daycare workers when they are not cooking or driving the buses.

One area we will partner with is the Red Cross. We will have each member of our staff get training in life rescue and other applicable first aid classes.

Our current staff consists of:

- 8 child care workers
- 2 cooks/child care workers
- 2 day managers
- 2 bus drivers/child care workers
- 1 accountant

We will also hire contractors to do various maintenance work as required.

Equipment

Transportation Bus

We will be purchasing a Blue Bird transportation bus. Our research has determined that Blue Bird is the best bus line based on customer satisfaction and safety requirements. Their line of Micro Bird small buses exceeds all requirements of Federal Motor Vehicle Safety Standards for school–bus constructed vehicles and is equipped with safety features such as a heavy–duty steel roll cage, purpose–built child restraint seats, a full–view outward opening entrance door and a special driver–view window. The seating capacity of the bus we will be purchasing is 10–20 people, including the driver.

Indoor Furniture

We will be buying all our indoor furniture from Little Tikes for the simple reason that they offer product warranties and insurance if any children are injured on their products. This is very important for our daycare, as it helps reduce the cost of insurance and provides our children with a safe and fun place to be.

Computers

We will have 12 desktop computers, all with the highest level of security features available from software developers. While there will be internet access, these computers will mostly be used to train children on the use of computers and to play educational games. Classes will be taught by the staff, and other computer use will be monitored by the staff. The computers will be maintained by the lease company as part of our lease agreement.

Outside Playground

We have chosen the Childscape Playgrounds for our outside play area equipment based on quality, price and warranty. We will be contacting them directly once we get financing in place to purchase various pieces.

Location Rental

We will work closely with our commercial real–estate agent to ensure the following requirements are met for our location:

- Centrally located
- Maximum rent of $1,200 per month
- Minimum 2,000 square feet
- 5 year lease, with all lease hold improvements paid by landlord
- Large fenced outdoor area to set up play equipment
- Just off major roads, allowing for easy access
- Low visible location, keeping it safer for children and staff
- Street level space (no second floors or basements)

Security

We will pay a monthly monitoring fee to a local security company. They will place security cameras throughout the childcare facility and will outfit the bus with wireless cameras. This will allow for management and staff to monitor all activity at the daycare. This will also allow parents to view their children remotely though a secure server they only have access to when their child is in care. When the child no longer is in our daycare, the parent's password will be disabled.

With the recent advances in technology, we will place a GPS watch on each child. The watch looks like a watch and keeps time like a watch, but it also acts as a tracking device so that we and the parents can know where their child is every minute of the day. These watches are safe for the child and can only be taken off by staff or remotely by the GPS tracking company via local or state police. This is included for all children in our care at no additional cost to families.

In–depth background checks will also be done on all potential staff.

Field trips will always be managed by one staff member per 8 children, in addition to the bus driver and one day manager. While this is not required by state laws, we will provide this for extra security for our children.

GROWTH STRATEGY

Our mission for the type of daycare we are opening is to have word of mouth transcend our success for future years. We are also of the mind that to start a business, you must first get the word out to potential clients.

To accomplish this task, we will offer free child safety classes where we will teach parents what they can do to keep their children safe. Local law enforcement and local media will be in attendance and this is where the parents will discover our new approach to running a daycare.

We will also try the traditional methods of advertising:

- Yellow pages advertisement

- Daily ad in classifieds of local newspapers

- Mailers to local businesses and subdivisions

FINANCIAL ANALYSIS

Start–Up Costs

Start–up costs are based on the assumption we will not have any revenue in the first three months of operation. Therefore we have determined that a start–up cost of $304,000 will be required prior to commencing operations. We will invest $75,000 of our own and seek the remainder in funding from banks and other sources.

Income

Based on our market review, we have determined that the size of the market we are entering has sufficient numbers to offer our company an opportunity to take a large market share. We project the first year gross annual sales will be $468,984 and our expenses will be $399,095 before taxes. Thus, our EBITA will be $49,525.

Based on a 5% increase in our fees coming in to year two, we will have projected revenue of $492,433 and EBITA of $121,975. This is an increase in EBITA of 246% over year one. We project that years three, four and five will have a 5% increases in revenue also.

One-year cash projection

Sources of cash

1. Personal funds	75,000
2. Loan proceeds	75,000
3. Cash receipts from business (net)	154,000
Total sources	**304,200**

Uses of cash

4. Equipment/Supplies	32,000
5. Vehicle purchase/Lease	4,320
6. Real estate	1,200
7. Fixtures	9,300
8. Security deposits (rent and utility)	9,000
9. Signs	9,200
10. Leasehold improvements	7,500
11. Cost of goods sold	52,360
12. Telephone and utilities	4,500
13. Rent	43,800
14. Business license fee	3,080
15. Insurance premiums	6,000
16. Office supplies	2,000
17. Legal and accounting	6,760
18. Advertising	9,000
19. Real estate taxes	3,700
20. Miscellaneous expense	6,000
21. Payroll taxes and benefits	9,240
22. Payroll wages (excluding withholdings)	46,200
23. Loan payments (principal and interest)	15,000
24. Owner's draw	24,840
Total uses	**305,200**
Net cash flow for the year (source minus uses)	**0**

Dentist's Office
Fremont Dental Office

31145 Brownell Blvd.
Fremont, California 90010

Gerald Rekve

Upon graduation from dental school, three partners took a unique approach to finding a dental office without incurring a lot of debt. This business plan outlines the steps they took to establish themselves in the industry.

EXECUTIVE SUMMARY

Joshua Williams, Eric Grey, and Rich Trame all had just graduated from dental school. All three were determined to open their own dental office. However, they knew this may not be possible due to large debt they were carrying from their education.

In discussions regarding the funding necessary to open a new dental office, the three students agreed they would call the local dental shops in the towns they grew up in. They were hoping there might be an opportunity to get sponsored by a local dentist who knew he/she was retiring in a few years, and was looking for a successor.

Joshua Williams made a call to his hometown of Fremont, which has a population of about 120,000 people. There are two dental offices already in practice; both are husband and wife teams. One of these offices is Fremont Dental Office; the owner (Don Snyder) is sixty years old and his wife is fifty–eight years old. After speaking with Joshua, Don Snyder invited Joshua and his partners to come up for the weekend.

Don Snyder told the partners that he and his wife had been planning their retirement for a few years and had actually hired a business broker to start looking for buyers. This process had started almost ten months ago, and resulted in a few offers. However, the offers were not close to the asking price.

Don offered that he would carry the financing for the partners, so they did not need to go to the bank to get funding. The only stipulation was that the interest rate charged for the loan would be 2% above market. The three partners said they needed some time to review the offer and get their partners' agreement in place. Don agreed and said he would hold the offer open to them for sixty days and would not take additional offers until they replied.

This is how this business plan came about. This plan was written to determine if there would be a large enough market to sustain all three partners and their growing families, while paying off this loan of $1,000,000. This deal included a turnkey dental office with equipment that was only three years old. The office had the most current x–ray equipment and surgical supplies.

MARKET ANALYSIS

Fremont is a city with a population of about 120,000 people. It is an older city and was founded in 1894. Over the years it has seen boom and bust economies. For the past ten years, the economy has been recovering from a long drought. However, recently the city was ranked in the top 100 for fastest growing cities. The farm sector which the city was dependant on for so many years is starting to be replaced by new economic industries.

These new industries are mostly related to the high tech sector. About six years ago, Technology USA set up a new manufacturing plant in the city. This plant employs over 1,200 people. Then Informtech saw the quality of production workers and opened an assembly plant that employs 800 people. While these numbers are small, the key to this change is important. In the last year, the local economic development manager has had over thirty requests from Fortune 500 companies hoping to start manufacturing or assembly shops in this region. This is a 250% increase in requests over the past five years.

The average household income in Fremont is $36,350 and the unemployment rate is only 5%. Based on our telephone surveys of local employers, over 69% of employers have a paid dental plan for employees. The other companies did not have a medical or dental plan, usually because they were still establishing the company or they simply could not afford to provide health care plans for their employees. We also determined that the companies that did offer dental plans to their staff employed over twenty employees. This is important because this means a higher percentage of the potential clients were covered by a dental plan. People who have a dental plan are 78% more likely to use the service, leading to more potential clients.

The average sale in Don's dental office was $198 plus x–ray costs; this average rose from $122 five years ago. This is because the fees charged by the dental offices are dictated by the insurance companies that pay these bills, not the dentist's office.

Since Don was already preparing to retire, he had started not accepting new clients. Instead, he would forward them to the other dentist in the city, who was overwhelmed with business. This office's waiting list was growing longer and potential clients were going to other cities to get this work done faster. In some cases they would drive one and half hours each way. The fact that clients had to travel so far confirmed that this was a great location. Instead of buying a new shop, they would acquire the existing shop with the cliental already in place.

Financial Analysis

The partners' management consultant told them that this was a great opportunity, but reminded them that the owner had been there for almost thirty–five years and had built up a great track record. The new owners would have to build up this same track record with the community. The consultant advised the partners to go back to the owner and make the following offer:

The partners would pay $700,000 for the business with a loan that carried no interest. If at any point the average revenue for the previous twelve months was not the same as the twelve months Don managed, the $700,000 would be reduced by the percentage of revenue reduction. This formula would only be used for the first twelve months. After this benchmark was achieved, the partners would pay off the remainder of the loan over a five year period.

The owner made one small addition to this offer. He proposed that if the revenue exceeds the $500,000 mark, he would get a bonus based on the same formula. The three partners accepted this and the deal was done.

BUSINESS STRATEGY

Operations

The transition from Don and his wife to the new owners took place over a thirty day period. Don and his wife worked side by side with the partners, helping clients as well making sure the partners would get a good foundation and start to their new dental office.

Because the office was a turnkey office, all the equipment was already in place and there would be no need to buy or replace any of the equipment.

There was a full–time assistant, and the partners agreed once they got up and running they would need to hire another full–time assistant. They also would hire an office manager to handle all the heavy paper work related to the insurance companies. Their market research determined there was a need in the city for an office that offered longer hours. Therefore, the partners expanded their hours from 9:00AM–5:00PM, Monday to Friday, to 7:00AM–7:00PM Monday to Saturday. These longer hours would allow them to grow the revenues and the profits for the business. It also meant they could increase their market share.

The dentist's office will be changing ownership in four weeks. All the required legal agreements will be signed and everything will be concluded. Our research determined that the average dental studio sells for 1.2 X gross revenues. Based on this figure, this purchase was right on the mark, and the fact that the partners were offered a good financing package from the owner was a bonus.

In order to facilitate the transfer of this business, the company will be set up as a joint practice, with each partner sharing in the company with 33 1/3 ownership and voting shares. All management decisions will go through board meetings which the partners will hold every two weeks for the first year, then once a month after that. Of course, the partners will be working very closely in a small office, so they can discuss issues at any time. It was agreed though, in order to run a professional office, they would leave all decisions which required in–depth talks or negotiation to the scheduled board meetings. This would allow for the management of the office to be smooth.

When the partners cannot get consensus, they will ask the management consultant for advice. This outside third party advice will be invaluable.

Advertising

The partners will follow the local state laws when it comes to advertising a dental office. They will join the state dental association; this will allow them to take part in joint advertising programs. They will run a larger ad in the Yellow Pages and they will include a photograph, so clients can become more aware of them. They will also include the name of Don's dental clinic and advertise with his logo. Since the partners needed to register a new phone number when they created a new business entity, they will have incoming phone calls transferred from the previous office number to the new office number for one year.

E–Commerce Website Producer
Internet Capabilities

941 Broshwell St.
Saint Paul, Minnesota 31214

Gerald Rekve

Internet Capabilities is an internet–based company which provides goods and services that are purchased and distributed over the World Wide Web.

Currently the main product that we offer is pre–made e–commerce websites, packaged as a ready–to–go Internet business for those wishing to work from home but need a product or service to sell.

EXECUTIVE SUMMARY

Market Analysis

In recent years there has been an explosion in the number of people who work from home, including employees of large corporations and small, independent business people.

Our product lines are designed to capture this new market, factoring in our easy–to–use templates.

We have thirty four different types of e–businesses for sale with over 300 different designs. Ninety percent of the businesses sold are fully automated, meaning that they do not require any maintenance, upkeep, or even order processing or fulfilling for the owner; very little PC knowledge is required. In addition, we provide the domain names as well as the hosting services.

At present we are in the capital attainment mode and will be focusing on securing funding for our operations, both an operating line of funding as well investment in capital equipment.

The founder has invested a great amount of time and resources to get the company to this stage. Due to the nature of our business, we feel our business will grow to new levels once the infrastructure is put in place. At present we have been operating out of our home while we put the systems in place.

Mission

We are a strong believer in do–it–yourself business building. What we mean by this is simple. If we can provide a market with a turnkey product that requires little expertise by the new owners, they will not only succeed in business, but they will also be very happy with the product we have sold them. In the end they will buy more products from us.

Our vision is to be the best online seller of this product and service. Internet Capabilities will work tirelessly to make every client our supporter.

Management Summary

President and CEO: Miyoshi Seto

Vice president: Lew Seto

As more personnel are added, managers will be appointed as the need arises.

FINANCIAL ANALYSIS

Funding

In order to market and expand our current product line, Internet Capabilities is seeking funding in the amount of $200,000. We will offer the standard market return on investment (ROI) on your investment.

Our current focus is toward moving into an office, purchasing office equipment and marketing previously developed products.

While interest has been high in our product line through word of mouth and online auctions, we would like to expand our specialized product line to a national market.

As Internet Capabilities grows and expands, our operational needs will also expand. To exploit these possibilities, television commercials and Internet advertising must be utilized at a considerable expense.

Therefore, management anticipates employing half of any funds received in marketing and advertising. Moving from a home business to an actual office will be necessary along with additional equipment and staff. These additions will be added gradually as business dictates.

Customer service will continue to be a main focus of all levels of employees. This commitment to customer service has made our company what it is today and will continue to make it successful in the future.

Expenses

Capital equipment and marketing expenses

Breakdown:

18 Computers	$ 20,000.00
9 Servers	$ 9,000.00
Domain registrar	$ 3,000.00
Cubicles and installation	$ 3,000.00
Chairs	$ 1,000.00
Software	$ 8,000.00
Lease (12 months)	$ 15,000.00
Miscellaneous	$ 1,000.00
Wages (4 months)	$ 40,800.00
Advertising and marketing	$ 99,200.00
Total	**$200,000.00**

GROWTH STRATEGY

Operations

We plan to take Internet Capabilities to the next level. Within the next six months we would like to lease an office space, purchase necessary equipment and servers, and hire employees in order to provide better service and handle more customers. This is part of a two–year expansion plan which includes opening an in–house advertising agency.

With a budget to hire customer service representatives and order fulfillment reps we will be able to provide more "personal" customer service via a 1–800 number or over the Internet with live help chat (already in place). Our order fulfillment representatives will be able to distribute the massive orders for website packages in a timely manner.

Advertising

Additionally, with a new advertising department we will have a more efficient and effective way of promoting our services and plan to profit from taking on new clients by providing Internet–based marketing for them as well.

We will have one of the most effective ways of advertising on the web. Five of the new employees we plan to hire will be software developers who will develop freeware and low–cost software which will allow us to send search results–related pop–up ads to computer users who have our software installed and have agreed to the terms according to their online behavior.

This is a highly effective means of reaching customers. Click–through rates are twenty to forty times higher than traditional banner ads because advertisers can reach consumers across the Web at exactly the right time in their buying cycle. Relevance is one of the most consistent drivers of successful advertising campaigns—especially in today's cluttered Internet environment. If a consumer is considering a purchase in a certain category, or knows she will be, information about that category becomes relevant and valuable. Other companies who use these exact methods such as "Save", "Advertising.com" and, "Gain" have each generated approximately $132 million in 2003.

By the end of 2006 we envision Internet Capabilities as an essential building block of the Internet.

Objectives

Within the First 4 Months

- Find and lease a location within Saint Paul, Minnesota

- Purchase and install equipment for customer service reps and order fulfillment reps

- Hire and train three customer service reps and four order fulfillment reps (one–week training)

- Deploy major marketing campaign by way of television commercials, newspaper and magazine ads, press release, and Internet marketing campaign (we will temporarily utilize the services of our soon to be competitors "Save" or "Gain")

Month 7

- Purchase and install equipment for two website designers (to keep the look of the e–businesses fresh and avoid the final product becoming dated)

- Hire and deploy web site designers to design sites specifically to be sold as e–businesses for Internet Capabilities. Use the designers to look for new types of products that can be added to our product offering

Month 10

- Hire three software developers to design our own advertising software along with the freeware and low–cost software for distribution

Month 15

- Begin the distribution of our freeware throughout the Internet by means of Cnet (download.com), through e–mail campaign, eBay, word of mouth, and as free "stickys" for other webmaster sites. "Stickys" are placed on a web site to attract visitors. They can distribute our products to their visitors for free.

Month 18

- Determine the number of people who have downloaded our products. Use this information to market our other products as well as look for new revenue opportunities.

PRODUCTS

Some examples of the Internet businesses that we sell are:

- Auction web sites

- Classifieds web sites

- Domain name registration web sites

- Search engine submission web sites

- e–book web sites

- Travel booking web sites

Because of our variety of businesses for sale, two thirds of our customers return as repeat customers. To help ensure the profitability of our customers we give them free marketing materials to help start them with their promotion.

Some of the free marketing materials that we offer to our customers include:

- Free search engine submission

- Built in meta tags

- Free web site banners

- Web rings

- Valuable marketing tips e–book

- List of sources where they can obtain leads for people who op–in

We provide people with a means to earn an income without all the normal hassle. The niche market of Internet Capabilities is high in demand and has very few competitors.

With our products we turn the at–home computer user into the Internet entrepreneur! We help other people reach their goals, while at the same time reaching our own.

Customers

As a home–based business, we are currently on a shoestring marketing budget; however, we are still able to attract a large amount of customers and traffic to our sites. This speaks volumes in terms of our potential growth opportunity with our product mix.

Studies have shown that women have become the majority of Web users and do the most on–line shopping in the United States. This fact is central to our business opportunity and our product mix.

According to the US Census in 2005, women became a slight majority of Web users in the United States for the first time in history (51 percent female vs. 49 percent male). Women make up almost half of the first–time Web buyers. It is believed that women will continue to flock to the on–line platform because it allows them to save time researching and buying what they want.

Stay–at–home parents are our main target market at present. Our service will allow them to make money from home while caring for their children at the same time.

In fact, this business was started while the founder was a stay–at–home mom. Now that her children are old enough, she is able to expand the business and help even more people. Her customers can benefit from her experiences.

Young entrepreneurial–spirited men between the ages of 19 and 35 are the secondary market. This group is categorized as highly energized with the ability to simultaneously work on multiple tasks.

These skills will allow them to manage the products they buy from us while at the same time working on other projects.

COMPANY HISTORY

We are a privately–held General C corporation currently operating out of a home office in Saint Paul, Minnesota.

Products & Services

Characteristics: completed, fully functional e–commerce web sites designed specifically to generate money on the internet. Most of the web sites sell internet products or products that can otherwise be fulfilled by a drop shipper. The web sites are sold as pre–made e–businesses for those looking to earn an income over the web.

How the service works: We do the time consuming part of finding a product to sell and building the web site. We provide the hosting services and domain name.

The only thing that the customer must do is promote their new business. To help them in this task, we provide free marketing materials to our customers including free search engine submission, web rings, marketing tips e–book, and links to other sites that provide free tools and information. In addition, the web sites come with meta tags already in place for search engine indexing.

The company founder started out by designing web sites for her friends and acquaintances. Word of mouth alone quickly expanded the business to the point where it provided a good income. Next, the web sites were sold on eBay; business was very good here, but competition is high. Finally, the founder built her own web site. Loyal eBay customers frequently visited and purchased from the web site, and this is the basis for the corporation.

We currently are on a limited marketing budget which only permits simple forms of advertising such as small email campaign and link exchanges. With funding we will be able to broaden our marketing and increase sales from $2,000 per month to an estimated $20,000 per month.

Product Description

We sell over 34 different types of e–businesses with over 300 different designs.

The product interface is extremely easy for customers to use. Most web sites are fully automated and only require customers to promote their sites. They can collect payment via paypal.com, which offers free accounts and secure merchant services so that they may accept payment via credit card or e–check.

For example, the auction web site contains scripts that allow users to register with the site for free. In order for them to sell their items, they must pay a nominal fee which can be automatically handled through paypal.

The scripts contained within the site allow users to upload pictures and item descriptions. It also allows member feedback and bidding. The owner of the web site does not have to do anything for the daily process to work and business will carry on without any maintenance.

Paypal integration is very powerful feature. The site's payment buttons are linked to paypal which processes the payments on a secure server into the customer's free account.

Product Life Cycle

Our products are entering growth stage. With enough funding, would like to help the products expand and add more services to our company, such as a mass Internet advertising department.

Because the Internet is only 10 years old, products produced for the Internet and sold on the Internet are still in the start up stage. While the internet has had a few bad days, we are confidant that the wave of the future is front of us; our products are well positioned to meet the needs of both our clients and the end users of our clients' products.

Entertainment Production, Distribution, and Performance Company

Mentonic Hero Inc.

2298 Rogers Ave.
Los Angeles, California 90023

Gerald Rekve

This probably needs a bit of an introduction—it is not your run–of–the–mill business plan. It is somewhat unconventional, a bit more 'flashy' than most, you say . . . but, you know what? I bet you will read it. It's slightly different, a bit innovative and certainly creative. You see, we had a difficult time conforming to the formal approach, and every so often, we slightly break the rules of business plan etiquette.

We wanted our business plan to convey that, and we wanted you to know our intentions . . . Someone or something comes along that makes us sit up and pay attention. Something that touches us at a level much deeper than routine . . . something that whispers to the soul because it holds value, honesty and integrity. Pay attention. This may be that something.

EXECUTIVE SUMMARY

Mentonic Hero Inc. is formed as an entertainment production, distribution and performance company specializing in the utilization and maximization of current entertainment business opportunities available—the worldwide reach of the 500 TV channels that has spurned a vacuum of need for TV Series. This demand is unrelenting for quality animation programming.

We currently have distribution agreements in place for the Asia market with a company called International Television in ASIA. We have an industry expert in place to write the show bible and the pilot script. The funding required for the first episode is $300,000; for production of 14 episodes, the cost will be in the range of $200,000 to $350,000. Producing all 26 episodes will require an investment of $6.5 million dollars.

With this level of investment needed, we will look at all venture proposals and offer competitive rates of return based on industry standards.

That being said, let's explain that the balance of this business plan may not follow all those revered rules of professional etiquette proffered by the 'experts.' We are a rather innovative and creative bunch, not given easily to the molding of the masses into narrow visions of 'should' and 'have to.' On the other hand, we have been around a while and thus gained insight and wisdom lending value to learned lessons and 'right' paths. There is immeasurable worth and undeniable clarity that comes from a good business plan. The proof, however, is whether it accurately describes, foretells and transmits the focus and objectives of the company itself. Time will tell, we assume, but perhaps you can judge for yourself if the following 'rings true' and holds significance for you.

Mentonic Hero offers consumers of a new variety of TV series; it also offers potential investors a planned return–on–investment opportunity with the potential for toys, video games, and other types of merchandising.

Such projects will enjoy the umbrella security, strategic relationships, beneficial knowledge and proficient talent provided by the holding company, Mentonic Hero.

Television Series Synopses

Mentonic Hero is a young boy in his early 20's and an unassuming, near–anonymous super hero. He appears to be a completely normal boy, aside from the fact that one of his arms is made of steel; at first glance, the arm appears to be a prosthetic. He walks with a jerky motion and each step is punctuated by a compressed air, assembly–line–apparatus–like sound.

The arm is actually equipped with an abundance of features and gadgetry that aid him in his heroic acts. Mentonic Hero's dream state is subject to real–time psychic visions, and many of his acts of heroism occur by him being awoken in the middle of the night. He then flies to the scene of the crime with the rocket launcher on his steel arm. His mother is also fitted with a steel arm, and the family dog, Hydro, has four steel legs. Aside from a wholesome family environment and attending school, Mentonic Hero shares a mutual infatuation with Gertrude, the young girl who lives next door, and has a passionate interest in roller derby. He also spends quality time with his unofficial surrogate father Hatch—a conspiracy theory spewing amputee and Vietnam veteran who lives in an apartment down the hall.

The accumulative effect of lost sleep due to late night rescue missions starts to interfere with Mentonic Hero's schooling, and he consults a sleep disorder specialist. The physician, a Dr. Eve L. Rains, is actually behind a recent epidemic making headlines throughout the story—a growing number of human beings who were inexplicably turned into human/animal hybrids (oxen, cats, rabbits, etc.). Dr. Rains runs a very sophisticated underground operation, and in this element goes by her villain alter ego name "Evila". Evila possesses the characteristics of a praying mantis, and conceals her bizarre appearance when conducting her practice as Dr. Rains. She is assisted in her cause to redefine mankind by a large staff of "Poodle Men"—full grown men who were transformed into poodles by Evila. They walk upright with chests slightly protruded, and are attired in black military–like uniforms that include insignias identifying their rank within the organization. When the Poodle Men are dispatched to abduct human specimens they don ski masks, gloves and sunglasses in order to blend in with civilization. Most of the Poodle Men's activities are underscored by a generous dose of humor, as they aspire to navy seal–type precision, but are more often bumbling.

Mentonic Hero begins to see Dr. Rains for treatment in the hopes she can help him sleep through his many demanding dream states. Through a chain of events, Mentonic Hero deduces that Dr. Rains is the mastermind behind the growing "animal people" epidemic, and he confronts her. She refutes the accusation, and the two have a dramatic exchange that results in Mentonic Hero vowing to bring her to justice, and Evila shutting down her "arms itimate" practice and going into hiding. Mentonic Hero continues to monitor the animal people developments and builds a liaison with a police detective, while Evila's Poodle Men keep a round–the–clock spy watch on Mentonic Hero so as to determine any threat level. After the Poodle Men conclude Mentonic Hero poses no serious threat, Evila instructs the Poodle Men to abduct Gertrude; she wishes to incite Mentonic Hero to become a true archrival so as to offset her relative boredom in the midst of her ascension to world domination. Gertrude is abducted and subsequently transformed into a virtual penguin. Mentonic Hero's dream state reveals this to him, and he flies into the night to rescue his beloved friend. Landing in the vicinity of Evila's compound, confused Mentonic Hero is helped to the exact location via a telepathic dialogue with a pigeon he crossed paths with earlier in the story. The two penetrate the highly secured headquarters and proceed to dismantle Evila's operation, climaxing in a giant fight scene with the Poodle Men that is reminiscent of Bruce Lee kung fu movies. In the final showdown, Evila spars with Mentonic Hero until he shatters her kneecap with his steel arm and she reduces herself to insect size and flees. Evila's chief confidant is more brains than brawn and impotently caves in to Mentonic Hero's demands for the "animal people" cure serum. Mentonic Hero rescues the penguin–faced Gertrude and the two share a touching moment and comical bit of kissing.

The final episode ends with Mentonic Hero watching the newly restored animal people being interviewed on TV with his mother, Hydro, Gertrude, Hatch, and the pigeon. The interviews include Evila's chief commander in human form via satellite from a federal prison cell. "Harry Queen", a Larry King caricature that monitors the animal people epidemic throughout the entire story, lambastes him for abandoning his post as France's diplomat to Guam to serve with Evila. (Before and after photos showing transition from dignitary to menacing "Poodle Man" are shown, etc.)

GROWTH STRATEGY

Objectives

Setting up our production company, we realized that along the way we will have more than one project and Mentonic Hero is just one of them. The investor will have access to other projects we produce; this will be based on a pre–negotiated agreement. The greater the return, the greater the investment.

Goals

1. Attract $200,000–$350,000 from outside investors

2. Secure an additional $6,500,000 to produce the complete package of films

The keys to our success include:

1. The strategic organization of creative endeavors into project format, allowing each project to be individually financed, developed, maintained and tracked according to its unique requirements and objectives. This provides the 'umbrella security and licensing' from Mentonic Hero Inc. but allows each project to live out its own singular existence. In addition, each project becomes a viable revenue source for Mentonic Hero Inc., dependent upon its own success and market worthiness. The multiple–project format also allows a broad diversity of effort and application to maximize the potential inherent in each market through individual projects. Finally, this format also dilutes the risk involved with each individual project for Mentonic Hero Inc. as a result of the separate funding secured for each project.

2. Development of multiple avenues of visibility for Mentonic Hero Inc. through strategic contacts, traditional advertising, digital TV satellite access and product development.

3. Strategic utilization of the unique pool of production and performance talent integral in the personnel makeup of Mentonic Hero Inc.

4. Excellence and commitment woven into every finished product and performance, thus creating the integrity Mentonic Hero Inc. shall possess.

COMPANY HISTORY

Mentonic Hero Inc. is a newly formed Limited Liability Company providing high–level expertise in the performance production industry. Mentonic Hero Inc. is not interested in competing with the major studios; we just want to find our own niche market. It has been created to fulfill the dreams and expectations of those people who desire their children to view quality TV and to satisfy the demand for such entertainment in the 500 Channel Universe.

Company Ownership

As a Limited Liability Company, ownership of Mentonic Hero Inc. is identified as belonging to its managers.

Summary of Start–up Costs

Start-up summary

	Start-up
Requirements	1,000,000
Start-up expenses	
Arms al	$ 200,000
Publications/membership	$ 20,000
Office equipment	$ 20,000
Consultants	$ 50,000
Insurance	$ 2,000
Website development/hosting	$ 100,000
Website management	$ 50,000
Expensed equipment	$ 10,000
Other	$ 20,000
Total start-up expenses	**$ 472,000**
Start-up assets needed	
Cash balance on starting date	$1,000,000
Other current assets	$ 0
Total current assets	$1,000,000
Long-term assets	$ 00
Total assets	$ 00
Total requirements	**$ 1,000,000**

OPERATIONS

Mentonic Hero Inc. will seek appropriate office space offering many benefits to the company:

- A close association with the entertainment industry
- Competent and professional production companies and studios
- Competent, experienced and professional studio and staff
- Marketing and distribution avenues through particularly strong ties to West Coast companies as well as to East Coast companies
- A burgeoning group of Internet–related companies providing services in the fields of graphics, Web–hosting, Web–marketing, CD reproduction and software distribution that will allow our TV series to be easily distributed
- Piggyback opportunities with both performers and their associated production companies

PRODUCTS & SERVICES

A savvy production group such as ours will weigh the performance, charisma, audience acceptance, production grasp and overall marketability of each animation project and incorporate only those peripheral 'products' that develop into viable components of the project.

This requires good judgment, extensive experience, and strong management ability, not to mention perhaps the most important and elusive capability ... that of 'reading' the market. Mentonic Hero Inc. encompasses individuals with separate and unique abilities lending themselves to this process. The overall excellence in this endeavor, however, rests in the comprehensive combined expertise of the principals of this company. Combined, we have backgrounds in the entertainment industry, business management, marketing, accounting, production, public relations and solid business application. These strengths point to an overall understanding of the marketability and viability of each 'product' considered.

Mentonic Hero Inc. offers services of varied structure and expandability:

- The complete packaging of a TV series project—comprehensive production work, extensive review, in–studio production work, arrangement and editing of film products, coordination of the manufacture and distribution of product, marketing of finished product, ongoing analysis of strategic placement and acceptance of product and performance, influential public relations efforts, follow–up and maximization of audience acceptability with additional strategies to further amplify recognition and revenue, and the coordination and management of live performances in correlation with the recorded product and market demand.

- Ultimately, the 'rainbow's end' outcome of such a project would be the negotiation with and resultant contractual sale or lease of the TV series to a major TV Studio or distribution company with international reach.

- A limited packaging of a TV series to result in a specific outcome or product; e.g., a pre–determined number of runs on TV (including, of course, all the above activities required to produce said TV series). Such packaging may or may not include distribution, marketing and coordination of live performances in conjunction with the produced TV series.

- The complete production and rendition of a desired performance or show including the appropriate above–mentioned activities.

- Contractual negotiation services on behalf of a TV series production staff.

- Coordination of strategic gratis appearances of actors/artists for public relations and marketing purposes.

- The development, maintenance, funding coordination and undertaking of any worthwhile and promising project as identified.

Services

Service fulfillment will be provided by principals of Mentonic Hero Inc. in coordination with the contributing contractors required to complete the products. Companies such as animation studios, animation software manufacturers, distribution houses, licensing firms, performance venues, traditional and online advertising groups, just to name a few, are regularly contracted to contribute to the finished product.

MARKET ANALYSIS

In today's technological world, we find a challenging and ever–expanding marketplace for almost any product or service. Such is the case for the services and products we plan to create. Through the worldwide reach of the Internet, innovative and resourceful companies can market their wares literally around the world. It is likely that someone in, say, South America would contact us to package and market them a TV series for their market.

Sample of advertising revenue from past TV series:

Show	1998–99 audience	Ad rate (30 seconds)
Touched	17 million	$ 275,000
Frasier	13 million	$ 475,000
Drew	10 million	$ 375,000
X-Files	8 million	$ 330,000
Simpsons	11 million	$ 290,000
Ally	6.5 million	$ 290,000

SOURCE: USA TV Sector Market Stats

Other Cartoon TV Series and Their Market Revenues

Pokemon

Pokemon, whether it is TV cartoons, movies, trading cards or one of the more than 1,000 associated products, has generated billions of dollars for its parent company, Nintendo, since its launch as a video game in early 1996. And the phenomenon is not confined to Japan. Led by the hero Satoshi and point man (monster) Pikachu, it swept across the world in just three years. Introduced to the US as a TV cartoon in September 1998, Pokemon generated an estimated $700 million dollars in retail sales in the following year.

The weekly cartoon became the top–rated kid's TV show and the video *Pokemon: Seaside Pikachu* topped the bestsellers list. Sociologists engage in serious debate about the educational value of kids' obsession with Pokemon cards. The logistics, tactics and pure arithmetic involved in pitting the various monsters, each with their own strengths and weaknesses, against each other certainly make kids use their brains. And the fact that the monsters don't die as a result of their battles—they just faint—is a welcome change from the usual cartoon carnage. But stories of schoolyard fights over cards and the kind of money changing hands—some cards are traded at over $100 dollars apiece—also cause concern.

Hello Kitty

The undisputed 'queen of cute' these days is Hello Kitty. Although she's been around for 25 years, her finest hour began in 1996. The girls who had made Kitty–chan a success back in the 1970's were now the baby–boomers with money to spend. Kitty's parent company Sanrio launched a series of pink satin keitai (cellular phone) pouches that became the only ones to be sold in the youth style centers of Tokyo and beyond.

When baby–faced pop star Kahala Tomomi announced that she was a Kitty–lah (Kitty groupie), sales went through the roof. New products were knocked out almost daily, anything from Kitty stickers and hair clips to Kitty cars—real cars for the girl who has everything, painted pink and with Kitty plastered all over. Sanrio even has its own theme park, Puroland, near Tokyo where you can meet Kitty and her friends including Peckle the Duck and Keroppi the Frog. She has even managed to spread her feline empire to Asia, Europe and the US, where Sanrio has 40 stores.

The little cat with no mouth (who incidentally was born in London to George and Mary White, has a twin sister Mimi, weighs the same as three apples and is stuck in the third grade) almost single–handedly helped Sanrio to increase profits by 1,300 percent in 1997.

Doraemon

Doraemon, the robot cat from the twenty–second century, and his human pal Nobita are the Japanese equivalent of Snoopy and Charlie Brown. Nobita is a classic 4th–grade underachiever who desperately wants to be liked but can't hit a baseball or even ride a bike and is always at the bottom of his class. Together with Doraemon and the other members of his neighborhood gang, he has adventures that entertain while gently educating its young audience. Doraemon's pouch is the source of all kinds of wonderful devices from the future that can be used—and abused—by Nobita to deal with his everyday problems. He also has a dokodemo–door through which the youngsters can visit anywhere in the world and, of course, a time machine.

Doraemon first appeared in a comic book by Fujimoto Hiroshi (1934–1996) in 1969 when he came back in time to save Nobita from his own future. Since then, in paperbacks (over 100 million copies sold), TV cartoons and over 20 movies, Doraemon has been the voice of reason guiding Nobita through one adventure after another. In a sense, Nobita represents all the youth of Japan and the lessons he learns are those faced by everyone in the rapidly developing world. The show airs at 7pm on Friday evenings.

Sazae–san

Less in the realm of cute are cartoon 'people' such as Sazae–san, Chibi Maruko and Crayon Shin–chan. These characters and their families represent different takes on Japanese life and culture. They encapsulate the generational changes of the postwar years as well as any sociological study could do. Perhaps the best loved and certainly the longest–running cartoon series is Sazae–san, shown at 6:30 on Sunday evenings. Sazae (a type of shellfish—like all the characters, her name is related to the sea) is a 23–year old housewife who lives with her parents, younger brother and sister, husband and baby son. At home, Sazae is surrounded by the usual electrical appliances, drawn to resemble the latest models by Toshiba, the show's sponsor! But otherwise life is firmly rooted in a world that is no more than a fading memory for today's Japanese.

The characters were created in a comic book by manga artist Hasegawa Machiko (1920–1992) shortly after World War II and have been on TV since 1969. Hasegawa was something of a recluse and the darker side of life in postwar Japan was part of her work.

But modern–day problems rarely intrude into the TV show and key features are the opening credits showing various scenic spots around the country and the timely inclusion of seasonal and festive elements. This, together with the always–polite language of the characters, makes the show excellent for students of Japan's language and culture. For Japanese, Sazae–san—like the Tora–san movie series—provides a chance to shake off the worries of work and school and soak in the warm glow of nostalgia.

Chibi Maruko–chan

Rooted more in the semi–rural Japan of the early 1970's, Chibi Maruko–chan (Little Miss Maruko) was originally created to appeal to the childhood memories of young women. As it turned out, its appeal was broader than that, with children the same age as the third–grade heroine tuning in and snapping up all the merchandising. The characters and humor are more rounded and endearing than those in Sazae-san. Maruko does what she can to avoid homework, takes advantage of her doting grandfather and squabbles with her sister. All ends well, of course, but never without a bit of embarrassment and comeuppance.

Created as a manga in 1986 by Sakura Momoko, the TV show was launched in 1990 and reached record–high ratings for a 30–minute animation. Apart from a one–year absence in 1993, the show has run ever since in the 6pm time slot before Sazae–san on Sunday evenings.

Crayon Shin–chan

The crazed antics of the 5–year old Crayon Shin–chan are a far cry from those of other animation characters. With a habit of dropping his pants, drinking his father's beer and mooning over centerfolds, Shin–chan (his full name is Shinnosuke) is a young Japanese Bart Simpson for the 90's if ever there was one.

His long–suffering parents are not much better and are usually shown indulging in vices of their own. It is often pointed out that the materialism and aimlessness of young Japanese today stems from the attitudes of their parents. Shin–chan seems to embody that kind of theory. It was a surprise hit when it was launched in the mid–1990's, the time when this kind of social criticism was beginning to become popular. This cartoon may not have the same level of popularity or stay on the air as long as Sazae–san or even the Simpsons, but in a way it does reflect the values of its time. The show airs in the 7:30pm time slot after Doraemon on Friday evenings.

Market Segmentation

Most important in our marketing approach will be the utilization of the contact and relationship base in the entertainment industry already established by the owners and key staff of our company.

Word–of–mouth advertising represents an important aspect, as well, with the quality of each project holding paramount value in the furtherance of our good reputation. Entertainers, by nature, are a conversant lot, and word–of–mouth advertising, although difficult to track and predict, can represent a major percentage of customer attraction.

Comprehensive utilization of the marketing opportunities offered through Internet usage will be the anchor for most of our marketing programs. The Mentonic Hero Inc. website will be a focal point where anyone interested in our services may migrate for further information and contact. References to the website will be incorporated into all collateral marketing pieces and campaigns.

Internet search engine placement using correct keywords and meta tags will be employed to attract a maximum number of visitors to our website. Regular evaluations of search engine placement activity will guide our continuing strategy.

Unlike marketing a specific brand of toothpaste where large numbers of purchases create cash flow and profitability, Mentonic Hero Inc. believes that word–of–mouth advertising, combined with the effective utilization of our website and traditional marketing avenues, will create enough business to carry us well into our second year of operation and beyond.

We are also aware of the power of major Broadcasting companies; if they put their marketing muscle behind a TV series, it will be quickly become a *Malcolm In the Middle* if it is produced well and has a strong story plot.

As we progress further into our future, we will focus on the strengths and factors that produced the most successful and rewarding projects and continue the incorporation of those factors into our day–to–day operations.

Traditional advertising will be continuously employed, but predominantly will serve as a support and recognition tool providing credibility but not necessarily bringing in the majority of our clients.

FINANCIAL ANALYSIS

In order to understand the industry costs, we have included some industry norms.

1. A two–hour TV movie costs between $4 million and $5 million; networks are willing to pay between $3.5 million and $4.5 million for most of these movies.

2. A single episode of a 60 minute dramatic program can cost as much as $2 million. Producers can lose $500 thousand to $750 thousand per episode when the program is licensed for network viewing.

You may be wondering why these costs are so high. Here are some reasons:

- Labor costs are high (union wage scales, overtime, huge salaries for stars)

- In dramas, location shooting rather than studio shooting is common—and more expensive.

- Series can be very expensive. When it was on the air in the 1980s, *Miami Vice*, for example, was one of the most expensive weekly series ever produced for TV. The producers were losing so much money on it that they threatened to move the production from Miami to California to save money. NBC increased its payments to the producers, but this did not significantly reduce the deficit.

These high costs have many consequences, including:

- The high cost of programming is one of the reasons there are so many situation comedies and reality programs (e.g., *Unsolved Mysteries*) on TV today. They are usually much cheaper than drama shows (such as *Law and Order* and *NYPD Blue*). Low cost entertainment/news shows such as *Entertainment Tonight*, *American Journal*, and *Hard Copy* are on for the same reason.

- Changes in production, notably shooting outside southern California. Vancouver, British Columbia is a common place these days for a lot of shooting. Union wages are much lower here than southern California; consequently, production costs can be as much as 20 percent less in Canada.

- High tech and action scenes from other films are often inserted into shows. Reusing the scenes saves money.

Even when losing money, producers persist for many reasons, including:

- Reruns. There is a very lucrative prospect of putting the show into reruns on local TV stations or cable networks if a sufficient number of episodes (usually about 100) are completed.

- Producers own the shows. When the shows are first broadcast on a network, the network only pays for the right to show the program 2 or 3 times. The producers can then sell the rights to others to show the program.

- The revenues from the secondary sales are almost all profit. The original costs have all already been paid.

- Most of the money will go to the producers (although some will go to the stars).

- Both local TV and some cable networks thrive on showing these "off network" reruns.

- Stripping. Instead of showing a single episode each week (as the networks do during the first run of a program), the station shows a different episode each day, five days a week. This is called stripping.

- The individual price per local station may not be terribly high for a show such as *Head of the Class*, but if 250 to 300 stations pay for the rights to show the program, the total amount of money that goes to the producer can be huge.

- Some reruns are enormously popular. When the *Cosby Show* first went into reruns in 1990, it frequently drew larger viewing audiences than new shows. The same has held true for *Seinfeld*. Reruns of *Seinfeld* have often been number one in their time slot, beating out new programming.

- Most series do not go into reruns, but enough do to make the industry profitable overall.

ADVERTISING

Reaching the Market

Successfully proffering your wares in the television industry is a delicate balance of offering a quality product and strategically placing that product where it can be seen and acquired. To a large extent the 'big boys' have the upper hand in reaching the masses. Unless you understand the audience and the idiosyncrasies inherent in that audience (and there are always idiosyncrasies), you may be one of those unfortunate many who spend large amounts of money appealing to the very people who could care less about your project and its associated product.

Strategy and Implementation

Mentonic Hero Inc. has this main project identified at present for immediate or near–future commencement. The sequence of initiation for this TV series is based on the strategic placement of product within the middle market of the TV industry. There is ample room in this market for successful operations such as Mentonic Hero Inc., offering enthusiastic audiences whom exhibit unusually high levels of loyalty to their favored TV series. Each new project will be designed to integrate with the previous one, while also penetrating new but kindred markets.

Initial Market Approach

Our plans are to secure the financing to develop a full–length episode; we will use this for marketing to the studios for placement in the TV season line up. We have a number of broadcast houses to meet with so, before we attempt to start to set up meeting, we want our first episode ready for showing.

There is already a niche market for this product in the United States with the vast range of channels on TV and the varied interest in different and unique shows, as well as selected areas overseas.

Successive Merchandising

Concurrent with the preparation of the Mentonic Hero project will be the initiation of other projects hitting more specialized markets. While not losing focus on our main TV series offering, the expansion of reach and market array will attract new films and series.

Here are a few of the potential merchandising opportunities that we will explore in order to add revenues to the company.

1. Branded interactive elements and features across multiple devices and platforms

2. TV program title music, stings and stabs as Ringtones—Mobi–tone

3. TV show or celebrity pictures/images sent to mobile, email or MMS—Mobi–pix

4. Programmer–related animated logos, characters, comic strips, etc. available for mobile, email or MMS—Mobi–logo

5. Karaoke tune and word text sent to mobile phone—Mobi–karaoke

6. Mobile, iTV and PC game sales or pay–per–play

7. Freebies/discounts via SMS, etc.

8. TV series soundtrack CDs

9. Sale of branded merchandise—T–shirts, toys, etc.

10. Downloading of video clips, etc.

11. Downloading of TV series audio clips/tracks, mobile stories, etc.

12. Broadband sales

13. Fanzine materials

14. Sale of videos

15. Sale of DVDs

16. Non–theatrical sales

17. Other sectors not listed at this time

BUSINESS STRATEGY

Pricing strategies, product sales forecasts, strategic partnerships, market penetration, and audience reception—all are individually dependent upon the unique aspects of the TV series and weigh heavily upon the techniques utilized for project implementation. Thus the strategy of separate financing for each project substantially benefits Mentonic Hero Inc. in establishing firm footing and stability for a project's performance and life.

The well–informed, cautious–but–enthusiastic planning of each project will provide for contingencies associated with both Mentonic Hero Inc. and the individual component. Identification of appropriate audiences, whether domestic or foreign, is key to a project's success.

There are receptive audiences in Japan who are eager for good animated TV series, while in the U.S., the same TV series would become just part of the pack and must vie desperately for recognition in a burgeoning genre.

Identification of audience, assessment of series reach, the strategic release of film, merchandising product, worldwide exposure through Internet concentration and well–placed, beneficially–crafted contracts with suppliers will provide Mentonic Hero Inc. a solid, firm footing upon which to build. The principals of this firm are not only well equipped to accomplish this type of strategic evaluation, but are endowed with various talents which, when combined, form a formidable and impressive knack for weighing and coordinating all components wisely to produce success.

COMPETITION

We happen to believe that there is no competition in the entertainment industry—only hard work, right marketing, skill in the delivery of a sound TV series, strategic placement of a finished product, maximization of audience acceptability…and then, the final ingredient—the benevolence of the entertainment gods. Or, as Bob Edgar often says, "The audience is like a big pie. Somewhere in that pie are those who like what I do. All I have to do is satisfy them, and I can enjoy my piece of the pie. The only one I'm in competition with is myself."

As a company we subscribe to this concept. It is not competition that creates a *Ren & Stempy*, or a *King of the Hill*, or a *Finding Nemo*. There does exist, however, the possibility that we may discover that new TV series concept that will be the best thing since Bugs Bunny.

What does create the new star in TV is the sometimes intangible but undeniable synchronicity of the 'right' script by the 'right' cartoon artist with the 'right' combination of production, distribution and marketing to result in the audience's recognition and acceptance of the 'rightful' reign of the newly–confirmed heir to fame.

We believe that those 'right' components can be applied to every project, thus resulting in a correlation of success and recognition within the parameters of that project. This does not mean we expect every project to produce a star. It does mean that we commit ourselves to the excellence and integrity of every project. We expect that most of our clients will hope for the full realization of their entertainment aspirations. We respect and honor their dreams and will perform to the best of our abilities to assist them in their endeavor. Each client will receive exactly what is represented as deliverable. We shall not, however, promise or guarantee any individual's fame or success. We leave that to the realm of those who deal in destiny.

We do believe that competing in the entertainment industry is enhanced and amplified through the following actions, each of which is an integral part of our overall service to each client:

•   Constant and mindful application of industry standards and state–of–the–art technologies. This requires the continuous, sometimes arduous, task of updating and educating oneself on industry developments and evolving techniques.

•   The ongoing maintenance of strategic industry contacts and relationships to ensure a broad understanding of the market and the ability to penetrate and utilize the industry to our benefit.

- Strong and knowledgeable business management to maximize the potential and profitability of each project and its associated artist/product.

- Continuous application of accurate accountability of all project components to ensure as much as possible the successful completion of each project and the satisfaction of each client and investor.

MANAGEMENT SUMMARY

The initial management team consists of two operational positions and three advisory/manager positions.

Organizational Structure

The operational positions within the company are president and vice president of administration. These positions carry full–time responsibilities for the ongoing daily operation of the company.

The advisory/manager positions are controller, company counsel and ambassador of goodwill. In the beginning, these positions carry part–time responsibilities dedicated to specialized functions necessary at times to fulfill the daily operation requirements of the company. As the scope of business enlarges, one or more of these individual positions may become full–time appointments.

General Staffing Company

GENRX LLC

7641 Highway 141
Saskatoon, Saskatchewan S7N 1M7

Gerald Rekve

GENRX LLC's mission is to be the best staffing firm in our region. Our focus will be to secure clients who may require our services on an ongoing basis.

EXECUTIVE SUMMARY

Business Strategy

GENRX LLC is opening a new general staffing company in 2006. Our area of focus is to be the best staffing firm in our region.

To begin, GENRX LLC will have six full–time staff, including the owner and five support staff to handle payroll, scheduling, and clients.

GENRX LLC will focus on the business sectors listed below. Other business sectors will be added as GENRX LLC matures and revenue potential for new sectors is increased.

- General labor

- Secretarial

- Specialized labor

- Manual labor

- Hourly or one day at a time

- Drop–in labor force

- Accounting staff

- Human Resource staff

- Technical staff

- Equipment operators

MARKET ANALYSIS

Saskatoon, Saskatchewan is a small market with only 240,000 people living in the city and one million living in the Province. There is another city 200 miles to the south named Regina with a population of 200,000. GENRX LLC will have an office in both locations.

There are 30,000 businesses that operate in the Province that are registered with the Government. Our focus will be to offer these business clients temporary staff as they require. While GENRX LLC will only focus our markets in Saskatoon and Regina, requests from clients outside these two markets will be reviewed to see if there is potential to make profits on an ongoing basis.

Marketing & Demographic Data

All information and charts are provided by the Saskatchewan Economic Development Authority.

Leading growth industries, Saskatoon, 2000

	Count	% of total
Business & professional services	190	27.09%
Personal & household services	109	16.01%
Traditional retail	77	11.31%
Building & construction related services	74	10.87%
Commercial service sector	65	9.43%
Health, wellness & education services	57	8.37%
Repair & maintenance services	39	5.73%
Automotive sales & service	27	3.96%
Manufacturing	18	2.64%
Services related to manufacturing, wholesale & transportation	17	2.50%
Wholesale industries	8	1.17%
Total	**681**	**100.00%**

Proportion of part time employees by suburban development area

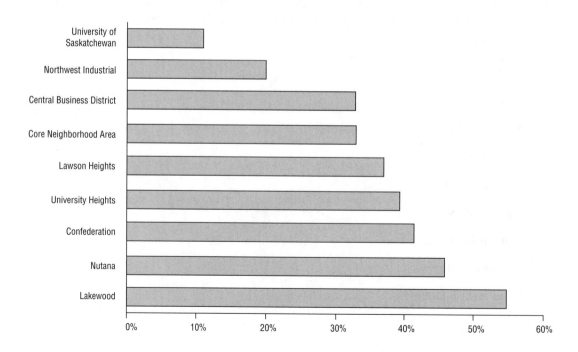

Competition

Our direct competitors in the market are Kelly Services, Labour Ready, Adecco, and Employment Network. Listed below are the areas where each one of these companies operate and the prices they charge.

Kelly Services

- Office & Administrative: $14–$18 per hour

- Customer Service: $11–$13 per hour

- Light Industrial: $12–$15 per hour

- Information Technology: $20–$36 per hour

- Scientific personnel: $25–$40 per hour

Labour Ready

- Construction: $14–$20 per hour

- Manufacturing: $12–$16 per hour

- Maintenance: $11–$14 per hour

- Farming: $14–$18 per hour

- Retail: $10–$12 per hour

- Transport: $16–$19 per hour

- Warehouse: $11–$13 per hour

- Hospitality: $10–$12 per hour

- Landscaping: $10–$12 per hour

- Horticulture: $10–$12 per hour

Adecco

- Temporary Staffing: $10–$12 per hour

- Payroll services: Rate quote on request

- Call centre: Rate quote on request

- Contract employment: Rate quote on request

- Permanent Staff Recruiting Service

Employment Network

- Construction: $13–$18 per hour

- Manufacturing: $15–$18 per hour

- Maintenance: $12–$13 per hour

- Farming: $11–$13 per hour

- Retail: $11–$13 per hour

- Transport: $13–$15 per hour

- Warehouse: $13–$14 per hour

- Hospitality: $11–$13 per hour

- Landscaping: $11–$14 per hour

Our Services & Pricing

- Construction: $10–$14 per hour

- Manufacturing: $10–$14 per hour

- Maintenance: $9.50–$11 per hour

- Farming: $11–$13 per hour

- Retail: $10–$11 per hour

- Transport: $14–$16 per hour

- Warehouse: $10–$12 per hour

- Hospitality: $10–$12 per hour

- Landscaping: $10–$12 per hour

- Horticulture: $10–$12 per hour

Growth Strategy

Our goal is to have a steady stream of staff to offer our clients. Our pricing strategy for the first 3 years is to make smaller margins for similar services that competitors offer. While doing this GENRX LLC will be able to win more contracts and build a steady revenue stream.

Our temporary staff will be paid above average wages and benefits. GENRX LLC will also go above the norm in the industry and offer medical and dental benefits to all temp staff who work 25 hours per week or more. While doing this will add to the bottom line cost of our company, it will help us achieve our long term goal of attracting top-of-the-line workers and therefore offering our clients the best talent.

Marketing our business will take the traditional approach. In addition, we will employ new marketing strategies to build and grow our business. GENRX LLC will place small ads in the yellow pages of both cities in which we operate. Additionally, we will place sustaining business-card-size ads in local newspapers.

Local Newspapers

Saskatoon Star Phoenix

- Annual Advertising budget of $7,000

- 35,000 paid circulation

- Daily newspaper

- MOPE Nadbank data reflects high business owner/manager readership

Regina Leader Post

- Annual Advertising budget of $5,000

- 31,000 paid circulation

- Daily newspaper

Prairie Dog Newspaper

- Annual Advertising budget of $4,000

- 25,000 paid circulation

- Weekly newspaper

Planet S

- Annual Advertising budget of $4,000

- 25,000 paid circulation

- Weekly newspaper

Radio Stations

- C95—Annual Advertising budget of $5,000

- CJME—Annual Advertising budget of $5,000

Building our new business will require spending on advertising and marketing. Over the course of the business start–up, however, we are confidant that going into years three and four, our advertising spending will be reduced because we will have built our number of clients and will not be required to continue to spend money to get awareness.

Business name recognition will be important to our business. We will use a variety of methods to get this awareness in addition to word of mouth and media events like charity sponsorships.

Charity sponsorships will be easy to find; all we need to do is offer free staffing in exchange for name coverage via the radio, newspaper or television. This will allow us to get more exposure for less than the cost of traditional advertising.

CUSTOMERS

Our focus will be to secure clients who may require our services on an ongoing basis. This will mean GENRX LLC will ask specific questions once a client calls our firm. These questions will gather key market research information that will help us identify the client's present needs *and* future needs. GENRX LLC will place all this information in the client's file for assessment.

List of Potential Sectors

- Manufacturing

- Retailing

- Construction

- Trucking (both long and short haul)

- Farming

- Office & Administrative

- Sales & Marketing

The industry norm is to charge a minimum of 25 percent for all work required to be done on the site by our staff. What this means is that if a client charged $10.00 per hour, then the worker gets $7.50 per hour and the staffing firm will get $2.50 per hour.

We do not feel this is fair for the worker or the client. Therefore, GENRX LLC will only charge 15 percent. This then will mean that for every $10.00 hour we charge a client, the staff person filling the position will make $8.50 per hour and $1.50 per hour will go to us.

This rate structure will also benefit the client, because we will be able to offer our clients the services of better staff than our competitors.

RISK FACTORS

There are risks in any business that starts from scratch, but having a solid business plan will be key to prepare for these risks.

One of our main risk factors is our competition. They are not likely to sit back and allow us to enter the market; in fact, we are confidant that they will match our pricing once it becomes apparent to them that they are losing business. Based on our review of the market, if we can win 5% of the market in the first year of business and then maintain it, we will be well positioned for future success.

We are very confidant that there is enough business for all of our competitors and us.

FINANCIAL ANALYSIS

Start–Up Expenses
Saskatoon Office

- Office Rental–$700 month
- Yellow pages–$250 month
- Telephone line & equipment–$400 month
- Internet–$75 month
- Office supplies–$1,000 (start up)
- Office supplies–$200 month
- Advertising–$5,000 (start up)
- Advertising–$500 month
- Office equipment—Computers, fax, copier, printers, etc–$5,000
- Desks, file cabinets etc.–$2,000
- Utilities–included in rent
- Parking–included in rent
- Leasehold improvements–included in rent
- First 3 months rent–free with 3 year lease
- Payroll and other software–$2,000

Regina Office

- Office Rental–$600 month
- Yellow pages–$250 month
- Telephone line & equipment–$400 month
- Internet–$75 month
- Office supplies–$1,000 (start up)
- Office supplies–$200 month
- Advertising–$4,000 (start up)
- Advertising–$400 month

- Office equipment—Computers, fax, copier, printers, etc.–$4,000

- Desks, file cabinets etc.–$1,500

- Utilities–included in rent

- Parking–included in rent

- Leasehold improvements–included in rent

- First 3 months rent–free with 3 year lease

- Payroll and other software–$1,000

We were able to negotiate with the landlord for three free months of rent per year we are in business. Our total start up expenses will amount to $31,500 (not including wages and salaries to our full time staff).

Our ongoing monthly expense will be $5,950 for both locations (not including wages).

Our wages for our full time staff will be expensed at the following rate:

- Manager owner—Monthly salary of $4,000

- 5 staff persons—$1,400 per month for each staff person and 5% of bookings for each client they sign to contracts.

Therefore our monthly staffing expense will be $11,000. Our total monthly company staff and office expense will be $16,950 per month.

Projected Income
We have determined that the in the first year we will set our goal to hire out an average of 30 staff per month for a total of 160 billable hours each at an average of $16.00 per hour.

Based on our estimates, we will average $11,520 per month in revenue. While this is less than our fixed costs, we have budgeted for the loss as a way to manage the risk.

Banking and Finance
Based on the required money to launch this business, the owner has invested $100,000 in cash.

Cash will be used to pay for all start–up expenses and monthly expenses as needed. Additionally this money will be used to secure an operating line of credit.

We have made an arrangement with the bank for an interest rate of five percent on the line of credit because we will maintain at least $50,000 in cash in the reserve.

The bank has also agreed to send us referrals if any of their business clients are in need of staff but cannot afford to hire full– or part–time staff by the traditional methods.

MANAGEMENT SUMMARY

Ben Worth—Owner/Manager
Ben has worked in the Human Resources sector for 20 years with four separate companies. These companies range from 40–employee firms all the way up to a 350–employee firm.

Over the course of the last seven years Ben started putting aside money for the business start–up because he always wanted to own his own company. His experience in the HR area has given Ben the ability to understand staffing needs and requirements. Furthermore, his direct experience with the general staffing companies in the area has given him a good understanding of our competitors as well the market in general.

Go–Cart Designer and Supplier

Speedy Go–Carts

342 Third St.
Ottawa, Ontario K1A0B1

Gerald Rekve

This company produces a go–cart that is equipped with a unique and patented braking system.

EXECUTIVE SUMMARY

Traditional go–carts are universally recognized to have multiple safety hazards, most notably caused by faulty braking systems. Speedy Go–Carts, with their unique and patented braking system, are the solution!

Sales of brand name go–carts have declined from about 5 million per year from ten years ago to about 4 million at present.

We feel the decline of the go–cart is due to its inherent safety hazards. If good, safe go–carts were available, the sport could be renewed and rejuvenated and the market could be dominated by the newer, safer go–cart.

Traditionally, most designers only utilized four wheels for their go–carts; this design inevitably leads to wheel skidding and flat spots, quickly destroying the wheels utilized for braking. Alternatives to this traditional design include hydraulic go–cart systems, but these are impossible to market because of their high cost.

Our unique go–cart model fulfills the crucial criteria of smooth and effective go–carts that are both simple and inexpensive to manufacture (only about $32–63 per go–cart). In spite of this, it has been difficult to introduce our go–cart prototype to manufacturers. We feel this is due to a number of different factors:

1. The information gets lost in the bureaucracies of those companies without reaching the decision–makers.

2. Most manufacturers have already been burned by trying to introduce poorly designed go–cart systems.

3. They are constantly being inundated by go–cart inventions that do not meet their criteria. This has resulted in a great skepticism regarding go–cart inventions.

4. Staff members that receive the information have no real incentive to put the ideas to the test.

5. The manufacturers have long–term production plans that they are very unwilling to interrupt.

Expert Opinions

Ben Clamtom, the buyer of go–carts for a major retailer (300 stores in Canada), tested the prototype and again confirmed the effectiveness of our go–cart system.

Ted Dansom, Vice President of OTHHO Sports in New York, has tested twenty–five different go–cart systems stated that the Speedy Go–Cart, "definitely works." In fact, his company made an offer for the exclusive rights to the invention that was proportionate to their small market share—about 100,000 per year. Unfortunately, this was too low for us to accept.

MARKET ANALYSIS

It is assumed that the reader of the following is aware of the obvious market need for go–carts equipped with a smooth and effective braking system, one that is far superior to the ineffective and hazardous rubber stoppers presently in use by all go–cart manufacturers.

It is also assumed that the reader is familiar with the invention titled "Four Wheel Mechanical Go–Carts System" and agrees that this is the best possible solution to the problem, and that therefore basic viability of this business opportunity is self evident.

The question that remains to be answered prior to receiving detailed quotes and information from manufacturers is, "What is the profit potential for this business opportunity?" This business plan seeks to answer this question.

Presently, there are approximately 20 go–cart manufacturers. The most well known brand names are sold primarily in large chain sporting good stores, while the other, smaller manufacturers are focused more on the local and specialized go–cart market.

Currently there are approximately 4 million brand name go–carts sold annually. This is a decline compared to the sales of 5 million brand name go–carts sold annually only 10–15 years ago. It is estimated that off–brand manufacturers sell an average 50,000 go–carts per year. Assuming this average holds, the off–brand go–cart market is currently at approximately one million go–carts annually.

The popularity of go–carts has declined somewhat since its peak and research shows that brand names have lost a lot of their market share to the specialized go–cart market. The two distinct markets are now somewhat overlapping as inexpensive go–carts manufactured by brand name manufacturers are appearing in some specialized stores. Brand name manufacturers are facing stiff competition and low profit margins in this new market.

The bottom line: NO MANUFACTURER HAS A DISTINCT ADVANTAGE IN THE MARKET.

Customers

The estimated worldwide customer base for go–carts is approximately one million people.

When anticipating what the market response will be when Speedy Go–Carts are introduced into both sporting goods and specialized stores, it seems both logical and reasonable to expect that the market response will be very positive—simply because it fills a very real market need. This is evidenced by the fact that so many inventors have spent millions of dollars on hundreds of patents in a quest to solve the braking problem for go–carts.

Faced with competition from such a superior go–cart, it is reasonable to assume that *all* manufacturers will lose a substantial portion of their market share. The resulting loss of market share will likely push some manufacturers into the red.

The totally unexploited, multi–million worldwide market of people that don't like to use go–carts because of safety concerns will immediately be accessible. Safe go–carts can also be extended from flat to steeper ground. This is expected to become popular also with experienced go–cart racers and will consequently open an additional unexploited market niche.

The bottom line: SPEEDY GO–CARTS HAVE OUTSTANDING MARKET POTENTIAL.

Competition

In spite of all the hundreds of patents issued so far for go–cart systems, not a single market success has been achieved. Research of previous patents provides an obvious reason. Of all the patented go–cart designs, none offers a safe and effective braking system.

The bottom line: THERE IS NO COMPETITION. SPEEDY GO CARTS ARE EQUIPPED WITH A SAFE AND EFFECTIVE BRAKING SYSTEM THAT IS OTHERWISE NOT AVAILABLE IN THE MARKET.

MARKETING & SALES

The Speedy Go–Cart Company will assume a position as global wholesaler of the new and unique go–cart. Creative marketing strategies will be associated with the new product launch, taking full advantage of the media attention received from well–planned publicity stunts on global sports TV channels, thereby significantly reducing marketing costs.

A targeted marketing campaign involving Internet marketing and all other media will coincide to maximize this exposure. By maintaining the momentum and marketing advantage gained, imitators trying to compete will be severely disadvantaged.

The bottom line: FREE PUBLICITY WILL CREATE THE LAUNCHING MOMENTUM REQUIRED.

Patent Protection

Patent rights are necessary in order to raise operating capital and to maximize the value of the company. However, patents only provide offensive rights, so the best way to discourage imitators and patent infringement is to rapidly dominate the market at a price that will not be profitable for others desiring to compete. Highly favorable international search and preliminary examination reports have been received from the European Patent Office.

The bottom line: THE MOST IMPORTANT KEY U.S. MARKET WILL BE COVERED BY BROAD, UNAVOIDABLE PATENT PROTECTION.

FINANCIAL ANALYSIS

Estimated Sales/Profits

All amounts are in Canadian dollars.

	Per soap box
Wholesale price	$450
Manufacturing cost	$350
Marketing, admin, operating and distribution costs	$50
Net profit	$50
Year 1	
Estimated sales	1 million carts
Estimated gross profit	$4 m
Estimated net profit	$2 m
Year 2	
Estimated sales	2.5 million carts
Estimated gross profit	$22 m
Estimated net profit	$15 m
Year 3	
Estimate sales	5 million carts
Estimated gross profit	$44 m
Estimated net profit	$28 m

Start–Up Costs

$1,500,000 Canadian is required in the initial startup phase.

Estimated expenses:

Engineering	$ 250,000
Tooling for test samples	$ 200,000
Manufacture test samples	$ 100,000
Testing	$ 190,000
Modification	$ 70,000
Manufacture 2nd test samples	$ 40,000
Test 2nd test samples	$ 70,000
Advertising/promotion	$ 230,000
Overhead/operating costs	$ 350,000

Production Phase Funding

Institutional funding and/or private investor capital will be sought as bridge funding that will be required to sustain the company operations through to profitability.

Home Inspection Company

Home Inspectors Are We

9123 Thornberry St.
Ann Arbor, Michigan 48103

Gerald Rekve

In today's real estate world there are a number of opportunities to start a business, but the area with the most profit potential is the area of home inspection.

EXECUTIVE SUMMARY

Growth Strategy

Our number one goal is to begin building long–term relationships with real estate agents in the region. The key to this strategy is to build trust as well as professionalism with our long–term goal of getting referrals from them. Referrals will be the key to our success in business. Following is our breakdown of the different types of referrals we will build.

1. Real estate agents

2. Home owners

3. Lawyers involved in real estate deals

4. Carpet cleaners

5. Home cleaners

6. Security companies

7. Moving and storage companies

8. Plumbing and electrical firms

9. Banks and mortgage brokers

10. Home renovation firms

11. Landscapers

12. Advertising mediums which sell or offer home improvements

For every referral we get, we are saving the cost of advertising to that client.

Yellow page advertising as well as real estate magazines will also be required to get a foothold into the market. We believe it is better to have an advertising plan that includes a smaller ad that runs on a more frequent basis than a larger ad that runs less frequently, so we will look for advertising opportunities accordingly.

FINANCIAL ANALYSIS

The start up costs to open a home inspection business

Home office	Free
Computer	$1,200
Software	$1,000
Office supplies	$ 300
Postal	$ 400
Legal	$ 450
Accounting	$ 50
Advertising	$ 500
Printed materials	$1,500
Desk	$ 200
Chair	$ 150
Fax	$ 125
Scanner	$ 100
Filing cabinet	$ 200
Shelves	$ 100
Cell phone	$ 150
City license fee	$ 100
Professional association fee	$ 150
Training in home inspection	$250–$1,000 (books, study course)
Liability insurance	$ 400
Auto lease	$ 400 month
Auto expenses	$ 500 month

BUSINESS STRATEGY

A home inspection is a thorough examination of the exterior and the interior of the house to determine the structural defects, broken or obsolete components, and damage due to water, wear and tear, and other conditions. As home inspectors, we are not responsible to fix or repair any of the property we are inspecting. We are only there to give our unbiased view for both the buyer and the seller of the unit.

Every time a house is bought or sold, a home inspection should be done. The most frequent buyer of the home inspection service is the home buyer, so this is the area to which we want to target our marketing dollars.

As a home inspector, it is not required to be an engineer. However, in order to be successful, training should be gained either via working in the industry or with a training course. It will add a great deal of creditability and real estate agents will be more likely refer clients to you. This being so, we plan to seek both practical and educational training.

There are several forms with which we must be familiar. The home inspector report is an itemization and summation of findings of the home with regard to the specific property. In addition, property condition forms are generally furnished to the seller by the real estate agent and ask the seller to fully disclose the all the defects about the home in writing. The home inspector compares this form with his report and provides the buyer a more accurate picture of the condition of the house.

Many states are currently formulating regulations to license and certify home inspectors. We will check with our state to determine the status of this requirement.

Gaining Experience

Before we open up shop, we will do the following to gain experience and build our skills.

We will ask ten to fifteen friends and relatives if we can give them a free home inspection. In doing so, we can hone our skills in the inspection business. We want to try to inspect the following types of homes, based on the year the home was built:

1940–1950	Inspect 10 homes
1950–1960	Inspect 7 homes
1960–1970	Inspect 10 homes
1970–1980	Inspect 5 homes
1980–1990	Inspect 10 homes
1990–2000+	Inspect 5 homes

We will also try to go to different new home building locations and watch how the homes are built; this will give us great insight to the new ways of building and the weakness of the old ways of building. Furthermore, new homebuilders can also give us a great deal of information on what to look for in a house, including the most common areas where houses are affected by poor workmanship.

FINANCIAL ANALYSIS

Fees

The average home inspector charges a fee of $190 to $500 for a typical inspection. The average time it takes to do an inspection varies; it can take from one hour to two and a half hours. Each job is quoted based on a estimated time it will take. We use $190 per hour as our minimum charge.

Basic home inspection fee	$ 190
With swimming pool	add $ 200
Environmental concerns	add $ 150
Multiple units	add $ 150 per unit
Farm or outside city limits	add $3.50 per mile
Insurance appraisal inspection certificate	add $ 100

Our market is quite large. Whenever a home is bought or sold, there should be a home inspection done; this means quite a lot of potential clients. Here is a formula to determine the market potential.

500 homes sold in a month, less 20 percent, divided by the number of home inspectors in the market.

If there were 4 the formula would look like this:

500 homes sold, less 20% = 400 homes. Divide 400 homes by 4 (the number of local inspectors), and each inspector could expect to service 100 homes per month. At an average cost of $200 per home, each inspector could expect to make $20,000 per month.

OPERATIONS

Equipment

As in many professions, there are tools and equipment of the trade. At the beginning we will not buy all tools required because some of them only need to be used on a rare occasion.

- Measuring tape. One 50 foot tape and one 100 foot tape.

- Binoculars. These are good for roof inspection if you cannot walk on the roof.

- Digital camera and photo equipment. Photos can be used for inspection report and records in case of liability issues. Digital images can be stored on a CD or our computer hard drive for future reference.

- Protective clothing. This is very important, not only to our health and our clothing, but also for our image. We plan to arrive in a suit, but will put on a white one piece protective jump suit with our logo before we begin the inspection work.

- Safety gear, including dust mask, goggles, helmet, gloves, and steel–toed boots.

- Electrical circuit tester.

- Voltage meter.

- Stud finder.

- High–powered flashlights. We will need a few different types including a small pocket or pen size, a medium size and a large size.

- Ladders. We will need a couple different types of ladders, including a step stool–type ladder, an 8 foot ladder, and a 20 to 30 foot expandable ladder. All of these will be attached to our van at all times.

- Gas leak detector. Some of the leaks that occur in a house are carbon monoxide and benign methane gas.

- Level.

- Market area maps. These will show land structure, grading and landscaping methods, etc.

- Moister meter.

- Screwdrivers and other hand tools to be kept in a tool belt.

- Mirrors. A small mirror and a large mirror, both with telescope capacity and a light, will help look in small or hard–to–reach areas.

- Thermometer. This can be used to measurer the recovery rate of the hot water heater.

- Toolbox or carrying case. This will be used for larger tools that will not fit in our tool belt.

- Business cards. We will have two types of business cards, both the standard card and a magnetic card with helpful info on it that the home owner can keep on their refrigerator for a long time.

Information Technology Personnel Agency

Revke IT Staffing

31 Wielfeld Hwy.
Detroit, Michigan 48202

Gerald Rekve

Rekve IT Staffing will provide additional services as well as support to a very specific field in the business sector. We will offer services to all IT sectors including computing, internet, and website design. Specifically we will offer: desktop support, software support, hardware support, network support, and infrastructure support.

EXECUTIVE SUMMARY

Rekve IT Staffing Inc. ("Rekve IT Staffing") was formed in 2005, when a market opportunity was identified by the owner of a Michigan–based computer repair and network consulting firm.

Mission

The goal of Rekve IT Staffing is to provide additional services as well as support to a very specific field in the business sector. We will hire contract staff to provide support in areas where the clients' staff is not qualified.

We will offer services to all IT sectors including computing, internet, website design and so on.

In order to begin this service, there will be little impact on our existing cash flows with exception of the start up marketing, advertising and additional resources required.

Company History

Rekve IT Staffing is a division of Bixby Computer Networks Inc. In 2005 Bixby Computer Networks had revenues of $1.5 million dollars and a staff of 8 people. They have been servicing the greater part of Detroit, Michigan for more than 15 years.

Bixby Computer Networks was founded by Jonathan Rekve after he graduated from technical college in the late 1980s. Jonathan found that his interest in owning his own company was more appealing than working for someone else. From the start, the business was lean on staff; over the years, though, it gradually hired more staff as the company required. Today with eight staff on board, the company is very profitable and has some long–term, big name clients on contract.

With the solid foundation that has been built up over 15 years, Mr. Rekve has allowed the expansion of Bixby Computer Networks into other areas that are of similar nature to the existing business model.

MARKET ANALYSIS

Computer networking in the Michigan market is like most markets in the world. There has been solid growth curve of the industry for the past 20 years. With the evolution of computing in the late 70s, the industry has not stopped.

The Detroit market is very competitive to say the least, with new companies starting almost on a daily basis. This has given existing firms like Bixby Computer Networks a run for their money. Competition this strong has also educated potential clients. Clients look for quality service and providers like us that have been around for while before committing to contracts. In fact, we have found smaller contracts (under $5,000) are typically from one–time clients and larger contracts (up to $50,000) are from existing clients or clients looking for a long–term solution and are thus willing to pay a little extra to get the quality they require. We feel that expanding into Rekve IT Staffing will just be an extension of our existing products and services.

Staffing in general over the years has taken many forms; we will be using the business model of knowledge–based staffing. The primary focus of knowledge–based staffing is to provide very specific solutions to issues and problems that clients currently face.

SERVICES

As mentioned earlier, we have identified a market niche that we feel is being underserved by existing vendors. We will be able to cross–sell services to fill this underserved area to both existing clients as well new clients.

We will offer the following staffing services to clients for daily, weekly, and monthly rates. Our contract staff may be at a client location for up to one year.

Our service will include all sectors of the IT industry in our region. Here is a list of a few of the areas; we will add more as they become relevant and cost effective.

- Desktop support
- Software support
- Hardware support
- Network support
- Infrastructure support

Each one of these areas can be broken down into many smaller departments; therefore, we will be required to hire specialist staff contract consultants as they become needed and available.

Desktop Support
This area will include the following departments:

- Upgrades
- Virus protection and recovery
- Software glitches
- Hardware configuration

Software Support
This area will include the following departments:

- Upgrades
- Virus protection and recovery

- Software glitches
- Software configuration

Hardware Support

This area will include the following departments:

- Router configuration
- Router troubleshooting
- Network devise troubleshooting
- Upgrades
- Recommendations
- Price quotes

Network Support

This area will include the following departments:

- Network configuration
- Devise setup
- Router configuration and setup
- Software installation
- Network troubleshooting
- Training existing staff to further troubleshoot network issues
- Purchase and installation of network devices

Infrastructure Support

This area will include the following departments:

- General infrastructure support
- Specific projects as needed

OPERATIONS

Workflow Process

Within our mandate of services, we will act to become an extension of staff for our clients. Rather than the client hiring full–time staff to complete functions within the company, the client will hire us on contract to complete the function. The IT staff of most companies are usually stretched to the limits. Our services will allow them to add help they need when they need it most.

Generally speaking, this is how our service will work; we will of course make required changes as the need arises. To begin, clients will contact us or one of our sales staff will put in a tender for services or solicit potential clients. Next, our staff manager will attend to the clients tender or request for pricing of services. This manager will then do a review of the required work and, based on this review, will estimate the hours/days/weeks required to complete the job. She will also look at which specialized skills will be necessary to properly complete the job based on the accepted and approved technological skills. With all this information now gathered, we will be able to offer a price quote to the client for the services required.

Filling Staffing Requests

When clients are in need of an Rekve IT Staffing employee, the first thing we will ask them to do is to determine the exact job duties and skills they will need the employee to perform. If the IT staffing employee will be replacing a career employee, we will ask the client if they will need the employee to perform the full scope of job duties or just a portion of the job functions. We may request a written job description with the duties they wish the Rekve IT Staffing employee to perform.

When we have that information, we can then determine the skills needed to perform the duties including such things as: what type of computer equipment (IBM or Macintosh) will be needed; software (WordPerfect, Microsoft Word, etc.); and what type of documents will be produced (manuscripts, letters, financial reports, etc.).

Furthermore, this information will allow us to classify the client job order using the Point Factor Systems and conduct an applicant search in the Rekve IT Staffing database for the best possible candidate.

Hours of Operation

Rekve IT Staffing is open from 8:00 am to 6:00 pm Monday through Friday to assist with client requests. We will also have a hotline number for after–hours support.

Orientation

To ensure that our staff have the best possible chances for success, we will ask clients to prepare for their arrival by doing such things as determining where they are going to sit, who will be supervising their work (if other than the stated supervisor), and who will be available to answer any questions they may have. We would like the employees to be given a brief introduction to other staff members in client office and be provided a brief overview of the office functions and instructions on job duties, departmental expectations, deadlines, and a lunch and break schedule. This preparation and information is crucial to avoid miscommunications and potential problems.

Overtime

Rekve IT staff will be available to work overtime when it is requested by their direct supervisor. The pay standards for overtime are the same as for career employees. Rekve IT Staffing employees are also paid shift differentials and premium overtime when authorized.

Employee Benefits

Employees of Rekve IT Staffing accrue vacation and sick leave by pay period. They are paid for holidays when they are on pay status before and after the holiday. They are eligible to receive CORE Medical benefits after three months service with Rekve IT Staffing. If an employee is hired into a career or casual position by a client department, all vacation and sick leave hours will be transferred to the new department upon notification.

Identification Badges

All Rekve IT Staffing Employees are required to wear I.D. Badges. The Rekve IT Staffing badges are not permanent badges with pictures; instead they are yellow in color and have the Rekve IT Staffing employee's name, the Client Department's Name, an Expiration Date, and signatures of both the Rekve IT Staffing employee and a client staff representative. These will be worn in addition to any identification or badges required by the client.

Rate and Billing Procedure

The recharge rate for Rekve IT Staffing employees is $75.00 per hour. Clients will be recharged according to the number of hours authorized on the Rekve IT Staffing employee's timesheet, which will require both the employee and client signatures. The client signature is imperative; it is our authorization to pay the Rekve IT Staffing employee and to recharge the client account for the number of hours indicated on the timesheet. Clients will receive recharge statements the first week of each month for IT staffing services undertaken in the preceding month.

Recruitment Process

Rekve IT Staffing actively recruits qualified applicants. We have a weekly posting in the Job Opportunities Bulletin and, when a special need is identified, we will advertise in local newspapers. Our most successful avenue of recruitment is by employee referral. Most of our applicants identify an Rekve IT Staffing employee as their first source of reference. Also, the staff at Rekve IT Staffing participates in job fairs, career days and professional organizations to find qualified applicants.

Application Process

All applicants are required to fill out a Rekve IT Staffing application detailing their work experience and history as well as a Skill Sheet, or self assessment. The information from these forms will then be entered into the Rekve IT Staffing database and reviewed by a member of the Rekve IT Staffing staff.

The criteria will also be used to screen applicants. Our screening process will prioritize the skills that have been determined to be in high demand when reviewing the job order requests from our client. Potential employees that possess those skills will be given priority and invited to a Rekve IT Staffing interview. Those that do not possess the needed skills will be sent a post card thanking them for their interest in the Rekve IT Staffing and indicating that their skills do not match our requirements at this time. They will be encouraged to inform us as they add to their education or skill level.

At the interview the applicant's work history and training will be discussed and their skill sheet will be reviewed in specific detail. Once the Rekve IT Staffing staff member determines that an applicant meets our skill requirements, the applicant's skills will be further evaluated to determine which level of assignment the applicant can be successfully placed. These evaluations will be determined by entering the applicant's experience and training into assessment software programs such as QWIZ for IBM and Mac Valuate for Macintosh. A general administrative skills evaluation program is also contained in the QWIZ package and is given to all applicants for such skills as typing speed, letter formatting, and, if applicable, 10 key, data, programming, transcription, and statistical skills. The applicant's scores will be entered into the Rekve IT Staffing database for future assignment skills matching.

Once it is determined the applicant is suitable for hire into Rekve IT Staffing, they will be given our Policy and Procedures Manual and our expectations and performance standards will be discussed. Two employment references will also be checked before an applicant is actually hired and placed on an assignment.

Checks and Balances

In addition to the reference checks on each applicant, Employee Evaluation Forms will be sent to the direct supervisor of all employees at the end of each assignment. Feedback will be sought in the following areas: Attendance, Punctuality, Skill, and Knowledge and Production; there will also be an area for additional supervisor comments. The evaluation form is *essential* to maintaining the quality of the employees in our program and the level of service we have promised our clients.

Hourly rates

Over time we may review and adjust these rates to reflect the current market conditions.

Department	Hourly rate
Analysis & design	$65
API's–standards/methods	$75
Architecture	$75
Auditing	$75
Certifications	$75
Data adminstration	$75
Data development	$75
Dev-client server	$75
Dev-mainframe	$75
Dev-mid range	$75
Dev-PC and desktop	$75
Dev-web	$75
Dev-wireless	$75
Development tools	$75
Enterprise change management	$75
ERP & packaged software	$75
Groupware	$75
Hardware/OS/sys admin	$75
Help desk and support	$75
Industries and apps	$75
IT management	$75
Networking	$75
Product management	$75
Project management	$75
QA & testing	$75
Security	$75
Support	$75
Tech trainers	$75
Technical writers	$75
Telecom	$75
Web analytics	$75

Our key areas of focus are listed below. As the company grows, we may add areas of opportunity or delete areas that are not profitable.

Business Applications

a. Business Application Delivery/Development

b. SAP Projects

c. E–Mail/Lotus Notes Delivery

d. Customer Relationship Management (CRM)

Data & Storage

a. Data Warehousing

b. Database/Data Administration

Infrastructure

a. Enterprise Architecture/Planning

b. Architecture Management

c. Infrastructure Development

d. Enterprise Infrastructure

Network and Systems Management

a. Network Operations

b. Systems Operations

c. Enterprise Operations

d. IT Support

e. Network Engineering

f. Systems Engineering

g. Enterprise Project Management

h. Inter/Intra/Extranet

Services and Outsourcing

a. Electronic Commerce/INet

b. Contingency Planning

c. Business/IT Alignment

Security

Security Management

COMPETITION

As mentioned above, we have a number of competitors in all of these sectors. For this purpose we will only mention the largest competitor.

Mitchell Technology Solutions

This is the largest competitor we have in the market. They have 60 contract staff on duty in all IT sectors and they advertise weekly for a variety of positions in the career section of the local newspaper.

They also use online career advertising services and have a number of postings for contract consultants. They have been around for 20 years and have a strong market position. They have a lot of strengths, but also have a few weaknesses including that fact that they do not pay their contract staff very well. Consequently, they have a high turnover rate in the contract consultants they employ. We have been able to exploit this weakness and have hired away some of their best staff.

GROWTH STRATEGY

Michigan has over 200,000 businesses listed with the state registration service. Of these businesses, there are 80,000 with employee counts over 50. These firms are the focus of our efforts—they are larger firms that are more likely to require our type of services. If we get one percent of the market, it will be enough to maintain our business for a long period of time.

Employment by Industry

Major Industry in the Detroit–area

Internationally known for automobile manufacturing and trade, the world headquarters of General Motors Corp. and Ford Motor Co. and the North American headquarters of DaimlerChrysler and Volkswagen are located in metro Detroit. The area ranks as a leader in the production of paints, non–electrical machinery and automation equipment, as well as pharmaceutical, rubber products, synthetic resins and garden seed. Other national and international corporations headquartered here include The Budd Company, American National Resources, Kelly Services, SBC, and Federal Mogul, plus pizza giants Domino's, Hungry Howie's and Little Caesars.

Agriculture, mining & natural resources	20,236
Manufacturing	419,871
Transportation, communication & utility	121,683
Wholesale trade	131,303
Retail trade	392,604
Finance, insurance & real estate	182,873
Services	915,743
Public administration	78,715
Total	**2,262,758**

SOURCE: Statistics from the *Southeast Michigan Council of Governments* as of 2000.

FINANCIAL ANALYSIS

Start Up Expenses

Because we are already in business, we will not have the same start–up expenses that others would have when starting a new business. All we will be doing is increasing our existing staff and resources to accommodate the new business. While the new business will be a separate entity, it will share our existing office location and materials.

We will be hiring three sales executives along with a sales manager and support staff. These staff will coordinate the flow of contracts and temp staff we place in the varieties of clients' locations.

Payroll for new company will be low compared to our existing operation.

- Manager—$30,000 annual salary and bonus component of 10% of all sales made

- Sales staff—$17,000 annual salary and bonus component of 10% of all sales made

- Support staff—$14,000 annual salary (one staff member to start)

- Individual contract staff we hire for placement are only paid on a per–job basis. This will amount to pay rates from $25–$36 per hour

We will also pay the following expenses:

- Travel expenses for manager and sales staff

- Auto allowance

- Gas reimbursement

- Meals for clients and sales staff on road

- Hotel

- Other travel not mentioned here

- Office supplies for presentations

- Laptop computers

- Cell phones

We are going to set up our staffing firm a little different than most; we will be actively going after clients we know who use this type of service and make sales calls right in their place of business.

With this hands–on approach we are confidant that we will meet our sales targets.

The best part of this add–on business is the fact that we will be getting our complete line of services put in front of new clients. All our sales material will have a good overview of the services we provide.

CONTRACT CONSULTANTS & STAFF

We have already lined up staff that will meet with our clients once we get the contracts. We have been recruiting staff for the past six months and have a number lined up.

This will make it easy for us to manage the clients we bring in, as we can fill the opening as soon as we win the contract.

CONCLUSION

The addition of information technology contract staff will be a positive force for our business. The growth potential will be allow us to diversify our business, while increasing profit and revenue streams.

Online Payment Services

Exactor Technologies, LLC

980 Floridian Way
Orlando, Florida 32812

Gerald Rekve

In 2006, Exactor Technologies, LLC was formed for the purpose of selling money orders and payment methods for online customers. Overall, our company can be characterized as a money service business. Our website allows buyers to send sellers money orders and payment methods online for auction payments using a Visa or MasterCard. We act as a middleman to facilitate this process easily, safely, and securely.

EXECUTIVE SUMMARY

Mission

Exactor Technologies, LLC's Mission is to provide innovative, practical and top–quality payment services that save time and improve the way people transact online. We believe our first responsibility is to the users who use our services. Our strong financial position will enable us to provide excellent customer service. In carrying out our day–to–day business we strive to:

1. Treat our employees with respect.

2. Follow the philosophy that our customers are the lifeline of our business model.

3. Be considered as a moral and ethical leader in our community.

We envision our business becoming a dominate online payment method in the next 3 years. Within the next 10 years, we envision our company being publicly traded on a stock exchange. By 2010, Exactor Technologies, LLC will be a highly visible company known as the best payment method online.

BUSINESS STRATEGY

For many years people have been limited to only one large company in this field—PayPal—and several other small companies that have included BidPay, StormPay, EMOCorp, and eGold. This small number of choices has been further limited for online merchants and consumers since the closure of both BidPay and EMOCorp.

The condition of the industry today is such that the Internet is becoming an integral part of people's daily lives and a tool for the development of the global economy. Online merchants have become the standard as well and norm for business startup and expansion of existing retailers.

We have just started development of a novel and proprietary website to integrate with online auction and merchant services such as eBay, Yahoo, Overstock, and other corporate websites to facilitate the selling of money orders and payment methods for online transactions.

The legal form of Exactor Technologies, LLC is Limited Liability Company residing in the State of Florida with Registered Agents in other states as required by Law. An LLC is suitable for smaller companies with restricted numbers of owners; furthermore, company "members" are protected from liability for acts and debts of the LLC and an LLC can elect to be taxed as a sole proprietor, partnership, S–corp, or corporation, providing much flexibility.

Now, Exactor Technologies, LLC is at a point where we are looking for investors in order to meet State requirements of $500,000 liquid assets to obtain a Money Services Business License in the State of Florida.

FINANCIAL ANALYSIS

Revenue projected for fiscal year 2007 without external funding is expected to be $5,475,000. Annual growth is projected to be exponential and at least double per year through 2009. We feel that within 4 years Exactor Technologies, LLC will be in a suitable position for further expansion and an initial public offering. Our objective at this time is to propel the company into a prominent market position.

Capital Requirements

According to the opportunities and requirements for Exactor Technologies, LLC described in this business plan, and based on what we feel are sound business assumptions, our initial capital requirements are for $500,000 by November 1, 2006.

To accomplish this goal we have developed a comprehensive plan to intensify and accelerate our marketing and sales activities, product development, services expansion, engineering, distribution and customer service. To implement our plans we require a loan or investment totaling $500,000 for the following purposes:

- Obtain a $300,000 bond for a State Money Services Business License,
- Maximize sales with an extensive click–based online advertising campaign to promote our services,
- Reinforce Customer Support services to handle the increased demands created by the influx of new orders and broader coverage of existing accounts,
- Augment company staff to support and sustain prolonged growth under the new marketing plan,
- Increase Research and Development to create additional follow–on products as well as to further fine–tune our competitive advantages.

We anticipate no additional investment requirements after the 2007 fiscal year. We pledge to reinvest all corporate profit minus employee salary and wages back within the company until year 2010.

Exit/Payback

The increase in profits generated by our website will allow us to have the funds to repay any loan and investors within 1–2 years.

Competitor's Fees

PayPal (standard rates) | U.S. domestic transactions (U.S.–U.S.) | International transaction (U.S.–Foreign country)
Fees to deposit/send money (buyer) | Free | Free
Fees to receive money | 2.9% + 30 cents | 3.9% + 30 cents

Storm Pay (non NetIBA rates) | U.S. domestic transactions (U.S.–U.S.) | International transaction (U.S.–Foreign country)
Fees to deposit/send money (buyer) | 3% | 3%
Fees to receive money | 6.9% + 69 cents | 6.9% + 69 cents

Our Proposed Fees

Exactor Technologies LLC proposed rates | U.S. domestic transactions (U.S.–U.S.) | International transaction (U.S.–foreign country)
Fees to deposit/send money (buyer) | 6% | 6%
Fees to receive money | 3% + 84 cents to mail/print money order | 3% + 84 cents to mail/print money order

Start-up requirements

Start-up expenses
Legal	$ 250
Stationery etc.	$ 100
Brochures	$ 125
Accountant	$ 75
Insurance	$ 150
Rent	$ 425
Research and development	$ 0
Expensed equipment	$ 500
Other	**$ 0**
Total start-up expenses	**$1,625**
Start-up assets needed	
Cash balance on starting date	$ 425
Other current assets	**$ 0**
Total current assets	**$ 425**
Long-term assets	**$ 0**
Total assets	**$ 425**
Total requirements	$ 2,050
Investment	
Owner investment	$ 2,050
Other	**$ 0**
Total investment	$ 2,050
Current liabilities	
Accounts payable	$ 0
Current borrowing	$ 0
Other current liabilities	**$ 0**
Current liabilities	$ 0
Long-term liabilities	**$ 0**
Total liabilities	$ 0
Loss at start-up	**($1,625)**
Total capital	**$ 425**
Total capital and liabilities	**$ 425**

General assumptions

	FY 2006	FY 2007	FY 2008
Plan month	1	2	3
Current interest rate	10.00%	10.00%	10.00%
Long-term interest rate	10.00%	10.00%	10.00%
Tax rate	25.42%	25.00%	25.42%
Sales on credit %	75.00%	75.00%	75.00%

Projected profit and loss

	FY 2006	FY 2007	FY 2008
Sales	$49,500	$90,000	$93,600
Direct cost of sales	$ 6,598	$11,997	$12,477
Other	$ 0	$ 0	$ 0
Total cost of sales	**$ 6,598**	**$11,997**	**$12,477**
Gross margin	**$42,902**	**$78,003**	**$81,123**
Gross margin %	86.67%	86.67%	86.67%
Expenses:			
Payroll	$ 0	$ 0	$ 0
Sales and marketing and other expenses	$ 2,475	$ 4,500	$ 4,680
Depreciation	$ 0	$ 0	$ 0
Leased equipment	$ 0	$ 0	$ 0
Utilities	$ 1,500	$ 125	$ 125
Insurance	$ 1,800	$ 2,000	$ 2,200
Rent	$ 5,100	$ 5,100	$ 5,100
Payroll taxes	$ 0	$ 0	$ 0
Other	$ 0	$ 0	$ 0
Total operating expenses	**$10,875**	**$11,725**	**$12,105**
Profit before interest and taxes	$32,027	$66,278	$69,018
Interest expense	$ 0	$ 0	$ 0
Taxes incurred	$ 8,008	$16,570	$17,542
Net profit	**$24,018**	**$49,709**	**$51,476**
Net profit/sales	**48.52%**	**55.23%**	**55.00%**

OPERATIONS

Management Summary

Most of our management team is in place; however, we require contractual customer service through an off–shore company to offer our customers online technical support. Our management team consists of: Jim Nash, President; Elisha Violet, Vice President of Legal Services; Jonathan Winston, Vice President of Finance; and Eileen Mary, Vice President of Operations.

Responsibilities
Jim Nash, President

Develops and maintains the vision of the company. Oversees marketing, product development, production and finance, customer service, etc. Approves all financial obligations. Seeks business opportunities and strategic alliances with other companies and organizations. Plans, develops, and establishes policies and objectives of business organization in accordance with board directives and company charter. Directs and coordinates financial programs to provide funding for new or continuing operations in order to maximize return on investments, and increase productivity.

Jonathan Winston, Vice President of Finance

Manages working capital including receivables, inventory, cash and marketable securities. Performs financial forecasting including capital budget, cash budget, pro forma financial statements, external financing requirements, and financial condition requirements.

Eileen Mary, Vice President of Operations

Directs manufacturing, raw materials procurement and management, field service, repair, and shipping/ receiving function. Oversees the company's facilities.

Elisha Violet, Vice President of Legal Services

Manages all legal matters pertaining to the company.

Board of Directors

An outside Board of Directors, including highly qualified business and industry professionals/experts, will assist our management team in making appropriate decisions and taking the most effective action; however, they will not be responsible for management decisions.

Stock Allocation

One thousand (1,000) shares of Exactor Technologies, LLC common stock has been authorized by the state of Florida. At this time 7,500 shares are outstanding, and have been allocated as shown below.

*   Jim Nash, President—70%

*   Elisha Violet, Vice President of Legal Services—10%

*   Jonathan Winston, Vice President of Finance—10%

*   Eileen Mary, Vice President of Operations—10%

Stock vests over 3 years from the date of employment. In addition, we plan to allocate 2006 shares of common stock for Employee Incentive stock options.

PRODUCTS

Exactor Technologies, LLC currently offers the ability for buyers to purchase money orders and payment methods online via www.ExactorTechnologies245.com. Our website implements integration with popular auction websites such as www.eBay.com, www.Yahoo.com, www.buysell–biz.com, and www.icibusiness.com, and also allows integration with other third party company websites.

Our website is currently in the testing and development stage.

Research and Development

In response to demonstrated needs of our market, new services are being developed to include improved wireless/mobile access, multiple languages, multiple currencies, non–auction money order sales, ACH transfers, and debit cards for instant access to cash. These new services are especially useful to customers who currently use our competitor's services. ACH transfers are especially useful to prospective PayPal and StormPay customers who can deposit funds into their bank account(s) without physically depositing a check/money order. Launches are scheduled to be deployed incrementally beginning with multiple language websites in late 2007.

Production and Delivery

The key factor in our services is the ability to maintain a large database online and handle thousands of simultaneous transactions quickly, effectively, and safely. Our website is being developed by an experienced off–shore Internet technology company located in India. Our website is being hosted in the United States with OLM on a cluster of Microsoft Windows 2009 Internet Information Servers hosting Microsoft SQL Server and Exchange Server. In addition we will be adding Oracle's newest server security to give us 400 Bit protection. By comparison, most banks now use 128 Bit protection.

Because of the anticipated rate of growth, we will need to expand our bandwidth and processing power by 2009, and will consider seeking a larger company to accommodate our growing technology needs. Our biggest advantage is our modular code that allows easy mobility to new technology platforms.

We anticipate that a significant amount of our transactions will be from eBay and third party websites. Statistics show that eBay averaged 15 million listings per day in 2006. Statistics also show that 28% of all eBay listings are completed and that the average aggregate selling price is $14 per item.

MARKET ANALYSIS

The e–commerce market is growing rapidly. There is an important need for companies to facilitate online transactions in a simple, safe, and secure manner. Currently, the market distribution is shared by two major companies, with PayPal considered the market leader. Statistics show that "PayPal has over 56 million accounts and more than 53,000 people who sign up for new access every day. PayPal deals in transactions totaling over $48 million in sales per day."

Customers

Exactor Technologies, LLC's target market includes eBay sellers and website operators. The typical customer of our products is someone who purchases products and services from online auction websites and online stores.

Competition

Companies that compete in this market are PayPal and StormPay.

All companies charge competitive rates.

Key factors have resulted in the present competitive position in the industry.

The ability to offer better rates to customers is contingent upon relationships with processing banks.

Pro forma cash flow

	FY 2006	FY 2007	FY 2008
Cash received			
Cash from operations:			
Cash sales	$12,375	$22,500	$ 23,400
Cash from receivables	$28,868	$60,744	$ 69,599
Subtotal cash from operations	**$41,243**	**$83,244**	**$ 92,999**
Expenditures			
Expenditures from operations:			
Cash spending	$ 2,548	$ 4,029	$ 4,184
Payment of accounts payable	$19,898	$34,498	$ 37,756
Subtotal spent on operations	**$22,446**	**$38,527**	**$ 41,940**
Net cash flow	**$18,796**	**$44,717**	**$ 51,060**
Cash balance	**$19,221**	**$63,938**	**$114,998**

Projected balance sheet

Assets	FY 2006	FY 2007	FY 2008
Current assets			
Cash	$19,221	$63,938	$114,998
Accounts receivable	$ 8,258	$15,014	$ 15,614
Other current assets	$ 0	$ 0	$ 0
Total current assets	**$27,479**	**$78,952**	**$130,612**
Long-term assets			
Long-term assets	$ 0	$ 0	$ 0
Accumulated depreciation	$ 0	$ 0	$ 0
Total long-term assets	$ 0	$ 0	$ 0
Total assets	**$27,479**	**$78,952**	**$130,612**
Liabilities and capital			
Current liabilities			
Accounts payable	$ 3,036	$ 4,800	$ 4,984
Current borrowing	$ 0	$ 0	$ 0
Other current liabilities	$ 0	$ 0	$ 0
Subtotal current liabilities	$ 3,036	$ 4,800	$ 4,984
Long-term liabilities	$ 0	$ 0	$ 0
Total liabilities	**$ 3,036**	**$ 4,800**	**$ 4,984**
Paid-in capital	$ 2,050	$ 2,050	$ 2,050
Retained earnings	($ 1,625)	$22,393	$ 72,102
Earnings	$24,018	$49,709	$ 51,476
Total capital	$24,443	$74,152	$125,628
Total liabilities and capital	**$27,479**	**$78,952**	**$130,612**
Net worth	**$24,443**	**$74,152**	**$125,628**

Our strategy for meeting the competition is offering a seller–oriented service. We guarantee no charge backs and guarantee delivery of funds. We also offer live online technical support, a feature our competitors lack.

Risk Factors

The top business risks that Exactor Technologies, LLC faces as it begins to enter the payment processing market are liquidity to cover rolling banking balances, website malfunctions and sabotage, compliance with state and federal laws, and maintaining a good working relationship with our processing banks and Visa/MasterCard.

MARKETING & SALES

Inquiries from prospective customers suggest that there is considerable demand for our services. Relationships with major banks and payment processors substantiate the fitness of Exactor Technologies, LLC for considerable growth and accomplishment in our industry.

Exactor Technologies, LLC's marketing strategy is to aggressively enhance, promote and support the fact that our services are seller–oriented, closely integrated with major auction websites, integrate easily with e–commerce websites, and are safe.

Partnerships

We plan to partner with an insurance company to offer Personal Property Protection for buyers to guarantee their online safety and equitable right to their products. It will also give us the ability to offer extended warranty coverage for products purchases through our website. We can generate lucrative commissions based on these partnerships.

Advertising

Our advertising and promotion strategy is to position Exactor Technologies, LLC as the leading service provider in the market.

We will utilize the following media and methods to drive our message home to our customers:

- Free news coverage

- Talk show freebees

- Google Adwords

- Auction site banners

- Referral credits

- Auto surf marketing

- Aggressive search engine placement

For the next 12 months, advertising and promotion will require $500,000. On an ongoing basis we will budget our advertising investment as 5% of total sales.

Public Relations

During 2006, Exactor Technologies, LLC will promote our service at major technology conferences such as eBay Live, CeBit, E3, and Comdex.

We will track, wherever possible, the incremental revenue generated from our advertising, promotion and publicity efforts.

OBJECTIVES

In order for Exactor Technologies, LLC to attain its vision in the manner described in our mission statement, the following primary strategic goals need to be achieved:

Corporate: By 2010 Exactor Technologies, LLC will become a publicly traded company.

Products: By 2008 Exactor Technologies, LLC will develop a method for users to access their cash via any ATM machine worldwide.

Sales: By mid–2006 Exactor Technologies, LLC will be offered as a payment method on thousands of users' eBay auctions and e–commerce vendor websites. We anticipate that our first 5 years of growth will be exponential.

- For 2006 total sales will exceed $5,750,000.

- For 2007 total sales will exceed $15,000,000.

- For 2008 total sales will exceed $30,000,000.

- For 2009 total sales will exceed $65,000,000.

Other major goal(s) to include:

- Understand customers, competition and industry

- Growth by fields of interest

- Balance people/management/business goals

- Operate at 50 vs. 5 employees

- Develop values and culture

We feel confident that the above goals can be reached. Two of our managers come from environments where they experienced managing a rapid growth high–tech development team.

During the next year, Exactor Technologies, LLC's organization will carry out the following specific objectives:

1. Launch online November 1, 2006.

2. Offer our website in multiple languages by January 1, 2007.

3. Offer ACH transfers by March 2007.

During the next year in order to help attain the primary goal of offering our website in multiple languages, Exactor Technologies, LLC's organization will carry out the following objectives:

1. Seek out and foreign language specialists by November, 2006.

2. Provide beta testing of foreign language sites by December, 2006.

Strategic Alliances

Exactor Technologies is working to form some very important relationships with major companies in the banking and insurance industry. Joint marketing with established companies will produce revenues, credibility, and market presence.

Exactor Technologies, LLC is pursuing joint marketing agreements with other organizations to further the name of Exactor Technologies, LLC's products in the banking market. Our plans include having them market or sell our products within their product line.

Exactor Technologies, LLC currently has a joint marketing relationship with Mastercard, Visa, and American Express, and we are in the process of engaging in agreements with major banks.

CONCLUSION

On paper, we are guaranteed to make money. Doing the math, if we only take between 0.5% to 1% of eBay's daily transaction, we will make a significant profit within the first year.

Online Woodworking Manufacturing & Retailing
U—nique Woodworking

4123 Reed Blvd.
Big River, Saskatchewan S7J 1G9

Gerald Rekve

EXECUTIVE SUMMARY

This business plan was written for a special needs person who has excellent woodworking skills. His wooden creations are marketed and sold online to help provide for his keeping and care.

Market Analysis

With the evolution of the internet, operating a business from remote regions allows anyone with a product an instant market.

Some of the most frequently purchased items over the internet are games and electronics. However, there are many niche areas that are viable as long as the fundamentals are correct.

Unique and well—made wood products are one of those niche areas. They are both easy to manufacture and highly profitable, as long as quality and cost of materials are closely monitored.

As a test, we posted a few custom wood products for sale on the internet. The result was phenomenal. The items sold quickly for a retail price that allowed both the retailers and the manufacturer to make a profit. In most cases, the retailer was able to sell the item for 30% more than a local retail store.

We also posted a few items on some auction websites to see if there was a market there as well. To our amazement, the items sold fairly quickly for the predetermined asking price. The only downside to this method of sales is the cost we had to pay to list the items and to receive payment for them. If the item did not sell, we were burdened with the cost of listing the item. If the item did sell, we were burdened with both the cost of listing the item and the cost of the common online payment systems.

These additional fees are important to consider. If, for example, we posted 100 items at an average cost of $1.50 per item, our listing cost for these 100 items would be $150.00 per 7–day period. Our cost to post the same items on the auction site would be $600.00 per month. Now let's consider that of the 100 items we list on the auction site, we sell 20% of the items. A percentage commission is then paid to the auction site for the sale of the item and the use the site's payment system. The total could result in an extra cost of 10% per item that sells.

Here is a detailed example:

- 400 items posted on website (100 per week)

- $600 per month posting fees ($1.50 per item)

- 20% of all items are sold, or a total of 80 items

- If each item sells for $29.00 and has a manufacturing cost of $7.00 per item, the profit would be $22.00 per item before fees

- Our total profit would be $1,760 before fees

- Less the 10% processing fee and posting fees, our net profit would be reduced to $984 for the month

This $984 looks reasonable, but we must also consider how much time it takes to manufacture, package and ship the items.

It took a total of 3 days to produce these 100 items. Based on this result, the maximum number of items that could be produced in any given month would be 660 items. At a retail price of $29.00, the revenue potential per month is $19,140.

We realize that working at maximum capacity every month will most likely not happen. Therefore we are planning to produce and sell at a rate of 30% of this maximum figure, or approximately 200 items per month. This figure is realistic for both manufacturing and sales.

Products

The products that we will produce for this business are as follows:

- Artist easels—all sizes and configurations

- Artist stretched canvases—custom and standard sizes

- Art boxes to carry art supplies

- Picture frames—pre–made, small sizes

As we go forward, we realize that this list may change—some of these products may no longer be viable or we may discover a market for additional products. Our main goal for any items we produce is to keep our manufacturing cost down, while producing good, quality items.

Equipment & Services Required

- Table saw

- Mitre saw

- Jig saw

- Band saw

- Scroll saw

- Compound mitre saw

- Sander—edge, table, palm, etc.

- Router table

- 2–in–1 air nail gun

- Exhaust ducting and air quality control

- Blades and saw supplies

- Table–top HD corner framers clamps

- Picture framing pneumatic nail gun
- Air dust collector and piping equipment
- Altos mat cutter
- Logan mat cutter
- Fletcher mat cutter
- Wood vice
- Lathe
- Wood shaper
- Bar clamps
- Wood chisels
- Ratchet clamps
- Jointer
- Planner
- Workshop counters—26 feet total
- Office desk
- Computer
- Printer
- CAD software
- Internet connection
- Accounts with all online auctions
- Various types of wood
- Cardboard for mailing
- Packing tape

OPERATIONS

Location

We will be setting up the business in a small town called Big River in Saskatchewan, Canada. The population is approximately 700 people and the town is about 100 miles away from the closest city (Prince Albert).

Here is a list of amenities the town has to offer:

- Two gas stations
- Four restaurants
- One food store
- Three convenience stores
- One lumber supply store
- One hardware store
- One electronics store

The major employer in the region is Weyerhaeuser Mill; it employs over 400 people from the region. The average salary is around $60,000. Mostly of a blue color demographic, the region has a vibrant economy.

Start up budget & costs

Table saw	$ 400
Miter saw	$ 250
Jig saw	$ 100
Band saw	$ 300
Scroll saw	$ 200
Compound miter saw	$ 400
Sander-edge, table, palm, etc.	$ 500
Router table	$ 250
2 in 1 air nail gun	$ 250
Exhaust ducting and air quality control	$ 500
Blades and saw supplies	$ 100
Table top HD corner framers clamps	$ 200
Picture framing pneumatic nail gun	$ 200
Air dust collector & piping equipment	$ 250
Altos mat cutter	$ 500
Logan mat cutter	$1,200
Fletcher mat cutter	$ 800
Wood vise	$ 200
Lathe	$ 400
Wood shaper	$ 300
Bar clamps	$ 200
Wood chisels	$ 300
Ratchet clamps	$ 300
Jointer	$ 300
Planner	$ 300
Workshop counters (26 feet total)	$ 200
Office desk	$ 300
Computer	$ 600
Printer	$ 200
CAD software	$ 300
Internet connection	$ 40
Various types of wood	$1,000
Cardboard for mailing	$ 100
Packing tape	$ 20

Leasehold improvements

Workshop	$4,000
Permits	$ 150
Power hook-up	$ 150
Natural gas hook up	$ 150
Taxes for town	$ 200
Business license	$ 100

MISSION

The main goal for this company will be to provide the owner with a source of reliable as well sustainable income for long period of time. If at any time the business grows to the point where it requires help, we will hire the required staff to do the work.

The products will change over time as we fine–tune the business; so will the areas where we practice business. It is our intention to run the sales arm of this business online, therefore allowing us to focus strictly on manufacturing and leaving the retailing up to the internet.

MARKETING & SALES

We will produce a series of products as samples. Over time, we will start listing them on our website and on online auctions. As the products sell, we will continue to add more items to our inventory list.

We will remove slow sellers or items that require too much effort for too little profit potential. Therefore, we will only produce products that are profitable.

As mentioned above, we will use the internet to sell 100% of our products. We will also accept sales to retailers who want to buy our products to resell in their store, as long as there is enough profit in it for us.

The items will be sold on the following internet sites:

- Our own website
- Yahoo Auctions
- Ebay auctions
- Amazon Auctions
- www.buysell–biz.com
- www.icibusiness.com
- Another 20 smaller online auctions services
- All the free classified websites we can find

COMPETITION

The competition for our products is fairly strong. If needed, we could reduce our price to beat the competition, thereby increasing our market share and sales. With our flexibility with top line pricing, we are very confidant that we will find a nice market that allows us to succeed and survive in this business.

Plumbing Service

Matt's Plumbing and Air Conditioning

4120 Highway 43
Gull Harbour, Florida 33994

Gerald Rekve

Once becoming a fully registered plumber, Matt Plank's employer approached him about opening a plumbing and air conditioning service location in the adjacent town. This business plan outlines the research and planning involved in this decision.

EXECUTIVE SUMMARY

Market Analysis

In 2004, Matt Plank had completed his journeyman's ticket and was now a fully registered plumber. His employer asked if he wanted to go into partnership with him and open a second location in the town close by. After hiring a management consultant to do research and market analysis on this business opportunity, Matt and his business partner decided to open a second location.

The strength of the business opportunity outweighed the risk of investment loss. Along with the help of the consultant, it was determined that there was also an opportunity for a retail store selling plumbing supplies and fixtures. This store would be share the same location as the plumbing company's office and would be built in conjunction with the office.

The plumbing business is built on trust. By showing their clients the investment they are willing to make in the market, the new owners will be able to grow their business from day one. The investment will come from the partners and a local bank, which has worked with the senior partner for over thirty years.

Customers

The town has a population of fifty thousand people and only one plumbing shop with six journeyman plumbers. The shop seems to be always behind on their work and the locals call out of town shops to complete projects.

The birth of the town happened in 1875, which makes the town over 130 years old. Therefore, many homes have an old infrastructure. The result of this is a steady stream of new business, for everything from new pipes to furnaces and complete renovations.

The medium income for the region is $54,000 and an average of 2.7 people per household. Based on 2003 statistics, the average home spent $350 per year on home plumbing repairs, including clogged pipes. This average does not include the major repairs like new furnaces and air conditioning repairs. The average price for these repairs is $2,500.

Upon review of the revenue that is generated from a town this size, it can be expected that we will generate approximately $300,000 in our first year, and then for each journeyman we hire, we will generate another $200,000.

The local town has already indicated they will give us three–year tax abatement; the reason for this is twofold. First, we will be constructing a 10,000 square foot building on a tax–zoned area for growth and development. Secondly, the town feels our services are desperately needed in the town, to better serve the region. We agree and feel we will prosper from this town.

Competition

Plumbing Shops

A few years ago, another plumbing shop was in business. However, the owner passed away, the crew was hired by the competing firm, and the shop closed. At the time, none of the crew wanted to start their own shop, because they were older and just wanted to keep their lives simple.

The local plumbing shop, who already has been in business for more than forty years, says our plan is great news. They already tell clients to call shops in other cities, if the clients need the work done sooner than the shop can achieve. The list below details the services offered by this shop.

Competitor's Services

- Water heaters
- Repairs
- Furnace repairs
- Air conditioner installation and repairs
- New home construction

Due to the limit in market competition, the local plumber can just about charge whatever he wants. The local market is captive to these rates. If clients want, they can hire plumbers from other regions and pay their travel fees. Travel fees are an average of $250, regardless of the type of job.

The current national average hourly rate for a plumber is $125 an hour; the local shop owner enjoys a rate of $150 an hour. Based on our research, we have determined that this rate will be our hourly rate. We do not want to get into a pricing war, so we will maintain all the same fees. The only area where we will be very competitive is service. We will offer 24/7 service at the same rate, with no off–peak hourly charges and only overtime charges for jobs that take longer than eight hours in one day.

Independent Service Providers

Most of the projects that are small tend to be done by untrained independent repairers. Based on our market research, we have determined that most clients are not happy with these untrained repairman. In most cases these clients had to call in a professional plumber to get the job done properly.

These contractors, while trying to do a great job for every sector, tend not to be trained in a specific home profession. This small community has gotten wise to these providers and only call on them when absolutely required. This will put us in the winning sector with these clients.

These independent providers charge anywhere from $30–$75 per hour. We do not feel these contractors will be a major competitor to us, as they have little impact on the only plumber in the market.

PRODUCTS & SERVICES

While we want to take this market by storm, we also want to be very careful to only offer clients the services and products in which we have expertise. This is part of our mission statement.

Services Offered

- New construction
- Furnace installation and repairs
- Air conditioning installation and repairs
- Bathroom renovations
- Kitchen renovations
- Water heater repair and replacement installation
- Fireplace installation

To separate ourselves from our competitors, we will also offer a full line of plumbing fixtures and supplies. This retail store will be a focus of our business, simply because it will show our clients that we know what we are doing. The store also will be a profit channel for our business. The local chain store will always be a major competitor for us. However our goal is to keep our prices fair and show our clients that it is still less expensive to use us, than to do it themselves or hire a third–party contractor who may not have the required training in this field.

The retail store will be beside the commercial division. The merchandise will house about 70% of the space. The office as well as the management will be based in the retail store, allowing the clients easy access to qualified staff. The store hours will be 8:00AM–6:00PM daily and Saturdays from 9:00AM–5:00PM.

OPERATIONS

Necessary Equipment

- Four vans for our service staff
- Tools for all services
- Three computers
- Three printers
- Two fax machines
- One POS system
- Four desks
- Three four–drawer filing cabinets
- Five racks for pipe retail supplies
- Store shelving as needed

Retail Store Inventory

We will inventory all basic items found in your typical retail store. While we have not supplied this list in this plan, we will supply the list for the banker's approval of the operating line of credit.

FINANCIAL ANALYSIS

Building of location—$400,000

Store fixtures—$40,000

Inventory—$160,000

Van maintenance—$30,000

Operating line of credit—$100,000

Special tools and equipment—$50,000

Total required operating funding—$780,000

Cash invested by partners is $100,000 with the balance coming from operating lines of credit and mortgage on building.

Monthly payroll is as follows:

Matt Plank—$5,000

Albert Wills—$1,000

Patricia Turk—$3,000

Journeyman—$4,800 x number of staff

Fixed monthly Costs

Van Fuel—$1,200

Van repairs—$200

Office Supplies—$200

Telephone—$250

Yellow Page Advertisement—$500

Utilities—$500

Staffing Personnel

- Matt Plank: CEO. Matt will run the day–to–day operations of the business. He will also go out on calls as required to service clients. Matt has just gotten his journeyman's ticket and is fully licensed.

- Albert Wills: Co–owner and silent partner. Albert will assist in the financial management of the company and will work two days a week in the store.

- Patricia Turk: Store manager and accountant. Patricia is Matt's wife and has an accounting degree and specializes in retail management. Patricia worked for a large hardware store for four years prior to taking on this role.

- Journeymen: Four journeymen will be hired; two will be transferred from the home location while the company ramps up.

BUSINESS STRATEGY

Matt's Plumbing and Air Conditioning will continue the alliance they already have with Breezy Air Conditioning and Furnaces, Inc. Also Matt's Plumbing and Air Conditioning will strike alliances with local new home manufacturers and home renovation firms. These will be negotiated and referral fees will be paid to these firms. Research on the market determined that there were no referral fees offered, and most of the time clients had to search out the trades individually. Our goal is to change this by working closely together with other firms looking to grow their business and who share our values for client services.

It may seem that retail shops need to provide niche products or services or be a "big box" in order to succeed. This being said, the trades can be a little different. It was found that one out of every ten clients left a "big box" home improvement store very disappointed with the shopping experience.

Here are some of the reasons:

- Store format is too large; a lot of walking was required
- Lack of staff presence (no one to ask advice of)
- Lost leader prices were good; however other items seemed to be higher

While our strategy is not to be everything to everybody, we will focus on our product lines and provide the best service to our clients as possible.

Some of the products we will sell in our store will be:

- Bathroom fixtures, sinks, toilets, bathtubs, etc.
- Jacuzzis and whirlpool tubs
- Saunas
- Hot tubs
- Air conditioners and furnaces
- Some electrical supplies related to plumbing
- Copper pipes and parts
- Plastic PVC pipes and parts
- Basic plumbing supplies

After we are established, we will hold Saturday morning teaching sessions for a small fee of $5 each. These sessions will focus on the do–it–yourself clients.

Initial Do–It–Yourself Class Topics

- Installing a tub surround
- Replacing kitchen or bathroom taps
- Unplugging clogged sinks
- Replacing a toilet
- Installing a hot tub
- Installing a bathroom in a basement

We will add and subtract classes as they are required; this will keep us in touch with the market. We will also work with local electricians to offer classes in electrical repair.

Our goal for this retail store will be one of total customer interaction. We strongly believe, and our market research maintains, that our clients will support our store based on the model we have outlined in this business plan.

Senior Care Facility

Hearts and Hopes Senior Home

2300 Oak Hollow Blvd.
Englewood, Florida 34224

Gerald Rekve

A woman familiar with managing a section of a hospital decided to transition to the independent care sector. This plan outlines the planning she underwent and steps she took to successfully establish her senior home.

EXECUTIVE SUMMARY

After working for five years in the management of a hospital wing, Patricia Millen decided it was time to move into her own business. When identified of the opportunity to own a care home, Patricia made the move to open this home. Coming from the medical field helped her; however, running a care home was more about running a business. Expenses can be high and, if not managed correctly, can be costly.

As part of the planning process, Patricia applied for the required license before she purchased a building or a land site. This was smart, considering without approval, you cannot operate this type of home.

MARKET ANALYSIS

Englewood has a population of 200,000 people. With the aging population as well as an increase in government grants, we have determined there was an opportunity to open a senior care facility in this area.

Right now there are only four of these types of facilities, with an average of 22 clients per site. After calls to each one, we identified there is a three month waiting list with over 100 names listed. The entire city has 27 adult care facilities and those have been at capacity for some time. The average client age is 69 years old, and their average stay is four years. There are three different levels of care. Most of these locations offer all levels of care. We have determined that in order to offer all levels of care, we will require a RN on staff 24/7.

In the area where we want locate, we have determined that with the age of the region, we would be required to buy a larger house and build adequate rooms on to it. This would not require a special city permit, because we have found out that this region is in real need for this type of service and the city is looking for qualified providers to offer these services. We applied and were approved for the license to operate a special care home in this geographic region.

FINANCIAL ANALYSIS

After researching the availiblity of government grants, we determined that there were a few for our region that we might qualify for. So we took the steps and applied for these grants and were approved for them. We applied for the home buying grant, and as a result, the federal government gave us a one time grant of $15,000 to put toward buying a home. We will also receive a $10,000 federally–funded grant each year for every RN hired. The state gave us a grant for all the required renovations to the house (i.e. wheelchair access, bathroom and kitchen access), which could be worth approximately $40,000.

The state also offers employers hiring any staff a special wage top–up for the first six months. This will include our business and we will receive a monthly check for each employee for the amount of $270.00.

OPERATIONS

Location

We have placed an offer on a 1,400 square foot bungalow with a detached garage. We will add a 1,000 square foot addition to the back of the home. This addition will take up only 50% of the back lawn, so there will still be plenty of room for clients to plant a garden and enjoy the outdoors.

The addition will add eight bedrooms to the home, making a total of 14 bedrooms for our clients. Because we will have staff on–site 24/7, we will have an additional bedroom designated for staff.

The home will contain all the appliances designed for special need clients. We have a security system and an emergency system. This facility is only one block from the fire department with four trucks and one ambulance. When there is a client emergency, the ambulance will be no more than five minutes away.

The front steps will be replaced with a front deck and wheelchair access. The front door will be replaced with a commercial size sliding door. The basement of the house has already been completed. It has two bedrooms and a bathroom, along with a living room and a storage/laundry room. We will move the laundry room to the main floor and put it in the new addition, allowing for ease of use for the staff. The rooms in the basement will house one staff person and the RN's room. We will not have any clients in the basement. We will put in games, card tables, and a foosball table to encourage clients to lounge in the basement. We will add a chair lift for the basement to transport clients up and down the steps as needed. This will allow everyone to enjoy the games and living room in the basement. We will also have a smaller living room on the main level.

The kitchen will be gutted and a larger kitchen with more commercial type appliances will be installed, while keeping in mind the need for clients to access the kitchen. Our goal is to have a free, easy going open policy for clients while respecting the safety of both the clients and the staff.

Community Support

Part of our goal is to offer our clients the best care and to assist them in keeping active. We will winterize the garage, allowing our clients to use the garage as a workshop. The workshop will only have smaller power tools and hand tools. If the clients require larger power tools to complete a job, we have made arrangements with a local handyman to use his shop. This handyman is strong supporter of all the care homes in the region and believes that people need to stay active. We don't have to pay anything for this service; we just need to make sure our insurance is properly written to cover us and our clients in the case of accidents, etc.

We have met will all the home owners within one block of the adult care home to tell them what we are doing. Every one of them was very supportive and signed a form giving us their support. This was very important for us, since ambulances will periodically come to our home to assist patients and they will have their sirens wailing.

Staffing

Our business is unlike most in that we require medical staff to work at our care home. Our staffing will contain a Registered Nurse (RN) who will work a twenty–five hour week and be on call as required. We have already hired a RN who had worked ten hours a week at a care home in the region. This will allow us to have a properly trained nurse on staff. Also, we will hire adult care providers from the local area; we have run some test ads and gotten a quite a few applicants that meet the state standards for experience and training.

Because our staff is key to our success, we will be offering them a various options for work. Since we are open 24/7, our work week consists of 168 hours in a week. If you divide this by forty hours, there are 4.2 full shifts in a week. We will hire four full–time staff to work forty hour rotating shifts, and we will hire six part–time staff to work 20–hour rotating shifts and on–call shifts.

Based on state laws and national laws, every hour that is worked over a forty–hour week is paid overtime. Therefore, if necessary, we will pay overtime.

Staffing Hours Worked and Wages Paid

- RN—25 hours per week @ $37 per hour
- Client staff—40 hours per week @ $14 per hour
- Client staff—20 hours per week @ $14 per hour
- Cleaning Staff—30 hours per week @ $9 per hour
- Accountant and Manager (Owner)—$40,000 per year + profits

MARKET ANALYSIS

Monthly Operating Expenses

- Taxes—$140
- Mortgage—$850
- Power—$200
- Natural Gas—$200
- Telephone—$100
- Cable TV/Internet—$100
- Food—$900
- Repairs and Maintenance—$140
- Bus—$599
- Fuel for Bus—$250

Competition

We have determined that this industry is not as competitive as most. In order to open this type of care home you need to get linked. The government also only approves a certain number of care homes based on population.

Growth Strategy

Start–up Schedule

1. Get licensed to operate home—completed
2. Buy home—will take one month

3. Renovate home—will take two months

4. Hire staff—will take one month

5. Bring in clients—will take three–four months from date of home purchase

Required Capital

- Money to buy home: $150,000

- Money to build addition: $40,000

- Money to buy required appliances: $10,000

- Operating line of credit: $50,000

- Money to lease a bus to transport clients: $599 per month

Necessary Furniture and Equipment

- Couch: 3

- Easy chairs: 10

- Coffee tables: 4

- Beds: 15

- Night tables: 15

- Chairs: 25

- Wall mirrors: 20

- Curtains: 25

- Stove: 1

- Refridgerator: 2

- Freezer: 2

- Book shelves: 20

- Large screen televisions: 2

- 12 inch televisions: 14

- Television stands: 20

- Barbeques: 3

- Kitchen tables: 2

- Basic cook and dinner ware

- Foosball table

- Pool table

- Card tables

- Power tools for the garage

- Lawn furniture

The benchmark of this facility is based on quality care of our clients. Since we have already been approved for this facility by the state, we are now putting together the financial package for the required banking units. This will allow us to get the funding required to move this project along.

We will have three telephones lines and phones. Each client will have the option of their own phone, and they will pay the installation fee and monthly costs.

Revenue Potential

We will charge our clients rent anywhere from $1,400–$3,000 per month, based on level of care required and identified by a doctor. This charge only covers the rent and food portions, and does not cover the other expenses incurred with this stay (i.e. medical devices, self–care products, clothing, etc.)

Based on this amount, our monthly revenue will be approximately 14 clients X $2,100 = $29,400 per month, or $352,800 per year.

Sports Bar and Grille

Stone Oak Sports Bar & Grille

1891 Ribersol Blvd.
Boerne, Michigan 43120

Staff at BusinessandMarketingPlans.com

This business plan secured $350,000 to help launch the first and "finest" sports bar in one of the fastest–growing areas in an upscale community. "Wow!" is one of the defining statements made by the banker who reviewed the well–researched, detailed plan, presented by a veteran restaurateur and a former law enforcement officer.

EXECUTIVE SUMMARY

Market Analysis

The Stone Oak Sports Bar & Grille will provide quality food in a quality atmosphere, along with excellent service, to become the first and finest sports bar in our area. The Stone Oak Sports Bar & Grille has been established out of a need to fill a niche in the Boerne, Michigan, market. Currently, there are no major chain restaurants located within one mile of our proposed location and there are only three bar licenses, like the one our restaurant has, in Boerne giving us a solid competitive advantage.

The Stone Oak Sports Bar & Grille does anticipate competition emerging in this area to meet demand. However, we hope to solidly establish ourselves in this market in a position of dominance by serving the best in food and entertainment. Furthermore, our strategic alliance with Nick Parro's Pizza will be vital to our success. Utilizing this cross promotion will give our restaurant a competitive advantage.

Today, Boerne is one of Michigan's fastest–growing cities, and is blossoming into a meticulously planned municipality. The population has mushroomed from 10,737 in 1995 to an estimated 96,000 today, with a new home completed almost every hour.

Commercial development is booming, as well, boosting sales tax revenues from $3.3 million in fiscal year 1996–97 to an estimated $23.3 million in 2003–04. The state's largest Wal–Mart Super Center, a sizeable Home Depot, Lowe's Home Improvement Center and Target are the anchor tenants of two power retail developments strategically situated at the intersection of the city's two main thoroughfares.

For the past three decades, the restaurant industry has consistently posted yearly sales gains. Today's consumers regard food prepared away from home as a necessity. Convenience, a need for socialization and gains in real disposable income has led consumers to spend more of their food dollars in restaurants.

Restaurant industry sales are expected to reach a record $476 billion in 900,000 restaurant locations in 2005, according to the National Restaurant Association's 2005 Restaurant Industry Forecast. The projected annual sales would mean a solid 4.9% increase over last year - and a total economic impact of over $1.2 trillion, highlighting the restaurant industry's critical role as a job creator in the nation's economy.

The restaurant industry is poised to add more than 1.8 million jobs over the next decade, with industry employment expected to rise from 12 million to 13.8 million by 2014, according to National Restaurant Association projections based on U.S. Bureau of Labor Statistics data. Despite modest growth during the challenging economic environment earlier this decade, the restaurant industry added an average of 260,000 new jobs a year for the last 10 years, statistics show. That steady growth in sales and jobs makes the industry the nation's largest private-sector employer. The industry's 12 million employees represent nearly 9% of total U.S. employment.

The Stone Oak Sports Bar & Grille is the best choice for quality, well–known food, exceptional service, and atmosphere. With the combined experience and knowledge of Mr. DiMuzio and Mr. Sturgeon, The Stone Oak Sports Bar & Grille will easily become a highly lucrative and successful organization.

Objectives

The Stone Oak Sports Bar & Grille's Main Objectives

- To secure funding in the amount of $350,000

- To achieve revenues in excess of $1,000,000 in the first fiscal year, increasing to $1,200,000 in the fifth fiscal year

Mission

The Stone Oak Sports Bar & Grille will deliver the first and finest sports bar in our area. We offer the best atmosphere with high quality food and excellent services while maintaining healthy profits and employing the best service–oriented people.

FINANCIAL ANALYSIS

Keys To Success

1. Provide Excellent Service

2. Quality Food

3. Superior Entertainment

Financial highlights

Stone Oak	FY1	FY2	FY3	FY4	FY5
Total income	$1,014,500	$1,075,370	$1,139,892	$1,208,286	$1,280,783
Gross profit	$ 758,259	$ 803,755	$ 851,980	$ 903,099	$ 957,285
Net profit	$ 199,233	$ 219,217	$ 250,941	$ 284,951	$ 321,400

ORGANIZATION

The Stone Oak Sports Bar & Grille is established out of a need. We realized the great potential for a high–quality facility in this area. Our success in the law enforcement arena and in the pizza restaurant business has positioned us for success along with the needed knowledge and experience.

Company Ownership

The Stone Oak Sports Bar & Grille is incorporated as Heartland Futures, a Limited Liability Company (LLC) in the state of Michigan. The ownership of the company is split between Henry DiMuzio (51%) and Nick Sturgeon (49%).

Company Facilities and Location

The Stone Oak Sports Bar & Grille will be leasing a 5,850 square–foot facility. We are estimating the leasehold improvement to cost approximately $270,000. In the restaurant business, location, location, and location are very important. We have selected a building in a prime location a half a mile west of the New Boerne Sports Complex (host to the best sporting events in town). The following information on the location and facilities was provided by Mercury Partners, Inc.

Use of Funds

In the table below, the Owner's Investment total consists of the start–up expenses and $200,000 in cash. All calculations presented in this plan are based on a $350,000 seven–year installment loan at 7.50% interest.

Use of funds	
Start-up expenses	
Liquor license (paid)	$ 93,000
Architectural fees (paid)	$ 20,000
Total start-up expenses	**$113,000**
Start-up assets	
Cash	$ 21,257
Food inventory	$ 7,502
Bar inventory	$ 21,240
Total current assets	**$ 50,000**
Long-term assets	
Equipment	$230,000
Leasehold improvements	$270,000
Total long-term assets	**$500,000**
Total assets	**$550,000**
Owner's equity	
Owner's Investment	$313,000
Total owner's equity	**$313,000**
Liabilities	
Current liabilities	
Total current liabilities	**$ 0**
Long-term liabilities	
Loan	$350,000
Total long-term liabilities	**$350,000**
Start-up expenses	($113,000)
Total liabilities and owner's equity	**$550,000**

PRODUCTS & SERVICES

The Stone Oak Sports Bar & Grille will provide quality food in a quality atmosphere along with excellent service. The idea behind our atmosphere, food and service is to fill a niche in the Boerne market.

We will be utilizing top–of–the–line audio and visual equipment for sports entertainment making us a choice location. We will not only be pulling customers in, but increasing their stay time and creating a community. The Stone Oak Sports Bar & Grille will be the first restaurant in this area with this type of equipment. Furthermore, our food will be quality, yet familiar (like an Applebee's, TGI Friday's, etc.) and our service will be exceptional. This company will tolerate nothing but the best.

Menu
The Stone Oak Sports Bar & Grille Menu
Appetizers

- Fried Calamari (choice of sweet or hot marinara sauce)

- Steamers by the Dozen (steamed clams served with drawn butter and Tabasco sauce)

- Mozzarella Sticks (8) (choice of sweet or hot marinara sauce)

- Chicken Fingers (6) (choice of 2 dipping sauces: BBQ, Honey Mustard, Sweet & Sour or Ranch)

- Potato Skins (6) (served with sour cream)

- Wings (12) Mild, Hot, or Insanely Hot (served with Ranch Dressing); available plain or BBQ

- Poppers (8)

- Fried Zucchini Basket (served with Ranch dressing)

- French Fries Basket (steak cut, string & seasoned curly)

- Onion Rings Basket

- Nachos Basket (served with sour cream, guacamole, salsa, and melted cheese)

- Quesadilla (choice of cheese, chicken or steak)

Food Items

- Half–pound Hamburgers and American Cheeseburgers (choice of one of 3 types of Fries or Onion Rings or Home Made Potato Salad) and standard Burger set–up of Lettuce, Tomato, Pickle and Red Onion. Additional items available for additional charge are: Cheddar cheese, Swiss cheese, Blue cheese, Monterrey Jack cheese, bacon, cooked onions, sauted mushrooms and avocado

- Bun Size Vienna Beef Hot Dogs (choice of one of 3 types of Fries or Onion Rings or Home Made Potato Salad and choice of either Chili, Sauer Kraut, Cheese Sauce, or Onions). Additional items available for additional charge are: tomato, cucumbers, relish or Italian–style cooked potatoes, peppers and onions

- 10 oz. Ribeye Steak Sandwich on toasted garlic bread (choice of one of 3 types of Fries or Onion Rings or Home Made Potato Salad and choice of either grilled onions or sauted mushrooms and one cheese)

- Our Famous Slow-Cooked Pork Ribs. One–half or whole slab with our secret family BBQ Dressing (choice of one of 3 types of Fries or Onion Rings or Homemade Potato Salad)

- 8 oz. Grilled Chicken Breast Sandwich (choice of one of 3 types of Fries or Onion Rings or Home Made Potato Salad and standard Chicken set–up of Lettuce, Tomato, Pickle and Red Onion). Additional items available for additional charge are: Cheddar cheese, Swiss cheese, Blue cheese, Monterrey Jack cheese, bacon, cooked onions, sauted mushrooms and avocado

- Chicken Fingers (8) Basket with dipping sauce (choice of one of 3 types of Fries or Onion Rings or Homemade Potato Salad and choice of 2 dipping sauces: BBQ, Honey Mustard, Sweet & Sour or Ranch Dressing)

- Italian Beef Sandwich with Au jus and melted Mozzarella Cheese (choice of one of 3 types of Fries or Onion Rings or Home Made Potato Salad or Potato Chips). Additional items available for additional charge are: grilled onions or sauted mushrooms

- Italian Sweet Sausage & Peppers Sub Sandwich (choice of one of 3 types of Fries or Onion Rings or Home Made Potato Salad or Potato Chips)

- Italian Sub Sandwich (Ham, Salami, Cappicola, & Provolone Cheese with shredded lettuce, tomato, onions and oil and vinegar). Choice of one of 3 types of Fries or Onion Rings or Home Made Potato Salad or Potato Chips. Mayo and italian dressings available

- Bacon, Lettuce, & Tomato (BLT) Sandwich on Toasted White or Wheat Bread (choice of one of 3 types of Fries or Onion Rings or Home Made Potato Salad or Potato Chips)

- Club Sandwich on Toasted White or Wheat Bread (Ham, Turkey, Bacon, American cheese, Lettuce & Tomato). Choice of one of 3 types of Fries or Onion Rings or Homemade Potato Salad or Potato Chips

Pasta

- Baked Lasagna

- Baked Ziti

- Ravioli

- Penne

- Angel Hair

Pizza

- Cheese

- Pepperoni

- Sausage

- Vegetable

- 10" personal Chicago Style pizza made by Nick's Pizza

Salads

- Spinach Salad: Baby Spinach with Boiled Eggs, Green Onions, and Bacon. Served with a sweetened cider vinegar dressing.

- Caesar Salad: Romaine Lettuce, Shredded Parmesan cheese & Anchovy filets, tossed with Caesar dressing and topped with toasted croutons.

- Grilled Chicken Caesar Salad: Sliced Seasoned Grilled 8 oz. Chicken Breast, Romaine Lettuce, Shredded Parmesan cheese and Anchovy filets, tossed with Caesar dressing.

- Buffalo Chicken Salad: Sliced Breaded 8 oz. Chicken Breast Basted in Hot or Mild Buffalo Sauce, over Romaine Lettuce with Blue cheese Dressing. Other dressing available upon request.

- Grilled Chicken Walnut Salad: Sliced Seasoned Grilled 8 oz. Chicken Breast, Romaine Lettuce, Sliced Granny Smith Apples & Candied Walnuts served with Balsamic Vinaigrette. Other dressing available upon request.

- Chef Salad: Mixed Green Lettuce, Sliced Ham, Sliced Turkey, Sliced Swiss cheese or Provolone cheese, Boiled Egg, Tomato Wedges and your choice of dressing.

Services

This business will be a mix of a family style and a corporate restaurant. By having owner operators present in the business operations, we are more aware of the business operations from quality food, good service, to customer satisfaction. Our staff will know we are serious and that we watch their service and the quality of the product that they serve. In addition, we believe the best restaurants are those that have an eye not only on weekly and monthly figures, but also know their daily figures and what goal they must reach.

The Stone Oak Sports Bar & Grille will focus mainly on meal counts, daily and weekly purchases, labor, and food and beverage costs. In slow times, we will reduce servers and kitchen personnel. Our two largest expenses are most likely food, labor and liquor costs. We will physically control our inventory and watch for the ability of food or beverages to be "walking out the door." Therefore, we will put periodic inventory counts in place to make sure the employees know we are watching.

Furthermore, in this economy the customer—more than ever—is looking not only for a quality product and great service, but a real value as well. We will keep in mind that once they have had just one bad experience, we may lose that customer for life! We will make sure the employees know the standards The Stone Oak Sports Bar & Grille are attaining.

SPORTS BAR AND GRILLE

For example, before every meal, as the wait staff is hearing the daily specials, we can make sure that the manager runs over some basic protocol tips, or ways to make the experience for our customer more enjoyable. At The Stone Oak Sports Bar & Grille we will train them to "up sell" and make recommendations, if so asked. There's nothing worse than a server who doesn't know the food that he or she is serving.

Finally, we understand that there are many ways to get our name in the news. From special dinner events to getting a review in the local paper, getting free publicity works great. We may consider many options like specials on holiday meals and sponsoring Chamber or local town events in non–peak hours.

OPERATIONS

In order to ensure successful operations many things will need to be categorized and codified to make sure we meet quality food and service standards. Utilizing checklists can guarantee that we are following the rules. The following is a short list of potential checklists we are developing:

- Service Checklist
- Purchasing Checklist
- Receiving Checklist
- Storage Checklist
- Preparation Checklist
- Cleaning Checklist (kitchen & storage)
- Bartender's Checklist
- Manager's Opening Checklist
- Manager's Shift Change Checklist
- Manager's Closing Checklist

Competition

Boerne is very unique with its liquor licenses. There are currently only two bar licenses, giving us a solid competitive advantage.

Our Three Competitors

- Benatar Lounge: It's mainly a biker/rocker bar with only 2,500 square feet. It doesn't serve food.
- Marathon Sports Bar: Another bar that doesn't serve food. It has one small TV, and is located in an undesirable side of the city.
- Armadillo Alley: This bar is 10 miles west of us, and is a country–western bar that doesn't serve food. It's also in a bad location.

We do anticipate competition emerging in this area to meet demand. We hope to establish ourselves in this market and in a position of dominance by serving food and entertainment, thus creating a quality experience.

There is competition in our area along the corporate lines of business as follows:

- Mariposa Mexican Restaurant
- TGI Friday's
- Applebee's
- Chili's

These "corporate" restaurants serve decent, quality food with average service. However, appealing to the sports market is something that isn't done. They do not create an atmosphere and entertainment since

142

BUSINESS PLANS HANDBOOK, Volume 12

their primary goal is table turnover. While we understand the importance of table turnover, we also understand the desire to be entertained, to have a drink, to sit and relax.

Sales Literature

One of the most important pieces of information is our menu. We will also be developing take home menus, putting door hangers on doors, doing local area direct mailing, and advertising in the *Boerne Independent* and *Boerne Today*.

Furthermore, our strategic alliance with Nick's Pizza will be very important. Utilizing cross promotion can give us a competitive advantage. We will serve his pizza in the bar and he will promote our restaurant on every pizza box. In addition, we will develop a full website that promotes the sports we will be showing, events taking place, menu specials, and promotional items. This website will even include coupons for slow times or lunch specials.

Sourcing and vendors

- Nick's Pizza
- Sysco
- United Beverage
- Northern Wine and Spirits
- Al's Beverages
- Brownsville Distributing
- Silver Eye Beverage
- Peroggi's Foods

Technology

We have a POS System in our budget. Currently, we are evaluating *Dinerware* from Positive Technologies. The following lists detail the benefits of this software system.

Ticket Handling

- Learn how to handle tickets in five minutes.
- The ticket shows all details, including choices and discounts.
- Instantly create a new ticket by simply choosing a menu item.
- Enter and pay for bar drinks quickly. No "fast bar" mode required.
- Split tickets.
- Share Items.
- Combine tickets.
- Add new people to a ticket at any time. Great for informal groups dining in the bar!
- Transfer tickets between servers.
- Change tables.
- One–touch item repeat is great for bartenders.
- Unlimited payments on a single ticket.
- Optional credit card integration.
- Ad–hoc ticket / table names.
- Hold and release items to control remote printing.

Order Routing

- *Dinerware* supports unlimited custom printers for Kitchen, Bar, Pizza, Hot Side, Cold Side, Wine Steward, and whatever else you need.

- Any item may print on any combination of printers when it is ordered.

- Choices can print at separate printers from their items; i.e. you could send the Side Salad to the Cold Side printer automatically.

- Items are not sent until all required choices have been made.

- Type a free–text Special Request for any item.

- If a printer malfunctions, it's easy to assign jobs to another printer temporarily.

- Items are sorted by Item Group at the kitchen printer, so you will see Appetizers before Entrees.

Menu Management

- Unlimited items and choices.

- No buttons to create. The order entry screens are created automatically.

- Quick adjustments from any terminal, anytime.

- Menu items can appear in multiple places.

- Unlimited Choices (aka Modifiers).

- Choices can affect item price by fixed amount or percentage.

- Use Item Groups to change the price of many items at once.

- Flexible taxation and revenue class options.

- Enter the cost of each item you sell for profit analysis.

Business Policies

- Unlimited, custom Void reasons.

- Create an unlimited number of custom discount types for gift certificates, coupons, promotions, employee perks, and happy hours

- Set up happy hours with a few mouse clicks, and turn them off the same way. The other software packages make you wrestle with an extremely complex and error–prone price schedule.

Reporting

- All data generated is kept in the database forever. You can generate history reports for any period, going as far back as you want.

- Instant, on–screen, daily sales and statistics are available at any time from any terminal, and print at the receipt printer.

- See the daily balance report for any server at any time. Servers can preview their own report at any time, and print it at the end of their shift.

- The "Blind Bartender" option allows you to restrict certain jobs from being able to view their daily report.

- View any report, at any time, from any Workstation. The other software packages force you to use a cumbersome "back office" program.

- *Dinerware* comes with dozens of useful reports, many with graphs.

- Reporting is expandable and customizable.

Another important technological consideration is our website, located at www.TheStoneOakSports-Bar.com. This can be important for promotional reasons and for customer connections. Feedback forms and much more can be utilized to be more intimate with our customers as well.

We will also be installing a surveillance system and ADT Monitoring. By using CCTV, we can keep our eyes on inventory and also make sure we are operating a safe and secure environment.

GROWTH STRATEGY

Location

Boerne was little more than a gas station and few small houses in 1938 when founder, Cecil M. Jacobs, a Finneytown lawyer and former state legislator turned real estate developer, subdivided the rural square–mile parcel into low–cost home sites for the area's agricultural workers, naming it after his New Hampshire hometown.

Today, it's one of Michigan's—and America's—fastest–growing cities blossoming into a meticulously planned metropolis. The population has mushroomed from 10,737 in 1995 to an estimated 96,000 today with a new home completed almost every hour.

There were nearly 5,000 single–family home starts in 2003, with more than 6,000 expected in 2004. Boasting 28 of Michigan's top 50 home builders, Boerne offers world–class resort retirement living in developments as well as award–winning, master–planned family communities.

Boerne, the once–sleepy square–mile farming community, is also offering millions in public funding to lure a professional sports team to town. A new aquatic center opened this summer with new parks, and a $1.7 million recreation center and a $1.5 million youth softball complex are in the budget for this fiscal year. In fact, $116 million of the city's $196 million 2004–05 budget is for capital projects such as a public safety building, fourth fire station, museum, water treatment plant expansion and road improvements. Yet, Boerne property tax rate ranks among the lowest in the state at .9101 per $100 of assessed valuation.

Commercial development is booming as well, boosting sales tax revenues from $3.3 million in fiscal year 1996–97 to an estimated $23.3 million in 2003–04. A Wal–Mart Supercenter, a sizeable Home Depot, Lowe's Home Improvement Center and Target are the anchor tenants of two power retail developments strategically situated at the intersection of the city's two main thoroughfares. Together, they feature more than 50 locally and nationally known retailers including Bed, Bath & Beyond, Barnes and Noble, Pier One Imports, Linens 'N Things, Red Lobster, Olive Garden and Starbuck's. Kohl's Department Store opened nearby and throughout the city more churches, gas stations, grocery and drug stores are cropping up.

The Earl Michaels Memorial Hospital nearly doubled in size in 2003 when it expanded to include women's services, labor and delivery, and a pediatric neonatal wing, and plans are progressing for a 2009 groundbreaking on a regional mall, auto mall, power center and lakefront home development along the nearby major interstate.

All the following data in the market analysis is taken from a within a five–mile radius of our proposed location—the corner of W. Cotton Rd. and Stone Oak Lane.

Executive Demographic Summary (Five–Mile Radius)

The population in this area is estimated to change from 63,083 to 105,173, resulting in a growth of 66.7% between 2000 and the current year. Over the next five years, the population is projected to grow by 32.1%. The current year median age for this population is 49.7, while the average age is 46.3. Five years from now, the median age is projected to be 45.1.

The number of households in this area is estimated to change from 28,989 to 44,436, resulting in an increase of 53.3% between 2000 and the current year. Over the next five years, the number of households is projected to increase by 29.4%. The average household income is estimated to be $60,951 for the current year.

Market Segmentations and Demographic Detail

Description	0.00–1.00 miles		0.00–3.00 miles		0.00–5.00 miles	
	Radius	%	Radius	%	Radius	%
Population						
2010 projection	21,048		82,273		138,977	
2005 estimate	15,036		61,187		105,173	
2000 census	7,188		34,016		63,083	
1990 census	324		9,764		28,922	
Growth 2005–2010	39.98%		34.46%		32.14%	
Growth 2000–2005	109.18%		79.88%		66.72%	
Growth 1991–2000	1,983.48%		248.38%		118.11%	
2005 Est. population by sex	15,036		61,187		105,173	
Male	7,470	49.68	29,545	48.29	51,285	48.76
Female	7,566	50.32	31,641	51.71	53,888	51.24
Male/female ratio	0.99		0.93		0.95	
2005 Est. population by age	15.036		61,187		105,173	
Age 0–4	1,778	11.82	4,325	7.07	7,640	7.26
Age 5–9	1,282	8.53	3,619	5.18	5,820	5.53
Age 10–14	1,153	7.67	2,870	4.69	5,363	5.10
Age 15–17	518	3.45	1,129	1.85	2,518	2.39
Age 18–20	285	1.90	914	1.49	2,405	2.29
Age 21–24	468	3.11	1,454	2.38	3,438	3.27
Age 25–34	3,243	21.57	8,295	13.56	12,936	12.30
Age 35–44	2,269	15.09	5,629	9.20	9,427	8.96
Age 45–49	604	4.02	1,647	2.69	3,224	3.07
Age 50–54	564	3.75	1,905	3.11	3,174	3.02
Age 55–59	661	4.40	3,597	5.88	5,243	4.99
Age 60–64	595	3.96	5,218	8.53	8,196	7.79
Age 65–74	999	6.64	12,064	19.72	19,782	18.81
Age 75–84	491	3.27	7,404	12.10	13,294	12.64
Age 85 and over	127	0.84	1,565	2.56	2,713	2.58
Age 16 and over	10,607	70.54	50,357	82.30	85,402	81.20
Age 18 and over	10,305	68.54	49,693	81.21	83,833	79.71
Age 21 and over	10,019	66.63	48,779	79.72	81,428	77.42
Age 65 and over	1,616	10.75	21,033	34.37	35,789	34.03
2005 Est. median age		31.27		53.05		49.71
2005 Est. average age		32.80		47.26		46.33
2005 Est. households by household income	5,791		27,481		44,436	
Income less that $15,000	274	4.73	1,606	5.84	3,196	7.19
Income $15,000–$24,999	346	5.97	2,175	7.91	4,177	9.40
Income $25,000–$34,999	508	8.77	3,267	11.89	5,876	13.22
Income $35,000–$49,999	1,105	19.08	5,380	19.58	8,910	20.05
Income $50,000–$74,999	1,779	30.72	7,607	27.68	11,533	25.95
Income $75,000–$99,999	960	16.58	3,882	14.13	5,385	12.12
Income $100,000–$149,999	580	10.02	2,509	9.13	3,737	8.41
Income $150,000–$249,999	195	3.37	737	2.68	1,156	2.60
Income $250,000–$499,999	32	0.55	259	0.94	358	0.81
Income $500,000 and more	11	0.19	58	0.21	107	0.24
2005 Est. average household income	$67,431		$64,251		$60,951	
2005 Est. median household income	$59,305		$54,313		$50,128	
2005 Est. per capita income	$25,970		$28,917		$25,799	

Exceptional Supply vs. Demand Analysis

Supply/demand analysis within one mile

Retail stores	Demand (consumer expenditures)	Supply (retail sales)	Opportunity gap/surplus
Foodservice and drinking places—722	24,324,197	491,635	23,832,562
Full-service restaurants—7221	10,029,566	87,577	9,941,989
Limited-service eating places—7222	10,376,686	404,058	9,972,628
Special foodservices—7223	1,845,469	0	1,845,469
Drinking places—alcoholic beverages—7224	2,072,476	0	2,072,476

Supply/demand analysis within three miles

Retail stores	Demand (consumer expenditures)	Supply (retail sales)	Opportunity gap/surplus
Foodservice and drinking places—722	108,845,683	55,053,922	53,791,761
Full-service restaurants—7221	44,921,845	39,274,401	5,647,444
Limited-service eating places—7222	45,951,723	15,367,786	30,583,937
Special foodservices—7223	8,195,393	0	8,195,393
Drinking places—alcoholic beverages—7224	9,776,722	411,735	9,364,987

Supply/demand analysis within five miles

Retail stores	Demand (consumer expenditures)	Supply (retail sales)	Opportunity gap/surplus
Foodservice and drinking places—722	170,650,757	62,953,974	107,696,783
Full-service restaurants—7221	70,402,708	40,279,887	30,122,821
Limited-service eating places—7222	72,192,444	21,716,768	50,475,676
Special foodservices—7223	12,873,986	17,375	12,856,611
Drinking places—alcoholic beverages—7224	15,181,619	939,944	14,241,675

Industry Analysis

The restaurant industry is poised to add more than 1.8 million jobs over the next decade, with industry employment expected to rise from 12 million to 13.8 million by 2014, according to National Restaurant Association projections based on U.S. Bureau of Labor Statistics data. Despite modest growth during the challenging economic environment earlier this decade, the restaurant industry added an average of 260,000 new jobs a year for the last 10 years, statistics show. That steady growth in sales and jobs makes the industry the nation's largest private–sector employer. The industry's 12 million employees represent nearly 9% of total U.S. employment.

For the past three decades, the restaurant industry has consistently posted yearly sales gains. Today's consumers regard food prepared away from home as a necessity. Convenience, a need for socialization and gains in real disposable income has led consumers to spend more of their food dollars in restaurants (*Let's Talk Business*, 2003).

More than 50% of all consumers visit a restaurant on their birthdays, making this the most popular occasion to eat out, followed by Mother's Day and Valentine's Day. More than four out of ten adults were restaurant patrons on a typical day in 1999. The average annual household expenditure for food away from home in 1998 was $2,030, or $812 per person. The restaurant–industry share of the food dollar today is 45.8%, compared with only 25% in 1955 (Mhef.org).

Industry Trends

Some of the key trends that are predicted for 2005 include:

- Greater use of technology and worker training as a means to boost productivity and efficiency. More than two–thirds of restaurant operators—including three out of four quick–service operators—say they are more productive than they were two years ago.

- Continued increased focus on healthy lifestyles and restaurants providing customers with balance, choice and customization. Surveys of both full–service and quick–service operators indicate that entre salads have increased in popularity more than many other menu items.

- Increased upgrades and improvements in decor with the help of new tax–depreciation rules. More than 54% of quick–service operators surveyed said they would dedicate a higher portion of their budget to remodeling in 2005, highlighting the focus on using ambiance and interior design to attract customers.

The National Restaurant Association research indicates that 25% of diners can be categorized as "adventurous," and are enthusiastic about trying new foods and ingredients. Most are between 30 and 60 years old, are educated and more likely to live in larger urban areas.

Restaurant industry sales are expected to reach a record $476 billion in 900,000 restaurant locations in 2005, according to the National Restaurant Association's 2005 Restaurant Industry Forecast. The projected annual sales would mean a solid 4.9% increase over last year—and a total economic impact of over $1.2 trillion, highlighting the restaurant industry's critical role as a job creator in the nation's economy.

"American consumers will spend almost 47% of their food dollar in the restaurant community in 2005," said Steven C. Anderson, president and chief executive officer of the National Restaurant Association. "The restaurant industry will serve as a driving force in our nation's economy by providing jobs to 12.2 million employees and continue providing a social oasis and convenience to communities nationwide as it posts its 14th consecutive year of real growth next year."

Competition Distribution

Within one mile there are no major chain competitors! The following are major chains within five miles:

Description	Totals
Total casual dining	2
Total casual dining fern bar	1
Applebee's	1
Total causal dining steak	1
Outback Steakhouse	1
Total midscale	5
Total midscale cafeteria	1
Luby's	1
Total midscale hotel	1
Quality Inn Restaurant	1
Total midscale Italian	2
Fazoli's	1
Streets of New York	1
Total midscale sandwich	1
Auntie Anne's Hand-Rolled Soft	1
Total QSR	31
Total QSR chicken	2
Chick-Fil-A	1
KFC (Kentucky Fried Chicken)	1
Total QSR fish	1
Long John Silver's	1
Total QSR hamburger	4
Burger King	1
Jack in the Box	1
McDonald's	1
Wendy's	1
Total QSR ice cream	1
Dairy Queen	
Total QSR Mexican	3
Del Taco	1
Rubio's Baja Grill	1
Taco Bell	1
Total QSR Oriental	1
Panda Express	1
Total QSR other sandwich	7
Arby's	1
Blimpie	1
Port of Subs	1
Quiznos	1
Subway	3
Total QSR other specialty	2
Starbucks Coffee	2
Total QSR pizza	4
Domino's Pizza	1
Peter Piper's Pizza	1
Pizza Hut	1
U S Pizza's	1
Total QSR retail	6
Chevron Gas Station Food Mart	2
Circle Food Stores	2
Diamond Shamrock Gas Station F	1
Quik Trip	1

BUSINESS STRATEGY

The Stone Oak Sports Bar & Grille believes there are several components of successful restaurant marketing. This isn't an all inclusive list, but some top strategic marketing issues include branding, positioning, due diligence, menu mix, and training.

Advertising

Branding

It's what customers, employees, vendors, the media and all other key constituents come to expect in dealing with our restaurant. Brand–building is closing the gap between what we promise and what we deliver. The Stone Oak Sports Bar & Grille believes a strong brand is one that has alignment between the promise and execution of quality food in a good atmosphere with high levels of service will be what we are known for.

Positioning

Positioning is an under–leveraged restaurant marketing component. Positioning is the place we will hold in the customers' mind relative to the competition (the cheaper choice, the higher quality choice, etc.) Effective positioning involves incorporation of our Unique Selling Proposition (USP). The Stone Oak Sports Bar & Grille is the best choice for quality, well–known food in our area. We also have the best service and coolest atmosphere. We are a unique service and product provider making the USP the one thing that only we can claim. It's a point of differentiation that the competition either cannot or does not claim.

Due Diligence

Restaurant marketing doesn't happen in a vacuum. We know that effective restaurant marketing must be built on a foundation of fact and knowledge about the market, our competition, our customers, our internal customers, financial history, marketing history, the industry, and outside forces that will impact our business. It's a lot to worry about, but our marketing has to factor these considerations into the overall strategy. Not even Coca–Cola can afford to market to everyone all the time, so effective market research and due diligence will help us be more effective in our marketing efforts.

Menu Analysis

Every six to twelve months, we'll want to conduct an analysis of our menu. This will include profitability analysis and competitive menu analysis. This will keep our menu fresh, relevant, and profitable. Also, we need to know specifically how each item on our menu is performing and also how it stacks up next to our top competition. We think of each item on our menu as a tenant leasing space and it has to earn its right to the space we've granted it.

Training

Marketing, human resources, operations and training are inextricably connected. Great marketing will just kill a bad operation faster. That's because if we send people into an operation that is performing at a B–level or below, people will have a bad experience and our money would be better spent on operation improvement rather than marketing. Training is a vital component of restaurant marketing. Our training will have to go beyond just employee orientation. We'll need an ongoing program that constantly improves and evolves our staff competencies. Also, we will include a restaurant marketing component in our training program so that we have a staff of ambassadors to help The Stone Oak Sports Bar & Grille's sales–building efforts.

Sales Building Strategy

Every effort we make to build sales falls into one of just four categories. Every promotion, advertisement, or offer will push one of the following four buttons:

- New Trial

- Frequency

- Check Average

- Party Size

New Trial

These are first–time customers buying from us for the first time. They will establish their opinion of our company during this first purchase and decide what percent of mind–share to award us in the future. New trial is the most expensive of the four sales–builders as acquisition costs are typically 7–10 times more costly to execute than the other sales builders. However, it is impossible to increase frequency, check average or party size without customers to start with. After a customer base has been established, however, it is advisable to focus considerable efforts on the sales builders listed below.

Frequency

Frequency is how often existing customers return to us for future purchases. Frequency is generated by developing enduring relationships and loyalty among customers. While it is rare to disagree that frequency is important, an alarming number of businesses fail to appropriate the needed mind–share and resources to developing successful programs. Customer loyalty programs will become critical once we establish our core clientele.

Check Average

Check average often refers to the total purchase for each transaction. In this instance, however, we are referring primarily to per person check average—the amount each guest or customer spends at purchase. Check averages can be built through price increases, suggestive selling programs, effective internal merchandising, and through add–ons or upgrades to name but a few techniques. The Stone Oak Sports Bar & Grille anticipates our check average to be between $15 and $19.99. We will make sure that the increase in check average remains consistent with our overall positioning strategy.

Party Size

As the name would suggest, Party Size refers to the number of people in each party. Do customers primarily visit alone, in groups of two, groups of five, or more? Whatever the number, we will devise programs that encourage customers to bring more of their friends with them for each visit. Examples of programs include bus drivers eat free, birthday clubs and refer–a–friend tactics. Encouraging party size turns customers into advocates and enlists them as part of your sales–building team. We will use the above definitions to constantly assure that we continually and effectively frame the challenges of growing our sales.

MARKETING & SALES

There are several rules of thumb and ratios in the restaurant industry and there are some for restaurant marketing as well. A typical restaurant should allocate 3% to 6% of sales to marketing. It's also a good idea to allocate this money proportionally to our sales volume. Meaning, if July is our busiest month, we will spend a proportionate amount on our restaurant's marketing budget in that month.

Fish where the fish are biting is one of The Stone Oak Sports Bar & Grille's marketing strategies. Some restaurant owners look at slow periods and think that's when they need to spend money to drive sales, so they spend a big chunk of cash trying to build a happy hour business and forgo building on top of their busy periods. Fact is, there is a reason people aren't coming in from 4 to 6 p.m. and we'll be sending valuable marketing dollars down a black hole if we try to build on slow periods. There are nearly one million restaurants in the United States and probably only 2% of them are busy from 4 to 6 p.m. Marketing can't change behavior; it can only influence existing behaviors. We will spend our marketing dollar where it will have the best return for our restaurant.

80% to 90% of restaurant marketing budgets are spent against new trial—getting a new customer to visit for the first time. This is the least effective place to spend our money. The majority of new trial efforts are spent against mass media advertising, which is costly and has dismal return on investment. The fact is, new customer acquisition is 7–10 times more expensive than building restaurant sales through increased frequency, check average and party size.

But restaurant marketing isn't always about what's most effective, more often, it's about what everyone else is doing. Restaurant operators see that their competitor is on television or in the yellow pages or on a billboard and think that they should be too. They do this without regard for what's working. Restaurant owners have to wear so many hats that sometimes they just do what's easiest—they write a check for mass media advertising and hope for the best. Mass media is often more about feeding ego than driving sales. It's also impossible for most companies to compete in a toe–to–toe battle with the big guys. We will be employing many effective guerrilla marketing techniques. Direct target flyers, networking within our community, delivering on our promise of quality, atmosphere, and service. We believe this can go much further. We do anticipate an initial advertising campaign in the local *Boerne Independent* and *Boerne Today*.

We know effective restaurant marketing isn't easy. It takes a lot of careful research, analysis and testing. It's also ever–evolving, which makes it even more difficult to master. The fact that effective restaurant marketing is difficult to master is what can give us the competitive advantage. We will resist the temptation to change everything at once or to go it all alone. We will start small and build our marketing competencies over time. In the beginning, we will do simple programs so we can execute them well and measure the results.

Marketing Tactics

We will immediately and directly be targeting much of the local residential area. We will target these customers directly through flyers, menu brochures, and other forms of cost effective distribution. Other strategic targets will include local businesses and the chamber of commerce to which we can offer open house lunches. It will be vital to network within the business community to increase our visibility.

Promotion Strategy

Our first promotional strategy principle will be as follows:

When we look at the community around us, it may seem as if our market is unlimited, but for most restaurants our market area generally extends to about a five–mile radius around our restaurant. The one–mile radius around our restaurant will receive 50% of our time and resources; up to three miles will receive an additional 30%; up to five miles an additional 16% to 18% and the outer limits a maximum of 2% to 4%.

Our second promotional strategy is as follows:

The real key to our success is dependent upon the relationship that we build with every one of our customers. How our customers "feel" about our restaurant services determines the strength of their patronage. The keys to creating fierce customer loyalty are to provide the highest quality food, outstanding customer service and personalized marketing. With proper planning and action, our restaurant will be the "Restaurant of First Choice" in our market area.

We will identify our market. This is done primarily through detailed mapping and gathering customer demographics. We will "saturate market" the homes of potential customers with door hangers about our restaurant and as they patronize us, we can enroll them in a "VIP Club" to gather their names and reward their loyalty. We will work extremely hard to build a customer database including at a minimum, their email address. We know that the customer groups that will show us the best return are within three miles around our restaurant.

The Stone Oak Sports Bar & Grille believes that next to e–mail, door hanging is by far the most effective and inexpensive way that we can distribute our marketing materials. But it is important that we set up procedures and processes so that the individuals who receive our materials actually want to receive them and don't perceive it as "garbage." If we do door hanging promotions correctly, very few people will be upset with the marketing materials from our restaurant. The materials that we hang on the door will have a professional appearance using full color pictures and text. Our goal is to do a quality job and distribute as many marketing pieces as we can by visiting as many homes and businesses as possible. This will be planned in every market segment around our restaurant which is referred to as "saturation marketing." It goes to everyone, except our current customers.

Promotional Timelines

- *At Startup:* At startup we will distribute flyers, hangers, do initial print media advertising and will strongly network within our community.

- *First 30 Days:* Begin marketing using our database. We will send out Bounce–Backs, Birthday Offers, and other Special Offers. We will establish an ongoing marketing program that delivers a consistent message and builds customer loyalty.

- *After 90 days:* Send out a more generous offer. If these customers have not bought from us for 90 days, then we can be assured that they are looking elsewhere to dine. When a customer does buy from us for a period of time and then stops, we know we will need to market to get them back. This is called marketing to "lost" or "lazy" customers and the goal is to get them back into our restaurant at least once a month.

- *After 120 days:* Send out an absolutely "FREE" offer with no strings attached. Focus and organization are the keys to strategic and tactical marketing.

Milestones

- Preliminary Research—Type—COMPLETE; Competitive Environment—COMPLETE; Location Research—COMPLETE

- Visit Other Restaurants and Conduct Onsite Research—COMPLETE

- Determine what restaurants are thriving—COMPLETE

- Begin Networking—ALL COMPLETE

- Preliminary Site Selection—COMPLETE

- Investigate Funding Strategies—COMPLETE

- Begin Preliminary Cost Structure Research—COMPLETE

- Design Preliminary Revenue Forecasts—COMPLETE

- Build Operational "Do" and "Don't" Strategies—COMPLETE

- Begin Determining Square Footage Requirements For—ALL COMPLETE

- Begin Recipe Design—COMPLETE

- Begin Building New/Used Equipment Contacts—COMPLETE

- Interview Restaurateurs—COMPLETE

- Interview Government Agencies—COMPLETE

- Interview Local People—COMPLETE

- Obtain Permits Information—COMPLETE

- Form Legal Entity—COMPLETE

- Personal Strength/Weakness Analysis—COMPLETE
- Find and Catalog Restaurant–based—ALL COMPLETE
- Outline Business Plan—COMPLETE
- Research Industry—COMPLETE
- Research Market—COMPLETE
- Focused Concept Design—In Progress
- Focused Menu and Recipe Design—In Progress
- Target Market Strategy Design—COMPLETE
- Begin Meeting with Real Estate Agents—COMPLETE
- Begin Meeting with Bankers—COMPLETE
- Expand Financial Projection—ALL COMPLETE
- Complete Recipes—In Progress
- Begin Price Research and Design—In Progress
- Begin Networking with Vendors—COMPLETE
- Meet with all Necessary ... (In Process)
- Join Trade Associations and Networking Forums—COMPLETE
- Finalize Advisor and Support Team—In Progress
- Finalize Financial Numbers—COMPLETE
- Finalize Business Plan—COMPLETE
- Set up restaurant's name and obtain taxpayer ID—In Progress
- Finalize Site Location—In Progress
- Begin working up plans with—In Progress
- Begin Business Plan Review Process—To be begun
- Begin Mapping the Restaurant Flow Plans—To be begun
- Finalize Equipment Needs—To be begun
- Begin Seeking Capital—In Progress
- Begin Location Negotiations—In Progress
- Do Final Business Plan Adjustments Due to Feedback—To be begun
- Obtain all Possible Financing and Capital—To be completed
- Begin Scheduling—To be begun
- Join Local Chamber of Commerce—In Progress
- Join National Restaurant Association—In Progress
- Begin Hardcore Community Networking—In Progress
- Begin Office Set–up—To be begun
- Determine Exact Small Ware Purchases—To be begun
- Final Menu Prices—To be begun

- Begin Development of Operations Manuals—To be begun

- Begin Development of Employee Handbooks—To be begun

- Manage and Monitor Construction Progression—To be begun

- Finish Office Set–Up (Including Bookkeeping and Accounting Systems)—To be begun

- Begin Feeding Family and Friends Menu Items—In Progress

- Begin Determining Hiring and Staffing Needs and Process—In Progress

- Begin Marketing, Advertising and Public Relations Plans—To be begun

- Begin Negotiations with Vendors and determine delivery schedules and terms—To be begun

- Order—To be begun

- Build Sourcing, Selection, Hiring, Training, Management—In Progress

- Continually Manage and Monitor Construction Progress—To be begun

- Put in All Orders for Food and Beverages to arrive three days before grand opening—To be begun

- Design all Cash handling procedures—To be begun

- Design all inventory procedures—To be begun

- Design all Checklists—To be begun

- Finalize Menu and Order Printing of Menus—To be begun

- Work with bank and arrange merchant accounts—To be begun

- Finalize Detailed Job Descriptions—To be begun

- Begin Executing People Plan—To be begun

- Ensure Facility Construction is Nearing Completion—To be done

- Set up all Utilities—To be begun

- Check Status of Permits and Licenses—To be begun

- Begin Pre–opening Countdown and PR campaign—To be begun

- Finalize all Operating Systems (Test all Systems)—To be begun

- Hire all Staff—To be begun

- Begin Staff Training—To be begun

- Ensure Construction is being Finished—To be begun

- Schedule Soft Grand Opening Date—To be begun

- Schedule VIP Grand Opening Date—To be begun

- Schedule Public Grand Opening Date—To be begun

- Hand Out Soft Grand Opening Date—To be begun

- Send out VIP Grand Opening Date—To be begun

- Begin Pre–Opening Advertising and Marketing—To be begun

- Construction—To be completed

- Equipment Schedule to Arrive—To be completed

- Equipment Installation—To be begun

- Equipment Testing—To be begun

- Small Wares Arrive—To be completed

- Begin Clean Up—To be completed

- Ensure Complete Small Wares Have Arrived—To be begun

- Follow Up to Ensure Licenses and Permits are Obtained and Displayed—To be completed

- Walk through Facilities with Construction Manager to Ensure Place is Complete

- Make any Plans with Construction Manager for Unsatisfactory Work—To be begun

- Ensure Food and Beverages Arrive on Schedule—To be begun

- Finalize Training for Soft Grand Opening—To be completed

- Soft Opening—To be completed

- Analyze Feedback—To be done

- Work with Staff to Make Necessary Changes or Focus on Weakness—To be done

- Prepare for VIP Grand Opening—To be begun

- Ensure that Unsatisfactory Construction Issues have been fixed—To be begun

- Make Sure all Items on All Checklists are Complete—To be completed

Strategic Alliances

Advisor List

1. Consultant: Brad E. Williams—Michigan Department of Liquor, Ret.

2. Attorney: Frank K. Ward

3. CPA: Earl V. Micks

4. Strategic Consultants: Hemmingway & Associates, Inc.

Revenue Forecast

The Revenue Forecast is based on industry averages from the National Restaurant Association, and Deloitte. Fiscal years two through five reflect 6% growth annually.

Annual revenue forcast

Stone Oak	FY 1	FY 2	FY 3	FY 4	FY 5
Beverages	$ 798,000	$ 845,880	$ 896,633	$ 950,431	$1,007,457
Food	$ 216,500	$ 229,490	$ 243,529	$ 257,855	$ 273,326
Total revenues	**$1,014,500**	**$1,075,370**	**$1,139,892**	**$1,208,286**	**$1,280,783**
Cost of goods sold					
Beverage	$ 189,126	$ 200,474	$ 212,502	$ 225,252	$ 238,767
Food	$ 67,115	$ 71,142	$ 75,410	$ 79,935	$ 84,731
Total cost of goods sold	**$ 256,241**	**$ 271,615**	**$ 287,912**	**$ 305,187**	**$ 323,498**

MANAGEMENT SUMMARY

Management Team

Henry DiMuzio

Mr. DiMuzio is a 10–year resident of Boerne. Up until just recently, he was in Law Enforcement since 1994 as a police officer and captain. He has the utmost integrity and respect for the law, and brings a good working knowledge of Michigan's Liquor Laws and procedures to this new business venture.

Prior to his Law Enforcement career, Mr. DiMuzio worked for a leading national beer distributor in New Jersey, as well as several bars and taverns in New York and New Jersey as a bartender and security personnel. This provides him with great insight into the liquor end of the business. Additionally, he was in the culinary arts for numerous years, working in Doubletree and Hilton Hotel chains as a line chef. This lends Mr. DiMuzio the experience of the back of the house—the kitchen.

Nick Sturgeon

Looking back to August 28, 1980, Mr. Sturgeon was in the eighth grade and was subsequently also the first day of his working life. He started as a newspaper carrier delivering newspapers to homes at 5 a.m. each and every morning until he was able to drive in 1983. This allowed him to work inside the newspaper distributing office. Mr. Sturgeon kept delivering newspapers until 1990 when he was rewarded with his own agency under contract until 1993.

It was then Mr. Sturgeon started to work part time at a friend's family pizza business located in downtown Detroit. He took interest to the point of opening his own, leaving the newspaper business after fifteen years. He opened his own pizza place on August 8, 1995, and was very successful.

In January 1999, Mr. Sturgeon saw the growth factor in Boerne and decided that life and business would be much more rewarding there. He moved his family there in May 2000. Shortly after relocating, he opened his first restaurant in Boerne. This restaurant consisted of 1,600 square feet, servicing a dining room and walk–ins as well as phone order pick–ups. Getting the staff organized allowed him to expand his business to nearby Greenbay Park in 2003.

The Greenbay Park location is currently operating with dine–in phone orders and walk–ins. This store is 1,800 square feet and also serves alcohol. Both Nick's stores keep busy and customer satisfaction is our best quality due to owner involvement. Employee turnaround is minimal, which makes operating much more adequate.

A third business which also brings his kitchen abilities to the new journey is currently Mr. Sturgeon's goal. This new venture will allow his Detroit food connections to bring unique foods to Boerne and keep a distance from competition. A third location or third business has been a personal goal for him in the past two years. Now the location, timing and a partner that is more dedicated than him, makes it all fall into place. It confirms that it is time to move forward just as he has in past decisions. Mr. Sturgeon has not had more than three different jobs in his entire life, so this decision is well thought–out.

Personnel Plan

Fiscal years two through five reflect a 5% increase in salaries and wages.

Annual personnel plan

Stone Oak	FY 1	FY 2	FY 3	FY 4	FY 5
Bartenders	$ 42,399	$ 44,519	$ 46,745	$ 49,083	$ 51,537
Wait-staff	$ 69,211	$ 72,671	$ 76,305	$ 80,120	$ 84,126
Kitchen staff	$ 93,112	$ 97,768	$102,656	$107,789	$113,179
Management	$ 64,015	$ 67,215	$ 70,576	$ 74,105	$ 77,810
Total payroll	**$268,737**	**$282,174**	**$296,283**	**$311,097**	**$326,652**

FINANCIAL ANALYSIS

Key financial indicators

Stone Oak	FY 1	FY 2	FY 3	FY 4	FY 5
Revenues	$1,014,500	$1,075,370	$1,139,892	$1,208,286	$1,280,783
Gross margin	$ 758,259	$ 803,755	$ 851,980	$ 903,099	$ 957,285
Operating expenses	$ 534,116	$ 562,695	$ 582,501	$ 603,172	$ 624,748

Annual pro forma profit and loss

Stone Oak	FY 1	FY 2	FY 3	FY 4	F Y5
Total income	$1,014,500	$1,075,370	$1,139,892	$1,208,286	$1,280,783
Cost of goods sold	$ 256,241	$ 271,615	$ 287,912	$ 305,187	$ 323,498
Gross profit	$ 758,259	$ 803,755	$ 851,980	$ 903,099	$ 957,285
Gross profit %	74.74%	74.74%	74.74%	74.74%	74.74%
Expenses:					
Payroll	$ 268,737	$ 282,174	$ 296,283	$ 311,097	$ 326,652
Depreciation	$ 71,429	$ 71,429	$ 71,429	$ 71,429	$ 71,429
Lease	$ 147,150	$ 151,565	$ 156,111	$ 160,795	$ 165,619
Satellite	$ 12,000	$ 12,240	$ 12,485	$ 12,734	$ 12,989
Electric	$ 12,000	$ 12,240	$ 12,485	$ 12,734	$ 12,989
Insurance	$ 8,400	$ 8,568	$ 8,739	$ 8,914	$ 9,092
Accounting	$ 4,800	$ 4,896	$ 4,994	$ 5,094	$ 5,196
Gas	$ 7,200	$ 7,344	$ 7,491	$ 7,641	$ 7,794
Phone/internet	$ 2,400	$ 2,448	$ 2,497	$ 2,547	$ 2,598
Supplies	$ 2,400	$ 2,448	$ 2,497	$ 2,547	$ 2,598
Advertising	$ 6,000	$ 6,120	$ 6,242	$ 6,367	$ 6,495
Maintenance & repairs	$ 1,200	$ 1,224	$ 1,248	$ 1,273	$ 1,299
Total operating expenses	$ 534,116	$ 562,695	$ 582,501	$ 603,172	$ 624,748
Profit before interest and taxes	$ 224,143	$ 241,059	$ 269,479	$ 299,926	$ 332,537
Interest expense	$ 24,910	$ 21,843	$ 18,537	$ 14,975	$ 11,137
Taxes incurred	$ 0	$ 0	$ 0	$ 0	$ 0
Net profit	$ 199,233	$ 219,217	$ 250,941	$ 284,951	$ 321,400
Net profit/sales	19.64%	20.39%	22.01%	23.58%	25.09%

Annual pro forma cash flow

Stone Oak	FY 1	FY 2	FY 3	FY 4	FY 5
Cash received					
Cash from operations:					
Revenues	**$1,014,500**	**$1,075,370**	**$1,139,892**	**$1,208,286**	**$1,280,783**
Expenditures					
Expenditures from operations					
Payroll	$ 268,737	$ 282,174	$ 296,283	$ 311,097	$ 326,652
Lease	$ 147,150	$ 151,565	$ 156,111	$ 160,795	$ 165,619
Satellite	$ 12,000	$ 12,240	$ 12,485	$ 12,734	$ 12,989
Electric	$ 12,000	$ 12,240	$ 12,485	$ 12,734	$ 12,989
Insurance	$ 8,400	$ 8,568	$ 8,739	$ 8,914	$ 9,092
Accounting	$ 4,800	$ 4,896	$ 4,994	$ 5,094	$ 5,196
Gas	$ 7,200	$ 7,344	$ 7,491	$ 7,641	$ 7,794
Phone/internet	$ 2,400	$ 2,448	$ 2,497	$ 2,547	$ 2,598
Supplies	$ 2,400	$ 2,448	$ 2,497	$ 2,547	$ 2,598
Advertising	$ 6,000	$ 6,120	$ 6,242	$ 6,367	$ 6,495
Maintenance & repairs	$ 1,200	$ 1,224	$ 1,248	$ 1,273	$ 1,299
Interest expense	$ 24,910	$ 21,843	$ 18,537	$ 14,975	$ 11,137
Cost of sales	$ 256,241	$ 271,615	$ 287,912	$ 305,187	$ 323,498
Subtotal spent on operations	$ 753,438	$ 784,725	$ 817,522	$ 851,906	$ 887,955
Additional cash spent					
Principle repayment of loan	$ 39,511	$ 42,578	$ 45,883	$ 49,445	$ 53,284
Subtotal cash spent	$ 792,949	$ 827,303	$ 863,406	$ 901,352	$ 941,239
Net cash flow	$ 221,551	$ 248,067	$ 276,486	$ 306,934	$ 339,544
Cash balance	$ 242,808	$ 490,876	$ 767,362	$1,074,296	$1,413,840

Pro forma balance sheet

Stone Oak	FY 1	FY 2	FY 3	FY 4	FY 5
Assets					
Current assets					
Cash	$242,808	$490,876	$ 767,362	$1,074,296	$1,413,840
Food inventory	$ 7,502	$ 7,502	$ 7,502	$ 7,502	$ 7,502
Bar inventory	$ 21,240	$ 21,240	$ 21,240	$ 21,240	$ 21,240
Total current assets	$271,551	$519,618	$ 796,105	$1,103,039	$1,442,583
Long-term assets					
Equipment	$230,000	$230,000	$ 230,000	$ 230,000	$ 230,000
Leasehold improvements	$270,000	$270,000	$ 270,000	$ 270,000	$ 270,000
Accumulated depreciation	$ 71,429	$142,857	$ 214,286	$ 285,714	$ 357,143
Total long-term assets	$428,571	$357,143	$ 285,714	$ 214,286	$ 142,857
Total assets	$700,123	$876,761	$1,081,819	$1,317,325	$1,585,440
Liabilities and owner's equity					
Current liabilities					
Current portion of debt	$ 42,578	$ 45,883	$ 49,445	$ 53,284	$ 57,421
Total current liabilities	$ 42,578	$ 45,883	$ 49,445	$ 53,284	$ 57,421
Long-term liabilities					
Loan	$267,911	$222,028	$ 172,583	$ 119,299	$ 61,878
Total liabilities	$310,489	$267,911	$ 222,028	$ 172,583	$ 119,299
Owner's investment	$313,000	$313,000	$ 313,000	$ 313,000	$ 313,000
Retained earnings	$ 76,633	$295,850	$ 546,791	$ 831,742	$1,153,142
Earnings	$189,633	$219,217	$ 250,941	$ 284,951	$ 321,400
Total owner's equity	$389,633	$608,850	$ 859,791	$1,144,742	$1,466,142
Total liabilities & owner's equity	$700,123	$876,761	$1,081,819	$1,317,325	$1,585,440

Sensitivity analysis

Stone Oak	FY 1	FY 2	FY 3	FY 4	FY 5
Revenues @80%					
Revenue	$ 811,600	$ 860,296	$ 911,914	$ 966,629	$1,024,626
COGS	$ 204,993	$ 217,292	$ 230,330	$ 244,150	$ 258,799
Payroll	$ 268,737	$ 282,174	$ 296,283	$ 311,097	$ 326,652
Fixed costs	$ 265,379	$ 280,521	$ 286,219	$ 292,075	$ 298,096
EBIT	**$ 72,492**	**$ 80,309**	**$ 99,083**	**$ 119,307**	**$ 141,080**
Revenues @90%					
Revenue	$ 913,050	$ 967,833	$1,025,903	$1,087,457	$1,152,705
COGS	$ 230,617	$ 244,454	$ 259,121	$ 274,668	$ 291,149
Payroll	$ 268,737	$ 282,174	$ 296,283	$ 311,097	$ 326,652
Fixed costs	$ 265,379	$ 280,521	$ 286,219	$ 292,075	$ 298,096
EBIT	**$ 148,317**	**$ 160,684**	**$ 184,281**	**$ 209,616**	**$ 236,808**
Revenues @100%					
Revenue	$1,014,500	$1,075,370	$1,139,892	$1,208,286	$1,280,783
COGS	$ 256,241	$ 271,615	$ 287,912	$ 305,187	$ 323,498
Payroll	$ 268,737	$ 282,174	$ 296,283	$ 311,097	$ 326,652
Fixed costs	$ 265,379	$ 280,521	$ 286,219	$ 292,075	$ 298,096
EBIT	**$ 224,143**	**$ 241,059**	**$ 269,479**	**$ 299,926**	**$ 332,537**
Revenues @110%					
Revenue	$1,115,950	$1,182,907	$1,253,881	$1,329,114	$1,408,861
COGS	$ 281,865	$ 298,777	$ 316,704	$ 335,706	$ 355,848
Payroll	$ 268,737	$ 282,174	$ 296,283	$ 311,097	$ 326,652
Fixed costs	$ 265,379	$ 280,521	$ 286,219	$ 292,075	$ 298,096
EBIT	**$ 299,969**	**$ 321,435**	**$ 354,677**	**$ 390,236**	**$ 428,265**
Revenues @120%					
Revenue	$1,217,400	$1,290,444	$1,367,871	$1,449,943	$1,536,939
COGS	$ 307,489	$ 325,939	$ 345,495	$ 366,225	$ 388,198
Payroll	$ 268,737	$ 282,174	$ 296,283	$ 311,097	$ 326,652
Fixed costs	$ 265,379	$ 280,521	$ 286,219	$ 292,075	$ 298,096
EBIT	**$ 375,795**	**$ 401,810**	**$ 439,875**	**$ 480,546**	**$ 523,993**

Monthly pro forma profit and loss

Stone Oak	Jul-06	Aug-06	Sep-06	Oct-06	Nov-06	Dec-06
Total income	$84,542	$84,542	$84,542	$84,542	$84,542	$84,542
Cost of goods sold	$21,353	$21,353	$21,353	$21,353	$21,353	$21,353
Gross profit	$63,188	$63,188	$63,188	$63,188	$63,188	$63,188
Gross profit %	74.74%	74.74%	74.74%	74.74%	74.74%	74.74%
Expenses:						
Payroll	$22,395	$22,395	$22,395	$22,395	$22,395	$22,395
Depreciation	$ 5,952	$ 5,952	$ 5,952	$ 5,952	$ 5,952	$ 5,952
Lease	$12,263	$12,263	$12,263	$12,263	$12,263	$12,263
Satellite	$ 1,000	$ 1,000	$ 1,000	$ 1,000	$ 1,000	$ 1,000
Electric	$ 1,000	$ 1,000	$ 1,000	$ 1,000	$ 1,000	$ 1,000
Insurance	$ 700	$ 700	$ 700	$ 700	$ 700	$ 700
Accounting	$ 400	$ 400	$ 400	$ 400	$ 400	$ 400
Gas	$ 600	$ 600	$ 600	$ 600	$ 600	$ 600
Phone/internet	$ 200	$ 200	$ 200	$ 200	$ 200	$ 200
Supplies	$ 200	$ 200	$ 200	$ 200	$ 200	$ 200
Advertising	$ 500	$ 500	$ 500	$ 500	$ 500	$ 500
Maintenance & repairs	$ 100	$ 100	$ 100	$ 100	$ 100	$ 100
Total operating expenses	$45,310	$45,310	$45,310	$45,310	$45,310	$45,310
Profit before Interest and taxes	$17,879	$17,879	$17,879	$17,879	$17,879	$17,879
Interest expense	$ 2,188	$ 2,168	$ 2,148	$ 2,127	$ 2,107	$ 2,087
Taxes incurred	$ 0	$ 0	$ 0	$ 0	$ 0	$ 0
Net profit	$15,691	$15,711	$15,731	$15,751	$15,771	$15,792
Net profit/sales	18.56%	18.58%	18.61%	18.63%	18.66%	18.68%

Stone Oak	Jan-07	Feb-07	Mar-07	Apr-07	May-07	Jun-07
Total income	$84,542	$84,542	$84,542	$84,542	$84,542	$84,542
Cost of goods sold	$21,353	$21,353	$21,353	$21,353	$21,353	$21,353
Gross profit	$63,188	$63,188	$63,188	$63,188	$63,188	$63,188
Gross profit %	74.74%	74.74%	74.74%	74.74%	74.74%	74.74%
Expenses:						
Payroll	$22,395	$22,395	$22,395	$22,395	$22,395	$22,395
Depreciation	$ 5,952	$ 5,952	$ 5,952	$5,952	$ 5,952	$ 5,952
Lease	$12,263	$12,263	$12,263	$12,263	$12,263	$12,263
Satellite	$ 1,000	$ 1,000	$ 1,000	$ 1,000	$ 1,000	$ 1,000
Electric	$ 1,000	$ 1,000	$ 1,000	$ 1,000	$ 1,000	$ 1,000
Insurance	$ 700	$ 700	$ 700	$ 700	$ 700	$ 700
Accounting	$ 400	$ 400	$ 400	$ 400	$ 400	$ 400
Gas	$ 600	$ 600	$ 600	$ 600	$ 600	$ 600
Phone/internet	$ 200	$ 200	$ 200	$ 200	$ 200	$ 200
Supplies	$ 200	$ 200	$ 200	$ 200	$ 200	$ 200
Advertising	$ 500	$ 500	$ 500	$ 500	$ 500	$ 500
Maintenance & repairs	$ 100	$ 100	$ 100	$ 100	$ 100	$ 100
Total operating expenses	$45,310	$45,310	$45,310	$45,310	$45,310	$45,310
Profit before interest and taxes	$17,879	$17,879	$17,879	$17,879	$17,879	$17,879
Interest expense	$ 2,066	$ 2,046	$ 2,025	$ 2,004	$ 1,983	$ 1,962
Taxes incurred	$ 0	$ 0	$ 0	$ 0	$ 0	$ 0
Net profit	$15,812	$15,833	$15,854	$15,875	$15,896	$15,917
Net profit/sales	18.70%	18.73%	18.75%	18.78%	18.80%	18.83%

Monthly pro forma cash flow

Stone Oak	Jul-06	Aug-06	Sep-06	Oct-06	Nov-06	Dec-06
Cash received						
Cash from operations:						
Revenues	**$84,542**	**$84,542**	**$84,542**	**$84,542**	**$ 84,542**	**$ 84,542**
Expenditures						
Expenditures from operations						
Payroll	$22,395	$22,395	$22,395	$22,395	$ 22,395	$ 22,395
Lease	$ 2,263	$12,263	$12,263	$12,263	$ 12,263	$ 12,263
Satellite	$ 1,000	$ 1,000	$ 1,000	$ 1,000	$ 1,000	$ 1,000
Electric	$ 1,000	$ 1,000	$ 1,000	$ 1,000	$ 1,000	$ 1,000
Insurance	$ 700	$ 700	$ 700	$ 700	$ 700	$ 700
Accounting	$ 400	$ 400	$ 400	$ 400	$ 400	$ 400
Gas	$ 600	$ 600	$ 600	$ 600	$ 600	$ 600
Phone/internet	$ 200	$ 200	$ 200	$ 200	$ 200	$ 200
Supplies	$ 200	$ 200	$ 200	$ 200	$ 200	$ 200
Advertising	$ 500	$ 500	$ 500	$ 500	$ 500	$ 500
Maintenance & repairs	$ 100	$ 100	$ 100	$ 100	$ 100	$ 100
Interest expense	$ 2,188	$ 2,168	$ 2,148	$ 2,127	$ 2,107	$ 2,087
Cost of sales	$21,353	$21,353	$21,353	$21,353	$ 21,353	$ 21,353
Subtotal spent on operations	$62,898	$62,878	$62,858	$62,838	$ 62,818	$ 62,798
Additional cash spent						
Principle repayment of loan	$ 3,181	$ 3,201	$ 3,221	$ 3,241	$ 3,261	$ 3,282
Subtotal cash spent	**$66,079**	**$66,079**	**$66,079**	**$66,079**	**$ 66,079**	**$ 66,079**
Net cash flow	**$18,463**	**$18,463**	**$18,463**	**$18,463**	**$ 18,463**	**$ 18,463**
Cash balance	**$39,720**	**$58,182**	**$76,645**	**$95,107**	**$113,570**	**$132,033**

Stone Oak	Jan-07	Feb-07	Mar-07	Apr-07	May-07	Jun-07
Cash received						
Cash from operations:						
Revenues	**$ 84,542**	**$ 84,542**	**$ 84,542**	**$ 84,542**	**$ 84,542**	**$ 84,542**
Expenditures						
Expenditures from operations						
Payroll	$ 22,395	$ 22,395	$ 22,395	$ 22,395	$ 22,395	$ 22,395
Lease	$ 12,263	$ 12,263	$ 12,263	$ 12,263	$ 12,263	$ 12,263
Satellite	$ 1,000	$ 1,000	$ 1,000	$ 1,000	$ 1,000	$ 1,000
Electric	$ 1,000	$ 1,000	$ 1,000	$ 1,000	$ 1,000	$ 1,000
Insurance	$ 700	$ 700	$ 700	$ 700	$ 700	$ 700
Accounting	$ 400	$ 400	$ 400	$ 400	$ 400	$ 400
Gas	$ 600	$ 600	$ 600	$ 600	$ 600	$ 600
Phone/internet	$ 200	$ 200	$ 200	$ 200	$ 200	$ 200
Supplies	$ 200	$ 200	$ 200	$ 200	$ 200	$ 200
Advertising	$ 500	$ 500	$ 500	$ 500	$ 500	$ 500
Maintenance & repairs	$ 100	$ 100	$ 100	$ 100	$ 100	$ 100
Interest expense	$ 2,066	$ 2,046	$ 2,025	$ 2,004	$ 1,983	$ 1,962
Cost of sales	$ 21,353	$ 21,353	$ 21,353	$ 21,353	$ 21,353	$ 21,353
Subtotal spent on operations	$ 62,777	$ 62,756	$ 62,736	$ 62,715	$ 62,694	$ 62,673
Additional cash spent						
Principle repayment of loan	$ 3,302	$ 3,323	$ 3,343	$ 3,364	$ 3,385	$ 3,407
Subtotal cash spent	**$ 66,079**	**$ 66,079**	**$ 66,079**	**$ 66,079**	**$ 66,079**	**$ 66,079**
Net cash flow	**$ 18,463**	**$ 18,463**	**$ 18,463**	**$ 18,463**	**$ 18,463**	**$ 18,463**
Cash balance	**$150,495**	**$168,958**	**$187,420**	**$205,883**	**$224,346**	**$242,808**

Sports Tournament Organizer

SCRAMBLE SPORTS TOURNAMENT SERIES

31 Stone School Dr.
Muncie, Indiana 47302

Brett Bachelier, Mark Chase, and Justin Renshaw

Our goal is to develop this company into a respected national tournament series encompassing both extreme and traditional sports, and to make this competition open to people of all ages and skill levels.

This business plan provides information relevant to the development of our national tournament series. It describes plans for our events, growth strategies, financial plans, the management team, and an analysis of the industry. It is meant to inform the reader about our company and its operations in years to come.

EXECUTIVE SUMMARY

Objectives

The Scramble Sports Tournament Series is a limited liability company headquartered in Muncie, Indiana. Our goal is to develop this company into a respected national tournament series encompassing both extreme and traditional sports, and to make this competition open to people of all ages and skill levels. We feel that by offering separate divisions for people of various age and skill levels in: Hockey, Soccer, Basketball, Volleyball, Skateboarding, In–Line Skating, and Biking in our first year of operation, with new sports to be added every year, we can tap into a large portion of the massive sports tournament marketplace.

In addition, by offering a vendor tradeshow, live bands, comfortable viewing areas, concessions, merchandise, and a fun family environment, we also hope to encourage spectators to attend our events as well. By enticing both athletes and spectators to attend our events, we will greatly increase our earning potential. We plan not only to charge athletes to compete in our events, but also to charge spectators to view and park at the events, vendors to showcase their merchandise at the events, sponsors to market products at the events, as well as selling concessions, photographs, merchandise, and tournament programs.

We also plan to form strategic partnerships with entities outside of the sporting industry in order to offer other unique competitions and contests which will broaden our customer base. In addition, we will also be partnering with an internet as well as a magazine media outlet so that we may push our content in front of our target market.

In the past our management team was able to start and successfully operate a national hockey tournament series, as well as a regional paintball tournament series. While this is a much larger project, we feel that we have a strong background in the sports tournament industry as well as the contacts and resources at our disposal to help us achieve our goal.

Mission

To become the amateur athletes' hub for knowledge, advancement, and competition.

The mission of the Scramble Sports Tournament Series is to form a respected national tournament series which will allow amateur athletes of various age and skill levels to learn, participate, improve skills, and compete in a variety of both traditional and extreme sports. In addition, contracts with vendors in each sport will provide the amateur athletes with an opportunity to discuss, watch, and learn about different aspects of each sport.

COMPANY HISTORY

The idea behind Scramble spurred from an observation that many athletes are interested in and passionate about a variety of sports; however, the majority of sports tournament series only offer a single sport in one location at a time. The idea behind Scramble is to offer a variety of sports in one single location so that athletes may not only participate in the sport which they are passionate about, but may also have the chance to watch and participate in other sports so that they may develop an understanding and respect for those sports as well.

Our management team observed that in the sports tournament marketplace there are an abundance of tournaments which offer a single sport at a single location, such as a local soccer tournament. In addition, there are a great deal of tournaments which offer a single sport at multiple locations throughout the year, such as a soccer tournament series, and there are a number of tournaments which offer multiple sports at different locations throughout the year, such as a soccer tournament in Muncie and a hockey tournament in Indianapolis.

This leaves a large void in the sports tournament marketplace. It seems that there are relatively few sports tournaments which offer multiple sports at the same location, such as a soccer and hockey tournament at one park. In addition, to take this idea one step further, there are even fewer, if any, sports tournaments which offer both traditional and extreme sports at the same location. This is the void in the sports tournament marketplace which we have identified and intend to fill.

Our design is to offer a multi sport tournament series, encompassing elements of both extreme and traditional sports, during the summer months when children are not in school and families are more able to travel. In our first year of operation we plan to offer eight regional tournaments taking place in major cities spread across the Midwest, as well as one national championship tournament in Muncie, centrally located in our Midwest region. In addition, during the off season we also plan to offer clinics as well as Sports Highlight tournaments that highlight and showcase each of the sports which we offer: Hockey, Soccer, Basketball, Volleyball, Skateboarding, In–Line Skating, and Biking.

Another big draw for our series will be the extensive vendor showcase. Our goal is to contract with one large vendor in each sport to attend our events and showcase their products as well as answer any questions that athletes may have, provide equipment assistance for athletes, and possibly even bring sponsored athletes to put on demonstrations and explain the intricacies of the various sports to aspiring athletes.

In addition, we also intend to contract with companies outside of the sporting industry so that we may peak other areas of interest at our events as well. While athletes and spectators are at our events we will have a relatively captive audience. Instead of ignoring this audience and forcing them to entertain themselves, or even worse, leave the venue for entertainment, we plan to contract with companies outside of the sporting industry to provide fun family–centered entertainment so that consumers with extra time will desire to remain at the venue and enjoy the atmosphere.

ORGANIZATION

The management team of the Scramble Tournament Series has a strong proven background in the sports tournament industry. One member of the management team, Bobby Risheo, along with his father, Thomas Risheo, was previously involved in starting, owning, and operating a national roller hockey tournament series. In addition, Bobby Risheo was also involved in starting and operating a regional paintball tournament series.

In 1997, the management team of Bobby and Thomas Risheo saw a market opportunity to run hockey tournaments at arenas during the night when the buildings would be otherwise closed and therefore generating no revenue. Due to prior relationships which the management team had with many local hockey rink owners, they were able to convince many local area rink owners to allow them access to the buildings during non–operating nighttime hours on the weekends.

During this time the management team ran a successful "All Night Hockey Tournament Series" at many venues throughout the Muncie area including: Number One Sports Complex located in Hartford City; The Rink located in Indianapolis; Ice Babies located in Muncie; and Wilbur Arena located in Fishers.

As the popularity of the series grew, the demand became too great to simply run the tournaments in the overnight fashion. There was simply not enough time to accommodate all of the teams that wished to participate in the series. Knowing that they had a loyal customer base in the Muncie marketplace, the management team decided to expand their tournaments from nighttime events to weekend–long tournaments and to change the name of the series from "Evening Hockey Tournament Series" to "Weekend Hockey Series."

With the new name and business model the team continued to promote their tournaments and continued to fill them to capacity. While running weekend–long events was much more difficult and time consuming than simply running one night events, the management team found that having consumers at the event for a longer period of time allowed for additional offerings and they were able to expand their revenue streams by offering concessions, merchandise, and even having side competitions when venues had the appropriate space required. These additional revenue streams, along with the additional capacity created by expanding the events from one night to an entire weekend, showed positive results on the company's financials.

With their new business model showing signs of success in the Muncie marketplace, the management team decided that expansion into other areas could be profitable as well. They began by taking the series to a regional level and offering similar events in Lansing, Michigan; Toledo, Ohio; Madison, Wisconsin; and Chicago, Illinois.

Upon success in these areas the management team decided to dream big and expanded the series to a national level by offering sixteen regional qualifying tournaments throughout the United States and a series national championship tournament located at the Number One Sports Complex in Hartford City.

While expanding to a national level continued to make the series even more popular and even more profitable, the management team had never intended to make the series their full–time career. Both members of the team had prior business careers which they wished to return to; therefore, in 2000 the team decided to exit the series via a buyout agreement with another national hockey tournament series whereby the buying series simply dissolved "Weekend Hockey Series" and shifted its clientele into their series.

Late in the year 2000 however Bobby Risheo once again decided to start and operate another tournament series, this time in the paintball industry. While working at a local paintball shop located in Indianapolis, *Total Paintball Madness*, Bobby had developed a close relationship with the owner. When the owner, Josh Doctor, decided to open playing fields in addition to the store, Bobby approached him with the offer to start, operate, and market a regional paintball tournament series at the new fields.

With most of the owner's time being tied up trying to manage the daily business of his store and his new playing fields, he did not have time to worry about a tournament series himself; however, he did think that it was a good idea. Therefore, he allowed Bobby, who had been working at the store for over a year at that point, to run the series. The structure was set up so that the field took a portion of the profits from each tournament and Bobby retained the rest of the profit himself. This worked out well for both parties since Bobby was not required to put up any capital to get the series off the ground, and Mr. Doctor was able to retain ownership and full rights to the series itself.

The buzz generated by the opening of the new fields combined with the marketing efforts of Bobby Risheo created an atmosphere which drew top paintball teams from around the region almost instantaneously. In fact, the first tournament held at the field drew approximately 35 teams, almost 25% more teams than expected and included teams traveling from as far as Knoxville, Tennessee and Chicago, Illinois—cities in which marketing campaigns were not even launched. While Bobby stepped down as tournament director late in 2004, the tournament series is still in operation today and remains one of the top regional paintball tournament series in the area.

BUSINESS STRATEGY

Currently the Scramble Sports Tournament Series is in the start–up phase. The major milestones which we feel we have accomplished towards bringing our business into fruition include:

- Having designed the format which we wish to operate by

- Identifying the sports which we intend to offer in our first season

- Setting a tentative schedule for the 2007–2008 calendar year

- Creating event outlines detailing how each of our various events will operate

- Designing sponsor and vendor packages

- Identifying strategic partnership opportunities

- Performing an analysis of the competition

- Analyzing the industry in which we will be operating

- Identifying various market segments for our tournament series

- Developing a marketing strategy to reach our various market segments

- Outlining the development milestones which we intend to accomplish in the future

Management Summary

Bobby B. Risheo—Owner/CEO

Bobby is a senior majoring in entrepreneurship in the Kelley Business School at Indiana University. Bobby's background in the sports industry is very extensive both as a participant and as a tournament operator. In addition to operating hockey and paintball tournaments, Bobby has participated in a great deal of sports tournaments. Bobby traveled throughout North America playing roller hockey tournaments for four years in addition to traveling around the United States playing paintball tournaments for three years. This extensive tournament knowledge has helped Bobby to understand what features of tournaments help to make them successful, as well as what features tend to lead to failure.

In addition to tournament experience, Bobby has also worked in the life insurance industry at his father's brokerage firm, Family Insurance Solutions. This has provided Bobby with the skills to work with complex database systems, allowed Bobby the opportunity to create and launch various marketing campaigns, as well as allowing Bobby the experience of personal selling.

After having started and operating two separate tournament series in two completely unrelated sports, Bobby came to realize that no matter what the sport may be, the format for running a tournament series remains similar. With this in mind he decided that if he were to create a format for running a national tournament series for a single sport, he might as well expand the idea and apply that same format to a number of different sports in order to create something which has never been done before.

Chad Bloom—Founding Member

Chad is a senior entrepreneurship student at the University of Michigan. In the past Chad has acted as a substitute manager for the Sports Park in Redford, Michigan where daily patron numbers often exceeded 300 people. Also, while working at the Sports Park, Chad helped to organize an annual Goofy Olympics in which nearly 400 children were separated by age groups and competed against one another in an attempt to win their division and be honored at the awards ceremony. Through his past experiences working at Sports Park Chad has gained the managerial and organizational skills necessary to direct and organize large groups of people.

In addition to large group organization, Chad has also dealt first–hand with sales, marketing, and quality control at his internship with Physicstone in 2005. During his time at Physicstone, Chad created accounts for new customers using ACT, which is a Windows–based business organizational tool. Chad also made sales calls to new customers and created Excel databases to organize seasonal mailers for the marketing department. Finally, Chad also called existing customers to ensure customer satisfaction and retention.

Will Reed—Founding Member

Will is a senior at Saint Louis University and is majoring in entrepreneurship. Will's career in leadership and management roles includes acting as a fleet coordinator for the Osage River Barge Company for the last one and a half years. During this time he has organized and deployed tug and barge operations on Lake of the Ozarks. This position also consisted of one on one customer relations that gave him first–hand personal selling experience.

Will has also acted as a boat and watercraft rental manager for The Barge Floating Restaurant where he coordinated all employee activities and contributed to his customers' overall experience with the company, providing an exciting and fulfilling experience for them. Will has been the Internal Vice President for Pi Kappa Alpha fraternity for the past year. His duties as Vice President include the organization of community service and philanthropy events, as well as conducting chapter meetings.

Will is very enthusiastic about, and has a broad range of experience and knowledge in, a wide variety of sports. He acted as captain of both his football and basketball team at Osage High School. Will's experiences in management and athletics have given him the skills necessary to organize people, events, and operations that are necessary to help Scramble reach its goals in the coming years. Furthermore, his leadership roles have given him the knowledge, influence, and charisma to help Scramble become the athlete's hub for knowledge, advancement, and competition.

SERVICES

Tournament Overview

In order to separate ourselves from the competition we plan to offer all seven of our sports in one location at the same time. Not only do we intend to offer all of our sports in one park, but we intend to strategically position our various sports playing surfaces close together (while still leaving room for comfortable viewing areas, vendor booths, sponsor displays and any other such desired space) so that spectators will be able to view a number of different sports without having to travel entirely across the venue.

Our design is to have two divisions in each sport which we intend to offer. The first division will be the competitive division and will consist of top athletes from around the Midwest in each sport. Athletes will be divided by age; however, the only other restriction will be that no professional athletes will be allowed to compete.

In order to entice these top athletes from around the country to participate in our tournament series, we will be working with vendors and sponsors to provide a variety of prizes which will be given to the winners of each division. In addition, we will be creating an atmosphere which will help these top players not only showcase their skills, but also improve them along the way. We will have high quality vendors in each sport on hand to answer any of the athletes' questions and offer advice and tips to help them rise to the top of their game.

The second division will be the recreational division. This division will consist of athletes who simply wish to try out a given sport, or who simply wish to play for fun, not on a competitive level. This division will not have any prizes for the winners, but rather participation prizes and prizes for things such as the 20th point of the day. The goal of this division is to give athletes of all ages a chance to participate in a sport which they have limited knowledge about or limited skill in, but yet wish to get the experience of playing the sport in an exciting venue the same way it is designed to be played by top athletes at a competitive level.

Format

In order to make this series available to more participants and accommodate more teams we have decided not to offer full sports games but rather scaled down versions of the sports. We feel that by offering scaled down versions of the sports with the same basic rules and principals but smaller playing surfaces, shorter game lengths and less participants on the court at a time we can not only accommodate more teams, but will also open the series up to groups of people who do not currently play on an organized team but are interested in becoming involved in a given sport.

In addition to offering full team registration, we will also offer the option to register as an individual and be placed on a team according to age and skill level. We feel that by allowing individuals as well as full teams to register we will greatly increase our draw and will be able to gain access to a great deal of individuals who would have otherwise not participated in the sports tournament marketplace.

In addition to allowing us to cater to a larger market, using a scaled down format also allows us a great deal of additional venue options. Since we will be using scaled down versions of playing surfaces rather than the much larger regulation size surfaces we will be able to purchase and transport our own playing surfaces. Since we will be utilizing our own playing surfaces for each sport we can select venues based on location as opposed to venues which can accommodate all of our sports. By choosing venues located in central areas we will provide participants and spectators easier access and less transportation problems, which should increase attendance.

Finally, using the scaled down format will provide for more exciting competition. Since the playing surface will be smaller than regulation, games should be much faster pace and result in higher scores. Higher scoring games usually result in greater fan interest and involvement and should produce a great deal of excitement. Since many spectators will be viewing new sports for the first time, this more exciting format should help to pique the interest of many new fans and help to generate cross interest among the sports.

Tournament Sports

In order to ensure that each sport receives the attention and publicity that is required to attain the highest possible standards within each individual sport, we have decided to start by offering four traditional team sports and three individual extreme sports. Each year we plan to add an additional traditional sport, as well as one or two additional extreme sports. This idea of starting small and slowly building will allow us to develop personal relationships with the vendors, athletes, and spectators related to each sport, as well as allowing us to expand into sporting events which our patrons are interested in. Our goal is to develop a loyal following that comes to all of our tournaments and to help them expand their horizons by offering events which they are interested in.

Hockey

Due to our management team's previous experience in the hockey tournament industry, hockey was the first sport which we decided to offer. Based on the past success that our management team had in running national hockey tournaments, we feel that this is a logical sport to offer. Due to our previous involvement in the hockey industry we have been able to redevelop many relationships with hockey vendors much more rapidly and with less effort than will be required in other sports.

In addition to our prior experience in the sport of hockey, we also see an opportunity in the street hockey tournament market due to the large void that now exists since the collapse of the NHL's street hockey series. Prior to the recent hockey strike the NHL sponsored a program called NHL Breakout. The NHL Breakout series was a street hockey tournament series that traveled around the country. Due to problems with the NHL, the league decided to stop running outside programs such as the NHL Breakout series. Now that the NHL is back in business, the league has decided not to reopen its Breakout series, but rather to lend its name to NARCH, the largest full scale roller hockey tournament series in North America.

While the NHL has already decided to sponsor another roller hockey league, the style of play between NHL Breakout and NARCH are drastically different. This means that all of the customers of the NHL Breakout series are currently without a league to participate in. We have decided to model many of the features of our league around the NHL Breakout model; however, we have decided to change the format some.

We intend to hold our competition on three small scale hockey rinks as opposed to the street as NHL Breakout did. We feel that holding the competition in an actual rink as opposed to on the street will make the tournament series stand out as something special and out of the ordinary as opposed to something that athletes could simply do at home. We will be purchasing three small-scale hockey rinks which will be 60 ft. long x 30 ft. wide x 42 in. high with a full net around the top. We feel that having three small-scale rinks setup outdoors will entice athletes and spectators alike to come watch a new version of street hockey come to life.

Our hockey games will consist of two six–minute halves with a continuously running clock. Game play will consist of two three–man teams with one goalie and up to two subs. Normal hockey and soccer fields will be identical and interchangeable street hockey rules will apply (rulebook will be available online as well as provided at registration); the head referee on the rink will have the final ruling on any discrepancies.

Soccer

Soccer has always been a very popular sport with international appeal; however, recent years have seen the popularity of soccer skyrocketing in the United States, especially among children.

Since the glorification of soccer stars such as David Beckham through outlets such as movies and tabloids, the sport has gained amazing popularity. Today pictures of soccer athletes grace the tops of billboards, movies, and even television shows. The trend has gone so far that one cable network recently began airing a series titled, "Soccer Players' Wives." With the popularity of soccer once again on the rise here in America, we feel that offering this world class sport with international appeal is a smart decision.

In addition to the growing popularity of soccer among Americans, the Hispanic population has always had a large involvement in the sport. While the Hispanic population of the Midwest is only roughly 22%, many soccer leagues find that a large portion of their participants are of Hispanic descent. In fact, more than 75% of the players in the Northern Nevada Soccer League are Hispanic, and the Hispanic population in northern Nevada is only roughly 19%. We feel that adding soccer to our mix of sports may generate some cultural diversity in our customer base, and we would like to encourage people from all different backgrounds to participate in our events.

In addition to providing some diversity among our customer base, soccer will prove to be helpful when it comes to expansion on both the west and east coasts as well as in the south. While the Hispanic population in the Midwest may only be 22%, 49% of the Hispanic population of the United States lives in either California or Texas, and 23% of Florida's population is Hispanic as well. In addition, the total Hispanic population in the United States grew 58% between 1990 and 2000. This was an increase of 13 million Hispanics in a period of 10 years. While this high percentage of Hispanics does not guarantee a successful soccer market in these regions, it would seem absurd not to offer soccer and ignore this fast growing market.

Much like hockey, we feel that in order to make the soccer competition stand out and have appeal we must make the soccer field special. We will be purchasing three soccer fields that will have dimensions identical to those of our hockey rinks, 60 ft. long x 30 ft wide x 42 in. high with a net around the top. Also, just like hockey, soccer will consist of two six–minute continuously running clock halves, and game play will consist of two teams with three players, one goalie and two subs. Normal indoor soccer rules will apply (rulebook will be available online as well as provided at registration) and the head referee on the field will have the final say in the event of any discrepancies.

Basketball

Basketball is a sport which offers great diversity. Basketball is enjoyed by people from many different walks of life, from the Ivy League college basketball teams to people playing basketball in the projects; it seems that people from all different backgrounds can find some common ground when it comes to the sport of basketball. Therefore, we feel that basketball is a great sport for us to offer in our first year of operation.

As it is easy to see from our unique mix of extreme and traditional sports, we are not simply trying to cater to one specific social group's taste in our tournament series, but rather trying to diversify our offerings and provide something that everyone can enjoy. By offering basketball as one of our sports in our first year of operation we hope to attract a diverse crowd which will add to the popularity of our tournament series.

Unlike soccer and hockey, we feel that basketball fans would not be attracted to a fancy court. We feel that basketball patrons enjoy the fact that basketball can be played anywhere, anytime, and by anybody.

In designing our basketball tournament series we have decided to take an approach similar to that of Hoop It Up and to simply use high quality portable basketball goals placed on pavement. We feel that using street basketball courts will set a certain tone to our basketball tournament series and will help to draw a diverse crowd of players as opposed to intimidating those players not used to playing in big gymnasiums.

Once again modeling ourselves after the Hoop It Up competition, our basketball games will be played in a half court format and will consist of a 30 minute run clock game which ends when either the time expires or one team reaches 20 points. Game play will consist of two teams of three players with two subs. Normal half court basketball rules will apply (rulebook will be available online as well as provided at registration) and the head referee on the court will have the final say in the event of a discrepancy.

Volleyball

Volleyball is a sport which can be enjoyed by people of all ages and skill levels. One of the main reasons that we decided to offer volleyball in our first year of operation is to illustrate that just because we are not offering separate men's and women's divisions does not mean that men and women cannot compete together. We intend for all of our sports to be coed; however, volleyball is one sport which we feel could easily be dominated by women.

While there are a great deal of talented women hockey, soccer, and basketball players, we feel that the number of skilled female volleyball players is more than likely higher than the number of skilled male players (at an amateur level in the age groups we intend to offer). We feel that the volleyball competition could provide an opportunity for an all women's team to defeat any coed and all male teams. While the idea of a female team winning the competition is not extraordinary, we feel that by offering female dominated sports such as volleyball we may be able to peak the interest of many women who would otherwise not be interested in sports tournaments. Once these women are at our events, perhaps another sport will peak their interest and we can once again generate some cross interest among the sports in a consumer who would have otherwise never put herself in a position to experience such an atmosphere.

In addition, volleyball is also a sport played by many couples. We feel that if parents are going to be taking their children to our tournament series and staying there all weekend with the child anyway, many parents may decide to enter the volleyball competition to provide themselves with something to do while their child is not competing. Since parents will be at the event already, it makes since to offer a sport which will cater to their taste.

Finally, volleyball also allows us a lot of creative venue opportunities. Volleyball can be played on practically any type of surface, and each different surface changes the game slightly Volleyball can be played on grass, sand, pavement, or in a gymnasium. Our goal is to continually switch the format of our volleyball tournaments to keep each one exciting. Some tournaments may involve beach volleyball while some may be played inside of a gymnasium. One of the great things about offering a sport such as volleyball is the diverse venue selections which will allow us to keep the competition interesting.

Our volleyball courts will consist of six high–quality portable volleyball nets. The volleyball game will be played by two teams of four players with up to two subs. Game play will consist of one 30–minute run clock time limit and games will end when either time expires, or one team reaches 11 points. Normal volleyball rules will apply based upon the type of playing surface being utilized at each given venue (rulebook will be available online as well as provided at registration), and the head referee on the court will have the final say regarding any discrepancies.

Skateboarding /In–line/Biking

We choose to offer this mixture of extreme sports in our first year of operation for a number of reasons. To begin, this mix provides a fairly diverse look at some of the different aspects and movements required by extreme sports. These three events were pioneers in the extreme sports category and although they may not receive quite as much press in recent times as some of the other extreme sports which have sprung onto the scene, they still remain staples of the extreme sports industry and should prove to form a great foundation for the extreme sports side of the tournament series.

In addition to the appeal of these sports, all of these sports also allow for the same structures to be used throughout the competition which will help to cut down on costs as well as space requirements. All of these sports utilize the same ramps and rails, meaning one course can be designed for all three sports. Also, all of these sports operate according to the same format so we will have less scheduling issues by running three sports with one format on the same course as opposed to running three separate formats on one course.

We will have three separate competitions in each sport for a total of nine overall extreme sports competitions. The format for the competitions is as follows:

Vert

- An extreme sports vert competition consists of every athlete making two 45-second runs in the qualifying round. In addition, the top ten athletes then qualify for the finals where each athlete makes three 45-second runs.

- An extreme sports vert best trick competition consists of one 45-minute jam session in which every rider performs as many tricks as possible in an attempt to impress the judges.

Street

- An extreme sports street competition consists of every athlete making three 75-second runs.

- An extreme sports street best trick competition consists of one 15-minute jam session in which every rider performs as many tricks as possible in an attempt to impress the judges.

Park

- An extreme sports park competition consists of every athlete making two 3-minute runs.

Each athlete registering to participate in one of the extreme sports will automatically be registered for all three competitions in that sport. Normal rules will apply for each sport (rulebook will be available online as well as provided at registration) and judges scores will be final determinants for all competitions.

Event Schedules and Outlines

Tournament Series Schedule

When developing a schedule for our tournament series we encountered a number of constraints which we had to consider. The following is a list of the constraints which we took into account along with the reasons why we felt it was important to consider these issues.

Desire to operate series tournaments during summer months

- Children are out of school

- Families are more able to travel

- Warm weather allows all sports to be played outside

Seasonal weather

- Need to hold certain sports outside in warm weather

- Ability to hold certain sports indoors

- Varying climates in selected cities

Travel logistics (map detailing travel routes included in appendix)

- Desire to draw maximum amount of patrons to events

- Minimize travel for both tournament staff and patrons

Sports appeal

- Venue availability for showcased sports

- Offer showcased sports in cities with a strong market

Clinic Event Outline

The first events which we intend to offer to kick off our national tournament series are two clinics. These clinics will serve multiple functions including:

- Providing individuals the opportunity to meet other people of their same age and skill level so that they can form teams to enter into our tournaments

- Helping athletes improve their abilities before the start of the series

- Building excitement and generating a buzz about the series

- Qualifying participants for the Officiate & Participate program of the tournament series

Since the clinics will be taking place in April, May and August, when children are still likely to be in school, we will operate the clinics according to the following schedule:

	Start	End	Usable hours
Friday	5:00 PM	10:00 PM	5
Saturday	12:00 PM	5:00 PM	5
Sunday	12:00 PM	5:00 PM	+ 5
			15 hours
			× 60 min.
			900 min.

The clinics will offer professional guidance from top athletes in each sport which will be offered in the tournament series. These clinics will be three-day-long events whereby on the first day athletes are evaluated as to their skill level and broken down into groups to practice various skills. On the second day athletes will continue training with professional athletes in their chosen sport. In addition, those athletes wishing to participate in the Officiate & Participate program of the tournament series will be given special refereeing classes. Finally, on the third day a small competition will be held whereby athletes are grouped into teams, based upon age and skill level so that teams are fair, and a mini tournament will be held. Athletes participating in the Officiate & Participate program will be observed while they referee games which they are not participating in so that they may be qualified to ref during the national tournament series.

In addition to the two clinics which will be held before the start of the national tournament series, we also intend to offer one clinic immediately following the conclusion of the national tournament series. This clinic also serves multiple functions including:

- Allowing teams that did not place as desired to improve their skills before the start of the next season

- Allowing participants to qualify for the Officiate & Participate program while they are still excited about the tournament series and before something else piques their interest

- Allowing us to kick off any new sports which we intend to offer by demonstrating and teaching them to participants thereby generating interest in the sports and allowing children eight months to practice before competition starts

Based on the amount of playing surfaces which we intend to purchase and the amount of time during which we plan to hold the clinics, we estimate that we will be able to accommodate roughly 100 athletes in each sport. We intend to charge $115 dollars, which is slightly less than the average clinic fees of $120–$150. In addition to charging less for our clinics, we are also providing three days of training from a professional in each sport, as well as allowing our athletes to qualify for the Officiate & Participate program of our national tournament series.

Series Tournament Event Outline

The series tournaments will consist of a full scale tournament being held in each of the sports which we offer. There will be seven individual sports tournaments taking place at one venue for the entire weekend.

Time constraints will be a big issue for our tournaments due to the volume of athletes that we will be trying to accommodate and the limited availability of the playing surfaces. In order to utilize as many hours of game time as possible, we will run our regional events based on the following schedule:

	Start	End	Usable hours
Friday	8:00 AM	10:00 PM	14
Saturday	7:00 AM	10:00 PM	15
Sunday	7:00 AM	8:00 PM	+ 13
			42 hours
			× 60 min.
			2,520 min.

This gives us a total of 42 usable hours, or 2,520 minutes, at any given playing surface assuming that the surface is lighted and continuously available for use. Based on this schedule we have developed the following constraints for each of the sports which we intend to offer in our first year of operation.

	Hockey	Soccer		Basketball	Volleyball
Halves	2	2			
Length of halve	× 6 min.	× 6 min.			
Time of game	12 min.	12 min.			
Warm-up	3 min.	3 min.	Time of game	30 min.	30 min.
Between halves	2 min.	2 min.	Warm-up	3 min.	3 min.
Between games	+ 3 min.	+ 3 min.	Between games	+ 2 min.	+ 2 min.
	20 min.	20 min.		35 min.	35 min.

Based on the above constraints and the number of playing surfaces which we intend to setup for each sport we will be able to accommodate games according to the following schedule:

	Hockey	Soccer	Basketball	Volleyball
Usable hours	2,520 min.	2,520 min.	2,520 min.	2,520 min.
Game length	/ 20 min.	/ 20 min.	/ 35 min.	/ 35 min.
Games accommodated	126	126	72	72
Number of courts	× 3	× 3	× 6	× 6
Games available	378	378	432	432

Based on the above schedule we are hoping to attract teams according to the following table:

	Hockey			Soccer	
Recreational teams	Age	Competitive teams	Recreational teams	Age	Competitive teams
12	10	12	12	10	12
12	12	12	12	12	12
12	14	12	12	14	12
12	16	12	12	16	12
6	18	6	6	18	6
6	Junior	6	6	Junior	6
6	Adult	6	6	Adult	6
66	**Total teams**	66	66	**Total teams**	66
	132			132	

	Basketball			Volleyball	
Recreational teams	Age	Competitive teams	Recreational teams	Age	Competitive teams
12	10	12	12	10	12
12	12	12	12	12	12
12	14	12	12	14	12
12	16	12	12	16	12
6	18	6	6	18	6
6	Junior	6	6	Junior	6
6	Silver	6	6	Silver	6
6	Gold	6	6	Gold	6
72	**Total teams**	72	72	**Total teams**	72
	144			144	

If each division with 12 teams plays two six–team round robin competitions with the winner of each round robin competition competing in one championship game to determine the winner of the division, each division will require thirty–one games. In addition, if each division with 6 teams plays one round robin competition with the top two teams competing in one championship game to determine the winner of the division, each division will require 16 games. Based on these constraints, the following number of games will be necessary.

	Hockey			Soccer	
Recreational teams	Age	Competitive teams	Recreational teams	Age	Competitive teams
31	10	31	31	10	31
31	12	31	31	12	31
31	14	31	31	14	31
31	16	31	31	16	31
16	18	16	16	18	16
16	Junior	16	16	Junior	16
16	Adult	16	16	Adult	16
172	**Total games**	172	172	**Total games**	172
	344			344	

	Basketball			Volleyball	
Recreational teams	Age	Competitive teams	Recreational teams	Age	Competitive teams
31	10	31	31	10	31
31	12	31	31	12	31
31	14	31	31	14	31
31	16	31	31	16	31
16	18	16	16	18	16
16	Junior	16	16	Junior	16
16	Silver	16	16	Silver	16
16	Gold	16	16	Gold	16
188	**Total games**	188	188	**Total games**	188
	376			376	

Based on the above information we have comprised the following table to illustrate how much extra court time we will have available in each sport.

	Hockey	Soccer	Basketball	Volleyball
Total games	344	344	376	376
Game length	× 20 min.	× 20 min.	× 35 min.	× 35 min.
Used hours	6,880 min.	6,880 min.	13,160 min.	13,160 min.
Usable hours	2,520 min.	2,520 min.	2,520 min.	2,520 min.
Number of courts	× 3	× 3	× 6	× 6
Total usable hours	7,560 min.	7,560 min.	15,120 min.	15,120 min.
Total usable hours	7,560 min.	7,560 min.	15,120 min.	15,120 min.
Used hours	− 6,880 min.	− 6,880 min.	−13,160 min.	−13,160 min.
Extra hours	680 min.	680 min.	1,960 min.	1,960 min.
	/ 60 min.	/ 60 min.	/ 60 min.	/ 60 min.
Extra hours	11.3 hrs.	11.3 hrs.	32.6 hrs.	32.6 hrs.

This extra time will be used for the skills competitions and awards ceremonies in each sport as well as providing a buffer should we fall behind schedule for any unforeseen reason.

The schedule for our extreme sports in our first year of operation will work a bit differently. Each of our extreme sports has a set amount of fixed time required as well as a certain amount of time that must be allocated to each athlete. The extreme sports will operate according to the following schedule:

	Vert			Street		Park
	Prelims	Finals	Best trick	Competition	Best trick	Competition
Length of run	45 sec.	45 sec.	45 min.	75 sec.	15 min.	180 sec.
Setup	+ 15 sec.	+ 15 sec.		+ 15 sec.		+ 15 sec.
Total time of run	1 min.	1 min.		90 sec.		195 sec.
Number of runs	× 2	× 3		× 3		× 2
Total time per skater	2 min.	3 min.		4.5 min.		6.5 min.
		× 10 athletes				
		30 min.				

Based upon this schedule, the extreme sports will require the following amount of fixed and variable time:

Fixed time		Variable time	
Vert finals	30 min.	Vert prelims	2 min.
Vert best trick	45 min.	Street competition	4.5 min.
Street best trick	15 min.	Park competition	6.5 min.
Total fixed time	90 min.	Time per athlete	13 min.

While the park competition requires the use of the entire skate park, the street and vert competitions may take place within the skate park at the same time. Based on this information the following table illustrates how many athletes can be accommodated in each of our extreme sports.

	Vert	Street
Usable hours	2,520 min.	2,520 min.
Total fixed time	− 75 min.	− 15 min.
Time remaining	2,445 min.	2,505 min.
Variable time	2 min.	4.5 min.
Park competition time	+ 6.5 min.	+ 6.5 min.
Total time	8.5 min.	11 min.
Time remaining	2,445 min.	2,505 min.
Total time	/ 8.5 min.	/ 11 min.
Total athletes accommodated	287	227
Total athletes accommodated	—	227
Number of extreme sports	/ —	/ 3
Total athletes per sport	—	75

National Championship Event Outline

Teams that qualify by placing in the top two at either a series tournament or a Sport Showcase tournament qualify to compete in the national championship. Due to the volume of athletes which we are estimating will be participating in our national championship event, we will need the ability to accommodate more teams in each sport; therefore, our national championship will be a four day event instead of a three day event as the regional tournaments are. The schedule for the national championship is as follows:

	Start	End	Usable hours
Thursday	8:00 AM	10:00 PM	14
Friday	7:00 AM	10:00 PM	15
Saturday	7:00 AM	10:00 PM	15
Sunday	7:00 AM	8:00 PM	+ 13
			57 hours
			× 60 min.
			3,420 min.

This gives us a total of 57 usable hours, or 3,420 minutes, at any given playing surface assuming that the surface is lighted and continuously available for use. We will no longer be limiting each division to a set number of teams but rather we will accommodate any qualifying teams that wish to participate and adjust the schedule accordingly. The following illustrates the maximum number of teams/individuals which could qualify to attend our national championship event:

	Hockey				Soccer	
Recreational teams	Age	Competitive teams		Recreational teams	Age	Competitive teams
18	10	18		18	10	18
18	12	18		18	12	18
18	14	18		18	14	18
18	16	18		18	16	18
18	18	18		18	18	18
18	Junior	18		18	Junior	18
18	Adult	18		18	Adult	18
126	**Total teams**	126		126	**Total teams**	126
	252				252	

	Basketball				Volleyball	
Recreational teams	Age	Competitive teams		Recreational teams	Age	Competitive teams
18	10	18		18	10	18
18	12	18		18	12	18
18	14	18		18	14	18
18	16	18		18	16	18
18	18	18		18	18	18
18	Junior	18		18	Junior	18
18	Silver	18		18	Silver	18
18	Gold	18		18	Gold	18
144	**Total teams**	144		144	**Total teams**	144
	288				288	

	Skateboarding				In-Line	
Recreational teams	Age	Competitive teams		Recreational teams	Age	Competitive teams
18	10	18		18	10	18
18	12	18		18	12	18
18	14	18		18	14	18
18	16	18		18	16	18
18	18	18		18	18	18
18	Adult	18		18	Adult	18
108	**Total teams**	108		108	**Total teams**	108
	216				216	

	Biking	
Recreational teams	Age	Competitive teams
18	10	18
18	12	18
18	14	18
18	16	18
18	18	18
18	Adult	18
108	**Total teams**	108
	216	

The following is a list of constraints on the number of games which we will be able to offer during our national championship.

	Hockey	Soccer	Basketball	Volleyball
Usable hours	3,420 min.	3,420 min.	3,420 min.	3,420 min.
Game length	/ 20 min.	/ 20 min.	/ 35 min.	/ 35 min.
Games accommodated	171	171	97	97
Number of courts	× 3	× 3	× 6	× 6
Games available	513	513	582	582

We will have to adjust the schedule for our national championship event based upon the number of qualifying teams that decide to participate. While we would like to see all of the qualifying teams compete in our national championship, this scenario is not likely. Some teams are likely to miss the event, thereby throwing off any type of schedule which we could develop. For this reason, we do not intend to create a detailed event outline for the national championship event until we have completed the registration process for this event.

Sports Highlight Tournament Outline
Sports Highlight tournaments will provide us with a way to highlight each sport offered in our tournament series. From September thru March we will offer one tournament per month, visiting each city on our series schedule, and showcasing a different sport in each city.

The Sports Highlight tournaments will be centered around a single showcased sport but will still offer a multi sport format. While all of the sports which we offer in our series may not be offered at every Sports Highlight tournament, every tournament will have a multi sport format. We will be selecting venues that accentuate the sport being showcased for that event, but will still accommodate other sports as well.

We will offer a combination of either one extreme sport and two traditional sports, or one traditional sport and three extreme sports. This format will allow us to accommodate the maximum number of participants in the sports which we will be showcasing. For example, when we offer soccer we will not offer hockey so that we may use all six of our rinks for the soccer competition. In addition, when we offer basketball and volleyball we will select venues which have extra courts in these sports so that we may accommodate more athletes.

The Sports Highlight tournaments will provide a fast track to the national competition. The tournaments will count as a national qualifier for the showcased sport, but not for any of the additional sports. This means that the top two teams competing in the showcased sport will automatically receive invitations to attend the national championship event.

Due to the fact that children will still be in school during the months when these events will be taking place, we will be forced to once again modify our schedule. For this reason the Sports Highlight tournaments will operate according to the following schedule:

	Start	End	Usable hours
Friday	5:00 AM	10:00 PM	5
Saturday	7:00 AM	10:00 PM	15
Sunday	7:00 AM	8:00 PM	+ 13
			33 hours
		×	60 min.
			1,980 min.

This gives us a total of 33 usable hours, or 1,980 minutes, at any given playing surface assuming that the surface is lighted and continuously available for use. Based on this information, the following is a list of constraints on the number of games which we will be able to offer during our Sports Highlight tournaments.

	Hockey	Soccer	Basketball	Volleyball
Usable hours	1,980 min.	1,980 min.	1,980 min.	1,980 min.
Game length	/ 20 min.	/ 20 min.	/ 35 min.	/ 35 min.
Games accommodated	99	99	56	56
Number of courts	× 6	× 6	× 12	× 12
Games available	594	594	678	678

Based on this information we will be registering teams based on the following schedule:

Hockey

Recreational teams	Age	Competitive teams
20	10	20
20	12	20
20	14	20
20	16	20
12	18	12
12	Junior	12
12	Adult	12
116	Total teams	116
	232	

Soccer

Recreational teams	Age	Competitive teams
20	10	20
20	12	20
20	14	20
20	16	20
12	18	12
12	Junior	12
12	Adult	12
116	Total teams	116
	232	

Basketball

Recreational teams	Age	Competitive teams
20	10	20
20	12	20
20	14	20
20	16	20
12	18	12
12	Junior	12
12	Silver	12
12	Gold	12
128	Total teams	128
	256	

Volleyball

Recreational teams	Age	Competitive teams
20	10	20
20	12	20
20	14	20
20	16	20
12	18	12
12	Junior	12
12	Silver	12
12	Gold	12
128	Total teams	128
	256	

If each division with 20 teams plays four 5–team round robin competitions with the winner of each round robin competition competing in one championship round robin to determine the winner of the division, each division will require forty six games. In addition, if each division with 12 teams plays two 6–team round robin competitions with the top two teams competing in one championship game to determine the winner of the division, each division will require thirty–one games. Based on these constraints, the following number of games will be necessary.

Hockey

Recreational teams	Age	Competitive teams
46	10	46
46	12	46
46	14	46
46	16	46
31	18	31
31	Junior	31
31	Adult	31
277	Total games	277
	554	

Soccer

Recreational teams	Age	Competitive teams
46	10	46
46	12	46
46	14	46
46	16	46
31	18	31
31	Junior	31
31	Adult	31
277	Total games	277
	554	

Basketball

Recreational teams	Age	Competitive teams
46	10	46
46	12	46
46	14	46
46	16	46
31	18	31
31	Junior	31
31	Silver	31
31	Gold	31
308	Total games	308
	616	

Volleyball

Recreational teams	Age	Competitive teams
46	10	46
46	12	46
46	14	46
46	16	46
31	18	31
31	Junior	31
31	Silver	31
31	Gold	31
308	Total games	308
	616	

Based on the above information we have comprised the following table to illustrate how much extra court time we will have available in each sport.

	Hockey	Soccer	Basketball	Volleyball
Total games	554	554	616	616
Game length	× 20 min.	× 20 min.	× 35 min.	× 35 min.
Used hours	11,080 min.	11,080 min.	21,560 min.	21,560 min.
Usable hours	1,980 min.	1,980 min.	1,980 min.	1,980 min.
Number of courts	× 6	× 6	× 12	× 12
Total Usable hours	11,880 min.	11,880 min.	23,760 min.	23,760 min.
Total Usable hours	11,880 min.	11,880 min.	23,760 min.	23,760 min.
Used hours	−11,080 min.	−11,080 min.	−21,560 min.	−21,560 min.
Extra hours	800 min.	800 min.	2,200 min.	2,200 min.
	/ 60 min.	/ 60 min.	/ 60 min.	/ 60 min.
Extra hours	13.3 hrs.	13.3 hrs.	36.6 hrs.	36.6 hrs.

As in the series tournaments, extra hours will be used for skills competitions, awards ceremonies, and will provide a buffer should we fall behind schedule for any unforeseen reason.

The following table shows how many athletes we will be able to accommodate in each sport of our extreme sports competition at our Sports Highlight tournaments.

	Vert	Street
Usable hours	1,980 min.	1,980 min.
Total fixed time	− 75 min.	− 15 min.
Time remaining	1,905 min.	1,965 min.
Variable time	2 min.	4.5 min.
Park competition time	+ 6.5 min.	+ 6.5 min.
Total time	8.5 min.	11 min.
Time remaining	1,905 min.	1,965 min.
Total time	/ 8.5 min.	/ 11 min.
Total athletes accommodated	—	178

FINANCIAL ANALYSIS

Revenue Streams

Entry Fees

Our first and most logical revenue stream will come in the form of entry fees paid by the athletes. We plan to collect entry fees based on the following schedule:

	Traditional sports		Extreme sports	
	Recreation	Competitive	Recreation	Competitive
Entry fee	$150	$200	$30	$150

In return for the entry fee, paid athletes will receive a t–shirt/jersey to be worn during the competition as well as prizes provided throughout the competition. In the recreational division, where entry fees are less and the competition is second to the fun of playing the sports, prizes will be awarded on a participation basis as well as creative competitions such as the 20th goal of the day, goalies receiving a shutout, and other such creative competitions.

In the competitive division, where entry fees are higher and the competition is more intense, we will be working with our vendors and sponsors to provide high quality prizes to teams that place in the top three in their division. We intend to offer the winning teams a combination of prizes that will total more than double the original cost of their entry fee.

By offering creative prizes in the recreational division, which allows teams the ability to win a prize even if they have no chance of winning the overall competition, we feel that we can really emphasize the importance of simply playing the sport and having fun. While we would like to see athletes improve and grow as a team, in the recreational division, where people simply sign up to play for fun, we want to keep players from becoming discouraged even if they do not do well in the competition. We want them to understand that just because they did not win the tournament does not mean that they cannot still have fun, win prizes, and come back and do it all over again at the next tournament.

In the competitive division however, we intend to stimulate the competition by offering desirable prizes for the top three teams in each division. In addition, we intend to offer the winning team in each division prizes worth double their entry fee. By doing this we hope to show teams that if they feel they have a chance to win the competitive division of one of our tournaments, not only could they have the fun of participating in the tournament and winning, but they could also benefit financially from the competition. Teams that place in the top three in the competitive division will receive prizes to help compensate them for their entry fees and will therefore essentially be competing in our tournaments for free.

Sponsors

After evaluating the format of our tournaments and clinics, the schedule by which we intend to operate, and our market segment, we have decided to offer the following sponsorship packages:

National			Local		
Number of sponsors	Level of sponsorship	Cost	Number of sponsors	Level of sponsorship	Cost
1	Platinum	$300,000	3	Gold	$10,000
3	Gold	$150,000	5	Silver	$ 5,000
5	Silver	$ 75,000	7	Bronze	$ 2,500

Based on the above table we plan to break our sponsors into two categories, national and local sponsors. National sponsors will sponsor our tournament series for an entire year and will travel with our series to each of our stops. Local sponsors will be sponsors that we pick up in each of the cities our series visits. The cost shown in the local category is the cost of sponsoring one of our events. Since our series will stop in each city multiple times however, sponsors will be encouraged to sponsor our events every time they visit the sponsor's city. In order to encourage this repeat sponsorship, sponsors willing to contract to sponsor each event we offer in their city will be entitled to a 10% discount off of the single tournament sponsor prices. (National sponsorship prices reflect a 20% discount off of the single tournament sponsor prices.)

Based on our evaluation of our tournament series format, the level of contact which we intend to have with our consumers, and numerous other factors, we have identified the following ways in which we can help our sponsors reach our consumers:

- Advertisements on t–shirt/jersey worn during game play

- Advertisements on playing surfaces

- Advertisements on scoreboards

- Advertisements on website

- Distribute sponsor's marketing materials with registration packets

- Provide sponsor's products as prizes

- Allocate space at events for sponsors to setup their own marketing materials

Customers

In order to identify companies which would provide a good fit as sponsors for our tournament series we must first describe the market segment which we intend to target. To begin, we will be offering age brackets in our competition that range from 9 years of age through adult; however, we will have twice as many athletes ranging in age from 9–17 as we will in the 18–adult age range. While this seems to suggest that our market segment will be composed of younger consumers, this is not necessarily true.

We will have twice as many 9–17 year old athletes; however, athletes in the 9–15 year old age range will still need to be accompanied by an adult since they will not be able to drive themselves to the events. In addition, it is our hope that we will entice a substantial amount of the athlete's friends and families to attend our events as well. This means that while it is likely that our mean market age is lower, we also intend to draw adults to our events as well, both in the form of athletes and spectators watching younger athletes compete.

Enticing both younger athletes and their parents to attend our events could have very positive results when it comes to attracting sponsors. As noted later in the market segment section of the business plan, teenagers today have higher disposable incomes than previous generations, bringing in an average of $125 of disposable income per week. While this figure may seem high, we must keep in mind that teenagers do not have the numerous bills incurred by adults, as well as the fact that children today are starting work sooner than previous generations.

While the average teenager in America may have a disposable income of $125 a week, this still does not mean that the teen will be the party responsible for making the purchasing decisions regarding this money, which provides the perfect opportunity for our tournament series. While families are at our tournaments we will have a relatively captive audience. We plan to schedule games far enough apart so that both athletes and spectators have time to enjoy all of our various offerings in between games, yet close enough together that they will not have time to leave the venue to partake in other forms of entertainment.

This provides us with a somewhat unique opportunity. We will have both teenagers, with this relatively high disposable income, as well as their parents, who are most likely in charge of the purchasing allocations of the disposable income, together at a single location with excess time on their hands. This means that a correctly engineered marketing campaign could reach both the end user of the product and the purchaser at the same time, while the two have time to discuss the situation and take action. From a marketing standpoint, this is a powerful statement.

In addition, athletes in the 18–adult age range are also great candidates for marketing campaigns as well. Considering that each of the athletes at one of our events has just spent somewhere around $50 simply to compete in the event, we can assume that these athletes have an above average disposable income. While these athletes may not be extremely wealthy, we can assume from the fact that they can afford to participate in leisurely activities such as sports tournaments that they have some disposable income to spend.

Sponsorship Opportunities

After defining our target market we considered companies which advertise in the sports market-place. We have identified the following product categories as possible sponsors for our tournament series.

- Car manufacturer: (Scion, Chevrolet, Nissan) With twice as many athletes in the 9–17 year old age brackets, who will be accompanied by their parents and families, we feel that we offer the perfect demographic for a car manufacturer. We have a captive audience in a perfect automobile purchasing age range accompanied by their parents and family members, who have a large say in the decision of what car a teenager purchases.

- Cell phone company: (Cingular, Sprint, Nextel) While almost everyone uses a cell phone in today's marketplace, the prime market for cell phone companies is teenagers. In addition, cell phone companies are currently pushing the option of family plans. With a captive market of teenagers and their families, our tournament series offers a great demographic to potential cellular company sponsors.

- Beverages (Red Bull, Coca–Cola, Gatorade) With the unique mix of sports which we will be offering in our tournament series we offer the ability for a beverage company to transcend the boundaries and reach both traditional and extreme sports athletes at one venue. In addition to reaching the athletes, reaching the purchaser of the groceries for the household, usually a parent, is also key for obtaining results. With the target market and the purchasers in one venue, beverage companies are presented with a unique opportunity.

- Gaming (IBM, Microsoft, Sony) With a target market which closely mirrors the market for sports tournaments, gaming companies could easily market to our consumers. A gaming company could set up a booth to allow athletes to try out their system and games during the time between sports games. In addition, the company could also get parents of gamers involved and provide information to them regarding some of the benefits of gaming.

- Hotels (Holiday Inn, Days Inn, Marriot) We will be offering our tournament series in eight different cities in our first year of operation before expanding to an even larger area and offering tournaments throughout the entire United States. While traveling from city to city participating in our tournaments our consumers will need to stay at hotels. We can offer the ability to secure a continuous customer base for a national hotel chain, or simply increase bookings for a weekend for a local hotel.

- Restaurants (Applebee's, Cracker Barrel, Subway) Once again, our series will operate in eight different cities in our first year before expanding throughout the United States. Athletes as well as spectators will need nourishment while in these cities and sponsoring our events offers a national restaurant chain the ability to secure a continuous customer base, or a local restaurant the ability to boost its sales for the weekend.

- Travel (Southwest Airlines, Enterprise Rental Car, Travelocity) From airfare to rental cars to ticketing agencies, our consumers will be traveling throughout the Midwest to participate in our tournaments in our first year of operation and throughout the entire United Stated soon thereafter. Sponsoring our tournament series offers travel companies the ability to exclusively market to this group of consumers who is sure to be traveling a great deal.

- Credit Card Companies (MasterCard, Visa, American Express) Credit card companies are constantly trying to sign up new members; however, many people simply throw away applications that arrive in the mail without ever opening them. Our events will provide credit card companies the ability to reach a diverse age group with extra time on their hands to fill out an application. In addition, many families will be attending our events together so the head of the household is likely to be in attendance to make any decisions on the matter.

- Music (Apple, Dell, Sony) Athletes love to listen to music to put them in the mood for competition. Since mp3 players have come to the marketplace, many athletes even listen to music while they are competing. Our events offer a mp3 manufacturer the ability to not only market their products, but also to bring in stations where athletes could pay a fee to download songs.

- Clothes (Nike, Adidas, Reebok) Fashion is important to people of all ages; however, athletes demand fashion with a certain level of functionality. Our tournament series offers the ability for a clothing manufacturer to market its goods to a very diverse crowd spread across seven different sports.

- Hygiene (Oxy, Proactive, Stridex) With a target market of young athletes, our tournament series offers companies in the hygiene industry the ability to reach their key demographic. Young athletes face many challenges when it comes to skin care and a hygiene company could help to educate both athletes and parents about skin care while also providing samples of their products to athletes right when they need them.

Vendors

In addition to our tournament sponsors, we would like to attract one major vendor in each sport to come to our events for a vendor tradeshow. Each vendor will have exclusive rights in their designated sport which could include features such as vendor logos on the playing surface, exclusive sale and use of the vendor's products at the events, as well as many other creative options. We will be looking for a total of seven vendors to accommodate each of our sports and will be charging a fee of $200,000 per vendor, as well as 5% of all vendor sales at the events.

Possible revenue streams which we have identified for vendors at our events include the sale of goods at the events as well as a charge for equipment tech support. In addition to these revenue streams however, vendors will also gain a tremendous amount of exposure and will have the ability to work with us to launch a variety of unique marketing campaigns.

For instance, we would like to work closely with each vendor to provide a number of creative sideshows at the events such as athletic demonstrations. Vendors will be encouraged to have any athletes which they have a relationship with come to the events and simply hang out, talk to aspiring athletes, watch games, provide tips, put on demonstrations, and so on. In addition, we would also encourage vendors to provide prizes at the events thereby further increasing their exposure and also putting their products in the consumers hands themselves.

Additional Revenue Streams

In addition to the revenue which we will generate from entry fees, sponsors and vendors, the following is a list of the additional revenue streams which we have identified for our business.

Tournament Program

We will be developing a tournament program that will be available before each event. This program will provide space for sponsors and vendors to advertise, showcase certain teams/individuals, explain different aspects of our various sports, show pictures of the winning teams from the last event, and so on. One program will be provided to each team in the registration packet and additional programs will be $3 each at the event as well as on our website.

Concessions

We will be subcontracting out concessions at the events to a non–profit group. We will be contacting groups such as the Boy Scouts to organize and manage all concession activity. We plan to collect 5% of the group's sales as another revenue stream. In an attempt to create a wholesome family environment however, no alcoholic beverages will be allowed on the premise. Food such as hamburgers, hotdogs, popcorn, pretzels, chips, soda, water, and sports drinks will be sold at various locations throughout the venue. Our goal for concessions is to keep the menu simple enough that our concessions sub contractors do not require any amenities such as running water or a stove. We plan for them to serve our customers with a barbeque grill and cooler. Our goal is not to serve our customers gourmet meals; we would simply like to provide them with food on the premises so that, should they choose, they will be able to remain at the event for a longer period of time without having to leave to obtain food.

Parking

Parking will be provided free of charge to athletes and coaches. Each athlete and coach will be given a special event parking tag which will allow them to park their vehicle in the lot for the duration of the tournament. Additional spectators without parking passes will however have to pay a small fee of $3 to park their vehicles for the entire event weekend. We feel that people are willing to pay a small amount for parking that is close to the tournament location. The extreme sports tournament Gravity Games currently charges $5 per day for parking. Our event–long parking is much cheaper than the gravity games, and offers a safe, close, and convenient location to the tournament.

Admission
Athletes and coaches will be provided with free entry into the venue. In addition, each team will be given five free passes and each individual athlete will be given two free passes. Outside of these, spectators will be charged a fee of $4 to enter the venue for the entire weekend.

Product Sales
T–shirts will be on sale in a number of different sizes, colors, and styles and will be available in pre–printed designs as well as available for personalization on the spot. Consumers will simply be able to choose from the preset templates which we will have loaded into our system, pick the color and size shirt they desire, and within minutes our technician will have their shirt ready for pickup. Some templates will even allow the consumer the ability to put their sport, team, name, and number on the shirt.

In addition, we will also be able to print any of the pictures taken at the event onto a T–shirt within minutes as well. If the athlete has not found a picture he or she likes, we will have a photographer on hand to take a picture which can then be printed onto a shirt within minutes. In addition to T–shirts, our website will offer options such as traditional pictures, coffee mugs, plaques and similar products with pictures printed on them. We will also have player cards available at the end of the series which will be similar to a professional sports card with the athlete's picture on the front and a full list of statistics on back.

Strategic Partnerships
In addition to paying sponsors and vendors, we also hope to form a number of strategic partnerships that will help our tournament series grow while providing a benefit to our partner company as well. The following is a list of the partnerships which we would like to have in place by the start of our first season.

• Media Partners: We will be partnering with one or more large media sources in order to get our content broadcast to the public. We would like to partner with one internet company such as America Online or Yahoo as well as one magazine company such as Sports Illustrated, which also has a children's sports magazine. We feel that by having a web presence as well as a hard copy media outlet we can better reach our diverse target market. Media partners such as these could vastly increase the exposure that our tournament series receives and prove to be incredibly helpful, especially during our transition to a national level. These outlets could help us to push our content to the public and could boost not only our athlete registration, but also our spectator turnout, thereby increasing the exposure of our sponsors and vendors and effectively helping us to recruit more companies in these areas. In return for the benefit which we receive we can offer these companies exclusive access to a demographic which closely resembles their target market so that they may market their services. We would effectively be inviting the media companies to all of our events and working with them to generate interest in both our tournament series and their media outlet. By increasing interest in our tournament series and convincing our customers to view our content provided by the media outlets we would effectively be increasing business for the media companies, as well as ourselves.

• Local Specialty Store Owners: We will be partnering with local specialty stores in each city we travel to. We will be approaching these local stores with a proposition to recruit teams for our tournament series. We will give each store a supply of registration flyers which will be color coded to allow us to identify which store an athlete was recruited by. Stores will be compensated 5% of the registration dollars generated by their colored registration flyers. Considering that local specialty store owners have: relationships with customers, mailing lists, relationships with sporting facilities, and most likely even have relationships with a number of sports teams, recruiting athletes to compete at our events should not pose a difficult task. We feel that this relationship will be very beneficial to both parties. We gain the local expertise and connections that the store has developed over time, and the store receives a 5% commission on any teams which sign up for our event based on the stores efforts.

- Photography/Magazine: Photography poses an interesting opportunity for us to get others involved in our tournament series. Rather than simply hiring photographers to take pictures at our events we plan to hold a competition. We plan on forming a strategic partnership with universities in each city where we are holding an event. We will be talking to these universities' photography and journalism departments. Our plan is to have students from each university come to the event held in their city to be event photographers for us. The photographers will photograph each team/individual before the first round of competition, as well as taking "action" pictures during the games. These pictures will then be for sale at the events themselves as well as on our website. In addition to taking pictures at the event we will also commission each university to create an event magazine. We will give all of the universities a guideline as to what materials are required to be in the magazine; however, we will be giving each university creative control over most aspects of the magazine design. At the end of the series we will have a competition to see which university created the best event magazine, and the winning university will receive a cash prize. We feel that using student photographers is beneficial because not only will it help to reduce our costs, as we will be paying student photographers much less than professional photography companies, but it will also get another group of people interested and hopefully excited about our tournament series. We plan to promote the photography/magazine contest much like another event being held as part of the series. In addition, we hope that it will help to illustrate that we are interested in giving back to the community. We want to give these students valuable experience in working with real life projects under time constraints. Since each magazine will be released at our next event, each university will only have one week to create and ship the magazine.

Officiate & Participate

Seeing as how we are not merely trying to provide a characteristic sports tournament atmosphere, but rather to help broaden athletes' horizons and help educate them on all the different aspects about any given sport, we will be offering a unique option to athletes of the competitive division. Assuming that many of these athletes will be very dedicated and knowledgeable about their sport of choice already, we would like to give them the opportunity to show this knowledge and save some money at the same time.

We will be offering a Officiate & Participate option to athletes of the competitive division. Should any of these athletes be interested in refereeing the recreational division, they may attend one of our three scheduled clinics in order to obtain the certification required to referee in the tournament series. During these clinics each athlete will receive instruction about refereeing, will be observed while refereeing actual games, and will be required to pass a test that will qualify them to referee in the tournament series.

In return for their services, which will include refereeing a set number of games at the tournament, these athletes will receive a $60 discount on their entry fee; however, in order to qualify for this discount, the referee must attend one of the three scheduled clinics and indicate their intent to participate in the program on their teams entry form so that we may clear up any scheduling conflicts which may result.

We feel that this is a very good program because it allows children to broaden their knowledge about sports, helps them feel a connection with the tournament series, and also allows them an opportunity to help with some of the cost, an area that is primarily dominated by parents.

Battle of the Bands

In order to promote the high–energy feel that we envision for our sports tournaments, we plan to host a regional "battle of the bands" contest. Currently, venues such as the X Games and Gravity Games feature bands to keep spectators and athletes pumped up for the tournament. In 2004, the Gravity Games brought in two high–energy bands, The Donnas, and Sum 41. We do not wish to spend a large amount of money on paying performers; however, we developed an idea for a battle of the bands competition.

We plan to bring in local and regional high–energy groups which will compete, based on audience applause, for a cash prize. The battle of the bands will take place in peak tournament hours, ensuring the most possible athletes and spectators.

Smaller bands are constantly trying to find new venues and outlets for their music to be heard, and our summer tournament events provide the perfect venue. We don't plan to drown out all conversation and team communication with music, but rather strategically place the band so that athletes and audience members will have the perfect soundtrack for the weekend. In the downtime between bands we plan to have a DJ play high–energy music over the stage's PA system.

COMPETITION

Amateur Athletic Union of the United States (AAU)

Many other sports tournaments and sports tournament series already exist, targeting many of the same athletes as we plan to. One competitor offering multiple sports competition is the Amateur Athletic Union of the United States (AAU). The AAU offers numerous tournaments and competitions throughout the year, acting as venues where amateur athletes can compete for fun in hopes of qualifying for the final event, the AAU Junior Olympics. The Junior Olympics started in Washington D.C. in 1967, offering two events: swimming and track & field. The Junior Olympics is currently the host of many amateur events including: baseball, baton twirling, beach volleyball, boys' basketball, cheerleading, dance, diving, field hockey, 7 on 7 football, girls' basketball, golf, gymnastics, indoor soccer, jump rope, lacrosse, karate, multi–events, power lifting, softball, swimming, table tennis, teakwood, track & field, trampoline & tumbling, weightlifting, and wrestling.

Hoop it Up

Hoop it Up is a 3 on 3 basketball tournament that runs during the summer months in the United States and Canada. Hoop it Up directly competes with our tournament series as the format for game play is very similar. In addition, the games are played outdoors with portable basketball goals, making for endless venue possibilities. There are 36 divisions consisting of competitive, recreational, adult male, youth male, and youth female. Hoop it Up also hosts camps throughout the year, which will be in direct competition with our sports clinics.

Street Soccer Cup USA

Street Soccer Cup is a 4 on 4 street soccer tournament series currently operating in Wichita, Philadelphia, Muncie, Detroit, Chicago, Springfield (IL), and Des Moines. The game is played on a street surface with specially designed walls to make game play more exciting. Street Soccer Cup USA is in direct competition with our tournament series, as we plan to offer 4 on 4 soccer games outdoors in small enclosed soccer fields, the same as Street Soccer Cup.

X Games

The X Games is the ESPN owned sports tournament for extreme sports, becoming the first large–scale extreme sports tournament in the world. The X Games started in 1994, and has been hosting a venue for extreme sports in the summer and winter seasons ever since. The X Games is a direct competitor to us because we will be offering three extreme sports in our tournament, with similar rules and judging standards as those used by the X Games. In the past, the X Games has proved a huge success, with the summer games drawing 235,000 people in 2005, and the winter games quickly growing to 160,000 in attendance. The attendance at the Winter X Games has grown 91% since 2002, showing that the extreme sports are drawing more and more people. As the market continues to grow, we feel that we can get into this market and expand on it through our tournament series and clinics.

Gravity Games

The gravity games are described as being "the ultimate action sports, lifestyle, and music festival" which tends to cater to the location of the games. In 2005, the gravity games were held in Swan River, in Perth, Australia. Due to the location, young sports such as kiteboarding and tow–in–surfing were part of the competition. Along with the new sports, the games also include skate, BMX, and in–line. The Gravity Games are a direct competitor to us, because currently, the Gravity Games are among the biggest amateur extreme sports tournaments in the nation. We are planning to offer the same three core extreme sports as the Gravity Games: skate, BMX, and inline. Again, the extreme sports market is young, growing, and popular, leaving many athletes without a large–scale venue to compete at. Our tournament will provide a larger scale event than any local tournament could do, and give athletes an opportunity to compete with others in their region at a competitive or recreational level.

Additional Competition

Since we are offering a variety of sporting events at our tournaments, our primary competition will come from multiple event tournaments, such as the AAU sponsored tournaments, X Games, and the Gravity Games. Although our primary focus of competition is on multiple event tournaments, we cannot ignore the threat of numerous other sports tournaments taking place almost non–stop through-out the year. Tournaments such as Hoop it Up and Street Soccer Cup USA provide a venue for an exciting, fast–paced version of basketball and soccer, respectively. This type of tournament is a large operation, and they are becoming more and more popular. Athletes are continually looking for a new venue at which they can compete, and new tournaments such as the Gravity Games are offering a little twist to the tournament feel, drawing in new crowds all the time.

Some sports tournaments are organized loosely, such as intramural basketball tournaments, drawing in local amateurs to compete for fun. Other tournaments are strictly structured with multiple sponsors and promotional campaigns, examples being any of the tournaments listed above. Despite the heavy competition in the sports tournament market, we feel that our unique mix of traditional and extreme sports offers a venue unlike any of those offered by the competition, allowing our tournament series to cater to more athletes and become a top sports tournament series in the United States.

Although much of our direct competition comes from sports tournaments, many sporting leagues exist which draw in athletes from all over. Local league competition can be extremely competitive, drawing in loyal athletes who have a strong desire to be the best in the league. These leagues, which exist primarily in the traditional sports, pose a large threat to us, as teams and individual athletes may choose to participate in league play rather than paying even more money to compete in a tournament.

In addition to other sports related events however, we must also consider any form of entertainment that piques the interest of young minds as indirect competition to our tournament series. American children in previous years have become increasingly lethargic and less willing to get outside and partake in any form of physical activity. With the creation of new video game formats that allow children to communicate with their friends through an internet connection as opposed to actually traveling to their homes, previous years have brought many problems with childhood obesity and a sense of complacency among youths in our country.

Recent years however have seen a decrease in this trend as many Americans seem to be on a lasting health craze. Due to national advertising campaigns produced by the government, various news stories, and many shocking health reports, Americans have once again begun to encourage their children to get outside for some activity. While the trend of children staying indoors all day is on a downward spiral, we must still consider any form of entertainment such as video games and movies a form of indirect competition.

Family vacations also act as a competitor to our business. Summer weekends are limited, and many families take advantage of the nice weather to travel. As a result, the Scramble Sports Tournament Series needs to consider the possibility that athletes and spectators may be lost due to vacations, and plan accordingly. Trends in traveling could be changing slightly as gas prices are at an all–time high, and people are traveling less as a result. In addition to gasoline prices rising, plane ticket prices are also rising. This is a threat to us as well, as we encourage athletes to compete in multiple tournaments and clinics in different cities. But, we feel that most people would be willing to drive a shorter distance to our tournaments, whether or not gas prices are higher.

Competitive Advantages

Sports provide an obvious market opportunity because many people like to play sports, and there are many sports that cannot be played alone. Therefore, people need someone to organize and provide them with an opportunity to play these sports. The question is, "Why would people pay the money to play in a sports tournament as opposed to organizing themselves, or paying less money to play in a local sports league?" The idea behind any sports tournament is that tournaments provide a much more exciting venue for people than merely playing locally. There is a certain thrill associated with playing in a sports tournament.

It is true that people could gather themselves to play soccer or basketball, or they could go to a local park to skateboard or bike, but for people who are really passionate about their sport, this is not enough. Some people are so engrossed in their sport of choice that merely playing it with their friends or even playing with others in a local league is not enough. These people want the opportunity to show off their skills and play against other top competitors across the nation. Sports tournaments give these athletes the opportunity to meet and compete against others who share their same love and desire to excel in their chosen sport.

We feel that Scramble is unlike any other sports tournament in the world, offering a unique mix of sports and attracting athletes and sponsors alike in order to successfully run and grow a new sports tournament in the United States. In addition to the unique structure of our tournament, we also have a great source of industry knowledge at our disposal, as well as many close sponsor connections that we will use to grow and promote the Scramble tournament series. The specific competitive advantages which we have identified are explained in detail below.

Unique mix of traditional and extreme sports

As we have stated many times earlier, our tournament offers both traditional and extreme sports for recreational and competitive athletes alike. The Junior Olympics is among our top competition, offering multiple sports, but not including any extreme sports in the mix of events offered. We feel that we are at an advantage by offering extreme sports because they will provide many new opportunities for both athletes and sponsors to pursue new interests. By combining both traditional and extreme sports, interest in each individual sport will increase and potentially inspire and influence many people to broaden their horizons.

The Olympics are starting to add some extreme sports such as snowboarding to their mix of sports and this is broadening their viewing spectrum by drawing in viewers and fans of these sports. However, at an amateur level the Junior Olympics has not caught on by adding any extreme sports into the mix. The Gravity Games offer many sports, some which may not be considered extreme, but they still don't offer a complete traditional and extreme mix. As a result, we feel that there is a huge opportunity that needs to be seized by combining traditional and extreme sports at both a recreational and competitive level, attracting athletes from all walks and avenues to one major sporting event.

Industry knowledge at our disposal

In addition to our passion and drive for the Scramble tournament series, we have an abundance of information and industry knowledge available to us. One advisor and potential investor that we have been meeting extensively with is Thomas Risheo.Thomas, along with the help of his son Bobby Risheo (the Owner/CEO of Scramble) has the experience of starting a successful and profitable national hockey tournament series which brought in sponsors and athletes from all over the United States. He is a great asset to our company, providing us with information for starting a sports tournament, and also acting as a mentor, insuring that we will not commit an obvious mistake or take the Scramble tournament series in a wrong direction.

Close Sponsor Connections

In order to make Scramble a reality we will require contributions from major sponsors and vendors. In order to build the Scramble tournament series to the successful level that we desire, we will not only need local sponsors, but also support from national sponsors and sporting goods vendors across the sports spectrum. Bauer/Nike, a major developer and producer of hockey equipment, has already expressed interest in becoming a vendor and contributing to our tournament series. Thomas Risheo has been in close contact with Bauer/Nike throughout the years and as a result was able to put us in contact with the hockey equipment giant. Bauer/Nike was excited to hear from us and has already sent us high quality equipment and gear as an example of equipment contributions they would be willing to donate for prizes at the Scramble tournament series. We feel that getting a connection with an industry leader such as Bauer/Nike will only help us to secure and land other contracts and deals with industry leaders in other sports. Bauer/Nike is the first potential vendor that we have been in contact with, but a full list of potential sponsors and vendors can be found in the primary revenue streams section of the business plan.

Market Opportunity

Our tournament series hopes not only to attract athletes who are looking for the excitement of competing at the top level in their sport, but also those athletes who simply love the sport in which they compete, even if they are not highly skilled. We intend to provide an atmosphere in which these athletes can learn what separates them from athletes at the top of their sport, and also to provide tips to help close this gap.

Many young athletes are simply interested in watching top athletes compete, and then trying to emulate them. We feel that by offering both a competitive and a recreational division we will give less talented athletes the ability to watch some of their more skilled counterparts and possibly learn a few things before they are scheduled to play.

MARKET ANALYSIS

The sports tournament industry is consistently profitable and always growing over time, as people continue to love sports. The average annual sales (based on over 18 million companies) for a company operating in the amateur sports tournament industry is $2,538,445 (Bizminer.com). As new sports continue to emerge, both children and adults become involved and excited about these new sports.

There are constantly new tournaments and venues that host these emerging new sports. Sports such as biking and aggressive inline skating are relatively new and have become popular in the last couple decades. Venues such as The X Games and Gravity Games cater to these new sports and provide a successful large–scale tournament.

The Scramble tournament series is combining two separate industries: traditional sports and extreme sports, enabling us to generate a profit in our beginning years of operations, in an industry that already proves to be good for startups. According to Bizmer.com, the average annual sales for a startup company in the amateur sports tournament industry are $242,000, based off of data from seven companies in the first three years of operation.

We plan to grow the Scramble tournament series every year by adding sports to ensure new and larger audiences for future years of operation. Our growth strategy will enable us to attract many different athletes and fans from all sports, traditional or extreme. As our growth continues, we will have to explore new venue opportunities to host so many additional sports. Our growth strategy can be found below in the business plan. As Scramble proves to be a safe, clean, unique and exciting tournament for amateur athletes, we will continue to grow a satisfied customer base that will return for years to come.

The market for the Scramble tournament series is large, and it is somewhat hard to define each and every possible consumer or participant. There are age categories for each amateur sport that we offer, providing a narrowed down group of people. On the other hand, it is much harder to define each and every group of people that may come as spectators to the Scramble tournaments. The diversity of the audience increases even more by combining the traditional and extreme sports into one tournament. The only thing that the overwhelming majority of people attending the tournaments have in common is the fact that they love sports. The various market segments are explained below.

Athletes competing in the tournament

The market for athletes competing in the Scramble tournament series is rather specific, as we provide age groups and requirements to compete. The athletes' age groups range from age 9 to adult, with the 9–17 age range having double the amount of athletes, with a recreational and competitive division offered in most age groups. We picked these age groups strategically, knowing that we can find amateur athletes in each of these age groups to fill up all possible time slots, thereby receiving the highest profit possible. In a recent article explaining teen spending in America, it is said that teens spend $159 billion each year. The article also explains that teens have a high disposable income, bringing in an average of $125 a week. Another article from the Sunday Tribune explains that teens today have a higher disposable income than generations before, buying mobile phones, iPods, clothes, stereos, and CDs. We feel with this recent trend towards more disposable income will only help our tournament series, bringing in athletes that are willing to pay higher amounts for entry fees, and more willing to compete in multiple tournaments or clinics throughout the year. Hoop it Up basketball tournaments offer age divisions ranging from age 8 to adult. Street Soccer Cup USA offers age divisions from under 6 all the way up to adult. The AAU offers age groups ranging from 8 years old to 18 years old at their events. With the amount of time we have allotted for our tournament series, we feel that the age divisions ranging from age 9 and up are appropriate. In addition, we feel that our target age of 9 to 17 is right on track to bring in the athletes with high disposable income.

Friends and Families of Athletes

We expect to see many spectators from the same age groups as outlined for the sports, as people will attend the tournament to watch their friends compete. At younger ages, children tend to be friends with each other, regardless of whether or not they play a sport together, and as a result, we plan to see many friends of athletes attending. In addition to the friends of athletes attending the Scramble tournaments, we also expect to see a great number of families, or family members, attending the tournaments as spectators and coaches. The vast majority of athletes will have family members, which are at the tournament as spectators, to watch their children participate. Families attending sporting events tend to spend money on many different things including: concessions, parking, photographs, magazines, clothing, and equipment. We expect to see much of our revenue coming from the families of the athletes, especially from the younger age divisions where a larger percentage of families will attend the events.

Families and other individuals

Finally, we expect to see many families and individuals that are not associated with athletes or vendors at the Scramble tournaments. We will be advertising in and around the cities where the Scramble tournament will be visiting, ensuring a market of spectators from all different ages. We plan to see a lot of families simply wanting to have something to do on a summer weekend. Also, we expect to see groups of children attending the tournament, again, looking for something to do. The Scramble tournament provides a safe and clean environment for children and adults alike, and we plan to advertise this aspect to parents who are letting their children attend the event as spectators.

Sponsors

Another market segment for our series includes national and local sponsors at each clinic and tournament. A complete sponsor section is described above, which details specific industries and companies within those industries that we would like to contract with. For example, Cingular is third on the list for the top sports advertisers, and they share a similar target market as us. The Scramble series would be a perfect place for Cingular to reach new potential cell phone users, while sticking to their sports advertising trend. Local sponsors may include a wide variety of businesses, ranging anywhere from a restaurant to a funeral home. We feel that we can provide local sponsors with a great marketing and advertising opportunity, encouraging the sponsors to pay for sponsorship of multiple events in their city.

Vendors

The Scramble series will generate revenue through vendors operating at the tournaments and clinics, creating another market segment. A significant amount of our income is scheduled to come from vendors, making this a very important segment. We plan to approach big-name, high quality vendors to participate in the Scramble series, as this will draw in more revenue and attract more athletes. The equipment used for game play in each sport will be provided by the vendors, and we hope to associate the Scramble series with quality names in each industry. For example, when a person thinks of quality products in the hockey industry, names such as Bauer/Nike, Easton, and CCM come to mind.

Although some of the market for the Scramble tournaments is unpredictable and variable, we feel that the most important target market is the athletes. If we can fill up all of the individual and team time slots, the Scramble tournament series will be profitable simply from athletes, and the athletes' friends and families. Word of mouth is a powerful form of marketing for sports tournaments in general, and we feel that a satisfied group of athletes will be a better marketing device than any advertising or promotional campaign. Satisfied athletes return to tournaments that they enjoy, and therefore, we will try everything within our power to make the Scramble tournament series an exciting, safe, and clean environment for everyone attending, ensuring customer retention for years to come.

MARKETING & SALES

Marketing Strategy

Since we are a startup company, our marketing strategy is set to be a little more intense in the first couple of years of operating as a major sports tournament series. In order to make Scramble a successful tournament series, we will first need to find enough teams to fill all of our competitive and recreational divisions for each sport. This will ensure maximum income and exposure in the first few years of operation. Since the tournament will be running in a variety of different locations and cities, we will need to construct an intensive marketing campaign at each location well in advance of the first tournament date.

Store Owners

We have observed that when children get involved in sports, they tend to surround their entire lives with that sport, constantly hanging out at sporting goods stores or specialty sports stores. As a result, storeowners have knowledge of many teams in their area, as well as a listing of teams in a particular sport. The store may even organize a sports tournament, whether it is on a local or regional level. This information is potentially a great asset to our company, as we plan to utilize a guerilla marketing campaign in each city prior to the start of the tournament series.

Color Coded Forms for Commission

Before the first year of operation, 7 or 8 employees of our tournament series will travel to each city on the tournament schedule, spending 14 days talking with major sports shops in each city that are associated with the sports we intend to offer. Our employees will talk to as many sports shops as the travel time will allow. We will provide each shop with tournament signup forms, which will be color-coded based on the specific store. When a team or individual sings up on a specific form, the store associated with that signup form will be paid a commission. In addition, the employee that gave the forms to the sport shop will be paid a commission. Bobby Risheo and possibly one other founding member will travel around to each city, building strong relationships with shop owners to promote our tournament series. The shop owners will then help us to secure teams for the first annual Scramble tournament series.

Guerilla Marketing

In addition to talking to shop owners, we plan to spend any additional time in each city talking with teams and coaches first hand. We plan to check out local practice areas so that we can establish a personal relationship with teams in an attempt to secure teams for the first year of the series. Most of all, we want to get people in key areas excited about our tournament, and we feel that the best way to do that is to talk with the coaches and teams first hand. If a kid hears one of our employees talk about how much the Scramble tournament series wants their team to compete, that kid is going to be a lot more excited than simply seeing a poster of the tournament hanging up. We feel that by directly speaking and interacting with potential teams and vendors, Scramble can hit the ground running and have a successful inaugural year.

Posters and Flyers

Although we would prefer to reach all potential teams and vendors personally, there is only so much time allocated for each city, resulting in missed opportunities. To counteract this situation, we will hang posters and give out flyers the entire time that we are in a certain city or region. If we can convince sports stores and shops to hang our posters and give out flyers promoting the tournament series, we feel that we can potentially find additional athletes to compete. Also, if we have previously developed a relationship with a shop where the poster is located, the storeowner will potentially be excited about the series and further promote our series to athletes and coaches alike.

Website

Each poster and flyer will also contain a URL address for the Scramble website. Our website will contain information about each event including: times, locations, and requirements for competing in each event. After the first event of our tournament series, the website will also include pictures and highlights from the previous events.

The website will also contain a section that will allow you to register for your events, and pay using a credit or debit card. We will offer a small variety of apparel featuring our tournament logo, which can also be paid for using a credit or debit card. Finally, we will also have any leftover tournament shirts just in case an athlete or spectator didn't get a chance to purchase one at the venue.

In addition, the website will also contain a section about the rules of every sport that we are offering at our tournament. Each rulebook will be in a downloadable PDF file. In addition, the website will have a video section, featuring highlights of current and past tournaments. We will also have a Webcam in the video section, which will feature live footage of the entire summer sports tournament series.

A full sponsor section will be on the website, giving potential sponsors for the national and local level a chance to check out pricing and sponsor benefits. Forms will be linked on the website, letting sponsors register online if desired.

Next, a section on the website will allow anyone to be put on our bi–monthly email list. The people on the email list will receive the latest tournament news and promotions and discounts on various things, such as entry fees and merchandise.

Finally we will have a section on the site about how to get involved with the tournament itself. You can fill out an application online to volunteer or apply for a position with the tournament series. Part time and full time positions will be listed on the website, and allow for us to draw employees and volunteers from all different cities throughout the region.

Word of Mouth
Finally, after the first few years of successful tournaments, we plan for a large amount of athletes and coaches contacting us through word–of–mouth marketing. The best advertising for our series will be from happy and satisfied athletes and coaches that competed in the tournament in previous years. Along with limited space for each sport, our tournament has limited time for teams to compete, which restricts the amount of teams that the Scramble tournament series can accommodate. We feel that word–of–mouth advertising, along with strong relationships developed early on, will provide the Scramble tournament series with plenty of potential teams and athletes in future years.

GROWTH STRATEGY

The Scramble tournament series will require a lot of work during the months that we are not in operation, especially in the months preceding the first year of operation. We have devised a series of phases that we will follow in order to prepare for, and to run the company in the first year of operation. Each phase is outlined in detail below.

Phase 1: Prior to First Year of Operation

1. Secure Venues: First, we will secure all of the venues that will be needed to operate the clinics, Sports Highlight tournaments, summer series tournaments, and finally the national championship tournament in Muncie, Indiana. We are currently researching venue opportunities around the country, attempting to find places that will offer accommodations for all of our traditional sports, as well as an area to build courses for the extreme sports.

2. Secure Vendors: In addition to securing sponsors, we must also find one major sports vendor in each sport which we intend to offer. Vendors will provide our series with revenue in the form of the initial vendor fee, as well as a 5% commission on all goods sold at the events. All seven vendors must be identified and contracted before the start of our first season as our extensive vendor showcase is one of the main spectator draws for our tournament series.

3. Secure Sponsors: In order to make our first year of operation a success, we will need sponsors to fill up our requirements for the platinum, gold, silver and bronze sponsor categories. The anticipated number of sponsors which we intend to attract in our first season can be found in the financial section of the business plan. Finding sponsors is a top priority, as they will bring in a great deal of revenue and prizes for the tournament.

Phase 2: Prior to First Year of Operation

1. Purchase/Build Equipment: The next stage of our development cycle will involve purchasing and/or renting all of the equipment for the first year of operation. The biggest pieces of equipment that we will need to provide will be the ramps, rails, and half pipe for the three extreme sports offered in the first year. Also, we will need to purchase materials to build a small wall around the hockey and soccer rinks, to keep flying pucks and balls in play. We plan to buy the raw materials to construct each and every piece of the course, reconstructing the entire course with the help of our volunteers and employees at each location. In addition to the extreme sports course, we will need flood lights for night events. Also, we will need to purchase a large amount of banquet tables and tents for athlete registration, concessions, and parking attendants. In order to travel between events, we plan to purchase trucks to transport our lights, tables, hockey and soccer equipment, and extreme sports course from venue to venue. The purchase of any additional supplies and raw materials, such as extension cords, portable toilets (if necessary) will be made during this stage in the development cycle.

2. Obtain Event/Liability Insurance for Venues: We are currently researching insurance costs for operating at different venues, as some venues have the ability to provide insurance to renters and some do not. Also, we have been in contact with an insurance company that has informed us of the possibility of obtaining outdoor tournament insurance in case of weather delays or cancellations.

Phase 3: First Season of Operation

1. Team Sign Up: The first step before running any clinics or tournaments must be to secure all of our athletes. We cannot expect to fill our age divisions and groups to 100% capacity in the first year; rather, our financial projections for year 1 assume a 70% capacity. Year 2 assumes an 85% capacity, and we predict to be at 100% capacity in year 3. Our primary method for teams to signup for the tournament is through our website, which features a section allowing teams to register and input all of their information online, including their payment. Teams will be asked on the website to input, if any, the color of the flyer or card from which they heard about the clinic or tournament. This will enable us to pay commission to the employee or volunteer responsible for distributing the flyer or card. Teams may also use the actual flyer, which will have a registration section, and mail the form and payment to our office in Muncie, Indiana.

2. Marketing/Advertising: While actively pursuing teams to participate in our first year of tournaments, we will also be advertising in tournament cities and surrounding areas. In phase 1, we are planning to secure a media partner, which can provide us with advertising and marketing through different mediums, such as internet, magazine or radio. In addition to the advertising and marketing through the media sponsor, we also plan to invest $40,000 in advertising before the first season of operation.

3. Transportation to Cities: In order to accommodate all of the equipment necessary to run such a large-scale operation, we will purchase 5 trucks with a closed cargo compartments, and 4 flat bed trailers which will be pulled by pickups. Based on weather charts and travel distances, we have devised a yearlong route that we will follow for our first year of operation. The weather charts and a map detailing the travel route which we plan to follow can be found in the appendix of this business plan.

4. Clinic/Tournament Set-Up: The set-up for each clinic and tournament will be rather extensive, as we have 7 sports to prepare for during the summer tournament series. We plan to have 25

employees setting up all necessary equipment for the summer tournaments, under the supervision of 3 high level managers, making sure the set–up runs smoothly. Set–up time will take 500 human hours for the summer series events, bringing the total set–up time to 20 hours.

5. Marketing in Cities of Operation: Although we do not plan to aggressively market our off–season tournaments and clinics during the operation of these events, we do plan to market our summer series in the city of operation, during the weekend of operation. This marketing campaign will require 10 employees who will aggressively travel around the city of operation putting up flyers, and promoting events such as a dunk contest, battle of the bands, and professional athletic demonstrations. We want to try and get the public in each city excited about our event, in hopes of starting a tradition where people look forward to our event each year.

6. Running Clinics/Tournaments: Running the clinics, off–season tournaments, summer series, and championship will all vary from each other in terms of employee numbers. The management and employee duties for each of these events will be basically the same, with the exception of the clinics. Labor costs for the summer series are roughly $50,000, and the off season tournaments demanding $25,000.

7. Equipment Tear Down: The takedown of all equipment used at the clinics or tournaments will require precise coordination between many employees. As with the set–up, we will require 25 employees to help with the tear down, being supervised by 3 managers. The total time for tear down of the summer series events is estimated to take a total of 25 hours. After the completion of phase one and two in the development cycle, the Scramble tournament series will be ready for the first season of operation. Our first event will be a clinic in Bloomington (April), followed by a clinic in Muncie (May) before the summer tournament series kicks off. The actual time allotted for this development cycle is yet to be determined, as we are not sure what the first year of operation will be. If we plan to start the tournament in the summer of 2007, we will have the time available from this current day until the first tournament of the series in the summer of 2007 for phases one and two. We feel that the summer of 2007 is the earliest that we could start the series, ensuring the tournament that we have envisioned. If we were forced to push back the start date to 2008, we will simply have more time for each one of the stages in phase one and two of the development cycle. The three phases described above outline what it takes for us to get through the first year of operation. We plan to have a phase four, which will include growing the tournament to a national level, and adding more sports in the process. As described earlier, the Hispanic population in places such as Florida, Texas, and California provide for much opportunity for the sport of soccer. Depending on the success of our series in the first year, we plan to expand nationally into different regions, slowly taking advantage of new markets. We also plan to add at least one traditional and extreme sport every year, further tapping into new markets, and expanding the size of our tournament series to a new level. We realize that a full–scale national tournament involves many risks, and for this reason, we are starting regionally and expanding based on the successes of our first year of operation.

RISK FACTORS

There are many risks associated with starting a major sporting tournament. The idea of competition and sporting events is not a new concept, and as a result, there are many existing competitors and tournaments already in place for every sport, including those we are offering in our mix. A list of potential risks to the Scramble tournament series, as well as our answers to those risks, follows:

- Not being able to secure enough teams for our first year of the tournament series. If we do not succeed in filling all time slots for every sport, we are losing out on registration money, and losing out on athletes who could potentially visit vendor booths and purchase concessions, photos, and other merchandise. We could also lose money if our city–to–city campaign fails, and we are spending traveling money, while not making the money back on new teams or sponsors. We are however not relying exclusively on our marketing efforts to provide all of the teams. In addition to the marketing campaigns which we are launching on our own, we will also be working with our strategic partners to locate teams. Strategic partnerships with local sporting good and specialty store owners should provide us with a large number of contacts which we can transition into clients.

- Other sporting events taking precedence over the Scramble tournament series. There are constantly sports tournaments occurring, ensuring that the Scramble tournament series will conflict with the schedules of athletes. If we fail to recognize another major tournament going on at the same time, we will lose out on athletes and sponsors for our tournament. In an effort to avoid two tournaments occurring at the same time and preventing athletes from being able to attend one of them, we must conduct extensive market research into the tournament schedules of our competitors and try to avoid scheduling our events opposite our competitors in our first year of operation. We are trying to build a strong tournament that will keep people coming back year after year, and minimizing the overlap of our tournament to others is a key strategy for our future success.

- Offering a mix of traditional and extreme sports. To our knowledge, a major tournament series offering traditional and extreme sports has never been attempted, and this poses a risk as we are attempting a completely new business venture. We feel that our tournament has created a niche market, attracting a mix of athletes which have never previously been brought together, but this mix may not be appealing to the coaches and/or athletes, resulting in a loss of participants. While we are prepared to make every effort to get this mix of sports to work well together and create cross interest between traditional and extreme sports, should this mix not work, we could easily modify our tournament structure and remain in operation. We could simply separate the extreme and traditional sports either at the same venue, or at entirely separate venues. While this would require a small amount of additional work on our part, we do not feel that separating the two sporting types would be out of the question should they fail to work well together.

- Offering seven sports in the first year of the tournament series. Many tournaments provide a venue for only one sport, and still prove to be a challenging event to manage. Starting with seven sports is a big step, one with big potential and also a large amount of risk. We may underestimate the volume of people attending, and the employees and volunteers necessary to make for a successful tournament. While operating a tournament of this magnitude will be a challenge, this is a risk which we have considered in every aspect of the design of our series. We decided to follow a growth strategy similar to that of the AAU Junior Olympics in that we are offering only a limited number of sports in our first year of operation, and we are planning to add between two and three additional sports every year. While this still leaves us offering seven sports in our first year of operation, we have an experienced management team, as well as an experienced mentor, and we feel that if we properly plan, we will be able to handle this difficult task.

FINANCIAL ANALYSIS

The Scramble Sports Tournament Series is tentatively scheduled to be operational in April of 2007, with our first event starting on April 27th in Bloomington, Indiana. One financial goal of the company is to turn a profit after our first season. This is planned and reflected in our financial statements as we plan to have a net income of $800,000 at the end of season one. In order to achieve this goal our most valuable assets will be our relationships with our sponsors/vendors and with our customers. Bringing these two groups of people together in an environment of learning and competition will not only help Scramble accomplish its financial goals, but will also bring athletic knowledge, advancement, and competition to all who participate in our events.

Request for Capital

Scramble is projecting to achieve a positive Net Income at the end of Season 1 while operating at only 70% revenue capacity and we intend to fund the operation with $1.4M in incremental stages. Though the financial statements show that all of Scramble's funding is in the preseason, in reality funding comes in 3 rounds. The current management team will contribute $140,000 in a bootstrap round lasting four months. The second round of funding will be a request for capital of $500,000 in the month of October. The final round of funding will be a request for capital of $1,000,000 in the month of March in order to purchase all fixed assets required for the first season of events.

Scramble offers these funding requests to investors with a passion for increasing the youth of America's athletic knowledge and ability. Potential investors also include vendors and sponsors as they will benefit directly from the success of the Scramble Sports Tournament Series.

Milestone phase 1		Milestone phase 2
Bootstrap June/September 2006 Hard cash establishment: $14,000	**Round 1** October/February 2006 Seed round advertising: $500,000	**Round 2** March 2006 - March 2007 Fixed asset purchases: $1,000,000
-Consult with and select venues in different cities where events will be held -Consulting with and establishing sponsor/ vendor relationships and strategic partnerships -Assemble full management team -Produce and distribute literature -Assemble sales team	-Finalize partnerships/relationships with sponsors/vendors -Finalize partnerships/relationships with event venues -Dispatch sales team -Establish legal and accounting relationships	-Purchase necessary transportation assets -Purchase necessary equipment for the events themselves -Begin operating and incurring costs associated with events in April.

General Financial Plan Assumptions

- Scramble will have a fiscal season starting at the beginning of April as this is the month of the first event. Upon the month before April, Scramble will have purchased all assets necessary to successfully implement all of the events, whether clinic or tournament, for the first full year's schedule.

- Preseason is established as being from the beginning of June of 2006 to March of 2007. No revenues will be earned in this point and time. The costs and expenditures associated with preseason are not reflected in the financial statements of year one.

- It is assumed, and displayed in the financial statements that during the first season's schedule, Scramble will be able to fill its team/individual slots per event to 70% of their capacity. The second season's events are assumed to be filled to 85% capacity. Events of season three, four, and five are assumed to be filled to their full capacities.

- Fixed assets purchased by Scramble will be transported from event to event with the company's own mode of transportation. Prices for travel/transportation of Scramble's equipment is heavily dependent on prices of fuel and the petroleum industry.

Revenue Assumptions

- There are ten sources of revenue for Scramble that are displayed in the financial statements: Entry Fee, Clinic Signup, Sponsor Revenue, Vendor Revenue, Program Sales, Event General Admission, Concessions, Parking, Magazine Sales and Photograph Sales.

- Entry fees, sponsorships, and vendor revenue comprise close to ninety percent of Scramble's Revenue, therefore, the company's success is heavily dependant on these three revenue streams.

- Concerning the smaller revenue streams, Scramble prescribes that a certain percentage of the population will purchase any one average item from the revenue streams. These percentages and cost of the average items are outlined in the financial statements under Secondary Revenue Streams.

- In projecting the attendance of the different events, several assumptions were made on the number of spectators a participant would draw to the event. It is thought by the management team, conservatively, that on average a participant would draw from 1.5–2.5 spectators per event depending on how close the event is filled to full capacity (whether we have filled all team slots).

- Since the various athletes will likely be present at the event during only the hours of and surrounding his/her own competitions, the management team can safely assume that the full attendance of an event will not be present all at one time, although the company does have the ability to accommodate the full attendance.

Sponsorship and Vendor Assumptions

- The management team concludes and displays in the financial statements that Scramble will have attracted one national Platinum Sponsor, one local and one national Gold Sponsor, one local and one national silver sponsor, and one local Bronze Sponsor to take part in the first season's schedule of events. Over the next four seasons the management team plans to fill all available unit packages for sponsorships.

- The management team assumes that in the first season it is possible to fill all available spaces for vendors. We feel that unlike sponsors, vendors will be readily willing to put their products up for prizes and display as they will have exclusive rights to their designated sport. Other benefits include vendor logos on the playing surface, exclusive sale and use of the vendor's products at the events, as well as many other creative options.

Preseason expenditure operating costs

Preseason expenditure breakdown

Fixed assets	Quantity	
Banquet tables	30	$ 2,000
Skatepark equipment	—	$ 75,000
Flood lights	20	$ 10,000
Tents	10	$ 20,000
Trucks/auto	5	$400,000
Trailers (Flatbed)	4	$ 50,000
Basketball goals	6	$ 3,000
Hockey nets	6	$ 3,000
Volleyball nets	6	$ 3,000
Stage	1	$ 20,000
Grandstands	15	$ 30,000
Soccer nets	6	$ 3,000
Hockey/soccer rinks	6	$120,000
Other equipment	—	$ 20,000
Office furniture & supplies	—	$ 15,000
Total equipment costs		**$774,000**
Buisness operations		
Advertising	—	$ 40,000
Travel	—	$ 40,000
Accounting	—	$ 10,000
Administrative salaries	—	$ 38,000
Legal fees	—	$ 30,000
Office expenses	—	$ 5,000
Utilities	—	$ 15,000
Literature production	—	$ 20,000
Payroll	—	$ 15,000
Office rent	—	$ 4,000
Office supplies	—	$ 3,000
Total other cost		**$220,000**
Total costs		**$994,000**

Income statement

Preseason—2007 season

Revenue	Preseason	April	May	June	July	Aug	Sept
Entry fee revenue	$ —	$ —	$ 80,000	$400,000	$160,000	$ 135,000	$ 45,000
Clinic revenue	$ —	$ 50,000	$ 55,000	$ —	$ —	$ 50,000	$ —
Sponsor revenue	$ —	$ 75,000	$ 75,000	$ 75,000	$ 75,000	$ 75,000	$ 75,000
Program revenue	$ —	$ 2,008	$ 2,515	$ 10,040	$ 4,016	$ 2,515	$ 2,424
Vendor revenue	$ —	$120,800	$120,800	$120,800	$120,800	$ 120,800	$120,800
Concessions revenue	$ —	$ 869	$ 4,312	$ 17,212	$ 6,885	$ 4,312	$ 2,494
General admission revenue	$ —	$ 518	$ 1,952	$ 7,172	$ 2,869	$ 1,952	$ 1,039
Photography revenue	$ —	$ 1,208	$ 5,989	$ 23,905	$ 9,562	$ 5,989	$ 3,464
Parking revenue	$ —	$ 217	$ 1,078	$ 4,303	$ 1,721	$ 1,484	$ 623
Magazine revenue	$ —	$ 1,546	$ 7,665	$ 30,598	$ 12,239	$ 10,553	$ 4,433
Total revenue	**$ —**	**$252,165**	**$354,310**	**$689,030**	**$393,092**	**$ 407,604**	**$255,277**
Cost of sales							
Payroll	$ 15,000	$ 77,000	$167,000	$450,000	$180,000	$ 167,000	$ 40,000
Office rent	$ 4,000	$ 1,000	$ 1,000	$ 1,000	$ 1,000	$ 1,000	$ 1,000
Venue rent	$ —	$ 15,000	$ 30,000	$ 80,000	$ 30,000	$ 30,000	$ 15,000
Prizes/awards	$ —	$ —	$ 10,000	$ 25,000	$ 10,000	$ 20,000	$ 5,000
Office supplies	$ 3,000	$ 1,000	$ 1,000	$ 3,000	$ 1,500	$ 3,000	$ 1,000
Sales commission	$ —	$ 4,500	$ 12,150	$ 36,000	$ 14,400	$ 16,650	$ 4,050
Total cost of sales	**$ 22,000**	**$ 98,500**	**$221,150**	**$595,000**	**$236,900**	**$ 237,650**	**$ 66,050**
Gross profit	**$ (22,000)**	**$158,165**	**$133,160**	**$ 94,030**	**$156,192**	**$ 169,954**	**$189,227**
Operating expense							
Advertising	$ 40,000	$ 5,000	$ 5,000	$ 5,000	$ 5,000	$ 5,000	$ 5,000
Other rentals	$ —	$ 3,333	$ 3,333	$ 3,333	$ 3,333	$ 3,333	$ 3,333
Travel	$ 40,000	$ 5,000	$ 10,000	$ 25,000	$ 10,000	$ 10,000	$ 5,000
Accounting	$ 10,000	$ 1,000	$ 1,000	$ 1,000	$ 1,000	$ 1,000	$ 1,000
Admin salaries	$ 38,000	$ 12,500	$ 12,500	$ 12,500	$ 12,500	$ 12,500	$ 12,500
Depreciation	$ —	$ 5,000	$ 5,000	$ 5,000	$ 5,000	$ 5,000	$ 5,000
General/event insurance	$ —	$ 15,000	$ 30,000	$ 75,000	$ 30,000	$ 30,000	$ 15,000
Legal fees	$ 30,000	$ 1,000	$ 1,000	$ 5,000	$ 1,000	$ 1,000	$ 1,000
Office expenses	$ 5,000	$ 1,000	$ 1,000	$ 1,000	$ 1,000	$ 1,000	$ 1,000
Utilities	$ 15,000	$ 2,000	$ 2,000	$ 2,000	$ 2,000	$ 2,000	$ 2,000
Literature production	$ 20,000	$ 2,000	$ 2,000	$ 2,000	$ 2,000	$ 2,000	$ 2,000
Total operating expense	**$ 198,000**	**$ 52,833**	**$ 72,833**	**$136,833**	**$ 72,833**	**$ 72,883**	**$ 52,883**
Total costs	**$ 220,000**	**$151,333**	**$293,983**	**$731,833**	**$309,733**	**$ 310,483**	**$118,883**
Operating income	**$(220,000)**	**$ 6,832**	**$ 60,327**	**$ (42,804)**	**$ 83,358**	**$ 97,121**	**$136,394**
Income tax	**$ —**	**$ 2,050**	**$ 18,098**	**$ (12,841)**	**$ 25,008**	**$ 29,136**	**$ 40,918**
Net income	**$(220,000)**	**$ 4,782**	**$ 42,229**	**$ (29,963)**	**$ 58,351**	**$ 67,985**	**$ 95,476**

(continued)

Income statement [CONTINUED]

Preseason—2007 season

Revenue	Oct	Nov	Dec	Jan	Feb	Mar	Year 1
Entry fee revenue	$ 45,000	$ 45,000	$ 45,000	$ 45,000	$ 45,000	$ 45,000	$1,090,000
Clinic revenue	$ —	$ —	$ —	$ —	$ —	$ —	$ 155,000
Sponsor revenue	$ 75,000	$ 75,000	$ 75,000	$ 75,000	$ 75,000	$ 75,000	$ 900,000
Program revenue	$ 2,424	$ 2,424	$ 2,424	$ 2,424	$ 2,424	$ 2,424	$ 38,066
Vendor revenue	$ 120,800	$ 120,800	$ 120,800	$ 120,800	$ 120,800	$ 120,800	$1,449,600
Concessions revenue	$ 2,494	$ 2,494	$ 2,494	$ 2,494	$ 2,494	$ 2,494	$ 51,045
General admission revenue	$ 1,039	$ 1,039	$ 1,039	$ 1,039	$ 1,039	$ 1,039	$ 21,735
Photography revenue	$ 3,464	$ 3,464	$ 3,464	$ 3,464	$ 3,464	$ 3,464	$ 70,896
Parking revenue	$ 623	$ 623	$ 623	$ 623	$ 623	$ 623	$ 13,167
Magazine revenue	$ 4,433	$ 4,433	$ 4,433	$ 4,433	$ 4,433	$ 4,433	$ 93,635
Total revenue	**$ 255,277**	**$ 255,277**	**$ 255,277**	**$ 255,277**	**$ 255,277**	**$ 255,277**	**$3,883,143**
Cost of sales							
Payroll	$ 40,000	$ 40,000	$ 40,000	$ 40,000	$ 40,000	$ 40,000	$1,321,000
Office rent	$ 1,000	$ 1,000	$ 1,000	$ 1,000	$ 1,000	$ 1,000	$ 12,000
Venue rent	$ 15,000	$ 15,000	$ 15,000	$ 15,000	$ 15,000	$ 15,000	$ 290,000
Prizes/awards	$ 5,000	$ 5,000	$ 5,000	$ 5,000	$ 5,000	$ 5,000	$ 250,000
Office supplies	$ 1,000	$ 1,000	$ 1,000	$ 1,000	$ 1,000	$ 1,000	$ 16,500
Sales commision	$ 4,050	$ 4,050	$ 4,050	$ 4,050	$ 4,050	$ 4,050	$ 112,050
Total cost of sales	$ 66,050	$ 66,050	$ 66,050	$ 66,050	$ 66,050	$ 66,050	$1,851,550
Gross profit	**$ 189,227**	**$ 189,227**	**$ 189,227**	**$ 189,227**	**$ 189,227**	**$ 189,227**	**$2,031,593**
Operating expense							
Advertising	$ 5,000	$ 5,000	$ 5,000	$ 5,000	$ 5,000	$ 5,000	$ 60,000
Other rentals	$ 3,333	$ 3,333	$ 3,333	$ 3,333	$ 3,333	$ 3,333	$ 40,000
Travel	$ 5,000	$ 5,000	$ 5,000	$ 5,000	$ 5,000	$ 5,000	$ 95,000
Accounting	$ 1,000	$ 1,000	$ 1,000	$ 1,000	$ 1,000	$ 1,000	$ 12,000
Admin salaries	$ 12,500	$ 12,500	$ 12,500	$ 12,500	$ 12,500	$ 12,500	$ 150,000
Depreciation	$ 5,000	$ 5,000	$ 5,000	$ 5,000	$ 5,000	$ 5,000	$ 60,000
General/Event insurance	$ 15,000	$ 15,000	$ 15,000	$ 15,000	$ 15,000	$ 28,000	$ 340,000
Legal fees	$ 1,000	$ 1,000	$ 1,000	$ 1,000	$ 1,000	$ 1,000	$ 16,000
Office expenses	$ 1,000	$ 1,000	$ 1,000	$ 1,000	$ 1,000	$ 1,000	$ 12,000
Utilities	$ 2,000	$ 2,000	$ 2,000	$ 2,000	$ 2,000	$ 2,000	$ 24,000
Literature production	$ 2,000	$ 2,000	$ 2,000	$ 2,000	$ 2,000	$ 2,000	$ 24,000
Total operating expense	**$ 52,833**	**$ 52,833**	**$ 52,833**	**$ 52,833**	**$ 52,833**	**$ 65,833**	$ 791,000
Total costs	**$ 118,883**	**$ 118,883**	**$ 118,883**	**$ 118,883**	**$ 118,883**	**$ 131,883**	
Operating income	**$ 136,394**	**$ 136,394**	**$ 136,394**	**$ 136,394**	**$ 136,394**	**$ 123,394**	**$1,240,593**
Income tax	**$ 40,918**	**$ 40,918**	**$ 40,918**	**$ 40,918**	**$ 40,918**	**$ 37,018**	**$ 372,178**
Net income	**$ 95,476**	**$ 95,476**	**$ 95,476**	**$ 95,476**	**$ 95,476**	**$ 86,376**	**$ 802,615**

Income statement

Season 1–5

Revenue	Season 1—'07	Season 2—'08	Season 3—'09	Season 4—'10	Season 5—'11
Entry fee revenue	$1,090,000	$1,250,000	$1,470,000	$1,690,500	$1,944,075
Clinic revenue	$ 155,000	$ 203,000	$ 240,000	$ 276,000	$ 317,400
Sponsor revenue	$ 900,000	$1,290,000	$1,880,000	$2,600,000	$3,175,000
Program revenue	$ 38,066	$ 45,679	$ 54,815	$ 65,777	$ 78,933
Vendor revenue	$1,449,600	$1,739,520	$2,087,424	$2,504,909	$3,005,891
Concessions revenue	$ 51,045	$ 30,000	$ 50,000	$ 60,000	$ 72,000
General admission revenue	$ 21,735	$ 16,000	$ 25,000	$ 30,000	$ 36,000
Photography revenue	$ 70,896	$ 38,000	$ 50,000	$ 60,000	$ 72,000
Parking revenue	$ 13,167	$ 18,000	$ 25,000	$ 30,000	$ 36,000
Magazine revenue	$ 93,635	$ 25,000	$ 40,000	$ 48,000	$ 57,600
Total revenue	**$3,883,143**	**$4,655,199**	**$5,922,239**	**$7,365,186**	**$8,794,898**
Cost of sales					
Payroll	$1,321,000	$1,585,200	$1,902,240	$2,282,688	$2,739,226
Office rent	$ 12,000	$ 14,400	$ 17,280	$ 20,736	$ 24,883
Venue rent	$ 290,000	$ 348,000	$ 417,600	$ 501,120	$ 601,344
Prizes/awards	$ 250,000	$ 300,000	$ 360,000	$ 432,000	$ 518,400
Office supplies	$ 16,500	$ 19,800	$ 23,760	$ 28,512	$ 34,214
Total cost of sales	**$1,851,550**	**$2,267,400**	**$2,720,880**	**$3,265,056**	**$3,918,067**
Gross profit	**$2,031,593**	**$2,387,799**	**$3,201,359**	**$4,100,130**	**$4,876,831**
Operating expense					
Advertising	$ 60,000	$ 72,000	$ 86,400	$ 103,680	$ 124,416
Sales commissions	$ 112,050	$ 134,460	$ 161,352	$ 193,622	$ 232,347
Travel	$ 95,000	$ 114,000	$ 136,800	$ 164,160	$ 196,992
Accounting	$ 12,000	$ 14,400	$ 17,280	$ 20,736	$ 24,883
Admin salaries	$ 150,000	$ 180,000	$ 216,000	$ 259,200	$ 311,040
Depreciation	$ 60,000	$ 60,000	$ 60,000	$ 60,000	$ 60,000
General/event insurance	$ 340,000	$ 408,000	$ 489,600	$ 587,520	$ 705,024
Legal fees	$ 16,000	$ 19,200	$ 23,040	$ 27,648	$ 33,178
Office expenses	$ 12,000	$ 14,400	$ 17,280	$ 20,736	$ 24,883
Utilities	$ 24,000	$ 28,800	$ 34,560	$ 41,472	$ 49,766
Literature production	$ 24,000	$ 28,800	$ 34,560	$ 41,472	$ 49,766
Total operating expense	**$ 791,000**	**$1,045,260**	**$1,242,312**	**$1,478,774**	**$1,762,529**
Total costs	**$2,642,550**	**$3,312,660**	**$3,963,192**	**$4,743,830**	**$5,680,596**
Operating income	**$1,240,593**	**$1,342,539**	**$1,959,047**	**$2,621,356**	**$3,114,302**
Income tax	**$ 372,178**	**$ 402,762**	**$ 587,714**	**$ 786,407**	**$ 934,291**
Net income	**$ 802,615**	**$ 939,777**	**$1,371,333**	**$1,834,949**	**$2,180,011**

Balance sheet and cash flows

Preseason and season 1

Balance sheet	Preseason	April	May	June	July	Aug	Sept
Current assets							
Cash	$ 646,000	$ 655,782	$ 703,011	$ 678,049	$ 741,400	$ 814,384	$ 914,860
Total current assets	**$ 646,000**	**$ 655,782**	**$ 703,011**	**$ 678,049**	**$ 741,400**	**$ 814,384**	**$ 914,860**
Long term assets							
Equipment	$ 739,000	$ 739,000	$ 739,000	$ 739,000	$ 739,000	$ 739,000	$ 739,000
Furniture and supplies	$ 35,000	$ 35,000	$ 35,000	$ 35,000	$ 35,000	$ 35,000	$ 35,000
Total long term assets	$ 774,000	$ 774,000	$ 774,000	$ 774,000	$ 774,000	$ 774,000	$ 774,000
Accumulated depreciation	$ —	$ 5,000	$ 10,000	$ 15,000	$ 20,000	$ 25,000	$ 30,000
Net long term assets	$ 774,000	$ 769,000	$ 764,000	$ 759,000	$ 754,000	$ 749,000	$ 744,000
Total assets	**$1,420,000**	**$1,424,782**	**$1,467,011**	**$1,437,049**	**$1,563,384**	**$1,563,384**	**$1,658,860**
Liabilities & owners' equity							
Long term debt	$ —	$ —	$ —	$ —	$ —	$ —	$ —
Total liabilities	**$ —**	**$ —**	**$ —**	**$ —**	**$ —**	**$ —**	**$ —**
Owner/stockholder equity							
Owner's stake in company	$1,640,000	$1,640,000	$1,640,000	$1,640,000	$1,640,000	$1,640,000	$1,640,000
Retained earnings	$ (220,000)	$ 4,782	$ 47,011	$ 17,049	$ 75,400	$ 143,384	$ 238,860
Total owners' equity	**$1,420,000**	**$1,644,782**	**$1,687,011**	**$1,687,049**	**$1,715,400**	**$1,783,384**	**$1,878,860**
Total liabilities & equity	**$1,420,000**	**$1,644,782**	**$1,687,011**	**$1,687,049**	**$1,715,400**	**$1,783,384**	**$1,878,860**
Cash flows							
Operations during the year:							
Net income after taxes	$ (220,000)	$ 4,782	$ 42,229	$ (29,963)	$ 58,351	$ 67,985	$ 95,476
Add depreciation	$ —	$ 5,000	$ 5,000	$ 5,000	$ 5,000	$ 5,000	$ 5,000
Cash from operations	$ (220,000)	$ 9,782	$ 47,229	$ (24,963)	$ 63,351	$ 72,985	$ 100,476
Paid in capital	$1,640,000	$ —	$ —	$ —	$ —	$ —	$ —
Cash from operations and financing	**$1,420,000**	**$ 9,782**	**$ 47,229**	**$ (24,963)**	**$ 63,351**	**$ 72,985**	**$ 100,476**
Applications of cash:							
Long term assets	$ 774,000	$ —	$ —	$ —	$ —	$ —	$ —
Dividends disbursed							
Increase/(Decrease) in cash	$ 646,000	$ 9,782	$ 47,229	$ (24,963)	$ 63,351	$ 72,985	$ 100,476
Change in cash balance:							
Beginning cash balance	$ —	$ 646,000	$ 655,782	$ 703,011	$ 678,049	$ 741,400	$ 814,384
Increase/(Decrease) in cash	$ 646,000	$ 9,782	$ 47,229	$ (24,963)	$ 63,351	$ 72,985	$ 100,476
Ending cash balance	**$ 646,000**	**$ 655,782**	**$ 703,011**	**$ 678,049**	**$ 741,400**	**$ 814,384**	**$ 914,860**

(continued)

Balance sheet and cash flows [CONTINUED]

Preseason and season 1

Balance sheet	Oct	Nov	Dec	Jan	Feb	Mar	Year 1
Current assets							
Cash	$1,015,336	$1,115,812	$1,216,288	$1,316,764	$1,417,239	$1,508,615	$1,508,615
Total current assets	**$1,015,336**	**$1,115,812**	**$1,216,288**	**$1,316,764**	**$1,417,239**	**$1,508,615**	**$1,508,615**
Long term assets							
Equipment	$ 739,000	$ 739,000	$ 739,000	$ 739,000	$ 739,000	$ 739,000	$ 739,000
Furniture and supplies	$ 35,000	$ 35,000	$ 35,000	$ 35,000	$ 35,000	$ 35,000	$ 35,000
Total long term assets	$ 774,000	$ 774,000	$ 774,000	$ 774,000	$ 774,000	$ 774,000	$ 774,000
Accumulated depreciation	$ 35,000	$ 40,000	$ 45,000	$ 50,000	$ 55,000	$ 60,000	$ 60,000
Net long term assets	$ 739,000	$ 734,000	$ 729,000	$ 724,000	$ 719,000	$ 714,000	$ 714,000
Total assets	**$1,754,336**	**$1,849,812**	**$1,945,288**	**$2,040,764**	**$2,136,239**	**$2,222,615**	**$2,222,615**
Liabilities & owners' equity							
Long term debt	$ —	$ —	$ —	$ —	$ —	$ —	$ —
Total liabilities	**$ —**	**$ —**	**$ —**	**$ —**	**$ —**	**$ —**	**$ —**
Owner/stockholder equity							
Owner's stake in company	$1,640,000	$1,640,000	$1,640,000	$1,640,000	$1,640,000	$1,640,000	$1,640,000
Retained earnings	$ 334,336	$ 429,812	$ 525,288	$ 620,764	$ 716,239	$ 802,615	$ 802,615
Total owners' equity	$1,974,336	$2,069,812	$2,165,288	$2,260,764	$2,356,239	$2,442,615	$2,442,615
Total liabilities & equity	**$1,974,336**	**$2,069,812**	**$2,165,288**	**$2,260,764**	**$2,356,239**	**$2,442,615**	**$2,442,615**
Cash flows							
Operations during the year:							
Net income after taxes	$ 95,476	$ 95,476	$ 95,476	$ 95,476	$ 95,476	$ 86,376	$ 802,615
Add depreciation	$ 5,000	$ 5,000	$ 5,000	$ 5,000	$ 5,000	$ 5,000	$ 60,000
Cash from operations	$ 100,476	$ 100,476	$ 100,476	$ 100,476	$ 100,476	$ 91,376	$ 862,615
Paid in capital	$ —	$ —	$ —	$ —	$ —	$ —	$1,120,000
Cash from operations and financing	**$ 100,476**	**$ 100,476**	**$ 100,476**	**$ 100,476**	**$ 100,476**	**$ 91,376**	**$1,982,615**
Applications of cash:							
Long term assets	$ —	$ —	$ —	$ —	$ —	$ —	$ —
Dividends disbursed							
Increase/(Decrease) in cash	$ 100,476	$ 100,476	$ 100,476	$ 100,476	$ 100,476	$ 91,376	$1,982,615
Change in cash balance:							
Beginning cash balance	$ 914,860	$1,015,336	$1,115,812	$1,216,288	$1,316,764	$1,417,239	$ —
Increase/(Decrease) in cash	$ 100,476	$ 100,476	$ 100,476	$ 100,476	$ 100,476	$ 91,376	$1,982,615
Ending cash balance	**$1,015,336**	**$1,115,812**	**$1,216,288**	**$1,316,764**	**$1,417,239**	**$1,508,615**	**$1,982,615**

Balance sheet

Assets	Season 1 2007	Season 2 2008	Season 3 2009	Season 4 2010	Season 5 2011
Current assets					
Cash	$1,508,615	$2,982,392	$4,413,725	$6,308,674	$8,548,685
Total current assets	$1,508,615	$2,982,392	$4,413,725	$6,308,674	$8,548,685
Long term assets					
Equipment	$ 739,000	$ 739,000	$ 739,000	$ 739,000	$ 739,000
Furniture and supplies	$ 35,000	$ 35,000	$ 35,000	$ 35,000	$ 35,000
Total long term assets	$ 774,000	$ 774,000	$ 774,000	$ 774,000	$ 774,000
Accumulated depreciation	$ 60,000	$ 120,000	$ 180,000	$ 240,000	$ 300,000
Net long term assets	$ 714,000	$ 654,000	$ 594,000	$ 534,000	$ 474,000
Total assets	**$2,222,615**	**$3,636,392**	**$5,007,725**	**$6,842,674**	**$9,022,685**
Liabilities & owners' equity					
Long term debt	$ —	$ —	$ —	$ —	$ —
Total liabilities	$ —	$ —	$ —	$ —	$ —
Owner/stockholder equity					
Owner's stake in company	$1,400,000	$1,400,000	$1,400,000	$1,400,000	$1,400,000
retained earnings	$ 802,615	$1,742,392	$3,113,725	$4,948,674	$7,128,685
Total owners' equity	$2,202,615	$3,142,392	$4,513,725	$6,348,674	$8,528,685
Total liabilities & equity	**$2,202,615**	**$3,142,392**	**$4,513,725**	**$6,348,674**	**$8,528,685**

Cash flows

	Season 1 2007	Season 2 2008	Season 3 2009	Season 4 2010	Season 5 2011
Operations during the year:					
Net income after taxes	$ 802,615	$ 939,777	$1,371,333	$1,834,949	$2,180,011
Add depreciation	$ 60,000	$ 60,000	$ 60,000	$ 60,000	$ 60,000
Cash from operations	$ 862,615	$ 999,777	$1,431,333	$1,894,949	$2,240,011
Paid in capital	$1,400,000	$ 0	$ 0	$ 0	$ 0
Cash from operations and financing	$2,262,615	$ 999,777	$1,431,333	$1,894,949	$2,240,011
Applications of cash:					
Long term assets	$ —	$ 0	$ 0	$ 0	$ 0
Dividends disbursed					
Increase/(decrease) in cash	$2,262,615	$ 999,777	$1,431,333	$1,894,949	$2,240,011
Change in cash balance	$ —	$ —	$ —	$ —	$ —
Beginning cash balance	$ —	$1,982,615	$2,982,392	$4,413,725	$6,308,674
Increase/(decrease) in cash	$2,262,615	$ 999,777	$1,431,333	$1,894,949	$2,240,011
Ending cash balance	$1,982,615	$2,982,392	$4,413,725	$6,308,674	$8,548,685

BUSINESS PLAN TEMPLATE

USING THIS TEMPLATE

A business plan carefully spells out a company's projected course of action over a period of time, usually the first two to three years after the start-up. In addition, banks, lenders, and other investors examine the information and financial documentation before deciding whether or not to finance a new business venture. Therefore, a business plan is an essential tool in obtaining financing and should describe the business itself in detail as well as all important factors influencing the company, including the market, industry, competition, operations and management policies, problem solving strategies, financial resources and needs, and other vital information. The plan enables the business owner to anticipate costs, plan for difficulties, and take advantage of opportunities, as well as design and implement strategies that keep the company running as smoothly as possible.

This template has been provided as a model to help you construct your own business plan. Please keep in mind that there is no single acceptable format for a business plan, and that this template is in no way comprehensive, but serves as an example.

The business plans provided in this section are fictional and have been used by small business agencies as models for clients to use in compiling their own business plans.

GENERIC BUSINESS PLAN

Main headings included below are topics that should be covered in a comprehensive business plan. They include:

Business Summary

Purpose
Provides a brief overview of your business, succinctly highlighting the main ideas of your plan.

Includes
- Name and Type of Business
- Description of Product/Service
- Business History and Development
- Location
- Market
- Competition
- Management

- Financial Information

- Business Strengths and Weaknesses

- Business Growth

Table of Contents

Purpose

Organized in an Outline Format, the Table of Contents illustrates the selection and arrangement of information contained in your plan.

Includes

- Topic Headings and Subheadings

- Page Number References

Business History and Industry Outlook

Purpose

Examines the conception and subsequent development of your business within an industry specific context.

Includes

- Start-up Information

- Owner/Key Personnel Experience

- Location

- Development Problems and Solutions

- Investment/Funding Information

- Future Plans and Goals

- Market Trends and Statistics

- Major Competitors

- Product/Service Advantages

- National, Regional, and Local Economic Impact

Product/Service

Purpose

Introduces, defines, and details the product and/or service that inspired the information of your business.

Includes

- Unique Features

- Niche Served

- Market Comparison

- Stage of Product/Service Development

- Production

- Facilities, Equipment, and Labor

- Financial Requirements

- Product/Service Life Cycle

- Future Growth

Market Examination

Purpose

Assessment of product/service applications in relation to consumer buying cycles.

Includes

- Target Market

- Consumer Buying Habits

- Product/Service Applications

- Consumer Reactions

- Market Factors and Trends

- Penetration of the Market

- Market Share

- Research and Studies

- Cost

- Sales Volume and Goals

Competition

Purpose

Analysis of Competitors in the Marketplace.

Includes

- Competitor Information

- Product/Service Comparison

- Market Niche

- Product/Service Strengths and Weaknesses

- Future Product/Service Development

Marketing

Purpose

Identifies promotion and sales strategies for your product/service.

Includes

- Product/Service Sales Appeal

- Special and Unique Features

- Identification of Customers

- Sales and Marketing Staff

- Sales Cycles

- Type of Advertising/Promotion

- Pricing

- Competition

- Customer Services

Operations

Purpose

Traces product/service development from production/inception to the market environment.

Includes

- Cost Effective Production Methods

- Facility

- Location

- Equipment

- Labor

- Future Expansion

Administration and Management

Purpose

Offers a statement of your management philosophy with an in-depth focus on processes and procedures.

Includes

- Management Philosophy

- Structure of Organization

- Reporting System

- Methods of Communication

- Employee Skills and Training

- Employee Needs and Compensation

- Work Environment

- Management Policies and Procedures

- Roles and Responsibilities

Key Personnel

Purpose

Describes the unique backgrounds of principle employees involved in business.

Includes

- Owner(s)/Employee Education and Experience

- Positions and Roles

- Benefits and Salary

- Duties and Responsibilities

- Objectives and Goals

Potential Problems and Solutions

Purpose

Discussion of problem solving strategies that change issues into opportunities.

Includes

- Risks

- Litigation

- Future Competition
- Economic Impact
- Problem Solving Skills

Financial Information

Purpose

Secures needed funding and assistance through worksheets and projections detailing financial plans, methods of repayment, and future growth opportunities.

Includes

- Financial Statements
- Bank Loans
- Methods of Repayment
- Tax Returns
- Start-up Costs
- Projected Income (3 years)
- Projected Cash Flow (3 Years)
- Projected Balance Statements (3 years)

Appendices

Purpose

Supporting documents used to enhance your business proposal.

Includes

- Photographs of product, equipment, facilities, etc.
- Copyright/Trademark Documents
- Legal Agreements
- Marketing Materials
- Research and or Studies
- Operation Schedules
- Organizational Charts
- Job Descriptions
- Resumes
- Additional Financial Documentation

Fictional Food Distributor

Commercial Foods, Inc.

This plan demonstrates how a partnership can have a positive impact on a new business. It demonstrates how two individuals can carve a niche in the specialty foods market by offering gourmet foods to upscale restaurants and fine hotels. This plan is fictional and has not been used to gain funding from a bank or other lending institution.

3003 Avondale Ave.
Knoxville, TN, 37920

STATEMENT OF PURPOSE

Commercial Foods, Inc. seeks a loan of $75,000 to establish a new business. This sum, together with $5,000 equity investment by the principals, will be used as follows:

- Merchandise inventory $25,000

- Office fixture/equipment $12,000

- Warehouse equipment $14,000

- One delivery truck $10,000

- Working capital $39,000

- Total $100,000

DESCRIPTION OF THE BUSINESS

Commercial Foods, Inc. will be a distributor of specialty food service products to hotels and upscale restaurants in the geographical area of a 50 mile radius of Knoxville. Richard Roberts will direct the sales effort and John Williams will manage the warehouse operation and the office. One delivery truck will be used initially with a second truck added in the third year. We expect to begin operation of the business within 30 days after securing the requested financing.

MANAGEMENT

A. Richard Roberts is a native of Memphis, Tennessee. He is a graduate of Memphis State University with a Bachelor's degree from the School of Business. After graduation, he worked for a major manufacturer of specialty food service products as a detail sales person for five years, and, for the past three years, he has served as a product sales manager for this firm.

B. John Williams is a native of Nashville, Tennessee. He holds a B.S. Degree in Food Technology from the University of Tennessee. His career includes five years as a product development chemist in gourmet food products and five years as operations manager for a food service distributor.

Both men are healthy and energetic. Their backgrounds complement each other, which will ensure the success of Commercial Foods, Inc. They will set policies together and personnel decisions will be made jointly. Initial salaries for the owners will be $1,000 per month for the first few years. The spouses of both principals are successful in the business world and earn enough to support the families.

They have engaged the services of Foster Jones, CPA, and William Hale, Attorney, to assist them in an advisory capacity.

PERSONNEL

The firm will employ one delivery truck driver at a wage of $8.00 per hour. One office worker will be employed at $7.50 per hour. One part-time employee will be used in the office at $5.00 per hour. The driver will load and unload his own trucks. Mr. Williams will assist in the warehouse operation as needed to assist one stock person at $7.00 per hour. An additional delivery truck and driver will be added the third year.

LOCATION

The firm will lease a 20,000 square foot building at 3003 Avondale Ave., in Knoxville, which contains warehouse and office areas equipped with two-door truck docks. The annual rental is $9,000. The building was previously used as a food service warehouse and very little modification to the building will be required.

PRODUCTS AND SERVICES

The firm will offer specialty food service products such as soup bases, dessert mixes, sauce bases, pastry mixes, spices, and flavors, normally used by upscale restaurants and nice hotels. We are going after a niche in the market with high quality gourmet products. There is much less competition in this market than in standard run of the mill food service products. Through their work experiences, the principals have contacts with supply sources and with local chefs.

THE MARKET

We know from our market survey that there are over 200 hotels and upscale restaurants in the area we plan to serve. Customers will be attracted by a direct sales approach. We will offer samples of our products and product application data on use of our products in the finished prepared foods. We will cultivate the chefs in these establishments. The technical background of John Williams will be especially useful here.

COMPETITION

We find that we will be only distributor in the area offering a full line of gourmet food service products. Other foodservice distributors offer only a few such items in conjunction with their standard product line. Our survey shows that many of the chefs are ordering products from Atlanta and Memphis because of a lack of adequate local supply.

SUMMARY

Commercial Foods, Inc. will be established as a foodservice distributor of specialty food in Knoxville. The principals, with excellent experience in the industry, are seeking a $75,000 loan to establish the business. The principals are investing $25,000 as equity capital.

The business will be set up as an S Corporation with each principal owning 50% of the common stock in the corporation.

FICTIONAL HARDWARE STORE

OSHKOSH HARDWARE, INC.

The following plan outlines how a small hardware store can survive competition from large discount chains by offering products and providing expert advice in the use of any product it sells. This plan is fictional and has not been used to gain funding from a bank or other lending institution.
123 Main St.
Oshkosh, WI, 54901

EXECUTIVE SUMMARY

Oshkosh Hardware, Inc. is a new corporation that is going to establish a retail hardware store in a strip mall in Oshkosh, Wisconsin. The store will sell hardware of all kinds, quality tools, paint, and housewares. The business will make revenue and a profit by servicing its customers not only with needed hardware but also with expert advice in the use of any product it sells.

Oshkosh Hardware, Inc. will be operated by its sole shareholder, James Smith. The company will have a total of four employees. It will sell its products in the local market. Customers will buy our products because we will provide free advice on the use of all of our products and will also furnish a full refund warranty.

Oshkosh Hardware, Inc. will sell its products in the Oshkosh store staffed by three sales representatives. No additional employees will be needed to achieve its short and long range goals. The primary short range goal is to open the store by October 1, 1994. In order to achieve this goal a lease must be signed by July 1, 1994 and the complete inventory ordered by August 1, 1994.

Mr. James Smith will invest $30,000 in the business. In addition, the company will have to borrow $150,000 during the first year to cover the investment in inventory, accounts receivable, and furniture and equipment. The company will be profitable after six months of operation and should be able to start repayment of the loan in the second year.

THE BUSINESS

The business will sell hardware of all kinds, quality tools, paint, and housewares. We will purchase our products from three large wholesale buying groups.

In general our customers are homeowners who do their own repair and maintenance, hobbyists, and housewives. Our business is unique in that we will have a complete line of all hardware items and will be able to get special orders by overnight delivery. The business makes revenue and profits by servicing our customers not only with needed hardware but also with expert advice in the use of any product we sell. Our major costs for bringing our products to market are cost of merchandise of 36%, salaries of $45,000, and occupancy costs of $60,000.

Oshkosh Hardware, Inc.'s retail outlet will be located at 1524 Frontage Road, which is in a newly developed retail center of Oshkosh. Our location helps facilitate accessibility from all parts of town and reduces our delivery costs. The store will occupy 7500 square feet of space. The major equipment involved in our business is counters and shelving, a computer, a paint mixing machine, and a truck.

THE MARKET

Oshkosh Hardware, Inc. will operate in the local market. There are 15,000 potential customers in this market area. We have three competitors who control approximately 98% of the market at present. We feel we can capture 25% of the market within the next four years. Our major reason for believing this is that our staff is technically competent to advise our customers in the correct use of all products we sell.

After a careful market analysis, we have determined that approximately 60% of our customers are men and 40% are women. The percentage of customers that fall into the following age categories are:

Under 16: 0%

17-21: 5%

22-30: 30%

31-40: 30%

41-50: 20%

51-60: 10%

61-70: 5%

Over 70: 0%

The reasons our customers prefer our products is our complete knowledge of their use and our full refund warranty.

We get our information about what products our customers want by talking to existing customers. There seems to be an increasing demand for our product. The demand for our product is increasing in size based on the change in population characteristics.

SALES

At Oshkosh Hardware, Inc. we will employ three sales people and will not need any additional personnel to achieve our sales goals. These salespeople will need several years experience in home repair and power tool usage. We expect to attract 30% of our customers from newspaper ads, 5% of our customers from local directories, 5% of our customers from the yellow pages, 10% of our customers from family and friends, and 50% of our customers from current customers. The most cost effect source will be current customers. In general our industry is growing.

MANAGEMENT

We would evaluate the quality of our management staff as being excellent. Our manager is experienced and very motivated to achieve the various sales and quality assurance objectives we have set. We will use a management information system that produces key inventory, quality assurance, and sales data on a weekly basis. All data is compared to previously established goals for that week, and deviations are the primary focus of the management staff.

GOALS IMPLEMENTATION

The short term goals of our business are:

1.   Open the store by October 1, 1994

2.   Reach our breakeven point in two months

3.   Have sales of $100,000 in the first six months

In order to achieve our first short term goal we must:

1.   Sign the lease by July 1, 1994

2.   Order a complete inventory by August 1, 1994

In order to achieve our second short term goal we must:

1.   Advertise extensively in Sept. and Oct.

2.   Keep expenses to a minimum

In order to achieve our third short term goal we must:

1.   Promote power tool sales for the Christmas season

2.   Keep good customer traffic in Jan. and Feb.

The long term goals for our business are:

1.   Obtain sales volume of $600,000 in three years

2.   Become the largest hardware dealer in the city

3.   Open a second store in Fond du Lac

The most important thing we must do in order to achieve the long term goals for our business is to develop a highly profitable business with excellent cash flow.

FINANCE

Oshkosh Hardware, Inc. Faces some potential threats or risks to our business. They are discount house competition. We believe we can avoid or compensate for this by providing quality products complimented by quality advice on the use of every product we sell. The financial projections we have prepared are located at the end of this document.

JOB DESCRIPTION-GENERAL MANAGER

The General Manager of the business of the corporation will be the president of the corporation. He will be responsible for the complete operation of the retail hardware store which is owned by the corporation. A detailed description of his duties and responsibilities is as follows.

Sales

Train and supervise the three sales people. Develop programs to motivate and compensate these employees. Coordinate advertising and sales promotion effects to achieve sales totals as outlined in budget. Oversee purchasing function and inventory control procedures to insure adequate merchandise at all times at a reasonable cost.

Finance

Prepare monthly and annual budgets. Secure adequate line of credit from local banks. Supervise office personnel to insure timely preparation of records, statements, all government reports, control of receivables and payables, and monthly financial statements.

Administration

Perform duties as required in the areas of personnel, building leasing and maintenance, licenses and permits, and public relations.

Organizations, Agencies, & Consultants

A listing of Associations and Consultants of interest to entrepreneurs, followed by the ten Small Business Administration Regional Offices, Small Business Development Centers, Service Corps of Retired Executives offices, and Venture Capital and Finance Companies.

ASSOCIATIONS

This section contains a listing of associations and other agencies of interest to the small business owner. Entries are listed alphabetically by organization name.

American Business Women's Association
9100 Ward Pkwy.
PO Box 8728
Kansas City, MO 64114-0728
(800)228-0007
E-mail: abwa@abwa.org
Website: http://www.abwa.org
Jeanne Banks, National President

American Franchisee Association
53 W Jackson Blvd., Ste. 1157
Chicago, IL 60604
(312)431-0545
E-mail: info@franchisee.org
Website: http://www.franchisee.org
Susan P. Kezios, President

American Independent Business Alliance
222 S Black Ave.
Bozeman, MT 59715
(406)582-1255
E-mail: info@amiba.net
Website: http://www.amiba.net
Jennifer Rockne, Director

American Small Businesses Association
206 E College St., Ste. 201
Grapevine, TX 76051
800-942-2722
E-mail: info@asbaonline.org
Website: http://www.asbaonline.org/

American Women's Economic Development Corporation
216 East 45th St., 10th Floor
New York, NY 10017
(917)368-6100
Fax: (212)986-7114
E-mail: info@awed.org
Website: http://www.awed.org
Roseanne Antonucci, Exec. Dir.

Association for Enterprise Opportunity
1601 N Kent St., Ste. 1101
Arlington, VA 22209
(703)841-7760
Fax: (703)841-7748
E-mail: aeo@assoceo.org
Website: http://
www.microenterpriseworks.org
Bill Edwards, Exec.Dir.

Association of Small Business Development Centers
c/o Don Wilson
8990 Burke Lake Rd.
Burke, VA 22015
(703)764-9850
Fax: (703)764-1234
E-mail: info@asbdc-us.org
Website: http://www.asbdc-us.org
Don Wilson, Pres./CEO

BEST Employers Association
2505 McCabe Way
Irvine, CA 92614
(949)253-4080
800-433-0088
Fax: (714)553-0883
E-mail: info@bestlife.com
Website: http://www.bestlife.com
Donald R. Lawrenz, CEO

Center for Family Business
PO Box 24219
Cleveland, OH 44124
(440)460-5409
E-mail: grummi@aol.com
Dr. Leon A. Danco, Chm.

Coalition for Government Procurement
1990 M St. NW, Ste. 400
Washington, DC 20036
(202)331-0975
E-mail: info@thecgp.org
Website: http://www.coalgovpro.org
Paul Caggiano, Pres.

Employers of America
PO Box 1874
Mason City, IA 50402-1874
(641)424-3187
800-728-3187
Fax: (641)424-1673
E-mail: employer@employerhelp.org
Website: http://www.employerhelp.org
Jim Collison, Pres.

Family Firm Institute
200 Lincoln St., Ste. 201
Boston, MA 02111
(617)482-3045
Fax: (617)482-3049
E-mail: ffi@ffi.org
Website: http://www.ffi.org
Judy L. Green, Ph.D., Exec.Dir.

Independent Visually Impaired Enterprisers
500 S 3rd St., Apt. H
Burbank, CA 91502
(818)238-9321
E-mail:
abazyn@bazyncommunications.com
http://www.acb.org/affiliates
Adris Bazyn, Pres.

International Association for Business Organizations
3 Woodthorn Ct., Ste. 12
Owings Mills, MD 21117
(410)581-1373
E-mail: nahbb@msn.com
Rudolph Lewis, Exec. Officer

International Council for Small Business
The George Washington University
School of Business and Public
Management
2115 G St. NW, Ste. 403
Washington, DC 20052
(202)994-0704
Fax: (202)994-4930
E-mail: icsb@gwu.edu
Website: http://www.icsb.org
Susan G. Duffy. Admin.

International Small Business Consortium
3309 Windjammer St.
Norman, OK 73072
E-mail: sb@isbc.com
Website: http://www.isbc.com

Kauffman Center for Entrepreneurial Leadership
4801 Rockhill Rd.
Kansas City, MO 64110-2046
(816)932-1000
E-mail: info@kauffman.org
Website: http://www.entreworld.org

National Alliance for Fair Competition
3 Bethesda Metro Center, Ste. 1100
Bethesda, MD 20814
(410)235-7116
Fax: (410)235-7116
E-mail: ampesq@aol.com
Tony Ponticelli, Exec.Dir.

National Association for the Self-Employed
PO Box 612067
DFW Airport
Dallas, TX 75261-2067
(800)232-6273
E-mail: mpetron@nase.org
Website: http://www.nase.org
Robert Hughes, Pres.

National Association of Business Leaders
4132 Shoreline Dr., Ste. J & H
Earth City, MO 63045
Fax: (314)298-9110
E-mail: nabl@nabl.com
Website: http://www.nabl.com/
Gene Blumenthal, Contact

National Association of Private Enterprise
PO Box 15550
Long Beach, CA 90815
888-224-0953
Fax: (714)844-4942

Website: http://www.napeonline.net
Laura Squiers, Exec.Dir.

National Association of Small Business Investment Companies
666 11th St. NW, Ste. 750
Washington, DC 20001
(202)628-5055
Fax: (202)628-5080
E-mail: nasbic@nasbic.org
Website: http://www.nasbic.org
Lee W. Mercer, Pres.

National Business Association
PO Box 700728
5151 Beltline Rd., Ste. 1150
Dallas, TX 75370
(972)458-0900
800-456-0440
Fax: (972)960-9149
E-mail: info@nationalbusiness.org
Website: http://
www.nationalbusiness.org
Raj Nisankarao, Pres.

National Business Owners Association
PO Box 111
Stuart, VA 24171
(276)251-7500
(866)251-7505
Fax: (276)251-2217
E-mail: membershipservices@nboa.org
Website: http://www.rvmdb.com.nboa
Paul LaBarr, Pres.

National Center for Fair Competition
PO Box 220
Annandale, VA 22003
(703)280-4622
Fax: (703)280-0942
E-mail: kentonp1@aol.com
Kenton Pattie, Pres.

National Family Business Council
1640 W. Kennedy Rd.
Lake Forest, IL 60045
(847)295-1040
Fax: (847)295-1898
E-mail: lmsnfbc@email.msn.com
Jogn E. Messervey, Pres.

National Federation of Independent Business
53 Century Blvd., Ste. 250
Nashville, TN 37214
(615)872-5800
800-NFIBNOW
Fax: (615)872-5353
Website: http://www.nfib.org
Jack Faris, Pres. and CEO

National Small Business Association
1156 15th St. NW, Ste. 1100
Washington, DC 20005
(202)293-8830
800-345-6728
Fax: (202)872-8543
E-mail: press@nsba.biz
Website: http://www.nsba.biz
Rob Yunich, Dir. of Communications

PUSH Commercial Division
930 E 50th St.
Chicago, IL 60615-2702
(773)373-3366
Fax: (773)373-3571
E-mail: info@rainbowpush.org
Website: http://www.rainbowpush.org
Rev. Willie T. Barrow, Co-Chm.

Research Institute for Small and Emerging Business
722 12th St. NW
Washington, DC 20005
(202)628-8382
Fax: (202)628-8392
E-mail: info@riseb.org
Website: http://www.riseb.org
Allan Neece, Jr., Chm.

Sales Professionals USA
PO Box 149
Arvada, CO 80001
(303)534-4937
888-736-7767
E-mail: salespro@salesprofessionals-usa.com
Website: http://www.salesprofessionals-usa.com
Sharon Herbert, Natl. Pres.

Score Association - Service Corps of Retired Executives
409 3rd St. SW, 6th Fl.
Washington, DC 20024
(202)205-6762
800-634-0245
Fax: (202)205-7636
E-mail: media@score.org
Website: http://www.score.org
W. Kenneth Yancey, Jr., CEO

Small Business and Entrepreneurship Council
1920 L St. NW, Ste. 200
Washington, DC 20036
(202)785-0238
Fax: (202)822-8118
E-mail: membership@sbec.org
Website: http://www.sbecouncil.org
Karen Kerrigan, Pres./CEO

Small Business in Telecommunications
1331 H St. NW, Ste. 500
Washington, DC 20005
(202)347-4511
Fax: (202)347-8607
E-mail: sbt@sbthome.org
Website: http://www.sbthome.org
Lonnie Danchik, Chm.

Small Business Legislative Council
1010 Massachusetts Ave. NW, Ste. 540
Washington, DC 20005
(202)639-8500
Fax: (202)296-5333
E-mail: email@sblc.org
Website: http://www.sblc.org
John Satagaj, Pres.

Small Business Service Bureau
554 Main St.
PO Box 15014
Worcester, MA 01615-0014
(508)756-3513
800-343-0939
Fax: (508)770-0528
E-mail: membership@sbsb.com
Website: http://www.sbsb.com
Francis R. Carroll, Pres.

Small Publishers Association of North America
1618 W COlorado Ave.
Colorado Springs, CO 80904
(719)475-1726
Fax: (719)471-2182
E-mail: span@spannet.org
Website: http://www.spannet.org
Scott Flora, Exec. Dir.

SOHO America
PO Box 941
Hurst, TX 76053-0941
800-495-SOHO
E-mail: soho@1sas.com
Website: http://www.soho.org

Structured Employment Economic Development Corporation
915 Broadway, 17th Fl.
New York, NY 10010
(212)473-0255
Fax: (212)473-0357
E-mail: info@seedco.org
Website: http://www.seedco.org
William Grinker, CEO

Support Services Alliance
107 Prospect St.
Schoharie, NY 12157
800-836-4772
E-mail: info@ssamembers.com

Website: http://www.ssainfo.com
Steve COle, Pres.

United States Association for Small Business and Entrepreneurship
975 University Ave., No. 3260
Madison, WI 53706
(608)262-9982
Fax: (608)263-0818
E-mail: jgillman@wisc.edu
Website: http://www.ususbe.org
Joan Gillman, Exec. Dir.

CONSULTANTS

This section contains a listing of consultants specializing in small business development. It is arranged alphabetically by country, then by state or province, then by city, then by firm name.

CANADA

Alberta

Common Sense Solutions
3405 16A Ave.
Edmonton, AB, Canada
(403)465-7330
Fax: (403)465-7380
E-mail: gcoulson@comsensesolutions.com
Website: http://www.comsensesolutions.com

Varsity Consulting Group
School of Business
University of Alberta
Edmonton, AB, Canada T6G 2R6
(780)492-2994
Fax: (780)492-5400
Website: http://www.bus.ualberta.ca/vcg

Viro Hospital Consulting
42 Commonwealth Bldg., 9912 - 106 St. NW
Edmonton, AB, Canada T5K 1C5
(403)425-3871
Fax: (403)425-3871
E-mail: rpb@freenet.edmonton.ab.ca

British Columbia

SRI Strategic Resources Inc.
4330 Kingsway, Ste. 1600
Burnaby, BC, Canada V5H 4G7
(604)435-0627
Fax: (604)435-2782

E-mail: inquiry@sri.bc.ca
Website: http://www.sri.com

Andrew R. De Boda Consulting
1523 Milford Ave.
Coquitlam, BC, Canada V3J 2V9
(604)936-4527
Fax: (604)936-4527
E-mail: deboda@intergate.bc.ca
Website: http://www.ourworld.compuserve.com/homepages/deboda

The Sage Group Ltd.
980 - 355 Burrard St.
744 W Haistings, Ste. 410
Vancouver, BC, Canada V6C 1A5
(604)669-9269
Fax: (604)669-6622

Tikkanen-Bradley
1345 Nelson St., Ste. 202
Vancouver, BC, Canada V6E 1J8
(604)669-0583
E-mail: webmaster@tikkanenbradley.com
Website: http://www.tikkanenbradley.com

Ontario

The Cynton Co.
17 Massey St.
Brampton, ON, Canada L6S 2V6
(905)792-7769
Fax: (905)792-8116
E-mail: cynton@home.com
Website: http://www.cynton.com

Begley & Associates
RR 6
Cambridge, ON, Canada N1R 5S7
(519)740-3629
Fax: (519)740-3629
E-mail: begley@in.on.ca
Website: http://www.in.on.ca/~begley/index.htm

CRO Engineering Ltd.
1895 William Hodgins Ln.
Carp, ON, Canada K0A 1L0
(613)839-1108
Fax: (613)839-1406
E-mail: J.Grefford@ieee.ca
Website: http://www.geocities.com/WallStreet/District/7401/

Task Enterprises
Box 69, RR 2 Hamilton
Flamborough, ON, Canada L8N 2Z7
(905)659-0153
Fax: (905)659-0861

HST Group Ltd.
430 Gilmour St.
Ottawa, ON, Canada K2P 0R8
(613)236-7303
Fax: (613)236-9893

Harrison Associates
BCE Pl.
181 Bay St., Ste. 3740
PO Box 798
Toronto, ON, Canada M5J 2T3
(416)364-5441
Fax: (416)364-2875

TCI Convergence Ltd. Management Consultants
99 Crown's Ln.
Toronto, ON, Canada M5R 3P4
(416)515-4146
Fax: (416)515-2097
E-mail: tci@inforamp.net
Website: http://tciconverge.com/
index.1.html

Ken Wyman & Associates Inc.
64B Shuter St., Ste. 200
Toronto, ON, Canada M5B 1B1
(416)362-2926
Fax: (416)362-3039
E-mail: kenwyman@compuserve.com

JPL Business Consultants
82705 Metter Rd.
Wellandport, ON, Canada L0R 2J0
(905)386-7450
Fax: (905)386-7450
E-mail: plamarch@freenet.npiec.on.ca

Quebec

The Zimmar Consulting Partnership Inc.
Westmount
PO Box 98
Montreal, QC, Canada H3Z 2T1
(514)484-1459
Fax: (514)484-3063

Saskatchewan

Trimension Group
No. 104-110 Research Dr.
Innovation Place, SK, Canada S7N 3R3
(306)668-2560
Fax: (306)975-1156
E-mail: trimension@trimension.ca
Website: http://www.trimension.ca

Corporate Management Consultants
PO Box 7570 Station Main
Saskatoon, SK, Canada, S7K 4L4

(306)343-8415
Fax: (650)618-2742
E-mail:
cmccorporatemanagement@shaw.ca
Website: http://www.Corporatemanage-
mentconsultants.com
Gerald Rekve

UNITED STATES

Alabama

Business Planning Inc.
300 Office Park Dr.
Birmingham, AL 35223-2474
(205)870-7090
Fax: (205)870-7103

Tradebank of Eastern Alabama
546 Broad St., Ste. 3
Gadsden, AL 35901
(205)547-8700
Fax: (205)547-8718
E-mail: mansion@webex.com
Website: http://www.webex.com/~tea

Alaska

AK Business Development Center
3335 Arctic Blvd., Ste. 203
Anchorage, AK 99503
(907)562-0335
Free: 800-478-3474
Fax: (907)562-6988
E-mail: abdc@gci.net
Website: http://www.abdc.org

Business Matters
PO Box 287
Fairbanks, AK 99707
(907)452-5650

Arizona

Carefree Direct Marketing Corp.
8001 E Serene St.
PO Box 3737
Carefree, AZ 85377-3737
(480)488-4227
Fax: (480)488-2841

Trans Energy Corp.
1739 W 7th Ave.
Mesa, AZ 85202
(480)827-7915
Fax: (480)967-6601
E-mail: aha@clean-air.org
Website: http://www.clean-air.org

CMAS
5125 N 16th St.
Phoenix, AZ 85016
(602)395-1001
Fax: (602)604-8180

Comgate Telemanagement Ltd.
706 E Bell Rd., Ste. 105
Phoenix, AZ 85022
(602)485-5708
Fax: (602)485-5709
E-mail: comgate@netzone.com
Website: http://www.comgate.com

Moneysoft Inc.
1 E Camelback Rd. #550
Phoenix, AZ 85012
Free: 800-966-7797
E-mail: mbray@moneysoft.com

Harvey C. Skoog
PO Box 26439
Prescott Valley, AZ 86312
(520)772-1714
Fax: (520)772-2814

LMC Services
8711 E Pinnacle Peak Rd., No. 340
Scottsdale, AZ 85255-3555
(602)585-7177
Fax: (602)585-5880
E-mail: louws@earthlink.com

Sauerbrun Technology Group Ltd.
7979 E Princess Dr., Ste. 5
Scottsdale, AZ 85255-5878
(602)502-4950
Fax: (602)502-4292
E-mail: info@sauerbrun.com
Website: http://www.sauerbrun.com

Gary L. McLeod
PO Box 230
Sonoita, AZ 85637
Fax: (602)455-5661

Van Cleve Associates
6932 E 2nd St.
Tucson, AZ 85710
(520)296-2587
Fax: (520)296-3358

California

Acumen Group Inc.
(650)949-9349
Fax: (650)949-4845
E-mail: acumen-g@ix.netcom.com
Website: http://pw2.netcom.
com/~janed/acumen.html

On-line Career and Management Consulting
420 Central Ave., No. 314
Alameda, CA 94501
(510)864-0336
Fax: (510)864-0336
E-mail: career@dnai.com
Website: http://www.dnai.com/~career

Career Paths-Thomas E. Church & Associates Inc.
PO Box 2439
Aptos, CA 95001
(408)662-7950
Fax: (408)662-7955
E-mail: church@ix.netcom.com
Website: http://www.careerpaths-tom.com

Keck & Co. Business Consultants
410 Walsh Rd.
Atherton, CA 94027
(650)854-9588
Fax: (650)854-7240
E-mail: info@keckco.com
Website: http://www.keckco.com

Ben W. Laverty III, PhD, REA, CEI
4909 Stockdale Hwy., Ste. 132
Bakersfield, CA 93309
(661)283-8300
Free: 800-833-0373
Fax: (661)283-8313
E-mail: cstc@cstcsafety.com
Website: http://www.cstcsafety.com/cstc

Lindquist Consultants-Venture Planning
225 Arlington Ave.
Berkeley, CA 94707
(510)524-6685
Fax: (510)527-6604

Larson Associates
PO Box 9005
Brea, CA 92822
(714)529-4121
Fax: (714)572-3606
E-mail: ray@consultlarson.com
Website: http://www.consultlarson.com

Kremer Management Consulting
PO Box 500
Carmel, CA 93921
(408)626-8311
Fax: (408)624-2663
E-mail: ddkremer@aol.com

W and J PARTNERSHIP
PO Box 2499
18876 Edwin Markham Dr.

Castro Valley, CA 94546
(510)583-7751
Fax: (510)583-7645
E-mail: wamorgan@wjpartnership.com
Website: http://www.wjpartnership.com

JB Associates
21118 Gardena Dr.
Cupertino, CA 95014
(408)257-0214
Fax: (408)257-0216
E-mail: semarang@sirius.com

House Agricultural Consultants
PO Box 1615
Davis, CA 95617-1615
(916)753-3361
Fax: (916)753-0464
E-mail: infoag@houseag.com
Website: http://www.houseag.com/

3C Systems Co.
16161 Ventura Blvd., Ste. 815
Encino, CA 91436
(818)907-1302
Fax: (818)907-1357
E-mail: mark@3CSysCo.com
Website: http://www.3CSysCo.com

Technical Management Consultants
3624 Westfall Dr.
Encino, CA 91436-4154
(818)784-0626
Fax: (818)501-5575
E-mail: tmcrs@aol.com

RAINWATER-GISH & Associates, Business Finance & Development
317 3rd St., Ste. 3
Eureka, CA 95501
(707)443-0030
Fax: (707)443-5683

Global Tradelinks
451 Pebble Beach Pl.
Fullerton, CA 92835
(714)441-2280
Fax: (714)441-2281
E-mail: info@globaltradelinks.com
Website: http://www.globaltradelinks.com

Strategic Business Group
800 Cienaga Dr.
Fullerton, CA 92835-1248
(714)449-1040
Fax: (714)525-1631

Burnes Consulting
20537 Wolf Creek Rd.
Grass Valley, CA 95949
(530)346-8188

Free: 800-949-9021
Fax: (530)346-7704
E-mail: kent@burnesconsulting.com
Website: http://www.burnesconsulting.com

Pioneer Business Consultants
9042 Garfield Ave., Ste. 312
Huntington Beach, CA 92646
(714)964-7600

Beblie, Brandt & Jacobs Inc.
16 Technology, Ste. 164
Irvine, CA 92618
(714)450-8790
Fax: (714)450-8799
E-mail: darcy@bbjinc.com
Website: http://198.147.90.26

Fluor Daniel Inc.
3353 Michelson Dr.
Irvine, CA 92612-0650
(949)975-2000
Fax: (949)975-5271
E-mail: sales.consulting@fluordaniel.com
Website: http://www.fluordanielconsulting.com

MCS Associates
18300 Von Karman, Ste. 710
Irvine, CA 92612
(949)263-8700
Fax: (949)263-0770
E-mail: info@mcsassociates.com
Website: http://www.mcsassociates.com

Inspired Arts Inc.
4225 Executive Sq., Ste. 1160
La Jolla, CA 92037
(619)623-3525
Free: 800-851-4394
Fax: (619)623-3534
E-mail: info@inspiredarts.com
Website: http://www.inspiredarts.com

The Laresis Companies
PO Box 3284
La Jolla, CA 92038
(619)452-2720
Fax: (619)452-8744

RCL & Co.
PO Box 1143
737 Pearl St., Ste. 201
La Jolla, CA 92038
(619)454-8883
Fax: (619)454-8880

Comprehensive Business Services
3201 Lucas Cir.
Lafayette, CA 94549
(925)283-8272

Fax: (925)283-8272

The Ribble Group
27601 Forbes Rd., Ste. 52
Laguna Niguel, CA 92677
(714)582-1085
Fax: (714)582-6420
E-mail: ribble@deltanet.com

Norris Bernstein, CMC
9309 Marina Pacifica Dr. N
Long Beach, CA 90803
(562)493-5458
Fax: (562)493-5459
E-mail: norris@ctecomputer.com
Website: http://foodconsultants.com/
bernstein/

Horizon Consulting Services
1315 Garthwick Dr.
Los Altos, CA 94024
(415)967-0906
Fax: (415)967-0906

Brincko Associates Inc.
1801 Avenue of the Stars, Ste. 1054
Los Angeles, CA 90067
(310)553-4523
Fax: (310)553-6782

Rubenstein/Justman Management Consultants
2049 Century Park E, 24th Fl.
Los Angeles, CA 90067
(310)282-0800
Fax: (310)282-0400
E-mail: info@rjmc.net
Website: http://www.rjmc.net

F.J. Schroeder & Associates
1926 Westholme Ave.
Los Angeles, CA 90025
(310)470-2655
Fax: (310)470-6378
E-mail: fjsacons@aol.com
Website: http://www.mcninet.com/
GlobalLook/Fjschroe.html

Western Management Associates
5959 W Century Blvd., Ste. 565
Los Angeles, CA 90045-6506
(310)645-1091
Free: (888)788-6534
Fax: (310)645-1092
E-mail: gene@cfoforrent.com
Website: http://www.cfoforrent.com

Darrell Sell and Associates
Los Gatos, CA 95030
(408)354-7794
E-mail: darrell@netcom.com

Leslie J. Zambo
3355 Michael Dr.
Marina, CA 93933
(408)384-7086
Fax: (408)647-4199
E-mail: 104776.1552@compuserve.com

Marketing Services Management
PO Box 1377
Martinez, CA 94553
(510)370-8527
Fax: (510)370-8527
E-mail: markserve@biotechnet.com

William M. Shine Consulting Service
PO Box 127
Moraga, CA 94556-0127
(510)376-6516

Palo Alto Management Group Inc.
2672 Bayshore Pky., Ste. 701
Mountain View, CA 94043
(415)968-4374
Fax: (415)968-4245
E-mail: mburwen@pamg.com

BizplanSource
1048 Irvine Ave., Ste. 621
Newport Beach, CA 92660
Free: 888-253-0974
Fax: 800-859-8254
E-mail: info@bizplansource.com
Website: http://www.bizplansource.com
Adam Greengrass, President

The Market Connection
4020 Birch St., Ste. 203
Newport Beach, CA 92660
(714)731-6273
Fax: (714)833-0253

Muller Associates
PO Box 7264
Newport Beach, CA 92658
(714)646-1169
Fax: (714)646-1169

International Health Resources
PO Box 329
North San Juan, CA 95960-0329
(530)292-1266
Fax: (530)292-1243
Website: http://
www.futureofhealthcare.com

NEXUS - Consultants to Management
PO Box 1531
Novato, CA 94948
(415)897-4400
Fax: (415)898-2252
E-mail: jimnexus@aol.com

Aerospcace.Org
PO Box 28831
Oakland, CA 94604-8831
(510)530-9169
Fax: (510)530-3411
Website: http://www.aerospace.org

Intelequest Corp.
722 Gailen Ave.
Palo Alto, CA 94303
(415)968-3443
Fax: (415)493-6954
E-mail: frits@iqix.com

McLaughlin & Associates
66 San Marino Cir.
Rancho Mirage, CA 92270
(760)321-2932
Fax: (760)328-2474
E-mail: jackmcla@msn.com

Carrera Consulting Group, a division of Maximus
2110 21st St., Ste. 400
Sacramento, CA 95818
(916)456-3300
Fax: (916)456-3306
E-mail: central@carreraconsulting.com
Website: http://
www.carreraconsulting.com

Bay Area Tax Consultants and Bayhill Financial Consultants
1150 Bayhill Dr., Ste. 1150
San Bruno, CA 94066-3004
(415)952-8786
Fax: (415)588-4524
E-mail: baytax@compuserve.com
Website: http://www.baytax.com/

AdCon Services, LLC
8871 Hillery Dr.
Dan Diego, CA 92126
(858)433-1411
E-mail: adam@adconservices.com
Website: http://www.adconservices.com
Adam Greengrass

California Business Incubation Network
101 W Broadway, No. 480
San Diego, CA 92101
(619)237-0559
Fax: (619)237-0521

G.R. Gordetsky Consultants Inc.
11414 Windy Summit Pl.
San Diego, CA 92127
(619)487-4939
Fax: (619)487-5587
E-mail: gordet@pacbell.net

Freeman, Sullivan & Co.
131 Steuart St., Ste. 500
San Francisco, CA 94105
(415)777-0707
Free: 800-777-0737
Fax: (415)777-2420
Website: http://www.fsc-research.com

Ideas Unlimited
2151 California St., Ste. 7
San Francisco, CA 94115
(415)931-0641
Fax: (415)931-0880

Russell Miller Inc.
300 Montgomery St., Ste. 900
San Francisco, CA 94104
(415)956-7474
Fax: (415)398-0620
E-mail: rmi@pacbell.net
Website: http://www.rmisf.com

PKF Consulting
425 California St., Ste. 1650
San Francisco, CA 94104
(415)421-5378
Fax: (415)956-7708
E-mail: callahan@pkfc.com
Website: http://www.pkfonline.com

Welling & Woodard Inc.
1067 Broadway
San Francisco, CA 94133
(415)776-4500
Fax: (415)776-5067

Highland Associates
16174 Highland Dr.
San Jose, CA 95127
(408)272-7008
Fax: (408)272-4040

ORDIS Inc.
6815 Trinidad Dr.
San Jose, CA 95120-2056
(408)268-3321
Free: 800-446-7347
Fax: (408)268-3582
E-mail: ordis@ordis.com
Website: http://www.ordis.com

Stanford Resources Inc.
20 Great Oaks Blvd., Ste. 200
San Jose, CA 95119
(408)360-8400
Fax: (408)360-8410
E-mail: sales@stanfordsources.com
Website: http://
www.stanfordresources.com

Technology Properties Ltd. Inc.
PO Box 20250

San Jose, CA 95160
(408)243-9898
Fax: (408)296-6637
E-mail: sanjose@tplnet.com

Helfert Associates
1777 Borel Pl., Ste. 508
San Mateo, CA 94402-3514
(650)377-0540
Fax: (650)377-0472

Mykytyn Consulting Group Inc.
185 N Redwood Dr., Ste. 200
San Rafael, CA 94903
(415)491-1770
Fax: (415)491-1251
E-mail: info@mcgi.com
Website: http://www.mcgi.com

Omega Management Systems Inc.
3 Mount Darwin Ct.
San Rafael, CA 94903-1109
(415)499-1300
Fax: (415)492-9490
E-mail: omegamgt@ix.netcom.com

The Information Group Inc.
4675 Stevens Creek Blvd., Ste. 100
Santa Clara, CA 95051
(408)985-7877
Fax: (408)985-2945
E-mail: dvincent@tig-usa.com
Website: http://www.tig-usa.com

Cast Management Consultants
1620 26th St., Ste. 2040N
Santa Monica, CA 90404
(310)828-7511
Fax: (310)453-6831

Cuma Consulting Management
Box 724
Santa Rosa, CA 95402
(707)785-2477
Fax: (707)785-2478

The E-Myth Academy
131B Stony Cir., Ste. 2000
Santa Rosa, CA 95401
(707)569-5600
Free: 800-221-0266
Fax: (707)569-5700
E-mail: info@e-myth.com
Website: http://www.e-myth.com

Reilly, Connors & Ray
1743 Canyon Rd.
Spring Valley, CA 91977
(619)698-4808
Fax: (619)460-3892
E-mail: davidray@adnc.com

Management Consultants
Sunnyvale, CA 94087-4700
(408)773-0321

RJR Associates
1639 Lewiston Dr.
Sunnyvale, CA 94087
(408)737-7720
E-mail: bobroy@rjrassoc.com
Website: http://www.rjrassoc.com

Schwafel Associates
333 Cobalt Way, Ste. 21
Sunnyvale, CA 94085
(408)720-0649
Fax: (408)720-1796
E-mail: schwafel@ricochet.net
Website: http://www.patca.org

Staubs Business Services
23320 S Vermont Ave.
Torrance, CA 90502-2940
(310)830-9128
Fax: (310)830-9128
E-mail: Harry_L_Staubs@Lamg.com

Out of Your Mind...and Into the Marketplace
13381 White Sands Dr.
Tustin, CA 92780-4565
(714)544-0248
Free: 800-419-1513
Fax: (714)730-1414
E-mail: lpinson@aol.com
Website: http://www.business-plan.com

Independent Research Services
PO Box 2426
Van Nuys, CA 91404-2426
(818)993-3622

Ingman Company Inc.
7949 Woodley Ave., Ste. 120
Van Nuys, CA 91406-1232
(818)375-5027
Fax: (818)894-5001

Innovative Technology Associates
3639 E Harbor Blvd., Ste. 203E
Ventura, CA 93001
(805)650-9353

Grid Technology Associates
20404 Tufts Cir.
Walnut, CA 91789
(909)444-0922
Fax: (909)444-0922
E-mail: grid_technology@msn.com

Ridge Consultants Inc.
100 Pringle Ave., Ste. 580
Walnut Creek, CA 94596

(925)274-1990
Fax: (510)274-1956
E-mail: info@ridgecon.com
Website: http://www.ridgecon.com

Bell Springs Publishing
PO Box 1240
Willits, CA 95490
(707)459-6372
E-mail: bellsprings@sabernet
Website: http://www.bellsprings.com

Hutchinson Consulting and Appraisal
23245 Sylvan St., Ste. 103
Woodland Hills, CA 91367
(818)888-8175
Free: 800-977-7548
Fax: (818)888-8220
E-mail: r.f.hutchinson-cpa@worldnet.att.net

Colorado

Sam Boyer & Associates
4255 S Buckley Rd., No. 136
Aurora, CO 80013
Free: 800-785-0485
Fax: (303)766-8740
E-mail: samboyer@samboyer.com
Website: http://www.samboyer.com/

Ameriwest Business Consultants Inc.
PO Box 26266
Colorado Springs, CO 80936
(719)380-7096
Fax: (719)380-7096
E-mail: email@abchelp.com
Website: http://www.abchelp.com

GVNW Consulting Inc.
2270 La Montana Way
Colorado Springs, CO 80936
(719)594-5800
Fax: (719)594-5803
Website: http://www.gvnw.com

M-Squared Inc.
755 San Gabriel Pl.
Colorado Springs, CO 80906
(719)576-2554
Fax: (719)576-2554

Thornton Financial FNIC
1024 Centre Ave., Bldg. E
Fort Collins, CO 80526-1849
(970)221-2089
Fax: (970)484-5206

TenEyck Associates
1760 Cherryville Rd.
Greenwood Village, CO 80121-1503
(303)758-6129
Fax: (303)761-8286

Associated Enterprises Ltd.
13050 W Ceder Dr., Unit 11
Lakewood, CO 80228
(303)988-6695
Fax: (303)988-6739
E-mail: ael1@classic.msn.com

The Vincent Company Inc.
200 Union Blvd., Ste. 210
Lakewood, CO 80228
(303)989-7271
Free: 800-274-0733
Fax: (303)989-7570
E-mail: vincent@vincentco.com
Website: http://www.vincentco.com

Johnson & West Management Consultants Inc.
7612 S Logan Dr.
Littleton, CO 80122
(303)730-2810
Fax: (303)730-3219

Western Capital Holdings Inc.
10050 E Applwood Dr.
Parker, CO 80138
(303)841-1022
Fax: (303)770-1945

Connecticut

Stratman Group Inc.
40 Tower Ln.
Avon, CT 06001-4222
(860)677-2898
Free: 800-551-0499
Fax: (860)677-8210

Cowherd Consulting Group Inc.
106 Stephen Mather Rd.
Darien, CT 06820
(203)655-2150
Fax: (203)655-6427

Greenwich Associates
8 Greenwich Office Park
Greenwich, CT 06831-5149
(203)629-1200
Fax: (203)629-1229
E-mail: lisa@greenwich.com
Website: http://www.greenwich.com

Follow-up News
185 Pine St., Ste. 818
Manchester, CT 06040
(860)647-7542
Free: 800-708-0696
Fax: (860)646-6544
E-mail: Followupnews@aol.com

Lovins & Associates Consulting
309 Edwards St.

New Haven, CT 06511
(203)787-3367
Fax: (203)624-7599
E-mail: Alovinsphd@aol.com
Website: http://www.lovinsgroup.com

JC Ventures Inc.
4 Arnold St.
Old Greenwich, CT 06870-1203
(203)698-1990
Free: 800-698-1997
Fax: (203)698-2638

Charles L. Hornung Associates
52 Ned's Mountain Rd.
Ridgefield, CT 06877
(203)431-0297

Manus
100 Prospect St., S Tower
Stamford, CT 06901
(203)326-3880
Free: 800-445-0942
Fax: (203)326-3890
E-mail: manus1@aol.com
Website: http://www.RightManus.com

RealBusinessPlans.com
156 Westport Rd.
Wilton, CT 06897
(914)837-2886
E-mail: ct@realbusinessplans.com
Website: http://www.RealBusinessPlans.com
Tony Tecce

Delaware

Focus Marketing
61-7 Habor Dr.
Claymont, DE 19703
(302)793-3064

Daedalus Ventures Ltd.
PO Box 1474
Hockessin, DE 19707
(302)239-6758
Fax: (302)239-9991
E-mail: daedalus@mail.del.net

The Formula Group
PO Box 866
Hockessin, DE 19707
(302)456-0952
Fax: (302)456-1354
E-mail: formula@netaxs.com

Selden Enterprises Inc.
2502 Silverside Rd., Ste. 1
Wilmington, DE 19810-3740
(302)529-7113
Fax: (302)529-7442

E-mail: selden2@bellatlantic.net
Website: http://
www.seldenenterprises.com

District of Columbia

Bruce W. McGee and Associates
7826 Eastern Ave. NW, Ste. 30
Washington, DC 20012
(202)726-7272
Fax: (202)726-2946

McManis Associates Inc.
1900 K St. NW, Ste. 700
Washington, DC 20006
(202)466-7680
Fax: (202)872-1898
Website: http://www.mcmanis-mmi.com

Smith, Dawson & Andrews Inc.
1000 Connecticut Ave., Ste. 302
Washington, DC 20036
(202)835-0740
Fax: (202)775-8526
E-mail: webmaster@sda-inc.com
Website: http://www.sda-inc.com

Florida

BackBone, Inc.
20404 Hacienda Court
Boca Raton, FL 33498
(561)470-0965
Fax: 516-908-4038
E-mail: BPlans@backboneinc.com
Website: http://www.backboneinc.com
Charles Epstein, President

Whalen & Associates Inc.
4255 Northwest 26 Ct.
Boca Raton, FL 33434
(561)241-5950
Fax: (561)241-7414
E-mail: drwhalen@ix.netcom.com

E.N. Rysso & Associates
180 Bermuda Petrel Ct.
Daytona Beach, FL 32119
(386)760-3028
E-mail: erysso@aol.com

Virtual Technocrats LLC
560 Lavers Circle, #146
Delray Beach, FL 33444
(561)265-3509
E-mail: josh@virtualtechnocrats.com;
info@virtualtechnocrats.com
Website: http://
www.virtualtechnocrats.com
Josh Eikov, Managing Director

Eric Sands Consulting Services
6193 Rock Island Rd., Ste. 412
Fort Lauderdale, FL 33319
(954)721-4767
Fax: (954)720-2815
E-mail: easands@aol.com
Website: http://
www.ericsandsconsultig.com

Professional Planning Associates, Inc.
1975 E. Sunrise Blvd. Suite 607
Fort Lauderdale, FL 33304
(954)764-5204
Fax: 954-463-4172
E-mail: Mgoldstein@proplana.com
Website: http://proplana.com
Michael Goldstein, President

Host Media Corp.
3948 S 3rd St., Ste. 191
Jacksonville Beach, FL 32250
(904)285-3239
Fax: (904)285-5618
E-mail: msconsulting@compuserve.com
Website: http://
www.mediaservicesgroup.com

William V. Hall
1925 Brickell, Ste. D-701
Miami, FL 33129
(305)856-9622
Fax: (305)856-4113
E-mail: williamvhall@compuserve.com

F.A. McGee Inc.
800 Claughton Island Dr., Ste. 401
Miami, FL 33131
(305)377-9123

Taxplan Inc.
Mirasol International Ctr.
2699 Collins Ave.
Miami Beach, FL 33140
(305)538-3303

T.C. Brown & Associates
8415 Excalibur Cir., Apt. B1
Naples, FL 34108
(941)594-1949
Fax: (941)594-0611
E-mail: tcater@naples.net.com

RLA International Consulting
713 Lagoon Dr.
North Palm Beach, FL 33408
(407)626-4258
Fax: (407)626-5772

Comprehensive Franchising Inc.
2465 Ridgecrest Ave.
Orange Park, FL 32065
(904)272-6567

Free: 800-321-6567
Fax: (904)272-6750
E-mail: theimp@cris.com
Website: http://www.franchise411.com

Hunter G. Jackson Jr. - Consulting Environmental Physicist
PO Box 618272
Orlando, FL 32861-8272
(407)295-4188
E-mail: hunterjackson@juno.com

F. Newton Parks
210 El Brillo Way
Palm Beach, FL 33480
(561)833-1727
Fax: (561)833-4541

Avery Business Development Services
2506 St. Michel Ct.
Ponte Vedra Beach, FL 32082
(904)285-6033
Fax: (904)285-6033

Strategic Business Planning Co.
PO Box 821006
South Florida, FL 33082-1006
(954)704-9100
Fax: (954)438-7333
E-mail: info@bizplan.com
Website: http://www.bizplan.com

Dufresne Consulting Group Inc.
10014 N Dale Mabry, Ste. 101
Tampa, FL 33618-4426
(813)264-4775
Fax: (813)264-9300
Website: http://www.dcgconsult.com

Agrippa Enterprises Inc.
PO Box 175
Venice, FL 34284-0175
(941)355-7876
E-mail: webservices@agrippa.com
Website: http://www.agrippa.com

Center for Simplified Strategic Planning Inc.
PO Box 3324
Vero Beach, FL 32964-3324
(561)231-3636
Fax: (561)231-1099
Website: http://www.cssp.com

Georgia

Marketing Spectrum Inc.
115 Perimeter Pl., Ste. 440
Atlanta, GA 30346
(770)395-7244
Fax: (770)393-4071

Business Ventures Corp.
1650 Oakbrook Dr., Ste. 405
Norcross, GA 30093
(770)729-8000
Fax: (770)729-8028

Informed Decisions Inc.
100 Falling Cheek
Sautee Nacoochee, GA 30571
(706)878-1905
Fax: (706)878-1802
E-mail: skylake@compuserve.com

Tom C. Davis & Associates, P.C.
3189 Perimeter Rd.
Valdosta, GA 31602
(912)247-9801
Fax: (912)244-7704
E-mail: mail@tcdcpa.com
Website: http://www.tcdcpa.com/

Illinois

TWD and Associates
431 S Patton
Arlington Heights, IL 60005
(847)398-6410
Fax: (847)255-5095
E-mail: tdoo@aol.com

Management Planning Associates Inc.
2275 Half Day Rd., Ste. 350
Bannockburn, IL 60015-1277
(847)945-2421
Fax: (847)945-2425

Phil Faris Associates
86 Old Mill Ct.
Barrington, IL 60010
(847)382-4888
Fax: (847)382-4890
E-mail: pfaris@meginsnet.net

Seven Continents Technology
787 Stonebridge
Buffalo Grove, IL 60089
(708)577-9653
Fax: (708)870-1220

Grubb & Blue Inc.
2404 Windsor Pl.
Champaign, IL 61820
(217)366-0052
Fax: (217)356-0117

ACE Accounting Service Inc.
3128 N Bernard St.
Chicago, IL 60618
(773)463-7854
Fax: (773)463-7854

AON Consulting Worldwide
200 E Randolph St., 10th Fl.
Chicago, IL 60601
(312)381-4800
Free: 800-438-6487
Fax: (312)381-0240
Website: http://www.aon.com

FMS Consultants
5801 N Sheridan Rd., Ste. 3D
Chicago, IL 60660
(773)561-7362
Fax: (773)561-6274

Grant Thornton
800 1 Prudential Plz.
130 E Randolph St.
Chicago, IL 60601
(312)856-0001
Fax: (312)861-1340
E-mail: gtinfo@gt.com
Website: http://www.grantthornton.com

Kingsbury International Ltd.
5341 N Glenwood Ave.
Chicago, IL 60640
(773)271-3030
Fax: (773)728-7080
E-mail: jetlag@mcs.com
Website: http://www.kingbiz.com

MacDougall & Blake Inc.
1414 N Wells St., Ste. 311
Chicago, IL 60610-1306
(312)587-3330
Fax: (312)587-3699
E-mail: jblake@compuserve.com

James C. Osburn Ltd.
6445 N. Western Ave., Ste. 304
Chicago, IL 60645
(773)262-4428
Fax: (773)262-6755
E-mail: osburnltd@aol.com

Tarifero & Tazewell Inc.
211 S Clark
Chicago, IL 60690
(312)665-9714
Fax: (312)665-9716

Human Energy Design Systems
620 Roosevelt Dr.
Edwardsville, IL 62025
(618)692-0258
Fax: (618)692-0819

China Business Consultants Group
931 Dakota Cir.
Naperville, IL 60563
(630)778-7992
Fax: (630)778-7915

E-mail: cbcq@aol.com

Center for Workforce Effectiveness
500 Skokie Blvd., Ste. 222
Northbrook, IL 60062
(847)559-8777
Fax: (847)559-8778
E-mail: office@cwelink.com
Website: http://www.cwelink.com

Smith Associates
1320 White Mountain Dr.
Northbrook, IL 60062
(847)480-7200
Fax: (847)480-9828

Francorp Inc.
20200 Governors Dr.
Olympia Fields, IL 60461
(708)481-2900
Free: 800-372-6244
Fax: (708)481-5885
E-mail: francorp@aol.com
Website: http://www.francorpinc.com

Camber Business Strategy Consultants
1010 S Plum Tree Ct
Palatine, IL 60078-0986
(847)202-0101
Fax: (847)705-7510
E-mail: camber@ameritech.net

Partec Enterprise Group
5202 Keith Dr.
Richton Park, IL 60471
(708)503-4047
Fax: (708)503-9468

Rockford Consulting Group Ltd.
Century Plz., Ste. 206
7210 E State St.
Rockford, IL 61108
(815)229-2900
Free: 800-667-7495
Fax: (815)229-2612
E-mail: rligus@RockfordConsulting.com
Website: http://
www.RockfordConsulting.com

RSM McGladrey Inc.
1699 E Woodfield Rd., Ste. 300
Schaumburg, IL 60173-4969
(847)413-6900
Fax: (847)517-7067
Website: http://www.rsmmcgladrey.com

A.D. Star Consulting
320 Euclid
Winnetka, IL 60093
(847)446-7827
Fax: (847)446-7827
E-mail: startwo@worldnet.att.net

ORGANIZATIONS, AGENCIES, & CONSULTANTS

Indiana

Modular Consultants Inc.
3109 Crabtree Ln.
Elkhart, IN 46514
(219)264-5761
Fax: (219)264-5761
E-mail: sasabo5313@aol.com

Midwest Marketing Research
PO Box 1077
Goshen, IN 46527
(219)533-0548
Fax: (219)533-0540
E-mail: 103365.654@compuserve

Ketchum Consulting Group
8021 Knue Rd., Ste. 112
Indianapolis, IN 46250
(317)845-5411
Fax: (317)842-9941

MDI Management Consulting
1519 Park Dr.
Munster, IN 46321
(219)838-7909
Fax: (219)838-7909

Iowa

McCord Consulting Group Inc.
4533 Pine View Dr. NE
PO Box 11024
Cedar Rapids, IA 52410
(319)378-0077
Fax: (319)378-1577
E-mail: smmccord@hom.com
Website: http://www.mccordgroup.com

Management Solutions L.C.
3815 Lincoln Pl. Dr.
Des Moines, IA 50312
(515)277-6408
Fax: (515)277-3506
E-mail: wasunimers@uswest.net

Grandview Marketing
15 Red Bridge Dr.
Sioux City, IA 51104
(712)239-3122
Fax: (712)258-7578
E-mail: eandrews@pionet.net

Kansas

Assessments in Action
513A N Mur-Len
Olathe, KS 66062
(913)764-6270
Free: (888)548-1504
Fax: (913)764-6495
E-mail: lowdene@qni.com

Website: http://www.assessments-in-action.com

Maine

Edgemont Enterprises
PO Box 8354
Portland, ME 04104
(207)871-8964
Fax: (207)871-8964

Pan Atlantic Consultants
5 Milk St.
Portland, ME 04101
(207)871-8622
Fax: (207)772-4842
E-mail: pmurphy@maine.rr.com
Website: http://www.panatlantic.net

Maryland

Clemons & Associates Inc.
5024-R Campbell Blvd.
Baltimore, MD 21236
(410)931-8100
Fax: (410)931-8111
E-mail: info@clemonsmgmt.com
Website: http://www.clemonsmgmt.com

Imperial Group Ltd.
305 Washington Ave., Ste. 204
Baltimore, MD 21204-6009
(410)337-8500
Fax: (410)337-7641

Leadership Institute
3831 Yolando Rd.
Baltimore, MD 21218
(410)366-9111
Fax: (410)243-8478
E-mail: behconsult@aol.com

Burdeshaw Associates Ltd.
4701 Sangamore Rd.
Bethesda, MD 20816-2508
(301)229-5800
Fax: (301)229-5045
E-mail: jstacy@burdeshaw.com
Website: http://www.burdeshaw.com

Michael E. Cohen
5225 Pooks Hill Rd., Ste. 1119 S
Bethesda, MD 20814
(301)530-5738
Fax: (301)530-2988
E-mail: mecohen@crosslink.net

World Development Group Inc.
5272 River Rd., Ste. 650
Bethesda, MD 20816-1405
(301)652-1818
Fax: (301)652-1250

E-mail: wdg@has.com
Website: http://www.worlddg.com

Swartz Consulting
PO Box 4301
Crofton, MD 21114-4301
(301)262-6728

Software Solutions International Inc.
9633 Duffer Way
Gaithersburg, MD 20886
(301)330-4136
Fax: (301)330-4136

Strategies Inc.
8 Park Center Ct., Ste. 200
Owings Mills, MD 21117
(410)363-6669
Fax: (410)363-1231
E-mail: strategies@strat1.com
Website: http://www.strat1.com

Hammer Marketing Resources
179 Inverness Rd.
Severna Park, MD 21146
(410)544-9191
Fax: (305)675-3277
E-mail: info@gohammer.com
Website: http://www.gohammer.com

Andrew Sussman & Associates
13731 Kretsinger
Smithsburg, MD 21783
(301)824-2943
Fax: (301)824-2943

Massachusetts

Geibel Marketing and Public Relations
PO Box 611
Belmont, MA 02478-0005
(617)484-8285
Fax: (617)489-3567
E-mail: jgeibel@geibelpr.com
Website: http://www.geibelpr.com

Bain & Co.
2 Copley Pl.
Boston, MA 02116
(617)572-2000
Fax: (617)572-2427
E-mail: corporate.inquiries@bain.com
Website: http://www.bain.com

Mehr & Co.
62 Kinnaird St.
Cambridge, MA 02139
(617)876-3311
Fax: (617)876-3023
E-mail: mehrco@aol.com

Monitor Company Inc.
2 Canal Park
Cambridge, MA 02141
(617)252-2000
Fax: (617)252-2100
Website: http://www.monitor.com

Information & Research Associates
PO Box 3121
Framingham, MA 01701
(508)788-0784

Walden Consultants Ltd.
252 Pond St.
Hopkinton, MA 01748
(508)435-4882
Fax: (508)435-3971
Website: http://
www.waldenconsultants.com

Jeffrey D. Marshall
102 Mitchell Rd.
Ipswich, MA 01938-1219
(508)356-1113
Fax: (508)356-2989

Consulting Resources Corp.
6 Northbrook Park
Lexington, MA 02420
(781)863-1222
Fax: (781)863-1441
E-mail: res@consultingresources.net
Website: http://
www.consultingresources.net

Planning Technologies Group L.L.C.
92 Hayden Ave.
Lexington, MA 02421
(781)778-4678
Fax: (781)861-1099
E-mail: ptg@plantech.com
Website: http://www.plantech.com

Kalba International Inc.
23 Sandy Pond Rd.
Lincoln, MA 01773
(781)259-9589
Fax: (781)259-1460
E-mail: info@kalbainternational.com
Website: http://
www.kalbainternational.com

VMB Associates Inc.
115 Ashland St.
Melrose, MA 02176
(781)665-0623
Fax: (425)732-7142
E-mail: vmbinc@aol.com

The Company Doctor
14 Pudding Stone Ln.
Mendon, MA 01756

(508)478-1747
Fax: (508)478-0520

Data and Strategies Group Inc.
190 N Main St.
Natick, MA 01760
(508)653-9990
Fax: (508)653-7799
E-mail: dsginc@dsggroup.com
Website: http://www.dsggroup.com

The Enterprise Group
73 Parker Rd.
Needham, MA 02494
(617)444-6631
Fax: (617)433-9991
E-mail: lsacco@world.std.com
Website: http://www.enterprise-group.com

PSMJ Resources Inc.
10 Midland Ave.
Newton, MA 02458
(617)965-0055
Free: 800-537-7765
Fax: (617)965-5152
E-mail: psmj@tiac.net
Website: http://www.psmj.com

Scheur Management Group Inc.
255 Washington St., Ste. 100
Newton, MA 02458-1611
(617)969-7500
Fax: (617)969-7508
E-mail: smgnow@scheur.com
Website: http://www.scheur.com

I.E.E.E., Boston Section
240 Bear Hill Rd., 202B
Waltham, MA 02451-1017
(781)890-5294
Fax: (781)890-5290

Business Planning and Consulting Services
20 Beechwood Ter.
Wellesley, MA 02482
(617)237-9151
Fax: (617)237-9151

Michigan

Walter Frederick Consulting
1719 South Blvd.
Ann Arbor, MI 48104
(313)662-4336
Fax: (313)769-7505

Fox Enterprises
6220 W Freeland Rd.
Freeland, MI 48623
(517)695-9170

Fax: (517)695-9174
E-mail: foxjw@concentric.net
Website: http://www.cris.com/~foxjw

G.G.W. and Associates
1213 Hampton
Jackson, MI 49203
(517)782-2255
Fax: (517)782-2255

Altamar Group Ltd.
6810 S Cedar, Ste. 2-B
Lansing, MI 48911
(517)694-0910
Free: 800-443-2627
Fax: (517)694-1377

Sheffieck Consultants Inc.
23610 Greening Dr.
Novi, MI 48375-3130
(248)347-3545
Fax: (248)347-3530
E-mail: cfsheff@concentric.net

Rehmann, Robson PC
5800 Gratiot
Saginaw, MI 48605
(517)799-9580
Fax: (517)799-0227
Website: http://www.rrpc.com

Francis & Co.
17200 W 10 Mile Rd., Ste. 207
Southfield, MI 48075
(248)559-7600
Fax: (248)559-5249

Private Ventures Inc.
16000 W 9 Mile Rd., Ste. 504
Southfield, MI 48075
(248)569-1977
Free: 800-448-7614
Fax: (248)569-1838
E-mail: pventuresi@aol.com

JGK Associates
14464 Kerner Dr.
Sterling Heights, MI 48313
(810)247-9055
Fax: (248)822-4977
E-mail: kozlowski@home.com

Minnesota

Health Fitness Corp.
3500 W 80th St., Ste. 130
Bloomington, MN 55431
(612)831-6830
Fax: (612)831-7264

Consatech Inc.
PO Box 1047

Burnsville, MN 55337
(612)953-1088
Fax: (612)435-2966

Robert F. Knotek
14960 Ironwood Ct.
Eden Prairie, MN 55346
(612)949-2875

DRI Consulting
7715 Stonewood Ct.
Edina, MN 55439
(612)941-9656
Fax: (612)941-2693
E-mail: dric@dric.com
Website: http://www.dric.com

Markin Consulting
12072 87th Pl. N
Maple Grove, MN 55369
(612)493-3568
Fax: (612)493-5744
E-mail: markin@markinconsulting.com
Website: http://
www.markinconsulting.com

**Minnesota Cooperation Office
for Small Business & Job
Creation Inc.**
5001 W 80th St., Ste. 825
Minneapolis, MN 55437
(612)830-1230
Fax: (612)830-1232
E-mail: mncoop@msn.com
Website: http://www.mnco.org

Enterprise Consulting Inc.
PO Box 1111
Minnetonka, MN 55345
(612)949-5909
Fax: (612)906-3965

Amdahl International
724 1st Ave. SW
Rochester, MN 55902
(507)252-0402
Fax: (507)252-0402
E-mail: amdahl@best-service.com
Website: http://www.wp.com/
amdahl_int

Power Systems Research
1365 Corporate Center Curve,
2nd Fl.
St. Paul, MN 55121
(612)905-8400
Free: (888)625-8612
Fax: (612)454-0760
E-mail: Barb@Powersys.com
Website: http://www.powersys.com

Missouri

Business Planning and Development Corp.
4030 Charlotte St.
Kansas City, MO 64110
(816)753-0495
E-mail: humph@bpdev.demon.co.uk
Website: http://www.bpdev.demon.co.uk

CFO Service
10336 Donoho
St. Louis, MO 63131
(314)750-2940
E-mail: jskae@cfoservice.com
Website: http://www.cfoservice.com

Nebraska

**International Management Consulting
Group Inc.**
1309 Harlan Dr., Ste. 205
Bellevue, NE 68005
(402)291-4545
Free: 800-665-IMCG
Fax: (402)291-4343
E-mail: imcg@neonramp.com
Website: http://www.mgtconsulting.com

**Heartland Management Consulting
Group**
1904 Barrington Pky.
Papillion, NE 68046
(402)339-2387
Fax: (402)339-1319

Nevada

The DuBois Group
865 Tahoe Blvd., Ste. 108
Incline Village, NV 89451
(775)832-0550
Free: 800-375-2935
Fax: (775)832-0556
E-mail: DuBoisGrp@aol.com

New Hampshire

Wolff Consultants
10 Buck Rd.
Hanover, NH 03755
(603)643-6015

BPT Consulting Associates Ltd.
12 Parmenter Rd., Ste. B-6
Londonderry, NH 03053
(603)437-8484
Free: (888)278-0030
Fax: (603)434-5388
E-mail: bptcons@tiac.net
Website: http://www.bptconsulting.com

New Jersey

Bedminster Group Inc.
1170 Rte. 22 E
Bridgewater, NJ 08807
(908)500-4155
Fax: (908)766-0780
E-mail: info@bedminstergroup.com
Website: http://
www.bedminstergroup.com
Fax: (202)806-1777
Terry Strong, Acting Regional Dir.

Delta Planning Inc.
PO Box 425
Denville, NJ 07834
(913)625-1742
Free: 800-672-0762
Fax: (973)625-3531
E-mail: DeltaP@worldnet.att.net
Website: http://deltaplanning.com

Kumar Associates Inc.
1004 Cumbermeade Rd.
Fort Lee, NJ 07024
(201)224-9480
Fax: (201)585-2343
E-mail: mail@kumarassociates.com
Website: http://kumarassociates.com

John Hall & Company Inc.
PO Box 187
Glen Ridge, NJ 07028
(973)680-4449
Fax: (973)680-4581
E-mail: jhcompany@aol.com

Market Focus
PO Box 402
Maplewood, NJ 07040
(973)378-2470
Fax: (973)378-2470
E-mail: mcss66@marketfocus.com

Vanguard Communications Corp.
100 American Rd.
Morris Plains, NJ 07950
(973)605-8000
Fax: (973)605-8329
Website: http://www.vanguard.net/

ConMar International Ltd.
1901 US Hwy. 130
North Brunswick, NJ 08902
(732)940-8347
Fax: (732)274-1199

KLW New Products
156 Cedar Dr.
Old Tappan, NJ 07675
(201)358-1300
Fax: (201)664-2594

E-mail: lrlarsen@usa.net
Website: http://
www.klwnewproducts.com

PA Consulting Group
315A Enterprise Dr.
Plainsboro, NJ 08536
(609)936-8300
Fax: (609)936-8811
E-mail: info@paconsulting.com
Website: http://www.pa-consulting.com

Aurora Marketing Management Inc.
66 Witherspoon St., Ste. 600
Princeton, NJ 08542
(908)904-1125
Fax: (908)359-1108
E-mail: aurora2@voicenet.com
Website: http://
www.auroramarketing.net

Smart Business Supersite
88 Orchard Rd., CN-5219
Princeton, NJ 08543
(908)321-1924
Fax: (908)321-5156
E-mail: irv@smartbiz.com
Website: http://www.smartbiz.com

Tracelin Associates
1171 Main St., Ste. 6K
Rahway, NJ 07065
(732)381-3288

Schkeeper Inc.
130-6 Bodman Pl.
Red Bank, NJ 07701
(732)219-1965
Fax: (732)530-3703

Henry Branch Associates
2502 Harmon Cove Twr.
Secaucus, NJ 07094
(201)866-2008
Fax: (201)601-0101
E-mail: hbranch161@home.com

Robert Gibbons & Company Inc.
46 Knoll Rd.
Tenafly, NJ 07670-1050
(201)871-3933
Fax: (201)871-2173
E-mail: crisisbob@aol.com

PMC Management Consultants Inc.
6 Thistle Ln.
Three Bridges, NJ 08887-0332
(908)788-1014
Free: 800-PMC-0250
Fax: (908)806-7287
E-mail: int@pmc-management.com

Website: http://www.pmc-management.com

R.W. Bankart & Associates
20 Valley Ave., Ste. D-2
Westwood, NJ 07675-3607
(201)664-7672

New Mexico

Vondle & Associates Inc.
4926 Calle de Tierra, NE
Albuquerque, NM 87111
(505)292-8961
Fax: (505)296-2790
E-mail: vondle@aol.com

InfoNewMexico
2207 Black Hills Rd., NE
Rio Rancho, NM 87124
(505)891-2462
Fax: (505)896-8971

New York

Powers Research and Training Institute
PO Box 78
Bayville, NY 11709
(516)628-2250
Fax: (516)628-2252
E-mail: powercocch@compuserve.com
Website: http://www.nancypowers.com

Consortium House
296 Wittenberg Rd.
Bearsville, NY 12409
(845)679-8867
Fax: (845)679-9248
E-mail: eugenegs@aol.com
Website: http://www.chpub.com

Progressive Finance Corp.
3549 Tiemann Ave.
Bronx, NY 10469
(718)405-9029
Free: 800-225-8381
Fax: (718)405-1170

Wave Hill Associates Inc.
2621 Palisade Ave., Ste. 15-C
Bronx, NY 10463
(718)549-7368
Fax: (718)601-9670
E-mail: pepper@compuserve.com

Management Insight
96 Arlington Rd.
Buffalo, NY 14221
(716)631-3319
Fax: (716)631-0203
E-mail:
michalski@foodserviceinsight.com

Website: http://
www.foodserviceinsight.com

Samani International Enterprises, Marions Panyaught Consultancy
2028 Parsons
Flushing, NY 11357-3436
(917)287-8087
Fax: 800-873-8939
E-mail: vjp2@biostrategist.com
Website: http://www.biostrategist.com

Marketing Resources Group
71-58 Austin St.
Forest Hills, NY 11375
(718)261-8882

Mangabay Business Plans & Development

Subsidiary of Innis Asset Allocation
125-10 Queens Blvd., Ste. 2202
Kew Gardens, NY 11415
(905)527-1947
Fax: 509-472-1935
E-mail: mangabay@mangabay.com
Website: http://www.mangabay.com
Lee Toh, Managing Partner

ComputerEase Co.
1301 Monmouth Ave.
Lakewood, NY 08701
(212)406-9464
Fax: (914)277-5317
E-mail: crawfordc@juno.com

Boice Dunham Group
30 W 13th St.
New York, NY 10011
(212)924-2200
Fax: (212)924-1108

Elizabeth Capen
27 E 95th St.
New York, NY 10128
(212)427-7654
Fax: (212)876-3190

Haver Analytics
60 E 42nd St., Ste. 2424
New York, NY 10017
(212)986-9300
Fax: (212)986-5857
E-mail: data@haver.com
Website: http://www.haver.com

The Jordan, Edmiston Group Inc.
150 E 52nd Ave., 18th Fl.
New York, NY 10022
(212)754-0710
Fax: (212)754-0337

KPMG International
345 Park Ave.
New York, NY 10154-0102
(212)758-9700
Fax: (212)758-9819
Website: http://www.kpmg.com

Mahoney Cohen Consulting Corp.
111 W 40th St., 12th Fl.
New York, NY 10018
(212)490-8000
Fax: (212)790-5913

Management Practice Inc.
342 Madison Ave.
New York, NY 10173-1230
(212)867-7948
Fax: (212)972-5188
Website: http://www.mpiweb.com

Moseley Associates Inc.
342 Madison Ave., Ste. 1414
New York, NY 10016
(212)213-6673
Fax: (212)687-1520

Practice Development Counsel
60 Sutton Pl. S
New York, NY 10022
(212)593-1549
Fax: (212)980-7940
E-mail: pwhaserot@pdcounsel.com
Website: http://www.pdcounsel.com

Unique Value International Inc.
575 Madison Ave., 10th Fl.
New York, NY 10022-1304
(212)605-0590
Fax: (212)605-0589

The Van Tulleken Co.
126 E 56th St.
New York, NY 10022
(212)355-1390
Fax: (212)755-3061
E-mail: newyork@vantulleken.com

Vencon Management Inc.
301 W 53rd St.
New York, NY 10019
(212)581-8787
Fax: (212)397-4126
Website: http://www.venconinc.com

Werner International Inc.
55 E 52nd, 29th Fl.
New York, NY 10055
(212)909-1260
Fax: (212)909-1273
E-mail: richard.downing@rgh.com
Website: http://www.wernertex.com

Zimmerman Business Consulting Inc.
44 E 92nd St., Ste. 5-B
New York, NY 10128
(212)860-3107
Fax: (212)860-7730
E-mail: ljzzbci@aol.com
Website: http://www.zbcinc.com

Overton Financial
7 Allen Rd.
Peekskill, NY 10566
(914)737-4649
Fax: (914)737-4696

Stromberg Consulting
2500 Westchester Ave.
Purchase, NY 10577
(914)251-1515
Fax: (914)251-1562
E-mail:
strategy@stromberg_consulting.com
Website: http://
www.stromberg_consulting.com

Innovation Management Consulting Inc.
209 Dewitt Rd.
Syracuse, NY 13214-2006
(315)425-5144
Fax: (315)445-8989
E-mail: missonneb@axess.net

M. Clifford Agress
891 Fulton St.
Valley Stream, NY 11580
(516)825-8955
Fax: (516)825-8955

Destiny Kinal Marketing Consultancy
105 Chemung St.
Waverly, NY 14892
(607)565-8317
Fax: (607)565-4083

Valutis Consulting Inc.
5350 Main St., Ste. 7
Williamsville, NY 14221-5338
(716)634-2553
Fax: (716)634-2554
E-mail: valutis@localnet.com
Website: http://
www.valutisconsulting.com

North Carolina

Best Practices L.L.C.
6320 Quadrangle Dr., Ste. 200
Chapel Hill, NC 27514
(919)403-0251
Fax: (919)403-0144
E-mail: best@best:in/class
Website: http://www.best-in-class.com

Norelli & Co.
Bank of America Corporate Ctr.
100 N Tyron St., Ste. 5160
Charlotte, NC 28202-4000
(704)376-5484
Fax: (704)376-5485
E-mail: consult@norelli.com
Website: http://www.norelli.com

North Dakota

Center for Innovation
4300 Dartmouth Dr.
PO Box 8372
Grand Forks, ND 58202
(701)777-3132
Fax: (701)777-2339
E-mail: bruce@innovators.net
Website: http://www.innovators.net

Ohio

Transportation Technology Services
208 Harmon Rd.
Aurora, OH 44202
(330)562-3596

Empro Systems Inc.
4777 Red Bank Expy., Ste. 1
Cincinnati, OH 45227-1542
(513)271-2042
Fax: (513)271-2042

Alliance Management International Ltd.
1440 Windrow Ln.
Cleveland, OH 44147-3200
(440)838-1922
Fax: (440)838-0979
E-mail: bgruss@amiltd.com
Website: http://www.amiltd.com

Bozell Kamstra Public Relations
1301 E 9th St., Ste. 3400
Cleveland, OH 44114
(216)623-1511
Fax: (216)623-1501
E-mail:
jfeniger@cleveland.bozellkamstra.com
Website: http://www.bozellkamstra.com

Cory Dillon Associates
111 Schreyer Pl. E
Columbus, OH 43214
(614)262-8211
Fax: (614)262-3806

Holcomb Gallagher Adams
300 Marconi, Ste. 303
Columbus, OH 43215

(614)221-3343
Fax: (614)221-3367
E-mail: riadams@acme.freenet.oh.us

Young & Associates
PO Box 711
Kent, OH 44240
(330)678-0524
Free: 800-525-9775
Fax: (330)678-6219
E-mail: online@younginc.com
Website: http://www.younginc.com

Robert A. Westman & Associates
8981 Inversary Dr. SE
Warren, OH 44484-2551
(330)856-4149
Fax: (330)856-2564

Oklahoma

Innovative Partners L.L.C.
4900 Richmond Sq., Ste. 100
Oklahoma City, OK 73118
(405)840-0033
Fax: (405)843-8359
E-mail: ipartners@juno.com

Oregon

INTERCON - The International Converting Institute
5200 Badger Rd.
Crooked River Ranch, OR 97760
(541)548-1447
Fax: (541)548-1618
E-mail:
johnbowler@crookedriverranch.com

Talbott ARM
HC 60, Box 5620
Lakeview, OR 97630
(541)635-8587
Fax: (503)947-3482

Management Technology Associates Ltd.
2768 SW Sherwood Dr, Ste. 105
Portland, OR 97201-2251
(503)224-5220
Fax: (503)224-5334
E-mail: lcuster@mta-ltd.com
Website: http://www.mgmt-tech.com

Pennsylvania

Healthscope Inc.
400 Lancaster Ave.
Devon, PA 19333
(610)687-6199
Fax: (610)687-6376
E-mail: health@voicenet.com

Website: http://www.healthscope.net/

Elayne Howard & Associates Inc.
3501 Masons Mill Rd., Ste. 501
Huntingdon Valley, PA 19006-3509
(215)657-9550

GRA Inc.
115 West Ave., Ste. 201
Jenkintown, PA 19046
(215)884-7500
Fax: (215)884-1385
E-mail: gramail@gra-inc.com
Website: http://www.gra-inc.com

Mifflin County Industrial Development Corp.
Mifflin County Industrial Plz.
6395 SR 103 N
Bldg. 50
Lewistown, PA 17044
(717)242-0393
Fax: (717)242-1842
E-mail: mcide@acsworld.net

Autech Products
1289 Revere Rd.
Morrisville, PA 19067
(215)493-3759
Fax: (215)493-9791
E-mail: autech4@yahoo.com

Advantage Associates
434 Avon Dr.
Pittsburgh, PA 15228
(412)343-1558
Fax: (412)362-1684
E-mail: ecocba1@aol.com

Regis J. Sheehan & Associates
Pittsburgh, PA 15220
(412)279-1207

James W. Davidson Company Inc.
23 Forest View Rd.
Wallingford, PA 19086
(610)566-1462

Puerto Rico

Diego Chevere & Co.
Metro Parque 7, Ste. 204
Metro Office
Caparra Heights, PR 00920
(787)774-9595
Fax: (787)774-9566
E-mail: dcco@coqui.net

Manuel L. Porrata and Associates
898 Munoz Rivera Ave., Ste. 201
San Juan, PR 00927
(787)765-2140

Fax: (787)754-3285
E-mail: m_porrata@manuelporrata.com
Website: http://manualporrata.com

South Carolina

Aquafood Business Associates
PO Box 13267
Charleston, SC 29422
(843)795-9506
Fax: (843)795-9477
E-mail: rraba@aol.com

Profit Associates Inc.
PO Box 38026
Charleston, SC 29414
(803)763-5718
Fax: (803)763-5719
E-mail: bobrog@awod.com
Website: http://www.awod.com/gallery/business/proasc

Strategic Innovations International
12 Executive Ct.
Lake Wylie, SC 29710
(803)831-1225
Fax: (803)831-1177
E-mail: stratinnov@aol.com
Website: http://www.strategicinnovations.com

Minus Stage
Box 4436
Rock Hill, SC 29731
(803)328-0705
Fax: (803)329-9948

Tennessee

Daniel Petchers & Associates
8820 Fernwood CV
Germantown, TN 38138
(901)755-9896

Business Choices
1114 Forest Harbor, Ste. 300
Hendersonville, TN 37075-9646
(615)822-8692
Free: 800-737-8382
Fax: (615)822-8692
E-mail: bz-ch@juno.com

RCFA Healthcare Management Services L.L.C.
9648 Kingston Pke., Ste. 8
Knoxville, TN 37922
(865)531-0176
Free: 800-635-4040
Fax: (865)531-0722
E-mail: info@rcfa.com
Website: http://www.rcfa.com

Growth Consultants of America
3917 Trimble Rd.
Nashville, TN 37215
(615)383-0550
Fax: (615)269-8940
E-mail: 70244.451@compuserve.com

Texas

Integrated Cost Management Systems Inc.
2261 Brookhollow Plz. Dr., Ste. 104
Arlington, TX 76006
(817)633-2873
Fax: (817)633-3781
E-mail: abm@icms.net
Website: http://www.icms.net

Lori Williams
1000 Leslie Ct.
Arlington, TX 76012
(817)459-3934
Fax: (817)459-3934

Business Resource Software Inc.
2013 Wells Branch Pky., Ste. 305
Austin, TX 78728
Free: 800-423-1228
Fax: (512)251-4401
E-mail: info@brs-inc.com
Website: http://www.brs-inc.com

Erisa Adminstrative Services Inc.
12325 Hymeadow Dr., Bldg. 4
Austin, TX 78750-1847
(512)250-9020
Fax: (512)250-9487
Website: http://www.cserisa.com

R. Miller Hicks & Co.
1011 W 11th St.
Austin, TX 78703
(512)477-7000
Fax: (512)477-9697
E-mail: millerhicks@rmhicks.com
Website: http://www.rmhicks.com

Pragmatic Tactics Inc.
3303 Westchester Ave.
College Station, TX 77845
(409)696-5294
Free: 800-570-5294
Fax: (409)696-4994
E-mail: ptactics@aol.com
Website: http://www.ptatics.com

Perot Systems
12404 Park Central Dr.
Dallas, TX 75251
(972)340-5000
Free: 800-688-4333

Fax: (972)455-4100
E-mail: corp.comm@ps.net
Website: http://www.perotsystems.com

ReGENERATION Partners
3838 Oak Lawn Ave.
Dallas, TX 75219
(214)559-3999
Free: 800-406-1112
E-mail: info@regeneration-partner.com
Website: http://www.regeneration-partners.com

High Technology Associates - Division of Global Technologies Inc.
1775 St. James Pl., Ste. 105
Houston, TX 77056
(713)963-9300
Fax: (713)963-8341
E-mail: hta@infohwy.com

MasterCOM
103 Thunder Rd.
Kerrville, TX 78028
(830)895-7990
Fax: (830)443-3428
E-mail: jmstubblefield@mastertraining.com
Website: http://www.mastertraining.com

PROTEC
4607 Linden Pl.
Pearland, TX 77584
(281)997-9872
Fax: (281)997-9895
E-mail: p.oman@ix.netcom.com

Alpha Quadrant Inc.
10618 Auldine
San Antonio, TX 78230
(210)344-3330
Fax: (210)344-8151
E-mail: mbussone@sbcglobal.net
Website:http://www.a-quadrant.com
Michele Bussone

Bastian Public Relations
614 San Dizier
San Antonio, TX 78232
(210)404-1839
E-mail: lisa@bastianpr.com
Website: http://www.bastianpr.com
Lisa Bastian CBC

Business Strategy Development Consultants
PO Box 690365
San Antonio, TX 78269
(210)696-8000
Free: 800-927-BSDC
Fax: (210)696-8000

Tom Welch, CPC
6900 San Pedro Ave., Ste. 147
San Antonio, TX 78216-6207
(210)737-7022
Fax: (210)737-7022
E-mail: bplan@iamerica.net
Website: http://www.moneywords.com

Utah

Business Management Resource
PO Box 521125
Salt Lake City, UT 84152-1125
(801)272-4668
Fax: (801)277-3290
E-mail: pingfong@worldnet.att.net

Virginia

Tindell Associates
209 Oxford Ave.
Alexandria, VA 22301
(703)683-0109
Fax: 703-783-0219
E-mail: scott@tindell.net
Website: http://www.tindell.net
Scott Lockett, President

Elliott B. Jaffa
2530-B S Walter Reed Dr.
Arlington, VA 22206
(703)931-0040
E-mail: thetrainingdoctor@excite.com
Website: http://www.tregistry.com/jaffa.htm

Koach Enterprises - USA
5529 N 18th St.
Arlington, VA 22205
(703)241-8361
Fax: (703)241-8623

Federal Market Development
5650 Chapel Run Ct.
Centreville, VA 20120-3601
(703)502-8930
Free: 800-821-5003
Fax: (703)502-8929

Huff, Stuart & Carlton
2107 Graves Mills Rd., Ste. C
Forest, VA 24551
(804)316-9356
Free: (888)316-9356
Fax: (804)316-9357
Website: http://www.wealthmgt.net

AMX International Inc.
1420 Spring Hill Rd. , Ste. 600
McLean, VA 22102-3006
(703)690-4100

Fax: (703)643-1279
E-mail: amxmail@amxi.com
Website: http://www.amxi.com

Charles Scott Pugh (Investor)
4101 Pittaway Dr.
Richmond, VA 23235-1022
(804)560-0979
Fax: (804)560-4670

John C. Randall and Associates Inc.
PO Box 15127
Richmond, VA 23227
(804)746-4450
Fax: (804)730-8933
E-mail: randalljcx@aol.com
Website: http://www.johncrandall.com

McLeod & Co.
410 1st St.
Roanoke, VA 24011
(540)342-6911
Fax: (540)344-6367
Website: http://www.mcleodco.com/

Salzinger & Company Inc.
8000 Towers Crescent Dr., Ste. 1350
Vienna, VA 22182
(703)442-5200
Fax: (703)442-5205
E-mail: info@salzinger.com
Website: http://www.salzinger.com

The Small Business Counselor
12423 Hedges Run Dr., Ste. 153
Woodbridge, VA 22192
(703)490-6755
Fax: (703)490-1356

Washington

Burlington Consultants
10900 NE 8th St., Ste. 900
Bellevue, WA 98004
(425)688-3060
Fax: (425)454-4383
E-mail:
partners@burlingtonconsultants.com
Website: http://
www.burlingtonconsultants.com

Perry L. Smith Consulting
800 Bellevue Way NE, Ste. 400
Bellevue, WA 98004-4208
(425)462-2072
Fax: (425)462-5638

St. Charles Consulting Group
1420 NW Gilman Blvd.
Issaquah, WA 98027
(425)557-8708
Fax: (425)557-8731

E-mail: info@stcharlesconsulting.com
Website: http://
www.stcharlesconsulting.com

Independent Automotive Training Services
PO Box 334
Kirkland, WA 98083
(425)822-5715
E-mail: ltunney@autosvccon.com
Website: http://www.autosvccon.com

Kahle Associate Inc.
6203 204th Dr. NE
Redmond, WA 98053
(425)836-8763
Fax: (425)868-3770
E-mail: randykahle@kahleassociates.com
Website: http://www.kahleassociates.com

Dan Collin
3419 Wallingord Ave N, No. 2
Seattle, WA 98103
(206)634-9469
E-mail: dc@dancollin.com
Website: http://members.home.net/
dcollin/

ECG Management Consultants Inc.
1111 3rd Ave., Ste. 2700
Seattle, WA 98101-3201
(206)689-2200
Fax: (206)689-2209
E-mail: ecg@ecgmc.com
Website: http://www.ecgmc.com

Northwest Trade Adjustment Assistance Center
900 4th Ave., Ste. 2430
Seattle, WA 98164-1001
(206)622-2730
Free: 800-667-8087
Fax: (206)622-1105
E-mail: matchingfunds@nwtaac.org
Website: http://www.taacenters.org

Business Planning Consultants
S 3510 Ridgeview Dr.
Spokane, WA 99206
(509)928-0332
Fax: (509)921-0842
E-mail: bpci@nextdim.com

West Virginia

Stanley & Associates Inc./ BusinessandMarketingPlans.com
1687 Robert C. Byrd Dr.
Beckley, WV 25801
(304)252-0324
Free: 888-752-6720

Fax: (304)252-0470
E-mail: cclay@charterinternet.com
Website: http://
www.BusinessandMarketingPlans.com
Christopher Clay

Wisconsin

White & Associates Inc.
5349 Somerset Ln. S
Greenfield, WI 53221
(414)281-7373
Fax: (414)281-7006
E-mail: wnaconsult@aol.com

SMALL BUSINESS ADMINISTRATION REGIONAL OFFICES

This section contains a listing of Small Business Administration offices arranged numerically by region. Service areas are provided. Contact the appropriate office for a referral to the nearest field office, or visit the Small Business Administration online at www.sba.gov.

Region 1

U.S. Small Business Administration
Region I Office
10 Causeway St., Ste. 812
Boston, MA 02222-1093
Phone: (617)565-8415
Fax: (617)565-8420
Serves Connecticut, Maine, Massachusetts, New Hampshire, Rhode Island, and Vermont.

Region 2

U.S. Small Business Administration
Region II Office
26 Federal Plaza, Ste. 3108
New York, NY 10278
Phone: (212)264-1450
Fax: (212)264-0038
Serves New Jersey, New York, Puerto Rico, and the Virgin Islands.

Region 3

U.S. Small Business Administration
Region III Office
Robert N C Nix Sr. Federal Building
900 Market St., 5th Fl.

Philadelphia, PA 19107
(215)580-2807
Serves Delaware, the District of
Columbia, Maryland, Pennsylvania,
Virginia, and West Virginia.

Region 4

U.S. Small Business Administration
Region IV Office
233 Peachtree St. NE
Harris Tower 1800
Atlanta, GA 30303
Phone: (404)331-4999
Fax: (404)331-2354
Serves Alabama, Florida, Georgia,
Kentucky, Mississippi, North Carolina,
South Carolina, and Tennessee.

Region 5

U.S. Small Business Administration
Region V Office
500 W. Madison St.
Citicorp Center, Ste. 1240
Chicago, IL 60661-2511
Phone: (312)353-0357
Fax: (312)353-3426
Serves Illinois, Indiana, Michigan,
Minnesota, Ohio, and Wisconsin.

Region 6

U.S. Small Business Administration
Region VI Office
4300 Amon Carter Blvd., Ste. 108
Fort Worth, TX 76155
Phone: (817)684-5581
Fax: (817)684-5588
Serves Arkansas, Louisiana, New Mexico,
Oklahoma, and Texas.

Region 7

U.S. Small Business Administration
Region VII Office
323 W. 8th St., Ste. 307
Kansas City, MO 64105-1500
Phone: (816)374-6380
Fax: (816)374-6339
Serves Iowa, Kansas, Missouri, and
Nebraska.

Region 8

U.S. Small Business Administration
Region VIII Office
721 19th St., Ste. 400
Denver, CO 80202
Phone: (303)844-0500
Fax: (303)844-0506

Serves Colorado, Montana, North
Dakota, South Dakota, Utah, and
Wyoming.

Region 9

U.S. Small Business Administration
Region IX Office
330 N Brand Blvd., Ste. 1270
Glendale, CA 91203-2304
Phone: (818)552-3434
Fax: (818)552-3440
Serves American Samoa, Arizona,
California, Guam, Hawaii, Nevada, and
the Trust Territory of the Pacific Islands.

Region 10

U.S. Small Business Administration
Region X Office
2401 Fourth Ave., Ste. 400
Seattle, WA 98121
Phone: (206)553-5676
Fax: (206)553-4155
Serves Alaska, Idaho, Oregon, and
Washington.

SMALL BUSINESS DEVELOPMENT CENTERS

*This section contains a listing of all Small
Business Development Centers, organized
alphabetically by state/U.S. territory, then
by city, then by agency name.*

Alabama

Alabama SBDC

UNIVERSITY OF ALABAMA
2800 Milan Court Suite 124
Birmingham, AL 35211-6908
Phone: 205-943-6750
Fax: 205-943-6752
E-Mail: wcampbell@provost.uab.edu
Website: http://www.asbdc.org
Mr. William Campbell Jr, State Director

Alaska

Alaska SBDC

UNIVERSITY OF ALASKA - ANCHORAGE
430 West Seventh Avenue, Suite 110
Anchorage, AK 99501
Phone: 907-274 -7232
Fax: 907-274-9524

E-Mail: anerw@uaa.alaska.edu
Website: http://www.aksbdc.org
Ms. Jean R. Wall, State Director

American Samoa

American Samoa SBDC

AMERICAN SAMOA COMMUNITY COLLEGE
P.O. Box 2609
Pago Pago, American Samoa 96799
Phone: 011-684-699-4830
Fax: 011-684-699-6132
E-Mail: htalex@att.net
Mr. Herbert Thweatt, Director

Arizona

Arizona SBDC

MARICOPA COUNTY COMMUNITY COLLEGE
2411 West 14th Street, Suite 132
Tempe, AZ 85281
Phone: 480-731-8720
Fax: 480-731-8729
E-Mail:
mike.york@domail.maricopa.edu
Website: http://
www.dist.maricopa.edu.sbdc
Mr. Michael York, State Director

Arkansas

Arkansas SBDC

UNIVERSITY OF ARKANSAS
2801 South University Avenue
Little Rock, AR 72204
Phone: 501-324-9043
Fax: 501-324-9049
E-Mail: jmroderick@ualr.edu
Website: http://asbdc.ualr.edu
Ms. Janet M. Roderick, State Director

California

California - San Francisco SBDC

Northern California SBDC Lead Center

HUMBOLDT STATE UNIVERSITY
Office of Economic Development
1 Harpst Street 2006A, Siemens Hall
Arcata, CA, 95521
Phone: 707-826-3922
Fax: 707-826-3206
E-Mail: gainer@humboldt.edu
Ms. Margaret A. Gainer, Regional
Director

California - Sacramento SBDC

CALIFORNIA STATE UNIVERSITY - CHICO
Chico, CA 95929-0765
Phone: 530-898-4598
Fax: 530-898-4734
E-Mail: dripke@csuchico.edu
Website: http://gsbdc.csuchico.edu
Mr. Dan Ripke, Interim Regional Director

California - San Diego SBDC

SOUTHWESTERN COMMUNITY COLLEGE DISTRICT
900 Otey Lakes Road
Chula Vista, CA 91910
Phone: 619-482-6388
Fax: 619-482-6402
E-Mail: dtrujillo@swc.cc.ca.us
Website: http://www.sbditc.org
Ms. Debbie P. Trujillo, Regional Director

California - Fresno SBDC

UC Merced Lead Center

UNIVERSITY OF CALIFORNIA - MERCED
550 East Shaw, Suite 105A
Fresno, CA 93710
Phone: 559-241-6590
Fax: 559-241-7422
E-Mail: crosander@ucmerced.edu
Website: http://sbdc.ucmerced.edu
Mr. Chris Rosander, State Director

California - Santa Ana SBDC

Tri-County Lead SBDC

CALIFORNIA STATE UNIVERSITY - FULLERTON
800 North State College Boulevard, LH640
Fullerton, CA 92834
Phone: 714-278-2719
Fax: 714-278-7858
E-Mail: vpham@fullerton.edu
Website: http://www.leadsbdc.org
Ms. Vi Pham, Lead Center Director

California - Los Angeles Region SBDC

LONG BEACH COMMUNITY COLLEGE DISTRICT
3950 Paramount Boulevard, Ste 101
Lakewood, CA 90712
Phone: 562-938-5004
Fax: 562-938-5030
E-Mail: ssloan@lbcc.edu

Ms. Sheneui Sloan, Interim Lead Center Director

Colorado

Colorado SBDC

OFFICE OF ECONOMIC DEVELOPMENT
1625 Broadway, Suite 170
Denver, CO 80202
Phone: 303-892-3864
Fax: 303-892-3848
E-Mail: Kelly.Manning@state.co.us
Website: http://www.state.co.us/oed/sbdc
Ms. Kelly Manning, State Director

Connecticut

Connecticut SBDC

UNIVERSITY OF CONNECTICUT
1376 Storrs Road, Unit 4094
Storrs, CT 06269-1094
Phone: 860-870-6370
Fax: 860-870-6374
E-Mail: richard.cheney@uconn.edu
Website: http://www.sbdc.uconn.edu
Mr. Richard Cheney, Interim State Director

Delaware

Delaware SBDC

DELAWARE TECHNOLOGY PARK
1 Innovation Way, Suite 301
Newark, DE 19711
Phone: 302-831-2747
Fax: 302-831-1423
E-Mail: Clinton.tymes@mvs.udel.edu
Website: http://www.delawaresbdc.org
Mr. Clinton Tymes, State Director

District of Columbia

District of Columbia SBDC

HOWARD UNIVERSITY
2600 6th Street, NW Room 128
Washington, DC 20059
Phone: 202-806-1550
Fax: 202-806-1777
E-Mail: hturner@howard.edu
Website: http://www.dcsbdc.com/
Mr. Henry Turner, Executive Director

Florida

Florida SBDC

UNIVERSITY OF WEST FLORIDA
401 East Chase Street, Suite 100

Pensacola, FL 32502
Phone: 850-473-7800
Fax: 850-473-7813
E-Mail: jcartwri@uwf.edu
Website: http://www.floridasbdc.com
Mr. Jerry Cartwright, State Director

Georgia

Georgia SBDC

UNIVERSITY OF GEORGIA
1180 East Broad Street
Athens, GA 30602
Phone: 706-542-6762
Fax: 706-542-6776
E-mail: aadams@sbdc.uga.edu
Website: http://www.sbdc.uga.edu
Mr. Allan Adams, Interim State Director

Guam

Guam Small Business Development Center

UNIVERSITY OF GUAM
Pacific Islands SBDC
P.O. Box 5014 - U.O.G. Station
Mangilao, GU 96923
Phone: 671-735-2590
Fax: 671-734-2002
E-mail: casey@pacificsbdc.com
Website: http://www.uog.edu/sbdc
Mr. Casey Jeszenka, Director

Hawaii

Hawaii SBDC

UNIVERSITY OF HAWAII - HILO
308 Kamehameha Avenue, Suite 201
Hilo, HI 96720
Phone: 808-974-7515
Fax: 808-974-7683
E-Mail: darrylm@interpac.net
Website: http://www.hawaii-sbdc.org
Mr. Darryl Mleynek, State Director

Idaho

Idaho SBDC

BOISE STATE UNIVERSITY
1910 University Drive
Boise, ID 83725
Phone: 208-426-3799
Fax: 208-426-3877
E-mail: jhogge@boisestate.edu
Website: http://www.idahosbdc.org
Mr. Jim Hogge, State Director

8888888

8888888888

888888

Illinois

Illinois SBDC

DEPARTMENT OF COMMERCE AND ECONOMIC OPPORTUNITY
620 E. Adams, S-4
Springfield, IL 62701
Phone: 217-524-5700
Fax: 217-524-0171
E-mail: mpatrilli@ildceo.net
Website: http://www.ilsbdc.biz
Mr. Mark Petrilli, State Director

Indiana

Indiana SBDC

INDIANA ECONOMIC DEVELOPMENT CORPORATION
One North Capitol, Suite 900
Indianapolis, IN 46204
Phone: 317-234-8872
Fax: 317-232-8874
E-mail: dtrocha@isbdc.org
Website: http://www.isbdc.org
Ms. Debbie Bishop Trocha, State Director

Iowa

Iowa SBDC

IOWA STATE UNIVERSITY
340 Gerdin Business Bldg.
Ames, IA 50011-1350
Phone: 515-294-2037
Fax: 515-294-6522
E-mail: jonryan@iastate.edu
Website: http://www.iabusnet.org
Mr. Jon Ryan, State Director

Kansas

Kansas SBDC

FORT HAYS STATE UNIVERSITY
214 SW Sixth Street, Suite 301
Topeka, KS 66603
Phone: 785-296-6514
Fax: 785-291-3261
E-mail: ksbdc.wkearns@fhsu.edu
Website: http://www.fhsu.edu/ksbdc
Mr. Wally Kearns, State Director

Kentucky

Kentucky SBDC

UNIVERSITY OF KENTUCKY
225 Gatton College of Business
Economics Building
Lexington, KY 40506-0034
Phone: 859-257-7668
Fax: 859-323-1907
E-mail: lrnaug0@pop.uky.edu
Website: http://www.ksbdc.org
Ms. Becky Naugle, State Director

Louisiana

Louisiana SBDC

UNIVERSITY OF LOUISIANA - MONROE

College of Business Administration
700 University Avenue
Monroe, LA 71209
Phone: 318-342-5506
Fax: 318-342-5510
E-mail: wilkerson@ulm.edu
Website: http://www.lsbdc.org
Ms. Mary Lynn Wilkerson, State Director

Maine

Maine SBDC

UNIVERSITY OF SOUTHERN MAINE
96 Falmouth Street P.O. Box 9300
Portland, ME 04103
Phone: 207-780-4420
Fax: 207-780-4810
E-mail: jrmassaua@maine.edu
Website: http://www.mainesbdc.org
Mr. John Massaua, State Director

Maryland

Maryland SBDC

UNIVERSITY OF MARYLAND
7100 Baltimore Avenue, Suite 401
College Park, MD 20742
Phone: 301-403-8300
Fax: 301-403-8303
E-mail: rsprow@mdsbdc.umd.edu
Website: http://www.mdsbdc.umd.edu
Ms. Renee Sprow, State Director

Massachusetts

Massachusetts SBDC

UNIVERSITY OF MASSACHUSETTS
School of Management, Room 205
Amherst, MA 01003-4935
Phone: 413-545-6301
Fax: 413-545-1273
E-mail: gep@msbdc.umass.edu
Website: http://msbdc.som.umass.edu
Ms. Georgianna Parkin, State Director

Michigan

Michigan SBTDC

GRAND VALLEY STATE UNIVERSITY
510 West Fulton Avenue
Grand Rapids, MI 49504
Phone: 616-331-7485
Fax: 616-331-7389
E-mail: lopuckic@gvsu.edu
Website: http://www.misbtdc.org
Ms. Carol Lopucki, State Director

Minnesota

Minnesota SBDC

MINNESOTA SMALL BUSINESS DEVELOPMENT CENTER
1st National Bank Building
332 Minnesota Street, Suite E200
St. Paul, MN 55101-1351
Phone: 651-297-5773
Fax: 651-296-5287
E-mail: michael.myhre@state.mn.us
Website: http://www.mnsbdc.com
Mr. Michael Myhre, State Director

Mississippi

Mississippi SBDC

UNIVERSITY OF MISSISSIPPI
B-19 Jeanette Phillips Drive
P.O. Box 1848
University, MS 38677
Phone: 662-915-5001
Fax: 662-915-5650
E-mail: wgurley@olemiss.edu
Website: http://www.olemiss.edu/depts/mssbdc
Mr. Doug Gurley, Jr., State Director

Missouri

Missouri SBDC

UNIVERSITY OF MISSOURI
1205 University Avenue, Suite 300
Columbia, MO 65211
Phone: 573-882-1348
Fax: 573-884-4297
E-mail: summersm@missouri.edu
Website: http://www.mo-sbdc.org/index.shtml
Mr. Max Summers, State Director

Montana

Montana SBDC

DEPARTMENT OF COMMERCE
301 South Park Avenue, Room 114 / P.O.
Box 200505
Helena, MT 59620
Phone: 406-841-2746
Fax: 406-444-1872
E-mail: adesch@state.mt.us
Website: http://commerce.state.mt.us/
brd/BRD_SBDC.html
Ms. Ann Desch, State Director

Nebraska

Nebraska SBDC

UNIVERSITY OF NEBRASKA - OMAHA
60th & Dodge Street, CBA Room 407
Omaha, NE 68182
Phone: 402-554-2521
Fax: 402-554-3473
E-mail: rbernier@unomaha.edu
Website: http://nbdc.unomaha.edu
Mr. Robert Bernier, State Director

Nevada

Nevada SBDC

UNIVERSITY OF NEVADA - RENO
Reno College of Business
Administration, Room 411
Reno, NV 89557-0100
Phone: 775-784-1717
Fax: 775-784-4337
E-mail: males@unr.edu
Website: http://www.nsbdc.org
Mr. Sam Males, State Director

New Hampshire

New Hampshire SBDC

UNIVERSITY OF NEW HAMPSHIRE
108 McConnell Hall
Durham, NH 03824-3593
Phone: 603-862-4879
Fax: 603-862-4876
E-mail: Mary.Collins@unh.edu
Website: http://www.nhsbdc.org
Ms. Mary Collins, State Director

New Jersey

New Jersey SBDC

RUTGERS UNIVERSITY
49 Bleeker Street
Newark, NJ 07102-1993

Phone: 973-353-5950
Fax: 973-353-1110
E-mail: bhopper@njsbdc.com
Website: http://www.njsbdc.com/home
Ms. Brenda Hopper, State Director

New Mexico

New Mexico SBDC

SANTA FE COMMUNITY COLLEGE
6401 Richards Avenue
Santa Fe, NM 87505
Phone: 505-428-1362
Fax: 505-471-9469
E-mail: rmiller@santa-fe.cc.nm.us
Website: http://www.nmsbdc.org
Mr. Roy Miller, State Director

New York

New York SBDC

STATE UNIVERSITY OF NEW YORK
SUNY Plaza, S-523
Albany, NY 12246
Phone: 518-443-5398
Fax: 518-443-5275
E-mail: j.king@nyssbdc.org
Website: http://www.nyssbdc.org
Mr. Jim King, State Director

North Carolina

North Carolina SBDTC

UNIVERSITY OF NORTH CAROLINA
5 West Hargett Street, Suite 600
Raleigh, NC 27601
Phone: 919-715-7272
Fax: 919-715-7777
E-mail: sdaugherty@sbtdc.org
Website: http://www.sbtdc.org
Mr. Scott Daugherty, State Director

North Dakota

North Dakota SBDC

UNIVERSITY OF NORTH DAKOTA
1600 E. Century Avenue, Suite 2
Bismarck, ND 58503
Phone: 701-328-5375
Fax: 701-328-5320
E-mail:
christine.martin@und.nodak.edu
Website: http://www.ndsbdc.org
Ms. Christine Martin-Goldman, State
Director

Ohio

Ohio SBDC

**OHIO DEPARTMENT OF
DEVELOPMENT**
77 South High Street
Columbus, OH 43216
Phone: 614-466-5102
Fax: 614-466-0829
E-mail: mabraham@odod.state.oh.us
Website: http://www.ohiosbdc.org
Ms. Michele Abraham, State Director

Oklahoma

Oklahoma SBDC

**SOUTHEAST OKLAHOMA STATE
UNIVERSITY**
517 University, Box 2584, Station A
Durant, OK 74701
Phone: 580-745-7577
Fax: 580-745-7471
E-mail: gpennington@sosu.edu
Website: http://www.osbdc.org
Mr. Grady Pennington, State Director

Oregon

Oregon SBDC

LANE COMMUNITY COLLEGE
99 West Tenth Avenue, Suite 390
Eugene, OR 97401-3021
Phone: 541-463-5250
Fax: 541-345-6006
E-mail: carterb@lanecc.edu
Website: http://www.bizcenter.org
Mr. William Carter, State Director

Pennsylvania

Pennsylvania SBDC

UNIVERSITY OF PENNSYLVANIA

The Wharton School
3733 Spruce Street
Philadelphia, PA 19104-6374
Phone: 215-898-1219
Fax: 215-573-2135
E-mail: ghiggins@wharton.upenn.edu
Website: http://pasbdc.org
Mr. Gregory Higgins, State Director

Puerto Rico

Puerto Rico SBDC

**INTER-AMERICAN UNIVERSITY OF
PUERTO RICO**
416 Ponce de Leon Avenue, Union Plaza,
Seventh Floor

Hato Rey, PR 00918
Phone: 787-763-6811
Fax: 787-763-4629
E-mail: cmarti@prsbdc.org
Website: http://www.prsbdc.org
Ms. Carmen Marti, Executive Director

Rhode Island

Rhode Island SBDC

BRYANT UNIVERSITY
1150 Douglas Pike
Smithfield, RI 02917
Phone: 401-232-6923
Fax: 401-232-6933
E-mail: adawson@bryant.edu
Website: http://www.risbdc.org
Ms. Diane Fournaris, Interim State
Director

South Carolina

South Carolina SBDC

UNIVERSITY OF SOUTH CAROLINA

College of Business Administration
1710 College Street
Columbia, SC 29208
Phone: 803-777-4907
Fax: 803-777-4403
E-mail: lenti@moore.sc.edu
Website: http://scsbdc.moore.sc.edu
Mr. John Lenti, State Director

South Dakota

South Dakota SBDC

UNIVERSITY OF SOUTH DAKOTA
414 East Clark Street, Patterson Hall
Vermillion, SD 57069
Phone: 605-677-6256
Fax: 605-677-5427
E-mail: jshemmin@usd.edu
Website: http://www.sdsbdc.org
Mr. John S. Hemmingstad, State
Director

Tennessee

Tennessee SBDC

TENNESSEE BOARD OF REGENTS
1415 Murfreessboro Road, Suite 540
Nashville, TN 37217-2833
Phone: 615-898-2745
Fax: 615-893-7089
E-mail: pgeho@mail.tsbdc.org
Website: http://www.tsbdc.org
Mr. Patrick Geho, State Director

Texas

Texas-North SBDC

DALLAS COUNTY COMMUNITY COLLEGE
1402 Corinth Street
Dallas, TX 75215
Phone: 214-860-5835
Fax: 214-860-5813
E-mail: emk9402@dcccd.edu
Website: http://www.ntsbdc.org
Ms. Liz Klimback, Region Director

Texas-Houston SBDC

UNIVERSITY OF HOUSTON
2302 Fannin, Suite 200
Houston, TX 77002
Phone: 713-752-8425
Fax: 713-756-1500
E-mail: fyoung@uh.edu
Website: http://sbdcnetwork.uh.edu
Mr. Mike Young, Executive Director

Texas-NW SBDC

TEXAS TECH UNIVERSITY
2579 South Loop 289, Suite 114
Lubbock, TX 79423
Phone: 806-745-3973
Fax: 806-745-6207
E-mail: c.bean@nwtsbdc.org
Website: http://www.nwtsbdc.org
Mr. Craig Bean, Executive Director

Texas-South-West Texas Border Region SBDC

UNIVERSITY OF TEXAS - SAN ANTONIO
501 West Durango Boulevard
San Antonio, TX 78207-4415
Phone: 210-458-2742
Fax: 210-458-2464
E-mail: albert.salgado@utsa.edu
Website: http://www.iedtexas.org
Mr. Alberto Salgado, Region Director

Utah

Utah SBDC

SALT LAKE COMMUNITY COLLEGE
9750 South 300 West
Sandy, UT 84070
Phone: 801-957-3493
Fax: 801-957-3488
E-mail: Greg.Panichello@slcc.edu
Website:http://www.slcc.edu/sbdc
Mr. Greg Panichello, State Director

Vermont

Vermont SBDC

VERMONT TECHNICAL COLLEGE
PO Box 188, 1 Main Street
Randolph Center, VT 05061-0188
Phone: 802-728-9101
Fax: 802-728-3026
E-mail: lquillen@vtc.edu
Website: http://www.vtsbdc.org
Ms. Lenae Quillen-Blume, State Director

Virgin Islands

Virgin Islands SBDC

UNIVERSITY OF THE VIRGIN ISLANDS
8000 Nisky Center, Suite 720
St. Thomas, VI 00802-5804
Phone: 340-776-3206
Fax: 340-775-3756
E-mail: wbush@webmail.uvi.edu
Website: http://rps.uvi.edu/SBDC
Mr. Warren Bush, State Director

Virginia

Virginia SBDC

GEORGE MASON UNIVERSITY
4031 University Drive, Suite 200
Fairfax, VA 22030-3409
Phone: 703-277-7727
Fax: 703-352-8515
E-mail: jkeenan@gmu.edu
Website: http://www.virginiasbdc.org
Ms. Jody Keenan, Director

Washington

Washington SBDC

WASHINGTON STATE UNIVERSITY
534 E. Trent Avenue
P.O. Box 1495
Spokane, WA 99210-1495
Phone: 509-358-7765
Fax: 509-358-7764
E-mail: barogers@wsu.edu
Website: http://www.wsbdc.org
Mr. Brett Rogers, State Director

West Virginia

West Virginia SBDC

WEST VIRGINIA DEVELOPMENT OFFICE
Capital Complex, Building 6, Room 652
Charleston, WV 25301

Phone: 304-558-2960
Fax: 304-558-0127
E-mail: csalyer@wvsbdc.org
Website: http://www.wvsbdc.org
Mr. Conley Salyor, State Director

Wisconsin

Wisconsin SBDC

UNIVERSITY OF WISCONSIN
432 North Lake Street, Room 423
Madison, WI 53706
Phone: 608-263-7794
Fax: 608-263-7830
E-mail: erica.kauten@uwex.edu
Website: http://www.wisconsinsbdc.org
Ms. Erica Kauten, State Director

Wyoming

Wyoming SBDC

UNIVERSITY OF WYOMING
P.O. Box 3922
Laramie, WY 82071-3922
Phone: 307-766-3505
Fax: 307-766-3406
E-mail: DDW@uwyo.edu
Website: http://www.uwyo.edu/sbdc
Ms. Debbie Popp, Acting State Director

SERVICE CORPS OF RETIRED EXECUTIVES (SCORE) OFFICES

This section contains a listing of all SCORE offices organized alphabetically by state/U.S. territory, then by city, then by agency name.

Alabama

SCORE Office (Northeast Alabama)
1330 Quintard Ave.
Anniston, AL 36202
(256)237-3536

SCORE Office (North Alabama)
901 South 15th St, Rm. 201
Birmingham, AL 35294-2060
(205)934-6868
Fax: (205)934-0538

SCORE Office (Baldwin County)
29750 Larry Dee Cawyer Dr.
Daphne, AL 36526
(334)928-5838

SCORE Office (Shoals)
612 S. COurt
Florence, AL 35630
(256)764-4661
Fax: (256)766-9017
E-mail: shoals@shoalschamber.com

SCORE Office (Mobile)
600 S Court St.
Mobile, AL 36104
(334)240-6868
Fax: (334)240-6869

SCORE Office (Alabama Capitol City)
600 S. Court St.
Montgomery, AL 36104
(334)240-6868
Fax: (334)240-6869

SCORE Office (East Alabama)
601 Ave. A
Opelika, AL 36801
(334)745-4861
E-mail: score636@hotmail.com
Website: http://www.angelfire.com/sc/score636/

SCORE Office (Tuscaloosa)
2200 University Blvd.
Tuscaloosa, AL 35402
(205)758-7588

Alaska

SCORE Office (Anchorage)
510 L St., Ste. 310
Anchorage, AK 99501
(907)271-4022
Fax: (907)271-4545

Arizona

SCORE Office (Lake Havasu)
10 S. Acoma Blvd.
Lake Havasu City, AZ 86403
(520)453-5951
E-mail: SCORE@ctaz.com
Website: http://www.scorearizona.org/lake_havasu/

SCORE Office (East Valley)
Federal Bldg., Rm. 104
26 N. MacDonald St.
Mesa, AZ 85201
(602)379-3100
Fax: (602)379-3143
E-mail: 402@aol.com
Website: http://www.scorearizona.org/mesa/

SCORE Office (Phoenix)
2828 N. Central Ave., Ste. 800

Central & One Thomas
Phoenix, AZ 85004
(602)640-2329
Fax: (602)640-2360
E-mail: e-mail@SCORE-phoenix.org
Website: http://www.score-phoenix.org/

SCORE Office (Prescott Arizona)
1228 Willow Creek Rd., Ste. 2
Prescott, AZ 86301
(520)778-7438
Fax: (520)778-0812
E-mail: score@northlink.com
Website: http://www.scorearizona.org/prescott/

SCORE Office (Tucson)
110 E. Pennington St.
Tucson, AZ 85702
(520)670-5008
Fax: (520)670-5011
E-mail: score@azstarnet.com
Website: http://www.scorearizona.org/tucson/

SCORE Office (Yuma)
281 W. 24th St., Ste. 116
Yuma, AZ 85364
(520)314-0480
E-mail: score@C2i2.com
Website: http://www.scorearizona.org/yuma

Arkansas

SCORE Office (South Central)
201 N. Jackson Ave.
El Dorado, AR 71730-5803
(870)863-6113
Fax: (870)863-6115

SCORE Office (Ozark)
Fayetteville, AR 72701
(501)442-7619

SCORE Office (Northwest Arkansas)
Glenn Haven Dr., No. 4
Ft. Smith, AR 72901
(501)783-3556

SCORE Office (Garland County)
Grand & Ouachita
PO Box 6012
Hot Springs Village, AR 71902
(501)321-1700

SCORE Office (Little Rock)
2120 Riverfront Dr., Rm. 100
Little Rock, AR 72202-1747
(501)324-5893
Fax: (501)324-5199

SCORE Office (Southeast Arkansas)
121 W. 6th
Pine Bluff, AR 71601
(870)535-7189
Fax: (870)535-1643

California

SCORE Office (Golden Empire)
1706 Chester Ave., No. 200
Bakersfield, CA 93301
(805)322-5881
Fax: (805)322-5663

SCORE Office (Greater Chico Area)
1324 Mangrove St., Ste. 114
Chico, CA 95926
(916)342-8932
Fax: (916)342-8932

SCORE Office (Concord)
2151-A Salvio St., Ste. B
Concord, CA 94520
(510)685-1181
Fax: (510)685-5623

SCORE Office (Covina)
935 W. Badillo St.
Covina, CA 91723
(818)967-4191
Fax: (818)966-9660

SCORE Office (Rancho Cucamonga)
8280 Utica, Ste. 160
Cucamonga, CA 91730
(909)987-1012
Fax: (909)987-5917

SCORE Office (Culver City)
PO Box 707
Culver City, CA 90232-0707
(310)287-3850
Fax: (310)287-1350

SCORE Office (Danville)
380 Diablo Rd., Ste. 103
Danville, CA 94526
(510)837-4400

SCORE Office (Downey)
11131 Brookshire Ave.
Downey, CA 90241
(310)923-2191
Fax: (310)864-0461

SCORE Office (El Cajon)
109 Rea Ave.
El Cajon, CA 92020
(619)444-1327
Fax: (619)440-6164

SCORE Office (El Centro)
1100 Main St.
El Centro, CA 92243
(619)352-3681
Fax: (619)352-3246

SCORE Office (Escondido)
720 N. Broadway
Escondido, CA 92025
(619)745-2125
Fax: (619)745-1183

SCORE Office (Fairfield)
1111 Webster St.
Fairfield, CA 94533
(707)425-4625
Fax: (707)425-0826

SCORE Office (Fontana)
17009 Valley Blvd., Ste. B
Fontana, CA 92335
(909)822-4433
Fax: (909)822-6238

SCORE Office (Foster City)
1125 E. Hillsdale Blvd.
Foster City, CA 94404
(415)573-7600
Fax: (415)573-5201

SCORE Office (Fremont)
2201 Walnut Ave., Ste. 110
Fremont, CA 94538
(510)795-2244
Fax: (510)795-2240

SCORE Office (Central California)
2719 N. Air Fresno Dr., Ste. 200
Fresno, CA 93727-1547
(559)487-5605
Fax: (559)487-5636

SCORE Office (Gardena)
1204 W. Gardena Blvd.
Gardena, CA 90247
(310)532-9905
Fax: (310)515-4893

SCORE Office (Lompoc)
330 N. Brand Blvd., Ste. 190
Glendale, CA 91203-2304
(818)552-3206
Fax: (818)552-3323

SCORE Office (Los Angeles)
330 N. Brand Blvd., Ste. 190
Glendale, CA 91203-2304
(818)552-3206
Fax: (818)552-3323

SCORE Office (Glendora)
131 E. Foothill Blvd.

Glendora, CA 91740
(818)963-4128
Fax: (818)914-4822

SCORE Office (Grover Beach)
177 S. 8th St.
Grover Beach, CA 93433
(805)489-9091
Fax: (805)489-9091

SCORE Office (Hawthorne)
12477 Hawthorne Blvd.
Hawthorne, CA 90250
(310)676-1163
Fax: (310)676-7661

SCORE Office (Hayward)
22300 Foothill Blvd., Ste. 303
Hayward, CA 94541
(510)537-2424

SCORE Office (Hemet)
1700 E. Florida Ave.
Hemet, CA 92544-4679
(909)652-4390
Fax: (909)929-8543

SCORE Office (Hesperia)
16367 Main St.
PO Box 403656
Hesperia, CA 92340
(619)244-2135

SCORE Office (Holloster)
321 San Felipe Rd., No. 11
Hollister, CA 95023

SCORE Office (Hollywood)
7018 Hollywood Blvd.
Hollywood, CA 90028
(213)469-8311
Fax: (213)469-2805

SCORE Office (Indio)
82503 Hwy. 111
PO Drawer TTT
Indio, CA 92202
(619)347-0676

SCORE Office (Inglewood)
330 Queen St.
Inglewood, CA 90301
(818)552-3206

SCORE Office (La Puente)
218 N. Grendanda St. D.
La Puente, CA 91744
(818)330-3216
Fax: (818)330-9524

SCORE Office (La Verne)
2078 Bonita Ave.
La Verne, CA 91750

(909)593-5265
Fax: (714)929-8475

SCORE Office (Lake Elsinore)
132 W. Graham Ave.
Lake Elsinore, CA 92530
(909)674-2577

SCORE Office (Lakeport)
PO Box 295
Lakeport, CA 95453
(707)263-5092

SCORE Office (Lakewood)
5445 E. Del Amo Blvd., Ste. 2
Lakewood, CA 90714
(213)920-7737

SCORE Office (Long Beach)
1 World Trade Center
Long Beach, CA 90831

SCORE Office (Los Alamitos)
901 W. Civic Center Dr., Ste. 160
Los Alamitos, CA 90720

SCORE Office (Los Altos)
321 University Ave.
Los Altos, CA 94022
(415)948-1455

SCORE Office (Manhattan Beach)
PO Box 3007
Manhattan Beach, CA 90266
(310)545-5313
Fax: (310)545-7203

SCORE Office (Merced)
1632 N. St.
Merced, CA 95340
(209)725-3800
Fax: (209)383-4959

SCORE Office (Milpitas)
75 S. Milpitas Blvd., Ste. 205
Milpitas, CA 95035
(408)262-2613
Fax: (408)262-2823

SCORE Office (Yosemite)
1012 11th St., Ste. 300
Modesto, CA 95354
(209)521-9333

SCORE Office (Montclair)
5220 Benito Ave.
Montclair, CA 91763

SCORE Office (Monterey Bay)
380 Alvarado St.
PO Box 1770
Monterey, CA 93940-1770
(408)649-1770

SCORE Office (Moreno Valley)
25480 Alessandro
Moreno Valley, CA 92553

SCORE Office (Morgan Hill)
25 W. 1st St.
PO Box 786
Morgan Hill, CA 95038
(408)779-9444
Fax: (408)778-1786

SCORE Office (Morro Bay)
880 Main St.
Morro Bay, CA 93442
(805)772-4467

SCORE Office (Mountain View)
580 Castro St.
Mountain View, CA 94041
(415)968-8378
Fax: (415)968-5668

SCORE Office (Napa)
1556 1st St.
Napa, CA 94559
(707)226-7455
Fax: (707)226-1171

SCORE Office (North Hollywood)
5019 Lankershim Blvd.
North Hollywood, CA 91601
(818)552-3206

SCORE Office (Northridge)
8801 Reseda Blvd.
Northridge, CA 91324
(818)349-5676

SCORE Office (Novato)
807 De Long Ave.
Novato, CA 94945
(415)897-1164
Fax: (415)898-9097

SCORE Office (East Bay)
519 17th St.
Oakland, CA 94612
(510)273-6611
Fax: (510)273-6015
E-mail: webmaster@eastbayscore.org
Website: http://www.eastbayscore.org

SCORE Office (Oceanside)
928 N. Coast Hwy.
Oceanside, CA 92054
(619)722-1534

SCORE Office (Ontario)
121 West B. St.
Ontario, CA 91762
Fax: (714)984-6439

SCORE Office (Oxnard)
PO Box 867
Oxnard, CA 93032
(805)385-8860
Fax: (805)487-1763

SCORE Office (Pacifica)
450 Dundee Way, Ste. 2
Pacifica, CA 94044
(415)355-4122

SCORE Office (Palm Desert)
72990 Hwy. 111
Palm Desert, CA 92260
(619)346-6111
Fax: (619)346-3463

SCORE Office (Palm Springs)
650 E. Tahquitz Canyon Way Ste. D
Palm Springs, CA 92262-6706
(760)320-6682
Fax: (760)323-9426

SCORE Office (Lakeside)
2150 Low Tree
Palmdale, CA 93551
(805)948-4518
Fax: (805)949-1212

SCORE Office (Palo Alto)
325 Forest Ave.
Palo Alto, CA 94301
(415)324-3121
Fax: (415)324-1215

SCORE Office (Pasadena)
117 E. Colorado Blvd., Ste. 100
Pasadena, CA 91105
(818)795-3355
Fax: (818)795-5663

SCORE Office (Paso Robles)
1225 Park St.
Paso Robles, CA 93446-2234
(805)238-0506
Fax: (805)238-0527

SCORE Office (Petaluma)
799 Baywood Dr., Ste. 3
Petaluma, CA 94954
(707)762-2785
Fax: (707)762-4721

SCORE Office (Pico Rivera)
9122 E. Washington Blvd.
Pico Rivera, CA 90660

SCORE Office (Pittsburg)
2700 E. Leland Rd.
Pittsburg, CA 94565
(510)439-2181
Fax: (510)427-1599

SCORE Office (Pleasanton)
777 Peters Ave.
Pleasanton, CA 94566
(510)846-9697

SCORE Office (Monterey Park)
485 N. Garey
Pomona, CA 91769

SCORE Office (Pomona)
485 N. Garey Ave.
Pomona, CA 91766
(909)622-1256

SCORE Office (Antelope Valley)
4511 West Ave. M-4
Quartz Hill, CA 93536
(805)272-0087
E-mail: avscore@ptw.com
Website: http://www.score.av.org/

SCORE Office (Shasta)
737 Auditorium Dr.
Redding, CA 96099
(916)225-2770

SCORE Office (Redwood City)
1675 Broadway
Redwood City, CA 94063
(415)364-1722
Fax: (415)364-1729

SCORE Office (Richmond)
3925 MacDonald Ave.
Richmond, CA 94805

SCORE Office (Ridgecrest)
PO Box 771
Ridgecrest, CA 93555
(619)375-8331
Fax: (619)375-0365

SCORE Office (Riverside)
3685 Main St., Ste. 350
Riverside, CA 92501
(909)683-7100

SCORE Office (Sacramento)
9845 Horn Rd., 260-B
Sacramento, CA 95827
(916)361-2322
Fax: (916)361-2164
E-mail: sacchapter@directcon.net

SCORE Office (Salinas)
PO Box 1170
Salinas, CA 93902
(408)424-7611
Fax: (408)424-8639

SCORE Office (Inland Empire)
777 E. Rialto Ave.
Purchasing

San Bernardino, CA 92415-0760
(909)386-8278

SCORE Office (San Carlos)
San Carlos Chamber of Commerce
PO Box 1086
San Carlos, CA 94070
(415)593-1068
Fax: (415)593-9108

SCORE Office (Encinitas)
550 W. C St., Ste. 550
San Diego, CA 92101-3540
(619)557-7272
Fax: (619)557-5894

SCORE Office (San Diego)
550 West C. St., Ste. 550
San Diego, CA 92101-3540
(619)557-7272
Fax: (619)557-5894
Website: http://www.score-sandiego.org

SCORE Office (Menlo Park)
1100 Merrill St.
San Francisco, CA 94105
(415)325-2818
Fax: (415)325-0920

SCORE Office (San Francisco)
455 Market St., 6th Fl.
San Francisco, CA 94105
(415)744-6827
Fax: (415)744-6750
E-mail: sfscore@sfscore.
Website: http://www.sfscore.com

SCORE Office (San Gabriel)
401 W. Las Tunas Dr.
San Gabriel, CA 91776
(818)576-2525
Fax: (818)289-2901

SCORE Office (San Jose)
Deanza College
208 S. 1st. St., Ste. 137
San Jose, CA 95113
(408)288-8479
Fax: (408)535-5541

SCORE Office (Santa Clara County)
280 S. 1st St., Rm. 137
San Jose, CA 95113
(408)288-8479
Fax: (408)535-5541
E-mail: svscore@Prodigy.net
Website: http://www.svscore.org

SCORE Office (San Luis Obispo)
3566 S. Hiquera, No. 104
San Luis Obispo, CA 93401

(805)547-0779

SCORE Office (San Mateo)
1021 S. El Camino, 2nd Fl.
San Mateo, CA 94402
(415)341-5679

SCORE Office (San Pedro)
390 W. 7th St.
San Pedro, CA 90731
(310)832-7272

SCORE Office (Orange County)
200 W. Santa Anna Blvd., Ste. 700
Santa Ana, CA 92701
(714)550-7369
Fax: (714)550-0191
Website: http://www.score114.org

SCORE Office (Santa Barbara)
3227 State St.
Santa Barbara, CA 93130
(805)563-0084

SCORE Office (Central Coast)
509 W. Morrison Ave.
Santa Maria, CA 93454
(805)347-7755

SCORE Office (Santa Maria)
614 S. Broadway
Santa Maria, CA 93454-5111
(805)925-2403
Fax: (805)928-7559

SCORE Office (Santa Monica)
501 Colorado, Ste. 150
Santa Monica, CA 90401
(310)393-9825
Fax: (310)394-1868

SCORE Office (Santa Rosa)
777 Sonoma Ave., Rm. 115E
Santa Rosa, CA 95404
(707)571-8342
Fax: (707)541-0331
Website: http://www.pressdemo.com/
community/score/score.html

SCORE Office (Scotts Valley)
4 Camp Evers Ln.
Scotts Valley, CA 95066
(408)438-1010
Fax: (408)438-6544

SCORE Office (Simi Valley)
40 W. Cochran St., Ste. 100
Simi Valley, CA 93065
(805)526-3900
Fax: (805)526-6234

SCORE Office (Sonoma)
453 1st St. E

Sonoma, CA 95476
(707)996-1033

SCORE Office (Los Banos)
222 S. Shepard St.
Sonora, CA 95370
(209)532-4212

SCORE Office (Tuolumne County)
39 North Washington St.
Sonora, CA 95370
(209)588-0128
E-mail: score@mlode.com

SCORE Office (South San Francisco)
445 Market St., Ste. 6th Fl.
South San Francisco, CA 94105
(415)744-6827
Fax: (415)744-6812

SCORE Office (Stockton)
401 N. San Joaquin St., Rm. 215
Stockton, CA 95202
(209)946-6293

SCORE Office (Taft)
314 4th St.
Taft, CA 93268
(805)765-2165
Fax: (805)765-6639

SCORE Office (Conejo Valley)
625 W. Hillcrest Dr.
Thousand Oaks, CA 91360
(805)499-1993
Fax: (805)498-7264

SCORE Office (Torrance)
3400 Torrance Blvd., Ste. 100
Torrance, CA 90503
(310)540-5858
Fax: (310)540-7662

SCORE Office (Truckee)
PO Box 2757
Truckee, CA 96160
(916)587-2757
Fax: (916)587-2439

SCORE Office (Visalia)
113 S. M St,
Tulare, CA 93274
(209)627-0766
Fax: (209)627-8149

SCORE Office (Upland)
433 N. 2nd Ave.
Upland, CA 91786
(909)931-4108

SCORE Office (Vallejo)
2 Florida St.
Vallejo, CA 94590

(707)644-5551
Fax: (707)644-5590

SCORE Office (Van Nuys)
14540 Victory Blvd.
Van Nuys, CA 91411
(818)989-0300
Fax: (818)989-3836

SCORE Office (Ventura)
5700 Ralston St., Ste. 310
Ventura, CA 93001
(805)658-2688
Fax: (805)658-2252
E-mail: scoreven@jps.net
Website: http://www.jps.net/scoreven

SCORE Office (Vista)
201 E. Washington St.
Vista, CA 92084
(619)726-1122
Fax: (619)226-8654

SCORE Office (Watsonville)
PO Box 1748
Watsonville, CA 95077
(408)724-3849
Fax: (408)728-5300

SCORE Office (West Covina)
811 S. Sunset Ave.
West Covina, CA 91790
(818)338-8496
Fax: (818)960-0511

SCORE Office (Westlake)
30893 Thousand Oaks Blvd.
Westlake Village, CA 91362
(805)496-5630
Fax: (818)991-1754

Colorado

SCORE Office (Colorado Springs)
2 N. Cascade Ave., Ste. 110
Colorado Springs, CO 80903
(719)636-3074
Website: http://www.cscc.org/score02/index.html

SCORE Office (Denver)
US Custom's House, 4th Fl.
721 19th St.
Denver, CO 80201-0660
(303)844-3985
Fax: (303)844-6490
E-mail: score62@csn.net
Website: http://www.sni.net/score62

SCORE Office (Tri-River)
1102 Grand Ave.

Glenwood Springs, CO 81601
(970)945-6589

SCORE Office (Grand Junction)
2591 B & 3/4 Rd.
Grand Junction, CO 81503
(970)243-5242

SCORE Office (Gunnison)
608 N. 11th
Gunnison, CO 81230
(303)641-4422

SCORE Office (Montrose)
1214 Peppertree Dr.
Montrose, CO 81401
(970)249-6080

SCORE Office (Pagosa Springs)
PO Box 4381
Pagosa Springs, CO 81157
(970)731-4890

SCORE Office (Rifle)
0854 W. Battlement Pky., Apt. C106
Parachute, CO 81635
(970)285-9390

SCORE Office (Pueblo)
302 N. Santa Fe
Pueblo, CO 81003
(719)542-1704
Fax: (719)542-1624
E-mail: mackey@iex.net
Website: http://www.pueblo.org/score

SCORE Office (Ridgway)
143 Poplar Pl.
Ridgway, CO 81432

SCORE Office (Silverton)
PO Box 480
Silverton, CO 81433
(303)387-5430

SCORE Office (Minturn)
PO Box 2066
Vail, CO 81658
(970)476-1224

Connecticut

SCORE Office (Greater Bridgeport)
230 Park Ave.
Bridgeport, CT 06601-0999
(203)576-4369
Fax: (203)576-4388

SCORE Office (Bristol)
10 Main St. 1st. Fl.
Bristol, CT 06010
(203)584-4718
Fax: (203)584-4722

SCORE office (Greater Danbury)
246 Federal Rd.
Unit LL2, Ste. 7
Brookfield, CT 06804
(203)775-1151

SCORE Office (Greater Danbury)
246 Federal Rd., Unit LL2, Ste. 7
Brookfield, CT 06804
(203)775-1151

SCORE Office (Eastern Connecticut)
Administration Bldg., Rm. 313
PO 625
61 Main St. (Chapter 579)
Groton, CT 06475
(203)388-9508

SCORE Office (Greater Hartford County)
330 Main St.
Hartford, CT 06106
(860)548-1749
Fax: (860)240-4659
Website: http://www.score56.org

SCORE Office (Manchester)
20 Hartford Rd.
Manchester, CT 06040
(203)646-2223
Fax: (203)646-5871

SCORE Office (New Britain)
185 Main St., Ste. 431
New Britain, CT 06051
(203)827-4492
Fax: (203)827-4480

SCORE Office (New Haven)
25 Science Pk., Bldg. 25, Rm. 366
New Haven, CT 06511
(203)865-7645

SCORE Office (Fairfield County)
24 Beldon Ave., 5th Fl.
Norwalk, CT 06850
(203)847-7348
Fax: (203)849-9308

SCORE Office (Old Saybrook)
146 Main St.
Old Saybrook, CT 06475
(860)388-9508

SCORE Office (Simsbury)
Box 244
Simsbury, CT 06070
(203)651-7307
Fax: (203)651-1933

SCORE Office (Torrington)
23 North Rd.
Torrington, CT 06791
(203)482-6586

Delaware

SCORE Office (Dover)
Treadway Towers
PO Box 576
Dover, DE 19903
(302)678-0892
Fax: (302)678-0189

SCORE Office (Lewes)
PO Box 1
Lewes, DE 19958
(302)645-8073
Fax: (302)645-8412

SCORE Office (Milford)
204 NE Front St.
Milford, DE 19963
(302)422-3301

SCORE Office (Wilmington)
824 Market St., Ste. 610
Wilmington, DE 19801
(302)573-6652
Fax: (302)573-6092
Website: http://www.scoredelaware.com

District of Columbia

SCORE Office (George Mason University)
409 3rd St. SW, 4th Fl.
Washington, DC 20024
800-634-0245

SCORE Office (Washington DC)
1110 Vermont Ave. NW, 9th Fl.
Washington, DC 20043
(202)606-4000
Fax: (202)606-4225
E-mail: dcscore@hotmail.com
Website: http://www.scoredc.org/

Florida

SCORE Office (Desota County Chamber of Commerce)
16 South Velucia Ave.
Arcadia, FL 34266
(941)494-4033

SCORE Office (Suncoast/Pinellas)
Airport Business Ctr.
4707 - 140th Ave. N, No. 311
Clearwater, FL 33755
(813)532-6800
Fax: (813)532-6800

SCORE Office (DeLand)
336 N. Woodland Blvd.
DeLand, FL 32720
(904)734-4331
Fax: (904)734-4333

SCORE Office (South Palm Beach)
1050 S. Federal Hwy., Ste. 132
Delray Beach, FL 33483
(561)278-7752
Fax: (561)278-0288

SCORE Office (Ft. Lauderdale)
Federal Bldg., Ste. 123
299 E. Broward Blvd.
Ft. Lauderdale, FL 33301
(954)356-7263
Fax: (954)356-7145

SCORE Office (Southwest Florida)
The Renaissance
8695 College Pky., Ste. 345 & 346
Ft. Myers, FL 33919
(941)489-2935
Fax: (941)489-1170

SCORE Office (Treasure Coast)
Professional Center, Ste. 2
3220 S. US, No. 1
Ft. Pierce, FL 34982
(561)489-0548

SCORE Office (Gainesville)
101 SE 2nd Pl., Ste. 104
Gainesville, FL 32601
(904)375-8278

SCORE Office (Hialeah Dade Chamber)
59 W. 5th St.
Hialeah, FL 33010
(305)887-1515
Fax: (305)887-2453

SCORE Office (Daytona Beach)
921 Nova Rd., Ste. A
Holly Hills, FL 32117
(904)255-6889
Fax: (904)255-0229
E-mail: score87@dbeach.com

SCORE Office (South Broward)
3475 Sheridian St., Ste. 203
Hollywood, FL 33021
(305)966-8415

SCORE Office (Citrus County)
5 Poplar Ct.
Homosassa, FL 34446
(352)382-1037

SCORE Office (Jacksonville)
7825 Baymeadows Way, Ste. 100-B

Jacksonville, FL 32256
(904)443-1911
Fax: (904)443-1980
E-mail: scorejax@juno.com
Website: http://www.scorejax.org/

SCORE Office (Jacksonville Satellite)
3 Independent Dr.
Jacksonville, FL 32256
(904)366-6600
Fax: (904)632-0617

SCORE Office (Central Florida)
5410 S. Florida Ave., No. 3
Lakeland, FL 33801
(941)687-5783
Fax: (941)687-6225

SCORE Office (Lakeland)
100 Lake Morton Dr.
Lakeland, FL 33801
(941)686-2168

SCORE Office (St. Petersburg)
800 W. Bay Dr., Ste. 505
Largo, FL 33712
(813)585-4571

SCORE Office (Leesburg)
9501 US Hwy. 441
Leesburg, FL 34788-8751
(352)365-3556
Fax: (352)365-3501

SCORE Office (Cocoa)
1600 Farno Rd., Unit 205
Melbourne, FL 32935
(407)254-2288

SCORE Office (Melbourne)
Melbourne Professional Complex
1600 Sarno, Ste. 205
Melbourne, FL 32935
(407)254-2288
Fax: (407)245-2288

SCORE Office (Merritt Island)
1600 Sarno Rd., Ste. 205
Melbourne, FL 32935
(407)254-2288
Fax: (407)254-2288

SCORE Office (Space Coast)
Melbourn Professional Complex
1600 Sarno, Ste. 205
Melbourne, FL 32935
(407)254-2288
Fax: (407)254-2288

SCORE Office (Dade)
49 NW 5th St.
Miami, FL 33128
(305)371-6889

Fax: (305)374-1882
E-mail: score@netrox.net
Website: http://www.netrox.net/~score/

SCORE Office (Naples of Collier)
International College
2654 Tamiami Trl. E
Naples, FL 34112
(941)417-1280
Fax: (941)417-1281
E-mail: score@naples.net
Website: http://www.naples.net/clubs/
score/index.htm

SCORE Office (Pasco County)
6014 US Hwy. 19, Ste. 302
New Port Richey, FL 34652
(813)842-4638

SCORE Office (Southeast Volusia)
115 Canal St.
New Smyrna Beach, FL 32168
(904)428-2449
Fax: (904)423-3512

SCORE Office (Ocala)
110 E. Silver Springs Blvd.
Ocala, FL 34470
(352)629-5959

Clay County SCORE Office
Clay County Chamber of Commerce
1734 Kingsdey Ave.
PO Box 1441
Orange Park, FL 32073
(904)264-2651
Fax: (904)269-0363

SCORE Office (Orlando)
80 N. Hughey Ave.
Rm. 445 Federal Bldg.
Orlando, FL 32801
(407)648-6476
Fax: (407)648-6425

SCORE Office (Emerald Coast)
19 W. Garden St., No. 325
Pensacola, FL 32501
(904)444-2060
Fax: (904)444-2070

SCORE Office (Charlotte County)
201 W. Marion Ave., Ste. 211
Punta Gorda, FL 33950
(941)575-1818
E-mail: score@gls3c.com
Website: http://www.charlotte-
florida.com/business/scorepg01.htm

SCORE Office (St. Augustine)
1 Riberia St.
St. Augustine, FL 32084

(904)829-5681
Fax: (904)829-6477

SCORE Office (Bradenton)
2801 Fruitville, Ste. 280
Sarasota, FL 34237
(813)955-1029

SCORE Office (Manasota)
2801 Fruitville Rd., Ste. 280
Sarasota, FL 34237
(941)955-1029
Fax: (941)955-5581
E-mail: score116@gte.net
Website: http://www.score-suncoast.org/

SCORE Office (Tallahassee)
200 W. Park Ave.
Tallahassee, FL 32302
(850)487-2665

SCORE Office (Hillsborough)
4732 Dale Mabry Hwy. N, Ste. 400
Tampa, FL 33614-6509
(813)870-0125

SCORE Office (Lake Sumter)
122 E. Main St.
Tavares, FL 32778-3810
(352)365-3556

SCORE Office (Titusville)
2000 S. Washington Ave.
Titusville, FL 32780
(407)267-3036
Fax: (407)264-0127

SCORE Office (Venice)
257 N. Tamiami Trl.
Venice, FL 34285
(941)488-2236
Fax: (941)484-5903

SCORE Office (Palm Beach)
500 Australian Ave. S, Ste. 100
West Palm Beach, FL 33401
(561)833-1672
Fax: (561)833-1712

SCORE Office (Wildwood)
103 N. Webster St.
Wildwood, FL 34785

Georgia

SCORE Office (Atlanta)
Harris Tower, Suite 1900
233 Peachtree Rd., NE
Atlanta, GA 30309
(404)347-2442
Fax: (404)347-1227

SCORE Office (Augusta)
3126 Oxford Rd.
Augusta, GA 30909
(706)869-9100

SCORE Office (Columbus)
School Bldg.
PO Box 40
Columbus, GA 31901
(706)327-3654

SCORE Office (Dalton-Whitfield)
305 S. Thorton Ave.
Dalton, GA 30720
(706)279-3383

SCORE Office (Gainesville)
PO Box 374
Gainesville, GA 30503
(770)532-6206
Fax: (770)535-8419

SCORE Office (Macon)
711 Grand Bldg.
Macon, GA 31201
(912)751-6160

SCORE Office (Brunswick)
4 Glen Ave.
St. Simons Island, GA 31520
(912)265-0620
Fax: (912)265-0629

SCORE Office (Savannah)
111 E. Liberty St., Ste. 103
Savannah, GA 31401
(912)652-4335
Fax: (912)652-4184
E-mail: info@scoresav.org
Website: http://www.coastalempire.com/
score/index.htm

Guam

SCORE Office (Guam)
Pacific News Bldg., Rm. 103
238 Archbishop Flores St.
Agana, GU 96910-5100
(671)472-7308

Hawaii

SCORE Office (Hawaii, Inc.)
1111 Bishop St., Ste. 204
PO Box 50207
Honolulu, HI 96813
(808)522-8132
Fax: (808)522-8135
E-mail: hnlscore@juno.com

SCORE Office (Kahului)
250 Alamaha, Unit N16A

Kahului, HI 96732
(808)871-7711

SCORE Office (Maui, Inc.)
590 E. Lipoa Pkwy., Ste. 227
Kihei, HI 96753
(808)875-2380

Idaho

SCORE Office (Treasure Valley)
1020 Main St., No. 290
Boise, ID 83702
(208)334-1696
Fax: (208)334-9353

SCORE Office (Eastern Idaho)
2300 N. Yellowstone, Ste. 119
Idaho Falls, ID 83401
(208)523-1022
Fax: (208)528-7127

Illinois

SCORE Office (Fox Valley)
40 W. Downer Pl.
PO Box 277
Aurora, IL 60506
(630)897-9214
Fax: (630)897-7002

SCORE Office (Greater Belvidere)
419 S. State St.
Belvidere, IL 61008
(815)544-4357
Fax: (815)547-7654

SCORE Office (Bensenville)
1050 Busse Hwy. Suite 100
Bensenville, IL 60106
(708)350-2944
Fax: (708)350-2979

SCORE Office (Central Illinois)
402 N. Hershey Rd.
Bloomington, IL 61704
(309)644-0549
Fax: (309)663-8270
E-mail: webmaster@central-illinois-
score.org
Website: http://www.central-illinois-
score.org/

SCORE Office (Southern Illinois)
150 E. Pleasant Hill Rd.
Box 1
Carbondale, IL 62901
(618)453-6654
Fax: (618)453-5040

SCORE Office (Chicago)
Northwest Atrium Ctr.

500 W. Madison St., No. 1250
Chicago, IL 60661
(312)353-7724
Fax: (312)886-5688
Website: http://www.mcs.net/~bic/

SCORE Office (Chicago–Oliver Harvey College)
Pullman Bldg.
1000 E. 11th St., 7th Fl.
Chicago, IL 60628
Fax: (312)468-8086

SCORE Office (Danville)
28 W. N. Street
Danville, IL 61832
(217)442-7232
Fax: (217)442-6228

SCORE Office (Decatur)
Milliken University
1184 W. Main St.
Decatur, IL 62522
(217)424-6297
Fax: (217)424-3993
E-mail: charding@mail.millikin.edu
Website: http://www.millikin.edu/
academics/Tabor/score.html

SCORE Office (Downers Grove)
925 Curtis
Downers Grove, IL 60515
(708)968-4050
Fax: (708)968-8368

SCORE Office (Elgin)
24 E. Chicago, 3rd Fl.
PO Box 648
Elgin, IL 60120
(847)741-5660
Fax: (847)741-5677

SCORE Office (Freeport Area)
26 S. Galena Ave.
Freeport, IL 61032
(815)233-1350
Fax: (815)235-4038

SCORE Office (Galesburg)
292 E. Simmons St.
PO Box 749
Galesburg, IL 61401
(309)343-1194
Fax: (309)343-1195

SCORE Office (Glen Ellyn)
500 Pennsylvania
Glen Ellyn, IL 60137
(708)469-0907
Fax: (708)469-0426

SCORE Office (Greater Alton)
Alden Hall
5800 Godfrey Rd.
Godfrey, IL 62035-2466
(618)467-2280
Fax: (618)466-8289
Website: http://www.altonweb.com/
score/

SCORE Office (Grayslake)
19351 W. Washington St.
Grayslake, IL 60030
(708)223-3633
Fax: (708)223-9371

SCORE Office (Harrisburg)
303 S. Commercial
Harrisburg, IL 62946-1528
(618)252-8528
Fax: (618)252-0210

SCORE Office (Joliet)
100 N. Chicago
Joliet, IL 60432
(815)727-5371
Fax: (815)727-5374

SCORE Office (Kankakee)
101 S. Schuyler Ave.
Kankakee, IL 60901
(815)933-0376
Fax: (815)933-0380

SCORE Office (Macomb)
216 Seal Hall, Rm. 214
Macomb, IL 61455
(309)298-1128
Fax: (309)298-2520

SCORE Office (Matteson)
210 Lincoln Mall
Matteson, IL 60443
(708)709-3750
Fax: (708)503-9322

SCORE Office (Mattoon)
1701 Wabash Ave.
Mattoon, IL 61938
(217)235-5661
Fax: (217)234-6544

SCORE Office (Quad Cities)
622 19th St.
Moline, IL 61265
(309)797-0082
Fax: (309)757-5435
E-mail: score@qconline.com
Website: http://www.qconline.com/
business/score/

SCORE Office (Naperville)
131 W. Jefferson Ave.

Naperville, IL 60540
(708)355-4141
Fax: (708)355-8355

SCORE Office (Northbrook)
2002 Walters Ave.
Northbrook, IL 60062
(847)498-5555
Fax: (847)498-5510

SCORE Office (Palos Hills)
10900 S. 88th Ave.
Palos Hills, IL 60465
(847)974-5468
Fax: (847)974-0078

SCORE Office (Peoria)
124 SW Adams, Ste. 300
Peoria, IL 61602
(309)676-0755
Fax: (309)676-7534

SCORE Office (Prospect Heights)
1375 Wolf Rd.
Prospect Heights, IL 60070
(847)537-8660
Fax: (847)537-7138

SCORE Office (Quincy Tri-State)
300 Civic Center Plz., Ste. 245
Quincy, IL 62301
(217)222-8093
Fax: (217)222-3033

SCORE Office (River Grove)
2000 5th Ave.
River Grove, IL 60171
(708)456-0300
Fax: (708)583-3121

SCORE Office (Northern Illinois)
515 N. Court St.
Rockford, IL 61103
(815)962-0122
Fax: (815)962-0122

SCORE Office (St. Charles)
103 N. 1st Ave.
St. Charles, IL 60174-1982
(847)584-8384
Fax: (847)584-6065

SCORE Office (Springfield)
511 W. Capitol Ave., Ste. 302
Springfield, IL 62704
(217)492-4416
Fax: (217)492-4867

SCORE Office (Sycamore)
112 Somunak St.
Sycamore, IL 60178
(815)895-3456
Fax: (815)895-0125

SCORE Office (University)
Hwy. 50 & Stuenkel Rd. Ste. C3305
University Park, IL 60466
(708)534-5000
Fax: (708)534-8457

Indiana

SCORE Office (Anderson)
205 W. 11th St.
Anderson, IN 46015
(317)642-0264

SCORE Office (Bloomington)
Star Center
216 W. Allen
Bloomington, IN 47403
(812)335-7334
E-mail: wtfische@indiana.edu
Website: http://
www.brainfreezemedia.com/score527/

SCORE Office (South East Indiana)
500 Franklin St.
Box 29
Columbus, IN 47201
(812)379-4457

SCORE Office (Corydon)
310 N. Elm St.
Corydon, IN 47112
(812)738-2137
Fax: (812)738-6438

SCORE Office (Crown Point)
Old Courthouse Sq. Ste. 206
PO Box 43
Crown Point, IN 46307
(219)663-1800

SCORE Office (Elkhart)
418 S. Main St.
Elkhart, IN 46515
(219)293-1531
Fax: (219)294-1859

SCORE Office (Evansville)
1100 W. Lloyd Expy., Ste. 105
Evansville, IN 47708
(812)426-6144

SCORE Office (Fort Wayne)
1300 S. Harrison St.
Ft. Wayne, IN 46802
(219)422-2601
Fax: (219)422-2601

SCORE Office (Gary)
973 W. 6th Ave., Rm. 326
Gary, IN 46402
(219)882-3918

SCORE Office (Hammond)
7034 Indianapolis Blvd.
Hammond, IN 46324
(219)931-1000
Fax: (219)845-9548

SCORE Office (Indianapolis)
429 N. Pennsylvania St., Ste. 100
Indianapolis, IN 46204-1873
(317)226-7264
Fax: (317)226-7259
E-mail: inscore@indy.net
Website: http://www.score-indianapolis.org/

SCORE Office (Jasper)
PO Box 307
Jasper, IN 47547-0307
(812)482-6866

SCORE Office (Kokomo/Howard Counties)
106 N. Washington St.
Kokomo, IN 46901
(765)457-5301
Fax: (765)452-4564

SCORE Office (Logansport)
300 E. Broadway, Ste. 103
Logansport, IN 46947
(219)753-6388

SCORE Office (Madison)
301 E. Main St.
Madison, IN 47250
(812)265-3135
Fax: (812)265-2923

SCORE Office (Marengo)
Rt. 1 Box 224D
Marengo, IN 47140
Fax: (812)365-2793

SCORE Office (Marion/Grant Counties)
215 S. Adams
Marion, IN 46952
(765)664-5107

SCORE Office (Merrillville)
255 W. 80th Pl.
Merrillville, IN 46410
(219)769-8180
Fax: (219)736-6223

SCORE Office (Michigan City)
200 E. Michigan Blvd.
Michigan City, IN 46360
(219)874-6221
Fax: (219)873-1204

SCORE Office (South Central Indiana)
4100 Charleston Rd.
New Albany, IN 47150-9538
(812)945-0066

SCORE Office (Rensselaer)
104 W. Washington
Rensselaer, IN 47978

SCORE Office (Salem)
210 N. Main St.
Salem, IN 47167
(812)883-4303
Fax: (812)883-1467

SCORE Office (South Bend)
300 N. Michigan St.
South Bend, IN 46601
(219)282-4350
E-mail: chair@southbend-score.org
Website: http://www.southbend-score.org/

SCORE Office (Valparaiso)
150 Lincolnway
Valparaiso, IN 46383
(219)462-1105
Fax: (219)469-5710

SCORE Office (Vincennes)
27 N. 3rd
PO Box 553
Vincennes, IN 47591
(812)882-6440
Fax: (812)882-6441

SCORE Office (Wabash)
PO Box 371
Wabash, IN 46992
(219)563-1168
Fax: (219)563-6920

Iowa

SCORE Office (Burlington)
Federal Bldg.
300 N. Main St.
Burlington, IA 52601
(319)752-2967

SCORE Office (Cedar Rapids)
2750 1st Ave. NE, Ste 350
Cedar Rapids, IA 52401-1806
(319)362-6405
Fax: (319)362-7861
E:mail: score@scorecr.org
Website: http://www.scorecr.org

SCORE Office (Illowa)
333 4th Ave. S
Clinton, IA 52732
(319)242-5702

SCORE Office (Council Bluffs)
7 N. 6th St.
Council Bluffs, IA 51502
(712)325-1000

SCORE Office (Northeast Iowa)
3404 285th St.
Cresco, IA 52136
(319)547-3377

SCORE Office (Des Moines)
Federal Bldg., Rm. 749
210 Walnut St.
Des Moines, IA 50309-2186
(515)284-4760

SCORE Office (Ft. Dodge)
Federal Bldg., Rm. 436
205 S. 8th St.
Ft. Dodge, IA 50501
(515)955-2622

SCORE Office (Independence)
110 1st. St. east
Independence, IA 50644
(319)334-7178
Fax: (319)334-7179

SCORE Office (Iowa City)
210 Federal Bldg.
PO Box 1853
Iowa City, IA 52240-1853
(319)338-1662

SCORE Office (Keokuk)
401 Main St.
Pierce Bldg., No. 1
Keokuk, IA 52632
(319)524-5055

SCORE Office (Central Iowa)
Fisher Community College
709 S. Center
Marshalltown, IA 50158
(515)753-6645

SCORE Office (River City)
15 West State St.
Mason City, IA 50401
(515)423-5724

SCORE Office (South Central)
SBDC, Indian Hills Community College
525 Grandview Ave.
Ottumwa, IA 52501
(515)683-5127
Fax: (515)683-5263

SCORE Office (Dubuque)
10250 Sundown Rd.
Peosta, IA 52068
(319)556-5110

SCORE Office (Southwest Iowa)
614 W. Sheridan
Shenandoah, IA 51601
(712)246-3260

SCORE Office (Sioux City)
Federal Bldg.
320 6th St.
Sioux City, IA 51101
(712)277-2324
Fax: (712)277-2325

SCORE Office (Iowa Lakes)
122 W. 5th St.
Spencer, IA 51301
(712)262-3059

SCORE Office (Vista)
119 W. 6th St.
Storm Lake, IA 50588
(712)732-3780

SCORE Office (Waterloo)
215 E. 4th
Waterloo, IA 50703
(319)233-8431

Kansas

SCORE Office (Southwest Kansas)
501 W. Spruce
Dodge City, KS 67801
(316)227-3119

SCORE Office (Emporia)
811 Homewood
Emporia, KS 66801
(316)342-1600

SCORE Office (Golden Belt)
1307 Williams
Great Bend, KS 67530
(316)792-2401

SCORE Office (Hays)
PO Box 400
Hays, KS 67601
(913)625-6595

SCORE Office (Hutchinson)
1 E. 9th St.
Hutchinson, KS 67501
(316)665-8468
Fax: (316)665-7619

SCORE Office (Southeast Kansas)
404 Westminster Pl.
PO Box 886
Independence, KS 67301
(316)331-4741

SCORE Office (McPherson)
306 N. Main

PO Box 616
McPherson, KS 67460
(316)241-3303

SCORE Office (Salina)
120 Ash St.
Salina, KS 67401
(785)243-4290
Fax: (785)243-1833

SCORE Office (Topeka)
1700 College
Topeka, KS 66621
(785)231-1010

SCORE Office (Wichita)
100 E. English, Ste. 510
Wichita, KS 67202
(316)269-6273
Fax: (316)269-6499

SCORE Office (Ark Valley)
205 E. 9th St.
Winfield, KS 67156
(316)221-1617

Kentucky

SCORE Office (Ashland)
PO Box 830
Ashland, KY 41105
(606)329-8011
Fax: (606)325-4607

SCORE Office (Bowling Green)
812 State St.
PO Box 51
Bowling Green, KY 42101
(502)781-3200
Fax: (502)843-0458

SCORE Office (Tri-Lakes)
508 Barbee Way
Danville, KY 40422-1548
(606)231-9902

SCORE Office (Glasgow)
301 W. Main St.
Glasgow, KY 42141
(502)651-3161
Fax: (502)651-3122

SCORE Office (Hazard)
B & I Technical Center
100 Airport Gardens Rd.
Hazard, KY 41701
(606)439-5856
Fax: (606)439-1808

SCORE Office (Lexington)
410 W. Vine St., Ste. 290, Civic C
Lexington, KY 40507
(606)231-9902

Fax: (606)253-3190
E-mail: scorelex@uky.campus.mci.net

SCORE Office (Louisville)
188 Federal Office Bldg.
600 Dr. Martin L. King Jr. Pl.
Louisville, KY 40202
(502)582-5976

SCORE Office (Madisonville)
257 N. Main
Madisonville, KY 42431
(502)825-1399
Fax: (502)825-1396

SCORE Office (Paducah)
Federal Office Bldg.
501 Broadway, Rm. B-36
Paducah, KY 42001
(502)442-5685

Louisiana

SCORE Office (Central Louisiana)
802 3rd St.
Alexandria, LA 71309
(318)442-6671

SCORE Office (Baton Rouge)
564 Laurel St.
PO Box 3217
Baton Rouge, LA 70801
(504)381-7130
Fax: (504)336-4306

SCORE Office (North Shore)
2 W. Thomas
Hammond, LA 70401
(504)345-4457
Fax: (504)345-4749

SCORE Office (Lafayette)
804 St. Mary Blvd.
Lafayette, LA 70505-1307
(318)233-2705
Fax: (318)234-8671
E-mail: score302@aol.com

SCORE Office (Lake Charles)
120 W. Pujo St.
Lake Charles, LA 70601
(318)433-3632

SCORE Office (New Orleans)
365 Canal St., Ste. 3100
New Orleans, LA 70130
(504)589-2356
Fax: (504)589-2339

SCORE Office (Shreveport)
400 Edwards St.
Shreveport, LA 71101

(318)677-2536
Fax: (318)677-2541

Maine

SCORE Office (Augusta)
40 Western Ave.
Augusta, ME 04330
(207)622-8509

SCORE Office (Bangor)
Peabody Hall, Rm. 229
One College Cir.
Bangor, ME 04401
(207)941-9707

SCORE Office (Central & Northern Arroostock)
111 High St.
Caribou, ME 04736
(207)492-8010
Fax: (207)492-8010

SCORE Office (Penquis)
South St.
Dover Foxcroft, ME 04426
(207)564-7021

SCORE Office (Maine Coastal)
Mill Mall
Box 1105
Ellsworth, ME 04605-1105
(207)667-5800
E-mail: score@arcadia.net

SCORE Office (Lewiston-Auburn)
BIC of Maine-Bates Mill Complex
35 Canal St.
Lewiston, ME 04240-7764
(207)782-3708
Fax: (207)783-7745

SCORE Office (Portland)
66 Pearl St., Rm. 210
Portland, ME 04101
(207)772-1147
Fax: (207)772-5581
E-mail: Score53@score.maine.org
Website: http://www.score.maine.org/chapter53/

SCORE Office (Western Mountains)
255 River St.
PO Box 252
Rumford, ME 04257-0252
(207)369-9976

SCORE Office (Oxford Hills)
166 Main St.
South Paris, ME 04281
(207)743-0499

Maryland

SCORE Office (Southern Maryland)
2525 Riva Rd., Ste. 110
Annapolis, MD 21401
(410)266-9553
Fax: (410)573-0981
E-mail: score390@aol.com
Website: http://members.aol.com/score390/index.htm

SCORE Office (Baltimore)
The City Crescent Bldg., 6th Fl.
10 S. Howard St.
Baltimore, MD 21201
(410)962-2233
Fax: (410)962-1805

SCORE Office (Bel Air)
108 S. Bond St.
Bel Air, MD 21014
(410)838-2020
Fax: (410)893-4715

SCORE Office (Bethesda)
7910 Woodmont Ave., Ste. 1204
Bethesda, MD 20814
(301)652-4900
Fax: (301)657-1973

SCORE Office (Bowie)
6670 Race Track Rd.
Bowie, MD 20715
(301)262-0920
Fax: (301)262-0921

SCORE Office (Dorchester County)
203 Sunburst Hwy.
Cambridge, MD 21613
(410)228-3575

SCORE Office (Upper Shore)
210 Marlboro Ave.
Easton, MD 21601
(410)822-4606
Fax: (410)822-7922

SCORE Office (Frederick County)
43A S. Market St.
Frederick, MD 21701
(301)662-8723
Fax: (301)846-4427

SCORE Office (Gaithersburg)
9 Park Ave.
Gaithersburg, MD 20877
(301)840-1400
Fax: (301)963-3918

SCORE Office (Glen Burnie)
103 Crain Hwy. SE
Glen Burnie, MD 21061

(410)766-8282
Fax: (410)766-9722

SCORE Office (Hagerstown)
111 W. Washington St.
Hagerstown, MD 21740
(301)739-2015
Fax: (301)739-1278

SCORE Office (Laurel)
7901 Sandy Spring Rd. Ste. 501
Laurel, MD 20707
(301)725-4000
Fax: (301)725-0776

SCORE Office (Salisbury)
300 E. Main St.
Salisbury, MD 21801
(410)749-0185
Fax: (410)860-9925

Massachusetts

SCORE Office (NE Massachusetts)
100 Cummings Ctr., Ste. 101 K
Beverly, MA 01923
(978)922-9441
Website: http://www1.shore.net/~score/

SCORE Office (Boston)
10 Causeway St., Rm. 265
Boston, MA 02222-1093
(617)565-5591
Fax: (617)565-5598
E-mail: boston-score-20@worldnet.att.net
Website: http://www.scoreboston.org/

SCORE office (Bristol/Plymouth County)
53 N. 6th St., Federal Bldg.
Bristol, MA 02740
(508)994-5093

SCORE Office (SE Massachusetts)
60 School St.
Brockton, MA 02401
(508)587-2673
Fax: (508)587-1340
Website: http://www.metrosouthchamber.com/score.html

SCORE Office (North Adams)
820 N. State Rd.
Cheshire, MA 01225
(413)743-5100

SCORE Office (Clinton Satellite)
1 Green St.
Clinton, MA 01510
Fax: (508)368-7689

SCORE Office (Greenfield)
PO Box 898
Greenfield, MA 01302
(413)773-5463
Fax: (413)773-7008

SCORE Office (Haverhill)
87 Winter St.
Haverhill, MA 01830
(508)373-5663
Fax: (508)373-8060

SCORE Office (Hudson Satellite)
PO Box 578
Hudson, MA 01749
(508)568-0360
Fax: (508)568-0360

SCORE Office (Cape Cod)
Independence Pk., Ste. 5B
270 Communications Way
Hyannis, MA 02601
(508)775-4884
Fax: (508)790-2540

SCORE Office (Lawrence)
264 Essex St.
Lawrence, MA 01840
(508)686-0900
Fax: (508)794-9953

SCORE Office (Leominster Satellite)
110 Erdman Way
Leominster, MA 01453
(508)840-4300
Fax: (508)840-4896

SCORE Office (Bristol/Plymouth Counties)
53 N. 6th St., Federal Bldg.
New Bedford, MA 02740
(508)994-5093

SCORE Office (Newburyport)
29 State St.
Newburyport, MA 01950
(617)462-6680

SCORE Office (Pittsfield)
66 West St.
Pittsfield, MA 01201
(413)499-2485

SCORE Office (Haverhill-Salem)
32 Derby Sq.
Salem, MA 01970
(508)745-0330
Fax: (508)745-3855

SCORE Office (Springfield)
1350 Main St.
Federal Bldg.

Springfield, MA 01103
(413)785-0314

SCORE Office (Carver)
12 Taunton Green, Ste. 201
Taunton, MA 02780
(508)824-4068
Fax: (508)824-4069

SCORE Office (Worcester)
33 Waldo St.
Worcester, MA 01608
(508)753-2929
Fax: (508)754-8560

Michigan

SCORE Office (Allegan)
PO Box 338
Allegan, MI 49010
(616)673-2479

SCORE Office (Ann Arbor)
425 S. Main St., Ste. 103
Ann Arbor, MI 48104
(313)665-4433

SCORE Office (Battle Creek)
34 W. Jackson Ste. 4A
Battle Creek, MI 49017-3505
(616)962-4076
Fax: (616)962-6309

SCORE Office (Cadillac)
222 Lake St.
Cadillac, MI 49601
(616)775-9776
Fax: (616)768-4255

SCORE Office (Detroit)
477 Michigan Ave., Rm. 515
Detroit, MI 48226
(313)226-7947
Fax: (313)226-3448

SCORE Office (Flint)
708 Root Rd., Rm. 308
Flint, MI 48503
(810)233-6846

SCORE Office (Grand Rapids)
111 Pearl St. NW
Grand Rapids, MI 49503-2831
(616)771-0305
Fax: (616)771-0328
E-mail: scoreone@iserv.net
Website: http://www.iserv.net/
~scoreone/

SCORE Office (Holland)
480 State St.
Holland, MI 49423
(616)396-9472

SCORE Office (Jackson)
209 East Washington
PO Box 80
Jackson, MI 49204
(517)782-8221
Fax: (517)782-0061

SCORE Office (Kalamazoo)
345 W. Michigan Ave.
Kalamazoo, MI 49007
(616)381-5382
Fax: (616)384-0096
E-mail: score@nucleus.net

SCORE Office (Lansing)
117 E. Allegan
PO Box 14030
Lansing, MI 48901
(517)487-6340
Fax: (517)484-6910

SCORE Office (Livonia)
15401 Farmington Rd.
Livonia, MI 48154
(313)427-2122
Fax: (313)427-6055

SCORE Office (Madison Heights)
26345 John R
Madison Heights, MI 48071
(810)542-5010
Fax: (810)542-6821

SCORE Office (Monroe)
111 E. 1st
Monroe, MI 48161
(313)242-3366
Fax: (313)242-7253

SCORE Office (Mt. Clemens)
58 S/B Gratiot
Mt. Clemens, MI 48043
(810)463-1528
Fax: (810)463-6541

SCORE Office (Muskegon)
PO Box 1087
230 Terrace Plz.
Muskegon, MI 49443
(616)722-3751
Fax: (616)728-7251

SCORE Office (Petoskey)
401 E. Mitchell St.
Petoskey, MI 49770
(616)347-4150

SCORE Office (Pontiac)
Executive Office Bldg.
1200 N. Telegraph Rd.
Pontiac, MI 48341
(810)975-9555

SCORE Office (Pontiac)
PO Box 430025
Pontiac, MI 48343
(810)335-9600

SCORE Office (Port Huron)
920 Pinegrove Ave.
Port Huron, MI 48060
(810)985-7101

SCORE Office (Rochester)
71 Walnut Ste. 110
Rochester, MI 48307
(810)651-6700
Fax: (810)651-5270

SCORE Office (Saginaw)
901 S. Washington Ave.
Saginaw, MI 48601
(517)752-7161
Fax: (517)752-9055

SCORE Office (Upper Peninsula)
2581 I-75 Business Spur
Sault Ste. Marie, MI 49783
(906)632-3301

SCORE Office (Southfield)
21000 W. 10 Mile Rd.
Southfield, MI 48075
(810)204-3050
Fax: (810)204-3099

SCORE Office (Traverse City)
202 E. Grandview Pkwy.
PO Box 387
Traverse City, MI 49685
(616)947-5075
Fax: (616)946-2565

SCORE Office (Warren)
30500 Van Dyke, Ste. 118
Warren, MI 48093
(810)751-3939

Minnesota

SCORE Office (Aitkin)
Aitkin, MN 56431
(218)741-3906

SCORE Office (Albert Lea)
202 N. Broadway Ave.
Albert Lea, MN 56007
(507)373-7487

SCORE Office (Austin)
PO Box 864
Austin, MN 55912
(507)437-4561
Fax: (507)437-4869

SCORE Office (South Metro)
Ames Business Ctr.
2500 W. County Rd., No. 42
Burnsville, MN 55337
(612)898-5645
Fax: (612)435-6972
E-mail: southmetro@scoreminn.org
Website: http://www.scoreminn.org/southmetro/

SCORE Office (Duluth)
1717 Minnesota Ave.
Duluth, MN 55802
(218)727-8286
Fax: (218)727-3113
E-mail: duluth@scoreminn.org
Website: http://www.scoreminn.org

SCORE Office (Fairmont)
PO Box 826
Fairmont, MN 56031
(507)235-5547
Fax: (507)235-8411

SCORE Office (Southwest Minnesota)
112 Riverfront St.
Box 999
Mankato, MN 56001
(507)345-4519
Fax: (507)345-4451
Website: http://www.scoreminn.org/

SCORE Office (Minneapolis)
North Plaza Bldg., Ste. 51
5217 Wayzata Blvd.
Minneapolis, MN 55416
(612)591-0539
Fax: (612)544-0436
Website: http://www.scoreminn.org/

SCORE Office (Owatonna)
PO Box 331
Owatonna, MN 55060
(507)451-7970
Fax: (507)451-7972

SCORE Office (Red Wing)
2000 W. Main St., Ste. 324
Red Wing, MN 55066
(612)388-4079

SCORE Office (Southeastern Minnesota)
220 S. Broadway, Ste. 100
Rochester, MN 55901
(507)288-1122
Fax: (507)282-8960
Website: http://www.scoreminn.org/

SCORE Office (Brainerd)
St. Cloud, MN 56301

SCORE Office (Central Area)
1527 Northway Dr.
St. Cloud, MN 56301
(320)240-1332
Fax: (320)255-9050
Website: http://www.scoreminn.org/

SCORE Office (St. Paul)
350 St. Peter St., No. 295
Lowry Professional Bldg.
St. Paul, MN 55102
(651)223-5010
Fax: (651)223-5048
Website: http://www.scoreminn.org/

SCORE Office (Winona)
Box 870
Winona, MN 55987
(507)452-2272
Fax: (507)454-8814

SCORE Office (Worthington)
1121 3rd Ave.
Worthington, MN 56187
(507)372-2919
Fax: (507)372-2827

Mississippi

SCORE Office (Delta)
915 Washington Ave.
PO Box 933
Greenville, MS 38701
(601)378-3141

SCORE Office (Gulfcoast)
1 Government Plaza
2909 13th St., Ste. 203
Gulfport, MS 39501
(228)863-0054

SCORE Office (Jackson)
1st Jackson Center, Ste. 400
101 W. Capitol St.
Jackson, MS 39201
(601)965-5533

SCORE Office (Meridian)
5220 16th Ave.
Meridian, MS 39305
(601)482-4412

Missouri

SCORE Office (Lake of the Ozark)
University Extension
113 Kansas St.
PO Box 1405
Camdenton, MO 65020
(573)346-2644
Fax: (573)346-2694
E-mail: score@cdoc.net

Website: http://sites.cdoc.net/score/

Chamber of Commerce (Cape Girardeau)
PO Box 98
Cape Girardeau, MO 63702-0098
(314)335-3312

SCORE Office (Mid-Missouri)
1705 Halstead Ct.
Columbia, MO 65203
(573)874-1132

SCORE Office (Ozark-Gateway)
1486 Glassy Rd.
Cuba, MO 65453-1640
(573)885-4954

SCORE Office (Kansas City)
323 W. 8th St., Ste. 104
Kansas City, MO 64105
(816)374-6675
Fax: (816)374-6692
E-mail: SCOREBIC@AOL.COM
Website: http://www.crn.org/score/

SCORE Office (Sedalia)
Lucas Place
323 W. 8th St., Ste.104
Kansas City, MO 64105
(816)374-6675

SCORE office (Tri-Lakes)
PO Box 1148
Kimberling, MO 65686
(417)739-3041

SCORE Office (Tri-Lakes)
HCRI Box 85
Lampe, MO 65681
(417)858-6798

SCORE Office (Mexico)
111 N. Washington St.
Mexico, MO 65265
(314)581-2765

SCORE Office (Southeast Missouri)
Rte. 1, Box 280
Neelyville, MO 63954
(573)989-3577

SCORE office (Poplar Bluff Area)
806 Emma St.
Poplar Bluff, MO 63901
(573)686-8892

SCORE Office (St. Joseph)
3003 Frederick Ave.
St. Joseph, MO 64506
(816)232-4461

SCORE Office (St. Louis)
815 Olive St., Rm. 242
St. Louis, MO 63101-1569
(314)539-6970
Fax: (314)539-3785
E-mail: info@stlscore.org
Website: http://www.stlscore.org/

SCORE Office (Lewis & Clark)
425 Spencer Rd.
St. Peters, MO 63376
(314)928-2900
Fax: (314)928-2900
E-mail: score01@mail.win.org

SCORE Office (Springfield)
620 S. Glenstone, Ste. 110
Springfield, MO 65802-3200
(417)864-7670
Fax: (417)864-4108

SCORE office (Southeast Kansas)
1206 W. First St.
Webb City, MO 64870
(417)673-3984

Montana

SCORE Office (Billings)
815 S. 27th St.
Billings, MT 59101
(406)245-4111

SCORE Office (Bozeman)
1205 E. Main St.
Bozeman, MT 59715
(406)586-5421

SCORE Office (Butte)
1000 George St.
Butte, MT 59701
(406)723-3177

SCORE Office (Great Falls)
710 First Ave. N
Great Falls, MT 59401
(406)761-4434
E-mail: scoregtf@in.tch.com

SCORE Office (Havre, Montana)
518 First St.
Havre, MT 59501
(406)265-4383

SCORE Office (Helena)
Federal Bldg.
301 S. Park
Helena, MT 59626-0054
(406)441-1081

SCORE Office (Kalispell)
2 Main St.

Kalispell, MT 59901
(406)756-5271
Fax: (406)752-6665

SCORE Office (Missoula)
723 Ronan
Missoula, MT 59806
(406)327-8806
E-mail: score@safeshop.com
Website: http://missoula.bigsky.net/score/

Nebraska

SCORE Office (Columbus)
Columbus, NE 68601
(402)564-2769

SCORE Office (Fremont)
92 W. 5th St.
Fremont, NE 68025
(402)721-2641

SCORE Office (Hastings)
Hastings, NE 68901
(402)463-3447

SCORE Office (Lincoln)
8800 O St.
Lincoln, NE 68520
(402)437-2409

SCORE Office (Panhandle)
150549 CR 30
Minatare, NE 69356
(308)632-2133
Website: http://www.tandt.com/SCORE

SCORE Office (Norfolk)
3209 S. 48th Ave.
Norfolk, NE 68106
(402)564-2769

SCORE Office (North Platte)
3301 W. 2nd St.
North Platte, NE 69101
(308)532-4466

SCORE Office (Omaha)
11145 Mill Valley Rd.
Omaha, NE 68154
(402)221-3606
Fax: (402)221-3680
E-mail: infoctr@ne.uswest.net
Website: http://www.tandt.com/score/

Nevada

SCORE Office (Incline Village)
969 Tahoe Blvd.
Incline Village, NV 89451
(702)831-7327
Fax: (702)832-1605

SCORE Office (Carson City)
301 E. Stewart
PO Box 7527
Las Vegas, NV 89125
(702)388-6104

SCORE Office (Las Vegas)
300 Las Vegas Blvd. S, Ste. 1100
Las Vegas, NV 89101
(702)388-6104

SCORE Office (Northern Nevada)
SBDC, College of Business
Administration
Univ. of Nevada
Reno, NV 89557-0100
(702)784-4436
Fax: (702)784-4337

New Hampshire

SCORE Office (North Country)
PO Box 34
Berlin, NH 03570
(603)752-1090

SCORE Office (Concord)
143 N. Main St., Rm. 202A
PO Box 1258
Concord, NH 03301
(603)225-1400
Fax: (603)225-1409

SCORE Office (Dover)
299 Central Ave.
Dover, NH 03820
(603)742-2218
Fax: (603)749-6317

SCORE Office (Monadnock)
34 Mechanic St.
Keene, NH 03431-3421
(603)352-0320

SCORE Office (Lakes Region)
67 Water St., Ste. 105
Laconia, NH 03246
(603)524-9168

SCORE Office (Upper Valley)
Citizens Bank Bldg., Rm. 310
20 W. Park St.
Lebanon, NH 03766
(603)448-3491
Fax: (603)448-1908
E-mail: billt@valley.net
Website: http://www.valley.net/~score/

SCORE Office (Merrimack Valley)
275 Chestnut St., Rm. 618
Manchester, NH 03103

(603)666-7561
Fax: (603)666-7925

SCORE Office (Mt. Washington Valley)
PO Box 1066
North Conway, NH 03818
(603)383-0800

SCORE Office (Seacoast)
195 Commerce Way, Unit-A
Portsmouth, NH 03801-3251
(603)433-0575

New Jersey

SCORE Office (Somerset)
Paritan Valley Community College, Rte. 28
Branchburg, NJ 08807
(908)218-8874
E-mail: nj-score@grizbiz.com.
Website: http://www.nj-score.org/

SCORE Office (Chester)
5 Old Mill Rd.
Chester, NJ 07930
(908)879-7080

SCORE Office (Greater Princeton)
4 A George Washington Dr.
Cranbury, NJ 08512
(609)520-1776

SCORE Office (Freehold)
36 W. Main St.
Freehold, NJ 07728
(908)462-3030
Fax: (908)462-2123

SCORE Office (North West)
Picantinny Innovation Ctr.
3159 Schrader Rd.
Hamburg, NJ 07419
(973)209-8525
Fax: (973)209-7252
E-mail: nj-score@grizbiz.com
Website: http://www.nj-score.org/

SCORE Office (Monmouth)
765 Newman Springs Rd.
Lincroft, NJ 07738
(908)224-2573
E-mail: nj-score@grizbiz.com
Website: http://www.nj-score.org/

SCORE Office (Manalapan)
125 Symmes Dr.
Manalapan, NJ 07726
(908)431-7220

SCORE Office (Jersey City)
2 Gateway Ctr., 4th Fl.
Newark, NJ 07102

(973)645-3982
Fax: (973)645-2375

SCORE Office (Newark)
2 Gateway Center, 15th Fl.
Newark, NJ 07102-5553
(973)645-3982
Fax: (973)645-2375
E-mail: nj-score@grizbiz.com
Website: http://www.nj-score.org

SCORE Office (Bergen County)
327 E. Ridgewood Ave.
Paramus, NJ 07652
(201)599-6090
E-mail: nj-score@grizbiz.com
Website: http://www.nj-score.org/

SCORE Office (Pennsauken)
4900 Rte. 70
Pennsauken, NJ 08109
(609)486-3421

SCORE Office (Southern New Jersey)
4900 Rte. 70
Pennsauken, NJ 08109
(609)486-3421
E-mail: nj-score@grizbiz.com
Website: http://www.nj-score.org/

SCORE Office (Greater Princeton)
216 Rockingham Row
Princeton Forrestal Village
Princeton, NJ 08540
(609)520-1776
Fax: (609)520-9107
E-mail: nj-score@grizbiz.com
Website: http://www.nj-score.org/

SCORE Office (Shrewsbury)
Hwy. 35
Shrewsbury, NJ 07702
(908)842-5995
Fax: (908)219-6140

SCORE Office (Ocean County)
33 Washington St.
Toms River, NJ 08754
(732)505-6033
E-mail: nj-score@grizbiz.com
Website: http://www.nj-score.org/

SCORE Office (Wall)
2700 Allaire Rd.
Wall, NJ 07719
(908)449-8877

SCORE Office (Wayne)
2055 Hamburg Tpke.
Wayne, NJ 07470
(201)831-7788
Fax: (201)831-9112

New Mexico

SCORE Office (Albuquerque)
525 Buena Vista, SE
Albuquerque, NM 87106
(505)272-7999
Fax: (505)272-7963

SCORE Office (Las Cruces)
Loretto Towne Center
505 S. Main St., Ste. 125
Las Cruces, NM 88001
(505)523-5627
Fax: (505)524-2101
E-mail: score.397@zianet.com

SCORE Office (Roswell)
Federal Bldg., Rm. 237
Roswell, NM 88201
(505)625-2112
Fax: (505)623-2545

SCORE Office (Santa Fe)
Montoya Federal Bldg.
120 Federal Place, Rm. 307
Santa Fe, NM 87501
(505)988-6302
Fax: (505)988-6300

New York

SCORE Office (Northeast)
1 Computer Dr. S
Albany, NY 12205
(518)446-1118
Fax: (518)446-1228

SCORE Office (Auburn)
30 South St.
PO Box 675
Auburn, NY 13021
(315)252-7291

SCORE Office (South Tier Binghamton)
Metro Center, 2nd Fl.
49 Court St.
PO Box 995
Binghamton, NY 13902
(607)772-8860

SCORE Office (Queens County City)
12055 Queens Blvd., Rm. 333
Borough Hall, NY 11424
(718)263-8961

SCORE Office (Buffalo)
Federal Bldg., Rm. 1311
111 W. Huron St.
Buffalo, NY 14202
(716)551-4301

Website: http://www2.pcom.net/score/buf45.html

SCORE Office (Canandaigua)
Chamber of Commerce Bldg.
113 S. Main St.
Canandaigua, NY 14424
(716)394-4400
Fax: (716)394-4546

SCORE Office (Chemung)
333 E. Water St., 4th Fl.
Elmira, NY 14901
(607)734-3358

SCORE Office (Geneva)
Chamber of Commerce Bldg.
PO Box 587
Geneva, NY 14456
(315)789-1776
Fax: (315)789-3993

SCORE Office (Glens Falls)
84 Broad St.
Glens Falls, NY 12801
(518)798-8463
Fax: (518)745-1433

SCORE Office (Orange County)
40 Matthews St.
Goshen, NY 10924
(914)294-8080
Fax: (914)294-6121

SCORE Office (Huntington Area)
151 W. Carver St.
Huntington, NY 11743
(516)423-6100

SCORE Office (Tompkins County)
904 E. Shore Dr.
Ithaca, NY 14850
(607)273-7080

SCORE Office (Long Island City)
120-55 Queens Blvd.
Jamaica, NY 11424
(718)263-8961
Fax: (718)263-9032

SCORE Office (Chatauqua)
101 W. 5th St.
Jamestown, NY 14701
(716)484-1103

SCORE Office (Westchester)
2 Caradon Ln.
Katonah, NY 10536
(914)948-3907
Fax: (914)948-4645
E-mail: score@w-w-w.com
Website: http://w-w-w.com/score/

SCORE Office (Queens County)
Queens Borough Hall
120-55 Queens Blvd. Rm. 333
Kew Gardens, NY 11424
(718)263-8961
Fax: (718)263-9032

SCORE Office (Brookhaven)
3233 Rte. 112
Medford, NY 11763
(516)451-6563
Fax: (516)451-6925

SCORE Office (Melville)
35 Pinelawn Rd., Rm. 207-W
Melville, NY 11747
(516)454-0771

SCORE Office (Nassau County)
400 County Seat Dr., No. 140
Mineola, NY 11501
(516)571-3303
E-mail: Counse1998@aol.com
Website: http://members.aol.com/Counse1998/Default.htm

SCORE Office (Mt. Vernon)
4 N. 7th Ave.
Mt. Vernon, NY 10550
(914)667-7500

SCORE Office (New York)
26 Federal Plz., Rm. 3100
New York, NY 10278
(212)264-4507
Fax: (212)264-4963
E-mail: score1000@erols.com
Website: http://users.erols.com/score-nyc/

SCORE Office (Newburgh)
47 Grand St.
Newburgh, NY 12550
(914)562-5100

SCORE Office (Owego)
188 Front St.
Owego, NY 13827
(607)687-2020

SCORE Office (Peekskill)
1 S. Division St.
Peekskill, NY 10566
(914)737-3600
Fax: (914)737-0541

SCORE Office (Penn Yan)
2375 Rte. 14A
Penn Yan, NY 14527
(315)536-3111

SCORE Office (Dutchess)
110 Main St.
Poughkeepsie, NY 12601
(914)454-1700

SCORE Office (Rochester)
601 Keating Federal Bldg., Rm. 410
100 State St.
Rochester, NY 14614
(716)263-6473
Fax: (716)263-3146
Website: http://www.ggw.org/score/

SCORE Office (Saranac Lake)
30 Main St.
Saranac Lake, NY 12983
(315)448-0415

SCORE Office (Suffolk)
286 Main St.
Setauket, NY 11733
(516)751-3886

SCORE Office (Staten Island)
130 Bay St.
Staten Island, NY 10301
(718)727-1221

SCORE Office (Ulster)
Clinton Bldg., Rm. 107
Stone Ridge, NY 12484
(914)687-5035
Fax: (914)687-5015
Website: http://www.scoreulster.org/

SCORE Office (Syracuse)
401 S. Salina, 5th Fl.
Syracuse, NY 13202
(315)471-9393

SCORE Office (Utica)
SUNY Institute of Technology, Route 12
Utica, NY 13504-3050
(315)792-7553

SCORE Office (Watertown)
518 Davidson St.
Watertown, NY 13601
(315)788-1200
Fax: (315)788-8251

North Carolina

SCORE office (Asheboro)
317 E. Dixie Dr.
Asheboro, NC 27203
(336)626-2626
Fax: (336)626-7077

SCORE Office (Asheville)
Federal Bldg., Rm. 259
151 Patton

Asheville, NC 28801-5770
(828)271-4786
Fax: (828)271-4009

SCORE Office (Chapel Hill)
104 S. Estes Dr.
PO Box 2897
Chapel Hill, NC 27514
(919)967-7075

SCORE Office (Coastal Plains)
PO Box 2897
Chapel Hill, NC 27515
(919)967-7075
Fax: (919)968-6874

SCORE Office (Charlotte)
200 N. College St., Ste. A-2015
Charlotte, NC 28202
(704)344-6576
Fax: (704)344-6769
E-mail: CharlotteSCORE47@AOL.com
Website: http://www.charweb.org/business/score/

SCORE Office (Durham)
411 W. Chapel Hill St.
Durham, NC 27707
(919)541-2171

SCORE Office (Gastonia)
PO Box 2168
Gastonia, NC 28053
(704)864-2621
Fax: (704)854-8723

SCORE Office (Greensboro)
400 W. Market St., Ste. 103
Greensboro, NC 27401-2241
(910)333-5399

SCORE Office (Henderson)
PO Box 917
Henderson, NC 27536
(919)492-2061
Fax: (919)430-0460

SCORE Office (Hendersonville)
Federal Bldg., Rm. 108
W. 4th Ave. & Church St.
Hendersonville, NC 28792
(828)693-8702
E-mail: score@circle.net
Website: http://www.wncguide.com/score/Welcome.html

SCORE Office (Unifour)
PO Box 1828
Hickory, NC 28603
(704)328-6111

SCORE Office (High Point)
1101 N. Main St.
High Point, NC 27262
(336)882-8625
Fax: (336)889-9499

SCORE Office (Outer Banks)
Collington Rd. and Mustain
Kill Devil Hills, NC 27948
(252)441-8144

SCORE Office (Down East)
312 S. Front St., Ste. 6
New Bern, NC 28560
(252)633-6688
Fax: (252)633-9608

SCORE Office (Kinston)
PO Box 95
New Bern, NC 28561
(919)633-6688

SCORE Office (Raleigh)
Century Post Office Bldg., Ste. 306
300 Federal St. Mall
Raleigh, NC 27601
(919)856-4739
E-mail: jendres@ibm.net
Website: http://www.intrex.net/score96/score96.htm

SCORE Office (Sanford)
1801 Nash St.
Sanford, NC 27330
(919)774-6442
Fax: (919)776-8739

SCORE Office (Sandhills Area)
1480 Hwy. 15-501
PO Box 458
Southern Pines, NC 28387
(910)692-3926

SCORE Office (Wilmington)
Corps of Engineers Bldg.
96 Darlington Ave., Ste. 207
Wilmington, NC 28403
(910)815-4576
Fax: (910)815-4658

North Dakota

SCORE Office (Bismarck-Mandan)
700 E. Main Ave., 2nd Fl.
PO Box 5509
Bismarck, ND 58506-5509
(701)250-4303

SCORE Office (Fargo)
657 2nd Ave., Rm. 225
Fargo, ND 58108-3083
(701)239-5677

SCORE Office (Upper Red River)
4275 Technology Dr., Rm. 156
Grand Forks, ND 58202-8372
(701)777-3051

SCORE Office (Minot)
100 1st St. SW
Minot, ND 58701-3846
(701)852-6883
Fax: (701)852-6905

Ohio

SCORE Office (Akron)
1 Cascade Plz., 7th Fl.
Akron, OH 44308
(330)379-3163
Fax: (330)379-3164

SCORE Office (Ashland)
Gill Center
47 W. Main St.
Ashland, OH 44805
(419)281-4584

SCORE Office (Canton)
116 Cleveland Ave. NW, Ste. 601
Canton, OH 44702-1720
(330)453-6047

SCORE Office (Chillicothe)
165 S. Paint St.
Chillicothe, OH 45601
(614)772-4530

SCORE Office (Cincinnati)
Ameritrust Bldg., Rm. 850
525 Vine St.
Cincinnati, OH 45202
(513)684-2812
Fax: (513)684-3251
Website: http://
www.score.chapter34.org/

SCORE Office (Cleveland)
Eaton Center, Ste. 620
1100 Superior Ave.
Cleveland, OH 44114-2507
(216)522-4194
Fax: (216)522-4844

SCORE Office (Columbus)
2 Nationwide Plz., Ste. 1400
Columbus, OH 43215-2542
(614)469-2357
Fax: (614)469-2391
E-mail: info@scorecolumbus.org
Website: http://www.scorecolumbus.org/

SCORE Office (Dayton)
Dayton Federal Bldg., Rm. 505
200 W. Second St.

Dayton, OH 45402-1430
(513)225-2887
Fax: (513)225-7667

SCORE Office (Defiance)
615 W. 3rd St.
PO Box 130
Defiance, OH 43512
(419)782-7946

SCORE Office (Findlay)
123 E. Main Cross St.
PO Box 923
Findlay, OH 45840
(419)422-3314

SCORE Office (Lima)
147 N. Main St.
Lima, OH 45801
(419)222-6045
Fax: (419)229-0266

SCORE Office (Mansfield)
55 N. Mulberry St.
Mansfield, OH 44902
(419)522-3211

SCORE Office (Marietta)
Thomas Hall
Marietta, OH 45750
(614)373-0268

SCORE Office (Medina)
County Administrative Bldg.
144 N. Broadway
Medina, OH 44256
(216)764-8650

SCORE Office (Licking County)
50 W. Locust St.
Newark, OH 43055
(614)345-7458

SCORE Office (Salem)
2491 State Rte. 45 S
Salem, OH 44460
(216)332-0361

SCORE Office (Tiffin)
62 S. Washington St.
Tiffin, OH 44883
(419)447-4141
Fax: (419)447-5141

SCORE Office (Toledo)
608 Madison Ave, Ste. 910
Toledo, OH 43624
(419)259-7598
Fax: (419)259-6460

SCORE Office (Heart of Ohio)
377 W. Liberty St.
Wooster, OH 44691

(330)262-5735
Fax: (330)262-5745

SCORE Office (Youngstown)
306 Williamson Hall
Youngstown, OH 44555
(330)746-2687

Oklahoma

SCORE Office (Anadarko)
PO Box 366
Anadarko, OK 73005
(405)247-6651

SCORE Office (Ardmore)
410 W. Main
Ardmore, OK 73401
(580)226-2620

SCORE Office (Northeast Oklahoma)
210 S. Main
Grove, OK 74344
(918)787-2796
Fax: (918)787-2796
E-mail: Score595@greencis.net

SCORE Office (Lawton)
4500 W. Lee Blvd., Bldg. 100, Ste. 107
Lawton, OK 73505
(580)353-8727
Fax: (580)250-5677

SCORE Office (Oklahoma City)
210 Park Ave., No. 1300
Oklahoma City, OK 73102
(405)231-5163
Fax: (405)231-4876
E-mail: score212@usa.net

SCORE Office (Stillwater)
439 S. Main
Stillwater, OK 74074
(405)372-5573
Fax: (405)372-4316

SCORE Office (Tulsa)
616 S. Boston, Ste. 406
Tulsa, OK 74119
(918)581-7462
Fax: (918)581-6908
Website: http://www.ionet.net/~tulscore/

Oregon

SCORE Office (Bend)
63085 N. Hwy. 97
Bend, OR 97701
(541)923-2849
Fax: (541)330-6900

SCORE Office (Willamette)
1401 Willamette St.

PO Box 1107
Eugene, OR 97401-4003
(541)465-6600
Fax: (541)484-4942

SCORE Office (Florence)
3149 Oak St.
Florence, OR 97439
(503)997-8444
Fax: (503)997-8448

SCORE Office (Southern Oregon)
33 N. Central Ave., Ste. 216
Medford, OR 97501
(541)776-4220
E-mail: pgr134f@prodigy.com

SCORE Office (Portland)
1515 SW 5th Ave., Ste. 1050
Portland, OR 97201
(503)326-3441
Fax: (503)326-2808
E-mail: gr134@prodigy.com

SCORE Office (Salem)
416 State St. (corner of Liberty)
Salem, OR 97301
(503)370-2896

Pennsylvania

SCORE Office (Altoona-Blair)
1212 12th Ave.
Altoona, PA 16601-3493
(814)943-8151

SCORE Office (Lehigh Valley)
Rauch Bldg. 37
Lehigh University
621 Taylor St.
Bethlehem, PA 18015
(610)758-4496
Fax: (610)758-5205

SCORE Office (Butler County)
100 N. Main St.
PO Box 1082
Butler, PA 16003
(412)283-2222
Fax: (412)283-0224

SCORE Office (Harrisburg)
4211 Trindle Rd.
Camp Hill, PA 17011
(717)761-4304
Fax: (717)761-4315

SCORE Office (Cumberland Valley)
75 S. 2nd St.
Chambersburg, PA 17201
(717)264-2935

SCORE Office (Monroe County-Stroudsburg)
556 Main St.
East Stroudsburg, PA 18301
(717)421-4433

SCORE Office (Erie)
120 W. 9th St.
Erie, PA 16501
(814)871-5650
Fax: (814)871-7530

SCORE Office (Bucks County)
409 Hood Blvd.
Fairless Hills, PA 19030
(215)943-8850
Fax: (215)943-7404

SCORE Office (Hanover)
146 Broadway
Hanover, PA 17331
(717)637-6130
Fax: (717)637-9127

SCORE Office (Harrisburg)
100 Chestnut, Ste. 309
Harrisburg, PA 17101
(717)782-3874

SCORE Office (East Montgomery County)
Baederwood Shopping Center
1653 The Fairways, Ste. 204
Jenkintown, PA 19046
(215)885-3027

SCORE Office (Kittanning)
2 Butler Rd.
Kittanning, PA 16201
(412)543-1305
Fax: (412)543-6206

SCORE Office (Lancaster)
118 W. Chestnut St.
Lancaster, PA 17603
(717)397-3092

SCORE Office (Westmoreland County)
300 Fraser Purchase Rd.
Latrobe, PA 15650-2690
(412)539-7505
Fax: (412)539-1850

SCORE Office (Lebanon)
252 N. 8th St.
PO Box 899
Lebanon, PA 17042-0899
(717)273-3727
Fax: (717)273-7940

SCORE Office (Lewistown)
3 W. Monument Sq., Ste. 204
Lewistown, PA 17044

(717)248-6713
Fax: (717)248-6714

SCORE Office (Delaware County)
602 E. Baltimore Pike
Media, PA 19063
(610)565-3677
Fax: (610)565-1606

SCORE Office (Milton Area)
112 S. Front St.
Milton, PA 17847
(717)742-7341
Fax: (717)792-2008

SCORE Office (Mon-Valley)
435 Donner Ave.
Monessen, PA 15062
(412)684-4277
Fax: (412)684-7688

SCORE Office (Monroeville)
William Penn Plaza
2790 Mosside Blvd., Ste. 295
Monroeville, PA 15146
(412)856-0622
Fax: (412)856-1030

SCORE Office (Airport Area)
986 Brodhead Rd.
Moon Township, PA 15108-2398
(412)264-6270
Fax: (412)264-1575

SCORE Office (Northeast)
8601 E. Roosevelt Blvd.
Philadelphia, PA 19152
(215)332-3400
Fax: (215)332-6050

SCORE Office (Philadelphia)
1315 Walnut St., Ste. 500
Philadelphia, PA 19107
(215)790-5050
Fax: (215)790-5057
E-mail: score46@bellatlantic.net
Website: http://www.pgweb.net/score46/

SCORE Office (Pittsburgh)
1000 Liberty Ave., Rm. 1122
Pittsburgh, PA 15222
(412)395-6560
Fax: (412)395-6562

SCORE Office (Tri-County)
801 N. Charlotte St.
Pottstown, PA 19464
(610)327-2673

SCORE Office (Reading)
601 Penn St.
Reading, PA 19601
(610)376-3497

SCORE Office (Scranton)
Oppenheim Bldg.
116 N. Washington Ave., Ste. 650
Scranton, PA 18503
(717)347-4611
Fax: (717)347-4611

SCORE Office (Central Pennsylvania)
200 Innovation Blvd., Ste. 242-B
State College, PA 16803
(814)234-9415
Fax: (814)238-9686
Website: http://countrystore.org/
business/score.htm

SCORE Office (Monroe-Stroudsburg)
556 Main St.
Stroudsburg, PA 18360
(717)421-4433

SCORE Office (Uniontown)
Federal Bldg.
Pittsburg St.
PO Box 2065 DTS
Uniontown, PA 15401
(412)437-4222
E-mail: uniontownscore@lcsys.net

SCORE Office (Warren County)
315 2nd Ave.
Warren, PA 16365
(814)723-9017

SCORE Office (Waynesboro)
323 E. Main St.
Waynesboro, PA 17268
(717)762-7123
Fax: (717)962-7124

SCORE Office (Chester County)
Government Service Center, Ste. 281
601 Westtown Rd.
West Chester, PA 19382-4538
(610)344-6910
Fax: (610)344-6919
E-mail: score@locke.ccil.org

SCORE Office (Wilkes-Barre)
7 N. Wilkes-Barre Blvd.
Wilkes Barre, PA 18702-5241
(717)826-6502
Fax: (717)826-6287

SCORE Office (North Central Pennsylvania)
240 W. 3rd St., Rm. 227
PO Box 725
Williamsport, PA 17703
(717)322-3720
Fax: (717)322-1607
E-mail: score234@mail.csrlink.net
Website: http://www.lycoming.org/score/

SCORE Office (York)
Cyber Center
2101 Pennsylvania Ave.
York, PA 17404
(717)845-8830
Fax: (717)854-9333

Puerto Rico

SCORE Office (Puerto Rico & Virgin Islands)
PO Box 12383-96
San Juan, PR 00914-0383
(787)726-8040
Fax: (787)726-8135

Rhode Island

SCORE Office (Barrington)
281 County Rd.
Barrington, RI 02806
(401)247-1920
Fax: (401)247-3763

SCORE Office (Woonsocket)
640 Washington Hwy.
Lincoln, RI 02865
(401)334-1000
Fax: (401)334-1009

SCORE Office (Wickford)
8045 Post Rd.
North Kingstown, RI 02852
(401)295-5566
Fax: (401)295-8987

SCORE Office (J.G.E. Knight)
380 Westminster St.
Providence, RI 02903
(401)528-4571
Fax: (401)528-4539
Website: http://www.riscore.org

SCORE Office (Warwick)
3288 Post Rd.
Warwick, RI 02886
(401)732-1100
Fax: (401)732-1101

SCORE Office (Westerly)
74 Post Rd.
Westerly, RI 02891
(401)596-7761
800-732-7636
Fax: (401)596-2190

South Carolina

SCORE Office (Aiken)
PO Box 892
Aiken, SC 29802
(803)641-1111

800-542-4536
Fax: (803)641-4174

SCORE Office (Anderson)
Anderson Mall
3130 N. Main St.
Anderson, SC 29621
(864)224-0453

SCORE Office (Coastal)
284 King St.
Charleston, SC 29401
(803)727-4778
Fax: (803)853-2529

SCORE Office (Midlands)
Strom Thurmond Bldg., Rm. 358
1835 Assembly St., Rm 358
Columbia, SC 29201
(803)765-5131
Fax: (803)765-5962
Website: http://www.scoremidlands.org/

SCORE Office (Piedmont)
Federal Bldg., Rm. B-02
300 E. Washington St.
Greenville, SC 29601
(864)271-3638

SCORE Office (Greenwood)
PO Drawer 1467
Greenwood, SC 29648
(864)223-8357

SCORE Office (Hilton Head Island)
52 Savannah Trail
Hilton Head, SC 29926
(803)785-7107
Fax: (803)785-7110

SCORE Office (Grand Strand)
937 Broadway
Myrtle Beach, SC 29577
(803)918-1079
Fax: (803)918-1083
E-mail: score381@aol.com

SCORE Office (Spartanburg)
PO Box 1636
Spartanburg, SC 29304
(864)594-5000
Fax: (864)594-5055

South Dakota

SCORE Office (West River)
Rushmore Plz. Civic Ctr.
444 Mount Rushmore Rd., No. 209
Rapid City, SD 57701
(605)394-5311
E-mail: score@gwtc.net

SCORE Office (Sioux Falls)
First Financial Center
110 S. Phillips Ave., Ste. 200
Sioux Falls, SD 57104-6727
(605)330-4231
Fax: (605)330-4231

Tennessee

SCORE Office (Chattanooga)
Federal Bldg., Rm. 26
900 Georgia Ave.
Chattanooga, TN 37402
(423)752-5190
Fax: (423)752-5335

SCORE Office (Cleveland)
PO Box 2275
Cleveland, TN 37320
(423)472-6587
Fax: (423)472-2019

SCORE Office (Upper Cumberland Center)
1225 S. Willow Ave.
Cookeville, TN 38501
(615)432-4111
Fax: (615)432-6010

SCORE Office (Unicoi County)
PO Box 713
Erwin, TN 37650
(423)743-3000
Fax: (423)743-0942

SCORE Office (Greeneville)
115 Academy St.
Greeneville, TN 37743
(423)638-4111
Fax: (423)638-5345

SCORE Office (Jackson)
194 Auditorium St.
Jackson, TN 38301
(901)423-2200

SCORE Office (Northeast Tennessee)
1st Tennessee Bank Bldg.
2710 S. Roan St., Ste. 584
Johnson City, TN 37601
(423)929-7686
Fax: (423)461-8052

SCORE Office (Kingsport)
151 E. Main St.
Kingsport, TN 37662
(423)392-8805

SCORE Office (Greater Knoxville)
Farragot Bldg., Ste. 224
530 S. Gay St.
Knoxville, TN 37902

(423)545-4203
E-mail: scoreknox@ntown.com
Website: http://www.scoreknox.org/

SCORE Office (Maryville)
201 S. Washington St.
Maryville, TN 37804-5728
(423)983-2241
800-525-6834
Fax: (423)984-1386

SCORE Office (Memphis)
Federal Bldg., Ste. 390
167 N. Main St.
Memphis, TN 38103
(901)544-3588

SCORE Office (Nashville)
50 Vantage Way, Ste. 201
Nashville, TN 37228-1500
(615)736-7621

Texas

SCORE Office (Abilene)
2106 Federal Post Office and Court Bldg.
Abilene, TX 79601
(915)677-1857

SCORE Office (Austin)
2501 S. Congress
Austin, TX 78701
(512)442-7235
Fax: (512)442-7528

SCORE Office (Golden Triangle)
450 Boyd St.
Beaumont, TX 77704
(409)838-6581
Fax: (409)833-6718

SCORE Office (Brownsville)
3505 Boca Chica Blvd., Ste. 305
Brownsville, TX 78521
(210)541-4508

SCORE Office (Brazos Valley)
3000 Briarcrest, Ste. 302
Bryan, TX 77802
(409)776-8876
E-mail: 102633.2612@compuserve.com

SCORE Office (Cleburne)
Watergarden Pl., 9th Fl., Ste. 400
Cleburne, TX 76031
(817)871-6002

SCORE Office (Corpus Christi)
651 Upper North Broadway, Ste. 654
Corpus Christi, TX 78477
(512)888-4322
Fax: (512)888-3418

SCORE Office (Dallas)
6260 E. Mockingbird
Dallas, TX 75214-2619
(214)828-2471
Fax: (214)821-8033

SCORE Office (El Paso)
10 Civic Center Plaza
El Paso, TX 79901
(915)534-0541
Fax: (915)534-0513

SCORE Office (Bedford)
100 E. 15th St., Ste. 400
Ft. Worth, TX 76102
(817)871-6002

SCORE Office (Ft. Worth)
100 E. 15th St., No. 24
Ft. Worth, TX 76102
(817)871-6002
Fax: (817)871-6031
E-mail: fwbac@onramp.net

SCORE Office (Garland)
2734 W. Kingsley Rd.
Garland, TX 75041
(214)271-9224

SCORE Office (Granbury Chamber of Commerce)
416 S. Morgan
Granbury, TX 76048
(817)573-1622
Fax: (817)573-0805

SCORE Office (Lower Rio Grande Valley)
222 E. Van Buren, Ste. 500
Harlingen, TX 78550
(956)427-8533
Fax: (956)427-8537

SCORE Office (Houston)
9301 Southwest Fwy., Ste. 550
Houston, TX 77074
(713)773-6565
Fax: (713)773-6550

SCORE Office (Irving)
3333 N. MacArthur Blvd., Ste. 100
Irving, TX 75062
(214)252-8484
Fax: (214)252-6710

SCORE Office (Lubbock)
1205 Texas Ave., Rm. 411D
Lubbock, TX 79401
(806)472-7462
Fax: (806)472-7487

SCORE Office (Midland)
Post Office Annex
200 E. Wall St., Rm. P121
Midland, TX 79701
(915)687-2649

SCORE Office (Orange)
1012 Green Ave.
Orange, TX 77630-5620
(409)883-3536
800-528-4906
Fax: (409)886-3247

SCORE Office (Plano)
1200 E. 15th St.
PO Drawer 940287
Plano, TX 75094-0287
(214)424-7547
Fax: (214)422-5182

SCORE Office (Port Arthur)
4749 Twin City Hwy., Ste. 300
Port Arthur, TX 77642
(409)963-1107
Fax: (409)963-3322

SCORE Office (Richardson)
411 Belle Grove
Richardson, TX 75080
(214)234-4141
800-777-8001
Fax: (214)680-9103

SCORE Office (San Antonio)
Federal Bldg., Rm. A527
727 E. Durango
San Antonio, TX 78206
(210)472-5931
Fax: (210)472-5935

SCORE Office (Texarkana State College)
819 State Line Ave.
Texarkana, TX 75501
(903)792-7191
Fax: (903)793-4304

SCORE Office (East Texas)
RTDC
1530 SSW Loop 323, Ste. 100
Tyler, TX 75701
(903)510-2975
Fax: (903)510-2978

SCORE Office (Waco)
401 Franklin Ave.
Waco, TX 76701
(817)754-8898
Fax: (817)756-0776
Website: http://www.brc-waco.com/

SCORE Office (Wichita Falls)
Hamilton Bldg.
900 8th St.
Wichita Falls, TX 76307
(940)723-2741
Fax: (940)723-8773

Utah

SCORE Office (Northern Utah)
160 N. Main
Logan, UT 84321
(435)746-2269

SCORE Office (Ogden)
1701 E. Windsor Dr.
Ogden, UT 84604
(801)629-8613
E-mail: score158@netscape.net

SCORE Office (Central Utah)
1071 E. Windsor Dr.
Provo, UT 84604
(801)373-8660

SCORE Office (Southern Utah)
225 South 700 East
St. George, UT 84770
(435)652-7751

SCORE Office (Salt Lake)
310 S Main St.
Salt Lake City, UT 84101
(801)746-2269
Fax: (801)746-2273

Vermont

SCORE Office (Champlain Valley)
Winston Prouty Federal Bldg.
11 Lincoln St., Rm. 106
Essex Junction, VT 05452
(802)951-6762

SCORE Office (Montpelier)
87 State St., Rm. 205
PO Box 605
Montpelier, VT 05601
(802)828-4422
Fax: (802)828-4485

SCORE Office (Marble Valley)
256 N. Main St.
Rutland, VT 05701-2413
(802)773-9147

SCORE Office (Northeast Kingdom)
20 Main St.
PO Box 904
St. Johnsbury, VT 05819
(802)748-5101

Virgin Islands

SCORE Office (St. Croix)
United Plaza Shopping Center
PO Box 4010, Christiansted
St. Croix, VI 00822
(809)778-5380

SCORE Office (St. Thomas-St. John)
Federal Bldg., Rm. 21
Veterans Dr.
St. Thomas, VI 00801
(809)774-8530

Virginia

SCORE Office (Arlington)
2009 N. 14th St., Ste. 111
Arlington, VA 22201
(703)525-2400

SCORE Office (Blacksburg)
141 Jackson St.
Blacksburg, VA 24060
(540)552-4061

SCORE Office (Bristol)
20 Volunteer Pkwy.
Bristol, VA 24203
(540)989-4850

SCORE Office (Central Virginia)
1001 E. Market St., Ste. 101
Charlottesville, VA 22902
(804)295-6712
Fax: (804)295-7066

SCORE Office (Alleghany Satellite)
241 W. Main St.
Covington, VA 24426
(540)962-2178
Fax: (540)962-2179

SCORE Office (Central Fairfax)
3975 University Dr., Ste. 350
Fairfax, VA 22030
(703)591-2450

SCORE Office (Falls Church)
PO Box 491
Falls Church, VA 22040
(703)532-1050
Fax: (703)237-7904

SCORE Office (Glenns)
Glenns Campus
Box 287
Glenns, VA 23149
(804)693-9650

SCORE Office (Peninsula)
6 Manhattan Sq.

PO Box 7269
Hampton, VA 23666
(757)766-2000
Fax: (757)865-0339
E-mail: score100@seva.net

SCORE Office (Tri-Cities)
108 N. Main St.
Hopewell, VA 23860
(804)458-5536

SCORE Office (Lynchburg)
Federal Bldg.
1100 Main St.
Lynchburg, VA 24504-1714
(804)846-3235

SCORE Office (Greater Prince William)
8963 Center St
Manassas, VA 20110
(703)368-4813
Fax: (703)368-4733

SCORE Office (Martinsvile)
115 Broad St.
Martinsville, VA 24112-0709
(540)632-6401
Fax: (540)632-5059

SCORE Office (Hampton Roads)
Federal Bldg., Rm. 737
200 Grandby St.
Norfolk, VA 23510
(757)441-3733
Fax: (757)441-3733
E-mail: scorehr60@juno.com

SCORE Office (Norfolk)
Federal Bldg., Rm. 737
200 Granby St.
Norfolk, VA 23510
(757)441-3733
Fax: (757)441-3733

SCORE Office (Virginia Beach)
Chamber of Commerce
200 Grandby St., Rm 737
Norfolk, VA 23510
(804)441-3733

SCORE Office (Radford)
1126 Norwood St.
Radford, VA 24141
(540)639-2202

SCORE Office (Richmond)
Federal Bldg.
400 N. 8th St., Ste. 1150
PO Box 10126
Richmond, VA 23240-0126
(804)771-2400
Fax: (804)771-8018

E-mail: scorechapter12@yahoo.com
Website: http://www.cvco.org/score/

SCORE Office (Roanoke)
Federal Bldg., Rm. 716
250 Franklin Rd.
Roanoke, VA 24011
(540)857-2834
Fax: (540)857-2043
E-mail: scorerva@juno.com
Website: http://hometown.aol.com/
scorerv/Index.html

SCORE Office (Fairfax)
8391 Old Courthouse Rd., Ste. 300
Vienna, VA 22182
(703)749-0400

SCORE Office (Greater Vienna)
513 Maple Ave. West
Vienna, VA 22180
(703)281-1333
Fax: (703)242-1482

SCORE Office (Shenandoah Valley)
301 W. Main St.
Waynesboro, VA 22980
(540)949-8203
Fax: (540)949-7740
E-mail: score427@intelos.net

SCORE Office (Williamsburg)
201 Penniman Rd.
Williamsburg, VA 23185
(757)229-6511
E-mail: wacc@williamsburgcc.com

SCORE Office (Northern Virginia)
1360 S. Pleasant Valley Rd.
Winchester, VA 22601
(540)662-4118

Washington

SCORE Office (Gray's Harbor)
506 Duffy St.
Aberdeen, WA 98520
(360)532-1924
Fax: (360)533-7945

SCORE Office (Bellingham)
101 E. Holly St.
Bellingham, WA 98225
(360)676-3307

SCORE Office (Everett)
2702 Hoyt Ave.
Everett, WA 98201-3556
(206)259-8000

SCORE Office (Gig Harbor)
3125 Judson St.

Gig Harbor, WA 98335
(206)851-6865

SCORE Office (Kennewick)
PO Box 6986
Kennewick, WA 99336
(509)736-0510

SCORE Office (Puyallup)
322 2nd St. SW
PO Box 1298
Puyallup, WA 98371
(206)845-6755
Fax: (206)848-6164

SCORE Office (Seattle)
1200 6th Ave., Ste. 1700
Seattle, WA 98101
(206)553-7320
Fax: (206)553-7044
E-mail: score55@aol.com
Website: http://www.scn.org/civic/score-online/index55.html

SCORE Office (Spokane)
801 W. Riverside Ave., No. 240
Spokane, WA 99201
(509)353-2820
Fax: (509)353-2600
E-mail: score@dmi.net
Website: http://www.dmi.net/
score/

SCORE Office (Clover Park)
PO Box 1933
Tacoma, WA 98401-1933
(206)627-2175

SCORE Office (Tacoma)
1101 Pacific Ave.
Tacoma, WA 98402
(253)274-1288
Fax: (253)274-1289

SCORE Office (Fort Vancouver)
1701 Broadway, S-1
Vancouver, WA 98663
(360)699-1079

SCORE Office (Walla Walla)
500 Tausick Way
Walla Walla, WA 99362
(509)527-4681

SCORE Office (Mid-Columbia)
1113 S. 14th Ave.
Yakima, WA 98907
(509)574-4944
Fax: (509)574-2943
Website: http://www.ellensburg.com/
~score/

West Virginia

SCORE Office (Charleston)
1116 Smith St.
Charleston, WV 25301
(304)347-5463
E-mail: score256@juno.com

SCORE Office (Virginia Street)
1116 Smith St., Ste. 302
Charleston, WV 25301
(304)347-5463

SCORE Office (Marion County)
PO Box 208
Fairmont, WV 26555-0208
(304)363-0486

SCORE Office (Upper Monongahela Valley)
1000 Technology Dr., Ste. 1111
Fairmont, WV 26555
(304)363-0486
E-mail: score537@hotmail.com

SCORE Office (Huntington)
1101 6th Ave., Ste. 220
Huntington, WV 25701-2309
(304)523-4092

SCORE Office (Wheeling)
1310 Market St.
Wheeling, WV 26003
(304)233-2575
Fax: (304)233-1320

Wisconsin

SCORE Office (Fox Cities)
227 S. Walnut St.
Appleton, WI 54913
(920)734-7101
Fax: (920)734-7161

SCORE Office (Beloit)
136 W. Grand Ave., Ste. 100
PO Box 717
Beloit, WI 53511
(608)365-8835
Fax: (608)365-9170

SCORE Office (Eau Claire)
Federal Bldg., Rm. B11
510 S. Barstow St.
Eau Claire, WI 54701
(715)834-1573
E-mail: score@ecol.net
Website: http://www.ecol.net/~score/

SCORE Office (Fond du Lac)
207 N. Main St.
Fond du Lac, WI 54935

(414)921-9500
Fax: (414)921-9559

SCORE Office (Green Bay)
835 Potts Ave.
Green Bay, WI 54304
(414)496-8930
Fax: (414)496-6009

SCORE Office (Janesville)
20 S. Main St., Ste. 11
PO Box 8008
Janesville, WI 53547
(608)757-3160
Fax: (608)757-3170

SCORE Office (La Crosse)
712 Main St.
La Crosse, WI 54602-0219
(608)784-4880

SCORE Office (Madison)
505 S. Rosa Rd.
Madison, WI 53719
(608)441-2820

SCORE Office (Manitowoc)
1515 Memorial Dr.
PO Box 903
Manitowoc, WI 54221-0903
(414)684-5575
Fax: (414)684-1915

SCORE Office (Milwaukee)
310 W. Wisconsin Ave., Ste. 425
Milwaukee, WI 53203
(414)297-3942
Fax: (414)297-1377

SCORE Office (Central Wisconsin)
1224 Lindbergh Ave.
Stevens Point, WI 54481
(715)344-7729

SCORE Office (Superior)
Superior Business Center Inc.
1423 N. 8th St.
Superior, WI 54880
(715)394-7388
Fax: (715)393-7414

SCORE Office (Waukesha)
223 Wisconsin Ave.
Waukesha, WI 53186-4926
(414)542-4249

SCORE Office (Wausau)
300 3rd St., Ste. 200
Wausau, WI 54402-6190
(715)845-6231

SCORE Office (Wisconsin Rapids)
2240 Kingston Rd.

Wisconsin Rapids, WI 54494
(715)423-1830

Wyoming

SCORE Office (Casper)
Federal Bldg., No. 2215
100 East B St.
Casper, WY 82602
(307)261-6529
Fax: (307)261-6530

VENTURE CAPITAL & FINANCING COMPANIES

This section contains a listing of financing and loan companies in the United States and Canada. These listing are arranged alphabetically by country, then by state or province, then by city, then by organization name.

CANADA

Alberta

Launchworks Inc.
1902J 11th St., S.E.
Calgary, AB, Canada T2G 3G2
(403)269-1119
Fax: (403)269-1141
Website: http://www.launchworks.com
Investment Types: Start-up. Industry Preferences: Diversified. Geographic Preferences: Canada.

Native Venture Capital Company, Inc.
21 Artist View Point, Box 7
Site 25, RR 12
Calgary, AB, Canada T3E 6W3
(903)208-5380
Milt Pahl, President
Investment Types: Seed, startup, first stage, second stage, and leveraged buyout. Industry Preferences: Diversified. Geographic Preferences: Western Canada.

Miralta Capital Inc.
4445 Calgary Trail South
888 Terrace Plaza Alberta
Edmonton, AB, Canada T6H 5R7
(780)438-3535
Fax: (780)438-3129
Michael Welsh
Preferred Investment Size: $1,000,000 minimum. Investment Types: First and

second stage, and leveraged buyout. Industry Preferences: Diversified communications, computer related, electronics, consumer products, industrial products and equipment. Geographic Preferences: Canada.

Vencap Equities Alberta Ltd.
10180-101st St., Ste. 1980
Edmonton, AB, Canada T5J 3S4
(403)420-1171
Fax: (403)429-2541
Preferred Investment Size: $1,000,000 minimum. Investment Types: Start-up, first and second stage, control-block purchases, leveraged buyout, and mezzanine. Industry Preferences: Diversified. Geographic Preferences: Northwest, Rocky Mountain region, and Western Canada.

British Columbia

Discovery Capital
5th Fl., 1199 West Hastings
Vancouver, BC, Canada V6E 3T5
(604)683-3000
Fax: (604)662-3457
E-mail: info@discoverycapital.com
Website: http://www.discoverycapital.com
Investment Types: Early stage and start-up. Industry Preferences: Internet related. Geographic Preferences: Canada.

Greenstone Venture Partners
1177 West Hastings St.
Ste. 400
Vancouver, BC, Canada V6E 2K3
(604)717-1977
Fax: (604)717-1976
Website: http://www.greenstonevc.com
Investment Types: Diversified. Industry Preferences: Diversified. Geographic Preferences: Canada.

Growthworks Capital
2600-1055 West Georgia St.
Box 11170 Royal Centre
Vancouver, BC, Canada V6E 3R5
(604)895-7259
Fax: (604)669-7605
Website: http://www.wofund.com
Mike Philips
Preferred Investment Size: $330,000 to $3,300,000. Investment Types: Seed, start-up, first and second stage, balanced, joint ventures, mezzanine, private placement, research and development, and management buyout. Industry

Preferences: Diversified. Geographic Preferences: British Columbia

MDS Discovery Venture Management, Inc.
555 W. Eighth Ave., Ste. 305
Vancouver, BC, Canada V5Z 1C6
(604)872-8464
Fax: (604)872-2977
E-mail: info@mds-ventures.com
David Scott, President
Investment Types: Seed, research and development, startup, first and second stages. Industry Preferences: Biotechnology and communications. Geographic Preferences: Western Canada and Northwestern U.S.

Ventures West Management Inc.
1285 W. Pender St., Ste. 280
Vancouver, BC, Canada V6E 4B1
(604)688-9495
Fax: (604)687-2145
Website: http://www.ventureswest.com
Investment Types: Seed, research and development, startup, first and second stages. Industry Preferences: Diversified technology. Geographic Preferences: Northeast and Western U.S., Canada.

Nova Scotia

ACF Equity Atlantic Inc.
Purdy's Wharf Tower II
Ste. 2106
Halifax, NS, Canada B3J 3R7
(902)421-1965
Fax: (902)421-1808
David Wilson
Investment Types: Seed, start-up, first and second stage, balanced, mezzanine, and leveraged buyout. Industry Preferences: Diversified. Geographic Preferences: Canada.

Montgomerie, Huck & Co.
146 Bluenose Dr.
PO Box 538
Lunenburg, NS, Canada B0J 2C0
(902)634-7125
Fax: (902)634-7130
Christopher Huck
Preferred Investment Size: $300,000 to $500,000. Investment Types: First and second stage, leveraged buyout, mezzanine, and special situation. Industry Preferences: Diversified communications, computer related, and industrial machinery. Geographic Preferences: Canada.

Ontario

IPS Industrial Promotion Services Ltd.
60 Columbia Way, Ste. 720
Markham, ON, Canada L3R 0C9
(905)475-9400
Fax: (905)475-5003
Azim Lalani
Preferred Investment Size: $500,000 minimum. Investment Types: Control-block purchases, leveraged buyout, second stage, and special situation. Industry Preferences: Diversified. Geographic Preferences: U.S. and Canada.

Betwin Investments Inc.
Box 23110
Sault Ste. Marie, ON, Canada P6A 6W6
(705)253-0744
Fax: (705)253-0744
D.B. Stinson
Preferred Investment Size: $500,000 to $1,000,000. Investment Types: Second stage. Industry Preferences: Diversified. Geographic Preferences: U.S. and Canada.

Bailey & Company, Inc.
594 Spadina Ave.
Toronto, ON, Canada M5S 2H4
(416)921-6930
Fax: (416)925-4670
Preferred Investment Size: $500,000 to $1,000,000. Investment Types: Research and development, first stage, and special situations. Industry Preferences: Diversified technology. Geographic Preferences: No preference.

BCE Capital
200 Bay St.
South Tower, Ste. 3120
Toronto, ON, Canada M5J 2J2
(416)815-0078
Fax: (416)941-1073
Website: http://www.bcecapital.com
Preferred Investment Size: $350,000 to $2,000,000. Investment Types: Seed, start-up, early stage, expansion, and research and development. Industry Preferences: Communications, Internet related, electronics, and computer software and services. Geographic Preferences: Ontario and West

Castlehill Ventures
55 University Ave., Ste. 500
Toronto, ON, Canada M5J 2H7
(416)862-8574

Fax: (416)862-8875
Investment Types: Start-up. Industry
Preferences: Telecommunications and
computer related. Geographic
Preferences: Ontario, Canada.

CCFL Mezzanine Partners of Canada
70 University Ave.
Ste. 1450
Toronto, ON, Canada M5J 2M4
(416)977-1450
Fax: (416)977-6764
E-mail: info@ccfl.com
Website: http://www.ccfl.com
Paul Benson
Preferred Investment Size: $10,000,000.
Investment Types: Generalist PE.
Industry Preferences: Diversified.
Geographic Preferences: U.S. and
Canada.

Celtic House International
100 Simcoe St., Ste. 100
Toronto, ON, Canada M5H 3G2
(416)542-2436
Fax: (416)542-2435
Website: http://www.celtic-house.com
Investment Types: Early stage. Industry
Preferences: Computer software and
services, electronics, Internet related,
communications, and computer
hardware. Geographic Preferences: U.S.
and Canada.

Clairvest Group Inc.
22 St. Clair Ave. East
Ste. 1700
Toronto, ON, Canada M4T 2S3
(416)925-9270
Fax: (416)925-5753
Jeff Parr
Preferred Investment Size: $5,000,000
minimum. Investment Types: Balanced,
control-block purchases, later stage,
leveraged buyout, and special situation.
Industry Preferences: Diversified.
Geographic Preferences: U.S. and
Canada.

Crosbie & Co., Inc.
One First Canadian Place
9th Fl.
PO Box 116
Toronto, ON, Canada M5X 1A4
(416)362-7726
Fax: (416)362-3447
E-mail: info@crosbieco.com
Website: http://www.crosbieco.com
Investment Types: Acquisition, distressed
debt, expansion, generalist PE, later

stage, leveraged and management
buyouts, mezzanine, private placement,
recaps, special situations, and
turnarounds. Industry Preferences:
Diversified. Geographic Preferences:
Ontario, Canada.

Drug Royalty Corp.
Eight King St. East
Ste. 202
Toronto, ON, Canada M5C 1B5
(416)863-1865
Fax: (416)863-5161
Harry K. Loveys
Preferred Investment Size: $4,000,000 to
$5,000,000. Investment Types: Research
and development and special situation.
Industry Preferences: Biotechnology and
medical/health related. Geographic
Preferences: No preference.

Grieve, Horner, Brown & Asculai
8 King St. E, Ste. 1704
Toronto, ON, Canada M5C 1B5
(416)362-7668
Fax: (416)362-7660
Preferred Investment Size: $300,000 to
$500,000. Investment Types: Startup,
first and second stages. Industry
Preferences: Diversified. Geographic
Preferences: Entire U.S. and Canada.

Jefferson Partners
77 King St. West
Ste. 4010
PO Box 136
Toronto, ON, Canada M5K 1H1
(416)367-1533
Fax: (416)367-5827
Website: http://www.jefferson.com
Preferred Investment Size: $3,000,000 to
$10,000,000. Investment Types: Seed and
expansion. Industry Preferences:
Communications and media, software, and
Internet related. Geographic Preferences:
Northeastern U.S. and Canada.

J.L. Albright Venture Partners
Canada Trust Tower, 161 Bay St.
Ste. 4440
PO Box 215
Toronto, ON, Canada M5J 2S1
(416)367-2440
Fax: (416)367-4604
Website: http://www.jlaventures.com
Jon Prosser
Investment Types: First and second stage.
Industry Preferences: Internet related,
communications, and computer related.
Geographic Preferences: Canada.

McLean Watson Capital Inc.
One First Canadian Place
Ste. 1410
PO Box 129
Toronto, ON, Canada M5X 1A4
(416)363-2000
Fax: (416)363-2010
Website: http://www.mcleanwatson.com
Matt H. Lawton
Investment Types: First and second stage.
Industry Preferences: Diversified
communications, computer related, laser
related, and fiber optics. Geographic
Preferences: U.S. and Canada.

Middlefield Capital Fund
One First Canadian Place
85th Fl.
PO Box 192
Toronto, ON, Canada M5X 1A6
(416)362-0714
Fax: (416)362-7925
Website: http://www.middlefield.com
David Roode
Preferred Investment Size: $3,000,000
minimum. Investment Types: Second
stage, control-block purchases, industry
rollups, leveraged buyout, and
mezzanine. Industry Preferences:
Diversified. Geographic Preferences: U.S.
and Canada.

Mosaic Venture Partners
24 Duncan St.
Ste. 300
Toronto, ON, Canada M5V 3M6
(416)597-8889
Fax: (416)597-2345
Investment Types: Early stage. Industry
Preferences: Internet related. Geographic
Preferences: U.S. and Canada.

Onex Corp.
161 Bay St.
PO Box 700
Toronto, ON, Canada M5J 2S1
(416)362-7711
Fax: (416)362-5765
Anthony Munk
Preferred Investment Size: $10,000,000
minimum. Investment Types: Control-
block purchases, leveraged buyout, and
special situations. Industry Preferences:
Diversified. Geographic Preferences: U.S.
and Canada.

Penfund Partners Inc.
145 King St. West
Ste. 1920
Toronto, ON, Canada M5H 1J8

(416)865-0300
Fax: (416)364-6912
Website: http://www.penfund.com
David Collins
Preferred Investment Size: $667,000 to
$4,670,000. Investment Types: Generalist
PE, leveraged and management buyouts,
and mezzanine. Industry Preferences:
Diversified. Geographic Preferences:
Canada.

Primaxis Technology Ventures Inc.
1 Richmond St. West, 8th Fl.
Toronto, ON, Canada M5H 3W4
(416)313-5210
Fax: (416)313-5218
Website: http://www.primaxis.com
Investment Types: Seed and early stage.
Industry Preferences:
Telecommunications, electronics, and
manufacturing. Geographic Preferences:
Canada.

Priveq Capital Funds
240 Duncan Mill Rd., Ste. 602
Toronto, ON, Canada M3B 3P1
(416)447-3330
Fax: (416)447-3331
E-mail: priveq@sympatico.ca
Preferred Investment Size: $1,000,000
minimum. Investment Types: Industry
rollups, leveraged buyout, mezzanine,
recaps, second stage, and special
situation. Industry Preferences:
Diversified. Geographic Preferences: Mid
Atlantic, Midwest, Northeast, Northwest,
and Southeastern U.S.

Roynat Ventures
40 King St. West, 26th Fl.
Toronto, ON, Canada M5H 1H1
(416)933-2667
Fax: (416)933-2783
Website: http://www.roynatcapital.com
Bob Roy
Investment Types: Early stage and
expansion. Industry Preferences:
Diversified. Geographic Preferences:
Canada.

Tera Capital Corp.
366 Adelaide St. East, Ste. 337
Toronto, ON, Canada M5A 3X9
(416)368-1024
Fax: (416)368-1427
Investment Types: Balanced. Industry
Preferences: Computer related and
biotechnology. Geographic Preferences:
U.S. and Canada.

Working Ventures Canadian Fund Inc.
250 Bloor St. East, Ste. 1600
Toronto, ON, Canada M4W 1E6
(416)934-7718
Fax: (416)929-0901
Website: http://www.workingventures.ca
Preferred Investment Size: $334,000
minimum. Investment Types: No
preference. Industry Preferences:
Diversified. Geographic Preferences:
Ontario and Western Canada.

Quebec

Altamira Capital Corp.
202 University
Niveau de Maisoneuve, Bur. 201
Montreal, QC, Canada H3A 2A5
(514)499-1656
Fax: (514)499-9570
Preferred Investment Size: $1,000,000
minimum. Investment Types: First stage.
Industry Preferences: Diversified.
Geographic Preferences: No preference.

Federal Business Development Bank
Venture Capital Division
Five Place Ville Marie, Ste. 600
Montreal, QC, Canada H3B 5E7
(514)283-1896
Fax: (514)283-5455
Preferred Investment Size: $1,000,000.
Investment Types: Seed, start-up, first
and second stage, mezzanine, research
and development, and leveraged buyout.
Industry Preferences: Biotechnology;
Internet related; computer software,
hardware, and services. Geographic
Preferences: Canada

Hydro-Quebec Capitech Inc.
75 Boul, Rene Levesque Quest
Montreal, QC, Canada H2Z 1A4
(514)289-4783
Fax: (514)289-5420
Website: http://www.hqcapitech.com
Investment Types: Seed, start-up, early,
first and second stage, balanced,
expansion, and mezzanine. Industry
Preferences: Diversified. Geographic
Preferences: U.S. and Canada.

Investissement Desjardins
2 complexe Desjardins
C.P. 760
Montreal, QC, Canada H5B 1B8
(514)281-7131
Fax: (514)281-7808
Website: http://www.desjardins.com/id

Preferred Investment Size: $5,000,000
minimum. Investment Types: Start-up,
first and second stage, control-block
purchases, mezzanine, and leveraged
buyout. Industry Preferences:
Diversified. Geographic Preferences:
Quebec, Canada.

Marleau Lemire Inc.
One Place Ville-Marie, Ste. 3601
Montreal, QC, Canada H3B 3P2
(514)877-3800
Fax: (514)875-6415
Jean Francois Perrault
Preferred Investment Size: $3,000,000
minimum. Investment Types: Second
stage, mezzanine, leveraged buyout, and
special situation. Industry Preferences:
Diversified. Geographic Preferences:
Canada.

Speirs Consultants Inc.
365 Stanstead
Montreal, QC, Canada H3R 1X5
(514)342-3858
Fax: (514)342-1977
Derek Speirs
Preferred Investment Size: $1,000,000
minimum. Investment Types: Start-up,
first and second stage, control-block
purchases, industry rollups, leveraged
buyout, mezzanine, research and
development, and special situation.
Industry Preferences: Diversified.
Geographic Preferences: Canad

Tecnocap Inc.
4028 Marlowe
Montreal, QC, Canada H4A 3M2
(514)483-6009
Fax: (514)483-6045
Website: http://www.technocap.com
Preferred Investment Size: $1,000,000
minimum. Investment Types: Early stage
and expansion. Industry Preferences:
Diversified. Geographic Preferences:
Northeast and Southwest U.S., and
Central Canada.

Telsoft Ventures
1000, Rue de la Gauchetiere
Quest, 25eme Etage
Montreal, QC, Canada H3B 4W5
(514)397-8450
Fax: (514)397-8451
Investment Types: First and second stage,
and mezzanine. Industry Preferences:
Computer related. Geographic
Preferences: West Coast, and Western
Canada.

Saskatchewan

Saskatchewan Government Growth Fund
1801 Hamilton St., Ste. 1210
Canada Trust Tower
Regina, SK, Canada S4P 4B4
(306)787-2994
Fax: (306)787-2086
Rob M. Duguid, Vice President, Investing
Investment Types: Startup, first stage, second stage, and mezzanine. Industry Preferences: Diversified. Geographic Preferences: Western Canada.

UNITED STATES

Alabama

FHL Capital Corp.
600 20th Street North
Suite 350
Birmingham, AL 35203
(205)328-3098
Fax: (205)323-0001
Kevin Keck, Vice President
Preferred Investment Size: Between $500,000 and $1,000,000. Investment Types: Mezzanine, leveraged buyout, and special situations. Geographic Preferences: Southeast.

Harbert Management Corp.
One Riverchase Pkwy. South
Birmingham, AL 35244
(205)987-5500
Fax: (205)987-5707
Website: http://www.harbert.net
Charles Miller, Vice President
Preferred Investment Size: $5,000,000 to $25,000,000. Investment Types: Leveraged buyout, special situations and industry roll ups. Industry Preferences: Oil and gas not considered. Geographic Preferences: Entire U.S.

Jefferson Capital Fund
PO Box 13129
Birmingham, AL 35213
(205)324-7709
Preferred Investment Size: From $1,000,000. Investment Types: Leveraged buyout, special situations and control block purchases. Industry Preferences: Telephone communications; consumer leisure and recreational products;

consumer and industrial, medical and catalog specialty distribut

Private Capital Corp.
100 Brookwood Pl., 4th Fl.
Birmingham, AL 35209
(205)879-2722
Fax: (205)879-5121
William Acker, Vice President
Preferred Investment Size: $1,000,000 to $5,000,000. Investment Types: Startup, first stage, second stage, mezzanine, leveraged buyout, and special situations. Industry Preferences: Communications; computer related; industrial, and medical product distribution; electronic components

21st Century Health Ventures
One Health South Pkwy.
Birmingham, AL 35243
(256)268-6250
Fax: (256)970-8928
W. Barry McRae
Preferred Investment Size: $5,000,000. Investment Types: First stage, second stage, and leveraged buyout. Industry Preferences: Medical/Health related. Geographic Preferences: Entire U.S.

FJC Growth Capital Corp.
200 W. Side Sq., Ste. 340
Huntsville, AL 35801
(256)922-2918
Fax: (256)922-2909
William B. Noojin, President
Preferred Investment Size: $300,000 and $500,000. Investment Types: Mezzanine and second stage. Industry Preferences: Communications, electronics, hotels, and resort. Geographic Preferences: Southeast.

Hickory Venture Capital Corp.
301 Washington St. NW
Suite 301
Huntsville, AL 35801
(256)539-1931
Fax: (256)539-5130
E-mail: hvcc@hvcc.com
Website: http://www.hvcc.com
J. Thomas Noojin, President
Preferred Investment Size: $1,000,000 - $7,000,000. Investment Types: First stage, late stage, and leverage buyout. Industry Preferences: Communications, computer and Internet-related, energy, consumer, and biotechnology. Geographic Preferences: Southeast, Midwest, and Texas.

Southeastern Technology Fund
7910 South Memorial Pkwy., Ste. F
Huntsville, AL 35802
(256)883-8711
Fax: (256)883-8558
Preferred Investment Size: $500,000 to $5,000,000. Investment Types: Early, first and second stage, and expansion. Industry Preferences: Internet related, computer related, and communications. Geographic Preferences: Southeast.

Cordova Ventures
4121 Carmichael Rd., Ste. 301
Montgomery, AL 36106
(334)271-6011
Fax: (334)260-0120
Website: http://www.cordovaventures.com
Teo F. Dagi
Investment Types: Startup, early, second and late stage, and expansion. Industry Preferences: Diversified. Geographic Preferences: Southeast.

Small Business Clinic of Alabama/AG Bartholomew & Associates
PO Box 231074
Montgomery, AL 36123-1074
(334)284-3640
Preferred Investment Size: From $2,000,000. Investment Types: Startup, first stage, second stage, leveraged buyout, and special situations. Industry Preferences: Communications, computer related, consumer, distribution, industrial products and equipment, medical/health related, educa

Arizona

Miller Capital Corp.
4909 E. McDowell Rd.
Phoenix, AZ 85008
(602)225-0504
Fax: (602)225-9024
Website: http://www.themillergroup.com
Rudy R. Miller, Chairman and President
Preferred Investment Size: $1,000,000 to $20,000,000. Investment Types: First stage, second stage, and recapitalizations. Industry Preferences: Communications, computer-related, electronics, financial and business services, and consumer-related. Geographic Preferences: Entire U.S.

The Columbine Venture Funds
9449 North 90th St., Ste. 200
Scottsdale, AZ 85258

(602)661-9222
Fax: (602)661-6262
Preferred Investment Size: $300,000 -
$800,000. Investment Types: Seed,
research and development, startup, and
first stage. Industry Preferences:
Diversified technology. Geographic
Preferences: Southwest, Rocky
Mountains, and West Coast.

Koch Ventures
17767 N. Perimeter Dr., Ste. 101
Scottsdale, AZ 85255
(480)419-3600
Fax: (480)419-3606
Website: http://www.kochventures.com
Preferred Investment Size: $2,000,000 to
$10,000,000. Investment Types: Early
stage and expansion. Industry
Preferences: Electronics, Internet and
computer related, and communications.
Geographic Preferences: U.S.

McKee & Co.
7702 E. Doubletree Ranch Rd.
Suite 230
Scottsdale, AZ 85258
(480)368-0333
Fax: (480)607-7446
Mark Jazwin, Corporate Finance
Preferred Investment Size: From
$1,000,000. Investment Types: Second
stage, mezzanine, and leveraged buyout.
Industry Preferences: Communications,
computer related, consumer,
distribution, electronic components and
instrumentation, energy/natural
resources, biosensors, industrial pro

Merita Capital Ltd.
7350 E. Stetson Dr., Ste. 108-A
Scottsdale, AZ 85251
(480)947-8700
Fax: (480)947-8766
Investment Types: First and second stage,
mezzanine, and special situation.
Industry Preferences: Diversified.
Geographic Preferences: Western U.S.

**Valley Ventures / Arizona Growth
Partners L.P.**
6720 N. Scottsdale Rd., Ste. 208
Scottsdale, AZ 85253
(480)661-6600
Fax: (480)661-6262
Investment Types: Second stage,
mezzanine, and leveraged buyout.
Industry Preferences: Diversified.
Geographic Preferences: Southwest and
Rocky Mountains.

Estreetcapital.com
660 South Mill Ave., Ste. 315
Tempe, AZ 85281
(480)968-8400
Fax: (480)968-8480
Website: http://www.estreetcapital.com
Industry Preferences: Internet related.
Geographic Preferences: Entire U.S.

Coronado Venture Fund
PO Box 65420
Tucson, AZ 85728-5420
(520)577-3764
Fax: (520)299-8491
Preferred Investment Size: $100,000
$500,000. Investment Types: Seed,
startup, first and second stage. Industry
Preferences: Communications, computer
related, electronic components and
instrumentation, genetic engineering,
industrial products and equipment,
medical and health related

Arkansas

Arkansas Capital Corp.
225 South Pulaski St.
Little Rock, AR 72201
(501)374-9247
Fax: (501)374-9425
Website: http://www.arcapital.com
Private firm investing own capital.
Interested in financing expansion.

California

Sundance Venture Partners, L.P.
100 Clocktower Place, Ste. 130
Carmel, CA 93923
(831)625-6500
Fax: (831)625-6590
Preferred Investment Size: $800,000
minimum. Investment Types: First and
second stage, mezzanine, leveraged
buyout, and special situations. Industry
Preferences: No preference. Geographic
Preferences: Southwest and West Coast.

Westar Capital (Costa Mesa)
949 South Coast Dr., Ste. 650
Costa Mesa, CA 92626
(714)481-5160
Fax: (714)481-5166
E-mail: mailbox@westarcapital.com
Website: http://www.westarcapital.com
Alan Sellers, General Partner
Preferred Investment Size: $5,000,000 to
$10,000,000. Investment Types:
Leveraged buyouts, special situations,
control block purchases, and industry

roll ups. Industry Preferences:
Diversified. Geographic Preferences:
Northwest, Southwest, Rocky
Mountains, and West Coast.

Alpine Technology Ventures
20300 Stevens Creek Boulevard, Ste. 495
Cupertino, CA 95014
(408)725-1810
Fax: (408)725-1207
Website: http://www.alpineventures.com
Investment Types: Seed, startup, research
and development, first and second stage.
Industry Preferences: Internet-related,
communications, computer-related,
distribution, electronic components and
instrumentation, industrial products and
equipment.

Bay Partners
10600 N. De Anza Blvd.
Cupertino, CA 95014-2031
(408)725-2444
Fax: (408)446-4502
Website: http://www.baypartners.com
Bob Williams, General Partner
Preferred Investment Size: $5,000,000 to
$15,000,000. Investment Types: Seed and
startup. Industry Preferences: Internet,
communications, and computer related.
Geographic Preferences: National.

Novus Ventures
20111 Stevens Creek Blvd., Ste. 130
Cupertino, CA 95014
(408)252-3900
Fax: (408)252-1713
Website: http://www.novusventures.com
Dan Tompkins, Managing General
Partner
Preferred Investment Size: $500,000 to $1
Million. Investment Types: Start-up, first
and early stage, expansion, and buyouts.
Industry Preferences: Information
technology. Geographic Preferences:
Western U.S.

Triune Capital
19925 Stevens Creek Blvd., Ste. 200
Cupertino, CA 95014
(310)284-6800
Fax: (310)284-3290
Preferred Investment Size: $1,000,000
minimum. Investment Types: First,
second, and late stage; mezzanine;
control block; and special situations.
Industry Preferences: Diversified
technology. Geographic Preferences:
West Coast.

Acorn Ventures

268 Bush St., Ste. 2829
Daly City, CA 94014
(650)994-7801
Fax: (650)994-3305
Website: http://www.acornventures.com
Preferred Investment Size: $250,000
minimum. Investment Types: Seed, first
and second stage, and leveraged buyout.
Industry Preferences: Diversified.
Geographic Preferences: No preference.

Digital Media Campus

2221 Park Place
El Segundo, CA 90245
(310)426-8000
Fax: (310)426-8010
E-mail: info@thecampus.com
Website: http://
www.digitalmediacampus.com
Investment Types: Seed and early stage.
Industry Preferences: Entertainment and
leisure, sports, and media. Geographic
Preferences: U.S.

BankAmerica Ventures / BA Venture Partners

950 Tower Ln., Ste. 700
Foster City, CA 94404
(650)378-6000
Fax: (650)378-6040
Website: http://
www.baventurepartners.com
George Rossman
Preferred Investment Size: $1,000,000 to
$12,000,000. Investment Types: Startup,
first and second stage. Industry
Preferences: Computer and Internet
related, communications, medical
product distribution, electronic
components and instrumentation,
genetic engineering, and medical/heal

Starting Point Partners

666 Portofino Lane
Foster City, CA 94404
(650)722-1035
Website: http://
www.startingpointpartners.com
Preferred Investment Size: $100,000 to
$1,000,000. Investment Types: Early
stage. Industry Preferences: Diversified.
Geographic Preferences: U.S.

Opportunity Capital Partners

2201 Walnut Ave., Ste. 210
Fremont, CA 94538
(510)795-7000
Fax: (510)494-5439
Website: http://www.ocpcapital.com

Peter Thompson, Managing Partner
Preferred Investment Size: $100,000 to
$1,500,000. Investment Types: Second
stage, late stage, mezzanine, leveraged
buyout, and industry roll ups. Industry
Preferences: Internet related, consumer
related, communications, computer, and
medical/health related. Geographic
Preferences: E

Imperial Ventures Inc.

9920 S. La Cienega Boulevar, 14th Fl.
Inglewood, CA 90301
(310)417-5409
Fax: (310)338-6115
Preferred Investment Size: $500,000 to
$2,000,000. Investment Types: Second
stage and leveraged buyout. Industry
Preferences: Diversified. Geographic
Preferences: No preference.

Ventana Global (Irvine)

18881 Von Karman Ave., Ste. 1150
Irvine, CA 92612
(949)476-2204
Fax: (949)752-0223
Website: http://www.ventanaglobal.com
Scott A. Burri, Managing Director
Preferred Investment Size: $1,000,000
minimum. Investment Types: First and
second stage, seed, special situation, and
mezzanine. Industry Preferences:
Diversified technology. Geographic
Preferences: Southwest.

Integrated Consortium Inc.

50 Ridgecrest Rd.
Kentfield, CA 94904
(415)925-0386
Fax: (415)461-2726
Preferred Investment Size: $1,000,000.
Investment Types: First and second stage,
control-block purchases, industry
rollups, leveraged buyouts, and
mezzanine. Industry Preferences:
Entertainment and leisure, retail,
computer stores, franchises, food/
beverage, consumer products and ser

Enterprise Partners

979 Ivanhoe Ave., Ste. 550
La Jolla, CA 92037
(858)454-8833
Fax: (858)454-2489
Website: http://www.epvc.com
Preferred Investment Size: $1,000,000 to
$20,000,000. Investment Types: Early
stage. Industry Preferences: Diversified.
Geographic Preferences: Entire U.S.

Domain Associates

28202 Cabot Rd., Ste. 200
Laguna Niguel, CA 92677
(949)347-2446
Fax: (949)347-9720
Website: http://www.domainvc.com
Preferred Investment Size: $1,000,000 to
$20,000,000. Investment Types: Seed,
first stage and second stage, expansion,
private placement, research and
development, and balanced. Industry
Preferences: Electronics, computer,
biotechnology, and medical/health
related. Geographic Prefere

Cascade Communications Ventures

60 E. Sir Francis Drake Blvd., Ste. 300
Larkspur, CA 94939
(415)925-6500
Fax: (415)925-6501
Dennis Brush
Preferred Investment Size: $1,000,000 to
$5,000,000. Investment Types: Leveraged
buyout and special situations. Industry
Preferences: Communications and
franchises. Geographic Preferences:
Entire U.S and Canada.

Allegis Capital

One First St., Ste. Two
Los Altos, CA 94022
(650)917-5900
Fax: (650)917-5901
Website: http://www.allegiscapital.com
Robert R. Ackerman, Jr.
Investment Types: Seed and early stage.
Industry Preferences: Diversified.
Geographic Preferences: West Coast and
District of Columbia.

Aspen Ventures

1000 Fremont Ave., Ste. 200
Los Altos, CA 94024
(650)917-5670
Fax: (650)917-5677
Website: http://www.aspenventures.com
Alexander Cilento, Partner
Preferred Investment Size: $500,000 to
$3,500,000. Investment Policies: Equity.
Investment Types: Seed, and early stage.
Industry Preferences: Communications,
computer related, medical/health,
biotechnology, and electronics.
Geographic Preferences: West Coast.

AVI Capital L.P.

1 First St., Ste. 2
Los Altos, CA 94022
(650)949-9862
Fax: (650)949-8510

Website: http://www.avicapital.com
Brian J. Grossi, General Partner
Preferred Investment Size: $1,000,000 to
$2 million. Investment Policies: Equity
Only. Investment Types: Seed, startup,
first and second stage, and special
situations. Industry Preferences:
Computer hardware, software, and
services; Internet related;
communications; electronics; ener

Bastion Capital Corp.
1999 Avenue of the Stars, Ste. 2960
Los Angeles, CA 90067
(310)788-5700
Fax: (310)277-7582
E-mail: ga@bastioncapital.com
Website: http://www.bastioncapital.com
James Villanueva, Vice President
Preferred Investment Size: $10,000,000
minimum. Investment Types: Leveraged
buyout, special situations and control
block purchases. Industry Preferences:
Diversified. Geographic Preferences:
Entire U.S. and Canada.

Davis Group
PO Box 69953
Los Angeles, CA 90069-0953
(310)659-6327
Fax: (310)659-6337
Roger W. Davis, Chairman
Preferred Investment Size: $100,000
minimum. Investment Types: Early
stages, leveraged buyouts, and special
situations. Industry Preferences:
Diversified. Geographic Preferences:
International.

Developers Equity Corp.
1880 Century Park East, Ste. 211
Los Angeles, CA 90067
(213)277-0300
Investment Types: Seed, startup, and
leverage buyout. Industry Preferences:
Industrial products and machinery,
transportation, and real estate.

Far East Capital Corp.
350 S. Grand Ave., Ste. 4100
Los Angeles, CA 90071
(213)687-1361
Fax: (213)617-7939
E-mail: free@fareastnationalbank.com
Preferred Investment Size: $100,000 to
$300,000. Investment Types: First stage,
second stage, mezzanine, and special
situations. Industry Preferences:
Communications, computer and Internet
related, electronic components and

instrumentation, genetic engineering,
medical/health related

Kline Hawkes & Co.
11726 San Vicente Blvd., Ste. 300
Los Angeles, CA 90049
(310)442-4700
Fax: (310)442-4707
Website: http://www.klinehawkes.com
Robert M. Freiland, Partner
Preferred Investment Size: $4,000,000 to
$10,000,000. Investment Types: Second
and later stage, private placement, and
expansion. Industry Preferences:
Diversified technology. Geographic
Preferences: West Coast.

Lawrence Financial Group
701 Teakwood
PO Box 491773
Los Angeles, CA 90049
(310)471-4060
Fax: (310)472-3155
Larry Hurwitz
Preferred Investment Size: $500,000 to
$1,000,000. Investment Types: Second
stage. Industry Preferences: Diversified.
Geographic Preferences: West Coast.

Riordan Lewis & Haden
300 S. Grand Ave., 29th Fl.
Los Angeles, CA 90071
(213)229-8500
Fax: (213)229-8597
Jonathan Leach
Preferred Investment Size: $2,000,000
minimum. Investment Types: First and
second stage, start-up, leveraged buyouts,
and special situations. Industry
Preferences: Diversified. Geographic
Preferences: West Coast.

Union Venture Corp.
445 S. Figueroa St., 9th Fl.
Los Angeles, CA 90071
(213)236-4092
Fax: (213)236-6329
Preferred Investment Size: $300,000 to
$500,000. Investment Types: Second
stage, mezzanine, leveraged buyout, and
special situations. Industry Preferences:
Communications, computer related.
Geographic Preferences: National.

Wedbush Capital Partners
1000 Wilshire Blvd.
Los Angeles, CA 90017
(213)688-4545
Fax: (213)688-6642
Website: http://www.wedbush.com

Preferred Investment Size: $500,000
minimum. Investment Types: Second
stage, mezzanine, and leveraged buyouts.
Industry Preferences: Diversified
computer technology, consumer related,
distribution, and healthcare. Geographic
Preferences: West Coast.

Advent International Corp.
2180 Sand Hill Rd., Ste. 420
Menlo Park, CA 94025
(650)233-7500
Fax: (650)233-7515
Website: http://
www.adventinternational.com
Preferred Investment Size: $1,000,000
minimum. Investment Types: Startup,
first and second stage, mezzanine,
leveraged buyout, special situations,
recaps, and acquisitions. Industry
Preferences: Diversified. Geographic
Preferences: Entire U.S. and Canada.

Altos Ventures
2882 Sand Hill Rd., Ste. 100
Menlo Park, CA 94025
(650)234-9771
Fax: (650)233-9821
Website: http://www.altosvc.com
Investment Types: Start-up, seed, first
and second stage. Industry Preferences:
Internet and computer related, consumer
related, medical/health. Geographic
Preferences: West Coast.

Applied Technology
1010 El Camino Real, Ste. 300
Menlo Park, CA 94025
(415)326-8622
Fax: (415)326-8163
Ellie McCormack, Partner
Investment Types: Seed, startup, first and
second stage, research and development.
Industry Preferences: Diversified.
Geographic Preferences: Entire U.S.

APV Technology Partners
535 Middlefield, Ste. 150
Menlo Park, CA 94025
(650)327-7871
Fax: (650)327-7631
Website: http://www.apvtp.com
Preferred Investment Size: $2,000,000 to
$10,000,000. Investment Types: Early
stage. Industry Preferences: Diversified.
Geographic Preferences: Entire U.S.

August Capital Management
2480 Sand Hill Rd., Ste. 101
Menlo Park, CA 94025
(650)234-9900

Fax: (650)234-9910
Website: http://www.augustcap.com
Andrew S. Rappaport, General Partner
Preferred Investment Size: $1,000,000 to
$5,000,000. Investment Types: Startup,
first stage and special situations. Industry
Preferences: Communications, computer
related, distribution, and electronic
components and instrumentation.
Geographic Preferences: Northwest,
Southwest, Rocky

Baccharis Capital Inc.
2420 Sand Hill Rd., Ste. 100
Menlo Park, CA 94025
(650)324-6844
Fax: (650)854-3025
Michelle von Roedelbronn
Preferred Investment Size: $1,000,000
minimum. Investment Types: Startup,
first stage and second stage, mezzanine
and special situations. Industry
Preferences: Diversified. Geographic
Preferences: West Coast.

Benchmark Capital
2480 Sand Hill Rd., Ste. 200
Menlo Park, CA 94025
(650)854-8180
Fax: (650)854-8183
E-mail: info@benchmark.com
Website: http://www.benchmark.com
Investment Types: Seed, research and
development, startup, first and second
stage, and special situations. Industry
Preferences: Communications, computer
related, and electronic components and
instrumentation. Geographic
Preferences: Southwest and West Coast.

**Bessemer Venture Partners (Menlo
Park)**
535 Middlefield Rd., Ste. 245
Menlo Park, CA 94025
(650)853-7000
Fax: (650)853-7001
Website: http://www.bvp.com
Investment Types: Seed, research and
development, start-up, first stages,
leveraged buyout, special situations, and
expansion. Industry Preferences:
Communications, computer related,
consumer products, distribution, and
electronics. Geographic Preferences:
Entire U.S.

The Cambria Group
1600 El Camino Real Rd., Ste. 155
Menlo Park, CA 94025
(650)329-8600

Fax: (650)329-8601
Website: http://www.cambriagroup.com
Paul L. Davies, III, Managing Principal
Preferred Investment Size: $3,000,000.
Investment Types: Second stage,
mezzanine, leveraged buyout, special
situations, and control block purchases.
Industry Preferences: Diversified.
Geographic Preferences: Entire U.S.

Canaan Partners
2884 Sand Hill Rd., Ste. 115
Menlo Park, CA 94025
(650)854-8092
Fax: (650)854-8127
Website: http://www.canaan.com
Preferred Investment Size: $5,00,000 to
$20,000,000. Investment Types: First and
second stage, and expansion. Industry
Preferences: Diversified. Geographic
Preferences: Entire U.S.

Capstone Ventures
3000 Sand Hill Rd., Bldg. One, Ste. 290
Menlo Park, CA 94025
(650)854-2523
Fax: (650)854-9010
Website: http://www.capstonevc.com
Eugene J. Fischer
Preferred Investment Size: $500,000 to
$3,000,000. Investment Types: First and
second stage, early, and expansion.
Industry Preferences: Diversified high
technology. Geographic Preferences:
Diversified.

**Comdisco Venture Group (Silicon
Valley)**
3000 Sand Hill Rd., Bldg. 1, Ste. 155
Menlo Park, CA 94025
(650)854-9484
Fax: (650)854-4026
Preferred Investment Size: $300,000 to
$20,000,000. Investment Types: Seed,
startup, first and second stage. Industry
Preferences: Diversified. Geographic
Preferences: No preference.

Commtech International
535 Middlefield Rd., Ste. 200
Menlo Park, CA 94025
(650)328-0190
Fax: (650)328-6442
Preferred Investment Size: $300,000 to
$500,000. Investment Types: Seed and
start-up. Industry Preferences:
Diversified. Geographic Preferences:
West Coast.

Compass Technology Partners
1550 El Camino Real, Ste. 275

Menlo Park, CA 94025-4111
(650)322-7595
Fax: (650)322-0588
Website: http://
www.compasstechpartners.com
Leon Dulberger, General Partner
Investment Types: Mezzanine, leveraged
buyout, and special situations. Industry
Preferences: Diversified high technology.
Geographic Preferences: National.

Convergence Partners
3000 Sand Hill Rd., Ste. 235
Menlo Park, CA 94025
(650)854-3010
Fax: (650)854-3015
Website: http://
www.convergencepartners.com
Preferred Investment Size: $2,000,000 to
$10,000,000. Investment Types: Seed,
startup, research and development, early
and late stage, and mezzanine. Industry
Preferences: Communications, computer
related, electronic components and
instrumentation, and interactive media.
Geographic P

The Dakota Group
PO Box 1025
Menlo Park, CA 94025
(650)853-0600
Fax: (650)851-4899
E-mail: info@dakota.com
Stephen A. Meyer, General Partner
Preferred Investment Size: $300,000 to
$500,000. Investment Types: Early and
later stages, and special situations.
Industry Preferences: Diversified
computer and communications
technology, education, and publishing.
Geographic Preferences: National.

Delphi Ventures
3000 Sand Hill Rd.
Bldg. One, Ste. 135
Menlo Park, CA 94025
(650)854-9650
Fax: (650)854-2961
Website: http://www.delphiventures.com
Preferred Investment Size: $500,000
minimum. Investment Types: Seed,
startup, first and second stage. Industry
Preferences: Medical/health related,
Internet related, biotechnology,
computer software and services.
Geographic Preferences: Entire U.S.

El Dorado Ventures
2884 Sand Hill Rd., Ste. 121
Menlo Park, CA 94025

(650)854-1200
Fax: (650)854-1202
Website: http://
www.eldoradoventures.com
Preferred Investment Size: $500,000 to
$5,000,000. Investment Types: Seed,
startup, first and second stage. Industry
Preferences: Communications, computer
and Internet related, electronics, and
industrial products and equipment.
Geographic Preferences: West Coast.

Glynn Ventures

3000 Sand Hill Rd., Bldg. 4, Ste. 235
Menlo Park, CA 94025
(650)854-2215
John W. Glynn, Jr., General Partner
Preferred Investment Size: $300,000 to
$500,000. Investment Types: Start-up,
first and second stage, leveraged buyout,
and mezzanine. Industry Preferences:
Diversified computer and
communications technology, and
medical/health. Geographic Preferences:
East and West Coast.

Indosuez Ventures

2180 Sand Hill Rd., Ste. 450
Menlo Park, CA 94025
(650)854-0587
Fax: (650)323-5561
Website: http://
www.indosuezventures.com
Preferred Investment Size: $250,000 to
$1,500,000. Investment Types: Start-up,
first and second stage, and mezzanine.
Industry Preferences: Diversified.
Geographic Preferences: West Coast.

Institutional Venture Partners

3000 Sand Hill Rd., Bldg. 2, Ste. 290
Menlo Park, CA 94025
(650)854-0132
Fax: (650)854-5762
Website: http://www.ivp.com
Preferred Investment Size: $500,000
minimum. Investment Types: Seed,
startup, first and second stage, and
special situations. Industry Preferences:
Diversified. Geographic Preferences:
International.

Interwest Partners (Menlo Park)

3000 Sand Hill Rd., Bldg. 3, Ste. 255
Menlo Park, CA 94025-7112
(650)854-8585
Fax: (650)854-4706
Website: http://www.interwest.com
Preferred Investment Size: $2,000,000 to
$25,000,000. Investment Types: Seed,

research and development, startup, first
and second stage, expansion, and special
situations. Industry Preferences:
Diversified. Geographic Preferences:
Entire U.S.

**Kleiner Perkins Caufield & Byers
(Menlo Park)**

2750 Sand Hill Rd.
Menlo Park, CA 94025
(650)233-2750
Fax: (650)233-0300
Website: http://www.kpcb.com
Preferred Investment Size: $500,000.
Investment Types: Seed, start-up, first
and second stage. Industry Preferences:
Diversified. Geographic Preferences:
West Coast.

Magic Venture Capital LLC

1010 El Camino Real, Ste. 300
Menlo Park, CA 94025
(650)325-4149
Patrick Lynn
Preferred Investment Size: $100,000 to
$1,000,000. Investment Types: Seed,
start-up, first stage. Industry Preferences:
Medical/health related. Geographic
Preferences: West Coast.

Matrix Partners

2500 Sand Hill Rd., Ste. 113
Menlo Park, CA 94025
(650)854-3131
Fax: (650)854-3296
Website: http://www.matrixpartners.com
Andrew W. Verlahen, General Partner
Preferred Investment Size: $500,000 to
$1,000,000. Investment Types: Startup,
early, first and second stage, and
leveraged buyout. Industry Preferences:
Communications, computer related,
medical/health, and electronic
components and instrumentation.
Geographic Preferences: Entire U.S

Mayfield Fund

2800 Sand Hill Rd.
Menlo Park, CA 94025
(650)854-5560
Fax: (650)854-5712
Website: http://www.mayfield.com
Preferred Investment Size: $250,000
minimum. Investment Types: Seed,
startup, first and second stage, and
recapitalization. Industry Preferences:
Diversified. Geographic Preferences:
Northwest, Rocky Mountains, and West
Coast.

**McCown De Leeuw and Co. (Menlo
Park)**

3000 Sand Hill Rd., Bldg. 3, Ste. 290
Menlo Park, CA 94025-7111
(650)854-6000
Fax: (650)854-0853
Website: http://www.mdcpartners.com
Christopher Crosby, Principal
Preferred Investment Size: $40,000,000
minimum. Investment Types: Leveraged
buyout and special situations. Industry
Preferences: Diversified. Geographic
Preferences: Entire U.S.

Menlo Ventures

3000 Sand Hill Rd., Bldg. 4, Ste. 100
Menlo Park, CA 94025
(650)854-8540
Fax: (650)854-7059
Website: http://www.menloventures.com
H. DuBose Montgomery, General
Partner and Managing Director
Venture capital supplier. Provides start-
up and expansion financing to
companies with experienced
management teams, distinctive product
lines, and large growing markets.
Primary interest is in technology-
oriented, Internet, and computer related
companies. Investments range from
$5,00

Merrill Pickard Anderson & Eyre

2480 Sand Hill Rd., Ste. 200
Menlo Park, CA 94025
(650)854-8600
Fax: (650)854-0345
Preferred Investment Size: $1,000,000
maximum. Investment Types: Seed,
startup, first and second stage. Industry
Preferences: Diversified technology.
Geographic Preferences: No preference.

**New Enterprise Associates (Menlo
Park)**

2490 Sand Hill Rd.
Menlo Park, CA 94025
(650)854-9499
Fax: (650)854-9397
Website: http://www.nea.com
Ronald H. Kase, General Partner
Preferred Investment Size: $100,000
minimum. Investment Types: Seed, early,
startup, first and second stage, and
mezzanine. Industry Preferences:
Diversified technology. Geographic
Preferences: No preference.

Onset Ventures

2400 Sand Hill Rd., Ste. 150

Menlo Park, CA 94025
(650)529-0700
Fax: (650)529-0777
Website: http://www.onset.com
Preferred Investment Size: $100,000
minimum. Investment Types: Early stage.
Industry Preferences: Communications,
computer related, medical and health
related. Geographic Preferences: West
Coast.

Paragon Venture Partners
3000 Sand Hill Rd., Bldg. 1, Ste. 275
Menlo Park, CA 94025
(650)854-8000
Fax: (650)854-7260
Preferred Investment Size: $500,000 to
$1,500,000. Investment Types: Start-up,
seed, first and second stage, special
situation. Industry Preferences:
Diversified. Geographic Preferences: No
preference.

**Pathfinder Venture Capital Funds
(Menlo Park)**
3000 Sand Hill Rd., Bldg. 3, Ste. 255
Menlo Park, CA 94025
(650)854-0650
Fax: (650)854-4706
Jack K. Ahrens, II, Investment Officer
Preferred Investment Size: $2,00,000
minimum. Investment Types: Seed,
startup, first and second stage,
mezzanine, leveraged buyout, and special
situations. Industry Preferences:
Diversified technology. Geographic
Preferences: Entire U.S. and Canada.

Rocket Ventures
3000 Sandhill Rd., Bldg. 1, Ste. 170
Menlo Park, CA 94025
(650)561-9100
Fax: (650)561-9183
Website: http://www.rocketventures.com
Preferred Investment Size: $100,000 to
$5,000,000. Investment Types: Seed,
start-up, and early stage. Industry
Preferences: Communications, software,
and Internet related. Geographic
Preferences: West Coast.

Sequoia Capital
3000 Sand Hill Rd., Bldg. 4, Ste. 280
Menlo Park, CA 94025
(650)854-3927
Fax: (650)854-2977
E-mail: sequoia@sequoiacap.com
Website: http://www.sequoiacap.com
Investment Types: Early, seed, start-up,
first and second stage. Industry

Preferences: Diversified technology.
Geographic Preferences: Western U.S.
and international.

Sierra Ventures
3000 Sand Hill Rd., Bldg. 4, Ste. 210
Menlo Park, CA 94025
(650)854-1000
Fax: (650)854-5593
Website: http://www.sierraventures.com
Preferred Investment Size: $100,000
minimum. Investment Types: Seed,
startup, first and second stage,
recapitalization, and leveraged buyout.
Industry Preferences: Diversified.
Geographic Preferences: No preference.

Sigma Partners
2884 Sand Hill Rd., Ste. 121
Menlo Park, CA 94025-7022
(650)853-1700
Fax: (650)853-1717
E-mail: info@sigmapartners.com
Website: http://www.sigmapartners.com
Lawrence G. Finch, Partner
Investment Types: Seed, start-up, first
and second stage, special situation, recap,
and control block purchases. Industry
Preferences: Diversified technology.
Geographic Preferences: U.S.

Sprout Group (Menlo Park)
3000 Sand Hill Rd.
Bldg. 3, Ste. 170
Menlo Park, CA 94025
(650)234-2700
Fax: (650)234-2779
Website: http://www.sproutgroup.com
Investment Types: Seed, startup, first and
second stage, mezzanine, leveraged
buyout, and special situations. Industry
Preferences: Diversified technology.
Geographic Preferences: U.S. and foreign
countries.

TA Associates (Menlo Park)
70 Willow Rd., Ste. 100
Menlo Park, CA 94025
(650)328-1210
Fax: (650)326-4933
Website: http://www.ta.com
Michael C. Child, Managing Director
Preferred Investment Size: $20,000,000 to
$60,000,000. Investment Types: Control-
block purchases, leveraged buyout, and
special situations. Industry Preferences:
Diversified. Geographic Preferences: No
preference.

Thompson Clive & Partners Ltd.
3000 Sand Hill Rd., Bldg. 1, Ste. 185

Menlo Park, CA 94025-7102
(650)854-0314
Fax: (650)854-0670
E-mail: mail@tcvc.com
Website: http://www.tcvc.com
Greg Ennis, Principal
Preferred Investment Size: $500,000 to
$1,000,000. Investment Types: Early
stage, management buyouts, and special
situations. Industry Preferences:
Diversified computer and
communications technology, electronic
instrumentation, genetic engineering,
and medical/health. Geographic Pref

Trinity Ventures Ltd.
3000 Sand Hill Rd., Bldg. 1, Ste. 240
Menlo Park, CA 94025
(650)854-9500
Fax: (650)854-9501
Website: http://www.trinityventures.com
Lawrence K. Orr, General Partner
Preferred Investment Size: $5,000,000 to
$20,000,000. Investment Types: Early
stage. Industry Preferences:
Communications, computer and Internet
related, consumer products and services,
and electronics. Geographic Preferences:
Mid-Atlantic and Western U.S.

U.S. Venture Partners
2180 Sand Hill Rd., Ste. 300
Menlo Park, CA 94025
(650)854-9080
Fax: (650)854-3018
Website: http://www.usvp.com
William K. Bowes, Jr., Founding Partner
Preferred Investment Size: $500,000
minimum. Investment Types: Seed,
startup, first and second stage, and late
stage. Industry Preferences:
Communications, computer related,
consumer products and services,
distribution, electronics, and medical/
health related. Geographic Preferences:

USVP-Schlein Marketing Fund
2180 Sand Hill Rd., Ste. 300
Menlo Park, CA 94025
(415)854-9080
Fax: (415)854-3018
Website: http://www.usvp.com
Venture capital fund. Prefers specialty
retailing/consumer products companies.

Venrock Associates
2494 Sand Hill Rd., Ste. 200
Menlo Park, CA 94025
(650)561-9580
Fax: (650)561-9180

Website: http://www.venrock.com
Ted H. McCourtney, Managing General
Partner
Preferred Investment Size: $500,000
minimum. Investment Types: Seed,
research and development, startup, first
and second stage. Industry Preferences:
Diversified. Geographic Preferences: No
preference.

Brad Peery Capital Inc.
145 Chapel Pkwy.
Mill Valley, CA 94941
(415)389-0625
Fax: (415)389-1336
Brad Peery, Chairman
Preferred Investment Size: $100,000 to
$300,000. Investment Types: Second
stage financing. Industry Preferences:
Communications and media. Geographic
Preferences: Entire U.S.

Dot Edu Ventures
650 Castro St., Ste. 270
Mountain View, CA 94041
(650)575-5638
Fax: (650)325-5247
Website: http://
www.doteduventures.com
Investment Types: Early stage and seed.
Industry Preferences: Internet related.
Geographic Preferences: Entire U.S.

Forrest, Binkley & Brown
840 Newport Ctr. Dr., Ste. 480
Newport Beach, CA 92660
(949)729-3222
Fax: (949)729-3226
Website: http://www.fbbvc.com
Jeff Brown, Partner
Investment Policies: $1,000,000 to
$10,000,000. Investment Types: First
stage, second stage, expansion, and
balanced. Industry Preferences:
Communications, computer and Internet
related, consumer, electronic
components and instrumentation,
genetic engineering, industrial products
and

Marwit Capital LLC
180 Newport Center Dr., Ste. 200
Newport Beach, CA 92660
(949)640-6234
Fax: (949)720-8077
Website: http://www.marwit.com
Thomas W. Windsor, Vice President
Preferred Investment Size: $250,000
minimum. Investment Types:
Acquisition, control-block, leveraged

buyout, and mezzanine. Industry
Preferences: Software, transportation,
distribution, and manufacturing.
Geographic Preferences: Entire U.S.

**Kaiser Permanente / National Venture
Development**
1800 Harrison St., 22nd Fl.
Oakland, CA 94612
(510)267-4010
Fax: (510)267-4036
Website: http://www.kpventures.com
Preferred Investment Size: $500,000 to
$2,000,000. Investment Types: Balanced,
first and second stage, expansion, joint
ventures, and private placement.
Industry Preferences: Diversified.
Geographic Preferences: Entire U.S. and
Canada.

Nu Capital Access Group, Ltd.
7677 Oakport St., Ste. 105
Oakland, CA 94621
(510)635-7345
Fax: (510)635-7068
Preferred Investment Size: $500,000 to
$1,000,000. Investment Types: First and
second stages, leveraged buyouts,
industry rollups, and special situations.
Industry Preferences: Diversified
consumer products and services, food
and industrial product distribution.
Geographic Preference

Inman and Bowman
4 Orinda Way, Bldg. D, Ste. 150
Orinda, CA 94563
(510)253-1611
Fax: (510)253-9037
Preferred Investment Size: $1,000,000
minimum. Investment Types: Startup,
first and second stage, leveraged buyout,
and special situations. Industry
Preferences: Diversified technology.
Geographic Preferences: West Coast.

Accel Partners (San Francisco)
428 University Ave.
Palo Alto, CA 94301
(650)614-4800
Fax: (650)614-4880
Website: http://www.accel.com
Preferred Investment Size: $1,000,000
minimum. Investment Types: Seed,
startup, and early stage. Industry
Preferences: Communications, computer
related, medical/health, biotechnology,
and electronic components and
instrumentation. Geographic
Preferences: No preference.

Accenture Technology Ventures
1661 Page Mill Rd.
Palo Alto, CA 94304
Preferred Investment Size: $100,000
minimum. Investment Types: Seed,
startup, first and second stage. Industry
Preferences: Diversified. Geographic
Preferences: Entire U.S.

Advanced Technology Ventures
485 Ramona St., Ste. 200
Palo Alto, CA 94301
(650)321-8601
Fax: (650)321-0934
Website: http://www.atvcapital.com
Steven Baloff, General Partner
Investment Types: Startup, first stage,
second stage, and balanced. Industry
Preferences: Diversified. Geographic
Preferences: National.

Anila Fund
400 Channing Ave.
Palo Alto, CA 94301
(650)833-5790
Fax: (650)833-0590
Website: http://www.anila.com
Investment Types: Early stage. Industry
Preferences: Telecommunications and
Internet related. Geographic Preferences:
Entire U.S.

**Asset Management Company Venture
Capital**
2275 E. Bayshore, Ste. 150
Palo Alto, CA 94303
(650)494-7400
Fax: (650)856-1826
E-mail: postmaster@assetman.com
Website: http://www.assetman.com
Preferred Investment Size: $750,000
minimum. Investment Types: Seed,
startup, and first stage. Industry
Preferences: Diversified technology.
Geographic Preferences: Northeast, West
Coast.

**BancBoston Capital / BancBoston
Ventures**
435 Tasso St., Ste. 250
Palo Alto, CA 94305
(650)470-4100
Fax: (650)853-1425
Website: http://
www.bancbostoncapital.com
Preferred Investment Size: $1,000,000 to
$10,000,000. Investment Types: Seed,
early stage, acquisition, expansion, later
stage, management buyouts, and
recapitalizations. Industry Preferences:

Diversified. Geographic Preferences: Entire U.S. and Eastern Canada.

Charter Ventures

525 University Ave., Ste. 1400
Palo Alto, CA 94301
(650)325-6953
Fax: (650)325-4762
Website: http://
www.charterventures.com
Investment Types: Seed, startup, first and second stage, mezzanine, leveraged buyout, and special situations. Industry Preferences: Diversified. Geographic Preferences: No preference.

Communications Ventures

505 Hamilton Avenue, Ste. 305
Palo Alto, CA 94301
(650)325-9600
Fax: (650)325-9608
Website: http://www.comven.com
Clifford Higgerson, General Partner
Preferred Investment Size: $500,000 to $25,000,000. Investment Types: Seed, start-up, early, first, and second stage. Industry Preferences: Communications, Internet related, electronics, and computer related. Geographic Preferences: No preference.

HMS Group

2468 Embarcadero Way
Palo Alto, CA 94303-3313
(650)856-9862
Fax: (650)856-9864
Industry Preferences: Communications, computer related, electronics, and industrial products. Geographic Preferences: No preference.

Jafco America Ventures, Inc.

505 Hamilton Ste. 310
Palto Alto, CA 94301
(650)463-8800
Fax: (650)463-8801
Website: http://www.jafco.com
Andrew P. Goldfarb, Senior Managing Director
Preferred Investment Size: $500,000 minimum. Investment Types: First and second stage and mezzanine. Industry Preferences: Diversified technology. Geographic Preferences: No preference.

New Vista Capital

540 Cowper St., Ste. 200
Palo Alto, CA 94301
(650)329-9333
Fax: (650)328-9434
E-mail: fgreene@nvcap.com

Website: http://www.nvcap.com
Frank Greene
Investment Types: Seed, startup, first stage, second stage. Industry Preferences: Communications, computer related, electronics, and consumer related. Geographic Preferences: Western U.S., Rocky Mountains.

Norwest Equity Partners (Palo Alto)

245 Lytton Ave., Ste. 250
Palo Alto, CA 94301-1426
(650)321-8000
Fax: (650)321-8010
Website: http://www.norwestvp.com
Charles B. Lennin, Partner
Preferred Investment Size: $1,000,000 to $25,000,000. Investment Types: Seed, early and later stage, and expansion. Industry Preferences: Diversified. Geographic Preferences: No preference.

Oak Investment Partners

525 University Ave., Ste. 1300
Palo Alto, CA 94301
(650)614-3700
Fax: (650)328-6345
Website: http://www.oakinv.com
Preferred Investment Size: $250,000 to $5,000,000. Investment Types: Seed, startup, first stage, leveraged buyout, open market, control-block purchases, and special situations. Industry Preferences: communications, computer related, consumer restaurants and retailing, electronics, ge

Patricof & Co. Ventures, Inc. (Palo Alto)

2100 Geng Rd., Ste. 150
Palo Alto, CA 94303
(650)494-9944
Fax: (650)494-6751
Website: http://www.patricof.com
Preferred Investment Size: $5,000,000 minimum. Investment Types: Seed, startup, first and second stage, mezzanine, and leveraged buyout. Industry Preferences: Diversified. Geographic Preferences: No preference.

RWI Group

835 Page Mill Rd.
Palo Alto, CA 94304
(650)251-1800
Fax: (650)213-8660
Website: http://www.rwigroup.com
Preferred Investment Size: $500,000 to $4,000,000. Investment Types: Seed, start-up, first and second stage. Industry

Preferences: Diversified. Geographic Preferences: West Coast.

Summit Partners (Palo Alto)

499 Hamilton Ave., Ste. 200
Palo Alto, CA 94301
(650)321-1166
Fax: (650)321-1188
Website: http://
www.summitpartners.com
Christopher W. Sheeline
Preferred Investment Size: $1,500,000 minimum. Investment Types: First and second stage, mezzanine, leveraged buyout, special situations, and control block purchases. Industry Preferences: Diversified. Geographic Preferences: Entire U.S. and Canada.

Sutter Hill Ventures

755 Page Mill Rd., Ste. A-200
Palo Alto, CA 94304
(650)493-5600
Fax: (650)858-1854
E-mail: shv@shv.com

Vanguard Venture Partners

525 University Ave., Ste. 600
Palo Alto, CA 94301
(650)321-2900
Fax: (650)321-2902
Website: http://
www.vanguardventures.com
Donald F. Wood, Partner
Preferred Investment Size: $500,000 to $1,000,000. Investment Types: Early stages. Industry Preferences: Diversified computer and communications technology, genetic engineering, and electronics. Geographic Preferences: National.

Venture Growth Associates

2479 East Bayshore St., Ste. 710
Palo Alto, CA 94303
(650)855-9100
Fax: (650)855-9104
James R. Berdell, Managing Partner
Preferred Investment Size: $1,000,000 to $5,000,000. Investment Types: First and second stage, leveraged buyout, and mezzanine. Industry Preferences: Diversified technology, finance and consumer related. Geographic Preferences: West Coast.

Worldview Technology Partners

435 Tasso St., Ste. 120
Palo Alto, CA 94301
(650)322-3800
Fax: (650)322-3880

Website: http://www.worldview.com
Mike Orsak, General Partner
Investment Types: Seed, research and
development, startup, first stage, second
stage, mezzanine. Industry Preferences:
Diversified technology. Geographic
Preferences: National.

**Draper, Fisher, Jurvetson / Draper
Associates**
400 Seaport Ct., Ste.250
Redwood City, CA 94063
(415)599-9000
Fax: (415)599-9726
Website: http://www.dfj.com
J.B. Fox
Preferred Investment Size: $1,000,000 to
$5,000,000. Investment Types: Seed,
startup, and first stage. Industry
Preferences: Communications, computer
and Internet related, electronic
components and instrumentation.
Geographic Preferences: No preference.

Gabriel Venture Partners
350 Marine Pkwy., Ste. 200
Redwood Shores, CA 94065
(650)551-5000
Fax: (650)551-5001
Website: http://www.gabrielvp.com
Preferred Investment Size: $500,000 to
$7,000,000. Investment Types: Seed, early
and first stage. Industry Preferences:
Internet and computer related,
communications, and electronics.
Geographic Preferences: West Coast and
Mid Atlantic.

Hallador Venture Partners, L.L.C.
740 University Ave., Ste. 110
Sacramento, CA 95825-6710
(916)920-0191
Fax: (916)920-5188
E-mail: chris@hallador.com
Chris L. Branscum, Managing Director
Preferred Investment Size: $500,000 to
$1,000,000. Investment Types: Early and
later stages, and research and
development. Industry Preferences:
Diversified computer and
communications technology, and
electronic semiconductors. Geographic
Preferences: Western U.S.

Emerald Venture Group
12396 World Trade Dr., Ste. 116
San Diego, CA 92128
(858)451-1001
Fax: (858)451-1003

Website: http://
www.emeraldventure.com
Cherie Simoni
Preferred Investment Size: $100,000 to
$50,000,000. Investment Types: Start-up,
seed, first and second stage, leveraged
buyout, mezzanine, and research and
development. Industry Preferences:
Diversified. Geographic Preferences: No
preference.

Forward Ventures
9255 Towne Centre Dr.
San Diego, CA 92121
(858)677-6077
Fax: (858)452-8799
E-mail: info@forwardventure.com
Website: http://
www.forwardventure.com
Standish M. Fleming, Partner
Preferred Investment Size: $500,000 to
$10,000,000. Investment Types: Seed,
research and development, startup, first
and second stage, mezzanine, and private
placement. Industry Preferences:
Biotechnology, and medical/health
related. Geographic Preferences: Entire
U.S.

Idanta Partners Ltd.
4660 La Jolla Village Dr., Ste. 850
San Diego, CA 92122
(619)452-9690
Fax: (619)452-2013
Website: http://www.idanta.com
Preferred Investment Size: $500,000
minimum. Investment Types: Seed,
startup, first and second stage. Industry
Preferences: Diversified. Geographic
Preferences: Entire U.S.

Kingsbury Associates
3655 Nobel Dr., Ste. 490
San Diego, CA 92122
(858)677-0600
Fax: (858)677-0800
Preferred Investment Size: $500,000 to
$1,000,000. Investment Types: Start-up,
first and second stage. Industry
Preferences: Medical/health,
biotechnology, computer and Internet
related. Geographic Preferences: West
Coast.

Kyocera International Inc.
Corporate Development
8611 Balboa Ave.
San Diego, CA 92123
(858)576-2600
Fax: (858)492-1456

Preferred Investment Size: $300,000 to
$500,000. Investment Types: Second
stage. Industry Preferences: Diversified.
Geographic Preferences: Northeast,
Northwest, West Coast.

Sorrento Associates, Inc.
4370 LaJolla Village Dr., Ste. 1040
San Diego, CA 92122
(619)452-3100
Fax: (619)452-7607
Website: http://
www.sorrentoventures.com
Vincent J. Burgess, Vice President
Preferred Investment Size: $500,000 TO
$7,000,000. Investment Policies: Equity
only. Investment Types: Start-up, first
and second stage, leveraged buyout,
special situations, and control block
purchases. Industry Preferences:
Medicine, health, communications,
electronics, special ret

Western States Investment Group
9191 Towne Ctr. Dr., Ste. 310
San Diego, CA 92122
(619)678-0800
Fax: (619)678-0900
Investment Types: Seed, research and
development, startup, first stage,
leveraged buyout. Industry Preferences:
Computer related, consumer, electronic
components and instrumentation,
medical/health related. Geographic
Preferences: Western U.S.

Aberdare Ventures
One Embarcadero Center, Ste. 4000
San Francisco, CA 94111
(415)392-7442
Fax: (415)392-4264
Website: http://www.aberdare.com
Preferred Investment Size: $500,000 to
$7,000,000. Investment Types: Start-up,
first and second stage. Industry
Preferences: Diversified. Geographic
Preferences: Entire U.S.

Acacia Venture Partners
101 California St., Ste. 3160
San Francisco, CA 94111
(415)433-4200
Fax: (415)433-4250
Website: http://www.acaciavp.com
Brian Roberts, Senior Associate
Preferred Investment Size: $2,000,000 to
$10,000,000. Investment Types: Seed,
startup, first and second stage, mezzanine
and leveraged buyout. Industry
Preferences: Computer, and medical/

health related. Geographic Preferences: Entire U.S.

Access Venture Partners
319 Laidley St.
San Francisco, CA 94131
(415)586-0132
Fax: (415)392-6310
Website: http://
www.accessventurepartners.com
Robert W. Rees, II, Managing Director
Preferred Investment Size: $250,000 to $5 million. Investment Types: Seed, startup, and first stage. Industry Preferences: Internet related, biotechnology, communications, and computer software and services. Geographic Preferences: Southwest and Rocky Mountain region.

Alta Partners
One Embarcadero Center, Ste. 4050
San Francisco, CA 94111
(415)362-4022
Fax: (415)362-6178
E-mail: alta@altapartners.com
Website: http://www.altapartners.com
Jean Deleage, Partner
Preferred Investment Size: $1,000,000 to $10,000,000. Investment Types: Seed, startup, first and second stage, and mezzanine. Industry Preferences: Communications, computer related, distribution, electronic components and instrumentation, genetic engineering, industrial products and

Bangert Dawes Reade Davis & Thom
220 Montgomery St., Ste. 424
San Francisco, CA 94104
(415)954-9900
Fax: (415)954-9901
E-mail: bdrdt@pacbell.net
Lambert Thom, Vice President
Preferred Investment Size: $500,000 to $5,000,000. Investment Types: Second stage, mezzanine, leveraged buyout and special situations. Industry Preferences: Diversified. Geographic Preferences: No preference.

Berkeley International Capital Corp.
650 California St., Ste. 2800
San Francisco, CA 94108-2609
(415)249-0450
Fax: (415)392-3929
Website: http://www.berkeleyvc.com
Arthur I. Trueger, Chairman
Preferred Investment Size: $3,000,000 to $15,000,000. Investment Types: Second stage, mezzanine, leveraged buyout and

special situations. Industry Preferences: Communications, computer related, distribution, electronic components and instrumentation, industrial products and equipment

Blueprint Ventures LLC
456 Montgomery St., 22nd Fl.
San Francisco, CA 94104
(415)901-4000
Fax: (415)901-4035
Website: http://
www.blueprintventures.com
Preferred Investment Size: $3,000,000 to $10,000,000. Investment Types: Early stage. Industry Preferences: Communications and Internet related. Geographic Preferences: Entire U.S.

Blumberg Capital Ventures
580 Howard St., Ste. 401
San Francisco, CA 94105
(415)905-5007
Fax: (415)357-5027
Website: http://www.blumberg-capital.com
Mark Pretorius, Principal
Preferred Investment Size: $500,000 to $5,000,000. Investment Types: Seed, start-up, first and early stage, and expansion. Industry Preferences: Diversified. Geographic Preferences: Entire U.S.

Burr, Egan, Deleage, and Co. (San Francisco)
1 Embarcadero Center, Ste. 4050
San Francisco, CA 94111
(415)362-4022
Fax: (415)362-6178
Private venture capital supplier. Invests start-up, expansion, and acquisitions capital nationwide. Principal concerns are strength of the management team; large, rapidly expanding markets; and unique products for services. Past investments have been made in the fields of biotechnolo

Burrill & Company
120 Montgomery St., Ste. 1370
San Francisco, CA 94104
(415)743-3160
Fax: (415)743-3161
Website: http://www.burrillandco.com
David Collier, Managing Director
Preferred Investment Size: $500,000 to $5,000,000. Investment Types: Startup, first and second stage, and mezzanine.

Industry Preferences: Diversified. Geographic Preferences: No preference.

CMEA Ventures
235 Montgomery St., Ste. 920
San Francisco, CA 94401
(415)352-1520
Fax: (415)352-1524
Website: http://www.cmeaventures.com
Thomas R. Baruch, General Partner
Preferred Investment Size: $100,000 to $1,000,000. Investment Types: Seed, startup, first and second stage. Industry Preferences: Diversified high technology. Geographic Preferences: No preference.

Crocker Capital
1 Post St., Ste. 2500
San Francisco, CA 94101
(415)956-5250
Fax: (415)959-5710
Investment Types: Second stage, leveraged buyout, and start-up. Industry Preferences: Communications, medical/health related, consumer, retail, food/beverage, education, industrial materials, and manufacturing. Geographic Preferences: West Coast.

Dominion Ventures, Inc.
44 Montgomery St., Ste. 4200
San Francisco, CA 94104
(415)362-4890
Fax: (415)394-9245
Preferred Investment Size: $1,000,000 to $10,000,000. Investment Types: First and second stage, and mezzanine. Industry Preferences: Diversified. Geographic Preferences: No preference.

Dorset Capital
Pier 1
Bay 2
San Francisco, CA 94111
(415)398-7101
Fax: (415)398-7141
Website: http://www.dorsetcapital.com
Preferred Investment Size: $1,000,000 to $10,000,000. Investment Types: Second and later stage, expansion, generalist PE, leveraged and management buyouts. Industry Preferences: Consumer retail, food and beverage, and business services. Geographic Preferences: Entire U.S.

Gatx Capital
Four Embarcadero Center, Ste. 2200
San Francisco, CA 94904
(415)955-3200
Fax: (415)955-3449

Preferred Investment Size: $500,000 to $5,000,000. Investment Types: Early and later stages, and leveraged buyouts. Industry Preferences: Diversified technologies, forestry, and agriculture. Geographic Preferences: National and Canada.

IMinds
135 Main St., Ste. 1350
San Francisco, CA 94105
(415)547-0000
Fax: (415)227-0300
Website: http://www.iminds.com
Preferred Investment Size: $500,000 to $2,000,000. Investment Types: Seed, start-up, and early stage. Industry Preferences: Internet and computer related. Geographic Preferences: West Coast.

LF International Inc.
360 Post St., Ste. 705
San Francisco, CA 94108
(415)399-0110
Fax: (415)399-9222
Website: http://www.lfvc.com
Preferred Investment Size: $500,000 to $1,000,000. Investment Types: Control-block purchases, first and second stage, expansion, industry rollups, management buyouts, and special situations. Industry Preferences: Consumer related, retail. Geographic Preferences: Entire U.S.

Newbury Ventures
535 Pacific Ave., 2nd Fl.
San Francisco, CA 94133
(415)296-7408
Fax: (415)296-7416
Website: http://www.newburyven.com
Preferred Investment Size: $500,000 to $1,000,000. Investment Types: Early and later stages, and leveraged buyout. Industry Preferences: Diversified high technology. Geographic Preferences: Eastern and Western U.S. and Canada.

Quest Ventures (San Francisco)
333 Bush St., Ste. 1750
San Francisco, CA 94104
(415)782-1414
Fax: (415)782-1415
E-mail: ruby@crownadvisors.com
Lucien Ruby, General Partner
Preferred Investment Size: $100,000 maximum. Investment Types: Seed and special situations. Industry Preferences: Diversified. Geographic Preferences: No preference.

Robertson-Stephens Co.
555 California St., Ste. 2600
San Francisco, CA 94104
(415)781-9700
Fax: (415)781-2556
Website: http://www.omegaadventures.com
Private venture capital firm. Considers investments in any attractive merging-growth area, including product and service companies. Key preferences include health care, communications and technology, biotechnology, software, and information services. Maximum investment is $5 million.

Rosewood Capital, L.P.
One Maritime Plaza, Ste. 1330
San Francisco, CA 94111-3503
(415)362-5526
Fax: (415)362-1192
Website: http://www.rosewoodvc.com
Kevin Reilly, Vice President
Preferred Investment Size: $1,000,000 to $3,000,000. Investment Policies: Equity. Investment Types: Later stages, leveraged buyout, and special situations. Industry Preferences: Consumer and Internet related. Geographic Preferences: National.

Ticonderoga Capital Inc.
555 California St., No. 4950
San Francisco, CA 94104
(415)296-7900
Fax: (415)296-8956
Graham K Crooke, Partner
Preferred Investment Size: $5,000,000 maximum. Investment Types: Second stage, mezzanine, leveraged buyout, and consolidation strategies. Industry Preferences: Diversified. Geographic Preferences: Entire U.S. and Canada.

21st Century Internet Venture Partners
Two South Park
2nd Floor
San Francisco, CA 94107
(415)512-1221
Fax: (415)512-2650
Website: http://www.21vc.com
Shawn Myers
Preferred Investment Size: $5,000,000 maximum. Investment Types: Seed, research and development, startup, first and second stage, mezzanine, leveraged buyout, and special situations. Industry Preferences: Diversified. Geographic Preferences: Entire U.S. and Canada.

VK Ventures
600 California St., Ste.1700
San Francisco, CA 94111
(415)391-5600
Fax: (415)397-2744
David D. Horwich, Senior Vice President
Preferred Investment Size: $100,000 to $250,000. Investment Types: Second stage, mezzanine, and leveraged buyout. Industry Preferences: Diversified. Geographic Preferences: West Coast.

Walden Group of Venture Capital Funds
750 Battery St., Seventh Floor
San Francisco, CA 94111
(415)391-7225
Fax: (415)391-7262
Arthur Berliner
Preferred Investment Size: $1,000,000 to $7,000,000. Investment Types: Seed, startup, first and second stage. Industry Preferences: Diversified technology. Geographic Preferences: Entire U.S.

Acer Technology Ventures
2641 Orchard Pkwy.
San Jose, CA 95134
(408)433-4945
Fax: (408)433-5230
James C. Lu, Managing Director
Preferred Investment Size: $500,000 to $5,000,000. Investment Types: Seed, startup, first and second stage. Industry Preferences: Diversified. Geographic Preferences: Entire U.S. and Canada.

Authosis
226 Airport Pkwy., Ste. 405
San Jose, CA 95110
(650)814-3603
Website: http://www.authosis.com
Investment Types: Seed, first and second stage. Industry Preferences: Computer software. Geographic Preferences: Entire U.S.

Western Technology Investment
2010 N. First St., Ste. 310
San Jose, CA 95131
(408)436-8577
Fax: (408)436-8625
E-mail: mktg@westerntech.com
Investment Types: Seed, research and development, startup, first stage, second stage, mezzanine, leveraged buyout, and special situations. Industry Preferences: Diversified. Geographic Preferences: National.

Drysdale Enterprises
177 Bovet Rd., Ste. 600
San Mateo, CA 94402
(650)341-6336
Fax: (650)341-1329
E-mail: drysdale@aol.com
George M. Drysdale, President
Preferred Investment Size: $500,000 to
$5,000,000. Investment Types: First and
second stage, mezzanine, leveraged
buyout, and special situations. Industry
Preferences: Diversified. Geographic
Preferences: West Coast.

Greylock
2929 Campus Dr., Ste. 400
San Mateo, CA 94401
(650)493-5525
Fax: (650)493-5575
Website: http://www.greylock.com
Preferred Investment Size: $250,000
minimum. Investment Types: Seed, start-
up, early and first stage, and expansion.
Industry Preferences: Diversified.
Geographic Preferences: Entire U.S.

Technology Funding
2000 Alameda de las Pulgas, Ste. 250
San Mateo, CA 94403
(415)345-2200
Fax: (415)345-1797
Peter F. Bernardoni, Partner
Small business investment corporation.
Provides primarily late first-stage, early
second-stage, and mezzanine equity
financing. Also offers secured debt with
equity participation to venture capital
backed companies. Investments range
from $250,000 to $500,000.

2M Invest Inc.
1875 S. Grant St.
Suite 750
San Mateo, CA 94402
(650)655-3765
Fax: (650)372-9107
E-mail: 2minfo@2minvest.com
Website: http://www.2minvest.com
Preferred Investment Size: $500,000 to $5
million. Investment Types: Startup.
Industry Preferences: Communications,
computer related, electronic components
and instrumentation. Non-information
technology companies not considered.
Geographic Preferences: West Coast.

Phoenix Growth Capital Corp.
2401 Kerner Blvd.
San Rafael, CA 94901
(415)485-4569

Fax: (415)485-4663
E-mail: nnelson@phxa.com
Preferred Investment Size: $250,000 to
$1,000,000. Investment Types: First and
second stage, and mezzanine. Industry
Preferences: Communications, computer
related, consumer retailing, distribution,
electronics, genetic engineering, medical/
health related, education, publishing, and
t

NextGen Partners LLC
1705 East Valley Rd.
Santa Barbara, CA 93108
(805)969-8540
Fax: (805)969-8542
Website: http://
www.nextgenpartners.com
Preferred Investment Size: $100,000 to
$3,000,000. Investment Types: Seed,
start-up, first and second stage,
expansion, and research and
development. Industry Preferences:
Diversified. Geographic Preferences:
Entire U.S. and Canada.

Denali Venture Capital
1925 Woodland Ave.
Santa Clara, CA 95050
(408)690-4838
Fax: (408)247-6979
E-mail: wael@denaliventurecapital.com
Website: http://
www.denaliventurecapital.com
Preferred Investment Size: $100,000 to
$5,000,000. Investment Types: Early
stage. Industry Preferences: Medical/
health related. Geographic Preferences:
West Coast.

Dotcom Ventures LP
3945 Freedom Circle, Ste. 740
Santa Clara, CA 95045
(408)919-9855
Fax: (408)919-9857
Website: http://
www.dotcomventuresatl.com
Investment Types: Early, first stage,
and seed. Industry Preferences:
Telecommunications and Internet
related. Geographic Preferences:
Entire U.S.

Silicon Valley Bank
3003 Tasman
Santa Clara, CA 95054
(408)654-7400
Fax: (408)727-8728
Investment Types: Startup, first stage,
second stage, mezzanine. Industry

Preferences: Diversified. Geographic
Preferences: National.

Al Shugart International
920 41st Ave.
Santa Cruz, CA 95062
(831)479-7852
Fax: (831)479-7852
Website: http://www.alshugart.com
Investment Types: Seed, start-up, and
early stage. Industry Preferences:
Diversified. Geographic Preferences: U.S.

Leonard Mautner Associates
1434 Sixth St.
Santa Monica, CA 90401
(213)393-9788
Fax: (310)459-9918
Leonard Mautner
Preferred Investment Size: $100,000 to
$300,000. Investment Types: Seed, start-
up, first stage, and special situation.
Industry Preferences: Diversified.
Geographic Preferences: West Coast.

Palomar Ventures
100 Wilshire Blvd., Ste. 450
Santa Monica, CA 90401
(310)260-6050
Fax: (310)656-4150
Website: http://
www.palomarventures.com
Preferred Investment Size: $250,000 to
$15,000,000. Investment Types: Seed,
start-up, first and early stage, and
expansion. Industry Preferences:
Communications, Internet related,
computer software and services.
Geographic Preferences: West Coast and
Southwest.

Medicus Venture Partners
12930 Saratoga Ave., Ste. D8
Saratoga, CA 95070
(408)447-8600
Fax: (408)447-8599
Website: http://www.medicusvc.com
Fred Dotzler, General Partner
Preferred Investment Size: $100,000 to
$5,000,000. Investment Types: Early
stages. Industry Preferences: Genetic
engineering and healthcare industry.
Geographic Preferences: Western U.S.

Redleaf Venture Management
14395 Saratoga Ave., Ste. 130
Saratoga, CA 95070
(408)868-0800
Fax: (408)868-0810
E-mail: nancy@redleaf.com
Website: http://www.redleaf.com

Robert von Goeben, Director
Preferred Investment Size: $1,000,000 to
$4,000,000. Investment Policies: Equity.
Investment Types: Early and late stage.
Industry Preferences: Internet business
related. Geographic Preferences:
Northwest and Silicon Valley.

Artemis Ventures

207 Second St., Ste. E
3rd Fl.
Sausalito, CA 94965
(415)289-2500
Fax: (415)289-1789
Website: http://
www.artemisventures.com
Investment Types: Seed, first and second
stage. Industry Preferences: Internet and
computer related, electronics, and
various products. Geographic
Preferences: Northern U.S. and West
Coast.

Deucalion Venture Partners

19501 Brooklime
Sonoma, CA 95476
(707)938-4974
Fax: (707)938-8921
Preferred Investment Size: $500,000
minimum. Investment Types: Seed, start-
up, first and second stage. Industry
Preferences: Computer software,
biotechnology, education, energy
conservation, industrial machinery,
transportation, financial services, and
publishing. Geographic Preferen

Windward Ventures

PO Box 7688
Thousand Oaks, CA 91359-7688
(805)497-3332
Fax: (805)497-9331
Investment Types: Seed, startup, first
stage, second stage. Industry Preferences:
Communications, computer related,
electronic components and
instrumentation, genetic engineering,
industrial products and equipment,
medical and health related. Geographic
Preferences: West Coast.

National Investment Management, Inc.

2601 Airport Dr., Ste.210
Torrance, CA 90505
(310)784-7600
Fax: (310)784-7605
E-mail: robins621@aol.com
Preferred Investment Size: $1,000,000 to
$5,000,000. Investment Types: Leveraged
buyout. Industry Preferences: Consumer

products and retailing, distribution,
industrial products and equipment,
medical/health related, and publishing.
Real estate deals not considered.
Geographic Prefer

Southern California Ventures

406 Amapola Ave. Ste. 125
Torrance, CA 90501
(310)787-4381
Fax: (310)787-4382
Preferred Investment Size: $300,000 to
$1,000,000. Investment Types: Seed,
start-up, and first stage. Industry
Preferences: Communications, and
medical/health related. Geographic
Preferences: West Coast.

Sandton Financial Group

21550 Oxnard St., Ste. 300
Woodland Hills, CA 91367
(818)702-9283
Preferred Investment Size: $100,000 to
$250,000. Investment Types: Early and
later stages, and special situations.
Industry Preferences: No preference.
Geographic Preferences: National and
Canada.

Woodside Fund

850 Woodside Dr.
Woodside, CA 94062
(650)368-5545
Fax: (650)368-2416
Website: http://www.woodsidefund.com
Matthew Bolton, Analyst
Investment Types: Seed, startup, first
stage, second stage, and special
situations. Industry Preferences:
Diversified technology. Geographic
Preferences: Western U.S.

Colorado

Colorado Venture Management

Ste. 300
Boulder, CO 80301
(303)440-4055
Fax: (303)440-4636
Preferred Investment Size: $250,000 to
$1,000,000. Investment Types: Seed,
start-up, early, and first and second stage.
Industry Preferences: Diversified.
Geographic Preferences: Midwest and
Rocky Mountain region.

Dean & Associates

4362 Apple Way
Boulder, CO 80301
Fax: (303)473-9900

Investment Types: First stage, second
stage, and mezzanine. Industry
Preferences: Internet related. Geographic
Preferences: Western U.S.

Roser Ventures LLC

1105 Spruce St.
Boulder, CO 80302
(303)443-6436
Fax: (303)443-1885
Website: http://www.roserventures.com
Steven T. Joanis, Associate
Investment Types: Startup, first stage,
second stage, and special situations.
Industry Preferences: Communications,
computer related, distribution, electronic
components and instrumentation,
energy/natural resources, industrial
products and equipment, medical and
health related. Geog

Sequel Venture Partners

4430 Arapahoe Ave., Ste. 220
Boulder, CO 80303
(303)546-0400
Fax: (303)546-9728
E-mail: tom@sequelvc.com
Website: http://www.sequelvc.com
Kinney Johnson, Partner
Preferred Investment Size: $100,000 to
$5,000,000. Investment Types: Seed,
startup, and early stage. Industry
Preferences: Diversified technology.
Geographic Preferences: Rocky
Mountains.

New Venture Resources

445C E. Cheyenne Mtn. Blvd.
Colorado Springs, CO 80906-4570
(719)598-9272
Fax: (719)598-9272
Jeffrey M. Cooper, Managing Director
Preferred Investment Size: $100,000 to
$250,000. Investment Types: Seed and
startup. Industry Preferences: Diversified
technology. Geographic Preferences:
Southwest, rocky mountains.

The Centennial Funds

1428 15th St.
Denver, CO 80202-1318
(303)405-7500
Fax: (303)405-7575
Website: http://www.centennial.com
Preferred Investment Size: $250,000 to
$5,000,000. Investment Types: Seed,
startup, first and second stage, and
national consolidations. Industry
Preferences: Diversified. Geographic
Preferences: No preference.

Rocky Mountain Capital Partners
1125 17th St., Ste. 2260
Denver, CO 80202
(303)291-5200
Fax: (303)291-5327
Investment Types: Mezzanine and leveraged buyout. Industry Preferences: Diversified. Communications, computer related, consumer, distribution, electronic components and instrumentation, and industrial products and equipment. Geographic Preferences: Western U.S.

Sandlot Capital LLC
600 South Cherry St., Ste. 525
Denver, CO 80246
(303)893-3400
Fax: (303)893-3403
Website: http://www.sandlotcapital.com
Preferred Investment Size: $250,000 to $20,000,000. Investment Types: Seed, start-up, early and first stage, and special situation. Industry Preferences: Diversified. Geographic Preferences: U.S.

Wolf Ventures
50 South Steele St., Ste. 777
Denver, CO 80209
(303)321-4800
Fax: (303)321-4848
E-mail: businessplan@wolfventures.com
Website: http://www.wolfventures.com
David O. Wolf
Preferred Investment Size: $500,000 to $3,000,000. Investment Types: First stage, second stage, and special situations. Industry Preferences: Diversified. Geographic Preferences: Rocky mountains.

The Columbine Venture Funds
5460 S. Quebec St., Ste. 270
Englewood, CO 80111
(303)694-3222
Fax: (303)694-9007
Preferred Investment Size: $100,000 to $250,000. Investment Types: Seed, research and development, startup, and first stage. Industry Preferences: Diversified technology. Geographic Preferences: Southwest, Rocky Mountains, and West Coast.

Investment Securities of Colorado, Inc.
4605 Denice Dr.
Englewood, CO 80111
(303)796-9192
Preferred Investment Size: $100,000 to $300,000. Investment Types: Seed and

startup. Industry Preferences: Electronic components, industrial controls and sensors, healthcare industry. Geographic Preferences: Rocky Mountain area.

Kinship Partners
6300 S. Syracuse Way, Ste. 484
Englewood, CO 80111
(303)694-0268
Fax: (303)694-1707
E-mail: block@vailsys.com
Preferred Investment Size: $250,000 to $1,000,000. Investment Types: Seed, startup, and early stage. Industry Preferences: Diversified computer and communication technology, specialty retailing, genetic engineering, and healthcare. Geographic Preferences: Within two hours of office.

Boranco Management, L.L.C.
1528 Hillside Dr.
Fort Collins, CO 80524-1969
(970)221-2297
Fax: (970)221-4787
Preferred Investment Size: $100,000. Investment Types: Early and late stage. Industry Preferences: Agricultural and animal biotechnology. Geographic Preferences: Within two hours of office.

Aweida Ventures
890 West Cherry St., Ste. 220
Louisville, CO 80027
(303)664-9520
Fax: (303)664-9530
Website: http://www.aweida.com
Investment Types: Seed and first and second stage. Industry Preferences: Software, Internet related, and medical/health related. Geographic Preferences: West Coast.

Access Venture Partners
8787 Turnpike Dr., Ste. 260
Westminster, CO 80030
(303)426-8899
Fax: (303)426-8828
E-mail: robert.rees@juno.com
Robert W. Rees, Managing Director
Investment Types: Seed, startup, first stage, and special situations. Industry Preferences: Diversified. Geographic Preferences: Western and Midwestern U.S.

Connecticut

Medmax Ventures LP
1 Northwestern Dr., Ste. 203
Bloomfield, CT 06002

(860)286-2960
Fax: (860)286-9960
Noam Karstaedt
Preferred Investment Size: $500,000 minimum. Investment Types: Seed, start-up, first and second stage, and research and development. Industry Preferences: Biotechnology and medical/health related. Geographic Preferences: Northeast.

James B. Kobak & Co.
Four Mansfield Place
Darien, CT 06820
(203)656-3471
Fax: (203)655-2905
Preferred Investment Size: $100,000 maximum. Investment Types: First stage. Industry Preferences: Publishing. Geographic Preferences: National.

Orien Ventures
1 Post Rd.
Fairfield, CT 06430
(203)259-9933
Fax: (203)259-5288
Anthony Miadich, Managing General Partner
Preferred Investment Size: $500,000 minimum. Investment Types: Start-up, seed, early and first stage. Industry Preferences: Diversified technology. Geographic Preferences: No preference.

ABP Acquisition Corporation
115 Maple Ave.
Greenwich, CT 06830
(203)625-8287
Fax: (203)447-6187
Preferred Investment Size: $10,000,000 to $30,000,000. Investment Types: Leveraged buyout and acquisition. Industry Preferences: Diversified. Geographic Preferences: Mid Atlantic, Northeast, Ontario, and Quebec.

Catterton Partners
9 Greenwich Office Park
Greenwich, CT 06830
(203)629-4901
Fax: (203)629-4903
Website: http://www.cpequity.com
Andrew C. Taub
Preferred Investment Size: $5,000,000 minimum. Investment Types: First stage, second stage, leveraged buyout, and special situations. Industry Preferences: Consumer products and services, Internet related, biotechnology. Geographic Preferences: U.S. and Canada.

Consumer Venture Partners
3 Pickwick Plz.
Greenwich, CT 06830
(203)629-8800
Fax: (203)629-2019
E-mail: lcummin@consumer-venture.com
Linda Cummin, Business Manager
Preferred Investment Size: $10,000,000 minimum. Investment Types: Startup, first and second stage, and leveraged buyout. Industry Preferences: Internet related, consumer related. Geographic Preferences: Entire U.S.

Insurance Venture Partners
31 Brookside Dr., Ste. 211
Greenwich, CT 06830
(203)861-0030
Fax: (203)861-2745
Preferred Investment Size: $500,000 to $50,000,000. Investment Types: First and second stage, and leveraged buyouts. Industry Preferences: Insurance. Geographic Preferences: U.S.

The NTC Group
Three Pickwick Plaza
Ste. 200
Greenwich, CT 06830
(203)862-2800
Fax: (203)622-6538
Preferred Investment Size: $1,000,000 minimum. Investment Types: Seed, first stage, control-block purchases, and leveraged buyout. Industry Preferences: Electronic components, factory automation, and machinery. Geographic Preferences: Entire U.S.

Regulus International Capital Co., Inc.
140 Greenwich Ave.
Greenwich, CT 06830
(203)625-9700
Fax: (203)625-9706
E-mail: lee@chaossystems.com
Preferred Investment Size: $100,000 minimum. Investment Types: Start-up, seed, research and development. Industry Preferences: Computer software, industrial materials and machinery, and publishing. Geographic Preferences: National.

Axiom Venture Partners
City Place II
185 Asylum St., 17th Fl.
Hartford, CT 06103
(860)548-7799
Fax: (860)548-7797

Website: http://www.axiomventures.com
Preferred Investment Size: $2,000,000 to $5,000,000. Investment Types: Seed, early and later stages, and expansion. Industry Preferences: Communications, computer and Internet related, distribution, genetic engineering, medical/health related. Geographic Preferences: National.

Conning Capital Partners
City Place II
185 Asylum St.
Hartford, CT 06103-4105
(860)520-1289
Fax: (860)520-1299
E-mail: pe@conning.com
Website: http://www.conning.com
John B. Clinton, Executive Vice President
Preferred Investment Size: $5,000,000 to $35,000,000. Investment Types: Second and late stage, and expansion. Industry Preferences: Computer related, consumer related, and medical/health related. Geographic Preferences: National.

First New England Capital L.P.
100 Pearl St.
Hartford, CT 06103
(860)293-3333
Fax: (860)293-3338
E-mail: info@firstnewenglandcapital.com
Website: http://www.firstnewenglandcapital.com
Preferred Investment Size: $100,000 to $1,000,000. Investment Types: Mezzanine, expansion, and management buyouts. Industry Preferences: Communications, computer related, electronics, consumer related, and medical/health related. Geographic Preferences: Northeastern U.S.

Northeast Ventures
One State St., Ste. 1720
Hartford, CT 06103
(860)547-1414
Fax: (860)246-8755
Preferred Investment Size: $1,000,000 minimum. Investment Types: Secondary. Industry Preferences: Diversified. Geographic Preferences: National.

Windward Holdings
38 Sylvan Rd.
Madison, CT 06443
(203)245-6870
Fax: (203)245-6865
Preferred Investment Size: $300,000 minimum. Investment Types: Leveraged

buyouts, mezzanine, recaps, and special situations. Industry Preferences: Electronics, food/beverage, and industrial products. Geographic Preferences: Northeastern U.S.

Advanced Materials Partners, Inc.
45 Pine St.
PO Box 1022
New Canaan, CT 06840
(203)966-6415
Fax: (203)966-8448
E-mail: wkb@amplink.com
Preferred Investment Size: $500,000 to $25,000,000. Investment Types: Seed, start-up, early and late stage, leveraged buyout, research and development, and special situations. Industry Preferences: Diversified. Geographic Preferences: National and Canada.

RFE Investment Partners
36 Grove St.
New Canaan, CT 06840
(203)966-2800
Fax: (203)966-3109
Website: http://www.rfeip.com
James A. Parsons, General Partner
Preferred Investment Size: $15,000,000 minimum. Investment Policies: Prefer equity investments. Investment Types: Later stage, industry rollups, leveraged buyout, mezzanine, and special situations. Industry Preferences: Diversified. Geographic Preferences: Entire U.S.

Connecticut Innovations, Inc.
999 West St.
Rocky Hill, CT 06067
(860)563-5851
Fax: (860)563-4877
E-mail: pamela.hartley@ctinnovations.com
Website: http://www.ctinnovations.com
Preferred Investment Size: $50,000 minimum to $1,000,000. Investment Types: Start-up, first and second stage, joint ventures, and mezzanine. Industry Preferences: Diversified technology. Geographic Preferences: Northeast.

Canaan Partners
105 Rowayton Ave.
Rowayton, CT 06853
(203)855-0400
Fax: (203)854-9117
Website: http://www.canaan.com
Preferred Investment Size: $5,000,000 to $20,000,000. Investment Types: Early,

first, and second stage; and expansion. Industry Preferences: Diversified. Geographic Preferences: National.

Landmark Partners, Inc.
10 Mill Pond Ln.
Simsbury, CT 06070
(860)651-9760
Fax: (860)651-8890
Website: http://
www.landmarkpartners.com
James P. McConnell, Partner
Preferred Investment Size: $500,000 to $5,000,000. Investment Types: Seed, start-up, first and second stage, and special situations. Industry Preferences: Diversified technology. Geographic Preferences: U.S. and Canada.

Sweeney & Company
PO Box 567
Southport, CT 06490
(203)255-0220
Fax: (203)255-0220
E-mail: sweeney@connix.com
Preferred Investment Size: $1,000,000 minimum. Investment Types: Seed, research and development, startup, first stage, second stage, mezzanine, leveraged buyout, and special situations. Industry Preferences: Diversified. Geographic Preferences: Northeast U.S. and Eastern Canada.

Baxter Associates, Inc.
PO Box 1333
Stamford, CT 06904
(203)323-3143
Fax: (203)348-0622
Preferred Investment Size: $2,000,000 minimum. Investment Types: Seed, start-up, first stage, research and development, leveraged buyout, and special situations. Industry Preferences: Diversified. Geographic Preferences: National.

Beacon Partners Inc.
6 Landmark Sq., 4th Fl.
Stamford, CT 06901-2792
(203)359-5776
Fax: (203)359-5876
Preferred Investment Size: $300,000 to $1,000,000. Investment Types: First stage, second stage, mezzanine, and leveraged buyout. Industry Preferences: Diversified. Geographic Preferences: Northeast.

Collinson, Howe, and Lennox, LLC
1055 Washington Blvd., 5th Fl.
Stamford, CT 06901

(203)324-7700
Fax: (203)324-3636
E-mail: info@chlmedical.com
Website: http://www.chlmedical.com
Investment Types: Seed, research and development, start-up, and first stage. Industry Preferences: Medical/health related, biotechnology, and Internet related. Geographic Preferences: National.

Prime Capital Management Co.
550 West Ave.
Stamford, CT 06902
(203)964-0642
Fax: (203)964-0862
Preferred Investment Size: $300,000 to $800,000. Investment Types: First and second stage, and recaps. Industry Preferences: Diversified. Geographic Preferences: Northeast.

Saugatuck Capital Co.
1 Canterbury Green
Stamford, CT 06901
(203)348-6669
Fax: (203)324-6995
Website: http://
www.saugatuckcapital.com
Preferred Investment Size: $25,000,000 maximum. Investment Types: Leveraged buyout, acquisition, control-block purchases, expansion, later stage, and recaps. Industry Preferences: Diversified. Geographic Preferences: Entire U.S.

Soundview Financial Group Inc.
22 Gatehouse Rd.
Stamford, CT 06902
(203)462-7200
Fax: (203)462-7350
Website: http://www.sndv.com
Brian Bristol, Managing Director
Preferred Investment Size: $100,000 to $500,000. Investment Types: Second stage and mezzanine. Industry Preferences: Diversified information technology. Geographic Preferences: United States and Canada.

TSG Ventures, L.L.C.
177 Broad St., 12th Fl.
Stamford, CT 06901
(203)406-1500
Fax: (203)406-1590
Darryl Thompson
Preferred Investment Size: $30,000,000 minimum. Investment Types: Second stage and leveraged buyout. Industry

Preferences: Diversified. Geographic Preferences: Entire U.S. and Canada.

Whitney & Company
177 Broad St.
Stamford, CT 06901
(203)973-1400
Fax: (203)973-1422
Website: http://www.jhwhitney.com
Preferred Investment Size: $1,000,000. Investment Types: Leveraged buyout and expansion. Industry Preferences: Diversified technology. Geographic Preferences: No preference.

Cullinane & Donnelly Venture Partners L.P.
970 Farmington Ave.
West Hartford, CT 06107
(860)521-7811
Fax: (860)521-7911
Preferred Investment Size: $300,000 to $1,000,000. Investment Types: Seed, first and second stage, and recaps. Industry Preferences: Diversified. Geographic Preferences: Northeast.

The Crestview Investment and Financial Group
431 Post Rd. E, Ste. 1
Westport, CT 06880-4403
(203)222-0333
Fax: (203)222-0000
Norman Marland, Pres.
Preferred Investment Size: $500,000 to $3,000,000. Investment Types: Seed, research and development, first stage, second stage, and mezzanine. Industry Preferences: Diversified. Geographic Preferences: U.S. and Canada.

Marketcorp Venture Associates, L.P. (MCV)
274 Riverside Ave.
Westport, CT 06880
(203)222-3030
Fax: (203)222-3033
E. Bulkeley Griswold, General Partner
Preferred Investment Size: $500,000 to $1,000,000. Investment Types: First and second stage, mezzanine, and leveraged buyout. Industry Preferences: Consumer products and services, and computer services. Geographic Preferences: Entire U.S.

Oak Investment Partners (Westport)
1 Gorham Island
Westport, CT 06880
(203)226-8346
Fax: (203)227-0372

Website: http://www.oakinv.com
Preferred Investment Size: $250,000 to $5,000,000. Investment Types: Startup; early, first, second, and late stage; leveraged buyout; open market; control-block purchases; open market; and special situations. Industry Preferences: Diversified technology. Geographic Preferences: Natio

Oxford Bioscience Partners

315 Post Rd. W
Westport, CT 06880-5200
(203)341-3300
Fax: (203)341-3309
Website: http://www.oxbio.com
William Greenman
Preferred Investment Size: $500,000 to $5,000,000. Investment Types: Early and first stage, and research and development. Industry Preferences: Genetic engineering and medical/health related, computer related. Geographic Preferences: Entire U.S. and Canada.

Prince Ventures (Westport)

25 Ford Rd.
Westport, CT 06880
(203)227-8332
Fax: (203)226-5302
Preferred Investment Size: $500,000 to $1,000,000. Investment Types: Seed, startup, first and second stage, and leveraged buyout. Industry Preferences: Genetic engineering and medical/health related, computer software and services, industrial, and communications. Geographic Preferenc

LTI Venture Leasing Corp.

221 Danbury Rd.
Wilton, CT 06897
(203)563-1100
Fax: (203)563-1111
Website: http://www.ltileasing.com
Richard Livingston, Vice President
Preferred Investment Size: $500,000 to $2,000,000. Investment Types: Early, first, second, and late stage; mezzanine; and special situation. Industry Preferences: Communications, computer related, consumer, electronic components and instrumentation, industrial products and equipment,

Delaware

Blue Rock Capital

5803 Kennett Pike, Ste. A
Wilmington, DE 19807

(302)426-0981
Fax: (302)426-0982
Website: http://
www.bluerockcapital.com
Preferred Investment Size: $250,000 to $3,000,000. Investment Types: Seed, start-up, and first stage. Industry Preferences: Communication, Internet related, computer, semiconductors, and consumer related. Geographic Preferences: Northeast, Middle Atlantic.

District of Columbia

Allied Capital Corp.

1919 Pennsylvania Ave. NW
Washington, DC 20006-3434
(202)331-2444
Fax: (202)659-2053
Website: http://www.alliedcapital.com
Tricia Daniels, Sales & Marketing
Preferred Investment Size: $5,000,000 to $40,000,000. Investment Types: Mezzanine, leveraged buyout, acquisition, management buyouts, and recapitalization. Industry Preferences: Diversified. Geographic Preferences: No preference.

Atlantic Coastal Ventures, L.P.

3101 South St. NW
Washington, DC 20007
(202)293-1166
Fax: (202)293-1181
Website: http://www.atlanticcv.com
Preferred Investment Size: $300,000 minimum. Investment Types: Leveraged buyout, mezzanine, and special situations. Industry Preferences: Communication and computer related, and electronics. Geographic Preferences: East Coast.

Columbia Capital Group, Inc.

1660 L St. NW, Ste. 308
Washington, DC 20036
(202)775-8815
Fax: (202)223-0544
Erica Batie, Director of Investments
Preferred Investment Size: $100,000 to $250,000. Investment Types: First and second stage, and mezzanine. Industry Preferences: Communication and computer related, electronics, and biotechnology. Geographic Preferences: Mid Atlanic.

Core Capital Partners

901 15th St., NW
9th Fl.

Washington, DC 20005
(202)589-0090
Fax: (202)589-0091
Website: http://www.core-capital.com
Preferred Investment Size: $1,000,000 to $10,000,000. Investment Types: Start-up, first and second stage, expansion, and later stage. Industry Preferences: Diversified. Geographic Preferences: Mid Atlantic, Northeast, and Southeast.

Next Point Partners

701 Pennsylvania Ave. NW, Ste. 900
Washington, DC 20004
(202)661-8703
Fax: (202)434-7400
E-mail: mf@nextpoint.vc
Website: http://www.nextpointvc.com
Michael Faber, Managing General Partner
Investment Types: First and second stage. Industry Preferences: Communications, computer related, and electronic components. Geographic Preferences: National.

Telecommunications Development Fund

2020 K. St. NW
Ste. 375
Washington, DC 20006
(202)293-8840
Fax: (202)293-8850
Website: http://www.tdfund.com
Preferred Investment Size: $375,000 to $1,000,000. Investment Types: Seed, early stage, and expansion. Industry Preferences: Internet related, computer hardware/software and services, and communications. Geographic Preferences: Entire U.S.

Wachtel & Co., Inc.

1101 4th St. NW
Washington, DC 20005-5680
(202)898-1144
Preferred Investment Size: $100,000 to $300,000. Investment Types: Start-up, first and second stage, and recaps. Industry Preferences: Diversified. Geographic Preferences: East Coast.

Winslow Partners LLC

1300 Connecticut Ave. NW
Washington, DC 20036-1703
(202)530-5000
Fax: (202)530-5010
E-mail: winslow@winslowpartners.com
Robert Chartener, Partner

Investment Types: Later stage, acquisition, control-block purchases, expansion, management and leverage buyouts. Industry Preferences: Diversified. Geographic Preferences: Entire U.S.

Women's Growth Capital Fund
1054 31st St., NW
Ste. 110
Washington, DC 20007
(202)342-1431
Fax: (202)341-1203
Website: http://www.wgcf.com
Preferred Investment Size: $500,000 to $2,000,000. Investment Types: First, second, and later stage. Industry Preferences: Internet related, communications, and computer software and services. Geographic Preferences: Entire U.S.

Florida

Sigma Capital Corp.
22668 Caravelle Circle
Boca Raton, FL 33433
(561)368-9783
Preferred Investment Size: $100,000 to $300,000. Investment Types: Second stage. Industry Preferences: Diversified communication and computer, consumer products and services, distribution, electronics, genetic engineering, finance, and real estate. Geographic Preferences: Southeast.

North American Business Development Co., L.L.C.
111 East Las Olas Blvd.
Ft. Lauderdale, FL 33301
(305)463-0681
Fax: (305)527-0904
Website: http://www.northamericanfund.com
Robert Underwood
PIS $10,000,000 minimum. Investment Types: Leveraged buyout, special situations, control block purchases, industry roll ups, and small business with growth potential. Industry Preferences: No preference. Geographic Preferences: Southeast and Midwest.

Chartwell Capital Management Co. Inc.
1 Independent Dr., Ste. 3120
Jacksonville, FL 32202
(904)355-3519
Fax: (904)353-5833
E-mail: info@chartwellcap.com

Anthony Marinatos
Preferred Investment Size: $5,000,000 minimum. Investment Types: First stage, second stage and leveraged buyout. Industry Preferences: Diversified. Geographic Preferences: Northwest and Southeast.

CEO Advisors
1061 Maitland Center Commons
Ste. 209
Maitland, FL 32751
(407)660-9327
Fax: (407)660-2109
Preferred Investment Size: $300,000 to $500,000. Investment Types: Seed, start-up, first stage, and research and development. Industry Preferences: Diversified. Geographic Preferences: Southeast.

Henry & Co.
8201 Peters Rd., Ste. 1000
Plantation, FL 33324
(954)797-7400
June Knaudt
Preferred Investment Size: $500,000 to $1,000,000. Investment Types: First and second stage. Industry Preferences: Healthcare industry. Geographic Preferences: West Coast.

Avery Business Development Services
2506 St. Michel Ct.
Ponte Vedra, FL 32082
(904)285-6033
Preferred Investment Size: $2,000,000. Investment Types: Seed, research and development, startup, first stage, leveraged buyout, and special situations. Industry Preferences: Diversified. Geographic Preferences: National.

New South Ventures
5053 Ocean Blvd.
Sarasota, FL 34242
(941)358-6000
Fax: (941)358-6078
Website: http://www.newsouthventures.com
Preferred Investment Size: $300,000 to $3,000,000. Investment Types: Seed and early stage. Industry Preferences: Diversified. Geographic Preferences: Southeast.

Venture Capital Management Corp.
PO Box 2626
Satellite Beach, FL 32937
(407)777-1969

Preferred Investment Size: $100,000 to $300,000. Investment Types: First and second stage, and leveraged buyout. Industry Preferences: Diversified. Geographic Preferences: National.

Florida Capital Venture Ltd.
325 Florida Bank Plaza
100 W. Kennedy Blvd.
Tampa, FL 33602
(813)229-2294
Fax: (813)229-2028
Warren Miller
Preferred Investment Size: $500,000 minimum. Investment Types: Startup, first and second stage, leveraged buyout, and special situations. Industry Preferences: Diversified. Geographic Preferences: Southeast.

Quantum Capital Partners
339 South Plant Ave.
Tampa, FL 33606
(813)250-1999
Fax: (813)250-1998
Website: http://www.quantumcapitalpartners.com
Preferred Investment Size: $1,000,000 to $5,000,000. Investment Types: Expansion, later stage, and mezzanine. Industry Preferences: Diversified technology, medical/health, consumer, retail, financial and business services, and manufacturing. Geographic Preferences: Florida.

South Atlantic Venture Fund
614 W. Bay St.
Tampa, FL 33606-2704
(813)253-2500
Fax: (813)253-2360
E-mail: venture@southatlantic.com
Website: http://www.southatlantic.com
Donald W. Burton, Chairman and Managing Director
Preferred Investment Size: $1,500,000 minimum. Investment Types: First and second stage, special situations, expansion and control block purchases. Industry Preferences: Diversified. Geographic Preferences: Southeast, Middle Atlantic, and Texas.

LM Capital Corp.
120 S. Olive, Ste. 400
West Palm Beach, FL 33401
(561)833-9700
Fax: (561)655-6587
Website: http://www.lmcapitalsecurities.com

Preferred Investment Size: $5,000,000 minimum. Investment Types: Leveraged buyout. Industry Preferences: Diversified. Geographic Preferences: No preference.

Georgia

Venture First Associates
4811 Thornwood Dr.
Acworth, GA 30102
(770)928-3733
Fax: (770)928-6455
J. Douglas Mullins
Preferred Investment Size: $500,000 to $5,000,000. Investment Types: Seed, startup, first and second stage. Industry Preferences: Diversified technology and electronics. Geographic Preferences: Southeast.

Alliance Technology Ventures
8995 Westside Pkwy., Ste. 200
Alpharetta, GA 30004
(678)336-2000
Fax: (678)336-2001
E-mail: info@atv.com
Website: http://www.atv.com
Preferred Investment Size: $250,000 to $1,000,000. Investment Types: Seed, start-up, first and second stage. Industry Preferences: Diversified technology. Geographic Preferences: Southeast.

Cordova Ventures
2500 North Winds Pkwy., Ste. 475
Alpharetta, GA 30004
(678)942-0300
Fax: (678)942-0301
Website: http://www.cordovaventures.com
Teo F. Dagi
Preferred Investment Size: $250,000 to $4,000,000. Investment Policies: Equity and/or debt. Investment Types: Early and late stage, start-up, expansion, and balanced. Industry Preferences: Diversified. Geographic Preferences: Southeast.

Advanced Technology Development Fund
1000 Abernathy, Ste. 1420
Atlanta, GA 30328-5614
(404)668-2333
Fax: (404)668-2333
Preferred Investment Size: $500,000 to $1,500,000. Investment Types: Seed, start-up, first and second stage, and leveraged buyout. Industry Preferences:

Diversified. Geographic Preferences: No preference.

CGW Southeast Partners
12 Piedmont Center, Ste. 210
Atlanta, GA 30305
(404)816-3255
Fax: (404)816-3258
Website: http://www.cgwlp.com
Garrison M. Kitchen, Managing Partner
Preferred Investment Size: $25,000,000 to $200,000,000. Investment Types: Management buyout. Industry Preferences: Diversified. Geographic Preferences: Entire U.S.

Cyberstarts
1900 Emery St., NW
3rd Fl.
Atlanta, GA 30318
(404)267-5000
Fax: (404)267-5200
Website: http://www.cyberstarts.com
Investment Types: Seed and start-up. Industry Preferences: Internet and financial services. Geographic Preferences: Entire U.S.

EGL Holdings, Inc.
10 Piedmont Center, Ste. 412
Atlanta, GA 30305
(404)949-8300
Fax: (404)949-8311
Salvatore A. Massaro, Partner
Preferred Investment Size: $1,000,000 minimum. Investment Types: Mezzanine, leveraged buyout, industry roll ups, recapitalization, and second stage. Industry Preferences: Diversified. Geographic Preferences: Southeast and East Coast, Midwest.

Equity South
1790 The Lenox Bldg.
3399 Peachtree Rd. NE
Atlanta, GA 30326
(404)237-6222
Fax: (404)261-1578
Douglas L. Diamond, Managing Director
Preferred Investment Size: $2,000,000 to $3,000,000. Investment Types: Mezzanine, leveraged buyout, recapitalization, and control block purchases. Industry Preferences: Diversified. Geographic Preferences: Northeast, Southeast, and Southwest.

Five Paces
3400 Peachtree Rd., Ste. 200
Atlanta, GA 30326
(404)439-8300

Fax: (404)439-8301
Website: http://www.fivepaces.com
Investment Types: Balanced. Industry Preferences: Diversified. Geographic Preferences: Entire U.S.

Frontline Capital, Inc.
3475 Lenox Rd., Ste. 400
Atlanta, GA 30326
(404)240-7280
Fax: (404)240-7281
Preferred Investment Size: $1,000,000 minimum. Investment Types: First stage. Industry Preferences: Diversified communication and computer technology, consumer products and services, distribution, electronics, business and financial services, and publishing. Geographic Preferences: S

Fuqua Ventures LLC
1201 W. Peachtree St. NW, Ste. 5000
Atlanta, GA 30309
(404)815-4500
Fax: (404)815-4528
Website: http://www.fuquaventures.com
Investment Types: Early stage. Industry Preferences: Internet related, biotechnology, communications, and computer software and services. Geographic Preferences: Entire U.S.

Noro-Moseley Partners
4200 Northside Pkwy., Bldg. 9
Atlanta, GA 30327
(404)233-1966
Fax: (404)239-9280
Website: http://www.noro-moseley.com
Preferred Investment Size: $1,000,000 to $5,000,000. Investment Types: Startup, first and second stage, mezzanine, leveraged buyout, special situations, and control block purchases. Industry Preferences: Diversified. Geographic Preferences: Southeast.

Renaissance Capital Corp.
34 Peachtree St. NW, Ste. 2230
Atlanta, GA 30303
(404)658-9061
Fax: (404)658-9064
Larry Edler
Preferred Investment Size: $300,000 minimum. Investment Types: Second stage, mezzanine, and leveraged buyout. Industry Preferences: Diversified. Geographic Preferences: Southeast.

River Capital, Inc.
Two Midtown Plaza
1360 Peachtree St. NE, Ste. 1430

Atlanta, GA 30309
(404)873-2166
Fax: (404)873-2158
Jerry D. Wethington
Preferred Investment Size: $3,000,000 minimum. Investment Types: Mezzanine, recapitalization, and leveraged buyout. Industry Preferences: Diversified. Geographic Preferences: Southeast, Southwest, Midwest, and Middle Atlantic.

State Street Bank & Trust Co.
3414 Peachtree Rd. NE, Ste. 1010
Atlanta, GA 30326
(404)364-9500
Fax: (404)261-4469
Preferred Investment Size: $10,000,000 minimum. Investment Types: Leveraged buyout and special situations. Industry Preferences: Diversified technology. Geographic Preferences: National.

UPS Strategic Enterprise Fund
55 Glenlake Pkwy. NE
Atlanta, GA 30328
(404)828-8814
Fax: (404)828-8088
E-mail: jcacyce@ups.com
Website: http://www.ups.com/sef/sef_home
Preferred Investment Size: $1,000,000. Investment Types: Early and late stage. Industry Preferences: Diversified communication and computer technology. Geographic Preferences: United States and Canada.

Wachovia
191 Peachtree St. NE, 26th Fl.
Atlanta, GA 30303
(404)332-1000
Fax: (404)332-1392
Website: http://www.wachovia.com/wca
Preferred Investment Size: $5,000,000 to $15,000,000. Investment Types: Expansion, later stage, management buyouts, mezzanine, private placement, and recaps. Industry Preferences: Diversified. Geographic Preferences: Southeast.

Brainworks Ventures
4243 Dunwoody Club Dr.
Chamblee, GA 30341
(770)239-7447
Investment Types: Balanced and early and later stage. Industry Preferences: Telecommunications and computers. Geographic Preferences: Southeast.

First Growth Capital Inc.
Best Western Plaza, Ste. 105
PO Box 815
Forsyth, GA 31029
(912)781-7131
Fax: (912)781-0066
Preferred Investment Size: $100,000 to $300,000. Investment Types: Second stage and special situation. Industry Preferences: Diversified. Geographic Preferences: No preference.

Financial Capital Resources, Inc.
21 Eastbrook Bend, Ste. 116
Peachtree City, GA 30269
(404)487-6650
Preferred Investment Size: $5,000,000 minimum. Investment Types: Leveraged buyout. Industry Preferences: Machinery. Geographic Preferences: National.

Hawaii

HMS Hawaii Management Partners
Davies Pacific Center
841 Bishop St., Ste. 860
Honolulu, HI 96813
(808)545-3755
Fax: (808)531-2611
Preferred Investment Size: $500,000 to $1,500,000. Investment Types: Seed, start-up, first stage, and leveraged buyout. Industry Preferences: Internet related, communications, and consumer related. Geographic Preferences: Entire U.S.

Idaho

Sun Valley Ventures
160 Second St.
Ketchum, ID 83340
(208)726-5005
Fax: (208)726-5094
Preferred Investment Size: $5,000,000. Investment Types: Second stage, leveraged buyout, control-block purchases, and special situations. Industry Preferences: Diversified. Geographic Preferences: Entire U.S. and Canada.

Illinois

Open Prairie Ventures
115 N. Neil St., Ste. 209
Champaign, IL 61820
(217)351-7000
Fax: (217)351-7051
E-mail: inquire@openprairie.com

Website: http://www.openprairie.com
Dennis D. Spice, Managing Member
Preferred Investment Size: $250,000 to $2,500,000. Investment Types: Early stage. Industry Preferences: Diversified communication and computer technology, electronics, and genetic engineering. Geographic Preferences: Midwest.

ABN AMRO Private Equity
208 S. La Salle St., 10th Fl.
Chicago, IL 60604
(312)855-7079
Fax: (312)553-6648
Website: http://www.abnequity.com
David Bogetz, Managing Director
Preferred Investment Size: $10,000,000 maximum. Investment Types: Early stage and expansion. Industry Preferences: Diversified. Geographic Preferences: Entire U.S. and Canada.

Alpha Capital Partners, Ltd.
122 S. Michigan Ave., Ste. 1700
Chicago, IL 60603
(312)322-9800
Fax: (312)322-9808
E-mail: acp@alphacapital.com
William J. Oberholtzer, Vice President
Preferred Investment Size: $2,000,000 minimum. Investment Types: First and second stage, leveraged buyout, and special situations. Industry Preferences: Diversified. Geographic Preferences: Midwest.

Ameritech Development Corp.
30 S. Wacker Dr., 37th Fl.
Chicago, IL 60606
(312)750-5083
Fax: (312)609-0244
Craig Lee, Director
Preferred Investment Size: $5,000,000 minimum. Investment Types: Startup, first and second stage. Industry Preferences: Communications, computer related, and electronics. Geographic Preferences: Entire U.S.

Apex Investment Partners
225 W. Washington, Ste. 1450
Chicago, IL 60606
(312)857-2800
Fax: (312)857-1800
E-mail: apex@apexvc.com
Website: http://www.apexvc.com
Preferred Investment Size: $500,000 to $15,000,000. Investment Types: Early stage. Industry Preferences: Diversified

communication and computer technology, consumer products and services, industrial/energy, and electronics. Geographic Preferences: Entire U.S.

Arch Venture Partners
8725 W. Higgins Rd., Ste. 290
Chicago, IL 60631
(773)380-6600
Fax: (773)380-6606
Website: http://www.archventure.com
Steven Lazarus, Managing Director
Preferred Investment Size: $100,000 to $1,000,000. Investment Types: Seed, start-up, early stage. Industry Preferences: Diversified communication and computer technology, electronics, and genetic engineering. Geographic Preferences: National.

The Bank Funds
208 South LaSalle St., Ste. 1680
Chicago, IL 60604
(312)855-6020
Fax: (312)855-8910
Investment Types: Control-block purchases, later stage, leveraged buyout, second stage, and special situation. Industry Preferences: Diversified. Geographic Preferences: No preference.

Batterson Venture Partners
303 W. Madison St., Ste. 1110
Chicago, IL 60606-3309
(312)269-0300
Fax: (312)269-0021
Website: http://www.battersonvp.com
Preferred Investment Size: $500,000 to $3,000,000. Investment Types: Seed, startup, first and second stage. Industry Preferences: Diversified. Geographic Preferences: Entire U.S.

William Blair Capital Partners, L.L.C.
222 W. Adams St., Ste. 1300
Chicago, IL 60606
(312)364-8250
Fax: (312)236-1042
E-mail: privateequity@wmblair.com
Website: http://www.wmblair.com
Maureen Naddy, Office Manager
Preferred Investment Size: $5,000,000 minimum. Investment Types: First and early stage, acquisition and leveraged buyout. Industry Preferences: Communications, computer related, consumer, electronics, energy/natural resources, genetic engineering, and medical/health related. Geograph

Bluestar Ventures
208 South LaSalle St., Ste. 1020
Chicago, IL 60604
(312)384-5000
Fax: (312)384-5005
Website: http://www.bluestarventures.com
Preferred Investment Size: $1,000,000 to $3,000,000. Investment Types: Early, first, and second stage. Industry Preferences: Diversified. Geographic Preferences: Midwest.

The Capital Strategy Management Co.
233 S. Wacker Dr.
Box 06334
Chicago, IL 60606
(312)444-1170
Eric Von Bauer
Preferred Investment Size: $200,000 to $50,000,000. Investment Types: Various types. Industry Preferences: Diversified communication and computer technology, medical/health, industrial/energy, consumer products and services, distribution, electronics, and utilities. Geographic Prefer

DN Partners
77 West Wacker Dr., Ste. 4550
Chicago, IL 60601
(312)332-7960
Fax: (312)332-7979
Investment Types: Leveraged buyout. Industry Preferences: Communications, computer related, electronics, medical/health, consumer related, industrial products, transportation, financial services, publishing, and agriculture related. Geographic Preferences: U.S.

Dresner Capital Inc.
29 South LaSalle St., Ste. 310
Chicago, IL 60603
(312)726-3600
Fax: (312)726-7448
John Riddle
Preferred Investment Size: $500,000 to $1,000,000. Investment Types: Leveraged buyout, mezzanine, and second stage. Industry Preferences: Diversified. Geographic Preferences: No preference.

Eblast Ventures LLC
11 South LaSalle St., 5th Fl.
Chicago, IL 60603
(312)372-2600
Fax: (312)372-5621
Website: http://www.eblastventures.com

Preferred Investment Size: $100,000 to $500,000. Investment Types: Early, seed, start-up, and turnaround. Industry Preferences: Diversified. Geographic Preferences: Midwest.

Essex Woodlands Health Ventures, L.P.
190 S. LaSalle St., Ste. 2800
Chicago, IL 60603
(312)444-6040
Fax: (312)444-6034
Website: http://www.essexwoodlands.com
Marc S. Sandroff, General Partner
Preferred Investment Size: $1,000,000 to $12,000,000. Investment Types: Startup, early and second stage, private placement, and mezzanine. Industry Preferences: Healthcare, biotechnology, Internet related. Geographic Preferences: No preference.

First Analysis Venture Capital
233 S. Wacker Dr., Ste. 9500
Chicago, IL 60606
(312)258-1400
Fax: (312)258-0334
Website: http://www.firstanalysis.com
Bret Maxwell, CEO
Preferred Investment Size: $3,000,000 to $15,000,000. Investment Types: Early and later stage, and expansion. Industry Preferences: Diversified. Geographic Preferences: No preference.

Frontenac Co.
135 S. LaSalle St., Ste.3800
Chicago, IL 60603
(312)368-0044
Fax: (312)368-9520
Website: http://www.frontenac.com
Preferred Investment Size: $500,000 minimum. Investment Types: Start-up, first and second stage, leveraged buyout, special situation, and industry roll ups. Industry Preferences: Diversified. Geographic Preferences: Entire U.S.

GTCR Golder Rauner, LLC
6100 Sears Tower
Chicago, IL 60606
(312)382-2200
Fax: (312)382-2201
Website: http://www.gtcr.com
Bruce V. Rauner
Preferred Investment Size: $10,000,000 minimum. Investment Types: Leveraged buyout, acquisition, expansion, management buyouts, and recapitalization. Industry Preferences:

ORGANIZATIONS, AGENCIES, & CONSULTANTS

Diversified. Geographic Preferences: No preference.

High Street Capital LLC
311 South Wacker Dr., Ste. 4550
Chicago, IL 60606
(312)697-4990
Fax: (312)697-4994
Website: http://www.highstr.com
Preferred Investment Size: $2,000,000 to $10,000,000. Investment Types: Acquisition, control-block purchases, expansion, generalist PE, leveraged and management buyouts, recaps, and special situations. Industry Preferences: Diversified. Geographic Preferences: Entire U.S.

IEG Venture Management, Inc.
70 West Madison
Chicago, IL 60602
(312)644-0890
Fax: (312)454-0369
Website: http://www.iegventure.com
Preferred Investment Size: $100,000 to $500,000. Investment Types: Seed, startup, first and second stage. Industry Preferences: Diversified. Geographic Preferences: Midwest.

JK&B Capital
180 North Stetson, Ste. 4500
Chicago, IL 60601
(312)946-1200
Fax: (312)946-1103
E-mail: gspencer@jkbcapital.com
Website: http://www.jkbcapital.com
Preferred Investment Size: $5,000,000 to $20,000,000. Investment Types: Early and late stage, and expansion. Industry Preferences: Diversified. Geographic Preferences: National.

Kettle Partners L.P.
350 W. Hubbard, Ste. 350
Chicago, IL 60610
(312)329-9300
Fax: (312)527-4519
Website: http://www.kettlevc.com
Preferred Investment Size: $1,000,000 to $5,000,000. Investment Types: Early, first and second stage, seed, and start-up. Industry Preferences: Internet related, communications, computer related. Geographic Preferences: Entire U.S.

Lake Shore Capital Partners
20 N. Wacker Dr., Ste. 2807
Chicago, IL 60606
(312)803-3536
Fax: (312)803-3534

Preferred Investment Size: $1,000,000 to $10,000,000. Investment Types: First and second stage, mezzanine, and leveraged buyout. Industry Preferences: Diversified. Geographic Preferences: National.

LaSalle Capital Group Inc.
70 W. Madison St., Ste. 5710
Chicago, IL 60602
(312)236-7041
Fax: (312)236-0720
Anthony Pesavento
Preferred Investment Size: $1,000,000 minimum. Investment Types: Leveraged buyout and special situation. Industry Preferences: Entertainment and leisure, consumer products, industrial products, and machinery. Geographic Preferences: No preference.

Linc Capital, Inc.
303 E. Wacker Pkwy., Ste. 1000
Chicago, IL 60601
(312)946-2670
Fax: (312)938-4290
E-mail: bdemars@linccap.com
Martin E. Zimmerman, Chairman
Preferred Investment Size: $500,000 to $2,000,000. Investment Types: Seed, start-up, early and late stage, mezzanine, research and development, and special situations. Industry Preferences: Diversified communication and computer technology, electronics, and medical/health related. Ge

Madison Dearborn Partners, Inc.
3 First National Plz., Ste. 3800
Chicago, IL 60602
(312)895-1000
Fax: (312)895-1001
E-mail: invest@mdcp.com
Website: http://www.mdcp.com
Preferred Investment Size: $20,000,000 to $400,000,000. Investment Types: Start-up, early stage, leveraged buyout, special situations, and expansion. Industry Preferences: Diversified. Geographic Preferences: Entire U.S. and Canada.

Mesirow Private Equity Investments Inc.
350 N. Clark St.
Chicago, IL 60610
(312)595-6950
Fax: (312)595-6211
Website: http://www.meisrowfinancial.com

Preferred Investment Size: $4,000,000 to $10,000,000. Investment Types: Second stage, mezzanine, and leveraged buyout. Industry Preferences: Diversified. Geographic Preferences: Entire U.S.

Mosaix Ventures LLC
1822 North Mohawk
Chicago, IL 60614
(312)274-0988
Fax: (312)274-0989
Website: http://www.mosaixventures.com
Preferred Investment Size: $500,000 to $3,000,000. Investment Types: Early and later stage, and expansion. Industry Preferences: Medical/health related. Geographic Preferences: U.S.

Nesbitt Burns
111 West Monroe St.
Chicago, IL 60603
(312)416-3855
Fax: (312)765-8000
Website: http://www.harrisbank.com
I. David Burn
Investment Types: Control-block purchases, leveraged buyout, and special situation. Industry Preferences: Diversified. Geographic Preferences: U.S. and Canada.

Polestar Capital, Inc.
180 N. Michigan Ave., Ste. 1905
Chicago, IL 60601
(312)984-9090
Fax: (312)984-9877
E-mail: wl@polestarvc.com
Website: http://www.polestarvc.com
Preferred Investment Size: $250,000 to $1,000,000. Investment Policies: Primarily equity. Investment Types: Start-up, first and second stage. Industry Preferences: Communications, computer related. Geographic Preferences: Entire U.S.

Prince Ventures (Chicago)
10 S. Wacker Dr., Ste. 2575
Chicago, IL 60606-7407
(312)454-1408
Fax: (312)454-9125
Preferred Investment Size: $500,000 to $1,000,000. Investment Types: Seed, startup, first and second stage, leveraged buyout. Industry Preferences: Genetic engineering and medical/health related. Geographic Preferences: No preference.

Prism Capital
444 N. Michigan Ave.
Chicago, IL 60611

(312)464-7900
Fax: (312)464-7915
Website: http://www.prismfund.com
Investment Types: First and second stage, mezzanine, leveraged buyout, and special situations. Industry Preferences: Diversified technology. Geographic Preferences: National.

Third Coast Capital
900 N. Franklin St., Ste. 700
Chicago, IL 60610
(312)337-3303
Fax: (312)337-2567
E-mail: manic@earthlink.com
Website: http://www.thirdcoastcapital.com
Preferred Investment Size: $2,000,000 to $5,000,000. Industry Preferences: Telecommunications and fiber optics. Geographic Preferences: National.

Thoma Cressey Equity Partners
4460 Sears Tower, 92nd Fl.
233 S. Wacker Dr.
Chicago, IL 60606
(312)777-4444
Fax: (312)777-4445
Website: http://www.thomacressey.com
Investment Types: Early and later stage, leveraged buyouts, and recapitalization. Industry Preferences: Diversified. Geographic Preferences: U.S. and Canada.

Tribune Ventures
435 N. Michigan Ave., Ste. 600
Chicago, IL 60611
(312)527-8797
Fax: (312)222-5993
Website: http://www.tribuneventures.com
Frances McCaughan
Preferred Investment Size: $1,000,000 to $10,000,000. Investment Types: Early stage, expansion, first and second stage, seed, and start-up. Industry Preferences: Diversified. Geographic Preferences: Entire U.S.

Wind Point Partners (Chicago)
676 N. Michigan Ave., Ste. 330
Chicago, IL 60611
(312)649-4000
Website: http://www.wppartners.com
Preferred Investment Size: $10,000,000 to $60,000,000. Investment Types: Later stage, leveraged buyout, acquisition, expansion, and recapitalization. Industry

Preferences: Diversified. Geographic Preferences: Midwest.

Marquette Venture Partners
520 Lake Cook Rd., Ste. 450
Deerfield, IL 60015
(847)940-1700
Fax: (847)940-1724
Website: http://www.marquetteventures.com
Preferred Investment Size: $1,000,000 to $5,000,000. Investment Types: Startup, first and second stage. Industry Preferences: Diversified. Geographic Preferences: Mid Atlantic, Midwest, Rocky Mountain, and West Coast.

Duchossois Investments Limited, LLC
845 Larch Ave.
Elmhurst, IL 60126
(630)530-6105
Fax: (630)993-8644
Website: http://www.duchtec.com
Preferred Investment Size: $500,000 to $5,000,000. Investment Types: Early, first and second stage. Industry Preferences: Diversified. Communications and computer related. Geographic Preferences: National.

Evanston Business Investment Corp.
1840 Oak Ave.
Evanston, IL 60201
(847)866-1840
Fax: (847)866-1808
E-mail: t-parkinson@nwu.com
Website: http://www.ebic.com
Preferred Investment Size: $250,000 to $500,000. Investment Types: Early stages. Industry Preferences: Diversified communication and computer technology, consumer products and services, medical/health, electronics, and publishing. Geographic Preferences: Chicago metropolitan area.

Inroads Capital Partners L.P.
1603 Orrington Ave., Ste. 2050
Evanston, IL 60201-3841
(847)864-2000
Fax: (847)864-9692
Preferred Investment Size: $1,000,000 to $5,000,000. Investment Types: Expansion and later stage. Industry Preferences: Diversified. Geographic Preferences: Entire U.S.

The Cerulean Fund/WGC Enterprises
1701 E. Lake Ave., Ste. 170
Glenview, IL 60025
(847)657-8002

Fax: (847)657-8168
Walter G. Cornett, III, Managing Director
Preferred Investment Size: $5,000,000 minimum. Investment Types: Seed, start-up, leveraged buyout, special situations, control block purchases, and research and development. Industry Preferences: Diversified. Geographic Preferences: Midwest.

Ventana Financial Resources, Inc.
249 Market Sq.
Lake Forest, IL 60045
(847)234-3434
Preferred Investment Size: $5,000,000 minimum. Investment Types: Seed, start-up, first and second stage, research and development, leveraged buyout, and mezzanine. Industry Preferences: Diversified. Geographic Preferences: Midwest, Southeast, and Southwest.

Beecken, Petty & Co.
901 Warrenville Rd., Ste. 205
Lisle, IL 60532
(630)435-0300
Fax: (630)435-0370
E-mail: hep@bpcompany.com
Website: http://www.bpcompany.com
Preferred Investment Size: $2,000,000 to $12,000,000. Investment Types: Early, first, second, and late stage; expansion; management buyouts; private placement; recapitalization. Industry Preferences: Communications, computer related, genetic engineering, medical and health related. G

Allstate Private Equity
3075 Sanders Rd., Ste. G5D
Northbrook, IL 60062-7127
(847)402-8247
Fax: (847)402-0880
Preferred Investment Size: $5,000,000 minimum. Investment Types: Startup, first and second stage, mezzanine, leveraged buyout, and special situations. Industry Preferences: Diversified. Geographic Preferences: Entire U.S.

KB Partners
1101 Skokie Blvd., Ste. 260
Northbrook, IL 60062-2856
(847)714-0444
Fax: (847)714-0445
E-mail: keith@kbpartners.com
Website: http://www.kbpartners.com
Keith Bank, Managing Partner

ORGANIZATIONS, AGENCIES, & CONSULTANTS

Preferred Investment Size: $1,000,000 to $5,000,000. Investment Types: Seed, startup, and early, first and second stage. Industry Preferences: Diversified. Geographic Preferences: National.

Transcap Associates Inc.
900 Skokie Blvd., Ste. 210
Northbrook, IL 60062
(847)753-9600
Fax: (847)753-9090
Ira J. Ederson
Preferred Investment Size: $500,000 to $5,000,000. Investment Types: Mezzanine, second stage, and special situation. Industry Preferences: Diversified. Geographic Preferences: Entire U.S.

Graystone Venture Partners, L.L.C. / Portage Venture Partners
One Northfield Plaza, Ste. 530
Northfield, IL 60093
(847)446-9460
Fax: (847)446-9470
Website: http://www.portageventures.com
Mathew B. McCall, Vice President
Preferred Investment Size: $250,000 to $3,000,000. Investment Types: Early stage. Industry Preferences: Diversified communication and computer technology, consumer products and services, genetic engineering, and medical/health. Geographic Preferences: National.

Motorola Inc.
1303 E. Algonquin Rd.
Schaumburg, IL 60196-1065
(847)576-4929
Fax: (847)538-2250
Website: http://www.mot.com/mne
James Burke, New Business Development Manager
Investment Types: Startup, first and second stage. Industry Preferences: Diversified technology. Geographic Preferences: National.

Indiana

Irwin Ventures LLC
500 Washington St.
Columbus, IN 47202
(812)373-1434
Fax: (812)376-1709
Website: http://www.irwinventures.com
Preferred Investment Size: $750,000 to $1,250,000. Investment Types: Early and

first stage. Industry Preferences: Internet related and financial services. Geographic Preferences: Northeast and Northwest.

Cambridge Venture Partners
4181 East 96th St., Ste. 200
Indianapolis, IN 46240
(317)814-6192
Fax: (317)944-9815
Jean Wojtowicz, President
Preferred Investment Size: $100,000 maximum. Investment Types: Second stage, mezzanine, and leveraged buyout. Industry Preferences: No preference. Geographic Preferences: Midwest, within 200 miles of office.

CID Equity Partners
One American Square, Ste. 2850
Box 82074
Indianapolis, IN 46282
(317)269-2350
Fax: (317)269-2355
Website: http://www.cidequity.com
Chris Gough, Associate
Preferred Investment Size: $1,000,000 minimum. Investment Types: Start-up, early and first stage, industry rollups, leveraged buyout, and special situations. Industry Preferences: Diversified. Geographic Preferences: Midwest and Rocky Mountain region.

Gazelle Techventures
6325 Digital Way, Ste. 460
Indianapolis, IN 46278
(317)275-6800
Fax: (317)275-1101
Website: http://www.gazellevc.com
Preferred Investment Size: $2,000,000 maximum. Investment Types: Early and later stage. Industry Preferences: Diversified. Geographic Preferences: Indiana.

Monument Advisors Inc.
Bank One Center/Circle
111 Monument Circle, Ste. 600
Indianapolis, IN 46204-5172
(317)656-5065
Fax: (317)656-5060
Website: http://www.monumentadv.com
Preferred Investment Size: $500,000 to $7,000,000. Investment Types: Balanced, leveraged buyout, management buyouts, and mezzanine. Industry Preferences: Business services, distribution, and manufacturing. Geographic Preferences: Midwest and Southeast.

MWV Capital Partners
201 N. Illinois St., Ste. 300
Indianapolis, IN 46204
(317)237-2323
Fax: (317)237-2325
Website: http://www.mwvcapital.com
Garth Dickey, Managing Director
Preferred Investment Size: $1,000,000 to $5,000,000. Investment Types: Balanced, second and later stage. Industry Preferences: Diversified. Geographic Preferences: Midwest.

First Source Capital Corp.
100 North Michigan St.
PO Box 1602
South Bend, IN 46601
(219)235-2180
Fax: (219)235-2227
Eugene L. Cavanaugh, Vice President
Preferred Investment Size: $300,000 to $500,000. Investment Types: Second stage, mezzanine, leveraged buyout, and special situations. Industry Preferences: Diversified. Geographic Preferences: Midwest.

Iowa

Allsop Venture Partners
118 Third Ave. SE, Ste. 837
Cedar Rapids, IA 52401
(319)368-6675
Fax: (319)363-9515
Preferred Investment Size: $500,000 minimum. Investment Types: First stage, industry rollups, leveraged buyout, mezzanine, second stage, and special situation. Industry Preferences: Diversified. Geographic Preferences: Entire U.S.

InvestAmerica Investment Advisors, Inc.
101 2nd St. SE, Ste. 800
Cedar Rapids, IA 52401
(319)363-8249
Fax: (319)363-9683
Kevin F. Mullane, Vice President
Preferred Investment Size: $500,000 to $1,000,000. Investment Types: First and second stage, leveraged buyout, and special situations. Industry Preferences: Diversified. Geographic Preferences: Entire U.S.

Pappajohn Capital Resources
2116 Financial Center
Des Moines, IA 50309
(515)244-5746

Fax: (515)244-2346
Website: http://www.pappajohn.com
Joe Dunham, President
Preferred Investment Size: $500,000 to
$1,000,000. Investment Policies: Equity.
Investment Types: Seed, start-up, first
and second stage, leveraged buyout, and
special situations. Industry Preferences:
Diversified communication and
computer technology, electronics, genetic
engineerin

Berthel Fisher & Company Planning Inc.
701 Tama St.
PO Box 609
Marion, IA 52302
(319)497-5700
Fax: (319)497-4244
Investment Types: Later stage. Industry
Preferences: Diversified. Geographic
Preferences: Midwest.

Kansas

Enterprise Merchant Bank
7400 West 110th St., Ste. 560
Overland Park, KS 66210
(913)327-8500
Fax: (913)327-8505
Preferred Investment Size: $1,000,000
minimum. Investment Types: Second
stage, leveraged buyout, mezzanine, and
special situations. Geographic
Preferences: Midwest.

Kansas Venture Capital, Inc. (Overland Park)
6700 Antioch Plz., Ste. 460
Overland Park, KS 66204
(913)262-7117
Fax: (913)262-3509
E-mail: jdalton@kvci.com
John S. Dalton, President
Preferred Investment Size: $1,000,000
minimum. Investment Types: First and
second stage, mezzanine, and leveraged
buyout. Industry Preferences:
Diversified. Geographic Preferences:
Midwest.

Child Health Investment Corp.
6803 W. 64th St., Ste. 208
Shawnee Mission, KS 66202
(913)262-1436
Fax: (913)262-1575
Website: http://www.chca.com
Investment Types: Balanced, early stage,
first stage, seed, and start-up. Industry

Preferences: Diversified. Geographic
Preferences: Entire U.S.

Kansas Technology Enterprise Corp.
214 SW 6th, 1st Fl.
Topeka, KS 66603-3719
(785)296-5272
Fax: (785)296-1160
E-mail: ktec@ktec.com
Website: http://www.ktec.com
Preferred Investment Size: $300,000.
Investment Types: Seed, start-up,
research and development. Industry
Preferences: Diversified communication
and computer technology, electronics,
genetic engineering, and healthcare.
Geographic Preferences: Within two
hours of office.

Kentucky

Kentucky Highlands Investment Corp.
362 Old Whitley Rd.
London, KY 40741
(606)864-5175
Fax: (606)864-5194
Website: http://www.khic.org
Investment Types: Second stage, special
situation, and start-up. Industry
Preferences: Manufacturing. Geographic
Preferences: Kentucky.

Chrysalis Ventures, L.L.C.
1850 National City Tower
Louisville, KY 40202
(502)583-7644
Fax: (502)583-7648
E-mail: bobsany@chrysalisventures.com
Website: http://
www.chrysalisventures.com
Preferred Investment Size: $3,000,000 to
$5,000,000. Investment Types: Start-up,
first and second stage. Industry
Preferences: Diversified communication
and computer technology. Geographic
Preferences: Southeast and Midwest.

Humana Venture Capital
500 West Main St.
Louisville, KY 40202
(502)580-3922
Fax: (502)580-2051
E-mail: gemont@humana.com
George Emont, Director
Preferred Investment Size: $10,000,000
minimum. Investment Types: Seed, start-
up, first and second stage, leveraged
buyout, mezzanine, and research and
development. Industry Preferences:
Medical/health related, Internet and

computer related, and biotechnology.
Geographic Preferences:

Summit Capital Group, Inc.
6510 Glenridge Park Pl., Ste. 8
Louisville, KY 40222
(502)332-2700
Preferred Investment Size: $10,000,000 to
$40,000,000. Investment Types: Control-
block purchases, expansion, leveraged
and management buyouts. Industry
Preferences: Diversified. Geographic
Preferences: Southeast and Southwest.

Louisiana

Bank One Equity Investors, Inc.
451 Florida St.
Baton Rouge, LA 70801
(504)332-4421
Fax: (504)332-7377
Michael P. Kriby
Preferred Investment Size: $8,000,000
minimum. Investment Types: First and
second stage, mezzanine, leveraged
buyout, and special situations. Industry
Preferences: Diversified. Geographic
Preferences: Southeast and Southwest.

Advantage Capital Partners
LLE Tower
909 Poydras St., Ste. 2230
New Orleans, LA 70112
(504)522-4850
Fax: (504)522-4950
Website: http://www.advantagecap.com
Steven T. Stull, President
Preferred Investment Size: $1,000,000 to
$10,000,000. Investment Types: Seed,
start-up, early and second stage, and
mezzanine. Industry Preferences:
Diversified. Geographic Preferences:
North and Southeast, and Midwest.

Maine

CEI Ventures / Coastal Ventures LP
2 Portland Fish Pier, Ste. 201
Portland, ME 04101
(207)772-5356
Fax: (207)772-5503
Website: http://www.ceiventures.com
Investment Types: No preference.
Industry Preferences: Diversified.
Geographic Preferences: Entire U.S.

Commwealth Bioventures, Inc.
4 Milk St.
Portland, ME 04101
(207)780-0904
Fax: (207)780-0913

E-mail: cbi4milk@aol.com
Investment Types: Seed. Industry Preferences: Biotechnology based start-ups. Geographic Preferences: No preference.

Maryland

Annapolis Ventures LLC
151 West St., Ste. 302
Annapolis, MD 21401
(443)482-9555
Fax: (443)482-9565
Website: http://www.annapolisventures.com
Preferred Investment Size: $2,000,000 to $5,000,000. Investment Types: Later stage. Industry Preferences: Diversified. Geographic Preferences: Midwest, Northeast, and Southeast.

Delmag Ventures
220 Wardour Dr.
Annapolis, MD 21401
(410)267-8196
Fax: (410)267-8017
Website: http://www.delmagventures.com
Preferred Investment Size: $250,000 to $1,000,000. Investment Types: Early stage and seed. Industry Preferences: Diversified. Geographic Preferences: Mid Atlantic.

Abell Venture Fund
111 S. Calvert St., Ste. 2300
Baltimore, MD 21202
(410)547-1300
Fax: (410)539-6579
Website: http://www.abell.org
Investment Types: Early stage, expansion, first and second stage, and private placement. Industry Preferences: Internet related, electronics, communications, and medical/health related. Geographic Preferences: Maryland.

ABS Ventures (Baltimore)
1 South St., Ste. 2150
Baltimore, MD 21202
(410)895-3895
Fax: (410)895-3899
Website: http://www.absventures.com
Preferred Investment Size: $500,000 maximum. Investment Types: Startup, first and second stage, and mezzanine. Industry Preferences: Communications, computer related, genetic engineering, and medical/health related. Geographic Preferences: Entire U.S.

Anthem Capital, L.P.
16 S. Calvert St., Ste. 800
Baltimore, MD 21202-1305
(410)625-1510
Fax: (410)625-1735
Website: http://www.anthemcapital.com
Preferred Investment Size: $500,000 to $1,000,000. Investment Types: Early and later stage, mezzanine, and special situations. Industry Preferences: Diversified. Geographic Preferences: Middle Atlantic.

Catalyst Ventures
1119 St. Paul St.
Baltimore, MD 21202
(410)244-0123
Fax: (410)752-7721
Preferred Investment Size: $500,000 maximum. Investment Policies: Equity. Investment Types: Research and development, and early stage. Industry Preferences: Data communications, biotechnology, and medical related. Geographic Preferences: Middle Atlantic.

Maryland Venture Capital Trust
217 E. Redwood St., Ste. 2200
Baltimore, MD 21202
(410)767-6361
Fax: (410)333-6931
E-mail: rblank@mdbusiness.state.md.us
Preferred Investment Size: $1,000,000 to $5,000,000. Investment Types: Seed, startup, first and second stage. Industry Preferences: Diversified. Geographic Preferences: Maryland.

New Enterprise Associates (Baltimore)
1119 St. Paul St.
Baltimore, MD 21202
(410)244-0115
Fax: (410)752-7721
Website: http://www.nea.com
Frank A. Bonsal, Jr., Founding Partner
Preferred Investment Size: $100,000 minimum. Investment Types: Seed, startup, first and second stage, and mezzanine. Industry Preferences: Diversified. Geographic Preferences: Entire U.S.

T. Rowe Price Threshold Partnerships
100 E. Pratt St., 8th Fl.
Baltimore, MD 21202
(410)345-2000
Fax: (410)345-2800
Terral Jordan
Preferred Investment Size: $3,000,000 to $5,000,000. Investment Types:

Mezzanine and special situations. Industry Preferences: Diversified. Geographic Preferences: Entire U.S.

Spring Capital Partners
16 W. Madison St.
Baltimore, MD 21201
(410)685-8000
Fax: (410)727-1436
E-mail: mailbox@springcap.com
Robert M. Stewart
Preferred Investment Size: $2,000,000 minimum. Investment Types: Second stage, acquisition, industry rollups, mezzanine, and leveraged buyout. Industry Preferences: Diversified. Geographic Preferences: Mid-Atlantic.

Arete Corporation
3 Bethesda Metro Ctr., Ste. 770
Bethesda, MD 20814
(301)657-6268
Fax: (301)657-6254
Website: http://www.arete-microgen.com
Jill Wilmoth
Investment Types: Seed, start-up, first stage, and research and development. Industry Preferences: Alternative energy. Geographic Preferences: Entire U.S. and Canada.

Embryon Capital
7903 Sleaford Place
Bethesda, MD 20814
(301)656-6837
Fax: (301)656-8056
Preferred Investment Size: $300,000 to $1,000,000. Investment Types: Diversified. Industry Preferences: Diversified. Geographic Preferences: Entire U.S.

Potomac Ventures
7920 Norfolk Ave., Ste. 1100
Bethesda, MD 20814
(301)215-9240
Website: http://www.potomacventures.com
Preferred Investment Size: $400,000 to $1,000,000. Investment Types: Early stage. Industry Preferences: Internet related. Geographic Preferences: Mid Atlantic.

Toucan Capital Corp.
3 Bethesda Metro Center, Ste. 700
Bethesda, MD 20814
(301)961-1970
Fax: (301)961-1969
Website: http://www.toucancapital.com

Preferred Investment Size: $1,000,000 to $1,000,000. Investment Types: Early stage, seed, and start-up. Industry Preferences: Diversified. Geographic Preferences: Entire U.S.

Kinetic Ventures LLC
2 Wisconsin Cir., Ste. 620
Chevy Chase, MD 20815
(301)652-8066
Fax: (301)652-8310
Website: http://
www.kineticventures.com
Investment Types: Startup, first stage, second stage, and leveraged buyout. Industry Preferences: Diversified technology. Geographic Preferences: National.

Boulder Ventures Ltd.
4750 Owings Mills Blvd.
Owings Mills, MD 21117
(410)998-3114
Fax: (410)356-5492
Website: http://
www.boulderventures.com
Preferred Investment Size: $2,000,000 to $5,000,000. Investment Types: Early stage, expansion, first stage, and start-up. Industry Preferences: Diversified. Geographic Preferences: Entire U.S.

Grotech Capital Group
9690 Deereco Rd., Ste. 800
Timonium, MD 21093
(410)560-2000
Fax: (410)560-1910
Website: http://www.grotech.com
Frank A. Adams, President and CEO
Preferred Investment Size: $1,000,000 to $5,000,000. Investment Types: First and second stage, start-up, mezzanine, leveraged buyouts, and special situations. Industry Preferences: Diversified. Geographic Preferences: Southeast and Middle Atlantic.

Massachusetts

Adams, Harkness & Hill, Inc.
60 State St.
Boston, MA 02109
(617)371-3900
Tim McMahan, Managing Director
Preferred Investment Size: $1,000,000 minimum. Investment Types: Second stage, balanced, mezzanine, and special situation. Industry Preferences: Computer, consumer, electronics, business services, industrial products and

equipment, and medical. Geographic Preferences: Northeast.

Advent International
75 State St., 29th Fl.
Boston, MA 02109
(617)951-9400
Fax: (617)951-0566
Website: http://
www.adventinernational.com
Will Schmidt, Managing Director
Preferred Investment Size: $1,000,000 minimum. Investment Types: Seed, first and second stage, mezzanine, leveraged buyout, special situations, research and development, and acquisitions. Industry Preferences: Diversified. Geographic Preferences: Entire U.S. and Canada.

American Research and Development
30 Federal St.
Boston, MA 02110-2508
(617)423-7500
Fax: (617)423-9655
Maureen A. White, Administrative Manager
Preferred Investment Size: $100,000 minimum. Investment Types: Seed, startup, first and second stage. Industry Preferences: Diversified technology. Geographic Preferences: Northeast.

Ascent Venture Partners
255 State St., 5th Fl.
Boston, MA 02109
(617)270-9400
Fax: (617)270-9401
E-mail: info@ascentvp.com
Website: http://www.ascentvp.com
Leigh E. Michl, Managing Director
Investment Types: First stage and acquisition. Industry Preferences: Diversified. Geographic Preferences: Northeast.

Atlas Venture
222 Berkeley St.
Boston, MA 02116
(617)488-2200
Fax: (617)859-9292
Website: http://www.atlasventure.com
Preferred Investment Size: $500,000 to $20,000,000. Investment Types: Seed, start-up, research and development, first and second stage, mezzanine, and balanced. Industry Preferences: Communications, computer, genetic engineering, electronics, medical and health related. Geographic Pr

Axxon Capital
28 State St., 37th Fl.
Boston, MA 02109
(617)722-0980
Fax: (617)557-6014
Website: http://www.axxoncapital.com
Preferred Investment Size: $300,000 to $2,500,000. Investment Types: Balanced. Industry Preferences: Communications and media. Geographic Preferences: Northeast.

BancBoston Capital/BancBoston Ventures
175 Federal St., 10th Fl.
Boston, MA 02110
(617)434-2509
Fax: (617)434-6175
Website: http://
www.bancbostoncapital.com
Frederick M. Fritz, President
Preferred Investment Size: $1,000,000 to $100,000,000. Investment Types: Seed, early stage, acquisition, recaps, later stage, management buyouts, expansion, and mezzanine. Industry Preferences: Diversified. Geographic Preferences: Entire U.S. and Eastern Canada.

Boston Capital Ventures
Old City Hall
45 School St.
Boston, MA 02108
(617)227-6550
Fax: (617)227-3847
E-mail: info@bcv.com
Website: http://www.bcv.com
Alexander Wilmerding
Preferred Investment Size: $250,000 to $8,000,000. Investment Types: Startup, first and second stage, recaps, and leveraged buyouts. Industry Preferences: Diversified. Geographic Preferences: Entire U.S.

Boston Financial & Equity Corp.
20 Overland St.
PO Box 15071
Boston, MA 02215
(617)267-2900
Fax: (617)437-7601
E-mail: debbie@bfec.com
Deborah J. Monosson, Senior Vice President
Preferred Investment Size: $500,000 to $1,000,000. Investment Types: Seed, start-up, first and second stage, leveraged buyout, mezzanine, and research and development. Industry Preferences:

Diversified. Geographic Preferences: National.

Boston Millennia Partners
30 Rowes Wharf
Boston, MA 02110
(617)428-5150
Fax: (617)428-5160
Website: http://
www.millenniapartners.com
Dana Callow, Managing General Partner
Preferred Investment Size: $5,000,000 to
$25,000,000. Investment Policies: Equity.
Investment Types: First and second stage,
start-up, leveraged buyout, and
mezzanine. Industry Preferences:
Communication, computer related,
consumer services, electronics, genetic
engineering, medical,

Bristol Investment Trust
842A Beacon St.
Boston, MA 02215-3199
(617)566-5212
Fax: (617)267-0932
E-mail: bernardberkman@prodigy.net
Preferred Investment Size: $100,000
minimum. Investment Policies: Equity.
Investment Types: First and second stage,
and mezzanine. Industry Preferences:
Restaurants, retailing, consumer
distribution, medical/health, and real
estate. Geographic Preferences:
Northeast.

Brook Venture Management LLC
50 Federal St., 5th Fl.
Boston, MA 02110
(617)451-8989
Fax: (617)451-2369
Website: http://www.brookventure.com
Preferred Investment Size: $500,000 to
$2,500,000. Investment Types: Early and
first stage. Industry Preferences:
Diversified. Geographic Preferences:
Northeast.

Burr, Egan, Deleage, and Co. (Boston)
200 Clarendon St., Ste. 3800
Boston, MA 02116
(617)262-7770
Fax: (617)262-9779
Preferred Investment Size: $2,000,000.
Investment Types: No preference.
Industry Preferences: Communications,
computer, and medical/health related.
Geographic Preferences: Entire U.S.

Cambridge/Samsung Partners
One Exeter Plaza
Ninth Fl.

Boston, MA 02116
(617)262-4440
Fax: (617)262-5562
Aashish Kalra, Associate
Preferred Investment Size: $100,000
minimum. Investment Policies: Equity.
Investment Types: Early stage. Industry
Preferences: Diversified. Geographic
Preferences: National.

Chestnut Street Partners, Inc.
75 State St., Ste. 2500
Boston, MA 02109
(617)345-7220
Fax: (617)345-7201
E-mail: chestnut@chestnutp.com
Drew Zalkind, Senior Vice President
Preferred Investment Size: $100,000 to
$1,000,000. Investment Types: Seed,
research and development, startup, and
first stage. Industry Preferences:
Diversified. Geographic Preferences: No
preference.

Claflin Capital Management, Inc.
10 Liberty Sq., Ste. 300
Boston, MA 02109
(617)426-6505
Fax: (617)482-0016
Website: http://www.claflincapital.com
William Wilcoxson, General Partner
Preferred Investment Size: $100,000
minimum. Investment Types: Seed,
startup, and first stage. Industry
Preferences: Diversified. Geographic
Preferences: Northeast.

Copley Venture Partners
99 Summer St., Ste. 1720
Boston, MA 02110
(617)737-1253
Fax: (617)439-0699
Preferred Investment Size: $1,000,000
minimum. Investment Types: First and
second stage, and start-up. Industry
Preferences: Diversified. Geographic
Preferences: No preference.

**Corning Capital / Corning Technology
Ventures**
121 High Street, Ste. 400
Boston, MA 02110
(617)338-2656
Fax: (617)261-3864
Website: http://
www.corningventures.com
Preferred Investment Size: $100,000 to
$500,000. Investment Policies: Equity.
Investment Types: Early stage. Industry

Preferences: Diversified technology.
Geographic Preferences: Northeast.

Downer & Co.
211 Congress St.
Boston, MA 02110
(617)482-6200
Fax: (617)482-6201
E-mail: cdowner@downer.com
Website: http://www.downer.com
Charles W. Downer
Preferred Investment Size: $300,000 to
$500,000. Investment Types: Start-up,
first and second stage, and mezzanine.
Industry Preferences: Diversified.
Geographic Preferences: Northeastern
U.S. and Canada.

Fidelity Ventures
82 Devonshire St.
Boston, MA 02109
(617)563-6370
Fax: (617)476-9023
Website: http://
www.fidelityventures.com
Neal Yanofsky, Vice President
Preferred Investment Size: $1,000,000 to
$10,000,000. Investment Types: Startup,
first and second stage, leveraged buyout,
and special situations. Industry
Preferences: Diversified. Geographic
Preferences: Northeast.

Greylock Management Corp. (Boston)
1 Federal St.
Boston, MA 02110-2065
(617)423-5525
Fax: (617)482-0059
Chris Surowiec
Preferred Investment Size: $250,000
minimum. Investment Types: Seed,
startup, first and early stage, and
expansion. Industry Preferences:
Diversified. Geographic Preferences: No
preference.

Gryphon Ventures
222 Berkeley St., Ste.1600
Boston, MA 02116
(617)267-9191
Fax: (617)267-4293
E-mail: all@gryphoninc.com
Andrew J. Atkinson, Vice President
Preferred Investment Size: $1,000,000
minimum. Investment Types: Startup,
first stage, second stage. Industry
Preferences: Energy/natural resources,
genetic engineering, and industrial
products and equipment. Geographic
Preferences: National.

Halpern, Denny & Co.
500 Boylston St.
Boston, MA 02116
(617)536-6602
Fax: (617)536-8535
David P. Malm, Partner
Preferred Investment Size: $5,000,000 to
$40,000,000. Investment Types: First
stage, second stage, control-black
purchases, and leveraged buyouts.
Industry Preferences: Consumer related,
Internet and computer related,
communications, industrial/energy, and
medical/health. Geographic

Harbourvest Partners, LLC
1 Financial Center, 44th Fl.
Boston, MA 02111
(617)348-3707
Fax: (617)350-0305
Website: http://www.hvpllc.com
Kevin Delbridge, Managing Partner
Preferred Investment Size: $5,000,000
minimum. Investment Types: All types.
Industry Preferences: Diversified.
Geographic Preferences: No preference.

Highland Capital Partners
2 International Pl.
Boston, MA 02110
(617)981-1500
Fax: (617)531-1550
E-mail: info@hcp.com
Website: http://www.hcp.com
Keith Benjamin, General Partner
Preferred Investment Size: $500,000 to
$5,000,000. Investment Types: Seed,
startup, and early, first and second stage.
Industry Preferences: Communications,
computer and Internet related, genetic
engineering, and medical/health related.
Geographic Preferences: Entire U.S. and
Canada.

Lee Munder Venture Partners
John Hancock Tower T-53
200 Clarendon St.
Boston, MA 02103
(617)380-5600
Fax: (617)380-5601
Website: http://www.leemunder.com
Investment Types: Early, first, second,
and later stage; expansion; mezzanine;
seed; start-up; and special situation.
Industry Preferences: Diversified.
Geographic Preferences: East Coast, Mid
Atlantic, Northeast, and Southeast.

M/C Venture Partners
75 State St., Ste. 2500

Boston, MA 02109
(617)345-7200
Fax: (617)345-7201
Website: http://www.mcventurepartners.com
Matthew J. Rubins
Preferred Investment Size: $5,000,000 to
$20,000,000. Investment Types: Early
stage. Industry Preferences:
Communications, computer software
and services, Internet related. Geographic
Preferences: Entire U.S. and Canada.

Massachusetts Capital Resources Co.
420 Boylston St.
Boston, MA 02116
(617)536-3900
Fax: (617)536-7930
William J. Torpey, Jr., President
Preferred Investment Size: $500,000 to
$1,000,000. Investment Policies: Equity.
Investment Types: Second stage,
leveraged buyout, and mezzanine.
Industry Preferences: No preference.
Geographic Preferences: Northeast.

**Massachusetts Technology
Development Corp. (MTDC)**
148 State St.
Boston, MA 02109
(617)723-4920
Fax: (617)723-5983
E-mail: jhodgman@mtdc.com
Website: http://www.mtdc.com
John F. Hodgman, President
Preferred Investment Size: $200,000 to
$1,000,000. Investment Types: Early,
seed, and startup. Industry Preferences:
Diversified. Geographic Preferences:
Massachusetts.

New England Partners
One Boston Place, Ste. 2100
Boston, MA 02108
(617)624-8400
Fax: (617)624-8999
Website: http://www.nepartners.com
Christopher P. Young
Preferred Investment Size: $1,000,000 to
$5,000,000. Investment Types: Balanced,
early, and first and second stage. Industry
Preferences: Diversified. Geographic
Preferences: Entire U.S.

North Hill Ventures
Ten Post Office Square
11th Fl.
Boston, MA 02109
(617)788-2112
Fax: (617)788-2152

Website: http://www.northhillventures.com
Preferred Investment Size: $1,500,000 to
$7,000,000. Investment Types: Balanced,
expansion, and later and second stage.
Industry Preferences: Communications,
computer software, Internet related,
consumer and retail related, business
services, and financial services.
Geographic Prefer

OneLiberty Ventures
150 Cambridge Park Dr.
Boston, MA 02140
(617)492-7280
Fax: (617)492-7290
Website: http://www.oneliberty.com
Stephen J. McCullen, General Partner
Preferred Investment Size: $1,000,000 to
$8,000,000. Investment Policies: Equity.
Investment Types: Early and late stage.
Industry Preferences: Diversified
technology. Geographic Preferences:
Northeast.

Schroder Ventures
Life Sciences
60 State St., Ste. 3650
Boston, MA 02109
(617)367-8100
Fax: (617)367-1590
Website: http://www.shroderventures.com
Preferred Investment Size: $250,000
minimum. Investment Types: Balanced,
first stage, leveraged buyout, mezzanine,
second stage, special situation, and start-
up. Industry Preferences: Diversified.
Geographic Preferences: Entire U.S. and
Canada.

Shawmut Capital Partners
75 Federal St., 18th Fl.
Boston, MA 02110
(617)368-4900
Fax: (617)368-4910
Website: http://www.shawmutcapital.com
Daniel Doyle, Managing Director
Preferred Investment Size: $5,000,000
minimum. Investment Types: Startup,
first stage, second stage, mezzanine,
leveraged buyout, and special situations.
Industry Preferences: Financial services
and applications. Geographic
Preferences: Entire U.S. and Canada.

Solstice Capital LLC
15 Broad St., 3rd Fl.
Boston, MA 02109

(617)523-7733
Fax: (617)523-5827
E-mail: solticecapital@solcap.com
Henry Newman, Partner
Preferred Investment Size: $250,000 to
$1,000,000. Investment Types: Early and
seed. Industry Preferences: Diversified.
Geographic Preferences: Northeast,
Rocky Mountain, Southwest, West Coast.

Spectrum Equity Investors
One International Pl., 29th Fl.
Boston, MA 02110
(617)464-4600
Fax: (617)464-4601
Website: http://
www.spectrumequity.com
William Collatos, Managing General
Partner
Preferred Investment Size: $5,000,000
minimum. Investment Types: Balanced.
Industry Preferences: Communications
and computer related. Geographic
Preferences: U.S. and Canada.

Spray Venture Partners
One Walnut St.
Boston, MA 02108
(617)305-4140
Fax: (617)305-4144
Website: http://www.sprayventure.com
Preferred Investment Size: $50,000 to
$4,000,000. Investment Policies: Equity.
Investment Types: Seed, start-up, first
and second stage, and research and
development. Industry Preferences:
Medical and health related, and genetic
engineering. Geographic Preferences:
National.

The Still River Fund
100 Federal St., 29th Fl.
Boston, MA 02110
(617)348-2327
Fax: (617)348-2371
Website: http://www.stillriverfund.com
Preferred Investment Size: $300,000 to
$4,000,000. Investment Types: Early
stage, expansion, first and second stage,
seed, and start-up. Industry Preferences:
Diversified. Geographic Preferences:
Entire U.S.

Summit Partners
600 Atlantic Ave., Ste. 2800
Boston, MA 02210-2227
(617)824-1000
Fax: (617)824-1159
Website: http://
www.summitpartners.com

Christopher W. Sheeline
Preferred Investment Size: $1,500,000
minimum. Investment Types: First and
second stage, mezzanine, leveraged
buyout, special situations, and control
block purchases. Industry Preferences:
Diversified. Geographic Preferences:
Entire U.S. and Canada.

TA Associates, Inc. (Boston)
High Street Tower
125 High St., Ste. 2500
Boston, MA 02110
(617)574-6700
Fax: (617)574-6728
Website: http://www.ta.com
Brian Conway, Managing Director
Preferred Investment Size: $60,000,000
maximum. Investment Types: Leveraged
buyout, special situations, control block
purchases. Industry Preferences:
Diversified. Geographic Preferences: No
preference.

TVM Techno Venture Management
101 Arch St., Ste. 1950
Boston, MA 02110
(617)345-9320
Fax: (617)345-9377
E-mail: info@tvmvc.com
Website: http://www.tvmvc.com
Helmut Schuehsler, Partner
Investment Types: Seed, start-up, first
and early stage. Industry Preferences:
Diversified. Geographic Preferences:
Entire U.S.

UNC Ventures
64 Burough St.
Boston, MA 02130-4017
(617)482-7070
Fax: (617)522-2176
Preferred Investment Size: $500,000 to
$1,000,000. Investment Types: Leveraged
buyout, mezzanine, and second stage.
Industry Preferences: Radio and
television broadcasting, environmental
related, and financial services.
Geographic Preferences: Entire U.S.

**Venture Investment Management
Company (VIMAC)**
177 Milk St.
Boston, MA 02190-3410
(617)292-3300
Fax: (617)292-7979
E-mail: bzeisig@vimac.com
Website: http://www.vimac.com
Preferred Investment Size: $1,000,000 to
$7,000,000. Investment Types: Seed,

startup, first and second stage. Industry
Preferences: Diversified technology.
Geographic Preferences: Northeast U.S.
and Eastern Canada.

MDT Advisers, Inc.
125 Cambridge Park Dr.
Cambridge, MA 02140-2314
(617)234-2200
Fax: (617)234-2210
Website: http://www.mdtai.com
Michael E.A. O'Malley
Preferred Investment Size: $500,000 to
$5,000,000. Investment Types: Early stage
and expansion. Industry Preferences:
Diversified. Geographic Preferences:
Northeast.

TTC Ventures
One Main St., 6th Fl.
Cambridge, MA 02142
(617)528-3137
Fax: (617)577-1715
E-mail: info@ttcventures.com
Investment Types: Seed, startup, first
stage, second stage, and mezzanine.
Industry Preferences: Computer related.
Geographic Preferences: National.

Zero Stage Capital Co. Inc.
101 Main St., 17th Fl.
Cambridge, MA 02142
(617)876-5355
Fax: (617)876-1248
Website: http://www.zerostage.com
Paul Kelley, President
Preferred Investment Size: $10,000 to
$15,000,000. Investment Types: Early and
later stage. Industry Preferences:
Diversified technology. Geographic
Preferences: Entire U.S.

Atlantic Capital
164 Cushing Hwy.
Cohasset, MA 02025
(617)383-9449
Fax: (617)383-6040
E-mail: info@atlanticcap.com
Website: http://www.atlanticcap.com
Preferred Investment Size: $300,000 to
$500,000. Investment Types: Startup and
first stage. Industry Preferences:
Diversified. Geographic Preferences:
National.

Seacoast Capital Partners
55 Ferncroft Rd.
Danvers, MA 01923
(978)750-1300
Fax: (978)750-1301
E-mail: gdeli@seacoastcapital.com

Website: http://www.seacoastcapital.com
Gregory A. Hulecki
Preferred Investment Size: $3,000,000
minimum. Investment Policies: Loans
and equity investments. Investment
Types: Second stage, industry rollups,
leveraged buyout, mezzanine, and special
situations. Industry Preferences:
Diversified. Geographic Preferences:
National.

Sage Management Group

44 South Street
PO Box 2026
East Dennis, MA 02641
(508)385-7172
Fax: (508)385-7272
E-mail: sagemgt@capecod.net
Charles Bauer
Preferred Investment Size: $500,000 to
$1,000,000. Investment Policies: Equity.
Investment Types: First and second stage,
leveraged buyout, mezzanine, and special
situations. Industry Preferences:
Diversified technology. Geographic
Preferences: National.

Applied Technology

1 Cranberry Hill
Lexington, MA 02421-7397
(617)862-8622
Fax: (617)862-8367
Ellie McCormack, Analyst
Preferred Investment Size: $100,000 to
$2,000,000. Investment Types: Seed,
startup, first and second stage, leveraged
buyout, and research and development.
Industry Preferences: Diversified.
Geographic Preferences: Entire U.S.

Royalty Capital Management

5 Downing Rd.
Lexington, MA 02421-6918
(781)861-8490
Preferred Investment Size: $100,000 to
$300,000. Investment Types: Startup,
first stage, second stage, leveraged
buyout, and special situations. Industry
Preferences: Diversified. Geographic
Preferences: Northeast.

Argo Global Capital

210 Broadway, Ste. 101
Lynnfield, MA 01940
(781)592-5250
Fax: (781)592-5230
Website: http://www.gsmcapital.com
Investment Types: Balanced and
expansion. Industry Preferences:
Communications, computer, and

Internet related. Geographic Preferences:
No preference.

Industry Ventures

6 Bayne Lane
Newburyport, MA 01950
(978)499-7606
Fax: (978)499-0686
Website: http://
www.industryventures.com
Preferred Investment Size: $250,000 to
$2,000,000. Investment Types: Early,
first, and second stage; seed, start-up.
Industry Preferences: Wireless
communications, computer software,
Internet related, retail, and media.
Geographic Preferences: Mid Atlantic,
Northeast, West Coast.

Softbank Capital Partners

10 Langley Rd., Ste. 202
Newton Center, MA 02459
(617)928-9300
Fax: (617)928-9305
E-mail: clax@bvc.com
Gary Rieschel
Investment Types: Seed, startup, first
stage, second stage, mezzanine, leveraged
buyout, and special situations. Industry
Preferences: Communications and
Internet. Geographic Preferences: Entire
U.S. and Canada.

Advanced Technology Ventures (Boston)

281 Winter St., Ste. 350
Waltham, MA 02451
(781)290-0707
Fax: (781)684-0045
E-mail: info@atvcapital.com
Website: http://www.atvcapital.com
Preferred Investment Size: $15,000,000 to
$35,000,000. Investment Types: Startup,
first stage, second stage, and balanced.
Industry Preferences: Diversified.
Geographic Preferences: No preference.

Castile Ventures

890 Winter St., Ste. 140
Waltham, MA 02451
(781)890-0060
Fax: (781)890-0065
Website: http://www.castileventures.com
Preferred Investment Size: $100,000 to
$15,000,000. Investment Types: Early,
first, and second stage; seed; and start-
up. Industry Preferences:
Communications and media, and
Internet related. Geographic Preferences:
Mid Atlantic, Northeast, and Southeast.

Charles River Ventures

1000 Winter St., Ste. 3300
Waltham, MA 02451
(781)487-7060
Fax: (781)487-7065
Website: http://www.crv.com
Richard M. Burnes, Jr., General Partner
Preferred Investment Size: $1,000,000 to
$20,000,000. Investment Types: Seed,
startup, first and second stage. Industry
Preferences: Diversified. Geographic
Preferences: No preference.

Comdisco Venture Group (Waltham)

Totton Pond Office Center
400-1 Totten Pond Rd.
Waltham, MA 02451
(617)672-0250
Fax: (617)398-8099
Preferred Investment Size: $300,000 to
$20,000,000. Investment Types: Seed,
startup, first and second stage. Industry
Preferences: Diversified. Geographic
Preferences: National.

Marconi Ventures

890 Winter St., Ste. 310
Waltham, MA 02451
(781)839-7177
Fax: (781)522-7477
Website: http://www.marconi.com
Preferred Investment Size: $1,000,000 to
$10,000,000. Investment Types:
Balanced; first, second, and later stage;
and start-up. Industry Preferences:
Diversified. Geographic Preferences: U.S.
and Canada.

Matrix Partners

Bay Colony Corporate Center
1000 Winter St., Ste.4500
Waltham, MA 02451
(781)890-2244
Fax: (781)890-2288
Website: http://www.matrixpartners.com
Andrew Marcuvitz, General Partner
Preferred Investment Size: $500,000 to
$1,000,000. Investment Types: Startup,
first and second stage, and leveraged
buyout. Industry Preferences:
Diversified. Geographic Preferences:
Entire U.S.

North Bridge Venture Partners

950 Winter St. Ste. 4600
Waltham, MA 02451
(781)290-0004
Fax: (781)290-0999
E-mail: eta@nbvp.com

Preferred Investment Size: $2,000,000 to $3,000,000. Investment Types: Seed, research and development, startup, first and second stage. Industry Preferences: Communications, computer related, medical/health, and electronics. Geographic Preferences: Entire U.S. and Canada.

Polaris Venture Partners
Bay Colony Corporate Ctr.
1000 Winter St., Ste. 3500
Waltham, MA 02451
(781)290-0770
Fax: (781)290-0880
E-mail: partners@polarisventures.com
Website: http://www.polarisventures.com
Michael Hirschland
Preferred Investment Size: $250,000 to $15,000,000. Investment Types: Seed, startup, first and second stages. Industry Preferences: Information technology, medical and health related. Geographic Preferences: National.

Seaflower Ventures
Bay Colony Corporate Ctr.
1000 Winter St. Ste. 1000
Waltham, MA 02451
(781)466-9552
Fax: (781)466-9553
E-mail: moot@seaflower.com
Website: http://www.seaflower.com
Alexander Moot, Partner
Investment Types: Seed, research and development, startup, first and second stage, recaps, and strategic alliances. Industry Preferences: Diversified technology. Geographic Preferences: Eastern U.S. and Midwest.

Ampersand Ventures
55 William St., Ste. 240
Wellesley, MA 02481
(617)239-0700
Fax: (617)239-0824
E-mail: info@ampersandventures.com
Website: http://www.ampersandventures.com
Paul C. Zigman, Partner
Preferred Investment Size: $5,000,000 to $15,000,000. Investment Types: All types. Industry Preferences: Diversified. Geographic Preferences: No preference.

Battery Ventures (Boston)
20 William St., Ste. 200
Wellesley, MA 02481
(781)577-1000

Fax: (781)577-1001
Website: http://www.battery.com
David A. Hartwig
Preferred Investment Size: $3,000,000 to $35,000,000. Investment Types: Seed, startup, first and second stage, mezzanine, and leveraged buyout. Industry Preferences: Communications, computer, computer and communications distribution. Geographic Preferences: No preference.

Commonwealth Capital Ventures, L.P.
20 William St., Ste.225
Wellesley, MA 02481
(781)237-7373
Fax: (781)235-8627
Website: http://www.ccvlp.com
Preferred Investment Size: $500,000 to $5,000,000. Investment Policies: Equity. Investment Types: Seed, start-up, first stage, leveraged buyout, mezzanine, and special situation. Industry Preferences: Diversified communication and computer technology, consumer products and services,

Fowler, Anthony & Company
20 Walnut St.
Wellesley, MA 02481
(781)237-4201
Fax: (781)237-7718
Preferred Investment Size: $4,000,000 to $5,000,000. Investment Types: All types. Industry Preferences: Diversified. Geographic Preferences: Entire U.S. and Canada.

Gemini Investors
20 William St.
Wellesley, MA 02481
(781)237-7001
Fax: (781)237-7233
C. Redington Barrett, III, Managing Director
Investment Types: Second stage, mezzanine, leveraged buyout, and special situations. Industry Preferences: Diversified. Geographic Preferences: National.

Grove Street Advisors Inc.
20 William St., Ste. 230
Wellesley, MA 02481
(781)263-6100
Fax: (781)263-6101
Website: http://www.grovestreetadvisors.com
Preferred Investment Size: $1,000,000 to $7,500,000. Investment Types: First stage,

mezzanine, second stage, special situation, and start-up. Industry Preferences: Diversified. Geographic Preferences: U.S.

Mees Pierson Investeringsmaat B.V.
20 William St., Ste. 210
Wellesley, MA 02482
(781)239-7600
Fax: (781)239-0377
Dennis P. Cameron
Investment Types: First and second stage, and start-up. Industry Preferences: Diversified technology. Geographic Preferences: Entire U.S. and Canada.

Norwest Equity Partners
40 William St., Ste. 305
Wellesley, MA 02481-3902
(781)237-5870
Fax: (781)237-6270
Website: http://www.norwestvp.com
Charles B. Lennin
Preferred Investment Size: $1,000,000 to $25,000,000. Investment Types: Seed, early and later stage, and expansion. Industry Preferences: Diversified. Geographic Preferences: National.

Bessemer Venture Partners (Wellesley Hills)
83 Walnut St.
Wellesley Hills, MA 02481
(781)237-6050
Fax: (781)235-7576
E-mail: travis@bvpny.com
Website: http://www.bvp.com
Preferred Investment Size: $100,000 to $15,000,000. Investment Types: Seed, start-up, early stage, first and second stage, and expansion. Industry Preferences: Communications, computer related, consumer products, distribution, and electronics. Geographic Preferences: National.

Venture Capital Fund of New England
20 Walnut St., Ste. 120
Wellesley Hills, MA 02481-2175
(781)239-8262
Fax: (781)239-8263
E-mail: kjdvcfne3@aol.com
Kevin J. Dougherty, General Partner
Preferred Investment Size: $750,000 to $3,000,000. Investment Types: Startup, first and second stage. Industry Preferences: Diversified. Geographic Preferences: Northeast.

Prism Venture Partners
100 Lowder Brook Dr., Ste. 2500

Westwood, MA 02090
(781)302-4000
Fax: (781)302-4040
E-mail: dwbaum@prismventure.com
Preferred Investment Size: $2,000,000 to $10,000,000. Investment Types: Startup, first stage, second stage, and mezzanine. Industry Preferences: Communications, computer and Internet related, electronic components and instrumentation, medical and health. Geographic Preferences: U.S.

Palmer Partners LP
200 Unicorn Park Dr.
Woburn, MA 01801
(781)933-5445
Fax: (781)933-0698
John Shane
Preferred Investment Size: $250,000 to $1,000,000. Investment Types: Startup, first and second stage, and special situations. Industry Preferences: Communications, computer, energy/ natural resources, industrial, education, finance, and publishing. Geographic Preferences: Northeast, S

Michigan

Arbor Partners, L.L.C.
130 South First St.
Ann Arbor, MI 48104
(734)668-9000
Fax: (734)669-4195
Website: http://www.arborpartners.com
Preferred Investment Size: $250,000 minimum. Investment Policies: Equity. Investment Types: Early and expansion. Industry Preferences: Diversified technology. Geographic Preferences: Midwest.

EDF Ventures
425 N. Main St.
Ann Arbor, MI 48104
(734)663-3213
Fax: (734)663-7358
E-mail: edf@edfvc.com
Website: http://www.edfvc.com
Mary Campbell, Partner
Preferred Investment Size: $500,000 to $10,000,000. Investment Types: Seed, startup, first stage, second stage, expansion, and research and development. Industry Preferences: Diversified technology. Geographic Preferences: Midwest.

White Pines Management, L.L.C.
2401 Plymouth Rd., Ste. B
Ann Arbor, MI 48105
(734)747-9401
Fax: (734)747-9704
E-mail: ibund@whitepines.com
Website: http://www.whitepines.com
Preferred Investment Size: $1,000,000 to $4,000,000. Investment Types: Second stage, mezzanine, leveraged buyout, and special situations. Industry Preferences: Diversified. Geographic Preferences: Southeast and Midwest.

Wellmax, Inc.
3541 Bendway Blvd., Ste. 100
Bloomfield Hills, MI 48301
(248)646-3554
Fax: (248)646-6220
Preferred Investment Size: $100,000 to $1,000,000. Investment Policies: Equity. Investment Types: Start-up, early and late stage, leveraged buyout, and special situations. Industry Preferences: Diversified. Geographic Preferences: Midwest, Southeast.

Venture Funding, Ltd.
Fisher Bldg.
3011 West Grand Blvd., Ste. 321
Detroit, MI 48202
(313)871-3606
Fax: (313)873-4935
Monis Schuster, Vice President
Preferred Investment Size: $1,000,000 minimum. Investment Policies: Equity. Investment Types: Startup, seed, leveraged buyout, research and development, and special situations. Industry Preferences: Diversified. Geographic Preferences: National.

Investcare Partners L.P. / GMA Capital LLC
32330 W. Twelve Mile Rd.
Farmington Hills, MI 48334
(248)489-9000
Fax: (248)489-8819
E-mail: gma@gmacapital.com
Website: http://www.gmacapital.com
Malcolm Moss, Managing Director
Investment Types: Second stage and leveraged buyout. Industry Preferences: Medical and health related. Geographic Preferences: National.

Liberty Bidco Investment Corp.
30833 Northwestern Highway, Ste. 211
Farmington Hills, MI 48334
(248)626-6070

Fax: (248)626-6072
James Zabriskie, Vice President
Preferred Investment Size: $500,000 minimum. Investment Types: Second stage, leveraged buyout, mezzanine, and special situations. Industry Preferences: Diversified. Geographic Preferences: Midwestern U.S. and Ontario, Canada.

Seaflower Ventures
5170 Nicholson Rd.
PO Box 474
Fowlerville, MI 48836
(517)223-3335
Fax: (517)223-3337
E-mail: gibbons@seaflower.com
Website: http://www.seaflower.com
M. Christine Gibbons, Partner
Investment Types: Seed, research and development, startup, recaps, strategic alliances, first and second stage. Industry Preferences: Genetic engineering, industrial products and equipment, medical and health related. Geographic Preferences: Midwest, Northeast, and Mid Atlantic.

Ralph Wilson Equity Fund LLC
15400 E. Jefferson Ave.
Gross Pointe Park, MI 48230
(313)821-9122
Fax: (313)821-9101
Website: http:// www.RalphWilsonEquityFund.com
J. Skip Simms, President
Preferred Investment Size: $200,000 to $1,000,000. Investment Types: Balanced, early stage, expansion, and first and second stage. Industry Preferences: Diversified. Geographic Preferences: Entire U.S.

Minnesota

Development Corp. of Austin
1900 Eighth Ave., NW
Austin, MN 55912
(507)433-0346
Fax: (507)433-0361
E-mail: dca@smig.net
Website: http://www.spamtownusa.com
Preferred Investment Size: $100,000. Investment Types: Startup, seed, and first stage. Industry Preferences: Diversified. Geographic Preferences: No preference.

Northeast Ventures Corp.
802 Alworth Bldg.
Duluth, MN 55802
(218)722-9915

Fax: (218)722-9871
Greg Sandbulte, President
Preferred Investment Size: $100,000 to
$500,000. Investment Policies: Equity.
Investment Types: Startup, early and late
stage, mezzanine, leveraged buyout, and
research and development. Industry
Preferences: No preference. Geographic
Preferences: Midwest.

Medical Innovation Partners, Inc.
6450 City West Pkwy.
Eden Prairie, MN 55344-3245
(612)828-9616
Fax: (612)828-9596
Mark B. Knudson, Ph.D., Managing
Partner
Preferred Investment Size: $100,000 to
$5,000,000. Investment Types: Seed,
startup, and first stage. Industry
Preferences: Medical technology and
healthcare, and communications.
Geographic Preferences: Northwest and
Midwest.

St. Paul Venture Capital, Inc.
10400 Vicking Dr., Ste. 550
Eden Prairie, MN 55344
(612)995-7474
Fax: (612)995-7475
Website: http://www.stpaulvc.com
Preferred Investment Size: $500,000
minimum. Investment Types: Early stage.
Industry Preferences: Diversified.
Geographic Preferences: California,
Massachusetts, and Minnesota.

Cherry Tree Investments, Inc.
7601 France Ave. S, Ste. 150
Edina, MN 55435
(612)893-9012
Fax: (612)893-9036
Website: http://www.cherrytree.com
Sandy Trump
Preferred Investment Size: $100,000
minimum. Investment Types: Balanced
and early second stage. Industry
Preferences: Diversified. Geographic
Preferences: Midwest.

Shared Ventures, Inc.
6550 York Ave. S
Edina, MN 55435
(612)925-3411
Howard Weiner
Preferred Investment Size: $100,000 to
$300,000. Investment Types: First and
second stage, start-up, leveraged buyout,
control-block purchases, and special
situations. Industry Preferences:

Consumer, electronics, distribution,
energy/natural resources, industrial
products and equipme

Sherpa Partners LLC
5050 Lincoln Dr., Ste. 490
Edina, MN 55436
(952)942-1070
Fax: (952)942-1071
Website: http://www.sherpapartners.com
Preferred Investment Size: $250,000 to
$5,000,000. Investment Types: Early
stage. Industry Preferences:
Telecommunications, computer
software, and Internet related.
Geographic Preferences:
Midwest.

Affinity Capital Management
901 Marquette Ave., Ste. 1810
Minneapolis, MN 55402
(612)252-9900
Fax: (612)252-9911
Website: http://www.affinitycapital.com
Edson W. Spencer
Preferred Investment Size: $250,000 to
$1,100,000. Investment Types: Seed,
startup, first and second stage. Industry
Preferences: Medical/Health related,
Internet and computer related.
Geographic Preferences: Midwest.

Artesian Capital
1700 Foshay Tower
821 Marquette Ave.
Minneapolis, MN 55402
(612)334-5600
Fax: (612)334-5601
E-mail: artesian@artesian.com
Frank B. Bennett, President
Preferred Investment Size: $300,000 to
$500,000. Investment Types: Seed,
research and development, leveraged
buyout, and startup. Industry
Preferences: Diversified. Geographic
Preferences: Midwest.

Coral Ventures
60 S. 6th St., Ste. 3510
Minneapolis, MN 55402
(612)335-8666
Fax: (612)335-8668
Website: http://www.coralventures.com
Preferred Investment Size: $1,000,000 to
$11,000,000. Investment Types: Seed,
startup, first and second stage. Industry
Preferences: Diversified technology.
Geographic Preferences: No preference.

Crescendo Venture Management, L.L.C.
800 LaSalle Ave., Ste. 2250

Minneapolis, MN 55402
(612)607-2800
Fax: (612)607-2801
Website: http://
www.crescendoventures.com
Jeffrey R. Tollefson, Partner
Preferred Investment Size: $1,000,000 to
$5,000,000. Investment Types: Startup,
seed, early and late stage. Industry
Preferences: Diversified information
technology. Geographic Preferences: U.S.
and Canada.

Gideon Hixon Venture
1900 Foshay Tower
821 Marquette Ave.
Minneapolis, MN 55402
(612)904-2314
Fax: (612)204-0913
E-mail: bkwhitney@gideonhixon.com
Preferred Investment Size: $300,000 to
$500,000. Investment Policies: Equity.
Investment Types: Startup, seed, early
and late stage. Industry Preferences:
Diversified communication and
computer technology, medical/health,
and electronics. Geographic Preferences:
West Coast.

Norwest Equity Partners
3600 IDS Center
80 S. 8th St.
Minneapolis, MN 55402
(612)215-1600
Fax: (612)215-1601
Website: http://www.norwestvp.com
Charles B. Lennin, Partner
Preferred Investment Size: $1,000,000 to
$25,000,000. Investment Policies: Equity.
Investment Types: Seed, expansion, early
and later stage. Industry Preferences:
Diversified. Geographic Preferences:
National.

Oak Investment Partners (Minneapolis)
4550 Norwest Center
90 S. 7th St.
Minneapolis, MN 55402
(612)339-9322
Fax: (612)337-8017
Website: http://www.oakinv.com
Preferred Investment Size: $250,000 to
$5,000,000. Investment Types: Startup,
first stage, second and late stage,
leveraged buyout, control-block
purchases, open market, and special
situations. Industry Preferences:
Diversified. Geographic Preferences:
Entire U.S.

Pathfinder Venture Capital Funds (Minneapolis)
7300 Metro Blvd., Ste. 585
Minneapolis, MN 55439
(612)835-1121
Fax: (612)835-8389
E-mail: jahrens620@aol.com
Jack K. Ahrens, II, Investment Officer
Preferred Investment Size: $2,000,000 minimum. Investment Types: Seed, startup, first and second stage, mezzanine, leveraged buyouts, and special situations. Industry Preferences: Diversified. Geographic Preferences: Entire U.S. and Canada.

U.S. Bancorp Piper Jaffray Ventures, Inc.
800 Nicollet Mall, Ste. 800
Minneapolis, MN 55402
(612)303-5686
Fax: (612)303-1350
Website: http://
www.paperjaffreyventures.com
Preferred Investment Size: $250,000 minimum. Investment Types: Early and late stage, and mezzanine. Industry Preferences: Diversified. Geographic Preferences: Entire U.S.

The Food Fund, Ltd. Partnership
5720 Smatana Dr., Ste. 300
Minnetonka, MN 55343
(612)939-3950
Fax: (612)939-8106
John Trucano, Managing General Partner
Preferred Investment Size: $800,000 minimum. Investment Types: Startup, first and second stage, leveraged buyout, and special situations. Industry Preferences: Consumer related, industrial and energy, and electronics. Geographic Preferences: Entire U.S.

Mayo Medical Ventures
200 First St. SW
Rochester, MN 55905
(507)266-4586
Fax: (507)284-5410
Website: http://www.mayo.edu
Preferred Investment Size: $1,000,000 minimum. Investment Types: Early stage. Industry Preferences: Diversified. Geographic Preferences: Entire U.S.

Missouri

Bankers Capital Corp.
3100 Gillham Rd.

Kansas City, MO 64109
(816)531-1600
Fax: (816)531-1334
Lee Glasnapp, Vice President
Preferred Investment Size: $100,000 minimum. Investment Types: Leveraged buyout. Industry Preferences: Consumer product and electronics distribution, and industrial equipment and machinery. Geographic Preferences: Midwest.

Capital for Business, Inc. (Kansas City)
1000 Walnut St., 18th Fl.
Kansas City, MO 64106
(816)234-2357
Fax: (816)234-2952
Website: http://
www.capitalforbusiness.com
Hollis A. Huels
Preferred Investment Size: $500,000 to $5,000,000. Investment Types: Expansion, leveraged and management buyouts, and later stage. Industry Preferences: Diversified. Geographic Preferences: Midwest.

De Vries & Co. Inc.
800 West 47th St.
Kansas City, MO 64112
(816)756-0055
Fax: (816)756-0061
Preferred Investment Size: $500,000 minimum. Investment Types: Acquisition, expansion, later stage, leveraged and management buyout, mezzanine, private placement, recaps, and second stage. Industry Preferences: Diversified. Geographic Preferences: No preference.

InvestAmerica Venture Group Inc. (Kansas City)
Commerce Tower
911 Main St., Ste. 2424
Kansas City, MO 64105
(816)842-0114
Fax: (816)471-7339
Kevin F. Mullane, Vice President
Preferred Investment Size: $500,000 to $1,000,000. Investment Types: First and second stage, leveraged buyout, and special situations. Industry Preferences: Diversified. Geographic Preferences: Entire U.S.

Kansas City Equity Partners
233 W. 47th St.
Kansas City, MO 64112
(816)960-1771
Fax: (816)960-1777

Website: http://www.kcep.com
Preferred Investment Size: $2,000,000 to $8,000,000. Investment Types: Start-up, early stage, expansion, and joint ventures. Industry Preferences: Diversified. Geographic Preferences: Midwest.

Bome Investors, Inc.
8000 Maryland Ave., Ste. 1190
St. Louis, MO 63105
(314)721-5707
Fax: (314)721-5135
Website: http://
www.gatewayventures.com
Gregory R. Johnson
Preferred Investment Size: $500,000 to $1,000,000. Investment Types: Startup, early and late stage. Industry Preferences: Diversified. Geographic Preferences: Midwest.

Capital for Business, Inc. (St. Louis)
11 S. Meramac St., Ste. 1430
St. Louis, MO 63105
(314)746-7427
Fax: (314)746-8739
Website: http://
www.capitalforbusiness.com
Hollis A. Huels
Preferred Investment Size: $500,000 to $5,000,000. Investment Types: Expansion, leveraged and management buyouts, and later stage. Industry Preferences: Diversified. Geographic Preferences: Midwest.

Crown Capital Corp.
540 Maryville Centre Dr., Ste. 120
Saint Louis, MO 63141
(314)576-1201
Fax: (314)576-1525
Website: http://www.crown-cap.com
Investment Types: Control-block purchases, first stage, leveraged buyout, mezzanine, second stage, and special situation. Industry Preferences: Diversified. Geographic Preferences: Entire U.S. and Canada.

Gateway Associates L.P.
8000 Maryland Ave., Ste. 1190
St. Louis, MO 63105
(314)721-5707
Fax: (314)721-5135
John S. McCarthy, Managing General Partner
Preferred Investment Size: $1,000,000 minimum. Investment Types: Start-up, second stage, mezzanine, leveraged

buyout, special situations, control block purchases. Industry Preferences: Communications, computer related, electronics, and hospital and other institutional management. Geo

Harbison Corp.
8112 Maryland Ave., Ste. 250
Saint Louis, MO 63105
(314)727-8200
Fax: (314)727-0249
Keith Harbison
Preferred Investment Size: $500,000 minimum. Investment Types: Control-block purchases, leveraged buyout, and special situation. Industry Preferences: Diversified. Geographic Preferences: Mid Atlantic and Southeast; Ontario and Quebec, Canada.

Nebraska

Heartland Capital Fund, Ltd.
PO Box 642117
Omaha, NE 68154
(402)778-5124
Fax: (402)445-2370
Website: http://www.heartlandcapitalfund.com
John G. Gustafson, Vice President
Preferred Investment Size: $500,000 to $3,000,000. Investment Policies: Equity. Investment Types: First and second stage, and expansion. Industry Preferences: Diversified technology. Geographic Preferences: Southwest and Midwest.

Odin Capital Group
1625 Farnam St., Ste. 700
Omaha, NE 68102
(402)346-6200
Fax: (402)342-9311
Website: http://www.odincapital.com
Preferred Investment Size: $1,000,000 to $5,000,000. Investment Types: Early, first, and second stage, and expansion. Industry Preferences: Internet related and financial services. Geographic Preferences: U.S.

Nevada

Edge Capital Investment Co. LLC
1350 E. Flamingo Rd., Ste. 3000
Las Vegas, NV 89119
(702)438-3343
E-mail: info@edgecapital.net
Website: http://www.edgecapital.net
Preferred Investment Size: $500,000 to $15,000,000. Investment Types: Seed,

startup, first stage, second stage, mezzanine, leveraged buyout, and special situations. Industry Preferences: Diversified technology. Geographic Preferences: U.S. and Canada.

The Benefit Capital Companies Inc.
PO Box 542
Logandale, NV 89021
(702)398-3222
Fax: (702)398-3700
Robert Smiley
Preferred Investment Size: $2,500,000 minimum. Investment Types: Leveraged buyout and mezzanine. Industry Preferences: Diversified. Geographic Preferences: Entire U.S.

Millennium Three Venture Group LLC
6880 South McCarran Blvd., Ste. A-11
Reno, NV 89509
(775)954-2020
Fax: (775)954-2023
Website: http://www.m3vg.com
Preferred Investment Size: $500,000 to $2,000,000. Investment Types: Early stage, expansion, first stage, mezzanine, second stage, and seed. Industry Preferences: Diversified. Geographic Preferences: West Coast.

New Jersey

Alan I. Goldman & Associates
497 Ridgewood Ave.
Glen Ridge, NJ 07028
(973)857-5680
Fax: (973)509-8856
Alan Goldman
Preferred Investment Size: $500,000 minimum. Investment Types: Control-block purchases, leveraged buyout, mezzanine, second stage, and special situation. Industry Preferences: Diversified. Geographic Preferences: Entire U.S. and Canada.

CS Capital Partners LLC
328 Second St., Ste. 200
Lakewood, NJ 08701
(732)901-1111
Fax: (212)202-5071
Website: http://www.cs-capital.com
Preferred Investment Size: $500,000 to $3,000,000. Investment Types: Distressed debt, early stage, expansion, first and second stage, and turnaround. Industry Preferences: Internet and computer related, communications, and medical/

health related. Geographic Preferences: Entire U.S. a

Edison Venture Fund
1009 Lenox Dr., Ste. 4
Lawrenceville, NJ 08648
(609)896-1900
Fax: (609)896-0066
E-mail: info@edisonventure.com
Website: http://www.edisonventure.com
John H. Martinson, Managing Partner
Preferred Investment Size: $1,000,000 to $6,000,000. Investment Types: Early and later stage, expansion, and management buyouts. Industry Preferences: Diversified. Geographic Preferences: Northeast and Middle Atlantic.

Tappan Zee Capital Corp. (New Jersey)
201 Lower Notch Rd.
PO Box 416
Little Falls, NJ 07424
(973)256-8280
Fax: (973)256-2841
Jeffrey Birnberg, President
Preferred Investment Size: $100,000 to $250,000. Investment Types: Leveraged buyout. Industry Preferences: Diversified. Geographic Preferences: No preference.

The CIT Group/Venture Capital, Inc.
650 CIT Dr.
Livingston, NJ 07039
(973)740-5429
Fax: (973)740-5555
Website: http://www.cit.com
Preferred Investment Size: $3,000,000 minimum. Investment Types: First and second stage, mezzanine, and leveraged buyout. Industry Preferences: Diversified. Geographic Preferences: Entire U.S.

Capital Express, L.L.C.
1100 Valleybrook Ave.
Lyndhurst, NJ 07071
(201)438-8228
Fax: (201)438-5131
E-mail: niles@capitalexpress.com
Website: http://www.capitalexpress.com
Niles Cohen
Preferred Investment Size: $300,000 to $500,000. Investment Policies: Equity. Investment Types: Start-up, first and second stage, and recaps. Industry Preferences: Internet and consumer related, and publishing. Geographic Preferences: East Coast.

Westford Technology Ventures, L.P.
17 Academy St.
Newark, NJ 07102
(973)624-2131
Fax: (973)624-2008
Preferred Investment Size: $300,000 to $500,000. Investment Types: Startup, first and second stage. Industry Preferences: Diversified communication and computer technology, electronics, industrial products and equipment. Geographic Preferences: No preference.

Accel Partners
1 Palmer Sq.
Princeton, NJ 08542
(609)683-4500
Fax: (609)683-4880
Website: http://www.accel.com
Preferred Investment Size: $1,000,000 minimum. Investment Types: Seed, start-up and early stage. Industry Preferences: Diversified. Geographic Preferences: National.

Cardinal Partners
221 Nassau St.
Princeton, NJ 08542
(609)924-6452
Fax: (609)683-0174
Website: http://www.cardinalhealthpartners.com
Lisa Skeete Tatum, Associate
Preferred Investment Size: $1,000,000 to $8,000,000. Investment Types: Seed, startup, first and second stage. Industry Preferences: Diversified. Geographic Preferences: U.S. and Canada.

Domain Associates L.L.C.
One Palmer Sq., Ste. 515
Princeton, NJ 08542
(609)683-5656
Fax: (609)683-9789
Website: http://www.domainvc.com
Preferred Investment Size: $1,000,000 to $20,000,000. Investment Types: Seed, start-up, first and second stage, balanced, expansion, mezzanine, private placement, research and development, and late stage. Industry Preferences: Electronic components and instrumentation, genetic engine

Johnston Associates, Inc.
181 Cherry Valley Rd.
Princeton, NJ 08540
(609)924-3131
Fax: (609)683-7524
E-mail: jaincorp@aol.com

Preferred Investment Size: $500,000 to $5,000,000. Investment Types: Start-up and early stage. Industry Preferences: Science and healthcare industry. Geographic Preferences: Northeast.

Kemper Ventures
Princeton Forrestal Village
155 Village Blvd.
Princeton, NJ 08540
(609)936-3035
Fax: (609)936-3051
Richard Secchia, Partner
Investment Types: Seed, research and development, startup, first and second stage. Industry Preferences: Computer related, medical and health related, financial services. Geographic Preferences: National.

Penny Lane Parnters
One Palmer Sq., Ste. 309
Princeton, NJ 08542
(609)497-4646
Fax: (609)497-0611
Preferred Investment Size: $1,000,000. Investment Types: Recaps, second stage, and leveraged buyouts. Industry Preferences: Computer related, genetic engineering, medical/health related, and electronics. Geographic Preferences: Eastern U.S.

Early Stage Enterprises L.P.
995 Route 518
Skillman, NJ 08558
(609)921-8896
Fax: (609)921-8703
Website: http://www.esevc.com
Ronald R. Hahn, Managing Director
Preferred Investment Size: $250,000 to $1,000,000. Investment Types: Seed, start-up, and early stage. Industry Preferences: Diversified. Geographic Preferences: Mid Atlantic.

MBW Management Inc.
1 Springfield Ave.
Summit, NJ 07901
(908)273-4060
Fax: (908)273-4430
Preferred Investment Size: $1,000,000 minimum. Investment Types: First stage, leveraged buyout, second stage, special situation, and start-up. Industry Preferences: Diversified. Geographic Preferences: No preference.

BCI Advisors, Inc.
Glenpointe Center W.

Teaneck, NJ 07666
(201)836-3900
Fax: (201)836-6368
E-mail: info@bciadvisors.com
Website: http://www.bcipartners.com
Thomas J. Cusick, General Partner
Preferred Investment Size: $5,000,000 to $25,000,000. Investment Types: Expansion. Industry Preferences: Diversified. Geographic Preferences: Entire U.S.

Demuth, Folger & Wetherill / DFW Capital Partners
Glenpointe Center E., 5th Fl.
300 Frank W. Burr Blvd.
Teaneck, NJ 07666
(201)836-2233
Fax: (201)836-5666
Website: http://www.dfwcapital.com
Donald F. DeMuth, General Partner
Preferred Investment Size: $500,000 minimum. Investment Policies: Equity. Investment Types: Acquisition, control-block purchases, later stage, leveraged buyout, management buyout, recaps, and speical situations. Industry Preferences: Healthcare, computer, communication, diversified.

First Princeton Capital Corp.
189 Berdan Ave., No. 131
Wayne, NJ 07470-3233
(973)278-3233
Fax: (973)278-4290
Website: http://www.lytellcatt.net
Michael Lytell
Preferred Investment Size: $200,000 minimum. Investment Types: First and second stage, mezzanine, recaps, control-block purchases, and leveraged buyout. Industry Preferences: Diversified. Geographic Preferences: Northeast and East Coast.

Edelson Technology Partners
300 Tice Blvd.
Woodcliff Lake, NJ 07675
(201)930-9898
Fax: (201)930-8899
Website: http://www.edelsontech.com
Harry Edelson, Managing Partner
Preferred Investment Size: $500,000 to $1,000,000. Investment Types: Seed, startup, first and second stage, leveraged buyout, and mezzanine. Industry Preferences: Diversified. Geographic Preferences: No preference.

New Mexico

Bruce F. Glaspell & Associates

10400 Academy Rd. NE, Ste. 313
Albuquerque, NM 87111
(505)292-4505
Fax: (505)292-4258
Bruce Glaspell
Preferred Investment Size: $100,000 to
$5,000,000. Investment Types: Seed,
startup, first stage, second stage, late
stage, private placement, and expansion.
Industry Preferences: Diversified.
Geographic Preferences: Entire U.S. and
Canada.

High Desert Ventures, Inc.

6101 Imparata St. NE, Ste. 1721
Albuquerque, NM 87111
(505)797-3330
Fax: (505)338-5147
E-mail: zilenziger@aol.com
Preferred Investment Size: $500,000 to
$2,500,000. Investment Types: Startup
and early stage. Industry Preferences:
Diversified. Geographic Preferences:
Northeast and Southwest.

New Business Capital Fund, Ltd.

5805 Torreon NE
Albuquerque, NM 87109
(505)822-8445
Preferred Investment Size: $100,000.
Investment Policies: Equity. Investment
Types: Seed, startup, and first stage.
Industry Preferences: Diversified.
Geographic Preferences: No preference.

SBC Ventures

10400 Academy Rd. NE, Ste. 313
Albuquerque, NM 87111
(505)292-4505
Fax: (505)292-4528
Viviana Cloninger, General Partner
Preferred Investment Size: $300,000 to
$3,000,000. Investment Types: Seed,
research and development, startup, and
first stage. Industry Preferences:
Diversified. Geographic Preferences:
Entire U.S. and Canada.

Technology Ventures Corp.

1155 University Blvd. SE
Albuquerque, NM 87106
(505)246-2882
Fax: (505)246-2891
Beverly Bendicksen
Investment Types: Seed, startup, first and
second stage. Industry Preferences:

Diversified. Geographic Preferences:
Southwest.

New York

New York State Science & Technology Foundation

Small Business Technology Investment Fund

99 Washington Ave., Ste. 1731
Albany, NY 12210
(518)473-9741
Fax: (518)473-6876
E-mail: jvanwie@empire.state.ny.us
Preferred Investment Size: $100,000 to
$300,000. Investment Types: Seed,
startup, first and second stage. Industry
Preferences: Diversified technology.
Geographic Preferences: Northeast.

Rand Capital Corp.

2200 Rand Bldg.
Buffalo, NY 14203
(716)853-0802
Fax: (716)854-8480
Website: http://www.randcapital.com
Allen F. Grum, President and CEO
Preferred Investment Size: $25,000 to
$500,000. Investment Types: Second
stage. Industry Preferences: Diversified.
Geographic Preferences: Northeast and
Ontario, Canada.

Seed Capital Partners

620 Main St.
Buffalo, NY 14202
(716)845-7520
Fax: (716)845-7539
Website: http://www.seedcp.com
Investment Types: Early stage. Industry
Preferences: Diversified technology,
communications, and other products.
Geographic Preferences: Northeast.

Coleman Venture Group

5909 Northern Blvd.
PO Box 224
East Norwich, NY 11732
(516)626-3642
Fax: (516)626-9722
Preferred Investment Size: $100,000 to
$1,000,000. Investment Types: First stage,
recaps, seed, start-up, and special
situation. Industry Preferences:
Electronics and consumer products.
Geographic Preferences: Northeast and
West Coast, and Canada.

Vega Capital Corp.

45 Knollwood Rd.

Elmsford, NY 10523
(914)345-9500
Fax: (914)345-9505
Ronald Linden
Preferred Investment Size: $300,000
minimum. Investment Types: Second
stage, mezzanine, leveraged buyout, and
special situations. Industry Preferences:
Diversified. Geographic Preferences:
Northeast, Southeast, and Middle
Atlantic.

Herbert Young Securities, Inc.

98 Cuttermill Rd.
Great Neck, NY 11021
(516)487-8300
Fax: (516)487-8319
Herbert D. Levine, President
Preferred Investment Size: $1,000,000
minimum. Investment Types: First and
second stage, leveraged buyout,
mezzanine, and special situation.
Industry Preferences: Diversified
communications and computer
technology, consumer products and
services, electronics, genetic engineering,
hea

Sterling/Carl Marks Capital, Inc.

175 Great Neck Rd., Ste. 408
Great Neck, NY 11021
(516)482-7374
Fax: (516)487-0781
E-mail: stercrlmar@aol.com
Website: http://
www.serlingcarlmarks.com
Preferred Investment Size: $1,000,000 to
$2,000,000. Investment Types: Second
stage, expansion, management buyouts,
and mezzanine. Industry Preferences:
Consumer related; distribution
of electronics equipment, food
and industrial products; and
industrial equipment and machinery.
Geog

Impex Venture Management Co.

PO Box 1570
Green Island, NY 12183
(518)271-8008
Fax: (518)271-9101
Jay Banker
Preferred Investment Size: $1,000,000
minimum. Investment Types: First stage,
leveraged buyout, second stage, special
situation, and start-up. Industry
Preferences: Diversified. Geographic
Preferences: Mid Atlantic and Northeast,
and Quebec, Canada.

Corporate Venture Partners L.P.
200 Sunset Park
Ithaca, NY 14850
(607)257-6323
Fax: (607)257-6128
Preferred Investment Size: $500,000 to
$1,000,000. Investment Types: First stage.
Industry Preferences: Diversified.
Geographic Preferences: Northeast.

Arthur P. Gould & Co.
One Wilshire Dr.
Lake Success, NY 11020
(516)773-3000
Fax: (516)773-3289
Andrew Gould, Vice President
Preferred Investment Size: $5,000,000
minimum. Investment Types: Seed,
research and development, startup, first
stage, second stage, mezzanine, and
leveraged buyout. Industry Preferences:
Diversified. Geographic Preferences:
National.

Dauphin Capital Partners
108 Forest Ave.
Locust Valley, NY 11560
(516)759-3339
Fax: (516)759-3322
Website: http://www.dauphincapital.com
Preferred Investment Size: $1,000,000 to
$3,000,000. Investment Types: Balanced;
and early, first, second, and later stage.
Industry Preferences: Diversified
technology, education, and business
services. Geographic Preferences: Entire U.S.

550 Digital Media Ventures
555 Madison Ave., 10th Fl.
New York, NY 10022
Website: http://www.550dmv.com
Investment Types: Early stage. Industry
Preferences: Entertainment and leisure,
and media. Geographic Preferences:
Entire U.S.

Aberlyn Capital Management Co., Inc.
500 Fifth Ave.
New York, NY 10110
(212)391-7750
Fax: (212)391-7762
Lawrence Hoffman, Chairman and CEO
Preferred Investment Size: $25,000,000
minimum. Investment Types: Startup,
first and second stage, leveraged buyout,
and special situation. Industry
Preferences: Diversified computer
technology, food and beverage products,
genetic engineering, and healthcare.
Geographic Preferences:

Adler & Company
342 Madison Ave., Ste. 807
New York, NY 10173
(212)599-2535
Fax: (212)599-2526
Jay Nickse, Treasurer & Chief Financial
Officer
Investment Types: Startup, first and
second stage, leveraged buyout, and
control-block purchases. Industry
Preferences: Diversified. Geographic
Preferences: National.

Alimansky Capital Group, Inc.
605 Madison Ave., Ste. 300
New York, NY 10022-1901
(212)832-7300
Fax: (212)832-7338
Howard Duby, Managing Director
Preferred Investment Size: $2,000,000.
Investment Types: First stage, second
stage, mezzanine, leveraged buyout, and
special situations. Industry Preferences:
Diversified. Geographic Preferences:
Entire U.S. and Canada.

Allegra Partners
515 Madison Ave., 29th Fl.
New York, NY 10022
(212)826-9080
Fax: (212)759-2561
Preferred Investment Size: $1,000,000
minimum. Investment Types: First stage,
leveraged buyout, recaps, second stage,
and special situation. Industry
Preferences: Communications, computer
related, and consumer related.
Geographic Preferences: Mid Atlantic,
and Eastern and Western U.S

The Argentum Group
The Chyrsler Bldg.
405 Lexington Ave.
New York, NY 10174
(212)949-6262
Fax: (212)949-8294
Website: http://
www.argentumgroup.com
Walter H. Barandiaran, Managing Dir.
Preferred Investment Size: $10,000,000
minimum. Investment Types: Second
stage, mezzanine, leveraged buyout, and
special situations. Industry Preferences:
Diversified. Geographic Preferences:
Entire U.S.

Axavision Inc.
14 Wall St., 26th Fl.
New York, NY 10005
(212)619-4000

Fax: (212)619-7202
Preferred Investment Size: $100,000 to
$300,000. Investment Types: Seed and
start-up. Industry Preferences: Computer
services and software, Internet related,
and financial services. Geographic
Preferences: No preference.

Bedford Capital Corp.
18 East 48th St., Ste. 1800
New York, NY 10017
(212)688-5700
Fax: (212)754-4699
E-mail: info@bedfordnyc.com
Website: http://www.bedfordnyc.com
Nathan Bernstein
Preferred Investment Size: $100,000 to
$300,000. Investment Types: First and
second stage, industry rollups, recaps,
and leveraged buyout. Industry
Preferences: Diversified. Geographic
Preferences: Midwest.

Bloom & Co.
950 Third Ave.
New York, NY 10022
(212)838-1858
Fax: (212)838-1843
Jack S. Bloom, President
Preferred Investment Size: $3,000,000
minimum. Investment Types: Startup,
first and second stage, control-block
purchases, leveraged buyout, mezzanine,
and special situation. Industry
Preferences: No preference. Geographic
Preferences: No preference.

Bristol Capital Management
300 Park Ave., 17th Fl.
New York, NY 10022
(212)572-6306
Fax: (212)705-4292
Investment Types: Leveraged buyout,
mezzanine, second stage, and special
situation. Industry Preferences:
Communications, computer related,
electronics, medical/health related,
entertainment and leisure, retail, food/
beverage, consumer services, machinery,
and publishing. Geographic

Citicorp Venture Capital Ltd. (New York City)
399 Park Ave., 14th Fl.
Zone 4
New York, NY 10043
(212)559-1127
Fax: (212)888-2940
Preferred Investment Size: $5,000,000.
Investment Types: Leveraged buyout,

second stage, and special situations. Industry Preferences: Diversified. Geographic Preferences: No preference.

CM Equity Partners
135 E. 57th St.
New York, NY 10022
(212)909-8428
Fax: (212)980-2630
Preferred Investment Size: $2,000,000 minimum. Investment Types: First and second stage, start-up, mezzanine, leveraged buyout, special situations, and industry rollups. Industry Preferences: Diversified. Geographic Preferences: No preference.

Cohen & Co., L.L.C.
800 Third Ave.
New York, NY 10022
(212)317-2250
Fax: (212)317-2255
E-mail: nlcohen@aol.com
Neil L. Cohen, President
Preferred Investment Size: $10,000,000 minimum. Investment Types: Startup, seed, early and late stage, mezzanine, leveraged buyout, control-block purchases, and special situations. Industry Preferences: Communications, consumer, distribution, electronics, energy, and healthcare. Geog

Cornerstone Equity Investors, L.L.C.
717 5th Ave., Ste. 1100
New York, NY 10022
(212)753-0901
Fax: (212)826-6798
Website: http://www.cornerstone-equity.com
Mark Rossi, Senior Managing Director
Preferred Investment Size: $50,000,000 maximum. Investment Types: Leveraged buyout, and special situations. Industry Preferences: Diversified. Geographic Preferences: No preference.

CW Group, Inc.
1041 3rd Ave., 2nd fl.
New York, NY 10021
(212)308-5266
Fax: (212)644-0354
Website: http://www.cwventures.com
Christopher Fenimore
Preferred Investment Size: $100,000 to $5,000,000. Investment Types: Seed, research and development, startup, first and second stage, leveraged buyout, special situations, and control block purchases. Industry Preferences:

Specialize in the medical/health business and biotechnology.

DH Blair Investment Banking Corp.
44 Wall St., 2nd Fl.
New York, NY 10005
(212)495-5000
Fax: (212)269-1438
J. Morton Davis, Chairman
Preferred Investment Size: $100,000. Investment Types: Research and development, startup, first stage, and leveraged buyout. Industry Preferences: Diversified. Geographic Preferences: No preference.

Dresdner Kleinwort Capital
75 Wall St.
New York, NY 10005
(212)429-3131
Fax: (212)429-3139
Website: http://www.dresdnerkb.com
Richard Wolf, Partner
Preferred Investment Size: $5,000,000 minimum. Investment Types: Early and second stage, expansion, mezzanine, and leveraged buyout. Industry Preferences: Diversified. Geographic Preferences: National.

East River Ventures, L.P.
645 Madison Ave., 22nd Fl.
New York, NY 10022
(212)644-2322
Fax: (212)644-5498
Montague H. Hackett
Preferred Investment Size: $500,000 to $5,000,000. Investment Types: Early and late stage, and mezzanine. Industry Preferences: Diversified communication and computer technology, consumer services, and medical. Geographic Preferences: National.

Easton Hunt Capital Partners
641 Lexington Ave., 21st Fl.
New York, NY 10017
(212)702-0950
Fax: (212)702-0952
Website: http://www.eastoncapital.com
Investment Types: First stage, mezzanine, and special situations. Industry Preferences: Diversified. Geographic Preferences: Entire U.S.

Elk Associates Funding Corp.
747 3rd Ave., Ste. 4C
New York, NY 10017
(212)355-2449
Fax: (212)759-3338
Gary C. Granoff, Pres.

Preferred Investment Size: $100,000 to $300,000. Investment Types: Second stage and leveraged buyout. Industry Preferences: Radio and TV, consumer franchise businesses, hotel and resort areas, and transportation. Geographic Preferences: Southeast and Midwest.

EOS Partners, L.P.
320 Park Ave., 22nd Fl.
New York, NY 10022
(212)832-5800
Fax: (212)832-5815
E-mail: mfirst@eospartners.com
Website: http://www.eospartners.com
Mark L. First, Managing Director
Preferred Investment Size: $3,000,000. Investment Policies: Equity and equity-oriented debt. Investment Types: Industry rollups, leveraged buyout, mezzanine, second stage, and special situation. Industry Preferences: Diversified. Geographic Preferences: Entire United States and Canad

Euclid Partners
45 Rockefeller Plaza, Ste. 3240
New York, NY 10111
(212)218-6880
Fax: (212)218-6877
E-mail: graham@euclidpartners.com
Website: http://www.euclidpartners.com
Preferred Investment Size: $500,000 to $5,000,000. Investment Types: Startup, first and second stage. Industry Preferences: Internet related, computer software and services, genetic engineering, and medical/health related. Geographic Preferences: No preference.

Evergreen Capital Partners, Inc.
150 East 58th St.
New York, NY 10155
(212)813-0758
Fax: (212)813-0754
E-mail: rysmith@evergreencapital.com
Preferred Investment Size: $1,000,000 to $300,000,000. Investment Types: No preference. Industry Preferences: Diversified. Geographic Preferences: National.

Exeter Capital L.P.
10 E. 53rd St.
New York, NY 10022
(212)872-1172
Fax: (212)872-1198
E-mail: exeter@usa.net
Karen J. Watai, Partner

Preferred Investment Size: $1,000,000 minimum. Investment Policies: Loans and equity investments. Investment Types: Leveraged buyout, mezzanine, second stage, and special situation. Industry Preferences: Diversified. Geographic Preferences: National.

Financial Technology Research Corp.
518 Broadway
Penthouse
New York, NY 10012
(212)625-9100
Fax: (212)431-0300
E-mail: fintek@financier.com
Neal Bruckman, President
Preferred Investment Size: $300,000 to $500,000. Investment Types: Seed, research and development, startup, first stage, second stage, and special situations. Industry Preferences: Diversified. Geographic Preferences: Entire U.S. and Canada.

4C Ventures
237 Park Ave., Ste. 801
New York, NY 10017
(212)692-3680
Fax: (212)692-3685
Website: http://www.4cventures.com
Ted Hobart, Partner
Preferred Investment Size: $500,000 to $1,000,000. Investment Types: Seed, research and development, startup, first and second stage. Industry Preferences: Communications, computer related, and consumer. Geographic Preferences: Entire U.S. and Canada.

Fusient Ventures
99 Park Ave., 20th Fl.
New York, NY 10016
(212)972-8999
Fax: (212)972-9876
E-mail: info@fusient.com
Website: http://www.fusient.com
Preferred Investment Size: $500,000 to $3,000,000. Investment Types: Early and first stage, and seed. Industry Preferences: Internet, entertainment and leisure, and media. Geographic Preferences: U.S.

Generation Capital Partners
551 Fifth Ave., Ste. 3100
New York, NY 10176
(212)450-8507
Fax: (212)450-8550
Website: http://www.genpartners.com
Preferred Investment Size: $5,000,000. Investment Types: Startup, early and late

stage, and leveraged buyout. Industry Preferences: Diversified communications and computer technology, consumer products and services, and industrial products and equipment. Geographic Preferences: Unite

Golub Associates, Inc.
555 Madison Ave.
New York, NY 10022
(212)750-6060
Fax: (212)750-5505
Evelyn Mordechai, Vice President
Preferred Investment Size: $1,000,000 to $10,000,000. Investment Types: Second stage, mezzanine, leveraged buyout, recaps, and special situations. Industry Preferences: Diversified. Geographic Preferences: Eastern U.S.

Hambro America Biosciences Inc.
650 Madison Ave., 21st Floor
New York, NY 10022
(212)223-7400
Fax: (212)223-0305
Preferred Investment Size: $2,500,000 to $5,000,000. Investment Types: First and second stage, and special situations. Industry Preferences: Genetic engineering, chemicals and materials, and medical/health related. Geographic Preferences: Entire U.S.

Hanover Capital Corp.
505 Park Ave., 15th Fl.
New York, NY 10022
(212)755-1222
Fax: (212)935-1787
Michael Wainstein
Preferred Investment Size: $300,000 minimum. Investment Types: Leveraged buyout, mezzanine, and second stage. Industry Preferences: Diversified. Geographic Preferences: Entire U.S.

Harvest Partners, Inc.
280 Park Ave, 33rd Fl.
New York, NY 10017
(212)559-6300
Fax: (212)812-0100
Website: http://www.harvpart.com
Harvey Mallement
Preferred Investment Size: $15,000,000 to $100,000,000. Investment Types: Acquisition, leveraged buyout, management buyouts, private placements, special situations, and turnaround. Industry Preferences: Consumer products and services,

communications, distribution, fiberoptics, and me

Holding Capital Group, Inc.
10 E. 53rd St., 30th Fl.
New York, NY 10022
(212)486-6670
Fax: (212)486-0843
James W. Donaghy, President
Preferred Investment Size: $5,000,000. Investment Types: Leveraged buyout. Industry Preferences: No preference. Geographic Preferences: Entire U.S.

Hudson Venture Partners
660 Madison Ave., 14th Fl.
New York, NY 10021-8405
(212)644-9797
Fax: (212)644-7430
Website: http://www.hudsonptr.com
Marilyn Adler
Preferred Investment Size: $500,000 to $2,800,000. Investment Types: Seed, start-up, first and early stages, and expansion. Industry Preferences: Diversified. Geographic Preferences: Entire U.S.

IBJS Capital Corp.
1 State St., 9th Fl.
New York, NY 10004
(212)858-2018
Fax: (212)858-2768
George Zombeck, Chief Operating Officer
Preferred Investment Size: $2,000,000. Investment Types: Mezzanine, leveraged buyout, and special situations. Industry Preferences: Consumer products and services, and chemicals and materials. Geographic Preferences: Entire U.S.

InterEquity Capital Partners, L.P.
220 5th Ave.
New York, NY 10001
(212)779-2022
Fax: (212)779-2103
Website: http://www.interequity-capital.com
Preferred Investment Size: $1,000,000 to $3,000,000. Investment Types: First and second stage, mezzanine, leveraged buyout, and special situations. Industry Preferences: Diversified. Geographic Preferences: Entire U.S.

The Jordan Edmiston Group Inc.
150 East 52nd St., 18th Fl.
New York, NY 10022
(212)754-0710
Fax: (212)754-0337

Scott Peters
Preferred Investment Size: $1,000,000.
Investment Types: Leveraged buyout,
mezzanine, second stage, and special
situation. Industry Preferences:
Publishing. Geographic Preferences: No
preference.

Josephberg, Grosz and Co., Inc.
633 3rd Ave., 13th Fl.
New York, NY 10017
(212)974-9926
Fax: (212)397-5832
Richard Josephberg
Preferred Investment Size: $1,000,000 to
$30,000,000. Investment Types: Many
types including seed, research and
development, startup, first and second
stage, mezzanine, and leveraged buyout.
Industry Preferences: Diversified.
Geographic Preferences: Entire U.S.

J.P. Morgan Capital Corp.
60 Wall St.
New York, NY 10260-0060
(212)648-9000
Fax: (212)648-5002
Website: http://www.jpmorgan.com
Lincoln E. Frank, Chief Operating
Officer
Preferred Investment Size: $10,000,000
to $20,000,000. Investment Types:
Second stage and special situations.
Industry Preferences: Diversified.
Geographic Preferences: Entire U.S. and
Canada.

The Lambda Funds
380 Lexington Ave., 54th Fl.
New York, NY 10168
(212)682-3454
Fax: (212)682-9231
Preferred Investment Size: $200,000 to
$500,000. Investment Types: Early stage,
expansion, first and second stage, and
management buyout. Industry
Preferences: Diversified. Geographic
Preferences: Mid Atlantic, Northeast, and
West Coast.

Lepercq Capital Management Inc.
1675 Broadway
New York, NY 10019
(212)698-0795
Fax: (212)262-0155
Michael J. Connelly
Preferred Investment Size: $1,000,000 to
$10,000,000. Investment Types: Control-
block purchases, leveraged buyout, and
second stage. Industry Preferences:

Diversified. Geographic Preferences: No
preference.

Loeb Partners Corp.
61 Broadway, Ste. 2400
New York, NY 10006
(212)483-7000
Fax: (212)574-2001
Preferred Investment Size: $100,000.
Investment Types: Early stage,
acquisition, expansion, leveraged and
management buyout. Industry
Preferences: Diversified. Geographic
Preferences: National.

Madison Investment Partners
660 Madison Ave.
New York, NY 10021
(212)223-2600
Fax: (212)223-8208
Preferred Investment Size: $5,000,000.
Investment Types: Second stage,
leveraged buyout, and industry roll ups.
Industry Preferences: Diversified.
Geographic Preferences: National.

MC Capital Inc.
520 Madison Ave., 16th Fl.
New York, NY 10022
(212)644-0841
Fax: (212)644-2926
Shunichi Maeda
Preferred Investment Size: $1,000,000 to
$30,000,000. Investment Types:
Acquisition, expansion, first stage, fund
of funds, generalist PE, joint ventures,
later stage, leveraged buyout, private
placement, second stage, special
situation, and turnaround. Industry
Preferences: Communic

**McCown, De Leeuw and Co. (New
York)**
65 E. 55th St., 36th Fl.
New York, NY 10022
(212)355-5500
Fax: (212)355-6283
Website: http://www.mdcpartners.com
Christopher Crosby, Principal
Preferred Investment Size: $40,000,000
minimum. Investment Types: Leveraged
buyout and special situations. Industry
Preferences: Diversified. Geographic
Preferences: Entire U.S.

Morgan Stanley Venture Partners
1221 Avenue of the Americas, 33rd Fl.
New York, NY 10020
(212)762-7900
Fax: (212)762-8424
E-mail: msventures@ms.com

Website: http://www.msvp.com
Preferred Investment Size: $2,000,000.
Investment Types: Second stage,
mezzanine, leveraged buyout, and
industry roll ups. Industry Preferences:
Diversified technology. Geographic
Preferences: Entire U.S. and Canada.

Nazem and Co.
645 Madison Ave., 12th Fl.
New York, NY 10022
(212)371-7900
Fax: (212)371-2150
E-mail: nazem@msn.com
Fred F. Nazem, Managing General
Partner
Preferred Investment Size: $1,000,000
minimum. Investment Types: Seed,
startup, first and second stage,
mezzanine, leveraged buyout, and special
situations. Industry Preferences:
Diversified. Geographic Preferences: No
preference.

Needham Capital Management, L.L.C.
445 Park Ave.
New York, NY 10022
(212)371-8300
Fax: (212)705-0299
Website: http://www.needhamco.com
Joseph Abramoff
Preferred Investment Size: $1,000,000 to
$10,000,000. Investment Policies: Equity.
Investment Types: Expansion, later stage,
leveraged buyout, management buyout,
and mezzanine. Industry Preferences:
Diversified technology. Geographic
Preferences: National.

Norwood Venture Corp.
1430 Broadway, Ste. 1607
New York, NY 10018
(212)869-5075
Fax: (212)869-5331
E-mail: nvc@mail.idt.net
Website: http://www.norven.com
Mark Littell
Preferred Investment Size: $500,000 to
$1,000,000. Investment Types:
Mezzanine, leveraged buyout, and special
situations. Industry Preferences:
Diversified. Geographic Preferences:
National.

Noveltek Venture Corp.
521 Fifth Ave., Ste. 1700
New York, NY 10175
(212)286-1963
Preferred Investment Size: $1,000,000
minimum. Investment Types:

Control-block purchases, first stage, mezzanine, second stage, special situation, and start-up. Industry Preferences: Diversified. Geographic Preferences: Entire U.S. and Canada.

Paribas Principal, Inc.
787 7th Ave.
New York, NY 10019
(212)841-2005
Fax: (212)841-3558
Gary Binning
Preferred Investment Size: $50,000,000. Investment Types: Leveraged buyout, special situations, and control block purchases. Industry Preferences: Diversified. Geographic Preferences: Entire U.S.

Patricof & Co. Ventures, Inc. (New York)
445 Park Ave.
New York, NY 10022
(212)753-6300
Fax: (212)319-6155
Website: http://www.patricof.com
Preferred Investment Size: $500,000 minimum. Investment Types: Seed, startup, first and second stage, mezzanine, and leveraged buyout. Industry Preferences: Diversified. Geographic Preferences: No preference.

The Platinum Group, Inc.
350 Fifth Ave, Ste. 7113
New York, NY 10118
(212)736-4300
Fax: (212)736-6086
Website: http://www.platinumgroup.com
Michael Grant, Analyst
Investment Types: Startup, first stage, second stage, and leveraged buyout. Industry Preferences: Diversified. Geographic Preferences: National.

Pomona Capital
780 Third Ave., 28th Fl.
New York, NY 10017
(212)593-3639
Fax: (212)593-3987
Website: http://www.pomonacapital.com
Karen Macleod
Preferred Investment Size: $1,000,000 minimum. Investment Types: Various investment types. Industry Preferences: Diversified. Geographic Preferences: Entire U.S.

Prospect Street Ventures
10 East 40th St., 44th Fl.

New York, NY 10016
(212)448-0702
Fax: (212)448-9652
E-mail: wkohler@prospectstreet.com
Website: http://www.prospectstreet.com
Edward Ryeom, Vice President
Preferred Investment Size: $1,000,000 minimum. Investment Types: First and second stage, start-up, control-block purchases, recaps, and special situations. Industry Preferences: Internet related, computer software and services, computer hardware, and communications. Geographic Prefer

Regent Capital Management
505 Park Ave., Ste. 1700
New York, NY 10022
(212)735-9900
Fax: (212)735-9908
E-mail: ninamcle@aol.com
Richard Hochman, Managing Director
Preferred Investment Size: $3,500,000 minimum. Investment Types: Second stage, mezzanine, and leveraged buyout. Industry Preferences: Communications, consumer products and services. Geographic Preferences: National.

Rothschild Ventures, Inc.
1251 Avenue of the Americas, 51st Fl.
New York, NY 10020
(212)403-3500
Fax: (212)403-3652
Website: http://www.nmrothschild.com
Preferred Investment Size: $500,000 to $5,000,000. Investment Types: Seed, research and development, startup, first and second stage, mezzanine, and leveraged buyout. Industry Preferences: Diversified. Geographic Preferences: Entire U.S. and Canada.

Sandler Capital Management
767 Fifth Ave., 45th Fl.
New York, NY 10153
(212)754-8100
Fax: (212)826-0280
Preferred Investment Size: $20,000,000 minimum. Investment Policies: Equity. Investment Types: Seed, start-up, first and second stage, control-block purchases, leveraged buyout, mezzanine, research and development, and special situation. Industry Preferences: Diversified communicatio

Siguler Guff & Company
630 Fifth Ave., 16th Fl.
New York, NY 10111

(212)332-5100
Fax: (212)332-5120
Maria Boyazny, Associate
Investment Types: Startup, first stage, second stage, control-block purchases, mezzanine, leveraged buyout, and special situations. Industry Preferences: Diversified. Geographic Preferences: National.

Spencer Trask Ventures Inc.
535 Madison Ave.
New York, NY 10022
(212)355-5565
Fax: (212)751-3362
Website: http://www.spencertrask.com
A. Emerson Martin, II, Senior Managing Director
Preferred Investment Size: $3,000,000 minimum. Investment Types: Startup, first stage, second stage, and special situations. Industry Preferences: Diversified. Geographic Preferences: National.

Sprout Group (New York City)
277 Park Ave.
New York, NY 10172
(212)892-3600
Fax: (212)892-3444
E-mail: info@sproutgroup.com
Website: http://www.sproutgroup.com
Patrick J. Boroian, General Partner
Preferred Investment Size: $5,000,000 to $50,000,000. Investment Types: Seed, startup, first and second stage, mezzanine, leveraged buyout, and special situations. Industry Preferences: Diversified technology. Geographic Preferences: Entire U.S.

US Trust Private Equity
114 W.47th St.
New York, NY 10036
(212)852-3949
Fax: (212)852-3759
Website: http://www.ustrust.com/privateequity
Jim Ruler
Preferred Investment Size: $5,000,000 minimum. Investment Types: Early, first stage, and second stage. Industry Preferences: Diversified. Geographic Preferences: National.

Vencon Management Inc.
301 West 53rd St., Ste. 10F
New York, NY 10019
(212)581-8787
Fax: (212)397-4126

Website: http://www.venconinc.com
Ingrid Yang
Preferred Investment Size: $500,000 to $10,000,000. Investment Types: First and second stage, leveraged buyout, seed, special situation, and start-up. Industry Preferences: Diversified. Geographic Preferences: Entire U.S. and Canada.

Venrock Associates
30 Rockefeller Plaza, Ste. 5508
New York, NY 10112
(212)649-5600
Fax: (212)649-5788
Website: http://www.venrock.com
Preferred Investment Size: $500,000 minimum. Investment Types: Seed, research and development, startup, first and second stages. Industry Preferences: Diversified. Geographic Preferences: National.

Venture Capital Fund of America, Inc.
509 Madison Ave., Ste. 812
New York, NY 10022
(212)838-5577
Fax: (212)838-7614
E-mail: mail@vcfa.com
Website: http://www.vcfa.com
Dayton T. Carr, General Partner
Preferred Investment Size: $500,000 to $100,000,000. Investment Types: Secondary partnership interests. Industry Preferences: Does not consider tax shelters, real estate, or direct investments in companies. Geographic Preferences: Entire U.S.

Venture Opportunities Corp.
150 E. 58th St.
New York, NY 10155
(212)832-3737
Fax: (212)980-6603
E-mail: jerryvoc@aol.com
Jerry March
Preferred Investment Size: $2,000,000 minimum. Investment Types: Startup, first and second stage, mezzanine, leveraged buyout, and special situations. Industry Preferences: Diversified. Geographic Preferences: Entire U.S.

Warburg Pincus Ventures, Inc.
466 Lexington Ave., 11th Fl.
New York, NY 10017
(212)878-9309
Fax: (212)878-9200
Website: http://www.warburgpincus.com
Preferred Investment Size: $1,000,000 to $500,000,000. Investment Types: Many

types including seed, startup, first and second stage, mezzanine, leveraged buyouts, private placements, recaps, and special situations. Industry Preferences: Diversified. Geographic Preferences: U.S. and C

Wasserstein, Perella & Co. Inc.
31 W. 52nd St., 27th Fl.
New York, NY 10019
(212)702-5691
Fax: (212)969-7879
Perry W. Steiner
Investment Types: Leveraged buyout. Industry Preferences: Diversified. Geographic Preferences: National.

Welsh, Carson, Anderson, & Stowe
320 Park Ave., Ste. 2500
New York, NY 10022-6815
(212)893-9500
Fax: (212)893-9575
Patrick J. Welsh, General Partner
Preferred Investment Size: $25,000,000 minimum. Investment Types: Leveraged buyout and special situations. Industry Preferences: Computer related and medical/health related. Geographic Preferences: Entire U.S.

Whitney and Co. (New York)
630 Fifth Ave. Ste. 3225
New York, NY 10111
(212)332-2400
Fax: (212)332-2422
Website: http://www.jhwitney.com
Preferred Investment Size: $1,000,000. Investment Types: Leveraged buyout and expansion. Industry Preferences: Diversified technology. Geographic Preferences: No preference.

Winthrop Ventures
74 Trinity Place, Ste. 600
New York, NY 10006
(212)422-0100
Cyrus Brown
Preferred Investment Size: $1,000,000 minimum. Investment Types: Startup, early and late stage, and leveraged buyout. Industry Preferences: Diversified. Geographic Preferences: National.

The Pittsford Group
8 Lodge Pole Rd.
Pittsford, NY 14534
(716)223-3523
Preferred Investment Size: $100,000 to $300,000. Investment Types: Startup, first and second stage, and control-block

purchases. Industry Preferences: Diversified technology. Geographic Preferences: Eastern U.S. and Canada.

Genesee Funding
70 Linden Oaks, 3rd Fl.
Rochester, NY 14625
(716)383-5550
Fax: (716)383-5305
Preferred Investment Size: $200,000. Investment Types: Second stage, mezzanine, and leveraged buyout. Industry Preferences: Diversified. Geographic Preferences: Northeast.

Gabelli Multimedia Partners
One Corporate Center
Rye, NY 10580
(914)921-5395
Fax: (914)921-5031
E-mail: fsommer@gabelli.com
Preferred Investment Size: $250,000 to $500,000. Investment Policies: Equity. Investment Types: Seed, startup, first and second stage. Industry Preferences: Diversified communications. Geographic Preferences: Northeast.

Stamford Financial
108 Main St.
Stamford, NY 12167
(607)652-3311
Fax: (607)652-6301
Website: http://www.stamfordfinancial.com
Alexander C. Brosda
Preferred Investment Size: $1,000,000 to $2,500,000. Investment Types: Expansion and mezzanine. Industry Preferences: Diversified. Geographic Preferences: Entire U.S.

Northwood Ventures LLC
485 Underhill Blvd., Ste. 205
Syosset, NY 11791
(516)364-5544
Fax: (516)364-0879
E-mail: northwood@northwood.com
Website: http://www.northwoodventures.com
Paul Homer, Associate
Preferred Investment Size: $1,000,000 to $10,000,000. Investment Types: First and second stage, acquisition, expansion, leveraged buyout, private placement, special situations, and industry roll ups. Industry Preferences: Diversified. Geographic Preferences: Entire U.S. and Canada.

Exponential Business Development Co.
216 Walton St.
Syracuse, NY 13202-1227
(315)474-4500
Fax: (315)474-4682
E-mail: dirksonn@aol.com
Website: http://www.exponential-ny.com
Dirk E. Sonneborn, Partner
Preferred Investment Size: $100,000 to $600,000. Investment Types: Early and first stage. Industry Preferences: No preference. Geographic Preferences: New York.

Onondaga Venture Capital Fund Inc.
714 State Tower Bldg.
Syracuse, NY 13202
(315)478-0157
Fax: (315)478-0158
Irving Schwartz
Preferred Investment Size: $100,000 to $250,000. Investment Types: Expansion, later stage, and mezzanine. Industry Preferences: Diversified. Geographic Preferences: Mid Atlantic and Northeast.

Bessemer Venture Partners (Westbury)
1400 Old Country Rd., Ste. 109
Westbury, NY 11590
(516)997-2300
Fax: (516)997-2371
E-mail: bob@bvpny.com
Website: http://www.bvp.com
Investment Types: Seed, research and development, start-up, first stages, leveraged buyout, special situations, and expansion. Industry Preferences: Communications, computer related, consumer products, distribution, and electronics. Geographic Preferences: Entire U.S.

Ovation Capital Partners
120 Bloomingdale Rd., 4th Fl.
White Plains, NY 10605
(914)258-0011
Fax: (914)684-0848
Website: http://www.ovationcapital.com
Preferred Investment Size: $500,000 to $4,000,000. Investment Types: Early stage. Industry Preferences: Internet related. Geographic Preferences: Northeast.

North Carolina

Carolinas Capital Investment Corp.
1408 Biltmore Dr.
Charlotte, NC 28207
(704)375-3888

Fax: (704)375-6226
E-mail: ed@carolinacapital.com
Edward Goode
Preferred Investment Size: $200,000 to $1,000,000. Investment Types: Seed, research and development, leveraged buyout, startup, first and second stages. Industry Preferences: Communications, electronic components and instrumentation. Geographic Preferences: No preference.

First Union Capital Partners
1st Union Center, 12th Fl.
301 S. College St.
Charlotte, NC 28288-0732
(704)383-0000
Fax: (704)374-6711
Website: http://www.fucp.com
L. Watts Hamrick, III, Partner
Preferred Investment Size: $5,000,000 minimum. Investment Types: Seed, start-up, first and second stage, mezzanine, expansion, leveraged buyout, special situations, and control block purchases. Industry Preferences: Diversified. Geographic Preferences: No preference.

Frontier Capital LLC
525 North Tryon St., Ste. 1700
Charlotte, NC 28202
(704)414-2880
Fax: (704)414-2881
Website: http://www.frontierfunds.com
Preferred Investment Size: $500,000 to $3,000,000. Investment Types: Early stage and expansion. Industry Preferences: Telecommunications, computer related, electronics, and energy. Geographic Preferences: Mid Atlantic and Southeast.

Kitty Hawk Capital
2700 Coltsgate Rd., Ste. 202
Charlotte, NC 28211
(704)362-3909
Fax: (704)362-2774
Website: http://www.kittyhawkcapital.com
Stephen W. Buchanan, General Partner
Preferred Investment Size: $1,000,000 to $7,000,000. Investment Types: Expansion, first and early stage. Industry Preferences: Diversified. Geographic Preferences: Southeast.

Piedmont Venture Partners
One Morrocroft Centre
6805 Morisson Blvd., Ste. 380
Charlotte, NC 28211
(704)731-5200

Fax: (704)365-9733
Website: http://www.piedmontvp.com
Preferred Investment Size: $250,000 to $5,000,000. Investment Types: Early stage. Industry Preferences: Diversified. Geographic Preferences: Southeast.

Ruddick Investment Co.
1800 Two First Union Center
Charlotte, NC 28282
(704)372-5404
Fax: (704)372-6409
Richard N. Brigden, Vice President
Preferred Investment Size: $500,000 to $1,000,000. Investment Types: First and second stage, and mezzanine. Industry Preferences: Diversified. Geographic Preferences: Southeast.

The Shelton Companies Inc.
3600 One First Union Center
301 S. College St.
Charlotte, NC 28202
(704)348-2200
Fax: (704)348-2260
Preferred Investment Size: $1,000,000 to $10,000,000. Investment Types: Control-block purchases, leveraged buyouts, recaps, and second stage. Industry Preferences: Diversified. Geographic Preferences: Mid Atlantic, Midwest, Southeast, and Southwest.

Wakefield Group
1110 E. Morehead St.
PO Box 36329
Charlotte, NC 28236
(704)372-0355
Fax: (704)372-8216
Website: http://www.wakefieldgroup.com
Anna Nelson, Partner
Preferred Investment Size: $1,000,000 to $5,000,000. Investment Types: Early stage. Industry Preferences: Diversified. Geographic Preferences: Southeast.

Aurora Funds, Inc.
2525 Meridian Pkwy., Ste. 220
Durham, NC 27713
(919)484-0400
Fax: (919)484-0444
Website: http://www.aurorafunds.com
Preferred Investment Size: $250,000 to $1,500,000. Investment Types: Startup, seed, early and first stage. Industry Preferences: Diversified. Geographic Preferences: Eastern United States.

Intersouth Partners
3211 Shannon Rd., Ste. 610

Durham, NC 27707
(919)493-6640
Fax: (919)493-6649
E-mail: info@intersouth.com
Website: http://www.intersouth.com
Jonathan Perl
Preferred Investment Size: $2,000,000 to $10,000,000. Investment Types: Seed, startup, first and early stages. Industry Preferences: Diversified. Geographic Preferences: Southeast and Southwest.

Geneva Merchant Banking Partners
PO Box 21962
Greensboro, NC 27420
(336)275-7002
Fax: (336)275-9155
Website: http://www.genevamerchantbank.com
Preferred Investment Size: $1,000,000 to $7,000,000. Investment Types: Balanced, distressed debt, expansion, leveraged and management buyout, mezzanine, second stage, and special situation. Industry Preferences: Diversified. Geographic Preferences: Mid Atlantic, Midwest, and Southeas

The North Carolina Enterprise Fund, L.P.
3600 Glenwood Ave., Ste. 107
Raleigh, NC 27612
(919)781-2691
Fax: (919)783-9195
Website: http://www.ncef.com
Charles T. Closson, President and CEO
Preferred Investment Size: $2,000,000 minimum. Investment Policies: Equity. Investment Types: Startup, first stage, and mezzanine. Industry Preferences: Diversified. Geographic Preferences: North Carolina and Southeast.

Ohio

Senmend Medical Ventures
4445 Lake Forest Dr., Ste. 600
Cincinnati, OH 45242
(513)563-3264
Fax: (513)563-3261
Preferred Investment Size: $500,000 to $1,000,000. Investment Types: Second stage and mezzanine. Industry Preferences: Genetic engineering, medical and health related. Geographic Preferences: National.

The Walnut Group
312 Walnut St., Ste. 1151
Cincinnati, OH 45202

(513)651-3300
Fax: (513)929-4441
Website: http://www.thewalnutgroup.com
Preferred Investment Size: $500,000 to $5,000,000. Investment Types: Balanced. Geographic Preferences: Northeast.

Brantley Venture Partners
20600 Chagrin Blvd., Ste. 1150
Cleveland, OH 44122
(216)283-4800
Fax: (216)283-5324
Kevin J. Cook, Associate
Preferred Investment Size: $1,000,000 to $5,000,000. Investment Types: Industry rollups, seed, start-up, and first stage. Industry Preferences: Diversified. Geographic Preferences: Entire U.S.

Clarion Capital Corp.
1801 E. 9th St., Ste. 1120
Cleveland, OH 44114
(216)687-1096
Fax: (216)694-3545
Preferred Investment Size: $250,000 to $500,000. Investment Types: Early, first and second stage. Industry Preferences: Diversified. Geographic Preferences: East Coast, Midwest, and West Coast.

Crystal Internet Venture Fund, L.P.
1120 Chester Ave., Ste. 418
Cleveland, OH 44114
(216)263-5515
Fax: (216)263-5518
E-mail: jf@crystalventure.com
Website: http://www.crystalventure.com
Daniel Kellog, Partner
Preferred Investment Size: $1,000,000 to $6,000,000. Investment Policies: Equity. Investment Types: Balanced and early stage. Industry Preferences: Diversified communications and computer technology. Geographic Preferences: National.

Key Equity Capital Corp.
127 Public Sq., 28th Fl.
Cleveland, OH 44114
(216)689-3000
Fax: (216)689-3204
Website: http://www.keybank.com
Cindy J. Babitt
Preferred Investment Size: $1,000,000 minimum. Investment Policies: Willing to make equity investments. Investment Types: Expansion, industry rollups, leveraged buyout, second stage, and special situation. Industry Preferences:

Diversified. Geographic Preferences: National.

Morgenthaler Ventures
Terminal Tower
50 Public Square, Ste. 2700
Cleveland, OH 44113
(216)416-7500
Fax: (216)416-7501
Website: http://www.morgenthaler.com
Robert C. Belles, Jr., General Partner
Preferred Investment Size: $500,000 minimum. Investment Types: Startup, first and second stage, acquisition, leveraged and management buyout, special situations, and expansion. Industry Preferences: Diversified. Geographic Preferences: Entire U.S. and Ontario, Canada.

National City Equity Partners Inc.
1965 E. 6th St.
Cleveland, OH 44114
(216)575-2491
Fax: (216)575-9965
E-mail: nccap@aol.com
Website: http://www.nccapital.com
Carl E. Baldassarre, Managing Director
Preferred Investment Size: $1,000,000 to $20,000,000. Investment Types: Second stage, mezzanine, leveraged buyout, special situations, recaps, management buyouts, and expansion. Industry Preferences: Diversified. Geographic Preferences: Entire U.S.

Primus Venture Partners, Inc.
5900 LanderBrook Dr., Ste. 2000
Cleveland, OH 44124-4020
(440)684-7300
Fax: (440)684-7342
E-mail: info@primusventure.com
Website: http://www.primusventure.com
Jeffrey J. Milius, Investment Manager
Preferred Investment Size: $5,000,000 minimum. Investment Types: Early stage, startup, expansion and balanced. Industry Preferences: Diversified. Geographic Preferences: Entire U.S.

Banc One Capital Partners (Columbus)
150 East Gay St., 24th Fl.
Columbus, OH 43215
(614)217-1100
Fax: (614)217-1217
Suzanne B. Kriscunas, Managing Director
Preferred Investment Size: $1,000,000 minimum. Investment Types: Later stage, leveraged buyout, mezzanine,

industry rollups, and special situations. Industry Preferences: Diversified. Geographic Preferences: Entire U.S.

Battelle Venture Partners
505 King Ave.
Columbus, OH 43201
(614)424-7005
Fax: (614)424-4874
Preferred Investment Size: $500,000 to $1,000,000. Investment Types: Startup, first and second stage. Industry Preferences: Energy/natural resources, industrial products and equipment. Geographic Preferences: National.

Ohio Partners
62 E. Board St., 3rd Fl.
Columbus, OH 43215
(614)621-1210
Fax: (614)621-1240
E-mail: mcox@ohiopartners.com
Investment Types: Startup, first and second stage. Industry Preferences: Computer related. Geographic Preferences: Western U.S. and Midwest.

Capital Technology Group, L.L.C.
400 Metro Place North, Ste. 300
Dublin, OH 43017
(614)792-6066
Fax: (614)792-6036
E-mail: info@capitaltech.com
Website: http://www.capitaltech.com
Preferred Investment Size: $250,000 to $1,000,000. Investment Types: Seed, early and start-up. Industry Preferences: Diversified electronics, alternative energy, and Internet related. Geographic Preferences: National.

Northwest Ohio Venture Fund
4159 Holland-Sylvania R., Ste. 202
Toledo, OH 43623
(419)824-8144
Fax: (419)882-2035
E-mail: bwalsh@novf.com
Barry P. Walsh, Managing Partner
Preferred Investment Size: $250,000 minimum. Investment Types: Seed, early and late stage, leveraged buyout, mezzanine, research and development. Industry Preferences: Diversified. Geographic Preferences: Midwest.

Oklahoma

Moore & Associates
1000 W. Wilshire Blvd., Ste. 370
Oklahoma City, OK 73116
(405)842-3660

Fax: (405)842-3763
Preferred Investment Size: $500,000 minimum. Investment Types: Startup, first and second stage, mezzanine, and leveraged buyout. Industry Preferences: Diversified technology. Geographic Preferences: National.

Chisholm Private Capital Partners
100 West 5th St., Ste. 805
Tulsa, OK 74103
(918)584-0440
Fax: (918)584-0441
Website: http://www.chisholmvc.com
James Bode, General Partner
Preferred Investment Size: $1,000,000 to $4,000,000. Investment Types: Startup, early and late stage. Industry Preferences: Diversified communications and computer, consumer products and retailing, electronics, alternative energy, and medical. Geographic Preferences: Entire U.S.

Davis, Tuttle Venture Partners (Tulsa)
320 S. Boston, Ste. 1000
Tulsa, OK 74103-3703
(918)584-7272
Fax: (918)582-3404
Website: http://www.davistuttle.com
Preferred Investment Size: $5,000,000 minimum. Investment Types: First and second stage, mezzanine, and leveraged buyout. Industry Preferences: Diversified. Geographic Preferences: Southwest.

RBC Ventures
2627 E. 21st St.
Tulsa, OK 74114
(918)744-5607
Fax: (918)743-8630
K.Y. Vargas, Vice President
Preferred Investment Size: $2,000,000 minimum. Investment Policies: Equity. Investment Types: Control-block purchases, leveraged buyout, mezzanine, second stage, and special situations. Industry Preferences: Diversified transportation. Geographic Preferences: Southwest.

Oregon

Utah Ventures II LP
10700 SW Beaverton-Hillsdale Hwy., Ste. 548
Beaverton, OR 97005
(503)574-4125
E-mail: adishlip@uven.com

Website: http://www.uven.com
Preferred Investment Size: $1,000,000 to $7,000,000. Investment Types: Early stages. Industry Preferences: Diversified technology. Geographic Preferences: Northwest and Rocky Mountains.

Orien Ventures
14523 SW Westlake Dr.
Lake Oswego, OR 97035
(503)699-1680
Fax: (503)699-1681
Anthony Miadich, Managing General Partner
Preferred Investment Size: $500,000 minimum. Investment Types: Start-up, seed, early and first stage. Industry Preferences: Diversified technology. Geographic Preferences: No preference.

OVP Venture Partners (Lake Oswego)
340 Oswego Pointe Dr., Ste. 200
Lake Oswego, OR 97034
(503)697-8766
Fax: (503)697-8863
E-mail: info@ovp.com
Website: http://www.ovp.com
Preferred Investment Size: $1,000,000 to $10,000,000. Investment Types: Seed, startup, and early stage. Industry Preferences: Communications, computer and Internet related, electronics, genetic engineering, and medical health related. Geographic Preferences: Western U.S. and Western

Oregon Resource and Technology Development Fund
4370 NE Halsey St., Ste. 233
Portland, OR 97213-1566
(503)282-4462
Fax: (503)282-2976
Preferred Investment Size: $100,000 to $300,000. Investment Types: Seed, start-up, research and development. Industry Preferences: Biotechnology, electronics, computer software and services, and medical/health related. Geographic Preferences: West Coast.

Shaw Venture Partners
400 SW 6th Ave., Ste. 1100
Portland, OR 97204-1636
(503)228-4884
Fax: (503)227-2471
Website: http://www.shawventures.com
Preferred Investment Size: $250,000 to $3,000,000. Investment Types: Seed, startup, first and second stage, leveraged buyout, and special situations. Industry

Preferences: Diversified. Geographic Preferences: Northwest.

Pennsylvania

Mid-Atlantic Venture Funds

125 Goodman Dr.
Bethlehem, PA 18015
(610)865-6550
Fax: (610)865-6427
Website: http://www.mavf.com
Thomas A. Smith
Preferred Investment Size: $500,000 to $8,000,000. Investment Types: Seed, research and development, first and second stage, leveraged buyout. Industry Preferences: Diversified. Geographic Preferences: Middle Atlantic and Northeast.

Newspring Ventures

100 W. Elm St., Ste. 101
Conshohocken, PA 19428
(610)567-2380
Fax: (610)567-2388
Website: http://www.newsprintventures.com
Preferred Investment Size: $1,000,000 minimum. Investment Types: Early stage and expansion. Industry Preferences: Communications, computer related, medical products, industrial products, and business services. Geographic Preferences: Mid Atlantic.

Patricof & Co. Ventures, Inc.

455 S. Gulph Rd., Ste. 410
King of Prussia, PA 19406
(610)265-0286
Fax: (610)265-4959
Website: http://www.patricof.com
Preferred Investment Size: $500,000 minimum. Investment Types: Seed, startup, first and second stage, mezzanine, and leveraged buyout. Industry Preferences: Diversified. Geographic Preferences: No preference.

Loyalhanna Venture Fund

527 Cedar Way, Ste. 104
Oakmont, PA 15139
(412)820-7035
Fax: (412)820-7036
James H. Knowles, Jr.
Preferred Investment Size: $300,000 to $1,000,000. Investment Types: First and second stage, and leveraged buyout. Industry Preferences: No preference. Geographic Preferences: Entire U.S.

Innovest Group Inc.

2000 Market St., Ste. 1400
Philadelphia, PA 19103
(215)564-3960
Fax: (215)569-3272
Richard Woosnam
Preferred Investment Size: $500,000 to $1,000,000. Investment Types: First stage, leveraged buyout, recaps, second stage, special situation, and start-up. Industry Preferences: Diversified. Geographic Preferences: Mid Atlantic, Midwest, Northeast, and Southeast.

Keystone Venture Capital Management Co.

1601 Market St., Ste. 2500
Philadelphia, PA 19103
(215)241-1200
Fax: (215)241-1211
Website: http://www.keystonevc.com
Peter Ligeti
Preferred Investment Size: $2,000,000 to $5,000,000. Investment Types: First and second stage, balanced, and expansion. Industry Preferences: Diversified. Geographic Preferences: Middle Atlantic.

Liberty Venture Partners

2005 Market St., Ste. 200
Philadelphia, PA 19103
(215)282-4484
Fax: (215)282-4485
E-mail: info@libertyvp.com
Website: http://www.libertyvp.com
Thomas Morse
Preferred Investment Size: $3,000,000 to $7,000,000. Investment Types: Early stage and expansion. Industry Preferences: Diversified technology. Geographic Preferences: National.

Penn Janney Fund, Inc.

1801 Market St., 11th Fl.
Philadelphia, PA 19103
(215)665-4447
Fax: (215)557-0820
William Rulon-Miller
Preferred Investment Size: $1,000,000 minimum. Investment Types: Second stage, mezzanine, leveraged buyout, and special situations. Industry Preferences: Diversified. Geographic Preferences: Northeast, West Coast, and Middle Atlantic.

Philadelphia Ventures, Inc.

The Bellevue
200 S. Broad St.
Philadelphia, PA 19102

(215)732-4445
Fax: (215)732-4644
Walter M. Aikman, Managing Director
Preferred Investment Size: $500,000 maximum. Investment Types: Startup, first and second stage, mezzanine, and leveraged buyout. Industry Preferences: Diversified technology. Geographic Preferences: Entire U.S.

Birchmere Ventures Inc.

2000 Technology Dr.
Pittsburgh, PA 15219-3109
(412)803-8000
Fax: (412)687-8139
Website: http://www.birchmerevc.com
Investment Types: Early stage, expansion, first and later stage, and start-up. Industry Preferences: Diversified. Geographic Preferences: Mid Atlantic.

CEO Venture Fund

2000 Technology Dr., Ste. 160
Pittsburgh, PA 15219-3109
(412)687-3451
Fax: (412)687-8139
E-mail: ceofund@aol.com
Website: http://www.ceoventurefund.com
Ned Renzi, General Partner
Preferred Investment Size: $1,000,000 to $2,000,000. Investment Types: Startup, first stage, second stage, leveraged buyout, and special situations. Industry Preferences: Diversified technology. Geographic Preferences: Middle Atlantic states.

Innovation Works Inc.

2000 Technology Dr., Ste. 250
Pittsburgh, PA 15219
(412)681-1520
Fax: (412)681-2625
Website: http://www.innovationworks.org
Preferred Investment Size: $100,000 to $500,000. Investment Types: Early and first stage, seed, and start-up. Industry Preferences: Diversified technology. Geographic Preferences: Pennsylvania.

Keystone Minority Capital Fund L.P.

1801 Centre Ave., Ste. 201
Williams Sq.
Pittsburgh, PA 15219
(412)338-2230
Fax: (412)338-2224
Earl Hord, General Partner
Preferred Investment Size: $500,000 minimum. Investment Types: Startup,

first stage, second stage, mezzanine, and leveraged buyout. Industry Preferences: Diversified. Geographic Preferences: Middle Atlantic states.

Mellon Ventures, Inc.
One Mellon Bank Ctr., Rm. 3500
Pittsburgh, PA 15258
(412)236-3594
Fax: (412)236-3593
Website: http://
www.mellonventures.com
Preferred Investment Size: $2,000,000 to $25,000,000. Investment Types: Mezzanine, leveraged buyout, and special situations. Industry Preferences: Diversified. Geographic Preferences: National.

Pennsylvania Growth Fund
5850 Ellsworth Ave., Ste. 303
Pittsburgh, PA 15232
(412)661-1000
Fax: (412)361-0676
Barry Lhormer, Partner
Preferred Investment Size: $500,000 minimum. Investment Types: Leveraged buyout, mezzanine, second stage, and special situation. Industry Preferences: Diversified. Geographic Preferences: Middle Atlantic, Midwest, Northeast, and Southeast.

Point Venture Partners
The Century Bldg.
130 Seventh St., 7th Fl.
Pittsburgh, PA 15222
(412)261-1966
Fax: (412)261-1718
Kent Engelmeier, General Partner
Preferred Investment Size: $2,000,000. Investment Types: Startup, first stage, second stage, mezzanine, recaps, and leveraged buyout. Industry Preferences: Diversified. Geographic Preferences: Eastern and Midwestern U.S.

Cross Atlantic Capital Partners
5 Radnor Corporate Center, Ste. 555
Radnor, PA 19087
(610)995-2650
Fax: (610)971-2062
Website: http://www.xacp.com
Preferred Investment Size: $1,000,000 to $10,000,000. Investment Types: Balanced, early stage, expansion, seed, and start-up. Industry Preferences: Diversified. Geographic Preferences: Entire U.S.

Meridian Venture Partners (Radnor)
The Radnor Court Bldg., Ste. 140
259 Radnor-Chester Rd.
Radnor, PA 19087
(610)254-2999
Fax: (610)254-2996
E-mail: mvpart@ix.netcom.com
Kenneth E. Jones
Preferred Investment Size: $1,000,000 to $2,000,000. Investment Types: Second stage, leveraged buyout, and special situations. Industry Preferences: Diversified. Geographic Preferences: Entire U.S.

TDH
919 Conestoga Rd., Bldg. 1, Ste. 301
Rosemont, PA 19010
(610)526-9970
Fax: (610)526-9971
J.B. Doherty, Managing General Partner
Preferred Investment Size: $1,500,000 minimum. Investment Types: Startup, first and second stage, mezzanine, recaps, and leveraged buyout. Industry Preferences: Diversified. Geographic Preferences: Eastern U.S. and Midwest.

Adams Capital Management
500 Blackburn Ave.
Sewickley, PA 15143
(412)749-9454
Fax: (412)749-9459
Website: http://www.acm.com
Joel Adams, General Partner
Investment Types: Early and first stages. Industry Preferences: Diversified technology. Geographic Preferences: National.

S.R. One, Ltd.
Four Tower Bridge
200 Barr Harbor Dr., Ste. 250
W. Conshohocken, PA 19428
(610)567-1000
Fax: (610)567-1039
Barbara Dalton, Vice President
Preferred Investment Size: $500,000 to $5,000,000. Investment Types: Start-up, first and second stage, and late stage. Industry Preferences: Healthcare and genetic engineering, and computer software and services. Geographic Preferences: No preference.

Greater Philadelphia Venture Capital Corp.
351 East Conestoga Rd.
Wayne, PA 19087
(610)688-6829

Fax: (610)254-8958
Fred Choate, Manager
Preferred Investment Size: $100,000 to $300,000. Investment Types: First and second stage, leveraged buyout, mezzanine, and special situations. Industry Preferences: Diversified. Geographic Preferences: Middle Atlantic.

PA Early Stage
435 Devon Park Dr., Bldg. 500, Ste. 510
Wayne, PA 19087
(610)293-4075
Fax: (610)254-4240
Website: http://www.paearlystage.com
Preferred Investment Size: $100,000 to $10,000,000. Investment Types: Early, first, and second stage; seed; and start-up. Industry Preferences: Diversified. Geographic Preferences: Mid Atlantic.

The Sandhurst Venture Fund, L.P.
351 E. Constoga Rd.
Wayne, PA 19087
(610)254-8900
Fax: (610)254-8958
Preferred Investment Size: $500,000 to $1,000,000. Investment Types: Second stage, recaps, and leveraged buyout. Industry Preferences: Computer stores, disposable medical/health related, and industrial products. Geographic Preferences: East Coast and Middle Atlantic.

TL Ventures
700 Bldg.
435 Devon Park Dr.
Wayne, PA 19087-1990
(610)975-3765
Fax: (610)254-4210
Website: http://www.tlventures.com
Pam Strisofsky,
pstrisofsky@tlventures.com
Preferred Investment Size: $2,000,000 minimum. Investment Types: Seed and early stage. Industry Preferences: Diversified technology. Geographic Preferences: National.

Rockhill Ventures, Inc.
100 Front St., Ste. 1350
West Conshohocken, PA 19428
(610)940-0300
Fax: (610)940-0301
E-mail: chuck@rockhillventures.com
Preferred Investment Size: $1,000,000 to $2,000,000. Investment Types: Seed, research and development, startup, first and second stage, leveraged buyout, and

recaps. Industry Preferences: Genetic engineering and medical/health related. Geographic Preferences: Eastern U.S.

Puerto Rico

Advent-Morro Equity Partners
Banco Popular Bldg.
206 Tetuan St., Ste. 903
San Juan, PR 00902
(787)725-5285
Fax: (787)721-1735
Cyril L. Meduna, General Partner
Preferred Investment Size: $500,000 to $3,000,000. Investment Types: No preference. Industry Preferences: Diversified. Geographic Preferences: Puerto Rico.

North America Investment Corp.
Mercantil Plaza, Ste. 813
PO Box 191831
San Juan, PR 00919
(787)754-6178
Fax: (787)754-6181
Marcelino D. Pastrana-Torres, President
Preferred Investment Size: $25,000 to $250,000. Investment Types: Early stage and expansion. Industry Preferences: Consumer products and retailing, consumer distribution, industrial equipment, therapeutic equipment, real estate, and business services. Geographic Preferences: Puerto R

Rhode Island

Manchester Humphreys, Inc.
40 Westminster St., Ste. 900
Providence, RI 02903
(401)454-0400
Fax: (401)454-0403
Preferred Investment Size: $500,000 minimum. Investment Types: Leveraged and management buyouts. Industry Preferences: Diversified. Geographic Preferences: National.

Navis Partners
50 Kennedy Plaza, 12th Fl.
Providence, RI 02903
(401)278-6770
Fax: (401)278-6387
Website: http://www.navispartners.com
Rory B. Smith, General Partner
Preferred Investment Size: $20,000,000 to $75,000,000. Investment Policies: Equity. Investment Types: Acquisition, early and later stage, leveraged and management buyouts, recaps, and expansion. Industry

Preferences: Diversified. Geographic Preferences: U.S. and Canada.

South Carolina

Capital Insights, L.L.C.
PO Box 27162
Greenville, SC 29616-2162
(864)242-6832
Fax: (864)242-6755
E-mail: jwarner@capitalinsights.com
Website: http://www.capitalinsights.com
Preferred Investment Size: $500,000 to $5,000,000. Investment Policies: Equity. Investment Types: Early and late stage. Industry Preferences: Communications and consumer-related services. Geographic Preferences: Southeast.

Transamerica Mezzanine Financing
7 N. Laurens St., Ste. 603
Greenville, SC 29601
(864)232-6198
Fax: (864)241-4444
J. Phillip Falls, Investment Officer
Investment Types: Seed, startup, first stage, second stage, and mezzanine. Industry Preferences: Diversified technology. Geographic Preferences: Southeast.

Tennessee

Valley Capital Corp.
Krystal Bldg.
100 W. Martin Luther King Blvd., Ste. 212
Chattanooga, TN 37402
(423)265-1557
Fax: (423)265-1588
Faye Robinson
Preferred Investment Size: $200,000 minimum. Investment Types: Second stage, mezzanine, and leveraged buyout. Industry Preferences: Diversified. Geographic Preferences: Southeast.

Coleman Swenson Booth Inc.
237 2nd Ave. S
Franklin, TN 37064-2649
(615)791-9462
Fax: (615)791-9636
Website: http://www.colemanswenson.com
Larry H. Coleman, Ph.D., Managing Partner
Preferred Investment Size: $1,000,000 to $7,000,000. Investment Types: Seed, startup, first and second stage, and mezzanine. Industry Preferences:

Diversified. Geographic Preferences: No preference.

Capital Services & Resources, Inc.
5159 Wheelis Dr., Ste. 106
Memphis, TN 38117
(901)761-2156
Fax: (907)767-0060
Charles Y. Bancroft, Treasurer
Preferred Investment Size: $300,000 minimum. Investment Policies: Equity. Investment Types: Second stage, leveraged buyout, and special situations. Industry Preferences: Diversified. Geographic Preferences: United States and Canada.

Paradigm Capital Partners LLC
6410 Poplar Ave., Ste. 395
Memphis, TN 38119
(901)682-6060
Fax: (901)328-3061
Preferred Investment Size: $500,000 to $6,000,000. Investment Types: First and second stage, and seed. Industry Preferences: Diversified. Geographic Preferences: Southeast.

SSM Ventures
845 Crossover Ln., Ste. 140
Memphis, TN 38117
(901)767-1131
Fax: (901)767-1135
Website: http://www.ssmventures.com
R. Wilson Orr, III
Preferred Investment Size: $2,000,000 to $10,000,000. Investment Types: Startup, leveraged buyout, and expansion. Industry Preferences: Diversified. Geographic Preferences: Southeast and Southwest U.S.

Capital Across America L.P.
501 Union St., Ste. 201
Nashville, TN 37219
(615)254-1414
Fax: (615)254-1856
Website: http://www.capitalacrossamerica.com
Investment Types: Balanced. Industry Preferences: Diversified; women/minority-owned businesses. Geographic Preferences: Entire U.S.

Equitas L.P.
2000 Glen Echo Rd., Ste. 101
PO Box 158838
Nashville, TN 37215-8838
(615)383-8673
Fax: (615)383-8693

Preferred Investment Size: $500.000.
Investment Types: Second stage,
leveraged buyout, mezzanine, recaps, and
special situation. Industry Preferences:
Diversified. Geographic Preferences:
Southeast and Midwest.

Massey Burch Capital Corp.
One Burton Hills Blvd., Ste. 350
Nashville, TN 37215
(615)665-3221
Fax: (615)665-3240
E-mail: tcalton@masseyburch.com
Website: http://www.masseyburch.com
Lucious E. Burch, IV, Partner
Preferred Investment Size: $1,000,000 to
$5,000,000. Investment Types: Seed,
startup, early and first stage. Industry
Preferences: Communication and
computer related. Geographic
Preferences: Southeast.

Nelson Capital Corp.
3401 West End Ave., Ste. 300
Nashville, TN 37203
(615)292-8787
Fax: (615)385-3150
Preferred Investment Size: $500,000
minimum. Investment Types: First and
second stage, leveraged buyout, and
mezzanine. Industry Preferences:
Diversified. Geographic Preferences:
Southeast.

Texas

Phillips-Smith Specialty Retail Group
5080 Spectrum Dr., Ste. 805 W
Addison, TX 75001
(972)387-0725
Fax: (972)458-2560
E-mail: pssrg@aol.com
Website: http://www.phillips-smith.com
G. Michael Machens, General Partner
Preferred Investment Size: $1,000,000
minimum. Investment Types: Seed,
startup, first and second stage,
mezzanine, and leveraged buyout.
Industry Preferences: Retail and Internet
related. Geographic Preferences: Entire
U.S.

Austin Ventures, L.P.
701 Brazos St., Ste. 1400
Austin, TX 78701
(512)485-1900
Fax: (512)476-3952
E-mail: info@ausven.com
Website: http://www.austinventures.com
Joseph C. Aragona, General Partner

Preferred Investment Size: $1,000,000 to
$15,000,000. Investment Types: Seed,
startup, first and second stage, leveraged
buyout, and special situations. Industry
Preferences: Diversified. Geographic
Preferences: Southwest and Texas.

The Capital Network
3925 West Braker Lane, Ste. 406
Austin, TX 78759-5321
(512)305-0826
Fax: (512)305-0836
Preferred Investment Size: $100,000 to
$500,000. Investment Types: Seed, early
and late stage, leveraged buyout,
mezzanine, research and development,
and special situations. Industry
Preferences: Diversified. Geographic
Preferences: United States and Canada.

Techxas Ventures LLC
5000 Plaza on the Lake
Austin, TX 78746
(512)343-0118
Fax: (512)343-1879
E-mail: bruce@techxas.com
Website: http://www.techxas.com
Bruce Ezell, General Partner
Preferred Investment Size: $500,000 to
$5,000,000. Investment Types: Seed,
startup, first stage, second stage,
balanced, joint ventures, and special
situations. Industry Preferences:
Diversified technology. Geographic
Preferences: Texas.

Alliance Financial of Houston
218 Heather Ln.
Conroe, TX 77385-9013
(936)447-3300
Fax: (936)447-4222
Preferred Investment Size: $300,000 to
$500,000. Investment Types: Second
stage, mezzanine, leveraged buyout, and
special situations. Industry Preferences:
Sales, distribution, and manufacturing.
Geographic Preferences: Gulf states.

Amerimark Capital Corp.
1111 W. Mockingbird, Ste. 1111
Dallas, TX 75247
(214)638-7878
Fax: (214)638-7612
E-mail: amerimark@amcapital.com
Website: http://www.amcapital.com
Preferred Investment Size: $500,000
minimum. Investment Types: Second
stage, mezzanine, and leveraged buyout.
Industry Preferences: Diversified.
Geographic Preferences: National.

**AMT Venture Partners / AMT Capital
Ltd.**
5220 Spring Valley Rd., Ste. 600
Dallas, TX 75240
(214)905-9757
Fax: (214)905-9761
Website: http://www.amtcapital.com
Preferred Investment Size: $100,000 to
$500,000. Investment Types: First and
second stages, and expanion. Industry
Preferences: Industrial products and
equipment, electronic components and
instruments. Geographic Preferences:
National.

Arkoma Venture Partners
5950 Berkshire Lane, Ste. 1400
Dallas, TX 75225
(214)739-3515
Fax: (214)739-3572
E-mail: joelf@arkomavp.com
Joel Fontenot, Executive Vice President
Preferred Investment Size: $250,000 to
$2,500,000. Investment Policies: Equity.
Investment Types: Seed, start-up, early
and second stage, and expansion.
Industry Preferences: Communications,
computer, and electronics. Geographic
Preferences: Southwest.

Capital Southwest Corp.
12900 Preston Rd., Ste. 700
Dallas, TX 75230
(972)233-8242
Fax: (972)233-7362
Website: http://
www.capitalsouthwest.com
Howard Thomas, Investment Associate
Preferred Investment Size: $1,000,000 to
$6,000,000. Investment Types: First and
second stage, leveraged buyout,
acquisition, expansion, management
buyout, and late stage. Industry
Preferences: Diversified. Geographic
Preferences: Entire U.S.

Dali, Hook Partners
One Lincoln Center, Ste. 1550
5400 LBJ Freeway
Dallas, TX 75240
(972)991-5457
Fax: (972)991-5458
E-mail: dhook@hookpartners.com
Website: http://www.hookpartners.com
David J. Hook
Preferred Investment Size: $100,000 to
$5,000,000. Investment Types: Balanced,
first, and second stage. Industry
Preferences: Diversified. Geographic
Preferences: Southwest and West Coast.

HO2 Partners
Two Galleria Tower
13455 Noel Rd., Ste. 1670
Dallas, TX 75240
(972)702-1144
Fax: (972)702-8234
Website: http://www.ho2.com
Preferred Investment Size: $750,000 to
$3,000,000. Investment Types: First and
second stage, and seed. Industry
Preferences: Diversified technology.
Geographic Preferences: Texas.

Interwest Partners (Dallas)
2 Galleria Tower
13455 Noel Rd., Ste. 1670
Dallas, TX 75240
(972)392-7279
Fax: (972)490-6348
Website: http://www.interwest.com
Preferred Investment Size: $2,000,000 to
$25,000,000. Investment Types: Seed,
research and development, startup, first
and second stage, expansion, and special
situations. Industry Preferences:
Diversified. Geographic Preferences:
Entire U.S.

Kahala Investments, Inc.
8214 Westchester Dr., Ste. 715
Dallas, TX 75225
(214)987-0077
Fax: (214)987-2332
Lee R. Slaughter, Jr., President
Preferred Investment Size: $10,000,000
minimum. Investment Types:
Mezzanine, leveraged buyout, special
situations, control block purchases, and
industry roll ups. Industry Preferences:
Diversified. Geographic Preferences:
Southeast and Southwest.

MESBIC Ventures Holding Co.
2435 North Central Expressway, Ste. 200
Dallas, TX 75080
(972)991-1597
Fax: (972)991-4770
Website: http://www.mvhc.com
Jeff Schaefer
Preferred Investment Size: $1,000,000
minimum. Investment Policies: Loans
and/or equity. Investment Types:
Leveraged buyout, mezzanine, and
second stage. Industry Preferences:
Diversified. Geographic Preferences:
Southeast and Southwest.

North Texas MESBIC, Inc.
9500 Forest Lane, Ste. 430
Dallas, TX 75243

(214)221-3565
Fax: (214)221-3566
Preferred Investment Size: $300,000
minimum. Investment Types: Second
stage, mezzanine, and leveraged buyout.
Industry Preferences: Consumer food
and beverage products, restaurants,
retailing, consumer and food
distribution. Geographic Preferences:
Southwest.

Richard Jaffe & Company, Inc,
7318 Royal Cir.
Dallas, TX 75230
(214)265-9397
Fax: (214)739-1845
E-mail: rjaffe@pssi.net
Richard R. Jaffe, President
Preferred Investment Size: $100,000 to
$300,000. Investment Types: Startup,
first stage, leveraged buyouts, and special
situations. Industry Preferences:
Diversified. Geographic Preferences:
Southwest.

Sevin Rosen Management Co.
13455 Noel Rd., Ste. 1670
Dallas, TX 75240
(972)702-1100
Fax: (972)702-1103
E-mail: info@srfunds.com
Website: http://www.srfunds.com
John V. Jaggers, Partner
Preferred Investment Size: $500,000
minimum. Investment Types: Start-up,
early and first stage. Industry Preferences:
Diversified technology. Geographic
Preferences: Entire U.S.

Stratford Capital Partners, L.P.
300 Crescent Ct., Ste. 500
Dallas, TX 75201
(214)740-7377
Fax: (214)720-7393
E-mail: stratcap@hmtf.com
Michael D. Brown, Managing Partner
Preferred Investment Size: $1,000,000
minimum. Investment Policies: Equity,
sub debt with equity. Investment Types:
Expansion, later stage, acquisition,
leveraged and management buyout,
mezzanine, and recaps. Industry
Preferences: Diversified. Geographic
Preferences: National.

Sunwestern Investment Group
12221 Merit Dr., Ste. 935
Dallas, TX 75251
(972)239-5650
Fax: (972)701-0024

Preferred Investment Size: $500,000 to
$1,000,000. Investment Types: Second
stage, leveraged buyout, and special
situations. Industry Preferences:
Diversified. Geographic Preferences:
Southwest and West Coast.

Wingate Partners
750 N. St. Paul St., Ste. 1200
Dallas, TX 75201
(214)720-1313
Fax: (214)871-8799
Preferred Investment Size: $20,000,000
minimum. Investment Types: Leveraged
buyout and control block purchases.
Industry Preferences: Diversified.
Geographic Preferences: Entire U.S. and
Canada.

Buena Venture Associates
201 Main St., 32nd Fl.
Fort Worth, TX 76102
(817)339-7400
Fax: (817)390-8408
Website: http://www.buenaventure.com
Preferred Investment Size: $1,000,000 to
$50,000,000. Investment Types: Early,
first and second stage; seed; and start-up.
Industry Preferences: Diversified
technology, and health services.
Geographic Preferences: Entire U.S.

The Catalyst Group
3 Riverway, Ste. 770
Houston, TX 77056
(713)623-8133
Fax: (713)623-0473
E-mail: herman@thecatalystgroup.net
Website: http://
www.thecatalystgroup.net
Rick Herman, Partner
Preferred Investment Size: $1,000,000
minimum. Investment Types: Second
stage, mezzanine, leveraged buyout, and
control block purchases. Industry
Preferences: Diversified. Geographic
Preferences: No preference.

Cureton & Co., Inc.
1100 Louisiana, Ste. 3250
Houston, TX 77002
(713)658-9806
Fax: (713)658-0476
Stewart Cureton, Jr., President
Preferred Investment Size: $10,000,000
minimum. Investment Types: First and
second stage, leveraged buyout, and
special situations. Industry Preferences:
Diversified. Geographic Preferences:
Southwest.

Davis, Tuttle Venture Partners (Dallas)
8 Greenway Plaza, Ste. 1020
Houston, TX 77046
(713)993-0440
Fax: (713)621-2297
Website: http://www.davistuttle.com
Phillip Tuttle, Partner
Preferred Investment Size: $5,000,000
minimum. Investment Types: First and
second stage, mezzanine, and leveraged
buyout. Industry Preferences:
Diversified. Geographic Preferences:
Southwest.

Houston Partners
401 Louisiana, 8th Fl.
Houston, TX 77002
(713)222-8600
Fax: (713)222-8932
Preferred Investment Size: $500,000 to
$1,000,000. Investment Types: Start-up,
first and second stage, and expansion.
Industry Preferences: Diversified
industry preference. Geographic
Preferences: Entire U.S.

Southwest Venture Group
10878 Westheimer, Ste. 178
Houston, TX 77042
(713)827-8947
(713)461-1470
David M. Klausmeyer, Partner
Preferred Investment Size: $50,000,000
minimum. Investment Types:
Diversified. Industry Preferences:
Diversified. Geographic Preferences: U.S.
and Canada.

Triad Ventures

AM Fund
4600 Post Oak Place, Ste. 100
Houston, TX 77027
(713)627-9111
Fax: (713)627-9119
David Mueller
Preferred Investment Size: $800,000
maximum. Investment Types: First and
second stage, and mezzanine. Industry
Preferences: Medical, consumer,
computer-related. Geographic
Preferences: Southwest and Texas.

Ventex Management, Inc.
3417 Milam St.
Houston, TX 77002-9531
(713)659-7870
Fax: (713)659-7855
Preferred Investment Size: $1,000,000 to
$5,000,000. Investment Types: Second

stage, mezzanine, leveraged buyout, and
special situations. Industry Preferences:
Diversified. Geographic Preferences:
Southwest.

MBA Venture Group
1004 Olde Town Rd., Ste. 102
Irving, TX 75061
(972)986-6703
John Mason
Preferred Investment Size: $1,000,000
minimum. Investment Types: First stage,
leveraged buyout, mezzanine, research
and development, second stage, seed,
start-up. Industry Preferences:
Diversified. Geographic Preferences:
Entire U.S.

First Capital Group Management Co.
750 East Mulberry St., Ste. 305
PO Box 15616
San Antonio, TX 78212
(210)736-4233
Fax: (210)736-5449
Jeffrey P. Blanchard, Managing Partner
Preferred Investment Size: $1,000,000
minimum. Investment Types: First and
second stage, mezzanine, leveraged
buyout, and special situations. Industry
Preferences: Diversified. Geographic
Preferences: Southwest.

The Southwest Venture Partnerships
16414 San Pedro, Ste. 345
San Antonio, TX 78232
(210)402-1200
Fax: (210)402-1221
E-mail: swvp@aol.com
Preferred Investment Size: $500,000 to
$5,000,000. Investment Types: Startup,
first and second stage, and leveraged
buyout. Industry Preferences:
Diversified. Geographic Preferences:
Southwest.

Medtech International Inc.
1742 Carriageway
Sugarland, TX 77478
(713)980-8474
Fax: (713)980-6343
Dave Banker
Preferred Investment Size: $100,000 to
$500,000. Investment Types: First stage,
leveraged buyout, mezzanine, research
and development, second stage, seed,
special situation, and start-up. Industry
Preferences: Diversified. Geographic
Preferences: No preference.

Utah

**First Security Business Investment
Corp.**
15 East 100 South, Ste. 100
Salt Lake City, UT 84111
(801)246-5737
Fax: (801)246-5740
Preferred Investment Size: $300,000 to
$800,000. Investment Policies: Loans
and/or equity. Investment Types:
Leveraged buyout, mezzanine, and
second stage. Industry Preferences:
Diversified. Geographic Preferences:
West Coast, Rocky Mountains.

Utah Ventures II, L.P.
423 Wakara Way, Ste. 206
Salt Lake City, UT 84108
(801)583-5922
Fax: (801)583-4105
Website: http://www.uven.com
James C. Dreyfous, Managing General
Partner
Preferred Investment Size: $1,000,000 to
$7,000,000. Investment Types: Early
stage. Industry Preferences: Diversified
technology. Geographic Preferences:
Northwest and Rocky Mountain region.

Wasatch Venture Corp.
1 S. Main St., Ste. 1400
Salt Lake City, UT 84133
(801)524-8939
Fax: (801)524-8941
E-mail: mail@wasatchvc.com
Todd Stevens, Manager
Preferred Investment Size: $500,000 to
$2,000,000. Investment Policies: Equity
and debt. Investment Types: Early stage.
Industry Preferences: High technology.
Geographic Preferences: Western U.S.

Vermont

North Atlantic Capital Corp.
76 Saint Paul St., Ste. 600
Burlington, VT 05401
(802)658-7820
Fax: (802)658-5757
Website: http://
www.northatlanticcapital.com
Preferred Investment Size: $1,500,000
minimum. Investment Types: First and
second stage, mezzanine, and leveraged
buyout. Industry Preferences: Diversified
technology. Geographic Preferences:
Northeast.

Green Mountain Advisors Inc.
PO Box 1230
Quechee, VT 05059
(802)296-7800
Fax: (802)296-6012
Website: http://www.gmtcap.com
Michael Sweatman, President
Preferred Investment Size: $100,000 to
$500,000. Investment Types: Second
stage, expansion, and mezzanine.
Industry Preferences: Technology,
communications. Geographic
Preferences: Entire U.S.

Virginia

Oxford Financial Services Corp.
Alexandria, VA 22314
(703)519-4900
Fax: (703)519-4910
E-mail: oxford133@aol.com
J. Alden Philbrick
Preferred Investment Size: $1,000,000.
Investment Types: Seed, research and
development, startup, first stage, second
stage, and mezzanine. Industry
Preferences: Diversified technology.
Geographic Preferences: National.

Continental SBIC
4141 N. Henderson Rd.
Arlington, VA 22203
(703)527-5200
Fax: (703)527-3700
Michael W. Jones, Senior Vice President
Preferred Investment Size: $300,000 to
$5,000,000. Investment Types: No
preference. Industry Preferences:
Diversified. Geographic Preferences:
Northeast, Southeast, Middle Atlantic,
and Central Canada.

Novak Biddle Venture Partners
1750 Tysons Blvd., Ste. 1190
McLean, VA 22102
(703)847-3770
Fax: (703)847-3771
E-mail: roger@novakbiddle.com
Website: http://www.novakbiddle.com
Roger Novak, General Partner
Preferred Investment Size: $1,000,000 to
$5,000,000. Investment Types: Seed and
early stage. Industry Preferences:
Communications and computer related.
Geographic Preferences: Eastern U.S.

Spacevest
11911 Freedom Dr., Ste. 500
Reston, VA 20190
(703)904-9800

Fax: (703)904-0571
E-mail: spacevest@spacevest.com
Website: http://www.spacevest.com
Roger P. Widing, Managing Director
Preferred Investment Size: $250,000 to
$10,000,000. Investment Policies: Equity.
Investment Types: Early and late stage,
expansion, and mezzanine. Industry
Preferences: Diversified. Geographic
Preferences: U.S. and Canada.

Virginia Capital
1801 Libbie Ave., Ste. 201
Richmond, VA 23226
(804)648-4802
Fax: (804)648-4809
E-mail: webmaster@vacapital.com
Website: http://www.vacapital.com
Thomas E. Deardorff, Vice President
Investment Types: Acquisition, balanced,
expansion, and leveraged and
management buyouts. Industry
Preferences: Communications,
consumer, medical and health related.
Geographic Preferences: Mid Atlantic.

Calvert Social Venture Partners
402 Maple Ave. W
Vienna, VA 22180
(703)255-4930
Fax: (703)255-4931
E-mail: calven2000@aol.com
John May, Managing General Partner
Preferred Investment Size: $100,000 to
$700,000. Investment Types: First stages.
Industry Preferences: Diversified. Geographic
Preferences: Middle Atlantic states.

Fairfax Partners
8000 Towers Crescent Dr., Ste. 940
Vienna, VA 22182
(703)847-9486
Fax: (703)847-0911
E-mail: bgouldey@fairfaxpartners.com
Bruce K. Gouldey, Managing Director
Investment Types: Startup, first stage,
second stage, and leveraged buyout.
Industry Preferences: Computer related,
Medical and health related. Geographic
Preferences: Middle Atlantic States.

Global Internet Ventures
8150 Leesburg Pike, Ste. 1210
Vienna, VA 22182
(703)442-3300
Fax: (703)442-3388
Website: http://www.givinc.com
Preferred Investment Size: $500,000 to
$3,000,000. Investment Types: Early
stage. Industry Preferences:

Communications, computer, and
Internet related. Geographic Preferences:
Entire U.S.

Walnut Capital Corp. (Vienna)
8000 Towers Crescent Dr., Ste. 1070
Vienna, VA 22182
(703)448-3771
Fax: (703)448-7751
Preferred Investment Size: $300,000 to
$500,000. Investment Types: Startup,
first and second stage, mezzanine, and
leveraged buyout. Industry Preferences:
Diversified. Geographic Preferences: No
preference.

Washington

Encompass Ventures
777 108th Ave. NE, Ste. 2300
Bellevue, WA 98004
(425)486-3900
Fax: (425)486-3901
E-mail: info@evpartners.com
Website: http://
www.encompassventures.com
Preferred Investment Size: $300,000 to
$3,000,000. Investment Types: Research
and development, startup, first and
second stages. Industry Preferences:
Computer related, medical and health
related. Geographic Preferences: Western
U.S. and Canada.

Fluke Venture Partners
11400 SE Sixth St., Ste. 230
Bellevue, WA 98004
(425)453-4590
Fax: (425)453-4675
E-mail: gabelein@flukeventures.com
Website: http://www.flukeventures.com
Dennis Weston, Managing Director
Preferred Investment Size: $250,000 to
$2,500,000. Investment Types: Startup, seed,
first stage, second stage, expansion, and
mezzanine. Industry Preferences: Diversified.
Geographic Preferences: Northwest.

Pacific Northwest Partners SBIC, L.P.
15352 SE 53rd St.
Bellevue, WA 98006
(425)455-9967
Fax: (425)455-9404
Preferred Investment Size: $500,000
minimum. Investment Policies: Private
equity investments. Investment Types:
Seed, start-up, and early and first stage.
Industry Preferences: Diversified.
Geographic Preferences: Entire U.S.

Materia Venture Associates, L.P.
3435 Carillon Pointe
Kirkland, WA 98033-7354
(425)822-4100
Fax: (425)827-4086
Preferred Investment Size: $500,000 to
$1,000,000. Investment Types: Startup,
first and second stage, and mezzanine.
Industry Preferences: Advanced
industrial products and equipment.
Geographic Preferences: Entire U.S.

OVP Venture Partners (Kirkland)
2420 Carillon Pt.
Kirkland, WA 98033
(425)889-9192
Fax: (425)889-0152
E-mail: info@ovp.com
Website: http://www.ovp.com
Preferred Investment Size: $1,000,000 to
$10,000,000. Investment Types: Seed,
startup, early stage. Industry Preferences:
Diversified technology. Geographic
Preferences: Western U.S. and Canada.

Digital Partners
999 3rd Ave., Ste. 1610
Seattle, WA 98104
(206)405-3607
Fax: (206)405-3617
Website: http://www.digitalpartners.com
Preferred Investment Size: $250,000 to
$3,000,000. Investment Types: Early, first
and second stage, and seed. Industry
Preferences: Diversified technology.
Geographic Preferences: Northwest and
Western Canada.

Frazier & Company
601 Union St., Ste. 3300
Seattle, WA 98101
(206)621-7200
Fax: (206)621-1848
E-mail: jon@frazierco.com
Jon Gilbert, General Partner
Preferred Investment Size: $2,000,000 to
$3,000,000. Investment Types: No
preference. Industry Preferences: Diversified.
Geographic Preferences: National.

Kirlan Venture Capital, Inc.
221 First Ave. W, Ste. 108
Seattle, WA 98119-4223
(206)281-8610
Fax: (206)285-3451
E-mail: bill@kirlanventure.com
Website: http://www.kirlanventure.com
Preferred Investment Size: $300,000 to
$500,000. Investment Types: First stage,
second stage, and mezzanine. Industry

Preferences: Diversified technology.
Geographic Preferences: Western U.S.
and Canada.

Phoenix Partners
1000 2nd Ave., Ste. 3600
Seattle, WA 98104
(206)624-8968
Fax: (206)624-1907
E-mail: djohnsto@interserv.com
William B. Horne, Chief Financial
Officer
Preferred Investment Size: $2,000,000 to
$3,000,000. Investment Types: Seed,
research and development, startup, first
and second stage, and mezzanine.
Industry Preferences: Diversified.
Geographic Preferences: No preference.

Voyager Capital
800 5th St., Ste. 4100
Seattle, WA 98103
(206)470-1180
Fax: (206)470-1185
E-mail: info@voyagercap.com
Website: http://www.voyagercap.com
Erik Benson, Senior Associate
Preferred Investment Size: $5,000,000 to
$10,000,000. Investment Policies: Equity.
Investment Types: Startup, early and late
stage. Industry Preferences: Diversified
communications and computer related.
Geographic Preferences: West Coast and
Western Canada.

Northwest Venture Associates
221 N. Wall St., Ste. 628
Spokane, WA 99201
(509)747-0728
Fax: (509)747-0758
Website: http://www.nwva.com
Christopher Brookfield
Preferred Investment Size: $1,000,000 to
$2,000,000. Investment Types: Seed,
research and development, startup, first
stage, second stage, and mezzanine.
Industry Preferences: Diversified.
Geographic Preferences: Northwest and
Rocky Mountains.

Wisconsin

Venture Investors Management, L.L.C.
University Research Park
505 S. Rosa Rd.
Madison, WI 53719
(608)441-2700
Fax: (608)441-2727
E-mail: roger@ventureinvestors.com

Website: http://
www.ventureinvesters.com
Scott Button, Partner
Preferred Investment Size: $250,000 to
$1,000,000. Investment Types: Seed,
startup, first and second stage, mezzanine,
and special situations. Industry
Preferences: Diversified. Geographic
Preferences: Southeast and Midwest.

Capital Investments, Inc.
1009 West Glen Oaks Lane, Ste. 103
Mequon, WI 53092
(414)241-0303
Fax: (414)241-8451
E-mail:
dmayer@capitalinvestmentsinc.com
Website: http://
www.capitalinvestmentsinc.com
Preferred Investment Size: $500,000 to
$1,000,000. Investment Types: Second stage,
mezzanine, and leveraged buyout. Industry
Preferences: Diversified. Geographic
Preferences: Southwest and Midwest.

Future Value Venture, Inc.
2745 N. Martin Luther King Dr., Ste. 204
Milwaukee, WI 53212-2300
(414)264-2252
Fax: (414)264-2253
E-mail: fvvventures@aol.com
William Beckett, President
Preferred Investment Size: $100,000 to
$300,000. Investment Types: First and
second stage, start-up, and mezzanine.
Industry Preferences: No preference.
Geographic Preferences: Entire U.S.

Lubar and Co., Inc.
700 N. Water St., Ste. 1200
Milwaukee, WI 53202
(414)291-9000
Fax: (414)291-9061
David J. Lubar, Partner
Preferred Investment Size: $10,000,000
minimum. Investment Types: Second
stage, leveraged buyout, special
situations, and control block purchases.
Industry Preferences: Diversified.
Geographic Preferences: Midwest.

GCI
20875 Crossroads Cir., Ste. 100
Waukesha, WI 53186
(262)798-5080
Fax: (262)798-5087
Preferred Investment Size: $2,000,000
minimum. Investment Types: First stage,
second stage, and leveraged buyout. Industry
Preferences: Diversified technology.
Geographic Preferences: National.

Glossary of Small Business Terms

Absolute liability
Liability that is incurred due to product defects or negligent actions. Manufacturers or retail establishments are held responsible, even though the defect or action may not have been intentional or negligent.

ACE
See Active Corps of Executives

Accident and health benefits
Benefits offered to employees and their families in order to offset the costs associated with accidental death, accidental injury, or sickness.

Account statement
A record of transactions, including payments, new debt, and deposits, incurred during a defined period of time.

Accounting system
System capturing the costs of all employees and/or machinery included in business expenses.

Accounts payable
See Trade credit

Accounts receivable
Unpaid accounts which arise from unsettled claims and transactions from the sale of a company's products or services to its customers.

Active Corps of Executives (ACE)
A group of volunteers for a management assistance program of the U.S. Small Business Administration; volunteers provide one-on-one counseling and teach workshops and seminars for small firms.

ADA
See Americans with Disabilities Act

Adaptation
The process whereby an invention is modified to meet the needs of users.

Adaptive engineering
The process whereby an invention is modified to meet the manufacturing and commercial requirements of a targeted market.

Adverse selection
The tendency for higher-risk individuals to purchase health care and more comprehensive plans, resulting in increased costs.

Advertising
A marketing tool used to capture public attention and influence purchasing decisions for a product or service. Utilizes various forms of media to generate consumer response, such as flyers, magazines, newspapers, radio, and television.

Age discrimination
The denial of the rights and privileges of employment based solely on the age of an individual.

Agency costs
Costs incurred to insure that the lender or investor maintains control over assets while allowing the borrower or entrepreneur to use them. Monitoring and information costs are the two major types of agency costs.

Agribusiness
The production and sale of commodities and products from the commercial farming industry.

America Online
An online service which is accessible by computer modem. The service features Internet access, bulletin boards, online periodicals, electronic mail, and other services for subscribers.

Americans with Disabilities Act (ADA)
Law designed to ensure equal access and opportunity to handicapped persons.

Annual report
Yearly financial report prepared by a business that adheres to the requirements set forth by the Securities and Exchange Commission (SEC).

Antitrust immunity
Exemption from prosecution under antitrust laws. In the transportation industry, firms with antitrust immunity are permitted under certain conditions to set schedules and sometimes prices for the public benefit.

Applied research
Scientific study targeted for use in a product or process.

Asians
A minority category used by the U.S. Bureau of the Census to represent a diverse group that includes Aleuts, Eskimos, American Indians, Asian Indians, Chinese, Japanese, Koreans, Vietnamese, Filipinos, Hawaiians, and other Pacific Islanders.

Assets
Anything of value owned by a company.

Audit
The verification of accounting records and business procedures conducted by an outside accounting service.

Average cost
Total production costs divided by the quantity produced.

Balance Sheet
A financial statement listing the total assets and liabilities of a company at a given time.

Bankruptcy
The condition in which a business cannot meet its debt obligations and petitions a federal district court either for reorganization of its debts (Chapter 11) or for liquidation of its assets (Chapter 7).

Basic research
Theoretical scientific exploration not targeted to application.

Basket clause
A provision specifying the amount of public pension funds that may be placed in investments not included on a state's legal list (see separate citation).

BBS
See Bulletin Board Service

BDC
See Business development corporation

Benefit
Various services, such as health care, flextime, day care, insurance, and vacation, offered to employees as part of a hiring package. Typically subsidized in whole or in part by the business.

BIDCO
See Business and industrial development company

Billing cycle
A system designed to evenly distribute customer billing throughout the month, preventing clerical backlogs.

Birth
See Business birth

Blue chip security
A low-risk, low-yield security representing an interest in a very stable company.

Blue sky laws
A general term that denotes various states' laws regulating securities.

Bond
A written instrument executed by a bidder or contractor (the principal) and a second party (the surety or sureties) to assure fulfillment of the principal's obligations to a third party (the obligee or government) identified in the bond. If the principal's obligations are not met, the bond assures payment to the extent stipulated of any loss sustained by the obligee.

Bonding requirements
Terms contained in a bond (see separate citation).

Bonus
An amount of money paid to an employee as a reward for achieving certain business goals or objectives.

Brainstorming
A group session where employees contribute their ideas for solving a problem or meeting a company objective without fear of retribution or ridicule.

Brand name
The part of a brand, trademark, or service mark that can be spoken. It can be a word, letter, or group of words or letters.

Bridge financing
A short-term loan made in expectation of intermediateterm or long-term financing. Can be used when a company plans to go public in the near future.

Broker
One who matches resources available for innovation with those who need them.

Budget
An estimate of the spending necessary to complete a project or offer a service in comparison to cash-on-hand and expected earnings for the coming year, with an emphasis on cost control.

Bulletin Board Service (BBS)
An online service enabling users to communicate with each other about specific topics.

Business and industrial development company (BIDCO)
A private, for-profit financing corporation chartered by the state to provide both equity and long-term debt capital to small business owners (see separate citations for equity and debt capital).

Business birth
The formation of a new establishment or enterprise. The appearance of a new establishment or enterprise in the Small Business Data Base (see separate citation).

Business conditions
Outside factors that can affect the financial performance of a business.

Business contractions
The number of establishments that have decreased in employment during a specified time.

Business cycle
A period of economic recession and recovery. These cycles vary in duration.

Business death
The voluntary or involuntary closure of a firm or establishment. The disappearance of an establishment or enterprise from the Small Business Data Base (see separate citation).

Business development corporation (BDC)
A business financing agency, usually composed of the financial institutions in an area or state, organized to assist in financing businesses unable to obtain assistance through normal channels; the risk is spread among various members of the business development corporation, and interest rates may vary somewhat from those charged by member institutions. A venture capital firm in which shares of ownership are publicly held and to which the Investment Act of 1940 applies.

Business dissolution
For enumeration purposes, the absence of a business that was present in the prior time period from any current record.

Business entry
See Business birth

Business ethics
Moral values and principles espoused by members of the business community as a guide to fair and honest business practices.

Business exit
See Business death

Business expansions
The number of establishments that added employees during a specified time.

Business failure
Closure of a business causing a loss to at least one creditor.

Business format franchising
The purchase of the name, trademark, and an ongoing business plan of the parent corporation or franchisor by the franchisee.

Business license
A legal authorization issued by municipal and state governments and required for business operations.

Business name
Enterprises must register their business names with local governments usually on a "doing business as" (DBA) form. (This name is sometimes referred to as a "fictional name.") The procedure is part of the business licensing process and prevents any other business from using that same name for a similar business in the same locality.

Business norms
See Financial ratios

Business permit
See Business license

Business plan
A document that spells out a company's expected course of action for a specified period, usually including a detailed listing and analysis of risks and uncertainties. For the small business, it should examine the proposed products, the market, the industry, the management policies, the marketing policies, production needs, and financial needs. Frequently, it is used as a prospectus for potential investors and lenders.

Business proposal
See Business plan

Business service firm
An establishment primarily engaged in rendering services to other business organizations on a fee or contract basis.

Business start
For enumeration purposes, a business with a name or similar designation that did not exist in a prior time period.

Cafeteria plan
See Flexible benefit plan

Capacity
Level of a firm's, industry's, or nation's output corresponding to full practical utilization of available resources.

Capital
Assets less liabilities, representing the ownership interest in a business. A stock of accumulated goods, especially at a specified time and in contrast to income received during a specified time period. Accumulated goods devoted to production. Accumulated possessions calculated to bring income.

Capital expenditure
Expenses incurred by a business for improvements that will depreciate over time.

Capital gain
The monetary difference between the purchase price and the selling price of capital. Capital gains are taxed at a rate of 28% by the federal government.

Capital intensity
The relative importance of capital in the production process, usually expressed as the ratio of capital to labor but also sometimes as the ratio of capital to output.

Capital resource
The equipment, facilities and labor used to create products and services.

Caribbean Basin Initiative
An interdisciplinary program to support commerce among the businesses in the nations of the Caribbean Basin and the United States. Agencies involved include: the Agency for International Development, the U.S. Small Business Administration, the International Trade Administration of the U.S. Department of Commerce, and various private sector groups.

Catastrophic care
Medical and other services for acute and long-term illnesses that cost more than insurance coverage limits or that cost the amount most families may be expected to pay with their own resources.

CDC
See Certified development corporation

CD-ROM
Compact disc with read-only memory used to store large amounts of digitized data.

Certified development corporation (CDC)
A local area or statewide corporation or authority (for profit or nonprofit) that packages U.S. Small Business Administration (SBA), bank, state, and/or private money into financial assistance for existing business capital improvements. The SBA holds the second lien on its maximum share of 40 percent involvement. Each state has at least one certified development corporation. This program is called the SBA 504 Program.

Certified lenders
Banks that participate in the SBA guaranteed loan program (see separate citation). Such banks must have a good track record with the U.S. Small Business Administration (SBA) and must agree to certain conditions set forth by the agency. In return, the SBA agrees to process any guaranteed loan application within three business days.

Champion
An advocate for the development of an innovation.

Channel of distribution
The means used to transport merchandise from the manufacturer to the consumer.

Chapter 7 of the 1978 Bankruptcy Act
Provides for a court-appointed trustee who is responsible for liquidating a company's assets in order to settle outstanding debts.

Chapter 11 of the 1978 Bankruptcy Act
Allows the business owners to retain control of the company while working with their creditors to reorganize their finances and establish better business practices to prevent liquidation of assets.

Closely held corporation
A corporation in which the shares are held by a few persons, usually officers, employees, or others close to the management; these shares are rarely offered to the public.

Code of Federal Regulations
Codification of general and permanent rules of the federal government published in the Federal Register.

Code sharing
See Computer code sharing

Coinsurance
Upon meeting the deductible payment, health insurance participants may be required to make additional health care cost-sharing payments. Coinsurance is a payment of a fixed percentage of the cost of each service; copayment is usually a fixed amount to be paid with each service.

Collateral
Securities, evidence of deposit, or other property pledged by a borrower to secure repayment of a loan.

Collective ratemaking
The establishment of uniform charges for services by a group of businesses in the same industry.

Commercial insurance plan
See Underwriting

Commercial loans
Short-term renewable loans used to finance specific capital needs of a business.

Commercialization
The final stage of the innovation process, including production and distribution.

Common stock
The most frequently used instrument for purchasing ownership in private or public companies. Common stock generally carries the right to vote on certain corporate actions and may pay dividends, although it rarely does in venture investments. In liquidation, common stockholders are the last to share in the proceeds from the sale of a corporation's assets; bondholders and preferred shareholders have priority. Common stock is often used in firstround start-up financing.

Community development corporation
A corporation established to develop economic programs for a community and, in most cases, to provide financial support for such development.

Competitor
A business whose product or service is marketed for the same purpose/use and to the same consumer group as the product or service of another.

Computer code sharing
An arrangement whereby flights of a regional airline are identified by the two-letter code of a major carrier in the computer reservation system to help direct passengers to new regional carriers.

Consignment
A merchandising agreement, usually referring to secondhand shops, where the dealer pays the owner of an item a percentage of the profit when the item is sold.

Consortium
A coalition of organizations such as banks and corporations for ventures requiring large capital resources.

Consultant
An individual that is paid by a business to provide advice and expertise in a particular area.

Consumer price index
A measure of the fluctuation in prices between two points in time.

Consumer research
Research conducted by a business to obtain information about existing or potential consumer markets.

Continuation coverage
Health coverage offered for a specified period of time to employees who leave their jobs and to their widows, divorced spouses, or dependents.

Contractions
See Business contractions

Convertible preferred stock
A class of stock that pays a reasonable dividend and is convertible into common stock (see separate citation). Generally the convertible feature may only be exercised after being held for a stated period of time. This arrangement is usually considered second-round financing when a company needs equity to maintain its cash flow.

Convertible securities
A feature of certain bonds, debentures, or preferred stocks that allows them to be exchanged by the owner for another class of securities at a future date and in accordance with any other terms of the issue.

Copayment
See Coinsurance

Copyright
A legal form of protection available to creators and authors to safeguard their works from unlawful use or claim of ownership by others. Copyrights may be acquired for works of art, sculpture, music, and published or unpublished manuscripts. All copyrights should be registered at the Copyright Office of the Library of Congress.

Corporate financial ratios
The relationship between key figures found in a company's financial statement expressed as a numeric value. Used to evaluate risk and company performance. Also known as Financial averages, Operating ratios, and Business ratios.

Corporation
A legal entity, chartered by a state or the federal government, recognized as a separate entity having its own rights, privileges, and liabilities distinct from those of its members.

Cost containment
Actions taken by employers and insurers to curtail rising health care costs; for example, increasing employee cost sharing (see separate citation), requiring second opinions, or preadmission screening.

Cost sharing
The requirement that health care consumers contribute to their own medical care costs through deductibles and coinsurance (see separate citations). Cost sharing does not include the amounts paid in premiums. It is used to control utilization of services; for example, requiring a fixed amount to be paid with each health care service.

Cottage industry
Businesses based in the home in which the family members are the labor force and family-owned equipment is used to process the goods.

Credit Rating
A letter or number calculated by an organization (such as Dun & Bradstreet) to represent the ability and disposition of a business to meet its financial obligations.

Customer service
Various techniques used to ensure the satisfaction of a customer.

Cyclical peak
The upper turning point in a business cycle.

Cyclical trough
The lower turning point in a business cycle.

DBA
See Business name

Death
See Business death

Debenture
A certificate given as acknowledgment of a debt (see separate citation) secured by the general credit of the issuing corporation. A bond, usually without security, issued by a corporation and sometimes convertible to common stock.

Debt
Something owed by one person to another. Financing in which a company receives capital that must be repaid; no ownership is transferred.

Debt capital
Business financing that normally requires periodic interest payments and repayment of the principal within a specified time.

Debt financing
See Debt capital

Debt securities
Loans such as bonds and notes that provide a specified rate of return for a specified period of time.

Deductible
A set amount that an individual must pay before any benefits are received.

Demand shock absorbers
A term used to describe the role that some small firms play by expanding their output levels to accommodate a transient surge in demand.

Demographics
Statistics on various markets, including age, income, and education, used to target specific products or services to appropriate consumer groups.

Demonstration
Showing that a product or process has been modified sufficiently to meet the needs of users.

Deregulation
The lifting of government restrictions; for example, the lifting of government restrictions on the entry of new businesses, the expansion of services, and the setting of prices in particular industries.

Desktop Publishing
Using personal computers and specialized software to produce camera-ready copy for publications.

Disaster loans
Various types of physical and economic assistance available to individuals and businesses through the U.S. Small Business Administration (SBA). This is the only SBA loan program available for residential purposes.

Discrimination
The denial of the rights and privileges of employment based on factors such as age, race, religion, or gender.

Diseconomies of scale
The condition in which the costs of production increase faster than the volume of production.

Dissolution
See Business dissolution

Distribution
Delivering a product or process to the user.

Distributor
One who delivers merchandise to the user.

Diversified company
A company whose products and services are used by several different markets.

Doing business as (DBA)
See Business name

Dow Jones
An information services company that publishes the Wall Street Journal and other sources of financial information.

Dow Jones Industrial Average
An indicator of stock market performance.

Earned income
A tax term that refers to wages and salaries earned by the recipient, as opposed to monies earned through interest and dividends.

Economic efficiency
The use of productive resources to the fullest practical extent in the provision of the set of goods and services that is most preferred by purchasers in the economy.

Economic indicators
Statistics used to express the state of the economy. These include the length of the average work week, the rate of unemployment, and stock prices.

Economically disadvantaged
See Socially and economically disadvantaged

Economies of scale
See Scale economies

EEOC
See Equal Employment Opportunity Commission

8(a) Program
A program authorized by the Small Business Act that directs federal contracts to small businesses owned and operated by socially and economically disadvantaged individuals.

Electronic mail (e-mail)
The electronic transmission of mail via phone lines.

E-mail
See Electronic mail

Employee leasing
A contract by which employers arrange to have their workers hired by a leasing company and then leased back to them for a management fee. The leasing company typically assumes the administrative burden of payroll and provides a benefit package to the workers.

Employee tenure
The length of time an employee works for a particular employer.

Employer identification number
The business equivalent of a social security number. Assigned by the U.S. Internal Revenue Service.

Enterprise
An aggregation of all establishments owned by a parent company. An enterprise may consist of a single, independent establishment or include subsidiaries and other branches under the same ownership and control.

Enterprise zone
A designated area, usually found in inner cities and other areas with significant unemployment, where businesses receive tax credits and other incentives to entice them to establish operations there.

Entrepreneur
A person who takes the risk of organizing and operating a new business venture.

Entry
See Business entry

Equal Employment Opportunity Commission (EEOC)
A federal agency that ensures nondiscrimination in the hiring and firing practices of a business.

Equal opportunity employer
An employer who adheres to the standards set by the Equal Employment Opportunity Commission (see separate citation).

Equity
The ownership interest. Financing in which partial or total ownership of a company is surrendered in exchange for capital. An investor's financial return comes from dividend payments and from growth in the net worth of the business.

Equity capital
See Equity; Equity midrisk venture capital

Equity financing
See Equity; Equity midrisk venture capital

Equity midrisk venture capital
An unsecured investment in a company. Usually a purchase of ownership interest in a company that occurs in the later stages of a company's development.

Equity partnership
A limited partnership arrangement for providing start-up and seed capital to businesses.

Equity securities
See Equity

Equity-type
Debt financing subordinated to conventional debt.

Establishment
A single-location business unit that may be independent (a single-establishment enterprise) or owned by a parent enterprise.

Establishment and Enterprise Microdata File
See U.S. Establishment and Enterprise Microdata File

Establishment birth
See Business birth

Establishment Longitudinal Microdata File
See U.S. Establishment Longitudinal Microdata File

Ethics
See Business ethics

Evaluation
Determining the potential success of translating an invention into a product or process.

Exit
See Business exit

Experience rating
See Underwriting

Export
A product sold outside of the country.

Export license
A general or specific license granted by the U.S. Department of Commerce required of anyone wishing to export goods. Some restricted articles need approval from the U.S. Departments of State, Defense, or Energy.

Failure
See Business failure

Fair share agreement
An agreement reached between a franchisor and a minority business organization to extend business ownership to minorities by either reducing the amount of capital required or by setting aside certain marketing areas for minority business owners.

Feasibility study
A study to determine the likelihood that a proposed product or development will fulfill the objectives of a particular investor.

Federal Trade Commission (FTC)
Federal agency that promotes free enterprise and competition within the U.S.

Federal Trade Mark Act of 1946
See Lanham Act

Fictional name
See Business name

Fiduciary
An individual or group that hold assets in trust for a beneficiary.

Financial analysis
The techniques used to determine money needs in a business. Techniques include ratio analysis, calculation of return on investment, guides for measuring profitability, and break-even analysis to determine ultimate success.

Financial intermediary
A financial institution that acts as the intermediary between borrowers and lenders. Banks, savings and loan associations, finance companies, and venture capital companies are major financial intermediaries in the United States.

Financial ratios
See Corporate financial ratios; Industry financial ratios

Financial statement
A written record of business finances, including balance sheets and profit and loss statements.

Financing
See First-stage financing; Second-stage financing; Thirdstage financing

First-stage financing
Financing provided to companies that have expended their initial capital, and require funds to start full-scale manufacturing and sales. Also known as First-round financing.

Fiscal year
Any twelve-month period used by businesses for accounting purposes.

504 Program
See Certified development corporation

Flexible benefit plan
A plan that offers a choice among cash and/or qualified benefits such as group term life insurance, accident and health insurance, group legal services, dependent care assistance, and vacations.

FOB
See Free on board

Format franchising
See Business format franchising; Franchising

401(k) plan
A financial plan where employees contribute a percentage of their earnings to a fund that is invested in stocks, bonds, or money markets for the purpose of saving money for retirement.

Four Ps
Marketing terms referring to Product, Price, Place, and Promotion.

Franchising
A form of licensing by which the owner-the franchisor- distributes or markets a product, method, or service through affiliated dealers called franchisees. The product, method, or service being marketed is identified by a brand name, and the franchisor maintains control over the marketing methods employed. The franchisee is often given exclusive access to a defined geographic area.

Free on board (FOB)
A pricing term indicating that the quoted price includes the cost of loading goods into transport vessels at a specified place.

Frictional unemployment
See Unemployment

FTC
See Federal Trade Commission

Fulfillment
The systems necessary for accurate delivery of an ordered item, including subscriptions and direct marketing.

Full-time workers
Generally, those who work a regular schedule of more than 35 hours per week.

Garment registration number
A number that must appear on every garment sold in the U.S. to indicate the manufacturer of the garment, which may or may not be the same as the label under which the garment is sold. The U.S. Federal Trade Commission assigns and regulates garment registration numbers.

Gatekeeper
A key contact point for entry into a network.

GDP
See Gross domestic product

General obligation bond
A municipal bond secured by the taxing power of the municipality. The Tax Reform Act of 1986 limits the purposes for which such bonds may be issued and establishes volume limits on the extent of their issuance.

GNP
See Gross national product

Good Housekeeping Seal
Seal appearing on products that signifies the fulfillment of the standards set by the Good Housekeeping Institute to protect consumer interests.

Goods sector
All businesses producing tangible goods, including agriculture, mining, construction, and manufacturing businesses.

GPO
See Gross product originating

Gross domestic product (GDP)
The part of the nation's gross national product (see separate citation) generated by private business using resources from within the country.

Gross national product (GNP)
The most comprehensive single measure of aggregate economic output. Represents the market value of the total output of goods and services produced by a nation's economy.

Gross product originating (GPO)
A measure of business output estimated from the income or production side using employee compensation, profit income, net interest, capital consumption, and indirect business taxes.

HAL
See Handicapped assistance loan program

Handicapped assistance loan program (HAL)
Low-interest direct loan program through the U.S. Small Business Administration (SBA) for handicapped persons. The SBA requires that these persons demonstrate that their disability is such that it is impossible for them to secure employment, thus making it necessary to go into their own business to make a living.

Health maintenance organization (HMO)
Organization of physicians and other health care professionals that provides health services to subscribers and their dependents on a prepaid basis.

Health provider
An individual or institution that gives medical care. Under Medicare, an institutional provider is a hospital, skilled nursing facility, home health agency, or provider of certain physical therapy services.

Hispanic
A person of Cuban, Mexican, Puerto Rican, Latin American (Central or South American), European Spanish, or other Spanish-speaking origin or ancestry.

HMO
See Health maintenance organization

Home-based business
A business with an operating address that is also a residential address (usually the residential address of the proprietor).

Hub-and-spoke system
A system in which flights of an airline from many different cities (the spokes) converge at a single airport (the hub). After allowing passengers sufficient time to make connections, planes then depart for different cities.

Human Resources Management
A business program designed to oversee recruiting, pay, benefits, and other issues related to the company's work force, including planning to determine the optimal use of labor to increase production, thereby increasing profit.

Idea
An original concept for a new product or process.

Import
Products produced outside the country in which they are consumed.

Income
Money or its equivalent, earned or accrued, resulting from the sale of goods and services.

Income statement
A financial statement that lists the profits and losses of a company at a given time.

Incorporation
The filing of a certificate of incorporation with a state's secretary of state, thereby limiting the business owner's liability.

Incubator
A facility designed to encourage entrepreneurship and minimize obstacles to new business formation and growth, particularly for high-technology firms, by housing a number of fledgling enterprises that share an array of services, such as meeting areas, secretarial services, accounting, research library, on-site financial and management counseling, and word processing facilities.

Independent contractor
An individual considered self-employed (see separate citation) and responsible for paying Social Security taxes and income taxes on earnings.

Indirect health coverage
Health insurance obtained through another individual's health care plan; for example, a spouse's employersponsored plan.

Industrial development authority
The financial arm of a state or other political subdivision established for the purpose of financing economic development in an area, usually through loans to nonprofit organizations, which in turn provide facilities for manufacturing and other industrial operations.

Industry financial ratios
Corporate financial ratios averaged for a specified industry. These are used for comparison purposes and reveal industry trends and identify differences between the performance of a specific company and the performance of its industry. Also known as Industrial averages, Industry ratios, Financial averages, and Business or Industrial norms.

Inflation
Increases in volume of currency and credit, generally resulting in a sharp and continuing rise in price levels.

Informal capital
Financing from informal, unorganized sources; includes informal debt capital such as trade credit or loans from friends and relatives and equity capital from informal investors.

Initial public offering (IPO)
A corporation's first offering of stock to the public.

Innovation
The introduction of a new idea into the marketplace in the form of a new product or service or an improvement in organization or process.

Intellectual property
Any idea or work that can be considered proprietary in nature and is thus protected from infringement by others.

Internal capital
Debt or equity financing obtained from the owner or through retained business earnings.

Internet
A government-designed computer network that contains large amounts of information and is accessible through various vendors for a fee.

Intrapreneurship
The state of employing entrepreneurial principles to nonentrepreneurial situations.

Invention
The tangible form of a technological idea, which could include a laboratory prototype, drawings, formulas, etc.

IPO
See Initial public offering

Job description
The duties and responsibilities required in a particular position.

Job tenure
A period of time during which an individual is continuously employed in the same job.

Joint marketing agreements
Agreements between regional and major airlines, often involving the coordination of flight schedules, fares, and baggage transfer. These agreements help regional carriers operate at lower cost.

Joint venture
Venture in which two or more people combine efforts in a particular business enterprise, usually a single transaction or a limited activity, and agree to share the profits and losses jointly or in proportion to their contributions.

Keogh plan
Designed for self-employed persons and unincorporated businesses as a tax-deferred pension account.

Labor force
Civilians considered eligible for employment who are also willing and able to work.

Labor force participation rate
The civilian labor force as a percentage of the civilian population.

Labor intensity
The relative importance of labor in the production process, usually measured as the capital-labor ratio; i.e., the ratio of units of capital (typically, dollars of tangible assets) to the number of employees. The higher the capital-labor ratio exhibited by a firm or industry, the lower the capital intensity of that firm or industry is said to be.

Labor surplus area
An area in which there exists a high unemployment rate. In procurement (see separate citation), extra points are given to firms in counties that are designated a labor surplus area; this information is requested on procurement bid sheets.

Labor union
An organization of similarly-skilled workers who collectively bargain with management over the conditions of employment.

Laboratory prototype
See Prototype

LAN
See Local Area Network

Lanham Act
Refers to the Federal Trade Mark Act of 1946. Protects registered trademarks, trade names, and other service marks used in commerce.

Large business-dominated industry
Industry in which a minimum of 60 percent of employment or sales is in firms with more than 500 workers.

LBO
See Leveraged buy-out

Leader pricing
A reduction in the price of a good or service in order to generate more sales of that good or service.

Legal list
A list of securities selected by a state in which certain institutions and fiduciaries (such as pension funds, insurance companies, and banks) may invest. Securities not on the list are not eligible for investment. Legal lists typically restrict investments to high quality securities meeting certain specifications. Generally, investment is limited to U.S. securities and investment-grade blue chip securities (see separate citation).

Leveraged buy-out (LBO)
The purchase of a business or a division of a corporation through a highly leveraged financing package.

Liability
An obligation or duty to perform a service or an act. Also defined as money owed.

License
A legal agreement granting to another the right to use a technological innovation.

Limited partnerships
See Venture capital limited partnerships

Liquidity
The ability to convert a security into cash promptly.

Loans
See Commercial loans; Disaster loans; SBA direct loans; SBA guaranteed loans; SBA special lending institution categories Local Area Network (LAN) Computer networks contained within a single building or small area; used to facilitate the sharing of information.

Local development corporation
An organization, usually made up of local citizens of a community, designed to improve the economy of the area by inducing business and industry to locate and expand there. A local development corporation establishes a capability to finance local growth.

Long-haul rates
Rates charged by a transporter in which the distance traveled is more than 800 miles.

Long-term debt
An obligation that matures in a period that exceeds five years.

Low-grade bond
A corporate bond that is rated below investment grade by the major rating agencies (Standard and Poor's, Moody's).

Macro-efficiency
Efficiency as it pertains to the operation of markets and market systems.

Managed care
A cost-effective health care program initiated by employers whereby low-cost health care is made available to the employees in return for exclusive patronage to program doctors.

Management Assistance Programs
See SBA Management Assistance Programs

Management and technical assistance
A term used by many programs to mean business (as opposed to technological) assistance.

Mandated benefits
Specific treatments, providers, or individuals required by law to be included in commercial health plans.

Market evaluation
The use of market information to determine the sales potential of a specific product or process.

Market failure
The situation in which the workings of a competitive market do not produce the best results from the point of view of the entire society.

Market information
Data of any type that can be used for market evaluation, which could include demographic data, technology forecasting, regulatory changes, etc.

Market research
A systematic collection, analysis, and reporting of data about the market and its preferences, opinions, trends, and plans; used for corporate decision-making.

Market share
In a particular market, the percentage of sales of a specific product.

Marketing
Promotion of goods or services through various media.

Master Establishment List (MEL)
A list of firms in the United States developed by the U.S. Small Business Administration; firms can be selected by industry, region, state, standard metropolitan statistical area (see separate citation), county, and zip code.

Maturity
The date upon which the principal or stated value of a bond or other indebtedness becomes due and payable.

Medicaid (Title XIX)
A federally aided, state-operated and administered program that provides medical benefits for certain low income persons in need of health and medical care who are eligible for one of the government's welfare cash payment programs, including the aged, the blind, the disabled, and members of families with dependent

children where one parent is absent, incapacitated, or unemployed.

Medicare (Title XVIII)
A nationwide health insurance program for disabled and aged persons. Health insurance is available to insured persons without regard to income. Monies from payroll taxes cover hospital insurance and monies from general revenues and beneficiary premiums pay for supplementary medical insurance.

MEL
See Master Establishment List

MESBIC
See Minority enterprise small business investment corporation

MET
See Multiple employer trust

Metropolitan statistical area (MSA)
A means used by the government to define large population centers that may transverse different governmental jurisdictions. For example, the Washington, D.C. MSA includes the District of Columbia and contiguous parts of Maryland and Virginia because all of these geopolitical areas comprise one population and economic operating unit.

Mezzanine financing
See Third-stage financing

Micro-efficiency
Efficiency as it pertains to the operation of individual firms.

Microdata
Information on the characteristics of an individual business firm.

Mid-term debt
An obligation that matures within one to five years.

Midrisk venture capital
See Equity midrisk venture capital

Minimum premium plan
A combination approach to funding an insurance plan aimed primarily at premium tax savings. The employer self-funds a fixed percentage of estimated monthly claims and the insurance company insures the excess.

Minimum wage
The lowest hourly wage allowed by the federal government.

Minority Business Development Agency
Contracts with private firms throughout the nation to sponsor Minority Business Development Centers which provide minority firms with advice and technical assistance on a fee basis.

Minority Enterprise Small Business Investment Corporation (MESBIC)
A federally funded private venture capital firm licensed by the U.S. Small Business Administration to provide capital to minority-owned businesses (see separate citation).

Minority-owned business
Businesses owned by those who are socially or economically disadvantaged (see separate citation).

Mom and Pop business
A small store or enterprise having limited capital, principally employing family members.

Moonlighter
A wage-and-salary worker with a side business.

MSA
See Metropolitan statistical area

Multi-employer plan
A health plan to which more than one employer is required to contribute and that may be maintained through a collective bargaining agreement and required to meet standards prescribed by the U.S. Department of Labor.

Multi-level marketing
A system of selling in which you sign up other people to assist you and they, in turn, recruit others to help them. Some entrepreneurs have built successful companies on this concept because the main focus of their activities is their product and product sales.

Multimedia
The use of several types of media to promote a product or service. Also, refers to the use of several different types of media (sight, sound, pictures, text) in a CD-ROM (see separate citation) product.

Multiple employer trust (MET)
A self-funded benefit plan generally geared toward small employers sharing a common interest.

NAFTA
See North American Free Trade Agreement

NASDAQ
See National Association of Securities Dealers Automated Quotations

National Association of Securities Dealers Automated Quotations
Provides price quotes on over-the-counter securities as well as securities listed on the New York Stock Exchange.

National income
Aggregate earnings of labor and property arising from the production of goods and services in a nation's economy.

Net assets
See Net worth

Net income
The amount remaining from earnings and profits after all expenses and costs have been met or deducted. Also known as Net earnings.

Net profit
Money earned after production and overhead expenses (see separate citations) have been deducted.

Net worth
The difference between a company's total assets and its total liabilities.

Network
A chain of interconnected individuals or organizations sharing information and/or services.

New York Stock Exchange (NYSE)
The oldest stock exchange in the U.S. Allows for trading in stocks, bonds, warrants, options, and rights that meet listing requirements.

Niche
A career or business for which a person is well-suited. Also, a product which fulfills one need of a particular market segment, often with little or no competition.

Nodes
One workstation in a network, either local area or wide area (see separate citations).

Nonbank bank
A bank that either accepts deposits or makes loans, but not both. Used to create many new branch banks.

Noncompetitive awards
A method of contracting whereby the federal government negotiates with only one contractor to supply a product or service.

Nonmember bank
A state-regulated bank that does not belong to the federal bank system.

Nonprofit
An organization that has no shareholders, does not distribute profits, and is without federal and state tax liabilities.

Norms
See Financial ratios

North American Free Trade Agreement (NAFTA)
Passed in 1993, NAFTA eliminates trade barriers among businesses in the U.S., Canada, and Mexico.

NYSE
See New York Stock Exchange

Occupational Safety & Health Administration (OSHA)
Federal agency that regulates health and safety standards within the workplace.

Optimal firm size
The business size at which the production cost per unit of output (average cost) is, in the long run, at its minimum.

Organizational chart
A hierarchical chart tracking the chain of command within an organization.

OSHA
See Occupational Safety & Health Administration

Overhead
Expenses, such as employee benefits and building utilities, incurred by a business that are unrelated to the actual product or service sold.

Owner's capital
Debt or equity funds provided by the owner(s) of a business; sources of owner's capital are personal savings, sales of assets, or loans from financial institutions.

P & L
See Profit and loss statement

Part-time workers
Normally, those who work less than 35 hours per week. The Tax Reform Act indicated that part-time workers who work less than 17.5 hours per week may be excluded from health plans for purposes of complying with federal nondiscrimination rules.

Part-year workers
Those who work less than 50 weeks per year.

Partnership
Two or more parties who enter into a legal relationship to conduct business for profit. Defined by the U.S. Internal Revenue Code as joint ventures, syndicates, groups, pools, and other associations of two or more persons organized for profit that are not specifically classified in the IRS code as corporations or proprietorships.

Patent
A grant made by the government assuring an inventor the sole right to make, use, and sell an invention for a period of 17 years.

PC
See Professional corporation

Peak
See Cyclical peak

Pension
A series of payments made monthly, semiannually, annually, or at other specified intervals during the lifetime of the pensioner for distribution upon retirement. The term is sometimes used to denote the portion of the retirement allowance financed by the employer's contributions.

Pension fund
A fund established to provide for the payment of pension benefits; the collective contributions made by all of the parties to the pension plan.

Performance appraisal
An established set of objective criteria, based on job description and requirements, that is used to evaluate the performance of an employee in a specific job.

Permit
See Business license

Plan
See Business plan

Pooling
An arrangement for employers to achieve efficiencies and lower health costs by joining together to purchase group health insurance or self-insurance.

PPO
See Preferred provider organization

Preferred lenders program
See SBA special lending institution categories

Preferred provider organization (PPO)
A contractual arrangement with a health care services organization that agrees to discount its health care rates in return for faster payment and/or a patient base.

Premiums
The amount of money paid to an insurer for health insurance under a policy. The premium is generally paid periodically (e.g., monthly), and often is split between the employer and the employee. Unlike deductibles and coinsurance or copayments, premiums are paid for coverage whether or not benefits are actually used.

Prime-age workers
Employees 25 to 54 years of age.

Prime contract
A contract awarded directly by the U.S. Federal Government.

Private company
See Closely held corporation

Private placement
A method of raising capital by offering for sale an investment or business to a small group of investors (generally avoiding registration with the Securities and Exchange Commission or state securities registration agencies). Also known as Private financing or Private offering.

Pro forma
The use of hypothetical figures in financial statements to represent future expenditures, debts, and other potential financial expenses.

Proactive

Taking the initiative to solve problems and anticipate future events before they happen, instead of reacting to an already existing problem or waiting for a difficult situation to occur.

Procurement

A contract from an agency of the federal government for goods or services from a small business.

Prodigy

An online service which is accessible by computer modem. The service features Internet access, bulletin boards, online periodicals, electronic mail, and other services for subscribers.

Product development

The stage of the innovation process where research is translated into a product or process through evaluation, adaptation, and demonstration.

Product franchising

An arrangement for a franchisee to use the name and to produce the product line of the franchisor or parent corporation.

Production

The manufacture of a product.

Production prototype

See Prototype

Productivity

A measurement of the number of goods produced during a specific amount of time.

Professional corporation (PC)

Organized by members of a profession such as medicine, dentistry, or law for the purpose of conducting their professional activities as a corporation. Liability of a member or shareholder is limited in the same manner as in a business corporation.

Profit and loss statement (P & L)

The summary of the incomes (total revenues) and costs of a company's operation during a specific period of time. Also known as Income and expense statement.

Proposal

See Business plan

Proprietorship

The most common legal form of business ownership; about 85 percent of all small businesses are proprietorships. The liability of the owner is unlimited in this form of ownership.

Prospective payment system

A cost-containment measure included in the Social Security Amendments of 1983 whereby Medicare payments to hospitals are based on established prices, rather than on cost reimbursement.

Prototype

A model that demonstrates the validity of the concept of an invention (laboratory prototype); a model that meets the needs of the manufacturing process and the user (production prototype).

Prudent investor rule or standard

A legal doctrine that requires fiduciaries to make investments using the prudence, diligence, and intelligence that would be used by a prudent person in making similar investments. Because fiduciaries make investments on behalf of third-party beneficiaries, the standard results in very conservative investments. Until recently, most state regulations required the fiduciary to apply this standard to each investment. Newer, more progressive regulations permit fiduciaries to apply this standard to the portfolio taken as a whole, thereby allowing a fiduciary to balance a portfolio with higher-yield, higher-risk investments. In states with more progressive regulations, practically every type of security is eligible for inclusion in the portfolio of investments made by a fiduciary, provided that the portfolio investments, in their totality, are those of a prudent person.

Public equity markets

Organized markets for trading in equity shares such as common stocks, preferred stocks, and warrants. Includes markets for both regularly traded and nonregularly traded securities.

Public offering

General solicitation for participation in an investment opportunity. Interstate public offerings are supervised by the U.S. Securities and Exchange Commission (see separate citation).

Quality control
The process by which a product is checked and tested to ensure consistent standards of high quality.

Rate of return
The yield obtained on a security or other investment based on its purchase price or its current market price. The total rate of return is current income plus or minus capital appreciation or depreciation.

Real property
Includes the land and all that is contained on it.

Realignment
See Resource realignment

Recession
Contraction of economic activity occurring between the peak and trough (see separate citations) of a business cycle.

Regulated market
A market in which the government controls the forces of supply and demand, such as who may enter and what price may be charged.

Regulation D
A vehicle by which small businesses make small offerings and private placements of securities with limited disclosure requirements. It was designed to ease the burdens imposed on small businesses utilizing this method of capital formation.

Regulatory Flexibility Act
An act requiring federal agencies to evaluate the impact of their regulations on small businesses before the regulations are issued and to consider less burdensome alternatives.

Research
The initial stage of the innovation process, which includes idea generation and invention.

Research and development financing
A tax-advantaged partnership set up to finance product development for start-ups as well as more mature companies.

Resource mobility
The ease with which labor and capital move from firm to firm or from industry to industry.

Resource realignment
The adjustment of productive resources to interindustry changes in demand.

Resources
The sources of support or help in the innovation process, including sources of financing, technical evaluation, market evaluation, management and business assistance, etc.

Retained business earnings
Business profits that are retained by the business rather than being distributed to the shareholders as dividends.

Revolving credit
An agreement with a lending institution for an amount of money, which cannot exceed a set maximum, over a specified period of time. Each time the borrower repays a portion of the loan, the amount of the repayment may be borrowed yet again.

Risk capital
See Venture capital

Risk management
The act of identifying potential sources of financial loss and taking action to minimize their negative impact.

Routing
The sequence of steps necessary to complete a product during production.

S corporations
See Sub chapter S corporations

SBA
See Small Business Administration

SBA direct loans
Loans made directly by the U.S. Small Business Administration (SBA); monies come from funds appropriated specifically for this purpose. In general, SBA direct loans carry interest rates slightly lower than those in the private financial markets and are available only to applicants unable to secure private financing or an SBA guaranteed loan.

SBA 504 Program
See Certified development corporation

SBA guaranteed loans
Loans made by lending institutions in which the U.S. Small Business Administration (SBA) will pay a prior agreed-upon percentage of the outstanding principal in the event the borrower of the loan defaults. The terms of the loan and the interest rate are negotiated between the borrower and the lending institution, within set parameters.

SBA loans
See Disaster loans; SBA direct loans; SBA guaranteed loans; SBA special lending institution categories

SBA Management Assistance Programs
Classes, workshops, counseling, and publications offered by the U.S. Small Business Administration.

SBA special lending institution categories
U.S. Small Business Administration (SBA) loan program in which the SBA promises certified banks a 72-hour turnaround period in giving its approval for a loan, and in which preferred lenders in a pilot program are allowed to write SBA loans without seeking prior SBA approval.

SBDB
See Small Business Data Base

SBDC
See Small business development centers

SBI
See Small business institutes program

SBIC
See Small business investment corporation

SBIR Program
See Small Business Innovation Development Act of 1982

Scale economies
The decline of the production cost per unit of output (average cost) as the volume of output increases.

Scale efficiency
The reduction in unit cost available to a firm when producing at a higher output volume.

SCORE
See Service Corps of Retired Executives

SEC
See Securities and Exchange Commission

SECA
See Self-Employment Contributions Act

Second-stage financing
Working capital for the initial expansion of a company that is producing, shipping, and has growing accounts receivable and inventories. Also known as Second-round financing.

Secondary market
A market established for the purchase and sale of outstanding securities following their initial distribution.

Secondary worker
Any worker in a family other than the person who is the primary source of income for the family.

Secondhand capital
Previously used and subsequently resold capital equipment (e.g., buildings and machinery).

Securities and Exchange Commission (SEC)
Federal agency charged with regulating the trade of securities to prevent unethical practices in the investor market.

Securitized debt
A marketing technique that converts long-term loans to marketable securities.

Seed capital
Venture financing provided in the early stages of the innovation process, usually during product development.

Self-employed person
One who works for a profit or fees in his or her own business, profession, or trade, or who operates a farm.

Self-Employment Contributions Act (SECA)
Federal law that governs the self-employment tax (see separate citation).

Self-employment income
Income covered by Social Security if a business earns a net income of at least $400.00 during the year. Taxes are paid on earnings that exceed $400.00.

Self-employment retirement plan
See Keogh plan

Self-employment tax
Required tax imposed on self-employed individuals for the provision of Social Security and Medicare.

The tax must be paid quarterly with estimated income tax statements.

Self-funding
A health benefit plan in which a firm uses its own funds to pay claims, rather than transferring the financial risks of paying claims to an outside insurer in exchange for premium payments.

Service Corps of Retired Executives (SCORE)
Volunteers for the SBA Management Assistance Program who provide one-on-one counseling and teach workshops and seminars for small firms.

Service firm
See Business service firm

Service sector
Broadly defined, all U.S. industries that produce intangibles, including the five major industry divisions of transportation, communications, and utilities; wholesale trade; retail trade; finance, insurance, and real estate; and services.

Set asides
See Small business set asides

Short-haul service
A type of transportation service in which the transporter supplies service between cities where the maximum distance is no more than 200 miles.

Short-term debt
An obligation that matures in one year.

SIC codes
See Standard Industrial Classification codes

Single-establishment enterprise
See Establishment

Small business
An enterprise that is independently owned and operated, is not dominant in its field, and employs fewer than 500 people. For SBA purposes, the U.S. Small Business Administration (SBA) considers various other factors (such as gross annual sales) in determining size of a business.

Small Business Administration (SBA)
An independent federal agency that provides assistance with loans, management, and advocating interests before other federal agencies.

Small Business Data Base
A collection of microdata (see separate citation) files on individual firms developed and maintained by the U.S. Small Business Administration.

Small business development centers (SBDC)
Centers that provide support services to small businesses, such as individual counseling, SBA advice, seminars and conferences, and other learning center activities. Most services are free of charge, or available at minimal cost.

Small business development corporation
See Certified development corporation

Small business-dominated industry
Industry in which a minimum of 60 percent of employment or sales is in firms with fewer than 500 employees.

Small Business Innovation Development Act of 1982
Federal statute requiring federal agencies with large extramural research and development budgets to allocate a certain percentage of these funds to small research and development firms. The program, called the Small Business Innovation Research (SBIR) Program, is designed to stimulate technological innovation and make greater use of small businesses in meeting national innovation needs.

Small business institutes (SBI) program
Cooperative arrangements made by U.S. Small Business Administration district offices and local colleges and universities to provide small business firms with graduate students to counsel them without charge.

Small business investment corporation (SBIC)
A privately owned company licensed and funded through the U.S. Small Business Administration and private sector sources to provide equity or debt capital to small businesses.

Small business set asides
Procurement (see separate citation) opportunities required by law to be on all contracts under $10,000 or a certain percentage of an agency's total procurement expenditure.

Smaller firms
For U.S. Department of Commerce purposes, those firms not included in the Fortune 1000.

SMSA
See Metropolitan statistical area

Socially and economically disadvantaged
Individuals who have been subjected to racial or ethnic prejudice or cultural bias without regard to their qualities as individuals, and whose abilities to compete are impaired because of diminished opportunities to obtain capital and credit.

Sole proprietorship
An unincorporated, one-owner business, farm, or professional practice.

Special lending institution categories
See SBA special lending institution categories

Standard Industrial Classification (SIC) codes
Four-digit codes established by the U.S. Federal Government to categorize businesses by type of economic activity; the first two digits correspond to major groups such as construction and manufacturing, while the last two digits correspond to subgroups such as home construction or highway construction.

Standard metropolitan statistical area (SMSA)
See Metropolitan statistical area

Start-up
A new business, at the earliest stages of development and financing.

Start-up costs
Costs incurred before a business can commence operations.

Start-up financing
Financing provided to companies that have either completed product development and initial marketing or have been in business for less than one year but have not yet sold their product commercially.

Stock
A certificate of equity ownership in a business.

Stop-loss coverage
Insurance for a self-insured plan that reimburses the company for any losses it might incur in its health claims beyond a specified amount.

Strategic planning
Projected growth and development of a business to establish a guiding direction for the future. Also used to determine which market segments to explore for optimal sales of products or services.

Structural unemployment
See Unemployment

Sub chapter S corporations
Corporations that are considered noncorporate for tax purposes but legally remain corporations.

Subcontract
A contract between a prime contractor and a subcontractor, or between subcontractors, to furnish supplies or services for performance of a prime contract (see separate citation) or a subcontract.

Surety bonds
Bonds providing reimbursement to an individual, company, or the government if a firm fails to complete a contract. The U.S. Small Business Administration guarantees surety bonds in a program much like the SBA guaranteed loan program (see separate citation).

Swing loan
See Bridge financing

Target market
The clients or customers sought for a business' product or service.

Targeted Jobs Tax Credit
Federal legislation enacted in 1978 that provides a tax credit to an employer who hires structurally unemployed individuals.

Tax number
A number assigned to a business by a state revenue department that enables the business to buy goods without paying sales tax.

Taxable bonds
An interest-bearing certificate of public or private indebtedness. Bonds are issued by public agencies to finance economic development.

Technical assistance
See Management and technical assistance

Technical evaluation
Assessment of technological feasibility.

Technology
The method in which a firm combines and utilizes labor and capital resources to produce goods or services; the application of science for commercial or industrial purposes.

Technology transfer
The movement of information about a technology or intellectual property from one party to another for use.

Tenure
See Employee tenure

Term
The length of time for which a loan is made.

Terms of a note
The conditions or limits of a note; includes the interest rate per annum, the due date, and transferability and convertibility features, if any.

Third-party administrator
An outside company responsible for handling claims and performing administrative tasks associated with health insurance plan maintenance.

Third-stage financing
Financing provided for the major expansion of a company whose sales volume is increasing and that is breaking even or profitable. These funds are used for further plant expansion, marketing, working capital, or development of an improved product. Also known as Third-round or Mezzanine financing.

Time deposit
A bank deposit that cannot be withdrawn before a specified future time.

Time management
Skills and scheduling techniques used to maximize productivity.

Trade credit
Credit extended by suppliers of raw materials or finished products. In an accounting statement, trade credit is referred to as "accounts payable."

Trade name
The name under which a company conducts business, or by which its business, goods, or services are identified. It may or may not be registered as a trademark.

Trade periodical
A publication with a specific focus on one or more aspects of business and industry.

Trade secret
Competitive advantage gained by a business through the use of a unique manufacturing process or formula.

Trade show
An exhibition of goods or services used in a particular industry. Typically held in exhibition centers where exhibitors rent space to display their merchandise.

Trademark
A graphic symbol, device, or slogan that identifies a business. A business has property rights to its trademark from the inception of its use, but it is still prudent to register all trademarks with the Trademark Office of the U.S. Department of Commerce.

Translation
See Product development

Treasury bills
Investment tender issued by the Federal Reserve Bank in amounts of $10,000 that mature in 91 to 182 days.

Treasury bonds
Long-term notes with maturity dates of not less than seven and not more than twenty-five years.

Treasury notes
Short-term notes maturing in less than seven years.

Trend
A statistical measurement used to track changes that occur over time.

Trough
See Cyclical trough

UCC
See Uniform Commercial Code

UL
See Underwriters Laboratories

Underwriters Laboratories (UL)
One of several private firms that tests products and processes to determine their safety. Although various firms can provide this kind of testing service, many local and insurance codes specify UL certification.

Underwriting
A process by which an insurer determines whether or not and on what basis it will accept an application for

insurance. In an experience-rated plan, premiums are based on a firm's or group's past claims; factors other than prior claims are used for community-rated or manually rated plans.

Unfair competition

Refers to business practices, usually unethical, such as using unlicensed products, pirating merchandise, or misleading the public through false advertising, which give the offending business an unequitable advantage over others.

Unfunded accrued liability

The excess of total liabilities, both present and prospective, over present and prospective assets.

Unemployment

The joblessness of individuals who are willing to work, who are legally and physically able to work, and who are seeking work. Unemployment may represent the temporary joblessness of a worker between jobs (frictional unemployment) or the joblessness of a worker whose skills are not suitable for jobs available in the labor market (structural unemployment).

Uniform Commercial Code (UCC)

A code of laws governing commercial transactions across the U.S., except Louisiana. Their purpose is to bring uniformity to financial transactions.

Uniform product code (UPC symbol)

A computer-readable label comprised of ten digits and stripes that encodes what a product is and how much it costs. The first five digits are assigned by the Uniform Product Code Council, and the last five digits by the individual manufacturer.

Unit cost

See Average cost

UPC symbol

See Uniform product code

U.S. Establishment and Enterprise Microdata (USEEM) File

A cross-sectional database containing information on employment, sales, and location for individual enterprises and establishments with employees that have a Dun & Bradstreet credit rating.

U.S. Establishment Longitudinal Microdata (USELM) File

A database containing longitudinally linked sample microdata on establishments drawn from the U.S. Establishment and Enterprise Microdata file (see separate citation).

U.S. Small Business Administration 504 Program

See Certified development corporation

USEEM

See U.S. Establishment and Enterprise Microdata File

USELM

See U.S. Establishment Longitudinal Microdata File

VCN

See Venture capital network

Venture capital

Money used to support new or unusual business ventures that exhibit above-average growth rates, significant potential for market expansion, and are in need of additional financing to sustain growth or further research and development; equity or equity-type financing traditionally provided at the commercialization stage, increasingly available prior to commercialization.

Venture capital company

A company organized to provide seed capital to a business in its formation stage, or in its first or second stage of expansion. Funding is obtained through public or private pension funds, commercial banks and bank holding companies, small business investment corporations licensed by the U.S. Small Business Administration, private venture capital firms, insurance companies, investment management companies, bank trust departments, industrial companies seeking to diversify their investment, and investment bankers acting as intermediaries for other investors or directly investing on their own behalf.

Venture capital limited partnerships

Designed for business development, these partnerships are an institutional mechanism for providing capital for young, technology-oriented businesses. The investors' money is pooled and invested in money market assets until venture investments have been selected. The general partners are experienced investment managers who select and invest the equity and debt securities of firms with high growth potential and the ability to go public in the near future.

Venture capital network (VCN)
A computer database that matches investors with entrepreneurs.

WAN
See Wide Area Network

Wide Area Network (WAN)
Computer networks linking systems throughout a state or around the world in order to facilitate the sharing of information.

Withholding
Federal, state, social security, and unemployment taxes withheld by the employer from employees' wages; employers are liable for these taxes and the corporate umbrella and bankruptcy will not exonerate an employer from paying back payroll withholding. Employers should escrow these funds in a separate account and disperse them quarterly to withholding authorities.

Workers' compensation
A state-mandated form of insurance covering workers injured in job-related accidents. In some states, the state is the insurer; in other states, insurance must be acquired from commercial insurance firms. Insurance rates are based on a number of factors, including salaries, firm history, and risk of occupation.

Working capital
Refers to a firm's short-term investment of current assets, including cash, short-term securities, accounts receivable, and inventories.

Yield
The rate of income returned on an investment, expressed as a percentage. Income yield is obtained by dividing the current dollar income by the current market price of the security. Net yield or yield to maturity is the current income yield minus any premium above par or plus any discount from par in purchase price, with the adjustment spread over the period from the date of purchase to the date of maturity.

INDEX

Listings in this index are arranged alphabetically by business plan type, then alphabetically by business plan name. Users are provided with the volume number in which the plan appears.

Accounting Service
Marcus Accounting LLC, 7

Accounting Systems Consultants
Accounting Management Systems, 1

Adventure Travel Lodging Company
Cobra Travel Adventure Group, 11

Advertising Agency
BlueIsland.com, 8

Aerospace Supplier
Flatland Manufacturing, Inc., 1

Aftermarket Internet Applications
AutoAftermarket.com, 8

Aftermarket Skate Store
Pegasus Sports International, 8

Airlines
Puddle Jumpers Airlines, Inc., 6
SkyTrails Airlines, Ltd., 9

Art Glass Studio
Phyllis Farmington Art Glass, 6

Audio Production Service
Jack Cornwall Productions, 4

Auto Accessories and Detailing
Auto Accessories Unlimited, 3
J.E.M. Ventures, Inc., 3

Automobile Assembly
Dream Cars 2

Automotive Dealer Group
Pompei-Schmidt Auto Dealers Inc., 4

Automotive Repair Service
Collision Experts Inc., 10
LR Automotive, 4

Auto Sales Company
Mountain View Lease, LLC, 7

Bagel Shop
USA Bagels, 5

Beauty Salon
Salon Flora, 12

Bed & Breakfast
Aphrodite's Dream Bed & Breakfast, 6
Red Barron Bed & Breakfast, 1
Victoria Bed & Breakfast, 4

Bioterrorism Prevention Organization
Bioterrorism & Infections Prevention Organization, 10

Biscotti Bakery
Italian Eatery, The, 1

Bistro and Wine Bar
Wine Bistro, The, 10

Bottled Water Manufacturer
Sparkling Horizon Bottled Water, 4

Bowling Alley
Family Bowl, The, 7

Bread Bakery
Breadcrafter, 5

Brewpub
Hopstreet Brewery, 11

Bridal Salon
Megan's Bridal Boutique, 6

Business Consulting
Blake & Associates, 1
Koshu, 1

Business Development Firm
NKR Consulting, Inc., 9

Campground
California RV & Campgrounds, 12

Car Wash
ABC, Inc., 7
Dirt Buster, The, 1

J&A Ventures, Inc., 5
Platinum Carwash, 12

Caribbean Café
Calypso Café, 6

Carpet Cleaning Service
Carpet Chem Corporation, 3

Caviar Company
Caviar Delights, 9

Charity Youth Hockey Tournament
Lucky Pucks, 8

Chemical Manufacturer
Chemalyze, Inc., 8

Child Transportation Service
Kid Cart, 4

Chiropractic Office
Cole's Care Chiropractic, 6

Christmas Ornament Company
Scriptures for You, Inc., 6

Cigar Company
Smokescreen Cigars, 11

Cigar Shop
Holy Smokes, 5

Climbing Outfitter
Rockhound Outfitters, 5

Coatings Inspection Company
Professional Coatings Services, Inc. 10

Coffee Bean Plant/Exporter
Silvera & Sons Ltda., 7

Coffee House
Coffee Circus, 4

Coffee Roaster
Venezia Coffee Roasters, 4

Computer Matchmaking Service
Matchmate, Inc., 3

Computer Reseller
Computech Management, 5
Ellipse Technologies, Inc., 5

Computer Training Service Business
Enhanced Occupations Center, 9

Concert Promotions Company
Good Vibrations, Inc., 9

Concrete Coating Company
Techno–Coatings USA, 12

Condiment Manufacturer
Salvador Sauces, Inc., 6

Construction Development & Real Estate Firm
Black Pearl Development and Real Estate LLC, 11

Construction and Home Rehabilitation Company
Pedro's Construction, 11

Convenience Store & Bait Shop
The Dock Store, 8

Cookie Shop
Grandma Miller's Cookies and Muffins, 6

Counseling Center
Juniper Counseling Center, 9

Crane Service
Chesterfield Crane Service, 1

Creative Agency
Oceania Creative Print & Interactive, 8

Custodial Cleaning Company
Spic and Span, 12

Dance and Skate Outfitter
Arabesque Dance & Skate Shop, 3

Daycare Facility
Childhood Dreams Inc. , 12
Rachel's Clubhouse, 11
Ziggle Zag Zip Daycare/Childcare, 12

Dentist
Fremont Dental Office, 12
Stanley M. Kramer, DDS, LLC, 8

Desktop Publishing Company
Power Desk Top Publishing, Inc., 7

Detective Agency
Barr Detective Agency, 5

Dial-It Service
Callmaster, Inc., 3

Diaper Delivery
Diapers 'n More, 1

Direct Mail Outlet
Post Direct, 4

Discount Internet Securities Broker
E-Best-Trade.com, 8

Display Technology Company
TouchTop Technologies, Inc., 7

Dollar Store
Dollar Daze, 9

Dry Cleaner
A.Z. Ventures/Expert Cleaning, 3

E–Commerce Website Producer
Internet Capabilities, 12

Editorial Services & Consulting
Hilton & Associates, 1

Elder Care
Summer Gardens Residential Care Facility for the Ambulatory Elderly, 1

Electronic Document Security Company
GoldTrustMark.com, 9

Emu Ranch
Southwestern Emu Ranch, 4

Energy Solutions Company
Abaka Energy Solutions, 8

Engineering Management Consultant
Herman Livingston Consultants, 4

Entertainment Production, Distribution, and Performance Company
Mentonic Hero Inc. , 12

Equipment Rental
Rich Rentals, 1

Event Photography Service
brightroom, Inc., 10

Event Planning Company
Occasions, The Event Planning Specialists, 7

Fast Food
Pasta Express, 3
Pasta Now!, 3

Fertilizer & Commodity Chemicals Company
Agronix Organics, Inc., 10

Financial Services Company
Diamond Strategic Services, 7
Prisma Microfinance, Inc., 9

Fire Equipment Retailer
Gallagher's Fire Service, 5

Food, Diet, & Nutrition Company
Think Thin Weight Loss Corporation, 10

Food Processor
Rio Grande, 3

Framing/Antiques Store
Flora's Frames & Antiques, 1

Franchise Postal Service
Express Postal Center, 5

Freelance Editor
Scrivener, The, 2
Word for Word, 2

Freight Expediting
Gazelle Expediting Inc., 5

General Contracting Company
Smith Contracting Company, 7

General Staffing Company
GENRX LLC, 12

Gift Store
Crystal Creek Gifts, 5

Giftware Company
Jenni Frey Gifts, 11

Go–Cart Designer and Supplier
Speedy Go–Cart, 12

Golf Driving Range
Mountain Cedar Golf Club, 9

Golf Grip Manufacturer
ProGrip, 10

Gourmet Foods Company
Good Earth Foods Company, 8

Graffiti Removal Service
Graffiti, Inc., 3

Grocery Store
Viking Grocery Stores, 9

Hair Salon
Epiphany Salon, 6

Handmade Greeting Card Company
Heartsongs, 11

Handyman Service
"I'm the Man!" Handyman Services, 11

Healthcare Software Company
QuikMed Info., 7

Health Insurance Company
Southeast Healthplans, Inc., 6

Holistic Health Center
Holistic Choices, LLC, 10

Home Décor Products Manufacturer
Burton Decor, Inc., 10

Home Inspection Company
Home Inspectors Are We, 12

Homeless Shelter
Sister Joan of Arc Center, 11

Hotel Resort
Seven Elms Resort, 7

Housing Rehabilitation Company
Madison Builders, LLC, 10

Ice Cream Shop
Fran's Ice, 3

Import Boutique
Bellisimo Imports, Inc., 1

Import/Export Store
Central Import/Export, 9

Indoor Playground
Kid's World, 3

Information Technology Personnel Agency
Rekve IT Staffing, 12

Inn/Resort
Lighthouse Inn, The, 1

Interior Design Company
Make It Your Own Space Inc., 11

Interior Painting Service
Eyecatching Interiors LLC, 11

Internet & Network Security Solution Provider
Safety Net Canada, Inc., 10

Internet Bid Clearinghouse
Opexnet, LLC, 5

Internet Cafe
Wired Bean, 5

Internet Communications Service Provider
Appian Way Communications Network, Ltd., 9

Internet Consultant
Allen Consulting, 3
Worldwide Internet Marketing Services, 3

Internet Loyalty Program
Tunes4You, 11

Internet Marketplace
ABC Internet Marketplace, Inc., 8

Internet Services Portal Site
Net Solutions, 11

Internet Software Company
Poggle, Inc., 9

Internet Travel Agency Business
Memory Lane Cruises, 9

Investor Trading Software Company
Investor Trends, Inc., 6

Kennel
Best Friend Kennel, 2

Ladder Company
Jacks' Ladder Inc., 1

Leasing Company
Leasing Group, 8

Limited Liability Company
Northern Investments, LLC, 7

Litigation Services Company
Acme Litigation Company, 10

Magazine Publisher
GRAPEVINE, 1

Mailing List Service
Forest Mail Service, 3

Management Consulting Service
Salmon & Salmon, 3

Manufacturing Business
Fiber Optic Automation, Inc., 3

Marble Quarry
Vomarth Marble Quarry, 9

Marketing Communications Firm
Cornelius Marketing, 4

Marketing Consultancy
Meridian Consulting, 5
Simmons Marketing Associates, 3

Massage Therapists
MASSAGEWORKS, 11

Maternity Aid
Nest in Comfort, 2

Media Producer
Dynamic Video, 2
Dynamic Video (Revised), 2
Shalimar Films, Inc., 2

Medical Billing Company
Physicians 1st Billing and Claims, 7

Medical Equipment Producer
Mediquip, Inc., 6
Premium Therapy, LLC, 10

Men's Clothing Retailer
Van Schaack, 4

Mentally Disabled Care Facility
Welcome Home Organization, 11

Metal Shop
Krosnow Metal Works, 5

Microbrewery
Harbor Brewing Company, 2
Juniper Brewing Company, 2

Mobile Studio
CRS Mobile Studio, 2

Mortgage Company
National Mortgage, Inc., 7

Motorcycle Dealership and Racetrack
Zoom Motors, 11

Multilevel Marketing
RFM Enterprises, 3

Mural Company
Smith Ray Design, 10

Network Game Centers
PowerPlay Gaming, LLC, 10

Newsletter
Network Journal, 2
Network Journal (Revised), 2

Nightclub
Wild Oasis, 7

Nonprofit Youth Outreach Ministry
Life Works Cincinnati, 9

Novelty Shop
Great Pretender, The, 5

Nursery
Wonderland Nursery, 7

Office Furniture
Powerline of Northern Minnesota, 5

Online Consulting
Borderline Transmissions, Inc., 1

Online Customer Service Support
live e-care, Inc., 10

Online Government Contract Service
U.S.Consulting - GOV.COM, 4

Online Hospitality Service
Tinner Corp., 4

Online Job Service
CareerConnections.com, 8

Online Merchant
E-Return Solutions, 8

Online Mortgage Company
Valuable Mortgage, 11

Online Outdoor Company
Outdoorsman.com, 8

Online Payment Services
Exactor Technologies, LLC, 12

Online Publishing System
Moonbeam Publishing, 9

Online Woodworking Manufacturing & Retailing
U–nique Woodworking, 12

Outdoor Adventure Travel Company
RAD-Venture, 4

Paint Distributor
Eartham Distributors, 4

Paintball Sport Company
Paintball Sport Palace, 6

Painting Company
Ko-Bas Painting Company, 10

Parts Manufacturer
Zemens Metal Corporation, 5

Party Supply Store
Celebrations, 5

Pasta Franchise
Pasta Express, 5

Pharmaceutical Company
Pain Away, Inc., 3

Photo Framing
Talking Photo Technology, 2

Pizzeria
Coastal Pizza, 11
Pizza to Go, Inc., 6

Plastic Drum Company
River City Drum, Inc., 7

Plumbing Service
Jax Plumbing, 3
Matt's Plumbing and Air Conditioning, 12

Powder Coating Manufacturer
Brudder Coating Systems Inc., 4
Innovative Over Coast, 4

Printing Company
Master Printer and Partners Printing, 1
Printer Perfect, 1

Private Investigator
FBEyes, 11

Private Label Food Manufacturer
Clarence Pratt Enterprises, Inc., 6

Public Relations Firm
SHP & Associates Business Communications, 2

Publisher
Group Publishing, The, 6
Infoguide Inc., 1

Racing Parts Store
Southeast Racing Parts, 8

Real Estate Company
MSN Real Estate, 7

Real Estate Investment Company
Wolfe Partners, 6

Real Estate Renovation Company
ABC Corp., 6

Record Company
Reed Entertainment Corp., 4

Record Store
Hidden Treasure Records L.C., 6

Refrigerant Recovery
Road Runner Refrigerant Recovery System, 3

Restaurant
American Diner, 1
Butcher Hollow Bar BQ, 7

Kelly House Inn, 5
Peach Blossom Diner, 1
Rock Island Tavern, 5
Whistle Shop, The, 4

Restaurant (Nonprofit)
McMurphy's Grill, 1
Murphy's Grill, 2
Murphy's Grill (Revised), 2

Restaurant Franchise
Reuben's Deli, 2

Restaurant/Bar
Plugged Nickel, The, 2
Watering Hole, The, 2

Restaurant/Microbrewery
Homesteaders' Pub & Grub, 5

Retail & Commercial Design Firm
Future Designs, 4

Retail Art Furnishings Business
Wood Designs Gallery, 6

Retail Business Incubator
Acme Incubators, 9

Retail Clothing
Boston Rags Clothing Store, 9
Clothes as Art Inc., 1

Retail Florist
Designs by Linda, 1

Retail Tobacco/Magazines
Standard Tobacco & News, 1

Rock Climber's Store & Cafe
The Boulder Stop, 8

Roller Rink
Santiago Roller Rink, 7

Routing/Navigation Software Company
PATH Systems, Inc., 10

Rubber Adhesive Manufacturer
Shake Proof, 4

Salad Packaging
Lyons & Coyne, Inc., 1

Sandwich Shop
Romastrano Incorporated, 3

Science Information Website Company
e-Science Technologies, Inc., 9

Screen Print Drying Company
DLP, Inc., 7

Search Service
Searchers, The, 2

Senior Care Facility
Hearts and Hopes Senior Home, 12

Shave Ice Business
Ice Dreams, 6

Ski Resort
Mounjoy, LLC, 8

Skin Cream Formulator
LaBelle Industries, Inc., 9

Software Developer
Data Technologies Corporation, 1

Software Engineering & Management Company
Swiss Issue WebTools, 7

Special Needs Clothing Store
You Can Do It!, 7

Sports Bar
Stone Oak Sports Bar & Grille, 12
Take Five Sports Bar & Grill, 6

Sports Collectibles
Diamond Collection, Inc., 2

Sports Tournament Organizer
Scramble Sports Tournament Series, 12

Structural Engineering Consulting Firm
StructureAll Ltd., 8

Structural Genomics Software Provider
Pharmatech Genomics, 10

Student Services Consulting Firm
Grad Student Exchange Consultants International, 8

Taxi Service
Lakeview Taxi, 5

Teen Night Club
Ventures, 8

Television Childproofer
Television for Kids, 2

Toiletry Company
Verde, 1

Toy Company
Toys for a New Generation Inc., 1

Travel Agency
International Business Tours, 4

Travel Information Service
Traveling U.S. Inc., 4

Used Car Business
Budget Cars, 6

Video Production & Distribution Company
Kitamon Productions, 9

Video Service
Express Video Service, 3

Virtual Reality
Building Aids Inc., 1
CineMedia Studios, Inc., 1

Virtual Shopping
Click 'n Shop Inc., 2

Wireless Internet Service
Superior XL Internet, 7

Wireless Systems Integrator
SpongeShark, LLC, 9